Scala and Spark for Big Data Analytics

Explore the concepts of functional programming, data streaming, and machine learning

Md. Rezaul Karim
Sridhar Alla

BIRMINGHAM - MUMBAI

Scala and Spark for Big Data Analytics

First published: July 2017

Production reference: 2241017

Published by Packt Publishing Ltd.
Livery Place
35 Livery Street
Birmingham
B3 2PB, UK.

ISBN 978-1-78528-084-9

www.packtpub.com

Credits

Author

Md. Rezaul Karim
Sridhar Alla

Reviewer

Andrea Bessi
Sumit Pal

Commissioning Editor

Aaron Lazar

Acquisition Editor

Nitin Dasan

Content Development Editor

Vikas Tiwari

Technical Editor

Subhalaxmi Nadar

Copy Editor

Safis Editing

Project Coordinator

Ulhas Kambali

Proofreader

Safis Editing

Indexer

Rekha Nair

Cover Work

Melwyn D'sa

Production Coordinator

Melwyn D'sa

About the Authors

Md. Rezaul Karim is a research scientist at Fraunhofer FIT, Germany. He is also a PhD candidate at RWTH Aachen University, Aachen, Germany. He holds a BSc and an MSc in computer science. Before joining Fraunhofer FIT, he had been working as a researcher at the Insight Centre for data analytics, Ireland. Previously, he worked as a lead engineer with Samsung Electronics' distributed R&D centers in Korea, India, Vietnam, Turkey, and Bangladesh. Earlier, he worked as a research assistant in the Database Lab at Kyung Hee University, Korea, and as an R&D engineer with BMTech21 Worldwide, Korea. Even before that, he worked as a software engineer with i2SoftTechnology, Dhaka, Bangladesh.

He has more than 8 years of experience in the area of research and development, with a solid knowledge of algorithms and data structures in C/C++, Java, Scala, R, and Python-focused big data technologies: Spark, Kafka, DC/OS, Docker, Mesos, Zeppelin, Hadoop, and MapReduce, and deep learning technologies: TensorFlow, DeepLearning4j, and H2O-Sparking Water. His research interests include machine learning, deep learning, semantic web, linked data, big data, and bioinformatics. He is the author of the following book titles with *Packt*:

- *Large-Scale Machine Learning with Spark*
- *Deep Learning with TensorFlow*

I am very grateful to my parents, who have always encouraged me to pursue knowledge. I also want to thank my wife Saroar, son Shadman, elder brother Mamtaz, elder sister Josna, and friends, who have endured my long monologues about the subjects in this book, and have always been encouraging and listening to me. Writing this book was made easier by the amazing efforts of the open source community and the great documentation of many projects out there related to Apache Spark and Scala. Further more, I would like to thank the acquisition, content development, and technical editors of Packt (and others who were involved in this book title) for their sincere cooperation and coordination. Additionally, without the work of numerous researchers and data analytics practitioners who shared their expertise in publications, lectures, and source code, this book might not exist at all!

Sridhar Alla is a big data expert helping small and big companies solve complex problems, such as data warehousing, governance, security, real-time processing, high-frequency trading, and establishing large-scale data science practices. He is an agile practitioner as well as a certified agile DevOps practitioner and implementer. He started his career as a storage software engineer at Network Appliance, Sunnyvale, and then worked as the chief technology officer at a cyber security firm, eIQNetworks, Boston. His job profile includes the role of the director of data science and engineering at Comcast, Philadelphia. He is an avid presenter at numerous Strata, Hadoop World, Spark Summit, and other conferences. He also provides onsite/online training on several technologies. He has several patents filed in the US PTO on large-scale computing and distributed systems. He holds a bachelors degree in computer science from JNTU, Hyderabad, India, and lives with his wife in New Jersey.

Sridhar has over 18 years of experience writing code in Scala, Java, C, C++, Python, R and Go. He also has extensive hands-on knowledge of Spark, Hadoop, Cassandra, HBase, MongoDB, Riak, Redis, Zeppelin, Mesos, Docker, Kafka, ElasticSearch, Solr, H2O, machine learning, text analytics, distributed computing and high performance computing.

I would like to thank my wonderful wife, Rosie Sarkaria, for all the love and patience during the many months I spent writing this book as well as reviewing countless edits I made. I would also like to thank my parents Ravi and Lakshmi Alla all the support and encouragement they continue to bestow upon me. I am very grateful to the many friends especially Abrar Hashmi, Christian Ludwig who helped me bounce ideas and get clarity on the various topics. Writing this book was not possible without the fantastic larger Apache community and Databricks folks who are making Spark so powerful and elegant. Further, I would like to thank the acquisition, content development and technical editors of Packt Publishing (and others who were involved in this book title) for their sincere cooperation and coordination.

About the Reviewers

Andre Baianov is an economist-turned-software developer, with a keen interest in data
science. After a bachelor's thesis on data mining and a master's thesis on business
intelligence, he started working with Scala and Apache Spark in 2015. He is currently
working as a consultant for national and international clients, helping them build
reactive architectures, machine learning frameworks, and functional programming
backends.

To my wife: beneath our superficial differences, we share the same soul.

Sumit Pal is a published author with Apress for *SQL on Big Data - Technology,
Architecture and Innovations* and *SQL on Big Data - Technology, Architecture and
Innovations*. He has more than 22 years of experience in the software industry in
various roles, spanning companies from start-ups to enterprises.

Sumit is an independent consultant working with big data, data visualization, and
data science, and a software architect building end-to-end, data-driven analytic
systems.
He has worked for Microsoft (SQL Server development team), Oracle (OLAP
development team), and Verizon (big data analytics team) in a career spanning 22
years.
Currently, he works for multiple clients, advising them on their data architectures
and big data solutions, and does hands-on coding with Spark, Scala, Java, and
Python.
Sumit has spoken at the following big data conferences: Data Summit NY, May 2017;
Big Data Symposium, Boston, May 2017; Apache Linux Foundation, May 2016, in
Vancouver, Canada; and Data Center World, March 2016, in Las Vegas.

www.PacktPub.com

For support files and downloads related to your book, please visit www.PacktPub.com.

Did you know that Packt offers eBook versions of every book published, with PDF and ePub files available? You can upgrade to the eBook version at www.PacktPub.com and as a print book customer, you are entitled to a discount on the eBook copy. Get in touch with us at service@packtpub.com for more details.

At www.PacktPub.com, you can also read a collection of free technical articles, sign up for a range of free newsletters and receive exclusive discounts and offers on Packt books and eBooks.

https://www.packtpub.com/mapt

Get the most in-demand software skills with Mapt. Mapt gives you full access to all Packt books and video courses, as well as industry-leading tools to help you plan your personal development and advance your career.

Why subscribe?

- Fully searchable across every book published by Packt
- Copy and paste, print, and bookmark content
- On demand and accessible via a web browser

Customer Feedback

Thanks for purchasing this Packt book. At Packt, quality is at the heart of our editorial process. To help us improve, please leave us an honest review on this book's Amazon page at `https://www.amazon.com/dp/1785280848`.

If you'd like to join our team of regular reviewers, you can e-mail us at `customerreviews@packtpub.com`. We award our regular reviewers with free eBooks and videos in exchange for their valuable feedback. Help us be relentless in improving our products!

Table of Contents

Preface

The continued growth in data coupled with the need to make increasingly complex decisions against that data is creating massive hurdles that prevent organizations from deriving insights in a timely manner using traditional analytical approaches. The field of big data has become so related to these frameworks that its scope is defined by what these frameworks can handle. Whether you're scrutinizing the clickstream from millions of visitors to optimize online ad placements, or sifting through billions of transactions to identify signs of fraud, the need for advanced analytics, such as machine learning and graph processing, to automatically glean insights from enormous volumes of data is more evident than ever.

Apache Spark, the de facto standard for big data processing, analytics, and data sciences across all academia and industries, provides both machine learning and graph processing libraries, allowing companies to tackle complex problems easily with the power of highly scalable and clustered computers. Spark's promise is to take this a little further to make writing distributed programs using Scala feel like writing regular programs for Spark. Spark will be great in giving ETL pipelines huge boosts in performance and easing some of the pain that feeds the MapReduce programmer's daily chant of despair to the Hadoop gods.

In this book, we used Spark and Scala for the endeavor to bring state-of-the-art advanced data analytics with machine learning, graph processing, streaming, and SQL to Spark, with their contributions to MLlib, ML, SQL, GraphX, and other libraries.

We started with Scala and then moved to the Spark part, and finally, covered some advanced topics for big data analytics with Spark and Scala. In the appendix, we will see how to extend your Scala knowledge for SparkR, PySpark, Apache Zeppelin, and in-memory Alluxio. This book isn't meant to be read from cover to cover. Skip to a chapter that looks like something you're trying to accomplish or that simply ignites your interest.

Happy reading!

What this book covers

Chapter 1, *Introduction to Scala*, will teach big data analytics using the Scala-based APIs of Spark. Spark itself is written with Scala and naturally, as a starting point, we will discuss a brief introduction to Scala, such as the basic aspects of its history, purposes, and how to install Scala on Windows, Linux, and Mac OS. After that, the Scala web framework will be discussed in brief. Then, we will provide a comparative analysis of Java and Scala. Finally, we will dive into Scala programming to get started with Scala.

Chapter 2, *Object-Oriented Scala*, says that the object-oriented programming (OOP) paradigm provides a whole new layer of abstraction. In short, this chapter discusses some of the greatest strengths of OOP languages: discoverability, modularity, and extensibility. In particular, we will see how to deal with variables in Scala; methods, classes, and objects in Scala; packages and package objects; traits and trait linearization; and Java interoperability.

Chapter 3, *Functional Programming Concepts*, showcases the functional programming concepts in Scala. More specifically, we will learn several topics, such as why Scala is an arsenal for the data scientist, why it is important to learn the Spark paradigm, pure functions, and higher-order functions (HOFs). A real-life use case using HOFs will be shown too. Then, we will see how to handle exceptions in higher-order functions outside of collections using the standard library of Scala. Finally, we will look at how functional Scala affects an object's mutability.

Chapter4, *Collection APIs*, introduces one of the features that attract most Scala users-- the Collections API. It's very powerful and flexible, and has lots of operations coupled. We will also demonstrate the capabilities of the Scala Collection API and how it can be used in order to accommodate different types of data and solve a wide range of different problems. In this chapter, we will cover Scala collection APIs, types and hierarchy, some performance characteristics, Java interoperability, and Scala implicits.

Chapter 5, *Tackle Big Data - Spark Comes to the Party*, outlines data analysis and big data; we see the challenges that big data poses, how they are dealt with by distributed computing, and the approaches suggested by functional programming. We introduce Google's MapReduce, Apache Hadoop, and finally, Apache Spark, and see how they embraced this approach and these techniques. We will look into the evolution of Apache Spark: why Apache Spark was created in the first place and the value it can bring to the challenges of big data analytics and processing.

Chapter 6, *Start Working with Spark - REPL and RDDs,* covers how Spark works; then, we introduce RDDs, the basic abstractions behind Apache Spark, and see that they are simply distributed collections exposing Scala-like APIs. We will look at the deployment options for Apache Spark and run it locally as a Spark shell. We will learn the internals of Apache Spark, what RDDs are, DAGs and lineages of RDDs, Transformations, and Actions.

Chapter 7, *Special RDD Operations,* focuses on how RDDs can be tailored to meet different needs, and how these RDDs provide new functionalities (and dangers!) Moreover, we investigate other useful objects that Spark provides, such as broadcast variables and Accumulators. We will learn aggregation techniques, shuffling.

Chapter 8, *Introduce a Little Structure - SparkSQL,* teaches how to use Spark for the analysis of structured data as a higher-level abstraction of RDDs and how Spark SQL's APIs make querying structured data simple yet robust. Moreover, we introduce datasets and look at the differences between datasets, DataFrames, and RDDs. We will also learn to join operations and window functions to do complex data analysis using DataFrame APIs.

Chapter 9, *Stream Me Up, Scotty - Spark Streaming,* takes you through Spark Streaming and how we can take advantage of it to process streams of data using the Spark API. Moreover, in this chapter, the reader will learn various ways of processing real-time streams of data using a practical example to consume and process tweets from Twitter. We will look at integration with Apache Kafka to do real-time processing. We will also look at structured streaming, which can provide real-time queries to your applications.

Chapter 10, *Everything is Connected - GraphX,* in this chapter, we learn how many real-world problems can be modeled (and resolved) using graphs. We will look at graph theory using Facebook as an example, Apache Spark's graph processing library GraphX, VertexRDD and EdgeRDDs, graph operators, aggregateMessages, TriangleCounting, the Pregel API, and use cases such as the PageRank algorithm.

Chapter 11, *Learning Machine Learning - Spark MLlib and ML,* the purpose of this chapter is to provide a conceptual introduction to statistical machine learning. We will focus on Spark's machine learning APIs, called Spark MLlib and ML. We will then discuss how to solve classification tasks using decision trees and random forest algorithms and regression problem using linear regression algorithm. We will also show how we could benefit from using one-hot encoding and dimensionality reductions algorithms in feature extraction before training a classification model. In later sections, we will show a step-by-step example of developing a collaborative filtering-based movie recommendation system.

Chapter 12, *My Name is Bayes, Naive Bayes,* states that machine learning in big data is a radical combination that has created great impact in the field of research, in both academia and industry. Big data imposes great challenges on ML, data analytics tools, and algorithms to find the real value. However, making a future prediction based on these huge datasets has never been easy. Considering this challenge, in this chapter, we will dive deeper into ML and find out how to use a simple yet powerful method to build a scalable classification model and concepts such as multinomial classification, Bayesian inference, Naive Bayes, decision trees, and a comparative analysis of Naive Bayes versus decision trees.

Chapter 13, *Time to Put Some Order - Cluster Your Data with Spark MLlib,* gets you started on how Spark works in cluster mode with its underlying architecture. In previous chapters, we saw how to develop practical applications using different Spark APIs. Finally, we will see how to deploy a full Spark application on a cluster, be it with a pre-existing Hadoop installation or without.

Chapter 14, *Text Analytics Using Spark ML,* outlines the wonderful field of text analytics using Spark ML. Text analytics is a wide area in machine learning and is useful in many use cases, such as sentiment analysis, chat bots, email spam detection, natural language processing, and many many more. We will learn how to use Spark for text analysis with a focus on use cases of text classification using a 10,000 sample set of Twitter data. We will also look at LDA, a popular technique to generate topics from documents without knowing much about the actual text, and will implement text classification on Twitter data to see how it all comes together.

Chapter 15, *Spark Tuning,* digs deeper into Apache Spark internals and says that while Spark is great in making us feel as if we are using just another Scala collection, we shouldn't forget that Spark actually runs in a distributed system. Therefore, throughout this chapter, we will cover how to monitor Spark jobs, Spark configuration, common mistakes in Spark app development, and some optimization techniques.

Chapter 16, *Time to Go to ClusterLand - Deploying Spark on a Cluster,* explores how Spark works in cluster mode with its underlying architecture. We will see Spark architecture in a cluster, the Spark ecosystem and cluster management, and how to deploy Spark on standalone, Mesos, Yarn, and AWS clusters. We will also see how to deploy your app on a cloud-based AWS cluster.

Chapter 17, *Testing and Debugging Spark,* explains how difficult it can be to test an application if it is distributed; then, we see some ways to tackle this. We will cover how to do testing in a distributed environment, and testing and debugging Spark applications.

Chapter 18, *PySpark & SparkR,* covers the other two popular APIs for writing Spark code using R and Python, that is, PySpark and SparkR. In particular, we will cover how to get started with PySpark and interacting with DataFrame APIs and UDFs with PySpark, and then we will do some data analytics using PySpark. The second part of this chapter covers how to get started with SparkR. We will also see how to do data processing and manipulation, and how to work with RDD and DataFrames using SparkR, and finally, some data visualization using SparkR.

Chapter 19, *Advanced Machine Learning Best Practices,* provides theoretical and practical aspects of some advanced topics of machine learning with Spark. We will see how to tune machine learning models for optimized performance using grid search, cross-validation, and hyperparameter tuning. In a later section, we will cover how to develop a scalable recommendation system using ALS, which is an example of a model-based recommendation algorithm. Finally, a topic modelling application will be demonstrated as a text clustering technique

Appendix A, *Accelerating Spark with Alluxio,* shows how to use Alluxio with Spark to increase the speed of processing. Alluxio is an open source distributed memory storage system useful for increasing the speed of many applications across platforms, including Apache Spark. We will explore the possibilities of using Alluxio and how Alluxio integration will provide greater performance without the need to cache the data in memory every time we run a Spark job.

Appendix B, *Interactive Data Analytics with Apache Zeppelin,* says that from a data science perspective, interactive visualization of your data analysis is also important. Apache Zeppelin is a web-based notebook for interactive and large-scale data analytics with multiple backends and interpreters. In this chapter, we will discuss how to use Apache Zeppelin for large-scale data analytics using Spark as the interpreter in the backend.

Chapter 19 and *Appendices* are not present in the book but are available for download at the following link: https://www.packtpub.com/sites/default/files/downloads/ScalaandSparkforBigDataAnalytics_OnlineChapter_Appendices.pdf.

What you need for this book

All the examples have been implemented using Python version 2.7 and 3.5 on an Ubuntu Linux 64 bit, including the TensorFlow library version 1.0.1. However, in the book, we showed the source code with only Python 2.7 compatible. Source codes that are Python 3.5+ compatible can be downloaded from the Packt repository. You will also need the following Python modules (preferably the latest versions):

- Spark 2.0.0 (or higher)
- Hadoop 2.7 (or higher)
- Java (JDK and JRE) 1.7+/1.8+
- Scala 2.11.x (or higher)
- Python 2.7+/3.4+
- R 3.1+ and RStudio 1.0.143 (or higher)
- Eclipse Mars, Oxygen, or Luna (latest)
- Maven Eclipse plugin (2.9 or higher)
- Maven compiler plugin for Eclipse (2.3.2 or higher)
- Maven assembly plugin for Eclipse (2.4.1 or higher)

Operating system: Linux distributions are preferable (including Debian, Ubuntu, Fedora, RHEL, and CentOS) and to be more specific, for Ubuntu it is recommended to have a complete 14.04 (LTS) 64-bit (or later) installation, VMWare player 12, or Virtual box. You can run Spark jobs on Windows (XP/7/8/10) or Mac OS X (10.4.7+).

Hardware configuration: Processor Core i3, Core i5 (recommended), or Core i7 (to get the best results). However, multicore processing will provide faster data processing and scalability. You will need least 8-16 GB RAM (recommended) for a standalone mode and at least 32 GB RAM for a single VM--and higher for cluster. You will also need enough storage for running heavy jobs (depending on the dataset size you will be handling), and preferably at least 50 GB of free disk storage (for standalone word missing and for an SQL warehouse).

Who this book is for

Anyone who wishes to learn how to perform data analysis by harnessing the power of Spark will find this book extremely useful. No knowledge of Spark or Scala is assumed, although prior programming experience (especially with other JVM languages) will be useful in order to pick up the concepts quicker. Scala has been observing a steady rise in adoption over the past few years, especially in the fields of data science and analytics. Going hand in hand with Scala is Apache Spark, which is programmed in Scala and is widely used in the field of analytics. This book will help you leverage the power of both these tools to make sense of big data.

Conventions

In this book, you will find a number of text styles that distinguish between different kinds of information. Here are some examples of these styles and an explanation of their meaning. Code words in text, database table names, folder names, filenames, file extensions, pathnames, dummy URLs, user input, and Twitter handles are shown as follows: "The next lines of code read the link and assign it to the to the `BeautifulSoup` function."

A block of code is set as follows:

```
package com.chapter11.SparkMachineLearning
import org.apache.spark.mllib.feature.StandardScalerModel
import org.apache.spark.mllib.linalg.{ Vector, Vectors }
import org.apache.spark.sql.{ DataFrame }
import org.apache.spark.sql.SparkSession
```

When we wish to draw your attention to a particular part of a code block, the relevant lines or items are set in bold:

```
val spark = SparkSession
                .builder
                .master("local[*]")
                .config("spark.sql.warehouse.dir", "E:/Exp/")
                .config("spark.kryoserializer.buffer.max", "1024m")
                .appName("OneVsRestExample")
            .getOrCreate()
```

Any command-line input or output is written as follows:

```
$./bin/spark-submit --class com.chapter11.RandomForestDemo \
--master spark://ip-172-31-21-153.us-west-2.compute:7077 \
--executor-memory 2G \
--total-executor-cores 2 \
file:///home/KMeans-0.0.1-SNAPSHOT.jar \
file:///home/mnist.bz2
```

New termsand **important words** are shown in bold. Words that you see on the screen, for example, in menus or dialog boxes, appear in the text like this: "Clicking the **Next** button moves you to the next screen."

Warnings or important notes appear like this.

Tips and tricks appear like this.

Reader feedback

Feedback from our readers is always welcome. Let us know what you think about this book-what you liked or disliked. Reader feedback is important for us as it helps us develop titles that you will really get the most out of. To send us general feedback, simply e-mail feedback@packtpub.com, and mention the book's title in the subject of your message. If there is a topic that you have expertise in and you are interested in either writing or contributing to a book, see our author guide at www.packtpub.com/authors.

Customer support

Now that you are the proud owner of a Packt book, we have a number of things to help you to get the most from your purchase.

Downloading the example code

You can download the example code files for this book from your account at http://www.packtpub.com. If you purchased this book elsewhere, you can visit http://www.packtpub.com/support and register to have the files e-mailed directly to you. You can download the code files by following these steps:

1. Log in or register to our website using your e-mail address and password.
2. Hover the mouse pointer on the **SUPPORT** tab at the top.
3. Click on **Code Downloads & Errata**.
4. Enter the name of the book in the **Search** box.
5. Select the book for which you're looking to download the code files.
6. Choose from the drop-down menu where you purchased this book from.
7. Click on **Code Download**.

Once the file is downloaded, please make sure that you unzip or extract the folder using the latest version of:

- WinRAR / 7-Zip for Windows
- Zipeg / iZip / UnRarX for Mac
- 7-Zip / PeaZip for Linux

The code bundle for the book is also hosted on GitHub at https://github.com/PacktPublishing/Scala-and-Spark-for-Big-Data-Analytics. We also have other code bundles from our rich catalog of books and videos available at https://github.com/PacktPublishing/. Check them out!

Downloading the color images of this book

We also provide you with a PDF file that has color images of the screenshots/diagrams used in this book. The color images will help you better understand the changes in the output. You can download this file from https://www.packtpub.com/sites/default/files/downloads/ScalaandSparkforBigDataAnalytics_ColorImages.pdf

Errata

Although we have taken every care to ensure the accuracy of our content, mistakes do happen. If you find a mistake in one of our books-maybe a mistake in the text or the code-we would be grateful if you could report this to us. By doing so, you can save other readers from frustration and help us improve subsequent versions of this book. If you find any errata, please report them by visiting `http://www.packtpub.com/submit-errata`, selecting your book, clicking on the **Errata Submission Form** link, and entering the details of your errata. Once your errata are verified, your submission will be accepted and the errata will be uploaded to our website or added to any list of existing errata under the Errata section of that title. To view the previously submitted errata, go to `https://www.packtpub.com/books/content/support` and enter the name of the book in the search field. The required information will appear under the **Errata** section.

Piracy

Piracy of copyrighted material on the Internet is an ongoing problem across all media. At Packt, we take the protection of our copyright and licenses very seriously. If you come across any illegal copies of our works in any form on the Internet, please provide us with the location address or website name immediately so that we can pursue a remedy. Please contact us at `copyright@packtpub.com` with a link to the suspected pirated material. We appreciate your help in protecting our authors and our ability to bring you valuable content.

Questions

If you have a problem with any aspect of this book, you can contact us at `questions@packtpub.com`, and we will do our best to address the problem.

Introduction to Scala

"I'm Scala. I'm a scalable, functional and object-oriented programming language. I can grow with you and you can play with me by typing one-line expressions and observing the results instantly"

- Scala Quote

In last few years, Scala has observed steady rise and wide adoption by developers and practitioners, especially in the fields of data science and analytics. On the other hand, Apache Spark which is written in Scala is a fast and general engine for large-scale data processing. Spark's success is due to many factors: easy-to-use API, clean programming model, performance, and so on. Therefore, naturally, Spark has more support for Scala: more APIs are available for Scala compared to Python or Java; although, new Scala APIs are available before those for Java, Python, and R.

Now that before we start writing your data analytics program using Spark and Scala (part II), we will first get familiar with Scala's functional programming concepts, object oriented features and the Scala collection APIs in detail (part I). As a starting point, we will provide a brief introduction to Scala in this chapter. We will cover some basic aspects of Scala including it's history and purposes. Then we will see how to install Scala on different platforms including Windows, Linux, and Mac OS so that your data analytics programs can be written on your favourite editors and IDEs. Later in this chapter, we will provide a comparative analysis between Java and Scala. Finally, we will dive into Scala programming with some examples.

In a nutshell, the following topics will be covered:

- History and purposes of Scala
- Platforms and editors
- Installing and setting up Scala
- Scala: the scalable language

- Scala for Java programmers
- Scala for the beginners
- Summary

History and purposes of Scala

Scala is a general-purpose programming language that comes with support of `functional programming` and a strong `static type` system. The source code of Scala is intended to be compiled into `Java` bytecode, so that the resulting executable code can be run on `Java virtual machine` (JVM).

Martin Odersky started the design of Scala back in 2001 at the **École Polytechnique Fédérale de Lausanne (EPFL)**. It was an extension of his work on Funnel, which is a programming language that uses functional programming and Petri nets. The first public release appears in 2004 but with only on the Java platform support. Later on, it was followed by .NET framework in June 2004.

Scala has become very popular and experienced wide adoptions because it not only supports the object-oriented programming paradigm, but it also embraces the functional programming concepts. In addition, although Scala's symbolic operators are hardly easy to read, compared to Java, most of the Scala codes are comparatively concise and easy to read -e.g. Java is too verbose.

Like any other programming languages, Scala was prosed and developed for specific purposes. Now, the question is, why was Scala created and what problems does it solve? To answer these questions, Odersky said in his blog:

> *"The work on Scala stems from a research effort to develop better language support for component software. There are two hypotheses that we would like to validate with the Scala experiment. First, we postulate that a programming language for component software needs to be scalable in the sense that the same concepts can describe small as well as large parts. Therefore, we concentrate on mechanisms for abstraction, composition, and decomposition, rather than adding a large set of primitives, which might be useful for components at some level of scale but not at other levels. Second, we postulate that scalable support for components can be provided by a programming language which unifies and generalizes object-oriented and functional programming. For statically typed languages, of which Scala is an instance, these two paradigms were up to now largely separate."*

Nevertheless, pattern matching and higher order functions, and so on, are also provided in Scala, not to fill the gap between FP and OOP, but because they are typical features of functional programming. For this, it has some incredibly powerful pattern-matching features, which are an actor-based concurrency framework. Moreover, it has the support of the first- and higher-order functions. In summary, the name "Scala" is a portmanteau of scalable language, signifying that it is designed to grow with the demands of its users.

Platforms and editors

Scala runs on **Java Virtual Machine (JVM)**, which makes Scala a good choice for Java programmers too who would like to have a functional programming flavor in their codes. There are lots of options when it comes to editors. It's better for you to spend some time making some sort of a comparative study between the available editors because being comfortable with an IDE is one of the key factors for a successful programming experience. Following are some options to choose from:

- Scala IDE
- Scala plugin for Eclipse
- IntelliJ IDEA
- Emacs
- VIM

Scala support programming on Eclipse has several advantages using numerous beta plugins. Eclipse provides some exciting features such as local, remote, and high-level debugging facilities with semantic highlighting and code completion for Scala. You can use Eclipse for Java as well as Scala application development with equal ease. However, I would also suggest Scala IDE (`http://scala-ide.org/`)--it's a full-fledged Scala editor based on Eclipse and customized with a set of interesting features (for example, Scala worksheets, ScalaTest support, Scala refactoring, and so on).

The second best option, in my view, is the IntelliJ IDEA. The first release came in 2001 as the first available Java IDEs with advanced code navigation and refactoring capabilities integrated. According to the InfoWorld report (see at `http://www.infoworld.com/article/2683534/development-environments/infoworld-review--top-java-programming-tools.html`), out of the four top Java programming IDE (that is, Eclipse, IntelliJ IDEA, NetBeans, and JDeveloper), IntelliJ received the highest test center score of 8.5 out of 10.

The corresponding scoring is shown in the following figure:

InfoWorld Scorecard	Documentation and help system (15.0%)	Ease of use (30.0%)	Plug-in ecosystem (25.0%)	Java features (30.0%)	Overall Score (100%)
Eclipse 3.6	8.0	6.0	10.0	8.0	7.9 ★★★★★
JetBrains IntelliJ IDEA 9.0.3	7.0	9.0	8.0	9.0	8.5 ★★★★★
NetBeans 6.9	8.0	8.0	8.0	8.0	8.0 ★★★★★
Oracle JDeveloper Studio 11g (11.1.1.3.0)	9.0	8.0	5.0	8.0	7.4 ★★★★★

Figure 1: Best IDEs for Scala/Java developers

From the preceding figure, you may be interested in using other IDEs such as NetBeans and JDeveloper too. Ultimately, the choice is an everlasting debate among the developers, which means the final choice is yours.

Installing and setting up Scala

As we have already mentioned, Scala uses JVM, therefore make sure you have Java installed on your machine. If not, refer to the next subsection, which shows how to install Java on Ubuntu. In this section, at first, we will show you how to install Java 8 on Ubuntu. Then, we will see how to install Scala on Windows, Mac OS, and Linux.

Installing Java

For simplicity, we will show how to install Java 8 on an Ubuntu 14.04 LTS 64-bit machine. But for Windows and Mac OS, it would be better to invest some time on Google to know how. For a minimum clue for the Windows users: refer to this link for details `https://java.com/en/download/help/windows_manual_download.xml`.

Now, let's see how to install Java 8 on Ubuntu with step-by-step commands and instructions. At first, check whether Java is already installed:

```
$ java -version
```

If it returns `The program java cannot be found in the following packages`, Java hasn't been installed yet. Then you would like to execute the following command to get rid of:

```
$ sudo apt-get install default-jre
```

This will install the **Java Runtime Environment** (JRE). However, if you may instead need the **Java Development Kit** (JDK), which is usually needed to compile Java applications on Apache Ant, Apache Maven, Eclipse, and IntelliJ IDEA.

The Oracle JDK is the official JDK, however, it is no longer provided by Oracle as a default installation for Ubuntu. You can still install it using apt-get. To install any version, first execute the following commands:

```
$ sudo apt-get install python-software-properties
$ sudo apt-get update
$ sudo add-apt-repository ppa:webupd8team/java
$ sudo apt-get update
```

Then, depending on the version you want to install, execute one of the following commands:

```
$ sudo apt-get install oracle-java8-installer
```

After installing, don't forget to set the Java home environmental variable. Just apply the following commands (for the simplicity, we assume that Java is installed at `/usr/lib/jvm/java-8-oracle`):

```
$ echo "export JAVA_HOME=/usr/lib/jvm/java-8-oracle" >> ~/.bashrc
$ echo "export PATH=$PATH:$JAVA_HOME/bin" >> ~/.bashrc
$ source ~/.bashrc
```

Now, let's see the `Java_HOME` as follows:

```
$ echo $JAVA_HOME
```

You should observe the following result on Terminal:

```
/usr/lib/jvm/java-8-oracle
```

Now, let's check to make sure that Java has been installed successfully by issuing the following command (you might see the latest version!):

```
$ java -version
```

You will get the following output:

```
java version "1.8.0_121"
Java(TM) SE Runtime Environment (build 1.8.0_121-b13)
Java HotSpot(TM) 64-Bit Server VM (build 25.121-b13, mixed mode)
```

Excellent! Now you have Java installed on your machine, thus you're ready Scala codes once it is installed. Let's do this in the next few subsections.

Windows

This part will focus on installing Scala on the PC with Windows 7, but in the end, it won't matter which version of Windows you to run at the moment:

1. The first step is to download a zipped file of Scala from the official site. You will find it at `https://www.Scala-lang.org/download/all.html`. Under the other resources section of this page, you will find a list of the archive files from which you can install Scala. We will choose to download the zipped file for Scala 2.11.8, as shown in the following figure:

Archive	System	Size
scala-2.11.8.tgz	Mac OS X, Unix, Cygwin	27.35M
scala-2.11.8.msi	Windows (msi installer)	109.35M
scala-2.11.8.zip	Windows	27.40M
scala-2.11.8.deb	Debian	76.02M
scala-2.11.8.rpm	RPM package	108.16M
scala-docs-2.11.8.txz	API docs	46.00M
scala-docs-2.11.8.zip	API docs	84.21M
scala-sources-2.11.8.tar.gz	Sources	

Figure 2: Scala installer for Windows

2. After the downloading has finished, unzip the file and place it in your favorite folder. You can also rename the file Scala for navigation flexibility. Finally, a PATH variable needs to be created for Scala to be globally seen on your OS. For this, navigate to **Computer** | **Properties**, as shown in the following figure:

Figure 3: Environmental variable tab on windows

3. Select **Environment Variables** from there and get the location of the `bin` folder of Scala; then, append it to the `PATH` environment variable. Apply the changes and then press **OK**, as shown in the following screenshot:

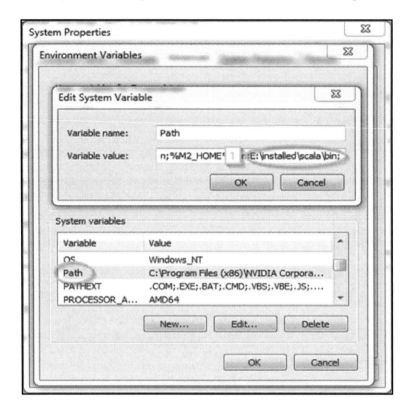

Figure 4: Adding environmental variables for Scala

4. Now, you are ready to go for the Windows installation. Open the CMD and just type `scala`. If you were successful in the installation process, then you should see an output similar to the following screenshot:

Figure 5: Accessing Scala from "Scala shell"

Mac OS

It's time now to install Scala on your Mac. There are lots of ways in which you can install Scala on your Mac, and here, we are going to mention two of them:

Using Homebrew installer

1. At first, check your system to see whether it has Xcode installed or not because it's required in this step. You can install it from the Apple App Store free of charge.

2. Next, you need to install `Homebrew` from the terminal by running the following command in your terminal:

```
$ /usr/bin/ruby -e "$(curl -fsSL
https://raw.githubusercontent.com/Homebrew/install/master/install)"
```

> Note: The preceding command is changed by the Homebrew guys from time to time. If the command doesn't seem to be working, check the Homebrew website for the latest incantation: `http://brew.sh/`.

3. Now, you are ready to go and install Scala by typing this command `brew install scala` in the terminal.

4. Finally, you are ready to go by simply typing Scala in your terminal (the second line) and you will observe the following on your terminal:

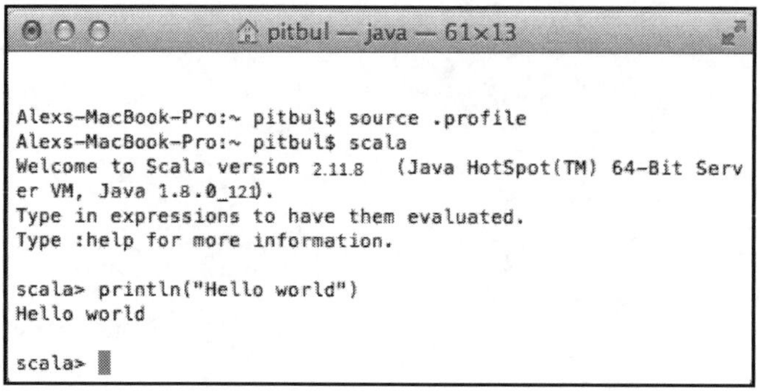

```
⊜ ○ ○                    ⌂ pitbul — java — 61×13

Alexs-MacBook-Pro:~ pitbul$ source .profile
Alexs-MacBook-Pro:~ pitbul$ scala
Welcome to Scala version 2.11.8   (Java HotSpot(TM) 64-Bit Serv
er VM, Java 1.8.0_121).
Type in expressions to have them evaluated.
Type :help for more information.

scala> println("Hello world")
Hello world

scala>
```

Figure 6: Scala shell on macOS

Installing manually

Before installing Scala manually, choose your preferred version of Scala and download the corresponding `.tgz` file of that version `Scala-verion.tgz` from `http://www.Scala-lang.org/download/`. After downloading your preferred version of Scala, extract it as follows:

```
$ tar xvf scala-2.11.8.tgz
```

Then, move it to `/usr/local/share` as follows:

```
$ sudo mv scala-2.11.8 /usr/local/share
```

Now, to make the installation permanent, execute the following commands:

```
$ echo "export SCALA_HOME=/usr/local/share/scala-2.11.8" >>
~/.bash_profile
$ echo "export PATH=$PATH: $SCALA_HOME/bin" >> ~/.bash_profile
```

That's it. Now, let's see how it can be done on Linux distributions like Ubuntu in the next subsection.

Linux

In this subsection, we will show you the installation procedure of Scala on the Ubuntu distribution of Linux. Before starting, let's check to make sure Scala is installed properly. Checking this is straightforward using the following command:

```
$ scala -version
```

If Scala is already installed on your system, you should get the following message on your terminal:

```
Scala code runner version 2.11.8 -- Copyright 2002-2016, LAMP/EPFL
```

Note that, during the writing of this installation, we used the latest version of Scala, that is, 2.11.8. If you do not have Scala installed on your system, make sure you install it before proceeding to the next step. You can download the latest version of Scala from the Scala website at http://www.scala-lang.org/download/ (for a clearer view, refer to *Figure 2*). For ease, let's download Scala 2.11.8, as follows:

```
$ cd Downloads/
$ wget https://downloads.lightbend.com/scala/2.11.8/scala-2.11.8.tgz
```

After the download has been finished, you should find the Scala tar file in the download folder.

 The user should first go into the Download directory with the following command: $ cd /Downloads/. Note that the name of the downloads folder may change depending on the system's selected language.

To extract the Scala tar file from its location or more, type the following command. Using this, the Scala tar file can be extracted from the Terminal:

```
$ tar -xvzf scala-2.11.8.tgz
```

Now, move the Scala distribution to the user's perspective (for example, /usr/local/scala/share) by typing the following command or doing it manually:

```
$ sudo mv scala-2.11.8 /usr/local/share/
```

Move to your home directory issue using the following command:

```
$ cd ~
```

Then, set the Scala home using the following commands:

```
$ echo "export SCALA_HOME=/usr/local/share/scala-2.11.8" >> ~/.bashrc
$ echo "export PATH=$PATH:$SCALA_HOME/bin" >> ~/.bashrc
```

Then, make the change permanent for the session by using the following command:

```
$ source ~/.bashrc
```

After the installation has been completed, you should better to verify it using the following command:

```
$ scala —version
```

If Scala has successfully been configured on your system, you should get the following message on your terminal:

```
Scala code runner version 2.11.8 -- Copyright 2002-2016, LAMP/EPFL
```

Well done! Now, let's enter into the Scala shell by typing the `scala` command on the terminal, as shown in the following figure:

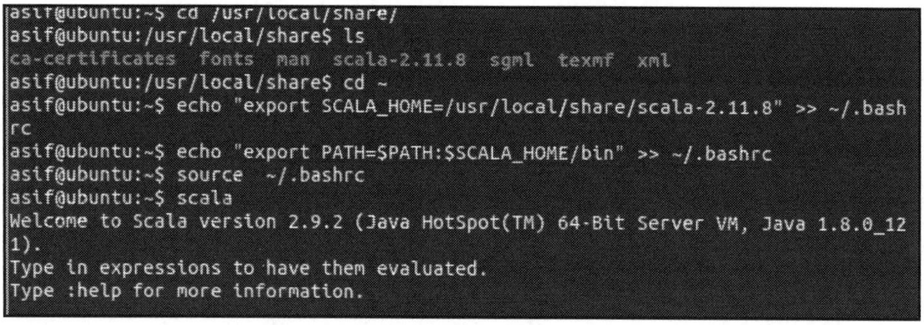

Figure 7: Scala shell on Linux (Ubuntu distribution)

Finally, you can also install Scala using the apt-get command, as follows:

```
$ sudo apt—get install scala
```

This command will download the latest version of Scala (that is, 2.12.x). However, Spark does not have support for Scala 2.12 yet (at least when we wrote this chapter). Therefore, we would recommend the manual installation described earlier.

Scala: the scalable language

The name Scala comes from a scalable language because Scala's concepts scale well to large programs. Some programs in other languages will take tens of lines to be coded, but in Scala, you will get the power to express the general patterns and concepts of programming in a concise and effective manner. In this section, we will describe some exciting features of Scala that Odersky has created for us:

Scala is object-oriented

Scala is a very good example of an object-oriented language. To define a type or behavior for your objects you need to use the notion of classes and traits, which will be explained later, in the next chapter. Scala doesn't support direct multiple inheritances, but to achieve this structure, you need to use Scala's extension of the **subclassing** and **mixing-based composition**. This will be discussed in later chapters.

Scala is functional

Functional programming treats functions like first-class citizens. In Scala, this is achieved with syntactic sugar and objects that extend traits (like *Function2*), but this is how functional programming is achieved in Scala. Also, Scala defines a simple and easy way to define **anonymous functions** (functions without names). It also supports higher-order functions and it allows nested functions. The syntax of these concepts will be explained in deeper details in the coming chapters.

Also, it helps you to code in an immutable way, and by this, you can easily apply it to parallelism with synchronization and concurrency.

Scala is statically typed

Unlike the other statically typed languages like Pascal, Rust, and so on, Scala does not expect you to provide redundant type information. You don't have to specify the type in most cases. Most importantly, you don't even need to repeat them again.

A programming language is called statically typed if the type of a variable is known at compile time: this also means that, as a programmer, you must specify what the type of each variable is. For example, Scala, Java, C, OCaml, Haskell, and C++, and so on. On the other hand, Perl, Ruby, Python, and so on are dynamically typed languages, where the type is not associated with the variables or fields, but with the runtime values.

The statically typed nature of Scala ensures that all kinds of checking are done by the compiler. This extremely powerful feature of Scala helps you find/catch most trivial bugs and errors at a very early stage, before being executed.

Scala runs on the JVM

Just like Java, Scala is also compiled into bytecode which can easily be executed by the JVM. This means that the runtime platforms of Scala and Java are the same because both generate bytecodes as the compilation output. So, you can easily switch from Java to Scala, you can and also easily integrate both, or even use Scala in your Android application to add a functional flavor.

Note that, while using Java code in a Scala program is quite easy, the opposite is very difficult, mostly because of Scala's syntactic sugar.

Also, just like the `javac` command, which compiles Java code into bytecode, Scala has the `scalas` command, which compiles the Scala code into bytecode.

Scala can execute Java code

As mentioned earlier, Scala can also be used to execute your Java code. Not just installing your Java code; it also enables you to use all the available classes from the Java SDK, and even your own predefined classes, projects, and packages right in the Scala environment.

Scala can do concurrent and synchronized processing

Some programs in other languages will take tens of lines to be coded, but in Scala, you will get the power to express the general patterns and concepts of programming in a concise and effective manner. Also, it helps you to code in an immutable way, and by this, you can easily apply it to parallelism with synchronization and concurrency.

Scala for Java programmers

Scala has a set of features that completely differ from Java. In this section, we will discuss some of these features. This section will be helpful for those who are from a Java background or are at least familiar with basic Java syntax and semantics.

All types are objects

As mentioned earlier, every value in Scala will look like an object. This statement means everything looks like an object, but some of them do not actually object and you will see the interpretation of this in the coming chapters (for example, the difference between the reference types and the primitive types still exists in Scala, but it hides it for the most part). For example, in Scala, strings are implicitly converted to collections of characters, but not in Java!

Type inference

If you are not familiar with the term, it is nothing but the deduction of types at compile time. Hold on, isn't that what dynamic typing means? Well, no. Notice that I said deduction of types; this is drastically different from what dynamically typed languages do, and another thing is, it is done at compile time and not runtime. Many languages have this built in, but the implementation varies from one language to another. This might be confusing at the beginning, but it will become clearer with code examples. Let's jump into the Scala REPL for some experimentation.

Scala REPL

The Scala REPL is a powerful feature that makes it more straightforward and concise to write Scala code on the Scala shell. **REPL** stands for **Read-Eval-Print-Loop** also called **the Interactive Interpreter**. This means it is a program for:

1. Reading the expressions you type in.
2. Evaluating the expression in step 1 using the Scala compiler.
3. Printing out the result of the evaluation in step 2.
4. Waiting (looping) for you to enter further expressions.

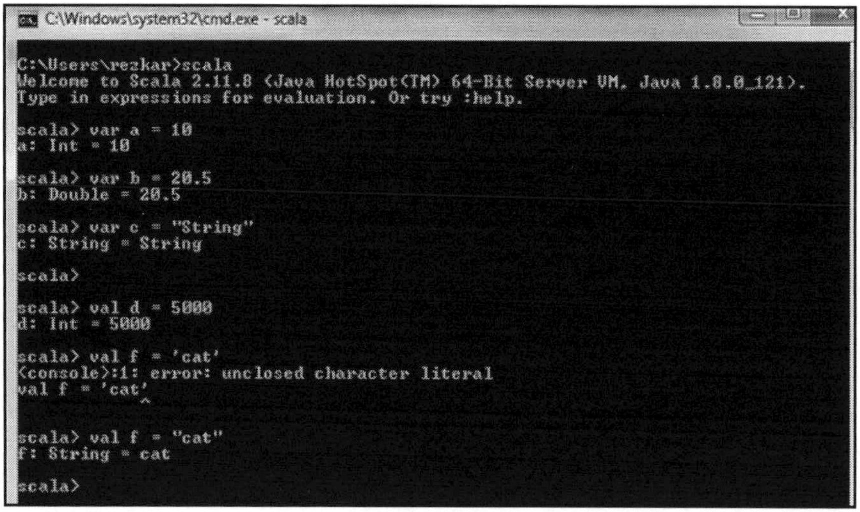

Figure 8: Scala REPL example 1

From the figure, it is evident that there is no magic, the variables are inferred automatically to the best types they deem fit at compile time. If you look even more carefully, when I tried to declare:

```
i:Int = "hello"
```

Then, the Scala shell throws an error saying the following:

```
<console>:11: error: type mismatch;
  found   : String("hello")
  required: Int
       val i:Int = "hello"
            ^
```

According to Odersky, *"Mapping a character to the character map over a RichString should again yield a RichString, as in the following interaction with the Scala REP"*. The preceding statement can be proved using the following line of code:

```
scala> "abc" map (x => (x + 1).toChar)
res0: String = bcd
```

However, if someone applies a method from `Char` to `Int` to a `String`, then what happens? In that case, Scala converts them, as a vector of integer also called immutable is a feature of Scala collection, as shown in *Figure 9*. We will look at the details on Scala collection API in `Chapter 4`, *Collections APIs*.

```
"abc" map (x => (x + 1))
res1: scala.collection.immutable.IndexedSeq[Int] = Vector(98, 99, 100)
```

Both static and instance methods of objects are also available. For example, if you declare x as a string `hello` and then try to access both the static and instance methods of objects x, they are available. In the Scala shell, type x then . and <tab> and then you will find the available methods:

```
scala> val x = "hello"
x: java.lang.String = hello
scala> x.re<tab>
reduce             reduceRight        replaceAll           reverse
reduceLeft         reduceRightOption  replaceAllLiterally
reverseIterator
reduceLeftOption   regionMatches      replaceFirst
reverseMap
reduceOption       replace            repr
scala>
```

Since this is all accomplished on the fly via reflection, even anonymous classes you've only just defined are equally accessible:

```
scala> val x = new AnyRef{def helloWord = "Hello, world!"}
x: AnyRef{def helloWord: String} = $anon$1@58065f0c
 scala> x.helloWord
    def helloWord: String
 scala> x.helloWord
 warning: there was one feature warning; re-run with -feature for
details
 res0: String = Hello, world!
```

The preceding two examples can be shown on the Scala shell, as follows:

```
scala> val i:Int = "hello"
<console>:11: error: type mismatch;
 found    : String("hello")
 required: Int
       val i:Int = "hello"
                   ^

scala> val x = "hello"
x: String = hello

scala> x.re
reduce              reduceRight          replaceAll            reverse
reduceLeft          reduceRightOption    replaceAllLiterally   reverseIterator
reduceLeftOption    regionMatches        replaceFirst          reverseMap
reduceOption        replace              repr

scala> val x = new AnyRef{def helloWord = "Hello, world!"}
x: AnyRef{def helloWord: String} = $anon$1@58065f0c

scala> x.helloWord
    def helloWord: String

scala> x.helloWord
warning: there was one feature warning; re-run with -feature for details
res0: String = Hello, world!

scala>
```

Figure 9: Scala REPL example 2

"So it turns out that map yields different types depending on what the result type of the passed function argument is!"

- Odersky

Nested functions

Why will you require a nested functions support in your programming language? Most of the time, we want to maintain our methods to be a few lines and avoid overly large functions. A typical solution for this in Java would be to define all these small functions on a class level, but any other method could easily refer and access them even though they are helper methods. The situation is different in Scala, so you can use define functions inside each other, and this way, prevent any external access to these functions:

```
def sum(vector: List[Int]): Int = {
  // Nested helper method (won't be accessed from outside this
function
  def helper(acc: Int, remaining: List[Int]): Int = remaining match {
```

```
    case Nil => acc
    case _   => helper(acc + remaining.head, remaining.tail)
  }
  // Call the nested method
  helper(0, vector)
}
```

We are not expecting you to understand these code snippets, which show the difference between Scala and Java.

Import statements

In Java, you can only import packages at the top of your code file, right after the packages statement. The situation is not the same in Scala; you can write your import statements almost anywhere inside your source file (for example, you can even write your import statements inside a class or a method). You just need to pay attention to the scope of your import statement, because it inherits the same scope of the members of your class or local variables inside your method. The _ (underscore) in Scala is used for wildcard imports, which is similar to the * (asterisk) that you would use in java:

```
// Import everything from the package math
import math._
```

You may also use these { } to indicate a set of imports from the same parent package, just in one line of code. In Java, you would use multiple lines of code to do so:

```
// Import math.sin and math.cos
import math.{sin, cos}
```

Unlike the Java, Scala does not have the concept of static imports. In other words, the concept of static doesn't exist in Scala. However, as a developer, obviously, you can import a member or more than one member of an object using a regular import statement. The preceding example already shows this, where we import the methods sin and cos from the package object named math. To demonstrate an example, the preceding code snippet can be defined from the Java programmer's perspective as follows:

```
import static java.lang.Math.sin;
import static java.lang.Math.cos;
```

Another beauty of Scala is that, in Scala, you can rename your imported packages as well. Alternatively, you can rename your imported packages to avoid the type conflicting with packages that have similar members. The following statement is valid in Scala:

```
// Import Scala.collection.mutable.Map as MutableMap
import Scala.collection.mutable.{Map => MutableMap}
```

Finally, you may want to exclude a member of packages for collisions or other purposes. For this, you can use a wildcard to do so:

```
// Import everything from math, but hide cos
import math.{cos => _, _}
```

Operators as methods

It's worth mentioning that Scala doesn't support the operator overloading. You might think that there are no operators at all in Scala.

An alternative syntax for calling a method taking a single parameter is the use of the infix syntax. The infix syntax provides you with a flavor just like you are applying an operator overloading, as like what you did in C++. For example:

```
val x = 45
val y = 75
```

In the following case, the + means a method in class Int. The following code is a non-conventional method calling syntax:

```
val add1 = x.+(y)
```

More formally, the same can be done using the infix syntax, as follows:

```
val add2 = x + y
```

Moreover, you can utilize the infix syntax. However, the method has only a single parameter, as follows:

```
val my_result = List(3, 6, 15, 34, 76) contains 5
```

There's one special case when using the infix syntax. That is, if the method name ends with a : (colon), then the invocation or call will be right associative. This means that the method is called on the right argument with the expression on the left as the argument, instead of the other way around. For example, the following is valid in Scala:

```
val my_list = List(3, 6, 15, 34, 76)
```

The preceding statement signifies that: `my_list.+:(5)` rather than `5.+:(my_list)` and more formally:

```
val my_result = 5 +: my_list
```

Now, let's look at the preceding examples on Scala REPL:

```
scala> val my_list = 5 +: List(3, 6, 15, 34, 76)
  my_list: List[Int] = List(5, 3, 6, 15, 34, 76)
scala> val my_result2 = 5+:my_list
  my_result2: List[Int] = List(5, 5, 3, 6, 15, 34, 76)
scala> println(my_result2)
  List(5, 5, 3, 6, 15, 34, 76)
scala>
```

In addition to the above, operators here are just methods, so that they can simply be overridden just like methods.

Methods and parameter lists

In Scala, a method can have multiple parameter lists or even no parameter list at all. On the other hand, in Java, a method always has one parameter list, with zero or more parameters. For example, in Scala, the following is the valid method definition (written in `currie notation`) where a method has two parameter lists:

```
def sum(x: Int)(y: Int) = x + y
```

The preceding method cannot be written as:

```
def sum(x: Int, y: Int) = x + y
```

A method, let's say `sum2`, can have no parameter list at all, as follows:

```
def sum2 = sum(2) _
```

Now, you can call the method `add2`, which returns a function taking one parameter. Then, it calls that function with the argument 5, as follows:

```
val result = add2(5)
```

Methods inside methods

Sometimes, you would like to make your applications, code modular by avoiding too long and complex methods. Scala provides you this facility to avoid your methods becoming overly large so that you can split them up into several smaller methods.

On the other hand, Java allows you only to have the methods defined at class level. For example, suppose you have the following method definition:

```
def main_method(xs: List[Int]): Int = {
  // This is the nested helper/auxiliary method
  def auxiliary_method(accu: Int, rest: List[Int]): Int = rest match {
    case Nil => accu
    case _   => auxiliary_method(accu + rest.head, rest.tail)
  }
}
```

Now, you can call the nested helper/auxiliary method as follows:

```
auxiliary_method(0, xs)
```

Considering the above, here's the complete code segment which is valid:

```
def main_method(xs: List[Int]): Int = {
  // This is the nested helper/auxiliary method
  def auxiliary_method(accu: Int, rest: List[Int]): Int = rest match {
    case Nil => accu
    case _   => auxiliary_method(accu + rest.head, rest.tail)
  }
   auxiliary_method(0, xs)
}
```

Constructor in Scala

One surprising thing about Scala is that the body of a Scala class is itself a constructor. However, Scala does so; in fact, in a more explicit way. After that, a new instance of that class is created and executed. Moreover, you can specify the arguments of the constructor in the class declaration line.

Consequently, the constructor arguments are accessible from all of the methods defined in that class. For example, the following class and constructor definition is valid in Scala:

```
class Hello(name: String) {
  // Statement executed as part of the constructor
  println("New instance with name: " + name)
  // Method which accesses the constructor argument
  def sayHello = println("Hello, " + name + "!")
}
```

The equivalent Java class would look like this:

```
public class Hello {
  private final String name;
  public Hello(String name) {
    System.out.println("New instance with name: " + name);
    this.name = name;
  }
  public void sayHello() {
    System.out.println("Hello, " + name + "!");
  }
}
```

Objects instead of static methods

As mentioned earlier, static does not exist in Scala. You cannot do static imports and neither can you cannot add static methods to classes. In Scala, when you define an object with the same name as the class and in the same source file, then the object is said to be the companion of that class. Functions that you define in this companion object of a class are like static methods of a class in Java:

```
class HelloCity(CityName: String) {
  def sayHelloToCity = println("Hello, " + CityName + "!")
}
```

This is how you can define a companion object for the class hello:

```
object HelloCity {
  // Factory method
  def apply(CityName: String) = new Hello(CityName)
}
```

The equivalent class in Java would look like this:

```
public class HelloCity {
  private final String CityName;
  public HelloCity(String CityName) {
    this.CityName = CityName;
  }
  public void sayHello() {
    System.out.println("Hello, " + CityName + "!");
  }
  public static HelloCity apply(String CityName) {
    return new Hello(CityName);
  }
}
```

So, lot's of verbose in this simple class, isn't there? The apply method in Scala is treated in a different way, such that you can find a special shortcut syntax to call it. This is the familiar way of calling the method:

```
val hello1 = Hello.apply("Dublin")
```

Here's the shortcut syntax that is equivalent to the one earlier:

```
val hello2 = Hello("Dublin")
```

Note that this only works if you used the apply method in your code because Scala treats methods that are named apply in this different way.

Traits

Scala provides a great functionality for you in order to extend and enrich your classes' behaviors. These traits are similar to the interface in which you define the function prototypes or signatures. So, with this, you can have mix-ins of functionality coming from different traits and, in this way, you enriched your classes' behavior. So, what's so good about traits in Scala? They enable the composition of classes from these traits, with traits being the building blocks. As always, let's look at in an example. This is how a conventional logging routine is set up in Java:

Note that, even though you can mix in any number of traits you want. Moreover, like Java, Scala does not have the support of multiple inheritances. However, in both Java and Scala, a subclass can only extend a single superclass. For example, in Java:

```
class SomeClass {
  //First, to have to log for a class, you must initialize it
  final static Logger log = LoggerFactory.getLogger(this.getClass());
```

```
    ...
    //For logging to be efficient, you must always check, if logging
level for current message is enabled
    //BAD, you will waste execution time if the log level is an error,
fatal, etc.
    log.debug("Some debug message");
    ...
    //GOOD, it saves execution time for something more useful
    if (log.isDebugEnabled()) { log.debug("Some debug message"); }
    //BUT looks clunky, and it's tiresome to write this construct every
time you want to log something.
  }
```

For a more detailed discussion, refer to this URL https://stackoverflow.com/
questions/963492/in-log4j-does-checking-isdebugenabled-before-logging-
improve-performance/963681#963681.

However, it's different with traits. It's very tiresome to always check for the log level
being enabled. It would be good, if you could write this routine once and reuse it
anywhere, in any class right away. Traits in Scala make this all possible. For example:

```
trait Logging {
  lazy val log = LoggerFactory.getLogger(this.getClass.getName)
  //Let's start with info level...
  ...
  //Debug level here...
  def debug() {
    if (log.isDebugEnabled) log.info(s"${msg}")
  }
  def debug(msg: => Any, throwable: => Throwable) {
    if (log.isDebugEnabled) log.info(s"${msg}", throwable)
  }
  ...
  //Repeat it for all log levels you want to use
}
```

If you look at the preceding code, you will see an example of using string starting
with s. This way, Scala offers the mechanism to create strings from your data called
String Interpolation.

String Interpolation, allows you to embed variable references directly in processed string literals. For example:

```
scala> val name = "John Breslin"
scala> println(s"Hello, $name") // Hello, John
Breslin.
```

Now, we can get an efficient logging routine in a more conventional style as a reusable block. To enable logging for any class, we just mix in our Logging trait! Fantastic! Now that's all it takes to add a logging feature to your class:

```
class SomeClass extends Logging {
  ...
  //With logging trait, no need for declaring a logger manually for
every class
  //And now, your logging routine is either efficient and doesn't
litter the code!

  log.debug("Some debug message")
  ...
}
```

It is even possible to mix-up multiple traits. For example, for the preceding trait (that is, Logging) you can keep extending in the following order:

```
trait Logging  {
  override def toString = "Logging "
}
class A extends Logging  {
  override def toString = "A->" + super.toString
}
trait B extends Logging  {
  override def toString = "B->" + super.toString
}
trait C extends Logging  {
  override def toString = "C->" + super.toString
}
class D extends A with B with C {
  override def toString = "D->" + super.toString
}
```

However, it is noted that a Scala class can extend multiple traits at once, but JVM classes can extend only one parent class.

Now, to invoke the above traits and classes, use `new D()` from Scala REPL, as shown in the following figure:

```
scala> trait Logging  { override def toString = "Logging " }
defined trait Logging

scala> class A extends Logging  { override def toString = "A->" + super.toString
}
defined class A

scala> trait B extends Logging  { override def toString = "B->" + super.toString
}
defined trait B

scala> trait C extends Logging  { override def toString = "C->" + super.toString
}
defined trait C

scala> class D extends A with B with C { override def toString = "D->" + super.t
oString }
defined class D

scala> new D()
res4: D = D->C->B->A->Logging

scala>
```

Figure 10: Mixing multiple traits

Everything has gone smoothly so far in this chapter. Now, let's move to a new section where we will discuss some topics for the beginner who wants to drive themselves into the realm of Scala programming.

Scala for the beginners

In this part, you will find that we assume that you have a basic understanding of any previous programming language. If Scala is your first entry into the coding world, then you will find a large set of materials and even courses online that explain Scala for beginners. As mentioned, there are lots of tutorials, videos, and courses out there.

There is a whole Specialization, which contains this course, on Coursera: `https://www.coursera.org/specializations/scala`. Taught by the creator of Scala, Martin Odersky, this online class takes a somewhat academic approach to teaching the fundamentals of functional programming. You will learn a lot about Scala by solving the programming assignments. Moreover, this specialization includes a course on Apache Spark. Furthermore, Kojo (`http://www. kogics.net/sf:kojo`) is an interactive learning environment that uses Scala programming to explore and play with math, art, music, animations, and games.

Your first line of code

As a first example, we will use the pretty common `Hello, world!` program in order to show you how to use Scala and its tools without knowing much about it. Let's open your favorite editor (this example runs on Windows 7, but can be run similarly on Ubuntu or macOS), say Notepad++, and type the following lines of code:

```scala
object HelloWorld {
  def main(args: Array[String]){
    println("Hello, world!")
  }
}
```

Now, save the code with a name, say `HelloWorld.scala`, as shown in the following figure:

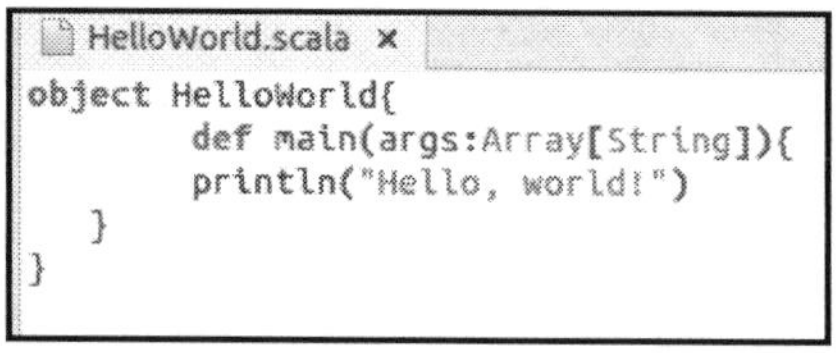

```
 HelloWorld.scala  ×
object HelloWorld{
        def main(args:Array[String]){
        println("Hello, world!")
    }
}
```

Figure 11: Saving your first Scala source code using Notepad++

Let's compile the source file as follows:

```
C:\>scalac HelloWorld.scala
 C:\>scala HelloWorld
 Hello, world!
 C:\>
```

I'm the hello world program, explain me well!

The program should be familiar to anyone who has some programming of experience. It has a main method which prints the string `Hello, world!` to your console. Next, to see how we defined the `main` function, we used the `def main()` strange syntax to define it. `def` is a Scala keyword to declare/define a method, and we will be covering more about methods and different ways of writing them in the next chapter. So, we have an `Array[String]` as an argument for this method, which is an array of strings that can be used for initial configurations of your program, and omit is valid. Then, we use the common `println()` method, which takes a string (or formatted one) and prints it to the console. A simple hello world has opened up many topics to learn; three in particular:

● Methods (covered in a later chapter)
● Objects and classes (covered in a later chapter)
● Type inference - the reason why Scala is a statically typed language - explained earlier

Run Scala interactively!

The `scala` command starts the interactive shell for you, where you can interpret Scala expressions interactively:

```
> scala
Welcome to Scala 2.11.8 (Java HotSpot(TM) 64-Bit Server VM, Java
1.8.0_121).
Type in expressions for evaluation. Or try :help.
scala>
scala> object HelloWorld {
     |    def main(args: Array[String]){
     |      println("Hello, world!")
     |    }
     | }
defined object HelloWorld
scala> HelloWorld.main(Array())
Hello, world!
scala>
```

The shortcut `:q` stands for the internal shell command `:quit`, used to exit the interpreter.

Compile it!

The scalac command, which is similar to javac command, compiles one or more Scala source files and generates a bytecode as output, which then can be executed on any Java Virtual Machine. To compile your hello world object, use the following:

```
> scalac HelloWorld.scala
```

By default, scalac generates the class files into the current working directory. You may specify a different output directory using the –d option:

```
> scalac –d classes HelloWorld.scala
```

However, note that the directory called classes must be created before executing this command.

Execute it with Scala command

The scala command executes the bytecode that is generated by the interpreter:

```
$ scala HelloWorld
```

Scala allows us to specify command options, such as the –classpath (alias –cp) option:

```
$ scala –cp classes HelloWorld
```

Before using the scala command to execute your source file(s), you should have a main method that acts as an entry point for your application. Otherwise, you should have an Object that extends Trait Scala.App, then all the code inside this object will be executed by the command. The following is the same Hello, world! example, but using the App trait:

```
#!/usr/bin/env Scala
object HelloWorld extends App {
  println("Hello, world!")
}
HelloWorld.main(args)
```

The preceding script can be run directly from the command shell:

```
./script.sh
```

Note: we assume here that the file `script.sh` has the execute permission:

```
$ sudo chmod +x script.sh
```

Then, the search path for the `scala` command is specified in the `$PATH` environment variable.

Summary

Throughout this chapter, you have learned the basics of the Scala programming language, its features, and available editor. We have also briefly discussed Scala and its syntax. We demonstrated the installation and setting up guidelines for beginners who are new to Scala programming. Later in the chapter, you learned how to write, compile, and execute a sample Scala code. Moreover, a comparative discussion about Scala and Java provided for those who are from a Java background. Here's a short comparison between Scala and Python:

Scala is statically typed, but Python is dynamically typed. Scala (mostly) embraces the functional programming paradigm, while Python doesn't. Python has a unique syntax that lacks most of the parentheses, while Scala (almost) always requires them. In Scala, almost everything is an expression; while this isn't true in Python. However, there are a few points on the upside that are seemingly convoluted. The type complexity is mostly optional. Secondly, according to the documentation provided by https://stackoverflow.com/questions/1065720/what-is-the-purpose-of-scala-programming-language/5828684#5828684, *Scala compiler is like free testing and documentation as cyclomatic complexity and lines of code escalate. When aptly implemented Scala can perform otherwise all but impossible operations behind consistent and coherent APIs.*

In next the chapter, we will discuss how to improve our experience on the basics to know how Scala implements the object oriented paradigm to allow building modular software systems.

2
Object-Oriented Scala

"The object-oriented model makes it easy to build up programs by accretion. What this often means, in practice, is that it provides a structured way to write spaghetti code."

- Paul Graham

In the previous chapter, we looked at how to get programming started with Scala. Well, if you're writing the procedural program that we followed in the previous chapter, you can enforce the code reusability by creating procedures or functions. However, if you continue working, consequently, your program gets longer, bigger, and more complex. At a certain point, you will not even have any other more simple way to organize the entire code before production.

On the contrary, the **object-oriented programming (OOP)** paradigm provides a whole new layer of abstraction. You can then modularize your code through defining OOP entities such as classes with related properties and methods. You can even define the relationship between those entities by utilizing inheritance or an interface. You can also group similar classes holding similar functionality together, as a helper class maybe; therefore, making your project suddenly feels more spacious and extensible. In short, the greatest strengths of OOP languages are discoverability, modularity, and extensibility.

Considering the preceding features of OOP languages, in this chapter, we will discuss the basic object-oriented features in Scala. In a nutshell, the following topics will be covered in this chapter:

- Variables in Scala
- Methods, classes, and objects in Scala
- Packages and package objects
- Traits and trait linearization
- Java Interoperability

Then, we will discuss pattern matching, which is a feature that comes from functional programming concepts. Moreover, we will discuss some built-in concepts in Scala, such as implicit and generics. Finally, we will discuss some widely used build tools that are needed for building our Scala applications into jars.

Variables in Scala

Before entering into the depth of OOP features, first, we need to know details about the different types of variables and data types in Scala. To declare a variable in Scala, you need to use `var` or `val` keywords. The formal syntax of declaring a variable in Scala is as follows:

```
val or var VariableName : DataType = Initial_Value
```

For example, let's see how can we declare two variables whose data types are explicitly specified as follows:

```
var myVar : Int = 50
val myVal : String = "Hello World! I've started learning Scala."
```

You can even just declare a variable without specifying the `DataType`. For example, let's see how to declare a variable using `val` or `var`, as follows:

```
var myVar = 50
val myVal = "Hello World! I've started learning Scala."
```

There are two types of variables in Scala: mutable and immutable that can be defined as follows:

- **Mutable:** The ones whose values you can change later
- **Immutable:** The ones whose values you cannot change once they have been set

In general, for declaring a mutable variable, a `var` keyword is used. On the other hand, for specifying an immutable variable, a `val` keyword is used. To show an example of using the mutable and immutable variables, let's consider the following code segment:

```
package com.chapter3.OOP
object VariablesDemo {
  def main(args: Array[String]) {
    var myVar : Int = 50
    valmyVal : String = "Hello World! I've started learning Scala."
```

```
        myVar = 90
        myVal = "Hello world!"
        println(myVar)
        println(myVal)
    }
}
```

The preceding code works fine until `myVar = 90`, since `myVar` is a mutable variable. However, if you try to change the value of the immutable variable (that is, `myVal`), as shown earlier, your IDE will show a compilation error saying reassignment to `val`, as follows:

```
S HamOrSpamDemo.scala    M DeepLearningwithH2O/po...    S AirlinesWithWeatherDem...    S
 1  package com.chapter3.OOP
 2
 3⊖ object VariablesDemo {
 4      def main(args: Array[String]) {
 5          var myVar : Int = 50;
 6          val myVal : String = "Hello World! I've started learning Scala.";
 7
 8          myVar = 90;
 9     ┌─────────────────────────────────────────────┐
10     │ Multiple markers at this line:               │
11     │                                              │
12     │    ▪ reassignment to val                     │
13     │    ▪ reassignment to val                     │
14     │  }                                           │
15  } └─────────────────────────────────────────────┘
```

Figure 1: Reassignment of immutable variables is not allowed in Scala variable scope

Don't worry looking at the preceding code with the object and method! We will discuss classes, methods, and objects later in this chapter, then things will become more clear.

In Scala variables, we can have three different scopes, depending on the place where you have declared them:

- **Fields:** These are variables that belong to an instance of a class of your Scala code. The fields are, therefore, accessible from inside every method in the object. However, depending on the access modifiers, fields can be accessible to instances of the other classes.

 As discussed earlier, object fields can be mutable or they can be immutable (based on the declaration types using either `var` or `val`). But, they can't be both at the same time.

- **Method arguments:** These are variables, and when the method is called, these can be used to pass the value inside a method. Method parameters are accessible only from inside the method. However, the objects being passed in may be accessible from the outside.

 It is to be noted that method parameters/arguments are always immutable, no matter what is/are the keyword(s) specified.

- **Local variables:** These variables are declared inside a method and are accessible from the inside the method itself. However, the calling code can access the returned value.

Reference versus value immutability

According to the section earlier, `val` is used to declare immutable variables, so can we change the values of these variables? Will it be similar to the final keyword in Java? To help us understand more about this, we will use the following code snippet:

```
scala> var testVar = 10
testVar: Int = 10

scala> testVar = testVar + 10
testVar: Int = 20

scala> val testVal = 6
testVal: Int = 6

scala> testVal = testVal + 10
<console>:12: error: reassignment to val
        testVal = testVal + 10
                ^

scala>
```

If you run the preceding code, an error at compilation time will be noticed, which will tell you that you are trying to reassign to a `val` variable. In general, mutable variables bring a performance advantage. The reason is that this is closer to how the computer behaves and because introducing immutable values forces the computer to create a whole new instance of an object whenever a change (no matter how small) to a particular instance is required

Data types in Scala

As mentioned, Scala is a JVM language, so it shares lots in common with Java. One of these commonalities is the data types; Scala shares the same data types with Java. In short, Scala has all the same data types as Java, with the same memory footprint and precision. As mentioned in `Chapter 1`, *Introduction to Scala*, objects are almost everywhere in Scala. and all data types are objects and you can call methods in them as follows:

Sr.No	Data Type and Description
1	**Byte**: 8 bit signed value. Ranges from -128 to 127
2	**Short**: 16 bit signed value. Ranges -32768 to 32767
3	**Int**: 32 bit signed value. Ranges -2147483648 to 2147483647
4	**Long**: 64 bit signed value. -9223372036854775808 to 9223372036854775807
5	**Float**: 32 bit IEEE 754 single-precision float
6	**Double**: 64 bit IEEE 754 double-precision float
7	**Char**: 16 bit unsigned Unicode character. Range from U+0000 to U+FFFF
8	**String**: A sequence of Chars
9	**Boolean**: Either the literal `true` or the literal `false`
10	**Unit**: Corresponds to no value
11	**Null**: Null or empty reference
12	**Nothing**: The subtype of every other type includes no values
13	**Any**: The supertype of any type any object is of type *Any*
14	**AnyRef**: The supertype of any reference type

Table 1: Scala data types. description. and range

All the data types listed in the preceding table are objects. However, note that there are no primitive types, as in Java. This means that you can call methods on an `Int`, `Long`, and so on.

```
val myVal = 20
//use println method to print it to the console you will also notice
that if will be inferred as Int
println(myVal + 10)
val myVal = 40
println(myVal * "test")
```

Now, you can start playing around with these variables. Let's get some ideas on how to initialize a variable and work on the type annotations.

Variable initialization

In Scala, it's a good practice to initialize the variables once declared. However, it is to be noted that uninitialized variables aren't necessarily nulls (consider types like `Int`, `Long`, `Double`, `Char`, and so on), and initialized variables aren't necessarily non-null (for example, `val s: String = null`). The actual reasons are that:

- In Scala, types are inferred from the assigned value. This means that a value must be assigned for the compiler to infer the type (how should the compiler consider this code: `val a`? Since a value isn't given, the compiler can't infer the type since it can't infer the type, it wouldn't know how to initialize it).
- In Scala, most of the time, you'll use `val`. Since these are immutable, you wouldn't be able to declare them and then initialize them afterward.

Although, Scala language requires you to initialize your instance variable before using it, Scala does not provide a default value for your variable. Instead, you have to set up its value manually using the wildcard underscore, which acts like a default value, as follows:

```scala
var name:String = _
```

Instead of using the names, such as `val1`, `val2` and so on, you can define your own names:

```scala
scala> val result = 6 * 5 + 8
result: Int = 38
```

You can use these names in subsequent expressions, as follows:

```scala
scala> 0.5 * result
res0: Double = 19.0
```

Type annotations

If you use a `val` or `var` keyword to declare a variable, its data type will be inferred automatically according to the value that you assigned to this variable. You also have the luxury of explicitly stating the data type of the variable at declaration time.

```
val myVal : Integer = 10
```

Now, let's look at some other aspects that will be needed while working with variables and data types in Scala. We will see how to work with type ascription and `lazy` variables.

Type ascription

Type ascription is used to tell the compiler what types you expect out of an expression, from all possible valid types. Consequently, a type is valid if it respects existing constraints, such as variance and type declarations, and it is either one of the types the expression it applies to "is a," or there's a conversion that applies in scope. So, technically, `java.lang.String` extends `java.lang.Object`, therefore any `String` is also an `Object`. For example:

```
scala> val s = "Ahmed Shadman"
s: String = Ahmed Shadman

scala> val p = s:Object
p: Object = Ahmed Shadman

scala>
```

Lazy val

The main characteristic of a `lazy val` is that the bound expression is not evaluated immediately, but once on the first access. Here's where the main difference between `val` and `lazy val` lies. When the initial access happens, the expression is evaluated and the result is bound to the identifier, the `lazy val`. On subsequent access, no further evaluation occurs, instead, the stored result is returned immediately. Let's see an interesting example:

```
scala> lazy val num = 1 / 0
num: Int = <lazy>
```

If you look at the preceding code in Scala REPL, you will notice that the code runs very well without throwing any errors, even though you divided an integer with 0! Let's see a better example:

```scala
scala> val x = {println("x") 20}
x
x: Int = 20

scala> x
res1: Int = 20
scala>
```

This works and, later on, you can access the value of variable x when required. These are just a few examples of using lazy val concepts. Interested readers should access this page for more details: https://blog.codecentric.de/en/2016/02/lazy-vals-scala-look-hood/.

Methods, classes, and objects in Scala

In the previous section, we saw how to work with Scala variables, different data types and their mutability and immutability, along with their usages scopes. However, in this section, to get the real flavor of the OOP concept, we are going to deal with methods, objects, and classes. These three features of Scala will help us understand the object-oriented nature of Scala and its features.

Methods in Scala

In this part, we are going to talk about methods in Scala. As you dive into Scala, you'll find that there are lots of ways to define methods in Scala. We will demonstrate them in some of these ways:

```scala
def min(x1:Int, x2:Int) : Int = {
  if (x1 < x2) x1 else x2
}
```

The preceding declaration of the method takes two variables and returns the smallest among them. In Scala, all the methods must start with the def keyword, which is then followed by a name for this method. Optionally, you can decide not to pass any parameters to the method or even decide not to return anything. You're probably wondering how the smallest value is returned, but we will get to this later. Also, in Scala, you can define methods without curly braces:

```
def min(x1:Int, x2:Int):Int= if (x1 < x2) x1 else x2
```

If your method has a small body, you can declare your method like this. Otherwise, it's preferred to use the curly braces in order to avoid confusion. As mentioned earlier, you can pass no parameters to the method if needed:

```
def getPiValue(): Double = 3.14159
```

A method with or without parentheses signals the absence or presence of a side effect. Moreover, it has a deep connection with the uniform access principle. Thus, you can also avoid the braces as follows:

```
def getValueOfPi : Double = 3.14159
```

There are also some methods which return the value by explicitly mentioning the return types. For example:

```
def sayHello(person :String) = "Hello " + person + "!"
```

It should be mentioned that the preceding code works due to the Scala compiler, which is able to infer the return type, just as with values and variables.

This will return `Hello` concatenated with the passed person name. For example:

```
scala> def sayHello(person :String) = "Hello " + person + "!"
sayHello: (person: String)String

scala> sayHello("Asif")
res2: String = Hello Asif!

scala>
```

The return in Scala

Before learning how a Scala method returns a value, let's recap the structure of a method in Scala:

```
def functionName ([list of parameters]) : [return type] = {
  function body
  value_to_return
}
```

For the preceding syntax, the return type could be any valid Scala data type and a list of parameters will be a list of variables separated by a comma and a list of parameters and return type is optional. Now, let's define a method that adds two positive integers and returns the result, which is also an integer value:

```
scala> def addInt( x:Int, y:Int ) : Int = {
     |           var sum:Int = 0
     |           sum = x + y
     |           sum
     |      }
addInt: (x: Int, y: Int)Int

scala> addInt(20, 34)
res3: Int = 54

scala>
```

If you now call the preceding method from the `main()` method with the real values, such as `addInt(10, 30)`, the method will return an integer value sum, which is equal to `40`. As using the keyword `return` is optional, the Scala compiler is designed such that the last assignment will be returned with the absence of the `return` keyword. As in this situation, the greater value will be returned:

```
scala> def max(x1 : Int , x2: Int)  = {
     |      if (x1>x2) x1 else x2
     | }
max: (x1: Int, x2: Int)Int

scala> max(12, 27)
res4: Int = 27

scala>
```

Well done! We have seen how to use variables and how to declare a method in Scala REPL. Now, its time to see how to encapsulate them inside Scala methods and classes. The next section discusses Scala objects.

Classes in Scala

Classes are considered as a blueprint and then you instantiate this class in order to create something that will actually be represented in memory. They can contain methods, values, variables, types, objects, traits, and classes which are collectively called **members**. Let's demonstrate this with the following example:

```
class Animal {
  var animalName = null
  var animalAge = -1
  def setAnimalName (animalName:String)  {
    this.animalName = animalName
  }
  def setAnaimalAge (animalAge:Int) {
    this.animalAge = animalAge
  }
  def getAnimalName () : String = {
    animalName
  }
  def getAnimalAge () : Int = {
    animalAge
  }
}
```

We have two variables `animalName` and `animalAge` with their setters and getters. Now, how do we use them to solve our purpose? Here come the usages of Scala objects. Now, we will discuss Scala objects, then we will trace back to our next discussion.

Objects in Scala

An **object** in Scala has a slightly different meaning than the traditional OOP one, and this difference should be explained. In particular, in OOP, an object is an instance of a class, while in Scala, anything that is declared as an object cannot be instantiated! The `object` is a keyword in Scala. The basic syntax for declaring an object in Scala is as follows:

```
object <identifier> [extends <identifier>] [{ fields, methods, and
classes }]
```

To understand the preceding syntax, let's revisit the hello world program:

```
object HelloWorld {
  def main(args : Array[String]){
    println("Hello world!")
  }
}
```

This hello world example is pretty similar to the Java ones. The only big difference is that the main method is not inside a class, but instead it's inside an object. In Scala, the keyword object can mean two different things:

- As in OOP, an object can represent an instance of a class
- A keyword for depicting a very different type of instance object called **Singleton**

Singleton and companion objects

In this subsection, we will see a comparative analysis between the singleton object in Scala and Java. The idea beneath the singleton pattern is to have an implementation that makes sure that only a single instance of a class can exist. Here's an example of the Singleton pattern in Java:

```
public class DBConnection {
  private static DBConnection dbInstance;
  private DBConnection() {
  }
  public static DBConnection getInstance() {
    if (dbInstance == null) {
      dbInstance = new DBConnection();
    }
    return dbInstance;
  }
}
```

The Scala object does a similar thing, and it's well taken care of by the compiler. Since there will be only one instance, there is no way for object creation here:

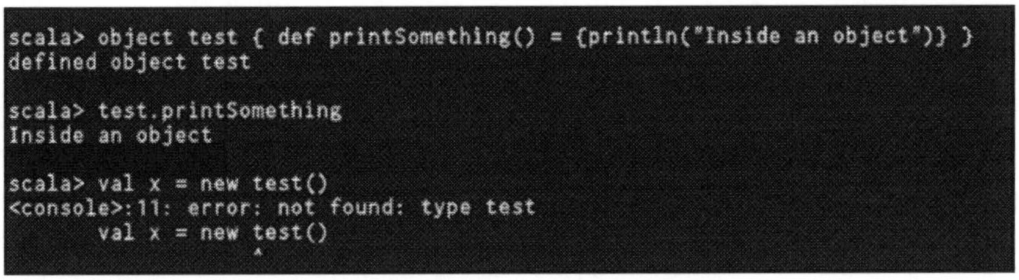

```
scala> object test { def printSomething() = {println("Inside an object")} }
defined object test

scala> test.printSomething
Inside an object

scala> val x = new test()
<console>:11: error: not found: type test
       val x = new test()
                   ^
```

Figure 3: Object creation in Scala

Companion objects

When a `singleton object` is named the same as a class, it is called a `companion object`. A companion object must be defined inside the same source file as the class. Let's demonstrate this with the example here:

```
class Animal {
  var animalName:String  = "notset"
  def setAnimalName(name: String) {
    animalName = name
  }
  def getAnimalName: String = {
    animalName
  }
  def isAnimalNameSet: Boolean = {
    if (getAnimalName == "notset") false else true
  }
}
```

The following is the way that you will call methods through the companion object (preferably with the same name - that is, `Animal`):

```
object Animal{
  def main(args: Array[String]): Unit= {
    val obj: Animal = new Animal
    var flag:Boolean  = false
    obj.setAnimalName("dog")
    flag = obj.isAnimalNameSet
    println(flag)  // prints true
    obj.setAnimalName("notset")
    flag = obj.isAnimalNameSet
    println(flag)   // prints false
  }
}
```

A Java equivalent would be very similar, as follows:

```java
public class Animal {
  public String animalName = "null";
  public void setAnimalName(String animalName) {
    this.animalName = animalName;
  }
  public String getAnimalName() {
    return animalName;
  }
  public boolean isAnimalNameSet() {
    if (getAnimalName() == "notset") {
      return false;
    } else {
      return true;
    }
  }

  public static void main(String[] args) {
    Animal obj = new Animal();
    boolean flag = false;
    obj.setAnimalName("dog");
    flag = obj.isAnimalNameSet();
    System.out.println(flag);
    obj.setAnimalName("notset");
    flag = obj.isAnimalNameSet();
    System.out.println(flag);
  }
}
```

Well done! So far, we have seen how to work with Scala objects and classes. However, working with the method for implementing and solving your data analytics problem is even more important. Thus, we will now see how to work with Scala methods in brief.

```scala
object RunAnimalExample {
  val animalObj = new Animal
  println(animalObj.getAnimalName) //prints the initial name
  println(animalObj.getAnimalAge) //prints the initial age
  // Now try setting the values of animal name and age as follows:
  animalObj.setAnimalName("dog") //setting animal name
  animalObj.setAnaimalAge(10) //seting animal age
  println(animalObj.getAnimalName) //prints the new name of the animal
  println(animalObj.getAnimalAge) //Prints the new age of the animal
}
```

The output is as follows:

```
notset
-1
dog
10
```

Now, let's have a brief overview on the accessibility and the visibility of the Scala classes in the next section.

Comparing and contrasting: val and final

Just like Java, the final keyword also exists in Scala, which works somehow similar to the val keyword. In order to differentiate between the val and final keywords in Scala, let's declare a simple animal class, as follows:

```
class Animal {
   val age = 2
}
```

As mentioned in Chapter 1, *Introduction to Scala*, while listing Scala features, Scala can override variables which don't exist in Java:

```
class Cat extends Animal{
   override val age = 3
   def printAge ={
     println(age)
   }
}
```

Now, before going deeper, a quick discussion on the keyword extends is a mandate. Refer to the following information box for details.

Using Scala, classes can be extensible. A subclass mechanism using the extends keyword makes it possible to *specialize* a class by inheriting all members of a given *superclass* and defining additional class members. Let's look at an example, as follows:

```
class Coordinate(xc: Int, yc: Int) {
val x: Int = xc
val y: Int = yc
def move(dx: Int, dy: Int): Coordinate = new
Coordinate(x + dx, y + dy)
}
class ColorCoordinate(u: Int, v: Int, c: String)
extends Coordinate(u, v) {
val color: String = c
def compareWith(pt: ColorCoordinate): Boolean = (pt.x
== x) && (pt.y == y) && (pt.color == color)
override def move(dx: Int, dy: Int): ColorCoordinate
= new ColorCoordinate(x + dy, y + dy, color)
}
```

However, if we declared the age variable as final in the Animal class, then the Cat class will not be able to override it, and it will give the following error. For this Animal example, you should have learned when to use the final keyword. Let's see an example of this:

```
scala> class Animal {
     |      final val age = 3
     | }
defined class Animal
scala> class Cat extends Animal {
     |      override val age = 5
     | }
<console>:13: error: overriding value age in class Animal of type
Int(3)
 value age cannot override final member
         override val age = 5
                  ^
scala>
```

Well done! To achieve the best encapsulation - also called information hiding - you should always declare methods with the least visibility that works. In the next subsection, we will learn how the access and visibility of classes, companion objects, packages, subclasses, and projects work.

Access and visibility

In this subsection, we will try to understand the access and visibility of Scala variables and different data types in the OOP paradigm. Let's have a look at access modifiers in Scala. A similar one for Scala:

Modifier	Class	Companion Object	Package	Subclass	Project
Default/No modifier	Yes	Yes	Yes	Yes	Yes
Protected	Yes	Yes	Yes	No	No
Private	Yes	Yes	No	No	No

Public members: Unlike a private and protected member, it is not required to specify the public keyword for public members. There is no explicit modifier for public members. Such members can be accessed from anywhere. For example:

```
class OuterClass { //Outer class
  class InnerClass {
    def printName() { println("My name is Asif Karim!") }
    class InnerMost { //Inner class
      printName() // OK
    }
  }
  (new InnerClass).printName() // OK because now printName() is public
}
```

Private members: A private member is visible only inside the class or object that contains the member definition. Let's see an example, as follows:

```
package MyPackage {
  class SuperClass {
    private def printName() { println("Hello world, my name is Asif
Karim!") }
  }
  class SubClass extends SuperClass {
    printName() //ERROR
  }
  class SubsubClass {
    (new SuperClass).printName() // Error: printName is not accessible
  }
}
```

Protected members: A protected member is only accessible from subclasses of the class in which the member is defined. Let's see an example, as follows:

```
package MyPackage {
  class SuperClass {
    protected def printName() { println("Hello world, my name is Asif
                                        Karim!") }
  }
  class SubClass extends SuperClass {
    printName()   //OK
  }
  class SubsubClass {
    (new SuperClass).printName() // ERROR: printName is not accessible
  }
}
```

Access modifiers in Scala can be augmented with qualifiers. A modifier of the form `private[X]` or `protected[X]` means that access is private or protected up to X, where X designates an enclosing package, class, or singleton object. Let's see an example:

```
package Country {
  package Professional {
    class Executive {
      private[Professional] var jobTitle = "Big Data Engineer"
      private[Country] var friend = "Saroar Zahan"
      protected[this] var secret = "Age"

      def getInfo(another : Executive) {
        println(another.jobTitle)
        println(another.friend)
        println(another.secret) //ERROR
        println(this.secret) // OK
      }
    }
  }
}
```

Here's a short note on the preceding code segment:

- Variable `jboTitle` will be accessible to any class within the enclosing package `Professional`
- Variable `friend` will be accessible to any class within the enclosing package `Country`
- Variable `secret` will be accessible only to the implicit object within instance methods (this) only

If you look at the preceding examples, we used the keyword `package`. However, we have not discussed this so far. But don't worry there will be a dedicated section later in this chapter. The constructor is a strong feature for any objected-oriented programming language. Scala is not an exception. Now, let's have a short overview of the constructor.

Constructors

The concept and the usage of constructors in Scala are a little different than what they are in C# or Java. There are two types of constructors in Scala - primary and auxiliary constructors. The primary constructor is the class's body, and it's parameter list appears right after the class name.

For example, the following code segment describes the way to use the primary constructor in Scala:

```
class Animal (animalName:String, animalAge:Int) {
  def getAnimalName () : String = {
    animalName
  }
  def getAnimalAge () : Int = {
    animalAge
  }
}
```

Now, to use the preceding constructor, this implementation is similar to the previous one, except there are no setters and getters. Instead, we can get the animal name and age, as here:

```
object RunAnimalExample extends App{
  val animalObj = new animal("Cat",-1)
  println(animalObj.getAnimalName)
  println(animalObj.getAnimalAge)
}
```

Parameters are given in the class definition time to represent constructors. If we declare a constructor, then we cannot create a class without providing the default values of the parameters that are specified in the constructor. Moreover, Scala allows the instantiation of an object without providing the necessary parameters to its constructor: this happens when all constructor arguments have a default value defined.

Although there is a constraint for using the auxiliary constructors, we are free to add as many additional auxiliary constructors as we want. An auxiliary constructor must, on the first line of its body, call either another auxiliary constructor that has been declared before it, or the primary constructor. To obey this rule, each auxiliary constructor will, either directly or indirectly, end up invoking the primary constructor.

For example, the following code segment demonstrates the use of the auxiliary constructor in Scala:

```
class Hello(primaryMessage: String, secondaryMessage: String) {
  def this(primaryMessage: String) = this(primaryMessage, "")
  // auxilary constructor
  def sayHello() = println(primaryMessage + secondaryMessage)
}
object Constructors {
  def main(args: Array[String]): Unit = {
    val hello = new Hello("Hello world!", " I'm in a trouble,
                          please help me out.")
    hello.sayHello()
  }
}
```

In the earlier setting, we included a secondary (that is, 2nd) message in the primary constructor. The primary constructor will instantiate a new `Hello` object. Method `sayHello()` will print the concatenated message.

 Auxiliary constructors: In Scala, defining one or more auxiliary constructors for a Scala class gives the consumers of the class different ways to create object instances. Define the auxiliary constructors as methods in the class with the name this. You can define multiple auxiliary constructors, but they must have different signatures (parameter lists). Also, each constructor must call one of the previously defined constructors.

Now let's peep into another important but relatively new concept in Scala, called **traits**. We will discuss this in the next section.

Traits in Scala

One of the new features in Scala is a trait, which is very similar to the notion of an interface in Java, except that it can also contain concrete methods. Although, Java 8 already has support for this.

On the other hand, traits are one of the new concepts in Scala. But the feature already exists in OOP. So, they look like abstract classes, except that they don't have constructors.

A trait syntax

You need to use the `trait` keyword in order to declare a trait and it should be followed by the trait name and body:

```
trait Animal {
  val age : Int
  val gender : String
  val origin : String
}
```

Extending traits

In order to extend traits or classes, you need to use the `extend` keyword. Traits cannot be instantiated because it may contain unimplemented methods. So, it's necessary to implement the abstract members in the trait:

```
trait Cat extends Animal{ }
```

A value class is not allowed to extend traits. To permit value classes to extend traits, universal traits are introduced, which extends for `Any`. For example, suppose that we have the following trait defined:

```
trait EqualityChecking {
  def isEqual(x: Any): Boolean
  def isNotEqual(x: Any): Boolean = !isEqual(x)
}
```

Now, to extend the preceding trait in Scala using the universal trait, we follow the following code segment:

```
trait EqualityPrinter extends Any {
   def print(): Unit = println(this)
}
```

So, what is the difference between an abstract class and the traits in Scala? As you have seen, an abstract class can have constructor parameters, type parameters, and multiple parameters. However, a trait in Scala can have only type parameters.

 A trait is fully interoperable if, and only if, it does not contain any implementation code. Furthermore, Scala traits are fully interoperable with Java interfaces in Scala 2.12. Because Java 8 allows method implementations in its interfaces, too.

There might be other cases for traits as well, for example, an abstract class can extend a trait or, if needed, any normal class (including the case classes) can extend an existing trait. For example, an abstract class can also extend traits:

```
abstract class Cat extends Animal { }
```

Lastly, a normal Scala class also can extend a Scala trait. Since classes are concrete, (that is, instances can be created), the abstract members of the trait should be implemented. In the next section, we will discuss the Java interoperability of Scala codes. Now let's peep into another important concept in every OOP, called **abstract classes**. We will discuss this in the next section.

Abstract classes

An abstract class in Scala can have constructor parameters as well as type parameters. An abstract class in Scala is fully interoperable with Java. In other words, it is possible to call them from Java code without any intermediate wrappers.

So, what is the difference between an abstract class and the traits in Scala? As you have seen, an abstract class can have constructor parameters, type parameters, and multiple parameters. However, a trait in Scala can have only type parameters. The following is a simple example of an abstract class:

```
abstract class Animal(animalName:String = "notset") {
   //Method with definition/return type
   def getAnimalAge
   //Method with no definition with String return type
   def getAnimalGender : String
```

```
    //Explicit way of saying that no implementation is present
    def getAnimalOrigin () : String {}
    //Method with its functionality implemented
    //Need not be implemented by subclasses, can be overridden if
  required
    def getAnimalName : String = {
      animalName
    }
  }
```

In order to extend this class by another one, we need to implement the unimplemented methods earlier getAnimalAge, getAnimalGender, and getAnimalOrigin. For getAnimalName, we can override it or not, since its implementation is already there.

Abstract classes and the override keyword

If you want to override a concrete method from the superclass, the override modifier is necessary. However, if you are implementing an abstract method, it is not strictly necessary to add the override modifier. Scala uses the override keyword to override a method from a parent class. For example, suppose you have the following abstract class and a method printContents() to print your message on the console:

```
abstract class MyWriter {
  var message: String = "null"
  def setMessage(message: String):Unit
  def printMessage():Unit
}
```

Now, add a concrete implementation of the preceding abstract class to print the contents on the console as follows:

```
class ConsolePrinter extends MyWriter {
  def setMessage(contents: String):Unit= {
    this.message = contents
  }

  def printMessage():Unit= {
    println(message)
  }
}
```

Secondly, if you want to create a trait to modify the behavior of the preceding concrete class, as follows:

```
trait lowerCase extends MyWriter {
  abstract override def setMessage(contents: String) = printMessage()
}
```

If you look at the preceding code segment carefully, you will find two modifiers (that is, abstract and override). Now, with the preceding setting, you can do the following to use the preceding class:

```
val printer:ConsolePrinter = new ConsolePrinter()
printer.setMessage("Hello! world!")
printer.printMessage()
```

In summary, we can add an override keyword in front of the method to work as expected.

Case classes in Scala

A **case** class is an instantiable class that includes several automatically generated methods. It also includes an automatically generated companion object with its own automatically generated methods. The basic syntax of a case class in Scala is as follows:

```
case class <identifier> ([var] <identifier>: <type>[, ... ]) [extends
<identifier>(<input parameters>)] [{ fields and methods }]
```

A case class can be pattern matched, and comes with the following methods already implemented the method hashCode (location/scope is a class), apply (location/scope is an object), copy (location/scope is a class), equals (location/scope is a class), toString (location/scope is a class), and unapply (location/scope is an object).

Like a plain class, a case class automatically define, getter methods for the constructor arguments. To get a practical insight about the preceding features or a case class, let's see the following code segment:

```
package com.chapter3.OOP
object CaseClass {
  def main(args: Array[String]) {
    case class Character(name: String, isHacker: Boolean) // defining
a
                              class if a person is a computer hacker
    //Nail is a hacker
    val nail = Character("Nail", true)
```

```
    //Now let's return a copy of the instance with any requested
changes
    val joyce = nail.copy(name = "Joyce")
    // Let's check if both Nail and Joyce are Hackers
    println(nail == joyce)
    // Let's check if both Nail and Joyce equal
    println(nail.equals(joyce))
    // Let's check if both Nail and Nail equal
    println(nail.equals(nail))
    // Let's the hasing code for nail
    println(nail.hashCode())
    // Let's the hasing code for nail
    println(nail)
    joyce match {
      case Character(x, true) => s"$x is a hacker"
      case Character(x, false) => s"$x is not a hacker"
    }
  }
}
```

The preceding code produces the following output:

```
false
false
true
-112671915
Character(Nail,true)
Joyce is a hacker
```

For the REPL and the output of the regular expression matching, if you execute the preceding code (except the `Object` and `main` method), you should be able to see the more interactive output as follows:

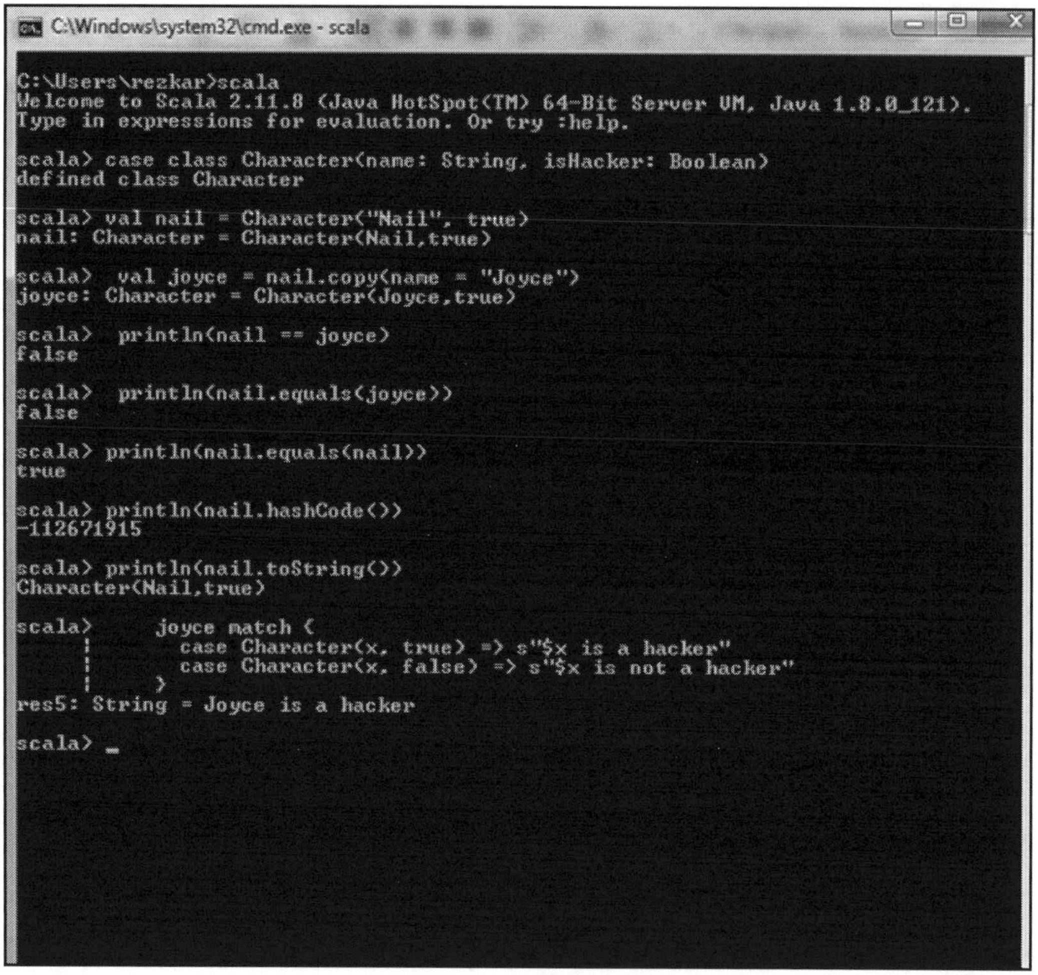

```
C:\Windows\system32\cmd.exe - scala

C:\Users\rezkar>scala
Welcome to Scala 2.11.8 (Java HotSpot(TM) 64-Bit Server VM, Java 1.8.0_121).
Type in expressions for evaluation. Or try :help.

scala> case class Character(name: String, isHacker: Boolean)
defined class Character

scala> val nail = Character("Nail", true)
nail: Character = Character(Nail,true)

scala>   val joyce = nail.copy(name = "Joyce")
joyce: Character = Character(Joyce,true)

scala>   println(nail == joyce)
false

scala>   println(nail.equals(joyce))
false

scala> println(nail.equals(nail))
true

scala> println(nail.hashCode())
-112671915

scala> println(nail.toString())
Character(Nail,true)

scala>      joyce match {
              case Character(x, true) => s"$x is a hacker"
              case Character(x, false) => s"$x is not a hacker"
            }
res5: String = Joyce is a hacker

scala> _
```

Figure 2: Scala REPL for case class

Packages and package objects

Just like Java, a package is a special container or object which contains/defines a set of objects, classes, and even packages. Every Scala file has the following automatically imported:

- `java.lang._`
- `scala._`
- `scala.Predef._`

The following is an example for basic imports:

```
// import only one member of a package
import java.io.File
// Import all members in a specific package
import java.io._
// Import many members in a single import statement
import java.io.{File, IOException, FileNotFoundException}
// Import many members in a multiple import statement
import java.io.File
import java.io.FileNotFoundException
import java.io.IOException
```

You can even rename a member while importing, and that's to avoid a collision between packages that have the same member name. This method is also called class alias:

```
import java.util.{List => UtilList}
import java.awt.{List => AwtList}
// In the code, you can use the alias that you have created
val list = new UtilList
```

As mentioned in Chapter 1, *Introduction to Scala*, you can also import all the members of a package, but some members are also called **member hiding**:

```
import java.io.{File => _, _}
```

If you tried this in the REPL, it just tells the compiler the full, canonical name of the defined class or object:

```
package fo.ba
class Fo {
  override def toString = "I'm fo.ba.Fo"
}
```

You can even use the style of defining packages in curly braces. You can have a single package and nested package means package within a package. For example, the following code segment defines a single package named `singlePackage` consisting of a single class named `Test`. The `Test` class, on the other hand, consists of a single method named `toString()`.

```
package singlePack {
  class Test { override def toString = "I am SinglePack.Test" }
}
```

Now, you can make the packaging nested. In other words, you can have more than one package in a nested way. For example, for the below case, we have two packages, namely `NestParentPack` and the `NestChildPack`, each containing their own classes.

```
package nestParentPack {
  class Test { override def toString = "I am NestParentPack.Test" }

  package nestChildPack {
    class TestChild { override def toString = "I am
nestParentPack.nestChildPack.TestChild" }
  }
}
```

Let's create a new object (let's name it `MainProgram`), in which we'll invoke the methods and classes we just defined:

```
object MainProgram {
  def main(args: Array[String]): Unit = {
    println(new nestParentPack.Test())
    println(new nestParentPack.nestChildPack.TestChild())
  }
}
```

You will find more examples on the internet that describe sophisticated use cases of packages and package objects. In the next section, we will discuss the Java interoperability of Scala codes.

Java interoperability

Java is one of the most popular languages, and many programmers learn Java programming as their first entrance to the programming world. The popularity of Java has increased since its initial release back in 1995. Java has gained in popularity for many reasons. One of them is the design of its platform, such that any Java code will be compiled to bytecode, which in turn runs on the JVM. With this magnificent feature, Java language to be being written once and run anywhere. So, Java is a cross-platform language.

Also, Java has lots of support from its community and lots of packages that will help you get your idea up and running with the help of these packages. Then comes Scala, which has lots of features that Java lacks, such as type inference and optional semicolon, immutable collections built right into Scala core, and lots more features (addressed in Chapter 1, *Introduction to Scala*). Scala also runs on the JVM, just like Java.

 Semicolon in Scala: Semicolons are exactly optional, and they are required when more lines of code should be written on a single line. That's probably the reason why the compiler doesn't complain if a semicolon is put at the end of a line: it is considered a piece of code followed by an empty piece of code that, coincidentally, lives on the same line.

As you can see that both Scala and Java run on the JVM, it makes sense to use them simultaneously in the same program without complaints from the compiler. Let's demonstrate this with an example. Consider the following Java code:

```java
ArrayList<String> animals = new ArrayList<String>();
animals.add("cat");
animals.add("dog");
animals.add("rabbit");
for (String animal : animals) {
  System.out.println(animal);
}
```

In order to write the same code in Scala, you can make use of Java packages. Let's translate the previous example into Scala with the help of using Java collections such as `ArrayList`:

```scala
import java.util.ArrayList
val animals = new ArrayList[String]
animals.add("cat")
```

```
animals.add("dog")
animals.add("rabbit")
for (animal <- animals) {
  println(animal)
}
```

The previous mix applies for the standard packages of Java, but you want to use libraries that aren't packaged with the standard libraries of Java, or even want to use your own classes. Then, you need to make sure that they lie in the classpath.

Pattern matching

One of the widely used features of Scala is pattern matching. Each pattern match has a set of alternatives, each of them starting with the case keyword. Each alternative has a pattern and expression(s), which will be evaluated if the pattern matches and the arrow symbol => separates pattern(s) from expression(s). The following is an example which demonstrates how to match against an integer:

```
object PatternMatchingDemo1 {
  def main(args: Array[String]) {
    println(matchInteger(3))
  }
  def matchInteger(x: Int): String = x match {
    case 1 => "one"
    case 2 => "two"
    case _ => "greater than two"
  }
}
```

You can run the preceding program by saving this file in `PatternMatchingDemo1.scala` and then using the following commands to run it. Just use the following command:

```
>scalac Test.scala
>scala Test
```

You will get the following output:

```
Greater than two
```

The cases statements are used as a function that maps integers to strings. The following is another example which matches against different types:

```
object PatternMatchingDemo2 {
  def main(args: Array[String]): Unit = {
    println(comparison("two"))
    println(comparison("test"))
    println(comparison(1))
  }
  def comparison(x: Any): Any = x match {
    case 1 => "one"
    case "five" => 5
    case _ => "nothing else"
  }
}
```

You can run this example by doing the same for the example earlier and will get the following output:

```
nothing else
nothing else
one
```

Pattern matching is a mechanism for checking a value against a pattern. A successful match can also deconstruct a value into its constituent parts. It is a more powerful version of the switch statement in Java, and it can likewise be used in place of a series of if...else statements. You can find more on pattern matching by referring to the official docs of Scala (URL: http://www.scala-lang.org/files/archive/spec/2.11/08-pattern-matching.html).

In the next section, we will discuss an important feature in Scala that enables us a value that can be passed automatically, so to speak, or a conversion from one type to another that is made automatically.

Implicit in Scala

Implicit is another exciting and powerful feature introduced by Scala, and it can refer to two different things:

- A value that can be automatically passed
- Automatic conversion from one type to another
- They can be used for extending the capabilities of a class

Actual automatic conversion can be accomplished with implicit def, as seen in the following example (supposing you are using the Scala REPL):

```
scala> implicit def stringToInt(s: String) = s.toInt
stringToInt: (s: String)Int
```

Now, having the preceding code in my scope, it's possible for me to do something like this:

```
scala> def add(x:Int, y:Int) = x + y
add: (x: Int, y: Int)Int

scala> add(1, "2")
res5: Int = 3
scala>
```

Even if one of the parameters passed to add() is a String (and add() would require you to provide two integers), having the implicit conversion in scope allows the compiler to automatically convert from String to Int. Obviously enough, this feature could be quite dangerous, because it makes the code less readable; moreover, once an implicit conversion is defined, it's not easy to tell the compiler when to use it and when to avoid using it.

The first type of implicit is a value that can automatically pass an implicit parameter. These parameters are passed while calling a method like any normal parameter, but Scala's compiler tries to fill them automatically. If Scala's compiler fails to automatically fill these parameters, it will complain. The following is an example to demonstrate the first type of implicit:

```
def add(implicit num: Int) = 2 + num
```

By this, you are asking the compiler to look for an implicit value for num, if not provided during calling the method. You can define implicit value to the compiler like this:

```
implicit val adder = 2
```

Then, we can simply call the function like this:

```
add
```

Here, no parameter is passed, so Scala's compiler will look for implicit value, which is 2, and then return 4 as the output of the method calling. However, a lot of other options have evolved a questions such as:

- Can a method contain both an explicit and an implicit parameter? The answer is YES. Let's see an example on Scala REPL:

```scala
scala> def helloWold(implicit a: Int, b: String) = println(a, b)
helloWold: (implicit a: Int, implicit b: String)Unit

scala> val i = 2
i: Int = 2

scala> helloWorld(i, implicitly)
(2,)

scala>
```

- Can a method contain more than one implicit parameter? The answer is YES. Let's see an example on Scala REPL:

```scala
scala> def helloWold(implicit a: Int, b: String) = println(a, b)
helloWold: (implicit a: Int, implicit b: String)Unit

scala> helloWold(i, implicitly)
(1,)

scala>
```

- Can an implicit parameter be explicitly provided? The answer is YES. Let's see an example on Scala REPL:

```scala
scala> def helloWold(implicit a: Int, b: String) = println(a, b)
helloWold: (implicit a: Int, implicit b: String)Unit

scala> helloWold(20, "Hello world!")
(20,Hello world!)
scala>
```

What happens if more implicits are contained in the same scope and how are implicits resolved? Is there any order to how implicits are resolved? To get to know the answer to these two questions, refer to this URL at http://stackoverflow.com/questions/9530893/good-example-of-implicit-parameter-in-scala.

In the next section, we will discuss generics in Scala with some examples.

Generic in Scala

Generic classes are classes which take a type as a parameter. They are particularly useful for collection classes. Generic classes can be used in everyday data structure implementation, such as stack, queue, linked list, and so on. We will see some examples.

Defining a generic class

Generic classes take a type as a parameter within square brackets []. One convention is to use the letter A as a type parameter identifier, though any parameter name may be used. Let's see a minimal example on Scala REPL, as follows:

```
scala> class Stack[A] {
    |           private var elements: List[A] = Nil
    |           def push(x: A) { elements = x :: elements }
    |           def peek: A = elements.head
    |           def pop(): A = {
    |             val currentTop = peek
    |             elements = elements.tail
    |             currentTop
    |           }
    |         }
defined class Stack
scala>
```

The preceding implementation of a `Stack` class takes any type A as a parameter. This means the underlying list, `var elements: List[A] = Nil` can only store elements of type A. The procedure def push only accepts objects of type A (note: `elements = x :: elements` reassigns elements to a new list created by prepending x to the current elements). Let's see an example of how to use the preceding class to implement a stack:

```
object ScalaGenericsForStack {
  def main(args: Array[String]) {
```

```
    val stack = new Stack[Int]
    stack.push(1)
    stack.push(2)
    stack.push(3)
    stack.push(4)
    println(stack.pop) // prints 4
    println(stack.pop) // prints 3
    println(stack.pop) // prints 2
    println(stack.pop) // prints 1
  }
}
```

The output is as follows:

```
4
3
2
1
```

The second use case could be implementing a linked list too. For instance, if Scala didn't have a linked-list class and you wanted to write your own, you could write the basic functionality like this:

```
class UsingGenericsForLinkedList[X] { // Create a user specific linked
list to print heterogenous values
  private class Node[X](elem: X) {
    var next: Node[X] = _
    override def toString = elem.toString
  }

  private var head: Node[X] = _

  def add(elem: X) { //Add element in the linekd list
    val value = new Node(elem)
    value.next = head
    head = value
  }

  private def printNodes(value: Node[X]) { // prining value of the
nodes
    if (value != null) {
      println(value)
      printNodes(value.next)
    }
  }
  def printAll() { printNodes(head) } //print all the node values at a
time
}
```

Now, let's see how could we use the preceding linked list implementation:

```scala
object UsingGenericsForLinkedList {
  def main(args: Array[String]) {
    // To create a list of integers with this class, first create an
    instance of it, with type Int:
    val ints = new UsingGenericsForLinkedList[Int]()
    // Then populate it with Int values:
    ints.add(1)
    ints.add(2)
    ints.add(3)
    ints.printAll()

    // Because the class uses a generic type, you can also create a
    LinkedList of String:
    val strings = new UsingGenericsForLinkedList[String]()
    strings.add("Salman Khan")
    strings.add("Xamir Khan")
    strings.add("Shah Rukh Khan")
    strings.printAll()

    // Or any other type such as Double to use:
    val doubles = new UsingGenericsForLinkedList[Double]()
    doubles.add(10.50)
    doubles.add(25.75)
    doubles.add(12.90)
    doubles.printAll()
  }
}
```

The output is as follows:

```
3
2
1
Shah Rukh Khan
Aamir Khan
Salman Khan
12.9
25.75
10.5
```

In summary, at the basic level, creating a generic class in Scala is just like creating a generic class in Java, with the exception of the brackets. Well! So far we have gotten to know some essential features to get started with an object-oriented programming language, Scala.

Although, we have not covered some other aspects, however, we still think that you can continue working. In Chapter 1, *Introduction to Scala*, we discussed what the available editors for Scala are. In the next section, we will see how to set up your build environment. More specifically, three build systems, like Maven, SBT, and Gradle will be covered.

SBT and other build systems

It's necessary to use a build tool for any enterprise software project. There are lots of build tools that you can choose from, such as Maven, Gradle, Ant, and SBT. A good choice of build tool is the one which will let you focus on coding rather than compilation complexities.

Build with SBT

Here, we are going to give a brief introduction to SBT. Before going any further, you need to install SBT using the installation method that fits your system from their official installations methods (URL: http://www.scala-sbt.org/release/docs/Setup.html).

So, let's begin with SBT to demonstrate the use of SBT in a terminal. For this build tool tutorial, we assume that your source code files are in a directory. You need to do the following:

1. Open the terminal and change path to that directory by using cd,
2. Create a build file called build.sbt.
3. Then, populate that build file with the following lines:

```
name := "projectname-sbt"
organization :="org.example"
scalaVersion :="2.11.8"
version := "0.0.1-SNAPSHOT"
```

Let's see the meaning of these lines:

- The `name` defines a name for your project. This name will be used in the generated jar files.
- The `organization` is a namespace that's used to prevent collisions between projects that have similar names.
- `scalaVersion` sets the version of Scala that you want to build against.
- `Version` specifies the current build version of your project and you can use `-SNAPSHOT` for versions that have not been released yet.

After creating this build file, you need to `run` the `sbt` command in your terminal and then a prompt starting with > will be opened for you. In this prompt, you can type `compile` in order to compile your Scala or Java source files in your code. Also, you can enter the command in the SBT prompt in order to run the program if it's runnable. Or you can use the package command in SBT prompt in order to generate a `.jar` file, which will exist in a subdirectory called `target`. To read more about SBT and more sophisticated examples, you can refer to the official site of SBT.

Maven with Eclipse

Using Eclipse as Scala IDE with Maven as a build tool is very easy and straightforward. In this section, we will demonstrate with screenshots how to use Scala with Eclipse and Maven. To be able to use Maven in Eclipse, you need to install its plugin, which will be different across different versions of Eclipse. After installing the Maven plugin, you will find that it doesn't support Scala directly. What we need to do in order to get this Maven plugin to support Scala projects is to install a connector called **m2eclipse-scala**.

If you paste this URL (`http://alchim31.free.fr/m2e-scala/update-site`) while trying to add new software to Eclipse, you will find that Eclipse understands the URL and suggests some plugins for you to add:

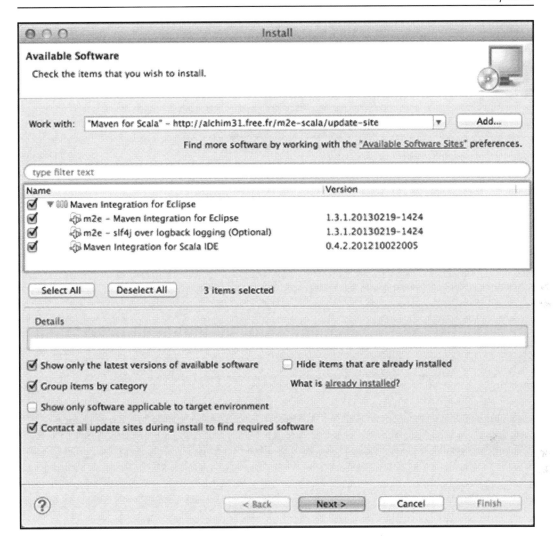

Figure 4: Installing Maven plugins on Eclipse to enable Maven build

After installing Maven and the connector for Scala support, we are going to create a new Scala Maven project. To create a new Scala Maven project, you need to navigate to **New** | **Project** | **Other** and then choose **Maven Project**. After this, select the option that has **net.alchim31.maven** as **Group Id**:

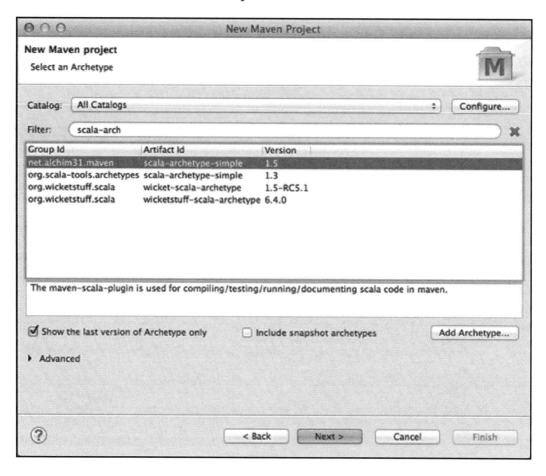

Figure 5: Creating a Scala Maven project on Eclipse

After this selection, you need to follow the wizard and enter the required values, such as **Group Id**, and so on. Then, hit **Finish** and, with this, you have created your first Scala project with Maven support in the workspace. In the project structure, you will find something called `pom.xml` where you can add all your dependencies and other things.

For more information about how to add dependencies to your project, you can refer to this link at `http://docs.scala-lang.org/tutorials/scala-with-maven.html`.

As a continuation of this section, we will show you how to build your Spark application written in Scala in the upcoming chapter.

Gradle with Eclipse

Gradle Inc. provides the Gradle tools and plugins for the Eclipse IDE. This tool allows you to create and import Gradle enabled projects into the Eclipse IDE. In addition, it allows you to run Gradle tasks and monitor the execution of the tasks.

The Eclipse project itself is called **Buildship**. The source code of this project is available on GitHub at `https://github.com/eclipse/Buildship`.

There are two options for installing Gradle plugins on Eclipse. These are as follows:

- Via the Eclipse Marketplace
- Via the Eclipse Update Manager

First, let's see how to install Buildship plugins for Grade build on Eclipse using Marketplace: **Eclipse** | **Help** | **Eclipse Marketplace**:

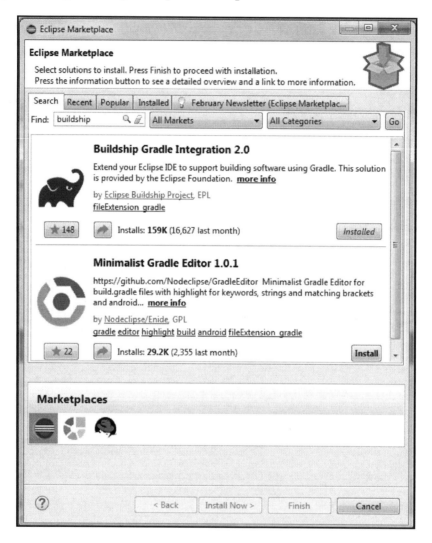

Figure 6: Installing Buildship plugins for Grade build on Eclipse using Marketplace

The second option for installing the Gradle plugins on Eclipse is from the **Help |
Install New Software...** menu path to install the Gradle tooling as shown in the
following figure:

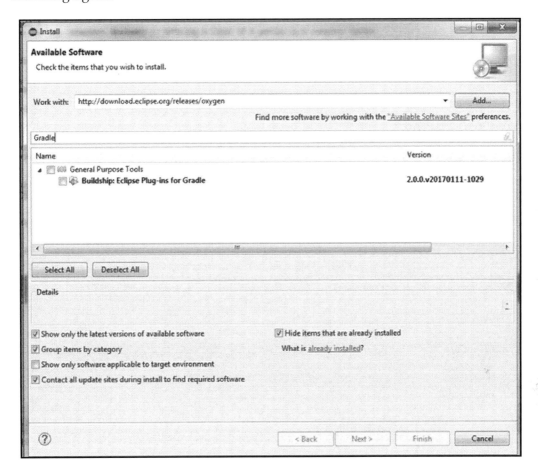

Figure 7: Installing Buildship plugins for Grade build on Eclipse using install new software

For example, the following URL can be used for Eclipse 4.6 (Neon)
release: `http://download.eclipse.org/releases/neon`.

Once you have installed the Gradle plugins by following any one of the methods described earlier, Eclipse Gradle helps you to set up Scala based Gradle projects: **File | New | Project | Select a wizard | Gradle | Gradle Project**.

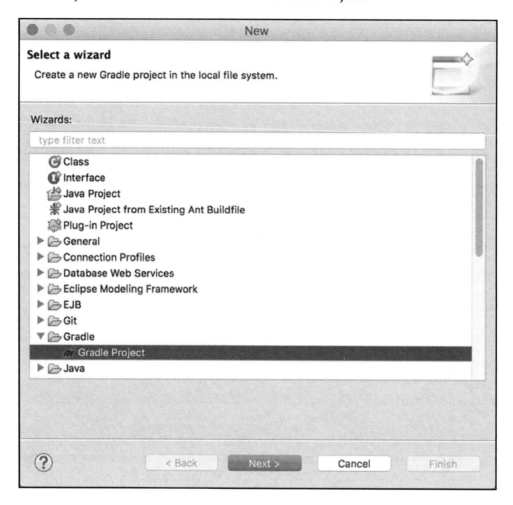

Figure 8: Creating a Gradle project on Eclipse

Now, if you press **Next>**, you will get the following wizard to specify the name of the project for your purpose:

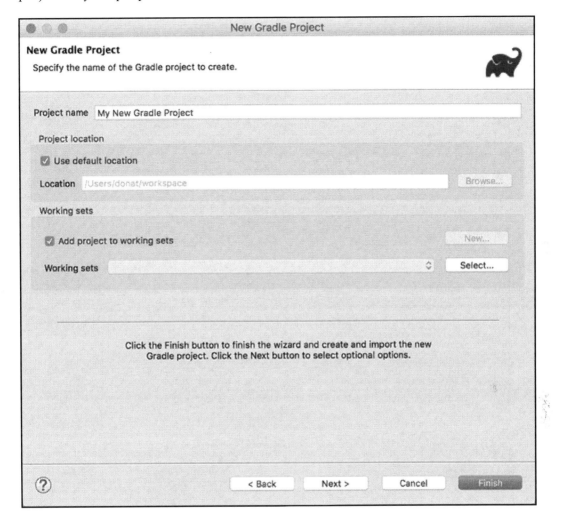

Figure 9: Creating a Gradle project on Eclipse specifying the project name

Finally, press the **Finish** button to create the project. Pressing the **Finish** button essentially triggers the Gradle `init --type java-library` command and imports the project. However, if you would like to get a preview of the configuration before the it is created, press **Next >** to get the following wizard:

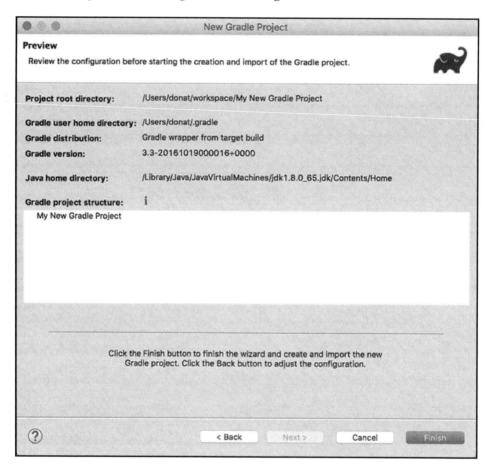

Figure 10: Preview of the configuration before it is created

Finally, you will see the following project structure on Eclipse. However, we will see how to build Spark applications using Maven, SBT, and Gradle in a later chapter. The reason is that, before starting your project, it is more important to learn Scala and Spark together.

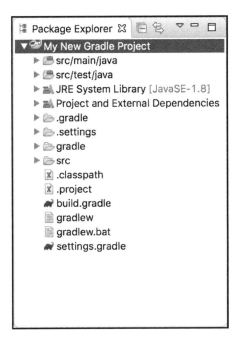

Figure 11: The project structure on Eclipse using Gradle

In this section, we have seen three build systems, including SBT, Maven, and Gradle. However, throughout the chapters, I will try to mainly use Maven because of its simplicity and better code compatibility. However, in later chapters, we will use SBT to create JARS from your Spark application.

Summary

Structuring code in a sane way, with classes and traits, enhances the reusability of your code with generics, and creates a project with standard and widespread tools. Improve on the basics to know how Scala implements the OO paradigm to allow the building of modular software systems. In this chapter, we discussed the basic object-oriented features in Scala, such as classes and objects, packages and package objects, traits, and trait linearization, Java interoperability, pattern matching, implicit, and generics. Finally, we discussed SBT and other build systems that will be needed to build our Spark application on Eclipse or any other IDEs.

In the next chapter, we will discuss what functional programming is and how Scala supports it. We will get to know why it matters and what the advantages of using functional concepts are. Continuing, you will learn pure functions, higher-order functions, Scala collections basics (map, flatMap, filter), for - comprehensions, monadic processing, and for extending higher-order functions outside of collections using the standard library of Scala.

Functional Programming Concepts

3

"Object-oriented programming makes code understandable by encapsulating moving parts. Functional programming makes code understandable by minimizing moving parts."

- Michael Feathers

Using Scala and Spark is a very good combination for learning big data analytics. However, along with the OOP paradigm, we also need to know-how why functional concepts are important for writing Spark applications that eventually analyze your data. As mentioned in the previous chapters, Scala supports two programming paradigms: the Object-Oriented Programming paradigm and the Functional programming concepts. In `Chapter 2`, *Object-Oriented Scala*, we explored the OOP paradigm in which we have seen how to represent real-world objects in blueprints (classes) and then instantiate them into objects having real memory representation.

In this chapter, we will focus on the second paradigm (i.e. functional programming). We will see what functional programming is and how Scala supports it, why it matters, and the related advantages of using this concept. More specifically, we will learn several topics, such as why Scala is an arsenal for the data scientist, why it is important to learn the Spark paradigm, pure functions, and **higher-order functions (HOFs)**. A real-life use case using HOF will also be shown in this chapter. Then, we will see how to handle exceptions in the higher-order functions outside collections using the standard library of Scala. Finally, we will learn how functional Scala affects an object's mutability.

In a nutshell, the following topics will be covered in this chapter:

- Introduction to functional programming
- Functional Scala for the data scientists
- Why functional programming and Scala are important for learning Spark?
- Pure functions and higher-order functions
- Using higher-order functions: A real-life use case
- Error handling in functional Scala
- Functional programming and data mutability

Introduction to functional programming

In computer science, `functional programming` (FP) is a programming paradigm and a unique style of building the structure and elements of computer programs. This uniqueness helps treat the computation as the evaluation of mathematical functions and avoids changing-state and mutable data. Thus, by using the FP concept, you can learn to code in your own style that ensures the immutability of your data. In other words, FP is about writing pure functions, about removing hidden inputs and outputs as far as we can, so that as much of our code as possible *just* describes a relationship between inputs and outputs.

This is not a new concept but the `Lambda Calculus`, which provides the basis of FP, was first introduced in the 1930s. However, in the realm of programming language, the term functional programming refers to a new style of declarative programming paradigm that means programming can be done with the help of control, declarations, or expressions instead of classical statements commonly used in an old programming language, such as C.

Advantages of functional programming

There are some exciting and cool features in FP paradigms such as `composition,` `pipelining,` and `higher order functions` that help to avoid writing unfunctional code. Alternatively, at least later on, this helps translate a unfunctional program into a functional style towards an imperative one. Finally, now let's see how we can define the term functional programming from the computer science perspective. Functional programming is a common computer science concept in which computations and the building structure of the program are treated as if you are evaluating mathematical functions that support immutable data and avoid state change. In functional programming, each function has the same mapping or output for the same input argument values.

With the need for a complex software comes the need for good structured programs and software that are not difficult to write and are debuggable. We also need to write extendable code that will save us programming costs in the future and can contribute to easy writing and debugging of the code; even more modular software that is easy to extend and requires less programming efforts. Due to the latter contribution of functional programming, modularity, functional programming is considered as a great advantage for software development.

In functional programming, there is a basic building block in its structure called functions without side effects (or at least very few) in most of your code. Without side effects, the order of evaluation really doesn't matter. When it comes to programming languages views, there are methods to force a particular order. In some FP languages (for example, eager languages such as Scheme), which have no evaluation order on arguments, you could nest these expressions in their own lambda forms as follows:

```
((lambda (val1)
  ((lambda (val2)
    ((lambda (val3) (/ (* val1 val2) val3))
      expression3)) ; evaluated third
      expression2))  ; evaluated second
    expression1)     ; evaluated first
```

In functional programming, writing mathematical functions in which the execution order doesn't matter usually makes your code more readable. Sometimes, one will argue that we need functions with side effects to be there as well. Actually, this is one of the major disadvantages of most functional programming languages since it's typically difficult to write functions that don't require any I/O; on the other hand, these function that requires I/O are difficult to implement in functional programming. From *Figure 1*, it can be seen that Scala is also a hybrid language that evolved by taking features from imperative languages such as Java and functional language such as Lisp.

But fortunately, here we are dealing with a mixed language in which object-oriented and functional programming paradigms are allowed and hence writing such functions that require I/O is quite easy. Functional programming also has major advantages over basic programming, such as comprehensions and caching.

One of the major advantages of functional programming is brevity because with functional programming you can write more compact and concise code. Also, concurrency is considered one of the major advantages, which is done more easily in functional programming. Therefore, functional languages such as Scala provide many other features and tools that encourage coders to make an entire paradigm shift to a more mathematical way of thinking.

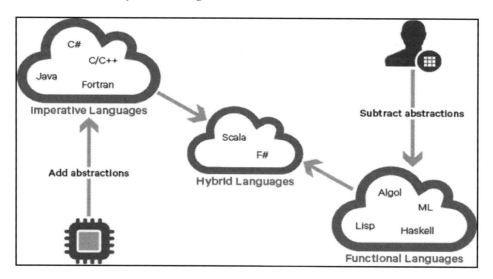

Figure 1: Shows a conceptual view of using functional programming concepts

By narrowing the focus to only a small number of composable abstract concepts, such as functions, function composition, and abstract algebra, FP concept provides several advantages over other paradigms. For example:

- **Closer alignment to mathematical thinking:** You tend to spell out your ideas in a format close to mathematical definitions rather than iterative programs.
- **No (or at least fewer) side effects:** Your functions do not influence other functions, which is great for concurrency and parallelization, and also for debugging.
- **Fewer lines of code without sacrificing conceptual clarity:** Lisp is more powerful than non-functional languages. Although it's true that you need to spend a greater proportion of your project thinking than writing, you will probably find that you are more productive eventually.

For these exciting features, functional programming achieves significant expressive power. For example, machine learning algorithms can take hundreds of lines of imperative code to implement yet they can be defined in just a handful of equations.

Functional Scala for the data scientists

For performing interactive data cleaning, processing, munging, and analysis, many data scientists use R or Python as their favorite tool. However, there are many data scientists who tend to get very attached to their favorite tool--that is, Python or R and try to solve all data analytics problems or jobs using that tool. Thus, introducing them to a new tool can be very challenging in most circumstances as the new tool has more syntax and a new set of patterns to learn before using the new tool to solve their purpose.

There are other APIs in Spark written in Python and R such as PySpark and SparkR respectively that allow you to use them from Python or R. However, most Spark books and online examples are written in Scala. Arguably, we think that learning how to work with Spark using the same language on which the Spark code has been written will give you many advantages over Java, Python, or R as a data scientist:

- Better performance and removes the data processing overhead
- Provides access to the latest and greatest features of Spark
- Helps to understand the Spark philosophy in a transparent way

Analyzing data means that you are writing Scala code to retrieve data from the cluster using Spark and its APIs (that is, SparkR, SparkSQL, Spark Streaming, Spark MLlib, and Spark GraphX). Alternatively, you're developing a Spark application using Scala to manipulate that data locally on your own machine. In both cases, Scala is your real friend and will pay you dividends in time.

Why FP and Scala for learning Spark?

In this section, we will discuss why we will learn Spark to solve our data analytics problem. We will then discuss why the functional programming concepts in Scala are particularly important to make data analysis easier for the data scientists. We will also discuss the Spark programming model and its ecosystem to make them clearer.

Why Spark?

Spark is a lightning fast cluster computing framework and is mainly designed for fast computations. Spark is based on the Hadoop MapReduce model and uses MapReduce in more forms and types of computation, such as interactive queries and stream processing. One of the main features of Spark is in-memory processing, which helps increase the performance and processing speed of an application. Spark supports a wide range of applications and workloads, such as the following:

- Batch-based applications
- Iterative algorithms that were not possible to run fast before
- Interactive query and streaming

Also, it doesn't require much time for you to learn Spark and implement it in your applications without the need to understand the inner details of concurrency and distributed systems. Spark was implemented in 2009 at AMPLab of UC Berkeley. In 2010, they decided to make it open source. Then, Spark became an Apache release in 2013 and since then Spark has been considered as the most famous/used Apache-released software. Apache Spark became very famous because of its features:

- **Fast computations**: Spark helps you to run applications that are faster than Hadoop because of its golden feature--in-memory processing.
- **Support for multiple programming languages**: Apache Spark provides wrappers and built-in APIs in different languages such as Scala, Java, Python, or even R.

- **More analytics**: As mentioned earlier, Spark supports MapReduce operations and it also supports more advanced analytics such as **machine learning (MLlib)**, data streaming, and algorithms for graph processing.

As mentioned earlier, Spark is built on top of the Hadoop software and you can deploy Spark in different ways:

- **Standalone cluster**: This means that Spark will run on top of **Hadoop Distributed File System (HDFS)** and space will actually be allocated to HDFS. Spark and MapReduce will run side by side to serve all the Spark jobs.
- **Hadoop YARN cluster**: This means that Spark simply runs on YARN without any root privileges or pre-installations.
- **Mesos cluster**: When a driver program creates a Spark job and starts assigning related tasks for scheduling, Mesos determines which computing nodes will handle which tasks. We assume that you have already configured and installed Mesos on your machine.
- **Deploy on pay-as-you-go cluster**: You can deploy Spark jobs in real cluster mode on AWS EC2. To make your applications run on Spark cluster mode and for better scalability, you can consider **Amazon Elastic Compute Cloud (EC2)** services as **Infrastructure as a Service (IaaS)** or **Platform as a Service (PaaS)**.

Refer to `Chapter 17`, *Time to Go to ClusterLand - Deploying Spark on a Cluster* and `Chapter 18`, *Testing and Debugging Spark* for how to deploy your data analytics application using Scala and Spark on a real cluster.

Scala and the Spark programming model

Spark programming starts with a dataset or a few, usually residing in some form of distributed and persistent storage such as HDFS. A typical RDD programming model that Spark provides can be described as follows:

- From an environment variable, Spark context (the Spark shell provides you with a Spark Context or you can make your own, this will be described later in this chapter) creates an initial data reference RDD object.
- Transform the initial RDD to create more RDD objects following the functional programming style (to be discussed later on).

- Send the code, algorithms, or applications from the driver program to the cluster manager nodes. Then, the cluster manager provides a copy to each computing node.
- Computing nodes hold a reference to the RDDs in their partition (again, the driver program also holds a data reference). However, computing nodes could have the input dataset provided by the cluster manager as well.
- After a transformation (via either narrow or wider transformation), the result to be generated is a brand new RDD, since the original one will not be mutated.
- Finally, the RDD object or more (specifically, data reference) is materialized through an action to dump the RDD into the storage.
- The driver program can ask the computing nodes for a chunk of results for the analysis or visualization of a program.

Wait! So far we have moved smoothly. We suppose you will ship your application code to the computing nodes in the cluster. Still, you will have to upload or send the input datasets to the cluster to be distributed among the computing nodes. Even during the bulk upload, you will have to transfer the data across the network. We also argue that the size of the application code and results are negligible or trivial. Another obstacle is if you want Spark to process the data at scale computation, it might require data objects to be merged from multiple partitions first. This means we will need to shuffle data among the worker/computing nodes that is usually done by `partition()`, `intersection()`, and `join()` transformation operations.

Scala and the Spark ecosystem

To provide more enhancement and additional big data processing capabilities, Spark can be configured and run on top of existing Hadoop-based clusters. The core APIs in Spark, on the other hand, are written in Java, Scala, Python, and R. Compared to MapReduce, with the more general and powerful programming model, Spark also provides several libraries that are part of the Spark ecosystems for additional capabilities for general-purpose data processing and analytics, graph processing, large-scale structured SQL, and **Machine Learning** (**ML**) areas.

The Spark ecosystem consists of the following components as shown (for details please refer Chapter 16, *Spark Tuning*):

- **Apache Spark core**: This is the underlying engine for the Spark platform on which all the other functionalities are built. Also, it's the one that provides in-memory processing.
- **Spark SQL**: As mentioned Spark core is the underlying engine and all the other components or features are built upon it. Spark SQL is the Spark component that provides support for different data structures (structured and semi-structured data).
- **Spark streaming**: This component is responsible for streaming data for analytics and converts them into mini batches that can be used later on for analytics.
- **MLlib (Machine Learning Library)**: MLlib is a machine learning framework that supports lots of ML algorithms in a distributed fashion.
- **GraphX**: A distributed graph framework built on top of Spark to express user-defined graph components in a parallel fashion.

As mentioned earlier, most functional programming languages allow the user to write nice, modular, and extensible code. Also, functional programming encourages safe ways of programming by writing functions that look like mathematical functions. Now, how did Spark make all the APIs work as a single unit? It was possible because of the advancement in the hardware and of course, the functional programming concepts. Since adding syntactic sugar to easily do lambda expressions is not sufficient to make a language functional, this is just the start.

Although the RDD concept in Spark works quite well, there are many use cases where it's a bit complicated due to its immutability. For the following example which is the classic example of calculating an average, make the source code robust and readable; of course, to reduce the overall cost, one does not want to first compute totals, then counts, even if the data is cached in the main memory.

```
val data: RDD[People] = ...
data.map(person => (person.name, (person.age, 1)))
.reduceByKey(_ |+| _)
.mapValues { case (total, count) =>
  total.toDouble / count
}.collect()
```

The DataFrames API (this will be discussed in the later chapters in detail) produces equally terse and readable code where the functional API fits well for most use cases and minimizes the MapReduce stages; there are many shuffles that can cost dramatically and the key reasons for this are as follows:

- Large code bases require static typing to eliminate trivial mistakes, such as *aeg* instead of *age* instantly
- Complex code requires transparent APIs to communicate design clearly
- 2x speed-ups in the DataFrames API via under-the-hood mutation can be equally achieved by encapsulating state via OOP and using mapPartitions and combineByKey
- Flexibility and Scala features are required to build functionality quickly

The combination of OOP and FP with Spark can make a pretty hard problem easier in Barclays. For example, in Barclays, recently an application called Insights Engine has been developed to execute an arbitrary number N of near-arbitrary SQL-like queries. The application can execute them in a way that can scale with increasing N.

Now let's talk about pure functions, higher order functions, and anonymous functions, which are the three important concepts in the functional programming of Scala.

Pure functions and higher-order functions

From the computer science perspective, functions can have many forms such as first order functions, higher-order functions, or pure functions. This is also true from the mathematics point of view. Using a higher-order function is a function one of the following can be performed:

- Takes one or more functions as arguments to do some operations
- Returns a function as its result

All other functions except the higher-order functions are first-order functions. However, from the mathematics point of view, higher-order functions are also called **operators** or **functionals**. On the other hand, if the return value of a function is only determined by its input and of course without observable side effects, it is called a **pure function**.

In this section, we will briefly discuss why and how to use different functional paradigms in Scala. Especially, pure functions, and higher-order functions will be discussed. At the end of this section, a brief overview of using anonymous functions will also be provided since this is used frequently while developing a Spark application using Scala.

Pure functions

One of the most important principles of functional programming is pure functions. So what are pure functions and why do we care about them? In this section, we will address this important feature of functional programming. One of the best practices of functional programming is to implement your programs such that the core of your program/application is made from pure functions and all the I/O functions or side effects such as network overhead and exceptions are in an exposed external layer.

So what are the benefits of pure functions? Pure functions are normally smaller than normal functions (although it depends on other factors such as programming language) and even easier to interpret and understand for the human brain because it looks like a mathematical function.

Yet, you might argue against this since most developers still find imperative programming more understandable! Pure functions are much easier to implement and test. Let's demonstrate this by an example. Suppose we have the following two separate functions:

```
def pureFunc(cityName: String) = s"I live in $cityName"
def notpureFunc(cityName: String) = println(s"I live in $cityName")
```

So in the previous two examples, if you want to test the `pureFunc` pure function, we just assert the return value that's coming from the pure function with what we are expecting based on our input such as:

```
assert(pureFunc("Dublin") == "I live in Dublin")
```

But on the other side, if we wanted to test our `notpureFunc` impure function then we need to redirect the standard output and then apply assertion on it. The next practical tip is that functional programming makes programmers more productive because, as mentioned earlier, pure functions are smaller and easier to write and you can easily compose them together. Also, the duplication of code is minimal and you can easily reuse your code. Now let's demonstrate this advantage with a better example. Consider these two functions:

```scala
scala> def pureMul(x: Int, y: Int) = x * y
pureMul: (x: Int, y: Int)Int

scala> def notpureMul(x: Int, y: Int) = println(x * y)
notpureMul: (x: Int, y: Int)Unit
```

However, there might be side effects of mutability; using a pure function (that is, without mutability) helps us reason about and test code:

```scala
def pureIncrease(x: Int) = x + 1
```

This one is advantageous and very easy to interpret and use. However, let's see another example:

```scala
varinc = 0
def impureIncrease() = {
  inc += 1
  inc
}
```

Now, consider how confusing this could be: what will be the output in a multithreaded environment? As you can see, we can easily use our pure function, `pureMul`, to multiply any sequence of numbers, unlike our `notpureMul` impure function. Let's demonstrate this by the following example:

```scala
scala> Seq.range(1,10).reduce(pureMul)
res0: Int = 362880
```

The complete code for the preceding examples can be shown as follows (methods were called using some real values):

```scala
package com.chapter3.ScalaFP

object PureAndNonPureFunction {
  def pureFunc(cityName: String) = s"I live in $cityName"
  def notpureFunc(cityName: String) = println(s"I live in $cityName")
  def pureMul(x: Int, y: Int) = x * y
  def notpureMul(x: Int, y: Int) = println(x * y)
  def main(args: Array[String]) {
```

```
    //Now call all the methods with some real values
    pureFunc("Galway") //Does not print anything
    notpureFunc("Dublin") //Prints I live in Dublin
    pureMul(10, 25) //Again does not print anything
    notpureMul(10, 25) // Prints the multiplicaiton -i.e. 250
    //Now call pureMul method in a different way
    val data = Seq.range(1,10).reduce(pureMul)
    println(s"My sequence is: " + data)
  }
}
```

The output of the preceding code is as follows:

```
I live in Dublin 250
My sequence is: 362880
```

As discussed earlier, you can consider pure functions as one of the most important features of functional programming and as a best practice; you need to build the core of your application using pure functions.

Functions versus methods:

In the programming realm, a **function** is a piece of code called by a name. Data (as an argument or as a parameter) can be passed to operate on and can return data (optionally). All data passed to a function is passed explicitly. A **method,** on the other hand, is also a piece of code that is called by a name too. However, a method is always associated with an object.

Sounds similar? Well! In most cases, a method is identical to a function except for two key differences:

1. A method is implicitly passed the object on which it was called.

2. A method is able to operate on data that is contained within the class.

It is already stated in the previous chapter that an object is an instance of a class--the class is the definition, the object is an instance of that data.

Now it's time to learn about higher-order functions. However, before that, we should learn one more important concept in functional Scala--**anonymous functions**. Through this, we will also learn how to use the lambda expression with functional Scala.

Anonymous functions

Sometimes in your code, you don't want to define a function prior to its usage, maybe because you will use it in one place. In functional programming, there's a type of function that is very suitable to this situation. It's called an anonymous function. Let's demonstrate the use of anonymous functions using the previous example of transferring money:

```
def TransferMoney(money: Double, bankFee: Double => Double): Double =
{
   money + bankFee(money)
}
```

Now, let's call the `TransferMoney()` method with some real value as follows:

```
TransferMoney(100, (amount: Double) => amount * 0.05)
```

Lambda expression:
As already stated, Scala supports first-class functions, which means functions can be expressed in function-literal syntax as well; functions can be represented by objects, called function values. Try the following expression, it creates a successor function for integers:
```
scala> var apply = (x:Int) => x+1
apply: Int => Int = <function1>
```
The apply variable is now a function that can be used in the usual way as follows:
```
scala> var x = apply(7)
x: Int = 8
```
What we have done here is simply use the core of a function: the argument list followed by the function arrow and the body of the function. This one is not black magic but a full-fledged function, only without a given name--that is, anonymous. If you define a function this way, there will be no way to refer to that function afterward and hence you couldn't call that function afterward because without a name it's an anonymous one. Also, we have a so-called **lambda expression**! It's just the pure, anonymous definition of a function.

The output of the preceding code is as follows:

```
105.0
```

So, in the previous example instead of declaring a separate `callback` function, we passed an anonymous function directly and it did the same job just like the `bankFee` function. You can also omit the type in the anonymous function and it will be directly inferred based on the passed argument like this:

```
TransferMoney(100, amount => amount * 0.05)
```

The output of the preceding code is as follows:

```
105.0
```

Let's demonstrate the previous example on the Scala shell as shown in the following screenshot:

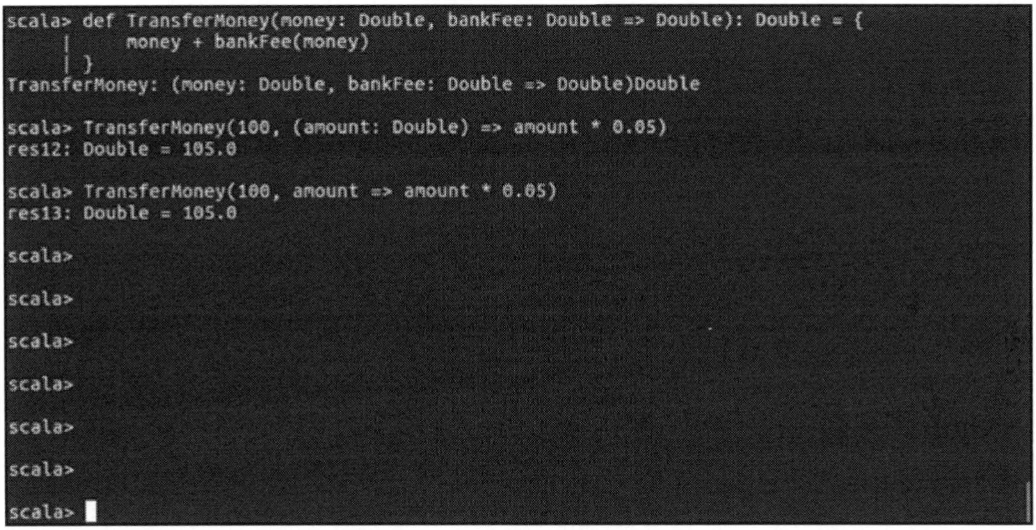

```
scala> def TransferMoney(money: Double, bankFee: Double => Double): Double = {
     |       money + bankFee(money)
     | }
TransferMoney: (money: Double, bankFee: Double => Double)Double

scala> TransferMoney(100, (amount: Double) => amount * 0.05)
res12: Double = 105.0

scala> TransferMoney(100, amount => amount * 0.05)
res13: Double = 105.0

scala>

scala>

scala>

scala>

scala>

scala>

scala>
```

Figure 6: Use of the anonymous function in Scala

Some programming languages that have functional support use the name lambda function instead of anonymous function.

Higher-order functions

In Scala's functional programming, you are allowed to pass functions as parameters and even return a function as a result from another function; this defines what are called higher-order functions.

Let's demonstrate this feature by an example. Consider the following function `testHOF` that takes another function `func` and then applies this function to its second argument value:

```scala
object Test {
  def main(args: Array[String]) {
    println( testHOF( paramFunc, 10) )
  }
  def testHOF(func: Int => String, value: Int) = func(value)
  def paramFunc[A](x: A) = "[" + x.toString() + "]"
}
```

After demonstrating the basics of Scala's functional programming, now we are ready to move to more complex cases of functional programming. As mentioned earlier, we can define a higher-order function as a function that accepts other functions as arguments and it returns them as a result. If you are coming from an object-oriented programming background, you will find it very a different approach, but it will become easier to understand as we go on.

Let's start by defining a simple function:

```scala
def quarterMaker(value: Int): Double = value.toDouble/4
```

The previous function is a very simple one. It's a function that accepts an Int value and then returns a quarter of this value in a `Double` type. Let's define another simple function:

```scala
def addTwo(value: Int): Int = value + 2
```

The second function `addTwo` is more trivial than the first one. It accepts an `Int` value and then adds 2 to it. As you can see, these two functions have something in common. Both of them accept `Int` and return another processed value that we can call `AnyVal`. Now, let's define a higher-order function that accepts another function among its parameters:

```
def applyFuncOnRange(begin: Int, end: Int, func: Int => AnyVal): Unit
= {
  for (i <- begin to end)
    println(func(i))
}
```

As you can see, the preceding function `applyFuncOnRange` accepts two `Int` values that work as a beginning and end to a sequence and it accepts a function that has the `Int => AnyVal` signature just like the previously defined simple functions (`quarterMakder` and `addTwo`). Now let's demonstrate our previous higher-order function by passing one of the two simple functions to it as a third argument (if you want to pass your own function then make sure that it has the same signature `Int => AnyVal`).

Scala syntax for loop with ranges: The simplest syntax of using a for loop with ranges in Scala is:
```
for( var x <- range ){
statement(s)
}
```
Here, the `range` could be a range of numbers and is represented as i to j or sometimes like i until j. The left-arrow ← operator is called a generator because it's generating individual values from a range. Let's see a concrete example of this feature:
```
object UsingRangeWithForLoop {
def main(args: Array[String]):Unit= {
var i = 0;
// for loop execution with a range
for( i <- 1 to 10){
println( "Value of i: " + i )
}
}
}
```

The output of the preceding code is as follows:
```
Value of i: 1
Value of i: 2
Value of i: 3
Value of i: 4
Value of i: 5
Value of i: 6
Value of i: 7
Value of i: 8
Value of i: 9
Value of i: 10
```

Let's first define our functions before starting to use them as shown in the following screenshot:

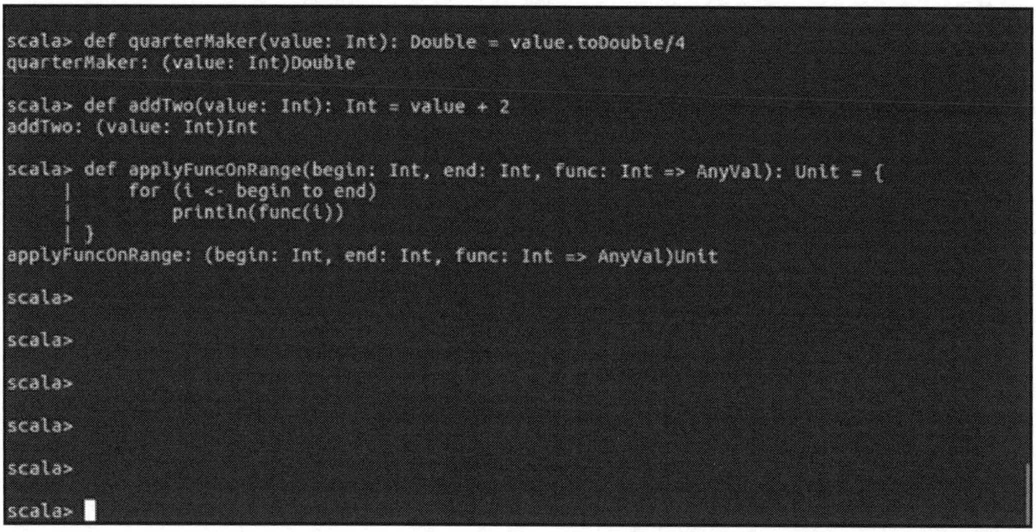

```
scala> def quarterMaker(value: Int): Double = value.toDouble/4
quarterMaker: (value: Int)Double

scala> def addTwo(value: Int): Int = value + 2
addTwo: (value: Int)Int

scala> def applyFuncOnRange(begin: Int, end: Int, func: Int => AnyVal): Unit = {
     |      for (i <- begin to end)
     |           println(func(i))
     | }
applyFuncOnRange: (begin: Int, end: Int, func: Int => AnyVal)Unit

scala>

scala>

scala>

scala>

scala>

scala>
```

Figure 2: An example of defining a higher-order function in Scala

Now, let's start by calling our higher-order function `applyFuncOnRange` and passing the `quarterMaker` function as a third argument:

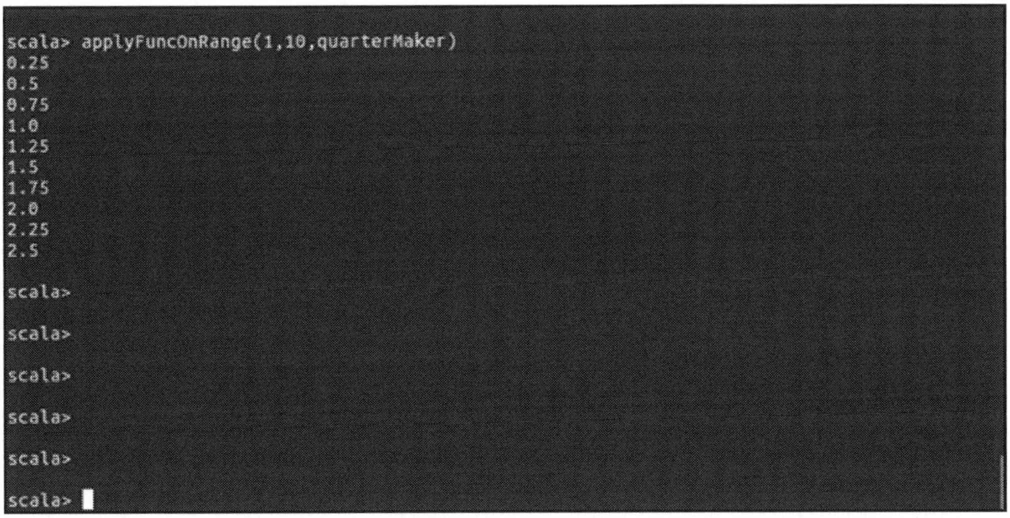

```
scala> applyFuncOnRange(1,10,quarterMaker)
0.25
0.5
0.75
1.0
1.25
1.5
1.75
2.0
2.25
2.5

scala>

scala>

scala>

scala>

scala>

scala>
```

Figure 3: Calling a higher-order function

We can even apply the other function `addTwo` since it has the same signature as shown in the following screenshot:

```
scala> applyFuncOnRange(1,10,addTwo)
3
4
5
6
7
8
9
10
11
12

scala>

scala>

scala>

scala>

scala>

scala>
```

Figure 4: An alternative way of calling a higher-order function

Before going into more examples, let's define what's called a callback function. A callback function is a function that can be passed as an argument to another function. Other functions are simply normal functions. Let's demonstrate more examples of using different callback functions. Consider the following higher-order function, which is responsible for transferring a specific amount of money from your account:

```
def TransferMoney(money: Double, bankFee: Double => Double): Double =
{
  money + bankFee(money)
}
def bankFee(amount: Double) = amount * 0.05
```

After calling the `TransferMoney` function on 100:

```
TransferMoney(100, bankFee)
```

The output of the preceding code is as follows:

```
105.0
```

From a functional programming point of view, this code is not ready to be integrated into the banking system because you need to apply different validations on the money parameters, such as it has to be positive and greater than the specific amount specified by the bank. However, here we are just demonstrating the use of high-order functions and callback functions.

So, this example works as follows: you want to transfer a specific amount of money to another bank account or money agent. The bank has a specific fee to be applied depending on the amount that you are transferring and here comes the role of the callback function. It takes the amount of money to transfer and applies the bank fee to it in order to come up with the total amount.

The `TransferMoney` function takes two parameters: the first one is the money to be transferred and the second one is a callback function with the signature `Double =>` `Double` that the function applies to the money argument to determine the bank fee over the transferred money.

```
scala> def bankFee(amount: Double) = amount * 0.05
bankFee: (amount: Double)Double

scala> def TransferMoney(money: Double, bankFee: Double => Double): Double = {
     |       money + bankFee(money)
     | }
TransferMoney: (money: Double, bankFee: Double => Double)Double

scala> TransferMoney(100, bankFee)
res2: Double = 105.0

scala>

scala>

scala>

scala>

scala>

scala>

scala>
```

Figure 5: Calling and giving extra power to the higher-order function

The complete source code of the preceding examples can be seen as follows (we called the methods using some real values):

```
package com.chapter3.ScalaFP
object HigherOrderFunction {
  def quarterMaker(value: Int): Double = value.toDouble / 4
  def testHOF(func: Int => String, value: Int) = func(value)
  def paramFunc[A](x: A) = "[" + x.toString() + "]"
  def addTwo(value: Int): Int = value + 2
  def applyFuncOnRange(begin: Int, end: Int, func: Int => AnyVal):
Unit = {
    for (i <- begin to end)
      println(func(i))
  }
  def transferMoney(money: Double, bankFee: Double => Double): Double
= {
    money + bankFee(money)
  }
  def bankFee(amount: Double) = amount * 0.05
  def main(args: Array[String]) {
    //Now call all the methods with some real values
```

```
        println(testHOF(paramFunc, 10)) // Prints [10]
        println(quarterMaker(20)) // Prints 5.0
        println(paramFunc(100)) //Prints [100]
        println(addTwo(90)) // Prints 92
        println(applyFuncOnRange(1, 20, addTwo)) // Prints 3 to 22 and ()
        println(TransferMoney(105.0, bankFee)) //prints 110.25
    }
}
```

The output of the preceding code is as follows:

```
[10]
5.0
[100]
92
3  4  5  6  7  8  9  10  11  12  13  14  15  16  1718  19  20  21  22  ()
110.25
```

By using callback functions, you are giving extra power to the higher-order function; so, it's a very powerful mechanism to make your program more elegant, flexible, and efficient.

Function as a return value

As mentioned, higher-order functions also support returning a function as a result. Let's demonstrate this by an example:

```
def transferMoney(money: Double) = {
  if (money > 1000)
    (money: Double) => "Dear customer we are going to add the
following
                       amount as Fee: "+money * 0.05
  else
    (money: Double) => "Dear customer we are going to add the
following
                       amount as Fee: "+money * 0.1
}
val returnedFunction = TransferMoney(1500)
returnedFunction(1500)
```

The preceding code segment will produce the following output:

Dear customer, we are going to add the following amount as Fee: 75.0

Let's run the previous example as shown in the following screenshot; it shows how to use the function as a return value:

```
scala> def TransferMoney(money: Double) = {
     |     if (money > 1000)
     |         (money: Double) => "Dear customer we are going to add the following amount as Fee
: "+money * 0.05
     |     else
     |         (money: Double) => "Dear customer we are going to add the following amount as Fee
: "+money * 0.1
     | }
TransferMoney: (money: Double)Double => String

scala> val returnedFunction = TransferMoney(1500)
returnedFunction: Double => String = <function1>

scala>
     | returnedFunction(1500)
res17: String = Dear customer we are going to add the following amount as Fee: 75.0

scala>

scala>

scala>

scala>
```

Figure 7: Function as a return value

The complete code of the preceding example can be seen as follows:

```
package com.chapter3.ScalaFP
object FunctionAsReturnValue {
  def transferMoney(money: Double) = {
    if (money > 1000)
      (money: Double) => "Dear customer, we are going to add following
                          amount as Fee: " + money * 0.05
    else
      (money: Double) => "Dear customer, we are going to add following
                          amount as Fee: " + money * 0.1
  }
  def main(args: Array[String]) {
    val returnedFunction = transferMoney(1500.0)
    println(returnedFunction(1500)) //Prints Dear customer, we are
                        going to add following amount as Fee: 75.0
  }
}
```

The output of the preceding code is as follows:

```
Dear customer, we are going to add following amount as Fee: 75.0
```

Now before stopping our discussion on HFO, let's see a real-life example, that is, currying using HFO.

Using higher-order functions

Suppose you work in a restaurant as a chef and one of your colleagues ask you a question: Implement a **HOF (higher-order function)** that performs currying. Looking for clues? Suppose you have the following two signatures for your HOF:

```
def curry[X,Y,Z](f:(X,Y) => Z) : X => Y => Z
```

Similarly, implement a function that performs uncurrying as follows:

```
def uncurry[X,Y,Z](f:X => Y => Z): (X,Y) => Z
```

Now, how could you use HOFs to perform the currying operation? Well, you could create a trait that encapsulates the signatures of two HOFs (that is, curry and uncurry) as follows:

```
trait Curry {
   def curry[A, B, C](f: (A, B) => C): A => B => C
   def uncurry[A, B, C](f: A => B => C): (A, B) => C
}
```

Now, you can implement and extend this trait as an object as follows:

```
object CurryImplement extends Curry {
   def uncurry[X, Y, Z](f: X => Y => Z): (X, Y) => Z = { (a: X, b: Y)
=> f(a)(b) }
   def curry[X, Y, Z](f: (X, Y) => Z): X => Y => Z = { (a: X) => { (b:
Y) => f(a, b) } }
}
```

Here I have implemented the uncurry first since it's easier. The two curly braces after the equals sign are an anonymous function literal for taking two arguments (that is, a and b of types X and Y respectively). Then, these two arguments can be used in a function that also returns a function. Then, it passes the second argument to the returned function. Finally, it returns the value of the second function. The second function literal takes one argument and returns a new function, that is, curry(). Eventually, it returns a function when called returns another function.

Now it comes: how to use the preceding object that extends the base trait in a real-life implementation. Here's an example:

```scala
object CurryingHigherOrderFunction {
  def main(args: Array[String]): Unit = {
    def add(x: Int, y: Long): Double = x.toDouble + y
    val addSpicy = CurryImplement.curry(add)
    println(addSpicy(3)(1L)) // prints "4.0"
    val increment = addSpicy(2)
    println(increment(1L)) // prints "3.0"
    val unspicedAdd = CurryImplement.uncurry(addSpicy)
    println(unspicedAdd(1, 6L)) // prints "7.0"
  }
}
```

In the preceding object and inside the main method:

- The `addSpicy` holds a function that takes a long as a type and adds 1 to it and then prints 4.0.
- The `increment` holds a function which takes a long as a type and adds 2 to it and finally prints 3.0.
- The `unspicedAdd` holds a function which adds 1 and takes a long as type. Finally, it prints 7.0.

The output of the preceding code is as follows:

```
4.0
3.0
7.0
```

In mathematics and computer science, currying is the technique of translating the evaluation of a function that takes multiple arguments (or a tuple of arguments) into evaluating a sequence of functions, each with a a single argument. Currying is related to, but not the same as, partial application:

Currying: Currying is useful in both practical and theoretical settings. In functional programming languages, and many others, it provides a way of automatically managing how arguments are passed to functions and exceptions. In theoretical computer science, it provides a way to study functions with multiple arguments in simpler theoretical models, which provide only one argument.

Uncurrying: Uncurrying is the dual transformation to currying, and can be seen as a form of defunctionalization. It takes a function `f` whose return value is another function `g` and yields a new function `f'` that takes as parameters the arguments for both `f` and `g`, and returns, as a result, the application of `f` and subsequently, `g`, to those arguments. The process can be iterated.

So far, we have seen how to deal with pure, higher-order, and anonymous functions in Scala. Now, let's have a brief overview on how to extend the higher-order function using `Throw`, `Try`, `Either`, and `Future` in the following section.

Error handling in functional Scala

So far, we focused on ensuring that the body of a Scala function does what it's supposed to and doesn't do anything else (that is, an error or exception). Now, in order to make use of any programming and to avoid producing error-prone code then you need to know how to catch exceptions and handle errors in this language. We will see how to extend higher-order functions outside collections using some special features of Scala such as `Try`, `Either`, and `Future`.

Failure and exceptions in Scala

At first, let's define what we mean by failures in general (source: `https://tersesystems.com/2012/12/27/error-handling-in-scala/`):

- **Unexpected internal failure**: The operation fails as the result of an unfulfilled expectation, such as a null pointer reference, violated assertions, or simply bad state
- **Expected internal failure**: The operation fails deliberately as a result of internal state, that is, a blacklist or circuit breaker
- **Expected external failure**: The operation fails because it is told to process some raw input, and will fail if the raw input cannot be processed
- **Unexpected external failure**: The operation fails because a resource that the system depends on is not there: there's a loose file handle, the database connection fails, or the network is down

Unfortunately, there are no concrete ways of stopping failures unless the failures are due to some manageable exceptions. On the other hand, Scala makes *checked versus unchecked* very simple: it doesn't have checked exceptions. All exceptions are unchecked in Scala, even `SQLException` and `IOException`, and so on. Now let's see how to handle such exceptions at least.

Throwing exceptions

A Scala method can throw an exception because of the unexpected workflow. You create an exception object and then you throw it with the throw keyword as follows. For example:

```
//code something
throw new IllegalArgumentException("arg 2 was wrong...");
//nothing will be executed from here.
```

Note that the primary goal of using exception handling is not to produce friendly messages but to exit the normal flow of your Scala program.

Catching exception using try and catch

Scala allows you to try/catch any exception in a single block and then perform pattern matching against it using case blocks. The basic syntax of using `try...catch` in Scala is as follows:

```
try
{
  // your scala code should go here
}
catch
{
  case foo: FooException => handleFooException(foo)
  case bar: BarException => handleBarException(bar)
  case _: Throwable => println("Got some other kind of exception")
}
finally
{
  // your scala code should go here, such as to close a database
connection
}
```

Thus, if you throw an exception, then you need to use the `try...catch` block in order to handle it nicely without crashing with an internal exception message:

```scala
package com.chapter3.ScalaFP
import java.io.IOException
import java.io.FileReader
import java.io.FileNotFoundException

object TryCatch {
  def main(args: Array[String]) {
    try {
      val f = new FileReader("data/data.txt")
    } catch {
      case ex: FileNotFoundException => println("File not found
exception")
      case ex: IOException => println("IO Exception")
    }
  }
}
```

If there's no file named `data.txt`, in the path/data under your project tree, you will experience `FileNotFoundException` as follows:

The output of the preceding code is as follows:

File not found exception

Now, let's have a brief example of using the `finally` clause in Scala to make the `try...catch` block complete.

Finally

Suppose you want to execute your code regardless of an exception being thrown or not, then you should use the `finally` clause. You can place it inside the `try` block as follows. Here is an example:

```scala
try {
    val f = new FileReader("data/data.txt")
  } catch {
    case ex: FileNotFoundException => println("File not found
exception")
  } finally { println("Dude! this code always executes") }
}
```

Now, here's the complete example of using try...catch...finally:

```
package com.chapter3.ScalaFP
import java.io.IOException
import java.io.FileReader
import java.io.FileNotFoundException

object TryCatch {
  def main(args: Array[String]) {
    try {
      val f = new FileReader("data/data.txt")
    } catch {
      case ex: FileNotFoundException => println("File not found
                                                  exception")
      case ex: IOException => println("IO Exception")
    } finally {
      println("Finally block always executes!")
    }
  }
}
```

The output of the preceding code is as follows:

```
File not found exception
Finally block always executes!
```

Next, we will discuss another powerful feature in Scala called Either.

Creating an Either

Either[X, Y] is an instance that contains either an instance of X or an instance of Y but not both. We call these subtypes left and right of Either. Creating an Either is trivial. But it's very powerful sometimes to use it in your program:

```
package com.chapter3.ScalaFP
import java.net.URL
import scala.io.Source
object Either {
  def getData(dataURL: URL): Either[String, Source] =
    if (dataURL.getHost.contains("xxx"))
      Left("Requested URL is blocked or prohibited!")
    else
      Right(Source.fromURL(dataURL))
  def main(args: Array[String]) {
    val either1 = getData(new URL("http://www.xxx.com"))
    println(either1)
```

```
        val either2 = getData(new URL("http://www.google.com"))
        println(either2)
    }
}
```

Now, if we pass any arbitrary URL that doesn't contain xxx then we will get a Scala.io.Source wrapped in a Right subtype. If the URL contains xxx, then we will get a String wrapped in a Left subtype. To make the preceding statement clearer, let's see the output of the preceding code segment:

Left(Requested URL is blocked or prohibited!) Right(non-empty iterator)

Next, we will explore another interesting feature of Scala called Future that is used to execute tasks in a non-blocking way. This is also a better way to handle the results when they finish.

Future

If you simply want to run tasks in a non-blocking way and need a way to handle the results when they finish, Scala provides you with Futures, for example, if you want to make multiple web service calls in a parallel fashion and work with the results after the web service handles all these calls. An example of using Future is provided in the following section.

Run one task, but block

The following example demonstrates how to create a Future and then block the sequence of execution in order to wait for its result. Creating Futures is trivial. You just need to pass it to the code that you want. The following example performs 2+2 in the future and then returns the results:

```
package com.chapter3.ScalaFP
import scala.concurrent.ExecutionContext.Implicits.global
import scala.concurrent.duration._
import scala.concurrent.{Await, Future}

object RunOneTaskbutBlock {
  def main(args: Array[String]) {
    // Getting the current time in Milliseconds
    implicit val baseTime = System.currentTimeMillis
    // Future creation
    val testFuture = Future {
```

```
      Thread.sleep(300)
      2 + 2
    }
    // this is the blocking part
    val finalOutput = Await.result(testFuture, 2 second)
    println(finalOutput)
  }
}
```

The `Await.result` method waits up to 2 seconds till the `Future` returns the result; if it doesn't return the result within 2 seconds, it throws the following exception you might want to handle or catch:

`java.util.concurrent.TimeoutException`

It's time to wrap up this chapter. However, I would like to take the chance to discuss an important view of mine about functional programming with Scala and object mutability.

Functional programming and data mutability

Pure functional programming is one of the best practices in functional programming and you should stick to it. Writing pure functions will make your programming life easier and you will be able to write code that's easy to maintain and extend. Also, if you want to parallelize your code then it will be easier to do so if you write pure functions.

If you're an FP purist, one drawback of using functional programming in Scala is that Scala supports both OOP and FP (see *Figure 1*), and therefore it's possible to mix the two coding styles in the same code base. In this chapter, we have seen several examples showing that writing pure functions is easy. However, combining them into a complete application is difficult. You might agree that advanced topics such as monads make FP intimidating.

I talked to many people and they think that the recursion doesn't feel reasonably natural. When you use immutable objects, you can never mutate them with something else. There aren't times when you are allowed to do that. That's the whole point of immutable objects! Sometimes what I have experienced is that a pure function and data input or output really mixes up. However, when you need to mutate, you can create a copy of the object containing your mutated field. Thus, theoretically, there's no need to *mix up*. Lastly, using only immutable values and recursion can potentially lead to performance problems in terms of CPU usage and RAM.

Summary

In this chapter, we have explored some functional programming concepts in Scala. We have seen what functional programming is and how Scala supports it, why it matters, and the advantages of using functional concepts. We have seen why learning FP concepts is important in learning the Spark paradigm. Pure functions, anonymous functions, and higher-order functions were discussed with suitable examples. Later in this chapter, we saw how to handle exceptions in the higher-order functions outside collections using the standard library of Scala. Finally, we discussed how functional Scala affects object mutability.

In the next chapter, we will provide an in-depth analysis on the Collections API, one of the most prominent features of the standard library.

4
Collection APIs

"That we become depends on what we read after all of the professors have finished with us. The greatest university of all is a collection of books."

- Thomas Carlyle

One of the features that attract most Scala users in its Collection APIs that are very powerful, flexible, and has lots of operations coupled with it. The wide range of operations will make your life easy dealing with any kind of data. We are going to introduce Scala collections APIs including their different types and hierarchies in order to accommodate different types of data and solve a wide range of different problems. In a nutshell, the following topics will be covered in this chapter:

- Scala collection APIs
- Types and hierarchies
- Performance characteristics
- Java interoperability
- Using Scala implicits

Scala collection APIs

The Scala collections are a well-understood and frequently used programming abstraction that can be distinguished between mutable and immutable collections. Like a mutable variable, a *mutable* collection can be changed, updated, or extended when necessary. However, like an immutable variable, *immutable* collections cannot be changed. Most collection classes to utilize them are located in the packages `scala.collection`, `scala.collection.immutable`, and `scala.collection.mutable`, respectively.

This extremely powerful feature of Scala provides you with the following facility to use and manipulate your data:

- **Easy to use**: For example, it helps you eliminate the interference between iterators and collection updates. As a result, a small vocabulary consisting of 20-50 methods should be enough to solve most of your collection problem in your data analytics solution.
- **Concise**: You can use functional operations with a light-weight syntax and combine operations and, at the end, you will feel like that you're using custom algebra.
- **Safe**: Helps you deal with most errors while coding.
- **Fast**: most collection objects are carefully tuned and optimized; this enables you data computation in a faster way.
- **Universal**: Collections enable you to use and perform the same operations on any type, anywhere.

In the next section, we will explore the types and associated hierarchies of Scala collection APIs. We will see several examples of using most features in the collection APIs.

Types and hierarchies

Scala collections are a well-understood and frequently-used programming abstraction that can be distinguished between mutable and immutable collections. Like a mutable variable, a mutable collection can be changed, updated, or extended when necessary. Like an immutable variable, immutable collections; cannot be changed. Most collection classes that utilize them are located in the packages `scala.collection`, `scala.collection.immutable`, and `scala.collection.mutable`, respectively.

The following hierarchical diagram (*Figure 1*) shows the Scala collections API hierarchy according to the official documentation of Scala. These all are either high-level abstract classes or traits. These have mutable as well as immutable implementations.

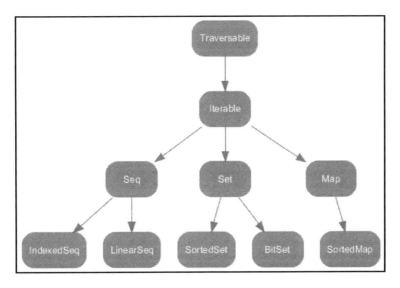

Figure 1: Collections under package scala.collection

Traversable

Traversable is the root of the collections' hierarchy. In Traversable, there are definitions for a wide range of operations that the Scala Collections API offers. There is only one abstract method in Traversable, which is the `foreach` method.

```
def foreach[U](f: Elem => U): Unit
```

This method is essential to all the operations contained in Traversable. If you have studied data structures, you will be familiar with traversing a data structure's elements and executing a function on each element. The `foreach` method does exactly so that, it traverses the elements in the collection and executes a function f on each element. As we mentioned, this is an abstract method and it was designed to have different definitions according to the underlying collection that will make use of it, to ensure highly optimized code for each collection.

Iterable

Iterable is the second root in the hierarchy diagram of the Scala collections API. It has an abstract method called iterator that must be implemented/defined in all other subcollections. It also implements the `foreach` method from the root, which is Traversable. But as we mentioned, all the descendent subcollections will override this implementation to make specific optimizations related to this subcollection.

Seq, LinearSeq, and IndexedSeq

A sequence has some differences from the usual Iterable, and it has a defined length and order. Seq has two sub-traits such as `LinearSeq` and `IndexedSeq`. Let's have a quick overview on them.

`LinearSeq` is a base trait for linear sequences. Linear sequences have reasonably efficient head, tail, and `isEmpty` methods. If these methods provide the fastest way to traverse the collection, a collection `Coll` that extends this trait should also extend `LinearSeqOptimized[A, Coll[A]]`. `LinearSeq` has three concrete methods:

- **isEmpty:** This checks if the list is empty or not
- **head**: This returns the first element in the list/sequence
- **tail**: This returns all the elements of the list but the first one. Each of the subcollections that inherit the `LinearSeq` will have its own implementation of these methods to ensure good performance. Two collections that inherit/extend are streams and lists.

 For more on this topic, refer to this URL at `http://www.scala-lang.org/api/current/scala/collection/LinearSeq.html`.

Finally, `IndexedSeq` has two methods that it's defined in terms of them:

- **Apply:** This finds elements by index.
- **length**: This returns the length of the sequence. Finding an element by its index requires well performing implementation by the subcollections. Two of these indexed sequences are `Vector` and `ArrayBuffer`.

Mutable and immutable

In Scala, you will find mutable and immutable collections. A collection can have a mutable implementation and an immutable implementation. That's the reason why, in Java, a List can't be both a LinkedList and an ArrayList, but List has a LinkedList implementation and an ArrayList implementation. The following figure shows all collections in the package scala.collection.immutable:

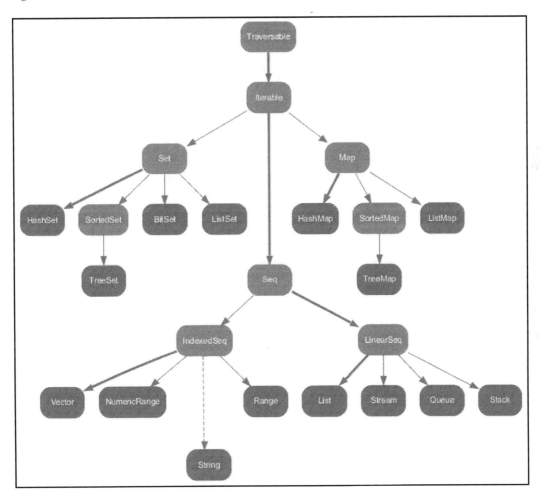

Figure 2: All collections in package scala.collection.immutable

Scala imports the immutable collections by default, and if you need to use a mutable one, then you need to import it yourself. Now to get a brief overview of all collections in package `scala.collection.mutable`, refer to the following diagram:

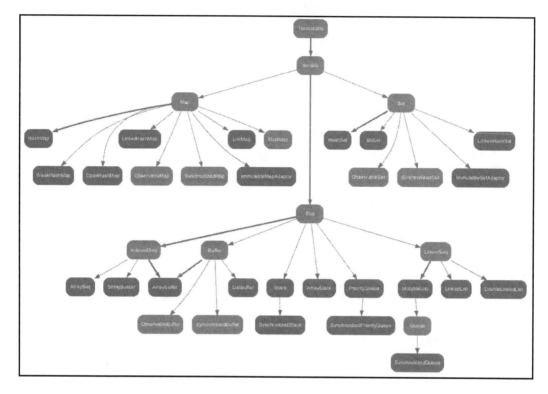

Figure 3: All collections in package Scala.collection.mutable

In every OOP and functional programming language, an array is an important collection package that helps us to store data objects so that, later on, we can access them very easily as well. In the next subsection, we will see a detailed discussion on arrays with some examples.

Arrays

An array is a mutable collection. In arrays, the order of the elements will be preserved and duplicated elements will be kept. Being mutable, you can change the value of any element of the array by accessing it by its index number. Let's demonstrate arrays with several examples. Use the following line of code to just declare a simple array:

```
val numbers: Array[Int] = Array[Int](1, 2, 3, 4, 5, 1, 2, 3, 3, 4, 5)
// A simple array
```

Now, print all the elements of the array:

```
println("The full array is: ")
  for (i <- numbers) {
    print(" " + i)
  }
```

Now, print a particular element: for example, element 3:

```
println(numbers(2))
```

Let's sum all the elements and print the sum:

```
var total = 0;
for (i <- 0 to (numbers.length - 1)) {
  total = total + numbers(i)
}
println("Sum: = " + total)
```

Finding the smallest element:

```
var min = numbers(0)
for (i <- 1 to (numbers.length - 1)) {
  if (numbers(i) < min) min = numbers(i)
}
println("Min is: " + min)
```

Finding the largest element:

```
var max = numbers(0);
for (i <- 1 to (numbers.length - 1)) {
  if (numbers(i) > max) max = numbers(i)
}
println("Max is: " + max)
```

Another way of creating and defining an array is using the `range ()` method that goes as follows:

```
//Creating array using range() method
var myArray1 = range(5, 20, 2)
var myArray2 = range(5, 20)
```

The preceding line of code means that I have created an array with elements between 5 and 20 with the range difference 2. If you don't specify the 3rd parameter, Scala will assume the range difference is:

```
//Creating array using range() method without range difference
var myArray1 = range(5, 20, 2)
```

Now, let's see how to access the elements as follows:

```
// Print all the array elements
for (x <- myArray1) {
  print(" " + x)
}
println()
for (x <- myArray2) {
  print(" " + x)
}
```

It's even possible to concatenate two arrays using the `concat ()` method as follows:

```
//Array concatenation
var myArray3 =  concat( myArray1, myArray2)
// Print all the array elements
for ( x <- myArray3 ) {
  print(" "+ x)
}
```

Note that for using the `range ()` and the `concat ()` method, you will need to import the Scala `Array` package as follows:

```
Import Array._
```

Lastly, it's even possible to define and use a multi-dimensional array as follows:

```
var myMatrix = ofDim[Int](4,4)
```

Now, first create a matrix using the preceding array as follows:

```
var myMatrix = ofDim[Int](4, 4)
// build a matrix
for (i <- 0 to 3) {
```

```
  for (j <- 0 to 3) {
    myMatrix(i)(j) = j
  }
}
println()
```

Print the earlier matrix as follows:

```
// Print two dimensional array
for (i <- 0 to 3) {
  for (j <- 0 to 3) {
    print(" " + myMatrix(i)(j))
  }
  println()
}
```

The complete source code of the previous example can be seen as follows:

```
package com.chapter4.CollectionAPI
import Array._
object ArrayExample {
  def main(args: Array[String]) {
    val numbers: Array[Int] = Array[Int](1, 2, 3, 4, 5, 1, 2, 3, 3, 4,
5)
    // A simple array
    // Print all the element of the array
    println("The full array is: ")
    for (i <- numbers) {
      print(" " + i)
    }
    //Print a particular element for example element 3
    println(numbers(2))
    //Summing all the elements
    var total = 0
    for (i <- 0 to (numbers.length - 1)) {
      total = total + numbers(i)
    }
    println("Sum: = " + total)
    // Finding the smallest element
    var min = numbers(0)
    for (i <- 1 to (numbers.length - 1)) {
      if (numbers(i) < min) min = numbers(i)
    }
    println("Min is: " + min)
    // Finding the largest element
    var max = numbers(0)
    for (i <- 1 to (numbers.length - 1)) {
      if (numbers(i) > max) max = numbers(i)
```

```
  }
  println("Max is: " + max)
  //Creating array using range() method
  var myArray1 = range(5, 20, 2)
  var myArray2 = range(5, 20)
  // Print all the array elements
  for (x <- myArray1) {
    print(" " + x)
  }
  println()
  for (x <- myArray2) {
    print(" " + x)
  }
  //Array concatenation
  var myArray3 = concat(myArray1, myArray2)
  // Print all the array elements
  for (x <- myArray3) {
    print(" " + x)
  }
  //Multi-dimensional array
  var myMatrix = ofDim[Int](4, 4)
  // build a matrix
  for (i <- 0 to 3) {
    for (j <- 0 to 3) {
      myMatrix(i)(j) = j
    }
  }
  println();
  // Print two dimensional array
  for (i <- 0 to 3) {
    for (j <- 0 to 3) {
      print(" " + myMatrix(i)(j))
    }
    println();
  }
  }
}
```

You will get the following output:

```
The full array is: 1 2 3 4 5 1 2 3 3 4 53
Sum: = 33
Min is: 1
Max is: 5
5 7 9 11 13 15 17 19 5 6 7 8 9 10 11 12 13 14 15 16 17 18 19 5 7 9 11
13 15 17 19 5 6 7 8 9 10 11 12 13 14 15 16 17 18 19
0 1 2 3
0 1 2 3
```

```
0 1 2 3
0 1 2 3
```

In Scala, lists preserve order, keep duplicated elements, and also check their immutability. Now, let's see some examples of using lists in Scala in the next subsection.

Lists

As discussed earlier, Scala provides mutable and immutable collections. The Immutable collections are imported by default, but if you need to use a mutable one you need to import yourself. A list is an immutable collections, and it can be used if you want order between the elements to be preserved and duplicates to be kept. Let's demonstrate an example and see how lists preserve order and keep duplicated elements, and also check its immutability:

```
scala> val numbers = List(1, 2, 3, 4, 5, 1, 2, 3, 4, 5)
numbers: List[Int] = List(1, 2, 3, 4, 5, 1, 2, 3, 4, 5)
scala> numbers(3) = 10
<console>:12: error: value update is not a member of List[Int]
numbers(3) = 10 ^
```

You can define lists using two different building blocks. `Nil` represents the tail of the `List` and, afterwards, an empty `List`. So, the preceding example can be rewritten as:

```
scala> val numbers = 1 :: 2 :: 3 :: 4 :: 5 :: 1 :: 2 :: 3:: 4:: 5 ::
Nil
numbers: List[Int] = List(1, 2, 3, 4, 5, 1, 2, 3,4, 5
```

Let's check lists with its method in the following detailed example:

```
package com.chapter4.CollectionAPI

object ListExample {
  def main(args: Array[String]) {
    // List of cities
    val cities = "Dublin" :: "London" :: "NY" :: Nil

    // List of Even Numbers
    val nums = 2 :: 4 :: 6 :: 8 :: Nil

    // Empty List.
    val empty = Nil

    // Two dimensional list
```

```
        val dim = 1 :: 2 :: 3 :: Nil ::
                  4 :: 5 :: 6 :: Nil ::
                  7 :: 8 :: 9 :: Nil :: Nil
        val temp = Nil
        // Getting the first element in the list
        println( "Head of cities : " + cities.head )

        // Getting all the elements but the last one
        println( "Tail of cities : " + cities.tail )

        //Checking if cities/temp list is empty
        println( "Check if cities is empty : " + cities.isEmpty )
        println( "Check if temp is empty : " + temp.isEmpty )
        val citiesEurope = "Dublin" :: "London" :: "Berlin" :: Nil
        val citiesTurkey = "Istanbul" :: "Ankara" :: Nil

        //Concatenate two or more lists with :::
        var citiesConcatenated = citiesEurope ::: citiesTurkey
        println( "citiesEurope ::: citiesTurkey : "+citiesConcatenated )
        // using the concat method
        citiesConcatenated = List.concat(citiesEurope, citiesTurkey)
        println( "List.concat(citiesEurope, citiesTurkey) : " +
                citiesConcatenated  )

    }
}
```

You will get the following output:

```
Head of cities : Dublin
Tail of cities : List(London, NY)
Check if cities is empty : false
Check if temp is empty : true
citiesEurope ::: citiesTurkey : List(Dublin, London, Berlin, Istanbul,
Ankara)
List.concat(citiesEurope, citiesTurkey) : List(Dublin, London, Berlin,
Istanbul, Ankara)
```

Now, let's see another quick overview of how to use sets in your Scala application in the next subsection.

Sets

A set is one of the most widely used collections. In sets order will not be preserved and sets don't allow duplicate elements. You can think of it as the mathematical notation of sets. Let's demonstrate this by an example, and we will see how sets don't preserve ordering and don't allow duplicates:

```scala
scala> val numbers = Set( 1, 2, 3, 4, 5, 1, 2, 3, 4, 5)
numbers: scala.collection.immutable.Set[Int] = Set(5, 1, 2, 3, 4)
```

The following source code shows the different uses of sets in a Scala program:

```scala
package com.chapter4.CollectionAPI
object SetExample {
  def main(args: Array[String]) {
    // Empty set of integer type
    var sInteger : Set[Int] = Set()
    // Set of even numbers
    var sEven : Set[Int] = Set(2,4,8,10)
    //Or you can use this syntax
    var sEven2 = Set(2,4,8,10)
    val cities = Set("Dublin", "London", "NY")
    val tempNums: Set[Int] = Set()
    //Finding Head, Tail, and checking if the sets are empty
    println( "Head of cities : " + cities.head )
    println( "Tail of cities : " + cities.tail )
    println( "Check if cities is empty : " + cities.isEmpty )
    println( "Check if tempNums is empty : " + tempNums.isEmpty )
    val citiesEurope = Set("Dublin", "London", "NY")
    val citiesTurkey = Set("Istanbul", "Ankara")
    // Sets Concatenation using ++ operator
    var citiesConcatenated = citiesEurope ++ citiesTurkey
    println( "citiesEurope ++ citiesTurkey : " + citiesConcatenated )
    //Also you can use ++ as a method
    citiesConcatenated = citiesEurope.++(citiesTurkey)
    println( "citiesEurope.++(citiesTurkey) : " + citiesConcatenated )
    //Finding minimum and maximum elements in the set
    val evenNumbers = Set(2,4,6,8)
    // Using the min and max methods
    println( "Minimum element in Set(2,4,6,8) : " + evenNumbers.min )
    println( "Maximum element in Set(2,4,6,8) : " + evenNumbers.max )
  }
}
```

You will get the following output:

```
Head of cities : Dublin
Tail of cities : Set(London, NY)
Check if cities is empty : false
Check if tempNums is empty : true
citiesEurope ++ citiesTurkey : Set(London, Dublin, Ankara, Istanbul,
NY)
citiesEurope.++(citiesTurkey) : Set(London, Dublin, Ankara, Istanbul,
NY)
Minimum element in Set(2,4,6,8) : 2
Maximum element in Set(2,4,6,8) : 8
```

From my personal experience while developing Spark applications using Java or Scala, I found very frequent uses of tuples, especially for grouping collections of elements without using any explicit classes. In the next subsection, we will see how to get started with Tuples in Scala.

Tuples

Scala tuples are used to combine a fixed number of items together. The ultimate target of this grouping is to help in the anonymous function and so that they can be passed around as a whole. The real difference with an array or list is that a tuple can hold objects of different types while maintaining the information of the type of each element, while a collection doesn't and uses, as the type, the common type (for instance, in the previous example, the type of that set would be Set[Any]).

From the computational point of view, Scala tuples are also immutable. In other words, Tuples do use a classes to store elements (for example, Tuple2, Tuple3, Tuple22, and so on).

The following is an example of a tuple holding an integer, a string, and the console:

```
val tuple_1 = (20, "Hello", Console)
```

Which is syntactic sugar (shortcut) for the following:

```
val t = new Tuple3(20, "Hello", Console)
```

Another example:

```
scala> val cityPop = ("Dublin", 2)
cityPop: (String, Int) = (Dublin,2)
```

There are no named accessors for you to access the tuple data but instead you need to use accessors that are based on the position and are 1-based not 0-based. For example:

```
scala> val cityPop = ("Dublin", 2)
cityPop: (String, Int) = (Dublin,2)

scala> cityPop._1
res3: String = Dublin

scala> cityPop._2
res4: Int = 2
```

Moreover, tuples can fit perfectly in pattern matching. For example:

```
cityPop match {
  case ("Dublin", population) => ...
  case ("NY", population) => ...
}
```

You can even use the special operator -> in order to write a compact syntax for 2-values tuples. For example:

```
scala> "Dublin" -> 2
res0: (String, Int) = (Dublin,2)
```

The following is a more detailed example to demonstrate tuple functionality:

```
package com.chapter4.CollectionAPI
object TupleExample {
  def main(args: Array[String]) {
    val evenTuple = (2,4,6,8)
    val sumTupleElements =evenTuple._1 + evenTuple._2 + evenTuple._3 +
evenTuple._4
    println( "Sum of Tuple Elements: "  + sumTupleElements )
    // You can also iterate over the tuple and print it's element
using the foreach method
    evenTuple.productIterator.foreach{ evenTuple =>println("Value = "
+ evenTuple )}
  }
}
```

You will get the following output:

```
Sum of Tuple Elements: 20 Value = 2 Value = 4 Value = 6 Value = 8
```

Now, let's delve into the world of using maps in Scala, these are widely used to hold basic datatypes.

Maps

A map is an `Iterable` consisting of pairs of keys and values (also named mappings or associations). A map is also one of the most widely used connections as it can be used to hold basic datatypes. For example:

```scala
scala> Map(1 -> 2)
res7: scala.collection.immutable.Map[Int,Int] = Map(1 -> 2)
scala> Map("X" -> "Y")
res8: scala.collection.immutable.Map[String,String] = Map(X -> Y)
```

Scala's `Predef` object offers an implicit conversion that lets you write `key -> value` as an alternate syntax for the `pair (key, value)`. For instance, `Map("a" -> 10, "b" -> 15, "c" -> 16)` means exactly the same as `Map(("a", 10), ("b", 15), ("c", 16))`, but reads better.

Moreover, a `Map` can be simply considered a collection of `Tuple2s`:

```scala
Map(2 -> "two", 4 -> "four")
```

The preceding line will be understood as:

```scala
Map((2, "two"), (4, "four"))
```

In the example, we can state that using `Map` a function can be stored, and this is the whole point of functions in a Functional Programming language: they are first-class citizens and can be used anywhere.

Suppose you have a method for finding the max element in an array as follows:

```scala
var myArray = range(5, 20, 2)
  def getMax(): Int = {
    // Finding the largest element
    var max = myArray(0)
    for (i <- 1 to (myArray.length - 1)) {
      if (myArray(i) > max)
        max = myArray(i)
    }
    max
  }
```

Now, let's map it such that using the `Map` the method can be stored:

```scala
scala> val myMax = Map("getMax" -> getMax())
scala> println("My max is: " + myMax )
```

Let's another of using maps as follows:

```scala
scala> Map( 2 -> "two", 4 -> "four")
res9: scala.collection.immutable.Map[Int,String] = Map(2 -> two, 4 ->
four)
scala> Map( 1 -> Map("X"-> "Y"))
res10:
scala.collection.immutable.Map[Int,scala.collection.immutable.Map[Stri
ng,String]] = Map(1 -> Map(X -> Y))
```

The following is a detailed example to demonstrate Map functionality:

```scala
package com.chapter4.CollectionAPI
import Array._

object MapExample {
  var myArray = range(5, 20, 2)
  def getMax(): Int = {
    // Finding the largest element
    var max = myArray(0)
    for (i <- 1 to (myArray.length - 1)) {
      if (myArray(i) > max)
        max = myArray(i)
    }
    max
  }

  def main(args: Array[String]) {
    val capitals = Map("Ireland" -> "Dublin", "Britain" -> "London",
    "Germany" -> "Berlin")

    val temp: Map[Int, Int] = Map()
    val myMax = Map("getMax" -> getMax())
    println("My max is: " + myMax )

    println("Keys in capitals : " + capitals.keys)
    println("Values in capitals : " + capitals.values)
    println("Check if capitals is empty : " + capitals.isEmpty)
    println("Check if temp is empty : " + temp.isEmpty)

    val capitals1 = Map("Ireland" -> "Dublin", "Turkey" -> "Ankara",
    "Egypt" -> "Cairo")
    val capitals2 = Map("Germany" -> "Berlin", "Saudi Arabia" ->
    "Riyadh")

    // Map concatenation using ++ operator
    var capitalsConcatenated = capitals1 ++ capitals2
    println("capitals1 ++ capitals2 : " + capitalsConcatenated)
```

```
    // use two maps with ++ as method
    capitalsConcatenated = capitals1.++(capitals2)
    println("capitals1.++(capitals2)) : " + capitalsConcatenated)

  }
}
```

You will get the following output:

```
My max is: Map(getMax -> 19)
Keys in capitals : Set(Ireland, Britain, Germany)
Values in capitals : MapLike(Dublin, London, Berlin)
Check if capitals is empty : false
Check if temp is empty : true
capitals1 ++ capitals2 : Map(Saudi Arabia -> Riyadh, Egypt -> Cairo,
Ireland -> Dublin, Turkey -> Ankara, Germany -> Berlin)
capitals1.++(capitals2)) : Map(Saudi Arabia -> Riyadh, Egypt -> Cairo,
Ireland -> Dublin, Turkey -> Ankara, Germany -> Berlin)
```

Now, let's take a quick overview of using option in Scala; this is basically a data container that can hold data.

Option

The Option type is used frequently in Scala programs, and you can compare this with the null value available in Java, which indicates no value. Scala Option [T] is a container for zero or one element for a given type. An Option [T] can be either a Some [T] or None object, which represents a missing value. For instance, the get method of Scala's Map produces Some (value) if a value corresponding to a given key has been found, or None if the given key is not defined in the Map.

The basic trait for an Option looks like this:

```
trait Option[T] {
  def get: A // Returns the option's value.
  def isEmpty: Boolean // Returns true if the option is None, false
  otherwise.
  def productArity: Int // The size of this product. For a product
  A(x_1, ..., x_k), returns k
  def productElement(n: Int): Any // The nth element of this product,
  0-based
  def exists(p: (A) => Boolean): Boolean // Returns true if this
option
  is nonempty
  def filter(p: (A) => Boolean): Option[A] // Returns this Option if
```

```
it
  is nonempty
  def filterNot(p: (A) => Boolean): Option[A] // Returns this Option
if
  it is nonempty or return None.
  def flatMap[B](f: (A) => Option[B]): Option[B] // Returns result of
  applying f to this Option's
  def foreach[U](f: (A) => U): Unit // Apply given procedure f to the
  option's value, if it is nonempty.
  def getOrElse[B >: A](default: => B): B // Returns the option's
value
  if the option is nonempty,
  def isDefined: Boolean // Returns true if the option is an instance
  of Some, false otherwise.
  def iterator: Iterator[A] // Returns a singleton iterator returning
  Option's value if it is nonempty
  def map[B](f: (A) => B): Option[B] // Returns a Some containing
  result of applying f to this Option's
  def orElse[B >: A](alternative: => Option[B]): Option[B] // Returns
  this Option if it is nonempty
  def orNull // Returns the option's value if it is nonempty,
              or null if it is empty.
}
```

For example, in the following code, we are trying to map and show some meagacities that are located in some countries such as India, Bangladesh, Japan, and USA:

```
object ScalaOptions {
  def main(args: Array[String]) {
    val megacity = Map("Bangladesh" -> "Dhaka", "Japan" -> "Tokyo",
    "India" -> "Kolkata", "USA" -> "New York")
    println("megacity.get( \"Bangladesh\" ) : " +
    show(megacity.get("Bangladesh")))
    println("megacity.get( \"India\" ) : " +
    show(megacity.get("India")))
  }
}
```

Now, to make the preceding code work, we need to have the show() method defined somewhere. Here, we can do it by Scala pattern matching using Option as follows:

```
def show(x: Option[String]) = x match {
  case Some(s) => s
  case None => "?"
}
```

Combining these as follows should print the accurate and desired result that we are expecting:

```
package com.chapter4.CollectionAPI
object ScalaOptions {
  def show(x: Option[String]) = x match {
    case Some(s) => s
    case None => "?"
  }
  def main(args: Array[String]) {
    val megacity = Map("Bangladesh" -> "Dhaka", "Japan" -> "Tokyo",
    "India" -> "Kolkata", "USA" -> "New York")
    println("megacity.get( \"Bangladesh\" ) : " +
    show(megacity.get("Bangladesh")))
    println("megacity.get( \"India\" ) : " +
    show(megacity.get("India")))
  }
}
```

You will get the following output:

```
megacity.get( "Bangladesh" ) : Dhaka
megacity.get( "India" ) : Kolkata
```

Using the getOrElse() method, it is possible to access a value or a default when no value is present. For example:

```
// Using getOrElse() method:
val message: Option[String] = Some("Hello, world!")
val x: Option[Int] = Some(20)
val y: Option[Int] = None
println("message.getOrElse(0): " + message.getOrElse(0))
println("x.getOrElse(0): " + x.getOrElse(0))
println("y.getOrElse(10): " + y.getOrElse(10))
```

You will get the following output:

```
message.getOrElse(0): Hello, world!
x.getOrElse(0): 20
y.getOrElse(10): 10
```

Moreover, using the isEmpty() method, you can check if the option is None or not. For example:

```
println("message.isEmpty: " + message.isEmpty)
println("x.isEmpty: " + x.isEmpty)
println("y.isEmpty: " + y.isEmpty)
```

Now, here's the complete program:

```
package com.chapter4.CollectionAPI
object ScalaOptions {
  def show(x: Option[String]) = x match {
    case Some(s) => s
    case None => "?"
  }
  def main(args: Array[String]) {
    val megacity = Map("Bangladesh" -> "Dhaka", "Japan" -> "Tokyo",
    "India" -> "Kolkata", "USA" -> "New York")
    println("megacity.get( \"Bangladesh\" ) : " +
    show(megacity.get("Bangladesh")))
    println("megacity.get( \"India\" ) : " +
    show(megacity.get("India")))

    // Using getOrElse() method:
    val message: Option[String] = Some("Hello, world")
    val x: Option[Int] = Some(20)
    val y: Option[Int] = None

    println("message.getOrElse(0): " + message.getOrElse(0))
    println("x.getOrElse(0): " + x.getOrElse(0))
    println("y.getOrElse(10): " + y.getOrElse(10))

    // Using isEmpty()
    println("message.isEmpty: " + message.isEmpty)
    println("x.isEmpty: " + x.isEmpty)
    println("y.isEmpty: " + y.isEmpty)
  }
}
```

You will get the following output:

```
megacity.get( "Bangladesh" ) : Dhaka
megacity.get( "India" ) : Kolkata
message.getOrElse(0): Hello, world
x.getOrElse(0): 20
y.getOrElse(10): 10
message.isEmpty: false
x.isEmpty: false
y.isEmpty: true
```

Let's take a look at other examples on when to use `Option`. For example, the `Map.get()` method uses `Option` in order to tell the user if the element that he tries to access exists or not. For example:

```scala
scala> val numbers = Map("two" -> 2, "four" -> 4)
numbers: scala.collection.immutable.Map[String,Int] = Map(two -> 2,
four -> 4)
scala> numbers.get("four")
res12: Option[Int] = Some(4)
scala> numbers.get("five")
res13: Option[Int] = None
```

Now, we will see how to use exists, which is used to check if a predicate holds for a subset of a set of elements in the Traversal collection.

Exists

Exists checks if a predicate holds for at least one element in the Traversable collection. For example:

```scala
def exists(p: ((A, B)) ⇒ Boolean): Boolean
```

Using the fat arrow: => is called the *right arrow, fat arrow,* or *rocket* and is used for passing parameters by name. That means the expression will be evaluated when a parameter is accessed. It is actually syntactic sugar for a zero parameter function `call: x: () => Boolean`. Let's see an example using this operator is as follows:

```scala
package com.chapter4.CollectionAPI
object UsingFatArrow {
def fliesPerSecond(callback: () => Unit) {
while (true) { callback(); Thread sleep 1000 }
}
def main(args: Array[String]): Unit= {
fliesPerSecond(() => println("Time and tide wait for
none but fly like arrows ..."))
}
}
```

You will get the following output:

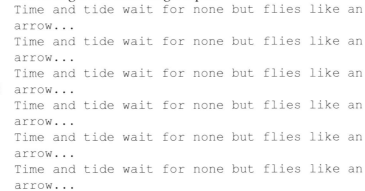

```
Time and tide wait for none but flies like an
arrow...
Time and tide wait for none but flies like an
arrow...
Time and tide wait for none but flies like an
arrow...
Time and tide wait for none but flies like an
arrow...
Time and tide wait for none but flies like an
arrow...
Time and tide wait for none but flies like an
arrow...
```

A detailed example can be seen in the following code as follows:

```scala
package com.chapter4.CollectionAPI

object ExistsExample {
  def main(args: Array[String]) {
    // Given a list of cities and now check if "Dublin" is included in
    the list
    val cityList = List("Dublin", "NY", "Cairo")
    val ifExisitsinList = cityList exists (x => x == "Dublin")
    println(ifExisitsinList)

    // Given a map of countries and their capitals check if Dublin is
    included in the Map
    val cityMap = Map("Ireland" -> "Dublin", "UK" -> "London")
    val ifExistsinMap =  cityMap exists (x => x._2 == "Dublin")
    println(ifExistsinMap)
  }
}
```

You will get the following output:

```
true
true
```

Note: Using the infix operator in Scala:

In the earlier example and in a subsequent section, we used the Scala infix notation. Suppose you would like to perform some operation with complex numbers and have a case class with an add method for adding two complex numbers:

```
case class Complex(i: Double, j: Double) {
    def plus(other: Complex): Complex = Complex(i + other.i, j +
other.j)
  }
```

Now in order to access the properties of this class, you need to create an object like this:

```
val obj = Complex(10, 20)
```

Moreover, suppose you have the following two complex numbers defined:

```
val a = Complex(6, 9)
 val b = Complex(3, -6)
```

Now to access the `plus()` method from the case class, you will do something like this:

```
val z = obj.plus(a)
```

This should give you output: `Complex(16.0,29.0)`. However, isn't it good if you just call the method like this:

```
val c = a plus b
```

And it really works like a charm. Here is the complete example:

```
package com.chapter4.CollectionAPI
 object UsingInfix {
   case class Complex(i: Double, j: Double) {
     def plus(other: Complex): Complex = Complex(i + other.i, j +
other.j)
   }
   def main(args: Array[String]): Unit = {
     val obj = Complex(10, 20)
     val a = Complex(6, 9)
     val b = Complex(3, -6)
     val c = a plus b
     val z = obj.plus(a)
     println(c)
     println(z)
   }
 }
```

The precedence of an infix operator: This is determined by the operator's first character. Characters are listed below in increasing order of precedence, with characters on the same line having the same precedence:

```
(all letters)
 |
 ^
 &
 = !
 < >
 :
 + -
 * / %
(all other special characters)
```

 General warning: Using the infix notation for calling regular, non-symbolic methods is discouraged and should be used only if it significantly increases readability. One example of a sufficiently motivated use of infix notation is matchers and other parts of the tests definition in `ScalaTest`.

Another interesting element in the Scala collection package is using `forall`. It is used to check if a predicate holds for each element in a `Traversable` collection. In the next subsection, we will see an example of it.

Forall

Forall checks if a predicate holds for each element in a `Traversable` collection. It can be defined formally as follows:

```
def forall (p: (A) ⇒ Boolean): Boolean
```

Let's see an example as follows:

```
scala> Vector(1, 2, 8, 10) forall (x => x % 2 == 0)
res2: Boolean = false
```

While writing Scala code for preprocessing especially, we often need to filter selected data objects. The filter feature of the Scala collection API is used for that. In the next sub-section, we will see an example of using filter.

Filter

`filter` selects all the elements that satisfy a specific predicate. It can be defined formally as follows:

```
def filter(p: (A) ⇒ Boolean): Traversable[A]
```

Let's see an example as follows:

```
scala> //Given a list of tuples (cities, Populations)
scala> // Get all cities that has population more than 5 million
scala> List(("Dublin", 2), ("NY", 8), ("London", 8)) filter (x =>x._2
>= 5)
res3: List[(String, Int)] = List((NY,8), (London,8))
```

A map is used to build a new collection or set of elements by traversing a function to all elements of the collection. In the next subsection, we will see an example of using Map.

Map

Map is used to build a new collection or set of elements by traversing a function to all elements of the collection. It can be defined formally as follows:

```
def map[B](f: (A) ⇒ B): Map[B]
```

Let's see an example as follows:

```
scala> // Given a list of integers
scala> // Get a list with all the elements square.
scala> List(2, 4, 5, -6) map ( x=> x * x)
res4: List[Int] = List(4, 16, 25, 36)
```

While using the collection API in Scala, you often need to select the nth elements of the list or array for example. In the next sub-section, we will explore examples of using take.

Take

Take is used to take the first n elements of a collection. The formal definition of using `take` is as follows:

```
def take(n: Int): Traversable[A]
```

Let's see an example as follows:

```
// Given an infinite recursive method creating a stream of odd
numbers.
def odd: Stream[Int] = {
  def odd0(x: Int): Stream[Int] =
    if (x%2 != 0) x #:: odd0(x+1)
    else odd0(x+1)
      odd0(1)
}// Get a list of the 5 first odd numbers.
odd take (5) toList
```

You will get the following output:

```
res5: List[Int] = List(1, 3, 5, 7, 9)
```

In Scala, if want to partition specific collections into a map of an other `Traversable` collection according to a specific partitioning function, you can use the `groupBy()` method. In the next subsection, we will show some examples of using `groupBy()`.

GroupBy

GroupBy is used to partition specific collections into a map of other Traversable collections according to a specific partitioning function. It can be defined formally as follows:

```
def groupBy[K](f: ((A, B)) ⇒ K): Map[K, Map[A, B]]
```

Let's see an example as follows:

```
scala> // Given a list of numbers
scala> // Group them as positive and negative numbers.
scala> List(1,-2,3,-4) groupBy (x => if (x >= 0) "positive" else
"negative")
res6: scala.collection.immutable.Map[String,List[Int]] = Map(negative
-> List(-2, -4), positive -> List(1, 3))
```

In Scala, if you want to select all the elements in a Traversable collection but the last one, you can use `init`. In the next subsection, we will see examples of it.

Init

`init` selects all the elements in a `Traversable` collection but the last one. It can be defined formally as follows:

```
def init: Traversable[A]
```

Let's see an example as follows:

```
scala> List(1,2,3,4) init
res7: List[Int] = List(1, 2, 3)
```

In Scala, if you want to select all elements except the first n elements, you should use drop. In the next subsection, we will see how to use drop.

Drop

`drop` is used to select all elements except the first n elements. It can be defined formally as follows:

```
def drop(n: Int): Traversable[A]
```

Let's see an example as follows:

```
// Drop the first three elements
scala> List(1,2,3,4) drop 3
res8: List[Int] = List(4)
```

In Scala, if you want take a set of elements until a predicate is satisfied, you should use `takeWhile`. In the next subsection, we will see how to use `takeWhile`.

TakeWhile

TakeWhile is used to take a set of elements until a predicate is satisfied. It can be defined formally as follows:

```
def takeWhile(p: (A) ⇒ Boolean): Traversable[A]
```

Let's see an example as follows:

```
// Given an infinite recursive method creating a stream of odd
numbers.
def odd: Stream[Int] = {
  def odd0(x: Int): Stream[Int] =
    if (x%2 != 0) x #:: odd0(x+1)
    else odd0(x+1)
      odd0(1)
}
// Return a list of all the odd elements until an element isn't less
then 9.
odd takeWhile (x => x < 9) toList
```

You will get the following output:

```
res11: List[Int] = List(1, 3, 5, 7)
```

In Scala, if you want to omit a set of elements till a predicate is satisfied, you should use `dropWhile`. We will see some examples of this in the next subsection.

DropWhile

`dropWhile` is used to omit a set of elements till a predicate is satisfied. It can be defined formally as follows:

```
def dropWhile(p: (A) ⇒ Boolean): Traversable[A]
```

Let's see an example as follows:

```
//Drop values till reaching the border between numbers that are
greater than 5 and less than 5
scala> List(2,3,4,9,10,11) dropWhile(x => x <5)
res1: List[Int] = List(9, 10, 11)
```

In Scala, if you want to use your **User Defined Functions** (UDF) such that it takes a function as an argument in the nested list and combines the output back together, `flatMap()` is a perfect candidate. We will see examples of using `flatMap()` in the next section.

FlatMap

FltatMap takes a function as an argument. The function given to `flatMap()` doesn't work on nested lists but it produces a new collection. It can be defined formally as follows:

```
def flatMap[B](f: (A) ⇒ GenTraversableOnce[B]): Traversable[B]
```

Let's see an example as follows:

```
//Applying function on nested lists and then combining output back
together
scala> List(List(2,4), List(6,8)) flatMap(x => x.map(x => x * x))
res4: List[Int] = List(4, 16, 36, 64)
```

We have just about finished covering the uses of Scala collection features. Also note that methods such as `Fold()`, `Reduce()`, `Aggregate()`, `Collect()`, `Count()`, `Find()`, and `Zip()` can be used to pass from one collection to another (for example, `toVector`, `toSeq`, `toSet`, `toArray`). However, we will see such examples in upcoming chapters. For the time being, it's time to see some performance characteristics of different Scala collection APIs.

Performance characteristics

In Scala, different collections have different performance characteristics and these performance characteristics are the reason you will prefer to choose one collection over the others. In this section, we will judge the performance characteristics of Scala collection objects from the operational and memory usage point of view. At the end of this section, we will provide some guidelines for selecting appropriate collection objects for your code and problem types.

Performance characteristics of collection objects

The following are the performance characteristics Scala Collections, based on the official documentation of Scala.

- **Const**: The operation takes only constant time.
- **eConst**: The operation takes effectively constant time, but this might depend on some assumptions such as the maximum length of a vector or the distribution of hash keys.
- **Linear**: The operation grows linearly with the collection size.
- **Log**: The operation grows logarithmically with the collection size.
- **aConst**: The operation takes the amortized constant time. Some invocations of the operation might take longer, but if many operations are performed on average only constant time per operation is taken.
- **NA**: Operation is not supported.

Performance characteristics of sequence types (immutable) are presented in the following table.

Immutable CO*	Head	Tail	Apply	Update	Prepend	Append	Insert
List	Const	Const	Linear	Linear	Const	Linear	NA
Stream	Const	Const	Linear	Linear	Const	Linear	NA
Vector	eConst	eConst	eConst	eConst	eConst	eConst	NA
Stack	Const	Const	Linear	Linear	Const	Linear	Linear
Queue	aConst	aConst	Linear	Linear	Const	Const	NA
Range	Const	Const	Const	NA	NA	NA	NA
String	Const	Linear	Const	Linear	Linear	Linear	NA

Table 1: Performance characteristics of sequence types (immutable) [*CO== Collection Object]

The following table shows the meaning of the operations described in **Table 1** and **Table 3** here:

Head	Is used to select the first few elements of an existing sequence.
Tail	Is used to select all elements except the first one and returns a new sequence.
Apply	Is used for indexing purposes.
Update	It is used as the functional update for immutable sequences. For the mutable sequence, it is a side-effecting update (with update for mutable sequences).
Prepend	It is used to add an element to the front of an existing sequence. A new sequence is produced for immutable sequences. For the mutable sequence, the existing one is modified.
Append	It is used to add an element at the end of an existing sequence. A new sequence is produced for immutable sequences. For a mutable sequence, the existing one is modified.
Insert	It is used to insert an element at an arbitrary position in an existing sequence. This can be done however directly for mutable sequences.

Table 2: The meaning of the operation described in table 1

Performance characteristics of sequence types (mutable) are shown in **Table 3** as follows:

Mutable CO*	Head	Tail	Apply	update	Prepend	Append	Insert
ArrayBuffer	Const	Linear	Const	Const	Linear	aConst	Linear
ListBuffer	Const	Linear	Linear	Linear	Const	Const	Linear
StringBuilder	Const	Linear	Const	Const	Linear	aCconst	Linear
MutableList	Const	Linear	Linear	Linear	Const	Const	Linear
Queue	Const	Linear	Linear	Linear	Const	Const	Linear
ArraySeq	Const	Linear	Const	Const	NA	NA	NA
Stack	Const	Linear	Linear	Linear	Const	Linear	Linear
ArrayStack	Const	Linear	Const	Const	aConst	Linear	Linear
Array	Const	Linear	Const	Const	NA	NA	NA

Table 3: Performance characteristics of sequence types (mutable) [*CO== Collection Object]

For more information about mutable collections and other types of collections, you can refer to this link (http://docs.scala-lang.org/overviews/collections/performance-characteristics.html).

Performance characteristics of set and map types are shown in the following table:

Collection types	Lookup	Add	Remove	Min
immutable	-	-	-	-
HashSet/HashMap	eConst	eConst	eConst	Linear
TreeSet/TreeMap	Log	Log	Log	Log
BitSet	Const	Linear	Linear	eConst*
ListMap	Linear	Linear	Linear	Linear
Collection types	Lookup	Add	Remove	Min
mutable	-	-	-	-
HashSet/HashMap	eConst	eConst	eConst	Linear
WeakHashMap	eConst	eConst	eConst	Linear
BitSet	Const	aConst	Const	eConst*
TreeSet	Log	Log	Log	Log

Table 4: Performance characteristics of set and map types [* applicable only if bits are densely packed]

The following table shows the meaning of each operation described in **Table 4**:

Operation	Meaning
Lookup	Is used to test whether an element is contained in a set. Secondly, it is also used to select a value associated with a particular key.
Add	It is used to add a new element to a set. Secondly, it is also used to add a new key/value pair to a map.
Remove	It is used to remove an element from a set or a key from a map.
Min	It is used to select the smallest element of the set or the smallest key of a map.

Table 5: The meaning of each operation described in Table 4

One of the basic performance metrics is the memory usage by a particular collection object. In the next section, we will provide some guidelines about how to measure these metrics based on memory usage.

Memory usage by collection objects

Sometimes, there are several benchmarking questions arrived for example: A `Lists` faster than `Vectors` for what you're doing or are `Vectors` faster than `Lists`? How much memory can you save using unboxed Arrays to store primitives? When you do performance tricks such as pre-allocating arrays or using a `while` loop instead of a `foreach` call, how much does it really matter? `var 1: List` or `val b: mutable.Buffer`? Memory usage can be estimated using different Scala benchmark codes, for example, refer to `https://github.com/lihaoyi/scala-bench`.

Table 6 here shows the estimated size (bytes) of the various immutable collections of 0-elements, 1- element, 4- elements, and powers of four all the way up to 1,048,576 elements. Although mostse are deterministic, these might be changed depending on your platform:

Size	0	1	4	16	64	256	1,024	4,069	16,192	65,536	262,144	1,048,576
Vector	56	216	264	456	1,512	5,448	21,192	84,312	334,440	1,353,192	5,412,168	21,648,072
Array[Object]	16	40	96	336	1,296	5,136	20,496	81,400	323,856	1,310,736	5,242,896	20,971,536
List	16	56	176	656	2,576	10,256	40,976	162,776	647,696	2,621,456	10,485,776	41,943,056
Stream (unforced)	16	160	160	160	160	160	160	160	160	160	160	160
Stream (forced)	16	56	176	656	2,576	10,256	40,976	162,776	647,696	2,621,456	10,485,776	41,943,056
Set	16	32	96	880	3,720	14,248	59,288	234,648	895,000	3,904,144	14,361,000	60,858,616
Map	16	56	176	1,648	6,800	26,208	109,112	428,592	1,674,568	7,055,272	26,947,840	111,209,368
SortedSet	40	104	248	824	3,128	12,344	49,208	195,368	777,272	3,145,784	12,582,968	50,331,704
Queue	40	80	200	680	2,600	10,280	41,000	162,800	647,720	2,621,480	10,485,800	41,943,080
String	40	48	48	72	168	552	2,088	8,184	32,424	131,112	524,328	2,097,192

Table 6: The estimated size (bytes) of the various collections

The following table shows the estimated size (bytes) of the array used in Scala with 0-elements, 1- element, 4- elements, and powers of four all the way up to 1,048,576 elements. Although mostse are deterministic, these might change depending on your platform:

Size	0	1	4	16	64	256	1,024	4,069	16,192	65,536	262,144	1,048,576
Array[Object]	16	40	96	336	1,296	5,136	20,496	81,400	323,856	1,310,736	5,242,896	20,971,536
Size	0	1	4	16	64	256	1,024	4,069	16,192	65,536	262,144	1,048,576
Array[Boolean]	16	24	24	32	80	272	1,040	4,088	16,208	65,552	262,160	1,048,592
Array[Byte]	16	24	24	32	80	272	1,040	4,088	16,208	65,552	262,160	1,048,592

Array[Short]	16	24	24	48	144	528	2,064	8,160	32,400	131,088	524,304	2,097,168
Array[Int]	16	24	32	80	272	1,040	4,112	16,296	64,784	262,160	1,048,592	4,194,320
Array[Long]	16	24	48	144	528	2,064	8,208	32,568	129,552	524,304	2,097,168	8,388,624
Boxed Array[Boolean]	16	40	64	112	304	1,072	4,144	16,328	64,816	262,192	1,048,624	4,194,352
Boxed Array[Byte]	16	40	96	336	1,296	5,136	8,208	20,392	68,880	266,256	1,052,688	4,198,416
Boxed Array[Short]	16	40	96	336	1,296	5,136	20,496	81,400	323,856	1,310,736	5,230,608	20,910,096
Boxed Array[Int]	16	40	96	336	1,296	5,136	20,496	81,400	323,856	1,310,736	5,242,896	20,971,536
Boxed Array[Long]	16	48	128	464	1,808	7,184	28,688	113,952	453,392	1,835,024	7,340,048	29,360,144

Table 7: The estimated size (bytes) of the arrays in Scala

However, this book does not set out to distinguish them in a broad way and hence we will omit any discussion on these topics. Refer to the following information box for further guidelines on these:

For very detailed benchmarking for Scala Collections with timed code, refer to this link on GitHub (`https://github.com/lihaoyi/scala-bench/tree/master/bench/src/main/scala/bench`).

As we mentioned in `Chapter 1`, *Introduction to Scala*, Scala has a very rich Collection API. The same applies for Java but there are lots of differences between the two Collection APIs. In the next section, we will see some examples on Java interoperability.

Java interoperability

As we mentioned earlier, Scala has very rich collection API. The same applies for Java but there are lots of differences between the two collection APIs. For example, both APIs have iterable, iterators, maps, sets, and sequences. But Scala has advantages; it pays more attention to immutable collections and provides more operations for you in order to produce another collection. Sometimes, you want to use or access Java collections or vice versa.

`JavaConversions` is no longer a sound choice. `JavaConverters` makes the conversion between Scala and Java collection explicit and you'll be much less likely to experience implicit conversions you didn't intend to use.

As a matter of fact, it's quite trivial to do so because Scala offers in an implicit way to convert between both APIs in the `JavaConversion` object. So, you might find bidirectional conversions for the following types:

```
Iterator              <=>      java.util.Iterator
Iterator              <=>      java.util.Enumeration
Iterable              <=>      java.lang.Iterable
Iterable              <=>      java.util.Collection
mutable.Buffer        <=>      java.util.List
mutable.Set           <=>      java.util.Set
mutable.Map           <=>      java.util.Map
mutable.ConcurrentMap <=>      java.util.concurrent.ConcurrentMap
```

In order to be able to use these kinds of conversion, you need to import them from the `JavaConversions` object. For example:

```
scala> import collection.JavaConversions._
import collection.JavaConversions._
```

By this, you have automatic conversions between Scala collections and their corresponding in Java:

```
scala> import collection.mutable._
import collection.mutable._
scala> val jAB: java.util.List[Int] = ArrayBuffer(3,5,7)
jAB: java.util.List[Int] = [3, 5, 7]
scala> val sAB: Seq[Int] = jAB
sAB: scala.collection.mutable.Seq[Int] = ArrayBuffer(3, 5, 7)
scala> val jM: java.util.Map[String, Int] = HashMap("Dublin" -> 2,
"London" -> 8)
jM: java.util.Map[String,Int] = {Dublin=2, London=8}
```

You can also try to convert other Scala collections into Java ones. For example:

```
Seq            =>     java.util.List
mutable.Seq    =>     java.utl.List
Set            =>     java.util.Set
Map            =>     java.util.Map
```

Java doesn't provide the functionality to distinguish between immutable and mutable collections. The `List` will be `java.util.List` where all attempts to mutate its elements will throw an `Exception`. The following is an example to demonstrate this:

```
scala> val jList: java.util.List[Int] = List(3,5,7)
jList: java.util.List[Int] = [3, 5, 7]
scala> jList.add(9)
java.lang.UnsupportedOperationException
```

```
    at java.util.AbstractList.add(AbstractList.java:148)
    at java.util.AbstractList.add(AbstractList.java:108)
    ... 33 elided
```

In Chapter 2, *Object-Oriented Scala*, we briefly discussed using implicits. However, we will provide a detailed discussion on using implicits in the next section.

Using Scala implicits

We have addressed implicits in the previous chapters, but here we are going to see more examples. Implicit parameters are very similar to default parameters but they use different mechanisms in order to find the default value.

An implicit parameter is one that is passed to a constructor or a method and is marked as implicit, which means that the compiler will search for an implicit value within the scope if you don't provide a value for this parameter. For example:

```
scala> def func(implicit x:Int) = print(x)
func: (implicit x: Int)Unit
scala> func
<console>:9: error: could not find implicit value for parameter x: Int
              func
              ^
scala> implicit val defVal = 2
defVal: Int = 2
scala> func(3)
3
```

Implicits are very useful for the collection API. For example, the collections API use implicit parameters to supply CanBuildFrom objects for many methods in these collections. This happens usually because users aren't concerned with these parameters.

One constraint is that you can't have more than one implicit keyword per method and it must be at the start of the parameter list. Here are some invalid examples:

```
scala> def func(implicit x:Int, y:Int)(z:Int) = println(y,x)
<console>:1: error: '=' expected but '(' found.
        def func(implicit x:Int, y:Int)(z:Int) = println(y,x)
                                        ^
```

Number of implicit parameters: Note that you can have more than one implicit parameter. But, you cannot have more than one group of implicit parameters.

The following is for more than 1 implicit parameter:

```
scala> def func(implicit x:Int, y:Int)(implicit z:Int, f:Int) =
println(x,y)
<console>:1: error: '=' expected but '(' found.
       def func(implicit x:Int, y:Int)(implicit z:Int, f:Int) =
println(x,y)
                                       ^
```

The final parameter list on a function can be identified or marked as implicit. This means the values will be taken from the context as they are being called. In other words, if there is no implicit value of the exact type in the scope, the source code using implicit will not be compiled. The reason is simple: since the implicit value must be resolved to a single value type, it would be a better idea to make the type specific to its purpose to avoid implicit clashes.

Moreover, you do not require methods to find an implicit. For example:

```
// probably in a library
class Prefixer(val prefix: String)
def addPrefix(s: String)(implicit p: Prefixer) = p.prefix + s
// then probably in your application
implicit val myImplicitPrefixer = new Prefixer("***")
addPrefix("abc")   // returns "***abc"
```

When your Scala compiler finds an expression of wrong types for the context it is feeding, it will look for an implicit function value instead for type-checking. So, the difference between your regular methods is that the one marked implicit will be inserted for you by the compiler when a `Double` is found but an `Int` is required. For example:

```
scala> implicit def doubleToInt(d: Double) = d.toInt
val x: Int = 42.0
```

The earlier code will work the same as:

```
scala> def doubleToInt(d: Double) = d.toInt
val x: Int = doubleToInt(42.0)
```

In the second we've inserted the conversion manually. At first, the compiler did this automatically. The conversion is required because of the type annotation on the left-hand side.

While working with data, we will often need to convert one type to another. Scala implicit type conversion gives us this facility. We will see several examples of it in the next section.

Implicit conversions in Scala

An implicit conversion from type S to type T is defined by an implicit value that has function type S => T, or by an implicit method convertible to a value of that type. Implicit conversions are applied in two situations (source: http://docs.scala-lang. org/tutorials/tour/implicit-conversions):

- If an expression e is of type S, and S does not conform to the expression's expected type T
- In a selection e.m with e of type S, if the selector m does not denote a member of S.

Well, we have seen how to use infix operator in Scala. Now, let's see some use cases of Scala implicit conversion. Suppose we have the following code segment:

```scala
class Complex(val real: Double, val imaginary: Double) {
  def plus(that: Complex) = new Complex(this.real + that.real,
this.imaginary + that.imaginary)
  def minus(that: Complex) = new Complex(this.real - that.real,
this.imaginary - that.imaginary)
  def unary(): Double = {
    val value = Math.sqrt(real * real + imaginary * imaginary)
    value
  }
  override def toString = real + " + " + imaginary + "i"
}
object UsingImplicitConversion {
  def main(args: Array[String]): Unit = {
    val obj = new Complex(5.0, 6.0)
    val x = new Complex(4.0, 3.0)
    val y = new Complex(8.0, -7.0)

    println(x) // prints 4.0 + 3.0i
    println(x plus y) // prints 12.0 + -4.0i
    println(x minus y) // -4.0 + 10.0i
    println(obj.unary) // prints 7.810249675906654
```

```
    }
  }
```

In the preceding code, we defined some methods for performing addition, subtraction, and a unary operation for complex numbers (that is, both real and imaginary numbers). Inside the `main()` method, we called these methods with real values. The output is given as follows:

```
4.0 + 3.0i
12.0 + -4.0i
-4.0 + 10.0i
7.810249675906654
```

But what if we want to support adding a normal number to a complex number, how would we do that? We could certainly overload our `plus` method to take a `Double` argument so that it's going to support the following expression.

```
val sum = myComplexNumber plus 6.5
```

For this, we can use Scala implicit conversion. It supports implicit conversion for both real and complex numbers for mathematical operation. So, we can just use that tuple as the parameter for our implicit conversion and convert it into a `Complex` refer to the following:

```
implicit def Tuple2Complex(value: Tuple2[Double, Double]) = new
Complex(value._1, value._2)
```

Alternatively, for double to complex conversion as follows:

```
implicit def Double2Complex(value : Double) = new Complex(value,0.0)
```

To take the advantage of this conversion, we need to import the following:

```
import ComplexImplicits._ // for complex numbers
import scala.language.implicitConversions // in general
```

Now, we can execute something like this on Scala REPL/IDE:

```
val z = 4 plus y
println(z) // prints 12.0 + -7.0i
val p = (1.0, 1.0) plus z
println(p) // prints 13.0 + -6.0i
```

You will get the following output:

```
12.0 + -7.0i
13.0 + -6.0i
```

The full source code for this example can be seen as follows:

```
package com.chapter4.CollectionAPI
import ComplexImplicits._
import scala.language.implicitConversions
class Complex(val real: Double, val imaginary: Double) {
  def plus(that: Complex) = new Complex(this.real + that.real,
this.imaginary + that.imaginary)
  def plus(n: Double) = new Complex(this.real + n, this.imaginary)
  def minus(that: Complex) = new Complex(this.real - that.real,
this.imaginary - that.imaginary)
  def unary(): Double = {
    val value = Math.sqrt(real * real + imaginary * imaginary)
    value
  }
  override def toString = real + " + " + imaginary + "i"
}
object ComplexImplicits {
  implicit def Double2Complex(value: Double) = new Complex(value, 0.0)
  implicit def Tuple2Complex(value: Tuple2[Double, Double]) = new
Complex(value._1, value._2)
}
object UsingImplicitConversion {
  def main(args: Array[String]): Unit = {
    val obj = new Complex(5.0, 6.0)
    val x = new Complex(4.0, 3.0)
    val y = new Complex(8.0, -7.0)
    println(x) // prints 4.0 + 3.0i
    println(x plus y) // prints 12.0 + -4.0i
    println(x minus y) // -4.0 + 10.0i
    println(obj.unary) // prints 7.810249675906654
    val z = 4 plus y
    println(z) // prints 12.0 + -7.0i
    val p = (1.0, 1.0) plus z
    println(p) // prints 13.0 + -6.0i
  }
}
```

We have now more or less covered Scala collection APIs. There are other features too, but page limitations prevented us from covering them. Interested readers who still want to explore this should refer to this page http://www.scala-lang.org/docu/files/collections-api/collections.html.

Summary

Throughout this chapter, we have seen many examples of using the Scala collections API. It's very powerful, flexible, and has lots of operations coupled with them. This wide range of operations will make your life easy dealing with any kind of data. We introduced the Scala collections API, and its different types and hierarchies. We also demonstrated the capabilities of the Scala collections API and how it can be used in order to accommodate different types of data and solve a wide range of different problems. In summary, you learned about types and hierarchies, performance characteristic, Java interoperability, and the usage of implicits. So, this is more or less the end of the learning Scala. However, you will keep on learning more advanced topics and operations using Scala through the following chapters.

In the next chapter, we will explore data analysis and big data to see the challenges that big data provides and how they are dealt via distributed computing and the approach suggested by functional programming. You will also learn about MapReduce, Apache Hadoop, and finally Apache Spark and see how they embrace this approach and these techniques.

5
Tackle Big Data – Spark Comes to the Party

An approximate answer to the right problem is worth a good deal more than an exact answer to an approximate problem.

- John Tukey

In this chapter, you learn about data analysis and big data; we see the challenges that big data provides and how they are dealt with. You will learn about distributed computing and the approach suggested by functional programming; we introduce Google's MapReduce, Apache Hadoop, and finally Apache Spark and see how they embrace this approach and these techniques.

In a nutshell, the following topics will be covered throughout this chapter:

- Introduction to data analytics
- Introduction to big data
- Distributed computing using Apache Hadoop
- Here comes Apache Spark

Introduction to data analytics

Data analytics is the process of applying qualitative and quantitative techniques when examining data with the goal of providing valuable insights. Using various techniques and concepts, data analytics can provide the means to explore the data **Exploratory Data Analysis (EDA)** as well as draw conclusions about the data **Confirmatory Data Analysis (CDA)**. EDA and CDA are fundamental concepts of data analytics, and it is important to understand the difference between the two.

EDA involves methodologies, tools, and techniques used to explore data with the intention of finding patterns in the data and relationships between various elements of the data. CDA involves methodologies, tools, and techniques used to provide an insight or conclusion on a specific question based on a hypothesis and statistical techniques or simple observation of the data.

A quick example to understand these ideas is that of a grocery store, which has asked you to give them ways to improve sales and customer satisfaction as well as keep the cost of operations low.

The following is a grocery store with aisles of various products:

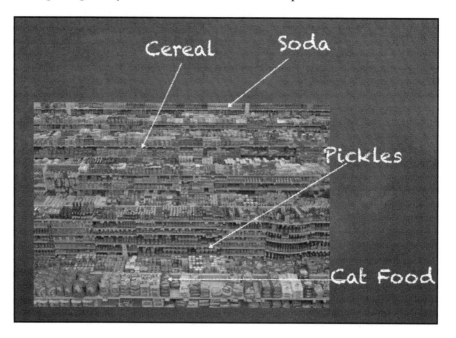

Assume that all sales at the grocery store are stored in some database and that you have access to the data for the last 3 months. Typically, businesses store data for years as you need sufficient data over a period of time to establish any hypothesis or observe any patterns. In this example, our goal is to perform better placement of products in various aisles based on how customers are buying the products. One hypothesis is that customers often buy products, that are both at eye level and also close together. For instance, if Milk is on one corner of the store and Yogurt is in other corner of the store, some customers might just choose either Milk or Yogurt and just leave the store, causing a loss of business. More adverse affects might result in customers choosing another store where products are better placed because if the feeling that *things are hard to find at this store*. Once that feeling sets in, it also percolates to friends and family eventually causing a bad social presence. This phenomenon is not uncommon in the real world causing some businesses to succeed while others fail while both seem to be very similar in products and prices.

There are many ways to approach this problem starting from customer surveys to professional statisticians to machine learning scientists. Our approach will be to understand what we can from just the sales transactions alone.

The following is an example of what the transactions might look like:

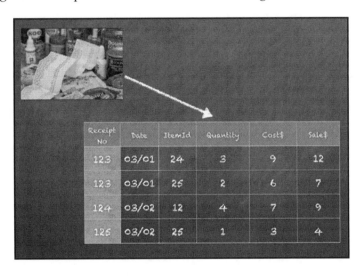

Receipt No	Date	ItemId	Quantity	Cost$	Sale$
123	03/01	24	3	9	12
123	03/01	25	2	6	7
124	03/02	12	4	7	9
125	03/02	25	1	3	4

The following are the steps you could follow as part of EDA:

1. Calculate *Average number of products bought per day = Total of all products sold in a day / Total number of receipts for the day.*
2. Repeat the preceding step for last 1 week, month, and quarter.

3. Try to understand if there is a difference between weekends and weekdays and also time of the day (morning, noon, and evening)
4. For each product, create a list of all other products to see which products are usually bought together (same receipt)
5. Repeat the preceding step for 1 day, 1 week, month, and quarter.
6. Try to determine which products should be placed closer together by the number of transactions (sorted in descending order).

Once we have completed the preceding 6 steps, we can try to reach some conclusions for CDA.

Let's assume this is the output we get:

Item	Day Of Week	Quantity
Milk	Sunday	1244
Bread	Monday	245
Milk	Monday	190

In this case, we could state that **Milk** is bought more on *weekends* so its better to increase the quantity and variety of Milk products over weekends. Take a look at the following table:

Item1	Item2	Quantity
Milk	Eggs	360
Bread	Cheese	335
Onions	Tomatoes	310

In this case, we could state that **Milk** and **Eggs** are bought by *more* customers in one purchase followed by **Bread** and **Cheese**. So, we could recommend that the store realigns the aisles and shelves to move **Milk** and **Eggs** *closer* to each other.

The two conclusions we have are:

- **Milk** is bought more on *weekends,* so it's better to increase the quantity and variety of Milk products over weekends.
- **Milk** and **Eggs** are bought by *more* customers in one purchase followed by **Bread** and **Cheese.** So, we could recommend that the store realigns the aisles and shelves to move **Milk** and **Eggs** *closer* to each other.

Conclusions are usually tracked over a period of time to evaluate the gains. If there is no significant impact on sales even after adopting the preceding two recommendations for 6 months, we simply invested in the recommendations which are not able to give you a good Return On Investment (ROI).

Similarly, you can also perform some analysis with respect to the Profit margin and pricing optimizations. This is why you will typically see a single item costing more than the average of multiple numbers of the same item bought. Buy one Shampoo for $7 or two bottles of Shampoo for $12.

Think about other aspects you can explore and recommend for the grocery store. For example, can you guess which products to position near checkout registers just based on fact that these have no affinity toward any particular product--chewing gum, magazines, and so on.

Data analytics initiatives support a wide variety of business uses. For example, banks and credit card companies analyze withdrawal and spending patterns to prevent fraud and identity theft. Advertising companies analyze website traffic to identify prospects with a high likelihood of conversion to a customer. Department stores analyze customer data to figure out if better discounts will help boost sales. Cell Phone operators can figure out pricing strategies. Cable companies are constantly looking for customers who are likely to churn unless given some offer or promotional rate to retain their customer. Hospitals and pharmaceutical companies analyze data to come up with better products and detect problems with prescription drugs or measure the performance of prescription drugs.

Inside the data analytics process

Data analytics applications involve more than just analyzing data. Before any analytics can be planned, there is also a need to invest time and effort in collecting, integrating, and preparing data, checking the quality of the data and then developing, testing, and revising analytical methodologies. Once data is deemed ready, data analysts and scientists can explore and analyze the data using statistical methods such as SAS or machine learning models using Spark ML. The data itself is prepared by data engineering teams and the data quality team checks the data collected. Data governance becomes a factor too to ensure the proper collection and protection of the data. Another not commonly known role is that of a Data Steward who specializes in understanding data to the byte, exactly where it is coming from, all transformations that occur, and what the business really needs from the column or field of data.

Various entities in the business might be dealing with addresses differently, **123 N Main St** as opposed to **123 North Main Street.** But, our analytics depends on getting the correct address field; otherwise both the addresses mentioned above will be considered different and our analytics will not have the same accuracy.

The analytics process starts with data collection based on what the analysts might need from the data warehouse, collecting all sorts of data in the organization (Sales, Marketing, Employee, Payroll, HR, and so on). Data stewards and the Governance team are important here to make sure the right data is collected and that any information deemed confidential or private is not accidentally exported out even if the end users are all employees.

 Social Security Numbers or full addresses might not be a good idea to include in analytics as this can cause a lot of problems to the organization.

Data quality processes must be established to make sure the data being collected and engineered is correct and will match the needs of the data scientists. At this stage, the main goal is to find and fix data quality problems that could affect the accuracy of analytical needs. Common techniques are profiling the data and cleansing the data to make sure that the information in a dataset is consistent, and also that any errors and duplicate records are removed.

Data from disparate source systems may need to be combined, transformed, and normalized using various data engineering techniques, such as distributed computing or MapReduce programming, Stream processing, or SQL queries, and then stored on Amazon S3, Hadoop cluster, NAS, or SAN storage devices or a traditional data warehouse such as Teradata. Data preparation or engineering work involves techniques to manipulate and organize the data for the planned analytics use.

Once we have the data prepared and checked for quality, and it is available for the Data scientists or analysts to use, the actual analytical work starts. A Data scientist can now build an analytical model using predictive modeling tools and languages such as SAS, Python, R, Scala, Spark, H2O, and so on. The model is initially run against a partial dataset to test its accuracy in the *training phase*. Several iterations of the training phase are common and expected in any analytical project. After adjustments at the model level, or sometimes going all the way to the Data Steward to get or fix some data being collected or prepared, the model output tends to get better and better. Finally, a stable state is reached when further tuning does not change the outcome noticeably; at this time, we can think of the model as being ready for production usage.

Now, the model can be run in production mode against the full dataset and generate outcomes or results based on how we trained the model. The choices made in building the analysis, either statistical or machine learning, directly affect the quality and the purpose of the model. You cannot look at the sales from groceries and figure out if Asians buy more milk than Mexicans as that needs additional elements from demographical data. Similarly, if our analysis was focused on customer experience (returns or exchanges of products) then it is based on different techniques and models than if we are trying to focus on revenue or up-sell customers.

 You will see various machine learning techniques in later chapters.

Analytical applications can thus be realized using several disciplines, teams, and skillsets. Analytical applications can be used to generate reports all the way to automatically triggering business actions. For example, you can simply create daily sales reports to be emailed out to all managers every day at 8 a.m. in the morning. But, you can also integrate with Business process management applications or some custom stock trading application to take action, such as buying, selling, or alerting on activities in the stock market. You can also think of taking in news articles or social media information to further influence the decisions to be made.

Data visualization is an important piece of data analytics and it's hard to understand numbers when you are looking at a lot of metrics and calculation. Rather, there is an increasing dependence on **Business Intelligence (BI)** tools, such as Tableau, QlikView, and so on, to explore and analyze data. Of course, large-scale visualization such as showing all Uber cars in the country or heat maps showing the water supply in New York City requires more custom applications or specialized tools to be built.

Managing and analyzing data has always been a challenge across many organizations of different sizes across all industries. Businesses have always struggled to find a pragmatic approach to capturing information about their customers, products, and services. When the company only had a handful of customers who bought a few of their items, it was not that difficult. It was not as big a challenge. But over time, companies in the markets started growing. Things have become more complicated. Now, we have branding Information and social media. We have things that are sold and bought over the Internet. We need to come up with different solutions. Web development, organizations, pricing, social networks, and segmentations; there's a lot of different data that we're dealing with that brings a lot more complexity when it comes to dealing, managing, organizing, and trying to gain some insight from the data.

Introduction to big data

As seen in the preceding section, data analytics incorporates techniques, tools, and methodologies to explore and analyze data to produce quantifiable outcomes for the business. The outcome could be a simple choice of a color to paint the storefront or more complicated predictions of customer behavior. As businesses grow, more and more varieties of analytics are coming into the picture. In 1980s or 1990s , all we could get was what was available in a SQL Data Warehouse; nowadays a lot of external factors are all playing an important role in influencing the way businesses run.

 Twitter, Facebook, Amazon, Verizon, Macy's, and Whole Foods are all companies that run their business using data analytics and base many of the decisions on it. Think about what kind of data they are collecting, how much data they might be collecting, and then how they might be using the data.

Let's look at our grocery store example seen earlier. What if the store starts expanding its business to set up 100s of stores. Naturally, the sales transactions will have to be collected and stored on a scale that is 100s of times more than the single store. But then, no business works independently any more. There is a lot of information out there starting from local news, tweets, yelp reviews, customer complaints, survey activities, competition from other stores, changing demographics, or the economy of the local area, and so on. All such additional data can help in better understanding customer behavior and revenue models.

For example, if we see increasing negative sentiment regarding the store parking facility, then we could analyze this and take corrective action such as validated parking or negotiating with the city public transportation department to provide more frequent trains or buses for better reach.

Such increasing quantity and a variety of data while provides better analytics also poses challenges to the business IT organization trying to store, process, and analyze all the data. It is, in fact, not uncommon to see TBs of data.

Every day, we create more than 2 quintillion bytes of data (2 Exa Bytes), and it is estimated that more than 90% of the data has been generated in the last few years alone.

1 KB = 1024 Bytes
1 MB = 1024 KB
1 GB = 1024 MB
1 TB = 1024 GB ~ 1,000,000 MB
1 PB = 1024 TB ~ 1,000,000 GB ~ 1,000,000,000 MB
1 EB = 1024 PB ~ 1,000,000 TB ~ 1,000,000,000 GB ~ 1,000,000,000,000 MB

Such large amounts of data since the 1990s, and the need to understand and make sense of the data, gave rise to the term *big data*.

The term big data, which spans computer science and statistics/econometrics, probably originated in the lunch-table conversations at Silicon Graphics in the mid-1990s, in which John Mashey figured prominently.

In 2001, Doug Laney, then an analyst at consultancy Meta Group Inc (which got acquired by Gartner) introduced the idea of 3Vs (variety, velocity, and volume). Now, we refer to 4 Vs instead of 3Vs with the addition of Veracity of data to the 3Vs.

4 Vs of big data

The following are the 4 Vs of big data used to describe the properties of big data.

Variety of Data

Data can be from weather sensors, car sensors, census data, Facebook updates, tweets, transactions, sales, and marketing. The data format is both structured and unstructured as well. Data types can also be different; binary, text, JSON, and XML.

Velocity of Data

Data can be obtained from a data warehouse, batch mode file archives, near real-time updates, or instantaneous real-time updates from the Uber ride you just booked.

Volume of Data

Data can be collected and stored for an hour, a day, a month, a year, or 10 years. The size of data is growing to 100s of TBs for many companies.

Veracity of Data

Data can be analyzed for actionable insights, but with so much data of all types being analyzed from across data sources, it is very difficult to ensure correctness and proof of accuracy.

The following are the 4 Vs of big data:

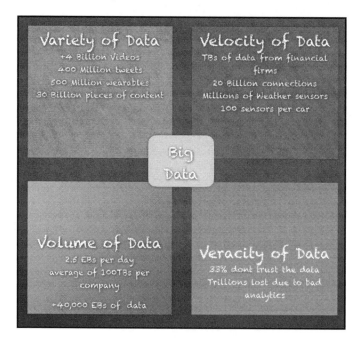

To make sense of all the data and apply data analytics to big data, we need to expand the concept of data analytics to operate at a much larger scale dealing with the 4 Vs of big data. This changes not only the tools, technologies, and methodologies used in analyzing data, but also the way we even approach the problem. If a SQL database was used for data in a business in 1999, now to handle the data for the same business we will need a distributed SQL database scalable and adaptable to the nuances of the big data space.

Big data analytics applications often include data from both internal systems and external sources, such as weather data or demographic data on consumers compiled by third-party information services providers. In addition, streaming analytics applications are becoming common in big data environments, as users look to do real-time analytics on data fed into Hadoop systems through Spark's Spark streaming module or other open source stream processing engines, such as Flink and Storm.

Early big data systems were mostly deployed on-premises particularly in large organizations that were collecting, organizing, and analyzing massive amounts of data. But cloud platform vendors, such as **Amazon Web Services (AWS)** and Microsoft, have made it easier to set up and manage Hadoop clusters in the cloud, as have Hadoop suppliers such as Cloudera and Hortonworks, which support their distributions of the big data framework on the AWS and Microsoft Azure clouds. Users can now spin up clusters in the cloud, run them for as long as needed, and then take them offline, with usage-based pricing that doesn't require ongoing software licenses.

Potential pitfalls that can trip up organizations on big data analytics initiatives include a lack of internal analytics skills and the high cost of hiring experienced data scientists and data engineers to fill the gaps.

The amount of data that's typically involved, and its variety, can cause data management issues in areas including data quality, consistency, and governance; also, data silos can result from the use of different platforms and data stores in a big data architecture. In addition, integrating Hadoop, Spark, and other big data tools into a cohesive architecture that meets an organization's big data analytics needs is a challenging proposition for many IT and analytics teams, which have to identify the right mix of technologies and then put the pieces together.

Distributed computing using Apache Hadoop

Our world is filled with devices starting from the smart refrigerator, smart watch, phone, tablet, laptops, kiosks at the airport, ATM dispensing cash to you, and many many more. We are able to do things we could not even imagine just a few years ago. Instagram, Snapchat, Gmail, Facebook, Twitter, and Pinterest are a few of the applications we are now so used to; it is difficult to imagine a day without access to such applications.

With the advent of Cloud computing, using a few clicks we are able to launch 100s if not, 1000s of machines in AWS, Azure (Microsoft), or Google Cloud among others and use immense resources to realize our business goals of all sorts.

Cloud computing has introduced us to the concepts of IaaS, PaaS, and SaaS, which gives us the ability to build and operate scalable infrastructures serving all types of use cases and business needs.

IaaS (Infrastructure as a Service) - Reliable-managed hardware is provided without the need for a Data center, power cords, Airconditioning, and so on.

PaaS (Platform as a Service) - On top of IaaS, managed platforms such as Windows, Linux , Databases and so on are provided.

SaaS (Software as a Service) - On top of SaaS, managed services such as SalesForce, `Kayak.com` and so on are provided to everyone.

Behind the scenes is the world of highly scalable distributed computing, which makes it possible to store and process PB (PetaBytes) of data.

1 ExaByte = 1024 PetaBytes (50 Million Blue Ray Movies)
1 PetaByte = 1024 Tera Bytes (50,000 Blue Ray Movies)
1 TeraByte = 1024 Giga Bytes (50 Blue Ray Movies)
Average size of 1 Blue Ray Disc for a Movie is ~ 20 GB

Now, the paradigm of Distributed Computing is not really a genuinely new topic and has been pursued in some shape or form over decades primarily at research facilities as well as by a few commercial product companies. **Massively Parallel Processing (MPP)** is a paradigm that was in use decades ago in several areas such as Oceanography, Earthquake monitoring, and Space exploration. Several companies such as Teradata also implemented MPP platforms and provided commercial products and applications. Eventually, tech companies such as Google and Amazon among others pushed the niche area of scalable distributed computing to a new stage of evolution, which eventually led to the creation of Apache Spark by Berkeley University.

Google published a paper on **Map Reduce (MR)** as well as **Google File System (GFS)**, which brought the principles of distributed computing to everyone. Of course, due credit needs to be given to Doug Cutting, who made it possible by implementing the concepts given in the Google white papers and introducing the world to Hadoop.

The Apache Hadoop Framework is an open source software framework written in Java. The two main areas provided by the framework are storage and processing. For Storage, the Apache Hadoop Framework uses **Hadoop Distributed File System (HDFS)**, which is based on the Google File System paper released on October 2003. For processing or computing, the framework depends on MapReduce, which is based on a Google paper on MR released in December 2004.

 The MapReduce framework evolved from V1 (based on Job Tracker and Task Tracker) to V2 (based on YARN).

Hadoop Distributed File System (HDFS)

HDFS is a software-based filesystem implemented in Java and sits on top of the native file system. The main concept behind HDFS is that it divides a file into blocks (typically 128 MB) instead of dealing with a file as a whole. This allowed many features such as distribution, replication, failure recovery, and more importantly distributed processing of the blocks using multiple machines.

 Block sizes can be 64 MB, 128 MB, 256 MB, or 512 MB, whatever suits the purpose. For a 1 GB file with 128 MB blocks, there will be 1024 MB / 128 MB = 8 blocks. If you consider replication factor of 3, this makes it 24 blocks.

HDFS provides a distributed storage system with fault tolerance and failure recovery. HDFS has two main components: name node and data node(s). Name node contains all the metadata of all content of the file system. Data nodes connect to the Name Node and rely on the name node for all metadata information regarding the content in the file system. If the name node does not know any information, data node will not be able to serve it to any client who wants to read/write to the HDFS.

The following is the HDFS architecture:

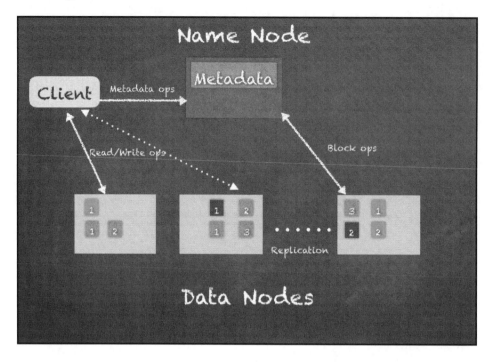

NameNode and DataNode are JVM processes so any machine that supports Java can run the NameNode or the DataNode process. There is only one NameNode (the second NameNode will be there too if you count the HA deployment) but 100s if not 1000s of DataNodes.

It is not advisable to have 1000s of DataNodes because all operations from all the DataNodes will tend to overwhelm the NameNode in a real production environment with a lot of data-intensive applications.

The existence of a single NameNode in a cluster greatly simplifies the architecture of the system. The NameNode is the arbitrator and repository for all HDFS metadata and any client, that wants to read/write data first contacts the NameNode for the metadata information. The data never flows directly through the NameNode, which allows 100s of DataNodes (PBs of data) to be managed by 1 NameNode.

HDFS supports a traditional hierarchical file organization with directories and files similar to most other filesystems. You can create, move, and delete files, and directories. The NameNode maintains the filesystem namespace and records all changes and the state of the filesystem. An application can specify the number of replicas of a file that should be maintained by HDFS and this information is also stored by the NameNode.

HDFS is designed to reliably store very large files in a distributed manner across machines in a large cluster of data nodes. To deal with replication, fault tolerance, as well as distributed computing, HDFS stores each file as a sequence of blocks.

The NameNode makes all decisions regarding the replication of blocks. This is mainly dependent on a Block report from each of the DataNodes in the cluster received periodically at a heart beat interval. A block report contains a list of all blocks on a DataNode, which the NameNode then stores in its metadata repository.

The NameNode stores all metadata in memory and serves all requests from clients reading from/writing to HDFS. However, since this is the master node maintaining all the metadata about the HDFS, it is critical to maintain consistent and reliable metadata information. If this information is lost, the content on the HDFS cannot be accessed.

For this purpose, HDFS NameNode uses a transaction log called the EditLog, which persistently records every change that occurs to the metadata of the filesystem. Creating a new file updates EditLog, so does moving a file or renaming a file, or deleting a file. The entire filesystem namespace, including the mapping of blocks to files and filesystem properties, is stored in a file called the `FsImage`. The **NameNode** keeps everything in memory as well. When a NameNode starts up, it loads the EditLog and the `FsImage` initializes itself to set up the HDFS.

The DataNodes, however, have no idea about the HDFS, purely relying on the blocks of data stored. DataNodes rely entirely on the NameNode to perform any operations. Even when a client wants to connect to read a file or write to a file, it's the NameNode that tells the client where to connect to.

HDFS High Availability

HDFS is a Master-Slave cluster with the NameNode as the master and the 100s, if not 1000s of DataNodes as slaves, managed by the master node. This introduces a **Single Point of Failure (SPOF)** in the cluster as if the Master NameNode goes down for some reason, the entire cluster is going to be unusable. HDFS 1.0 supports an additional Master Node known as the **Secondary NameNode** to help with recovery of the cluster. This is done by maintaining a copy of all the metadata of the filesystem and is by no means a Highly Available System requiring manual interventions and maintenance work. HDFS 2.0 takes this to the next level by adding support for full **High Availability (HA)**.

HA works by having two Name Nodes in an active-passive mode such that one Name Node is active and other is passive. When the primary NameNode has a failure, the passive Name Node will take over the role of the Master Node.

The following diagram shows how the active-passive pair of NameNodes will be deployed:

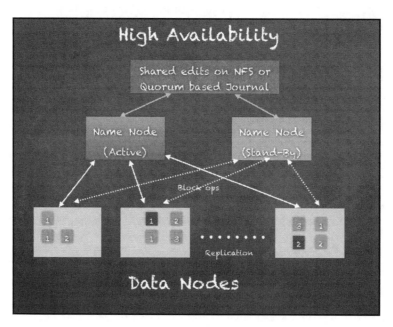

HDFS Federation

HDFS Federation is a way of using multiple name nodes to spread the filesystem namespace over. Unlike the first HDFS versions, which simply managed entire clusters using a single NameNode, which does not scale that well as the size of the cluster grows, HDFS Federation can support significantly larger clusters and horizontally scales the NameNode or name service using multiple federated name nodes. Take a look at the following diagram:

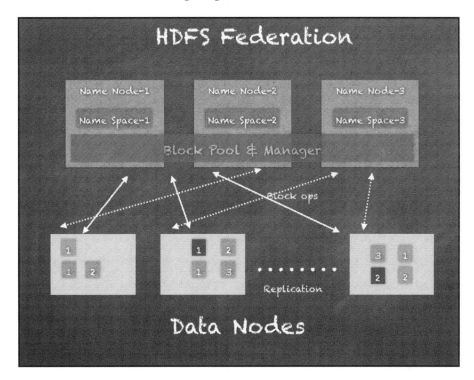

HDFS Snapshot

Hadoop 2.0 also added a new capability: taking a snapshot (read-only copy and copy-on-write) of the filesystem (data blocks) stored on the data nodes. Using Snapshots, you can take a copy of directories seamlessly using the NameNode's metadata of the data blocks. Snapshot creation is instantaneous and doesn't require interference with other regular HDFS operations.

The following is an illustration of how snapshot works on specific directories:

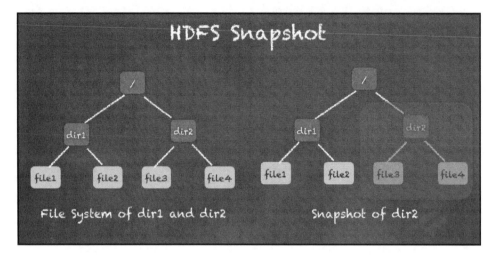

HDFS Read

Client connects to the NameNode and ask about a file using the name of the file. NameNode looks up the block locations for the file and returns the same to the client. The client can then connect to the DataNodes and read the blocks needed. NameNode does not participate in the data transfer.

The following is the flow of a read request from a client. First, the client gets the locations and then pulls the blocks from the DataNodes. If a DataNode fails in the middle, then the client gets the replica of the block from another DataNode.

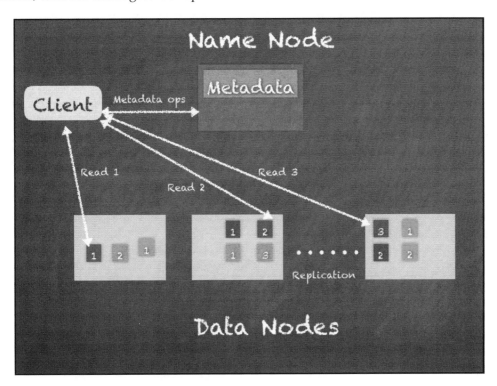

HDFS Write

The client connects to the NameNode and asks the NameNode to let it write to the HDFS. The NameNode looks up information and plans the blocks, the Data Nodes to be used to store the blocks, and the replication strategy to be used. The NameNode does not handle any data and only tells the client where to write. Once the first DataNode receives the block, based on the replication strategy, the NameNode tells the first DataNode where else to replicate. So, the DataNode that is received from client sends the block over to the second DataNode (where the copy of the block is supposed to be written to) and then the second DataNode sends it to a third DataNode (if replication-factor is 3).

The following is the flow of a write request from a client. First, the client gets the locations and then writes to the first DataNode. The DataNode that receives the block replicates the block to the DataNodes that should hold the replica copy of the block. This happens for all the blocks being written to from the client. If a DataNode fails in the middle, then the block gets replicated to another DataNode as determined by the NameNode.

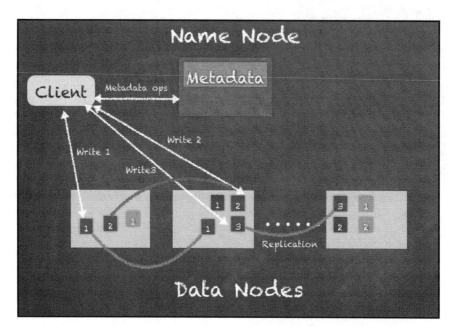

So far, we have seen how HDFS provides a distributed filesystem using blocks, the NameNode, and DataNodes. Once data is stored at a PB scale, it is also important to actually process the data to serve the various use cases of the business.

MapReduce framework was created in the Hadoop framework to perform distributed computation. We will look at this further in the next section.

MapReduce framework

MapReduce (**MR**) framework enables you to write distributed applications to process large amounts of data from a filesystem such as HDFS in a reliable and fault-tolerant manner. When you want to use the MapReduce Framework to process data, it works through the creation of a job, which then runs on the framework to perform the tasks needed.

A MapReduce job usually works by splitting the input data across worker nodes running **Mapper** tasks in a parallel manner. At this time, any failures that happen either at the HDFS level or the failure of a Mapper task are handled automatically to be fault-tolerant. Once the Mappers are completed, the results are copied over the network to other machines running **Reducer** tasks.

An easy way to understand this concept is to imagine that you and your friends want to sort out piles of fruit into boxes. For that, you want to assign each person the task of going through one raw basket of fruit (all mixed up) and separate out the fruit into various boxes. Each person then does the same with this basket of fruit.

In the end, you end up with a lot of boxes of fruit from all your friends. Then, you can assign a group to put the same kind of fruit together in a box, weight the box, and seal the box for shipping.

The following depicts the idea of taking fruit baskets and sorting the fruit by the type of fruit:

MapReduce framework consists of a single resource manager and multiple node managers (usually Node Managers coexist with the data nodes of HDFS). When an application wants to run, the client launches the application master, which then negotiates with the resource manager to get resources in the cluster in form of containers.

A container represents CPUs (cores) and memory allocated on a single node to be used to run tasks and processes. Containers are supervised by the node manager and scheduled by the resource manager.

Examples of containers:

1 core + 4 GB RAM

2 cores + 6 GB RAM

4 cores + 20 GB RAM

Some Containers are assigned to be Mappers and other to be Reducers; all this is coordinated by the application master in conjunction with the resource manager. This framework is called **Yet Another Resource Negotiator (YARN)**

The following is a depiction of YARN:

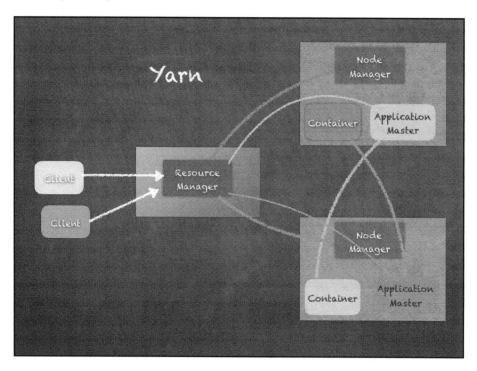

A classic example showing the MapReduce framework at work is the word count example. The following are the various stages of processing the input data, first splitting the input across multiple worker nodes and then finally generating the output counts of words:

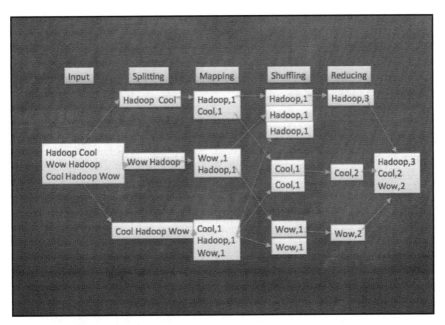

Though MapReduce framework is very successful all across the world and has been adopted by most companies, it does run into issues mainly because of the way it processes data. Several technologies have come into existence to try and make MapReduce easier to use such as Hive and Pig but the complexity remains.

Hadoop MapReduce has several limitations such as:

- Performance bottlenecks due to disk-based processing
- Batch processing doesn't serve all needs
- Programming can be verbose and complex
- Scheduling of the tasks is slow as there is not much reuse of resources
- No good way to do real-time event processing
- Machine learning takes too long as usually ML involves iterative processing and MR is too slow for this

Hive was created by Facebook as a SQL-like interface to MR. Pig was created by Yahoo with a scripting interface to MR. Moreover, several enhancements such as Tez (Hortonworks) and LLAP (Hive2.x) are in use, which makes use of in-memory optimizations to circumvent the limitations of MapReduce.

In the next section, we will look at Apache Spark, which has already solved some of the limitations of Hadoop technologies.

Here comes Apache Spark

Apache Spark is a unified distributed computing engine across different workloads and platforms. Spark can connect to different platforms and process different data workloads using a variety of paradigms such as Spark streaming, Spark ML, Spark SQL, and Spark GraphX.

Apache Spark is a fast in-memory data processing engine with elegant and expressive development APIs to allow data workers to efficiently execute streaming machine learning or SQL workloads that require fast interactive access to data sets. Apache Spark consists of Spark core and a set of libraries. The core is the distributed execution engine and the Java, Scala, and Python APIs offer a platform for distributed application development. Additional libraries built on top of the core allow workloads for streaming, SQL, Graph processing, and machine learning. Spark ML, for instance, is designed for data science and its abstraction makes data science easier.

Spark provides real-time streaming, queries, machine learning, and graph processing. Before Apache Spark, we had to use different technologies for different types of workloads, one for batch analytics, one for interactive queries, one for real-time streaming processing and another for machine learning algorithms. However, Apache Spark can do all of these just using Apache Spark instead of using multiple technologies that are not always integrated.

Using Apache Spark, all types of workload can be processed and Spark also supports Scala, Java, R, and Python as a means of writing client programs.

Apache Spark is an open-source distributed computing engine which has key advantages over the MapReduce paradigm:

- Uses in-memory processing as much as possible
- General purpose engine to be used for batch, real-time workloads
- Compatible with YARN and also Mesos
- Integrates well with HBase, Cassandra, MongoDB, HDFS, Amazon S3, and other file systems and data sources

Spark was created in Berkeley back in 2009 and was a result of the project to build Mesos, a cluster management framework to support different kinds of cluster computing systems. Take a look at the following table:

Version	Release date	Milestones
0.5	2012-10-07	First available version for non-production usage
0.6	2013-02-07	Point release with various changes
0.7	2013-07-16	Point release with various changes
0.8	2013-12-19	Point release with various changes
0.9	2014-07-23	Point release with various changes
1.0	2014-08-05	First production ready, backward-compatible release. Spark Batch, Streaming, Shark, MLLib, GraphX
1.1	2014-11-26	Point release with various changes
1.2	2015-04-17	Structured Data, SchemaRDD (subsequently evolved into DataFrames)
1.3	2015-04-17	API to provide a unified API to read from structured and semi-structured sources
1.4	2015-07-15	SparkR, DataFrame API, Tungsten improvements
1.5	2015-11-09	Point release with various changes
1.6	2016-11-07	Dataset DSL introduced
2.0	2016-11-14	DataFrames and Datasets API as fundamental layer for ML, Structured Streaming, SparkR improvements.
2.1	2017-05-02	Event time watermarks, ML, GraphX improvements

 2.2 has been released 2017-07-11 which has several improvements especially Structured Streaming which is now GA.

Spark is a platform for distributed computing that has several features:

- Transparently processes data on multiple nodes via a simple API
- Resiliently handles failures
- Spills data to disk as necessary though predominantly uses memory
- Java, Scala, Python, R, and SQL APIs are supported
- The same Spark code can run standalone, in Hadoop YARN, Mesos, and the cloud

 Scala features such as implicits, higher-order functions, structured types, and so on allow us to easily build DSL's and integrate them with the language.

Apache Spark does not provide a Storage layer and relies on HDFS or Amazon S3 and so on. Hence, even if Apache Hadoop technologies are replaced with Apache Spark, HDFS is still needed to provide a reliable storage layer.

 Apache Kudu provides an alternative to HDFS and there is already integration between Apache Spark and Kudu Storage layer, further decoupling Apache Spark and the Hadoop ecosystem.

Hadoop and Apache Spark are both popular big data frameworks, but they don't really serve the same purposes. While Hadoop provides distributed storage and a MapReduce distributed computing framework, Spark on the other hand is a data processing framework that operates on the distributed data storage provided by other technologies.

Spark is generally a lot faster than MapReduce because of the way it processes data. MapReduce operates on splits using Disk operations, Spark operates on the dataset much more efficiently than MapReduce, with the main reason behind the performance improvement in Apache Spark being the efficient off-heap in-memory processing rather than solely relying on disk-based computations.

 MapReduce's processing style can be sufficient if you were data operations and reporting requirements are mostly static and it is okay to use batch processing for your purposes, but if you need to do analytics on streaming data or your processing requirements need multistage processing logic, you will probably want to want to go with Spark.

There are three layers in the Spark stack. The bottom layer is the cluster manager, which can be standalone, YARN, or Mesos.

 Using local mode, you don't need a cluster manager to process.

In the middle, above the cluster manager, is the layer of Spark core, which provides all the underlying APIs to perform task scheduling and interacting with storage.

At the top are modules that run on top of Spark core such as Spark SQL to provide interactive queries, Spark streaming for real-time analytics, Spark ML for machine learning, and Spark GraphX for graph processing.

The three layers are as follows:

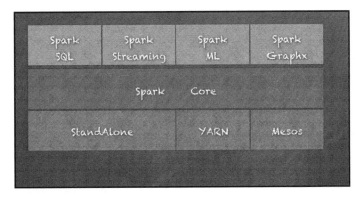

As seen in the preceding diagram, the various libraries such as Spark SQL, Spark streaming, Spark ML, and GraphX all sit on top of Spark core, which is the middle layer. The bottom layer shows the various cluster manager options.

Let's now look at each of the component briefly:

Spark core

Spark core is the underlying general execution engine for the Spark platform that all other functionality is built upon. Spark core contains basic Spark functionalities required for running jobs and needed by other components. It provides in-memory computing and referencing datasets in external storage systems, the most important being the **Resilient Distributed Dataset (RDD)**.

In addition, Spark core contains logic for accessing various filesystems, such as HDFS, Amazon S3, HBase, Cassandra, relational databases, and so on. Spark core also provides fundamental functions to support networking, security, scheduling, and data shuffling to build a high scalable, fault-tolerant platform for distributed computing.

We cover Spark core in detail in Chapter 6, *Start Working with Spark - REPL and RDDs* and Chapter 7, *Special RDD Operations*.

DataFrames and datasets built on top of RDDs and introduced with Spark SQL are becoming the norm now over RDDs in many use cases. RDDs are still more flexible in terms of handling totally unstructured data, but in future datasets, API might eventually become the core API.

Spark SQL

Spark SQL is a component on top of Spark core that introduces a new data abstraction called **SchemaRDD**, which provides support for structured and semi-structured data. Spark SQL provides functions for manipulating large sets of distributed, structured data using an SQL subset supported by Spark and Hive QL. Spark SQL simplifies the handling of structured data through DataFrames and datasets at a much more performant level as part of the Tungsten initative. Spark SQL also supports reading and writing data to and from various structured formats and data sources, files, parquet, orc, relational databases, Hive, HDFS, S3, and so on. Spark SQL provides a query optimization framework called **Catalyst** to optimize all operations to boost the speed (compared to RDDs Spark SQL is several times faster). Spark SQL also includes a Thrift server, which can be used by external systems to query data through Spark SQL using classic JDBC and ODBC protocols.

We cover Spark SQL in detail in Chapter 8, *Introduce a Little Structure - Spark SQL*.

Spark streaming

Spark streaming leverages Spark core's fast scheduling capability to perform streaming analytics by ingesting real-time streaming data from various sources such as HDFS, Kafka, Flume, Twitter, ZeroMQ, Kinesis, and so on. Spark streaming uses micro-batches of data to process the data in chunks and, uses a concept known as DStreams, Spark streaming can operate on the RDDs, applying transformations and actions as regular RDDs in the Spark core API. Spark streaming operations can recover from failure automatically using various techniques. Spark streaming can be combined with other Spark components in a single program, unifying real-time processing with machine learning, SQL, and graph operations.

 We cover Spark streaming in detail in the `Chapter 9`, *Stream Me Up, Scotty - Spark Streaming*.

In addition, the new Structured Streaming API makes Spark streaming programs more similar to Spark batch programs and also allows real-time querying on top of streaming data, which is complicated with the Spark streaming library before Spark 2.0+.

Spark GraphX

GraphX is a distributed graph processing framework on top of Spark. Graphs are data structures comprising vertices and the edges connecting them. GraphX provides functions for building graphs, represented as Graph RDDs. It provides an API for expressing graph computation that can model user-defined graphs by using the Pregel abstraction API. It also provides an optimized runtime for this abstraction. GraphX also contains implementations of the most important algorithms of graph theory, such as page rank, connected components, shortest paths, SVD++, and others.

 We cover Spark Graphx in detail in `Chapter 10`, *Everything is Connected - GraphX*.

A newer module known as GraphFrames is in development, which makes it easier to do Graph processing using DataFrame-based Graphs. GraphX is to RDDs what GraphFrames are to DataFrames/datasets. Also, this is currently separate from GraphX and is expected to support all the functionality of GraphX in the future, when there might be a switch over to GraphFrames.

Spark ML

MLlib is a distributed machine learning framework above Spark core and handles machine-learning models used for transforming datasets in the form of RDDs. Spark MLlib is a library of machine-learning algorithms providing various algorithms such as logistic regression, Naive Bayes classification, **Support Vector Machines (SVMs)**, decision trees, random forests, linear regression, **Alternating Least Squares (ALS)**, and k-means clustering. Spark ML integrates very well with Spark core, Spark streaming, Spark SQL, and GraphX to provide a truly integrated platform where data can be real-time or batch.

 We cover Spark ML in detail in `Chapter 11`, *Learning Machine Learning - Spark MLlib and ML*.

In addition, PySpark and SparkR are also available as means to interact with Spark clusters and use the Python and R APIs. Python and R integrations truly open up Spark to a population of Data scientists and Machine learning modelers as the most common languages used by Data scientists in general are Python and R. This is the reason why Spark supports Python integration and also R integration, so as to avoid the costly process of learning a new language of Scala. Another reason is that there might be a lot of existing code written in Python and R, and if we can leverage some of the code, that will improve the productivity of the teams rather than building everything again from scratch.

There is increasing popularity for, and usage of, notebook technologies such as Jupyter and Zeppelin, which make it significantly easier to interact with Spark in general, but particularly very useful in Spark ML where a lot of hypotheses and analysis are expected.

PySpark

PySpark uses Python-based `SparkContext` and Python scripts as tasks and then uses sockets and pipes to executed processes to communicate between Java-based Spark clusters and Python scripts. PySpark also uses `Py4J`, which is a popular library integrated within PySpark that lets Python interface dynamically with Java-based RDDs.

> Python must be installed on all worker nodes running the Spark executors.

The following is how PySpark works by communicating between Java processed and Python scripts:

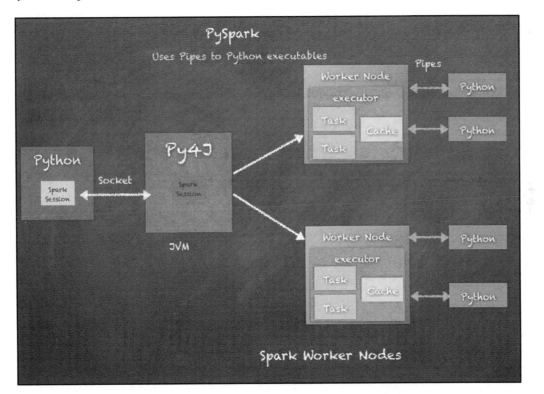

SparkR

SparkR is an R package that provides a light-weight frontend to use Apache Spark from R. SparkR provides a distributed data frame implementation that supports operations such as selection, filtering, aggregation, and so on. SparkR also supports distributed machine learning using MLlib. SparkR uses R-based SparkContext and R scripts as tasks and then uses JNI and pipes to executed processes to communicate between Java-based Spark clusters and R scripts.

R must be installed on all worker nodes running the Spark executors.

The following is how SparkR works by communicating between Java processed and R scripts:

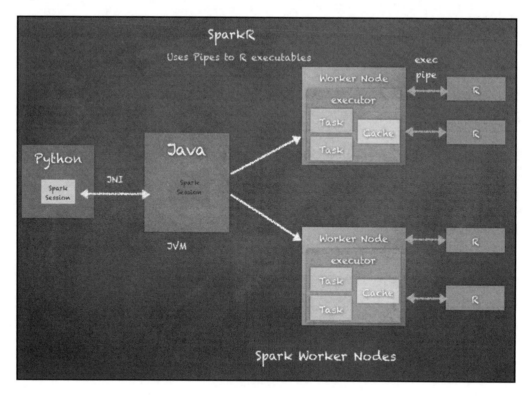

Summary

We explored the evolution of the Hadoop and MapReduce frameworks and discussed YARN, HDFS concepts, HDFS Reads and Writes, and key features as well as challenges. Then, we discussed the evolution of Apache Spark, why Apache Spark was created in the first place, and the value it can bring to the challenges of big data analytics and processing.

Finally, we also took a peek at the various components in Apache Spark, namely, Spark core, Spark SQL, Spark streaming, Spark GraphX, and Spark ML as well as PySpark and SparkR as a means of integrating Python and R language code with Apache Spark.

Now that we have seen big data analytics, the space and the evolution of the Hadoop Distributed computing platform, and the eventual development of Apache Spark along with a high-level overview of how Apache Spark might solve some of the challenges, we are ready to start learning Spark and how to use it in our use cases.

In the next chapter, we will delve more deeply into Apache Spark and start to look under the hood of how it all works in `Chapter 6`, *Start Working with Spark - REPL and RDDs*.

Start Working with Spark – 6
REPL and RDDs

"All this modern technology just makes people try to do everything at once."

- Bill Watterson

In this chapter, you will learn how Spark works; then, you will be introduced to RDDs, the basic abstractions behind Apache Spark, and you'll learn that they are simply distributed collections exposing Scala-like APIs. You will then see how to download Spark and how to make it run locally via the Spark shell.

In a nutshell, the following topics will be covered in this chapter:

- Dig deeper into Apache Spark
- Apache Spark installation
- Introduction to RDDs
- Using the Spark shell
- Actions and Transformations
- Caching
- Loading and Saving data

Dig deeper into Apache Spark

Apache Spark is a fast in-memory data processing engine with elegant and expressive development APIs to allow data workers to efficiently execute streaming machine learning or SQL workloads that require fast interactive access to datasets. Apache Spark consists of Spark core and a set of libraries. The core is the distributed execution engine and the Java, Scala, and Python APIs offer a platform for distributed application development.

Additional libraries built on top of the core allow the workloads for streaming, SQL, Graph processing, and machine learning. SparkML, for instance, is designed for Data science and its abstraction makes Data science easier.

In order to plan and carry out the distributed computations, Spark uses the concept of a job, which is executed across the worker nodes using Stages and Tasks. Spark consists of a driver, which orchestrates the execution across a cluster of worker nodes. The driver is also responsible for tracking all the worker nodes as well as the work currently being performed by each of the worker nodes.

Let's look into the various components a little more. The key components are the Driver and the Executors which are all JVM processes (Java processes):

- **Driver**: The Driver program contains the applications, main program. If you are using the Spark shell, that becomes the Driver program and the Driver launches the executors across the cluster and also controls the task executions.

- **Executor**: Next are the executors which are processes running on the worker nodes in your cluster. Inside the executor, the individual tasks or computations are run. There could be one or more executors in each worker node and, similarly, there could be multiple tasks inside each executor. When Driver connects to the cluster manager, the cluster manager assigns resources to run executors.

 The cluster manager could be a standalone cluster manager, YARN, or Mesos.

The **Cluster Manager** is responsible for the scheduling and allocation of resources across the compute nodes forming the cluster. Typically, this is done by having a manager process which knows and manages a cluster of resources and allocates the resources to a requesting process such as Spark. We will look at the three different cluster managers: standalone, YARN, and Mesos further down in the next sections.

The following is how Spark works at a high level:

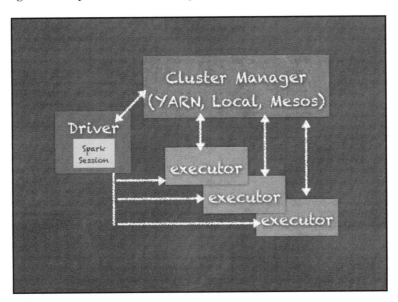

The main entry point to a Spark program is called the `SparkContext`. The `SparkContext` is inside the **Driver** component and represents the connection to the cluster along with the code to run the scheduler and task distribution and orchestration.

> In Spark 2.x, a new variable called `SparkSession` has been introduced. `SparkContext`, `SQLContext`, and `HiveContext` are now member variables of the `SparkSession`.

When you start the **Driver** program, the commands are issued to the cluster using the `SparkContext`, and then the **executors** will execute the instructions. Once the execution is completed, the **Driver** program completes the job. You can, at this point, issue more commands and execute more Jobs.

The ability to maintain and reuse the `SparkContext` is a key advantage of the Apache Spark architecture, unlike the Hadoop framework where every `MapReduce` job or Hive query or Pig Script starts entire processing from scratch for each task we want to execute that too using expensive disk instead of memory.

The `SparkContext` can be used to create RDDs, accumulators, and broadcast variables on the cluster. Only one `SparkContext` may be active per JVM/Java process. You must `stop()` the active `SparkContext` before creating a new one.

The **Driver** parses the code, and serializes the byte level code across to the executors to be executed. When we perform any computations, the computations will actually be done at the local level by each node, using in-memory processing.

The process of parsing the code and planning the execution is the key aspect implemented by the **Driver** process.

The following is how Spark **Driver** coordinates the computations across the cluster:

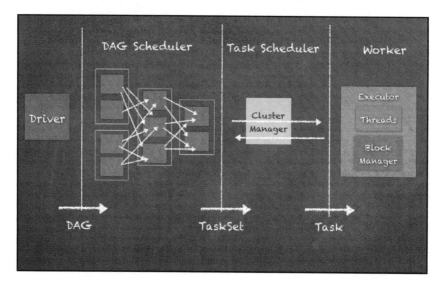

The **Directed Acyclic Graph (DAG)** is the secret sauce of Spark framework. The **Driver** process creates a DAG of tasks for a piece of code you try to run using the distributed processing framework. Then, the DAG is actually executed in stages and tasks by the task scheduler by communicating with the **Cluster Manager** for resources to run the executors. A DAG represents a job, and a job is split into subsets, also called stages, and each stage is executed as tasks using one core per task.

An illustration of a simple job and how the DAG is split into stages and tasks is shown in the following two illustrations; the first one shows the job itself, and the second diagram shows the stages in the job and the tasks:

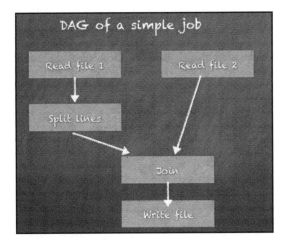

The following diagram now breaks down the job/DAG into stages and tasks:

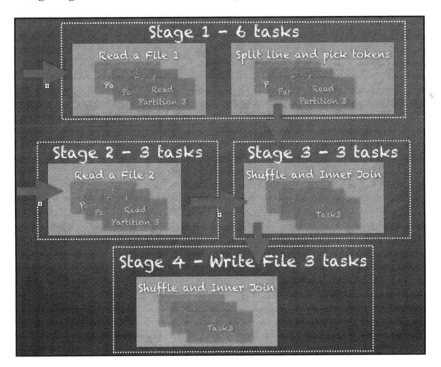

The number of stages and what the stages consist of is determined by the kind of operations. Usually, any transformation comes into the same stage as the one before, but every operation such as reduce or shuffle always creates a new stage of execution. Tasks are part of a stage and are directly related to the cores executing the operations on the executors.

If you use YARN or Mesos as the cluster manager, you can use dynamic YARN scheduler to increase the number of executors when more work needs to be done, as well as killing idle executors.

The driver, hence, manages the fault tolerance of the entire execution process. Once the job is completed by the Driver, the output can be written to a file, database, or simply to the console.

Remember that the code in the Driver program itself has to be completely serializable including all the variables and objects. The often seen exception is a not a serializable exception, which is a result of including global variables from outside the block.

Hence, the Driver process takes care of the entire execution process while monitoring and managing the resources used, such as executors, stages, and tasks, making sure everything is working as planned and recovering from failures such as task failures on executor nodes or entire executor nodes as a whole.

Apache Spark installation

Apache Spark is a cross-platform framework, which can be deployed on Linux, Windows, and a Mac Machine as long as we have Java installed on the machine. In this section, we will look at how to install Apache Spark.

Apache Spark can be downloaded from `http://spark.apache.org/downloads.html`

First, let's look at the pre-requisites that must be available on the machine:

- Java 8+ (mandatory as all Spark software runs as JVM processes)
- Python 3.4+ (optional and used only when you want to use PySpark)
- R 3.1+ (optional and used only when you want to use SparkR)
- Scala 2.11+ (optional and used only to write programs for Spark)

Spark can be deployed in three primary deployment modes, which we will look at:

- Spark standalone
- Spark on YARN
- Spark on Mesos

Spark standalone

Spark standalone uses a built-in scheduler without depending on any external scheduler such as YARN or Mesos. To install Spark in standalone mode, you have to copy the spark binary install package onto all the machines in the cluster.

In standalone mode, the client can interact with the cluster, either through spark-submit or Spark shell. In either case, the Driver communicates with the Spark master Node to get the worker nodes, where executors can be started for this application.

 Multiple clients interacting with the cluster create their own executors on the Worker Nodes. Also, each client will have its own Driver component.

The following is the standalone deployment of Spark using Master node and worker nodes:

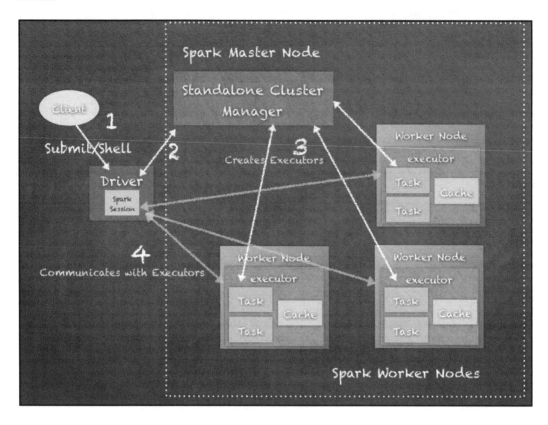

Let's now download and install Spark in standalone mode using a Linux/Mac:

1. Download Apache Spark from the link `http://spark.apache.org/downloads.html`:

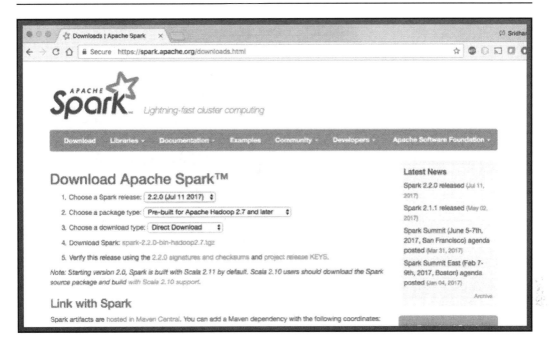

2. Extract the package in your local directory:

```
tar -xvzf spark-2.2.0-bin-hadoop2.7.tgz
```

3. Change directory to the newly created directory:

```
cd spark-2.2.0-bin-hadoop2.7
```

4. Set environment variables for JAVA_HOME and SPARK_HOME by implementing the following steps:

   1. JAVA_HOME should be where you have Java installed. On my Mac terminal, this is set as:

```
export JAVA_HOME=/Library/Java/JavaVirtualMachines/
        jdk1.8.0_65.jdk/Contents/Home/
```

   2. SPARK_HOME should be the newly extracted folder. On my Mac terminal, this is set as:

```
export SPARK_HOME= /Users/myuser/spark-2.2.0-bin-
        hadoop2.7
```

5. Run Spark shell to see if this works. If it does not work, check the JAVA_HOME and SPARK_HOME environment variable: `./bin/spark-shell`

6. You will now see the shell as shown in the following:

```
falcon:spark-2.2.0-bin-hadoop2.7 salla$ ./bin/spark-shell
Using Spark's default log4j profile:
Setting default log level to "WARN".
To adjust logging level use sc.setLogLevel(newLevel). For SparkR, use setLogLevel(newLevel).
17/07/15 15:05:37 WARN NativeCodeLoader: Unable to load native-hadoop library for your platform... using builtin-java classes where applicable
17/07/15 15:05:37 WARN Utils: Your hostname, falcon resolves to a loopback address: 127.0.0.1; using 192.168.1.253 instead (on interface en1)
17/07/15 15:05:37 WARN Utils: Set SPARK_LOCAL_IP if you need to bind to another address
17/07/15 15:05:56 WARN ObjectStore: Version information not found in metastore. hive.metastore.schema.verification is not enabled so recording the schema version 1.2.0
17/07/15 15:05:57 WARN ObjectStore: Failed to get database default, returning NoSuchObjectException
17/07/15 15:06:02 WARN ObjectStore: Failed to get database global_temp, returning NoSuchObjectException
Spark context Web UI available at http://192.168.1.253:4040
Spark context available as 'sc' (master = local[*], app id = local-1500145542037).
Spark session available as 'spark'.
Welcome to
      ____              __
     / __/__  ___ _____/ /__
    _\ \/ _ \/ _ `/ __/  '_/
   /___/ .__/\_,_/_/ /_/\_\   version 2.2.0
      /_/

Using Scala version 2.11.8 (Java HotSpot(TM) 64-Bit Server VM, Java 1.8.0_65)
Type in expressions to have them evaluated.
Type :help for more information.

scala>

scala>
```

5. You will see the Scala/ Spark shell at the end and now you are ready to interact with the Spark cluster:

```
scala>
```

Now, we have a Spark-shell connected to an automatically setup local cluster running Spark. This is the quickest way to launch Spark on a local machine. However, you can still control the workers/executors as well as connect to any cluster (standalone/YARN/Mesos). This is the power of Spark, enabling you to quickly move from interactive testing to testing on a cluster and subsequently deploying your jobs on a large cluster. The seamless integration offers a lot of benefits, which you cannot realize using Hadoop and other technologies.

You can refer to the official documentation in case you want to understand all the settings `http://spark.apache.org/docs/latest/`.

There are several ways to start the Spark shell as in the following snippet. We will see more options in a later section, showing Spark shell in more detail.:

- Default shell on local machine automatically picks local machine as master:

```
./bin/spark-shell
```

- Default shell on local machine specifying local machine as master with n threads:

```
./bin/spark-shell --master local[n]
```

- Default shell on local machine connecting to a specified spark master:

```
./bin/spark-shell --master spark://<IP>:<Port>
```

- Default shell on local machine connecting to a YARN cluster using client mode:

```
./bin/spark-shell --master yarn --deploy-mode client
```

- Default shell on local machine connecting to a YARN cluster using cluster mode:

```
./bin/spark-shell --master yarn --deploy-mode cluster
```

Spark Driver also has a Web UI, which helps you to understand everything about the Spark cluster, the executors running, the jobs and tasks, environment variables, and cache. The most important use, of course, is to monitor the jobs.

Launch the Web UI for the local Spark cluster at
http://127.0.0.1:4040/jobs/

The following is the Jobs tab in the Web UI:

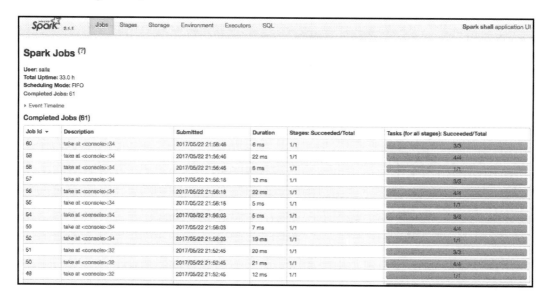

The following is the tab showing all the executors of the cluster:

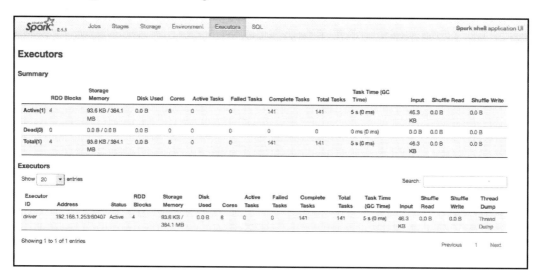

Spark on YARN

In YARN mode, the client communicates with YARN resource manager and gets containers to run the Spark execution. You can regard it as something like a mini Spark-cluster deployed just for you.

 Multiple clients interacting with the cluster create their own executors on the cluster nodes (node managers). Also, each client will have its own Driver component.

When running using YARN, Spark can run either in YARN-client mode or YARN-cluster mode.

YARN client mode

In YARN client mode, the Driver runs on a node outside the cluster (typically where the client is). Driver first contacts the resource manager requesting resources to run the Spark job. The resource manager allocates a container (container zero) and responds to the Driver. The Driver then launches the Spark application master in the container zero. The Spark application master then creates the executors on the containers allocated by the resource manager. The YARN containers can be on any node in the cluster controlled by node manager. So, all allocations are managed by resource manager.

Even the Spark application master needs to talk to resource manager to get subsequent containers to launch executors.

The following is the YARN-client mode deployment of Spark:

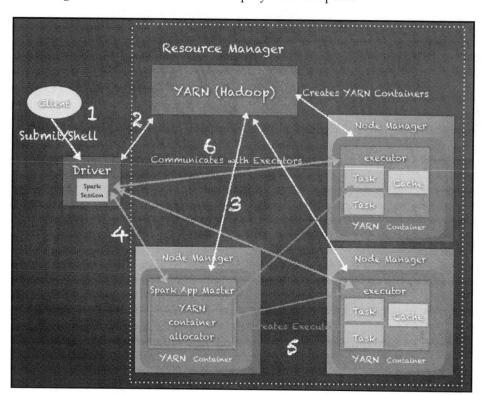

YARN cluster mode

In the YARN cluster mode, the Driver runs on a node inside the cluster (typically where the application master is). Client first contacts the resource manager requesting resources to run the Spark job. The resource manager allocates a container (container zero) and responds to the client. The client then submits the code to the cluster and then launches the Driver and Spark application master in the container zero. The Driver runs along with the application master and the Spark application master, and then creates the executors on the containers allocated by the resource manager. The YARN containers can be on any node in the cluster controlled by the node manager. So, all allocations are managed by the resource manager.

Even the Spark application master needs to talk to the resource manager to get subsequent containers to launch executors.

The following is the Yarn-cluster mode deployment of Spark:

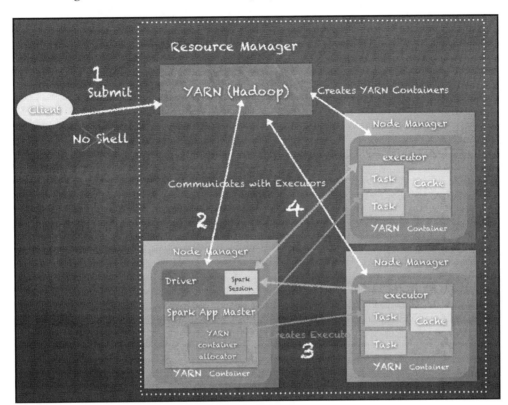

There is no shell mode in YARN cluster mode, since the Driver itself is running inside YARN.

Spark on Mesos

Mesos deployment is similar to Spark standalone mode and the Driver communicates with the Mesos Master, which then allocates the resources needed to run the executors. As seen in standalone mode, the Driver then communicates with the executors to run the job. Thus, the Driver in Mesos deployment first talks to the master and then secures the container's request on all the Mesos slave nodes.

When the containers are allocated to the Spark job, the Driver then gets the executors started up and then runs the code in the executors. When the Spark job is completed and Driver exits, the Mesos master is notified, and all the resources in the form of containers on the Mesos slave nodes are reclaimed.

 Multiple clients interacting with the cluster create their own executors on the slave nodes. Also, each client will have its own Driver component. Both client and cluster mode are possible just like YARN mode

The following is the mesos-based deployment of Spark depicting the **Driver** connecting to **Mesos Master Node**, which also has the cluster manager of all the resources on all the Mesos slaves:

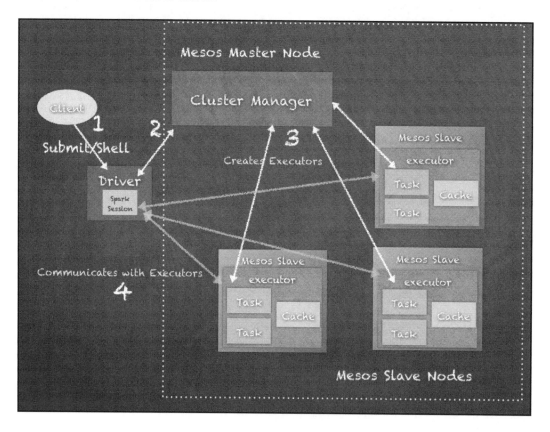

Introduction to RDDs

A **Resilient Distributed Dataset** (**RDD**) is an immutable, distributed collection of objects. Spark RDDs are resilient or fault tolerant, which enables Spark to recover the RDD in the face of failures. Immutability makes the RDDs read-only once created. Transformations allow operations on the RDD to create a new RDD but the original RDD is never modified once created. This makes RDDs immune to race conditions and other synchronization problems.

The distributed nature of the RDDs works because an RDD only contains a reference to the data, whereas the actual data is contained within partitions across the nodes in the cluster.

 Conceptually, a RDD is a distributed collection of elements spread out across multiple nodes in the cluster. We can simplify a RDD to better understand by thinking of a RDD as a large array of integers distributed across machines.

A RDD is actually a dataset that has been partitioned across the cluster and the partitioned data could be from **HDFS** (**Hadoop Distributed File System**), HBase table, Cassandra table, Amazon S3.

Internally, each RDD is characterized by five main properties:

- A list of partitions
- A function for computing each split
- A list of dependencies on other RDDs
- Optionally, a partitioner for key-value RDDs (for example, to say that the RDD is hash partitioned)
- Optionally, a list of preferred locations to compute each split on (for example, block locations for an HDFS file)

Take a look at the following diagram:

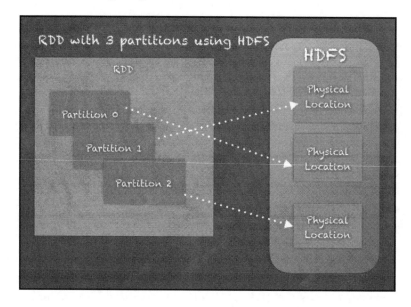

Within your program, the driver treats the RDD object as a handle to the distributed data. It is analogous to a pointer to the data, rather than the actual data used, to reach the actual data when it is required.

The RDD by default uses the hash partitioner to partition the data across the cluster. The number of partitions is independent of the number of nodes in the cluster. It could very well happen that a single node in the cluster has several partitions of data. The number of partitions of data that exist is entirely dependent on how many nodes your cluster has and the size of the data. If you look at the execution of tasks on the nodes, then a task running on an executor on the worker node could be processing the data which is available on the same local node or a remote node. This is called the locality of the data, and the executing task chooses the most local data possible.

The locality affects the performance of your job significantly. The order of preference of locality by default can be shown as
`PROCESS_LOCAL > NODE_LOCAL > NO_PREF > RACK_LOCAL > ANY`

There is no guarantee of how many partitions a node might get. This affects the processing efficiency of any executor, because if you have too many partitions on a single node processing multiple partitions, then the time taken to process all the partitions also grows, overloading the cores on the executor, and thus slowing down the entire stage of processing, which directly slows down the entire job. In fact, partitioning is one of the main tuning factors to improve the performance of a Spark job. Refer to the following command:

```
class RDD[T: ClassTag]
```

Let's look further into what an RDD will look like when we load data. The following is an example of how Spark uses different workers to load different partitions or splits of the data:

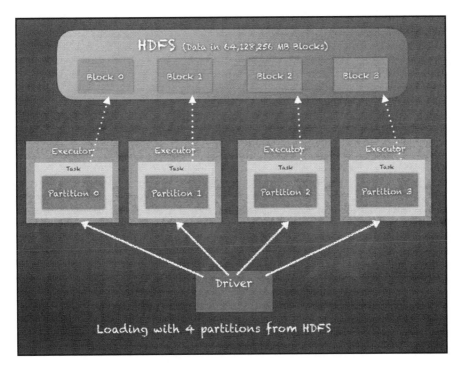

Loading with 4 partitions from HDFS

No matter how the RDD is created, the initial RDD is typically called the base RDD and any subsequent RDDs created by the various operations are part of the lineage of the RDDs. This is another very important aspect to remember, as the secret to fault tolerance and recovery is that the **Driver** maintains the lineage of the RDDs and can execute the lineage to recover any lost blocks of the RDDs.

The following is an example showing multiple RDDs created as a result of operations. We start with the **Base RDD,** which has 24 items and derive another RDD **carsRDD** that contains only items (3) which match cars:

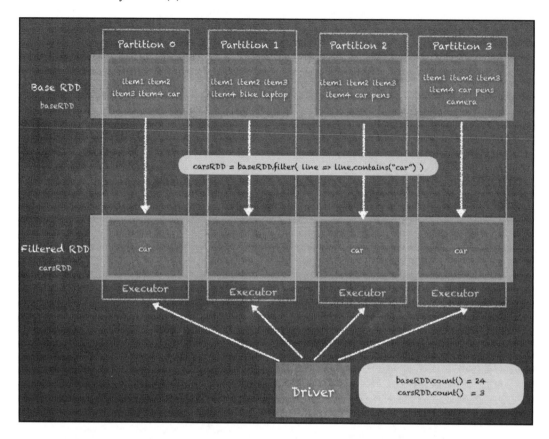

 The number of partitions does not change during such operations, as each executor applies the filter transformation in-memory, generating a new RDD partition corresponding to the original RDD partition.

Next, we will see how to create RDDs

RDD Creation

An RDD is the fundamental object used in Apache Spark. They are immutable collections representing datasets and have the inbuilt capability of reliability and failure recovery. By nature, RDDs create new RDDs upon any operation such as transformation or action. RDDs also store the lineage which is used to recover from failures. We have also seen in the previous chapter some details about how RDDs can be created and what kind of operations can be applied to RDDs.

An RDD can be created in several ways:

- Parallelizing a collection
- Reading data from an external source
- Transformation of an existing RDD
- Streaming API

Parallelizing a collection

Parallelizing a collection can be done by calling `parallelize()` on the collection inside the driver program. The driver, when it tries to parallelize a collection, splits the collection into partitions and distributes the data partitions across the cluster.

The following is an RDD to create an RDD from a sequence of numbers using the SparkContext and the `parallelize()` function. The `parallelize()` function essentially splits the Sequence of numbers into a distributed collection otherwise known as an RDD.

```scala
scala> val rdd_one = sc.parallelize(Seq(1,2,3))
rdd_one: org.apache.spark.rdd.RDD[Int] = ParallelCollectionRDD[0] at
parallelize at <console>:24

scala> rdd_one.take(10)
res0: Array[Int] = Array(1, 2, 3)
```

Reading data from an external source

A second method for creating an RDD is by reading data from an external distributed source such as Amazon S3, Cassandra, HDFS, and so on. For example, if you are creating an RDD from HDFS, then the distributed blocks in HDFS are all read by the individual nodes in the Spark cluster.

Each of the nodes in the Spark cluster is essentially doing its own input-output operations and each node is independently reading one or more blocks from the HDFS blocks. In general, Spark makes the best effort to put as much RDD as possible into memory. There is the capability to `cache` the data to reduce the input-output operations by enabling nodes in the spark cluster to avoid repeated reading operations, say from the HDFS blocks, which might be remote to the Spark cluster. There are a whole bunch of caching strategies that can be used within your Spark program, which we will examine later in a section for caching.

The following is an RDD of text lines loading from a text file using the Spark Context and the `textFile()` function. The `textFile` function loads the input data as a text file (each newline \n terminated portion becomes an element in the RDD). The function call also automatically uses HadoopRDD (shown in next chapter) to detect and load the data in the form of several partitions as needed, distributed across the cluster.

```scala
scala> val rdd_two = sc.textFile("wiki1.txt")
rdd_two: org.apache.spark.rdd.RDD[String] = wiki1.txt
MapPartitionsRDD[8] at textFile at <console>:24

scala> rdd_two.count
res6: Long = 9

scala> rdd_two.first
res7: String = Apache Spark provides programmers with an application
programming interface centered on a data structure called the
resilient distributed dataset (RDD), a read-only multiset of data
items distributed over a cluster of machines, that is maintained in a
fault-tolerant way.
```

Transformation of an existing RDD

RDDs, by nature, are immutable; hence, your RDDs could be created by applying transformations on any existing RDD. Filter is one typical example of a transformation.

The following is a simple `rdd` of integers and transformation by multiplying each integer by 2. Again, we use the `SparkContext` and parallelize function to create a sequence of integers into an RDD by distributing the Sequence in the form of partitions. Then, we use the `map()` function to transform the RDD into another RDD by multiplying each number by 2.

```scala
scala> val rdd_one = sc.parallelize(Seq(1,2,3))
rdd_one: org.apache.spark.rdd.RDD[Int] = ParallelCollectionRDD[0] at
parallelize at <console>:24

scala> rdd_one.take(10)
res0: Array[Int] = Array(1, 2, 3)

scala> val rdd_one_x2 = rdd_one.map(i => i * 2)
rdd_one_x2: org.apache.spark.rdd.RDD[Int] = MapPartitionsRDD[9] at map
at <console>:26

scala> rdd_one_x2.take(10)
res9: Array[Int] = Array(2, 4, 6)
```

Streaming API

RDDs can also be created via spark streaming. These RDDs are called Discretized Stream RDDs (DStream RDDs).

We will look at this further in `Chapter 9`, *Stream Me Up, Scotty - Spark Streaming*.

In the next section, we will create RDDs and explore some of the operations using Spark-Shell.

Using the Spark shell

Spark shell provides a simple way to perform interactive analysis of data. It also enables you to learn the Spark APIs by quickly trying out various APIs. In addition, the similarity to Scala shell and support for Scala APIs also lets you also adapt quickly to Scala language constructs and make better use of Spark APIs.

Spark shell implements the concept of **read-evaluate-print-loop** (**REPL**), which allows you to interact with the shell by typing in code which is evaluated. The result is then printed on the console, without needing to be compiled, so building executable code.

Start it by running the following in the directory where you installed Spark:

`./bin/spark-shell`

Spark shell launches and the Spark shell automatically creates the SparkSession and SparkContext objects. The SparkSession is available as a Spark and the SparkContext is available as sc.

spark-shell can be launched with several options as shown in the following snippet (the most important ones are in bold):

```
                ./bin/spark-shell --help
           Usage: ./bin/spark-shell [options]

                         Options:
   --master MASTER_URL spark://host:port, mesos://host:port, yarn, or
                          local.
      --deploy-mode DEPLOY_MODE Whether to launch the driver program
                    locally ("client") or
      on one of the worker machines inside the cluster ("cluster")
                      (Default: client).
   --class CLASS_NAME Your application's main class (for Java / Scala
                          apps).
           --name NAME A name of your application.
    --jars JARS Comma-separated list of local jars to include on the
                          driver
                and executor classpaths.
   --packages Comma-separated list of maven coordinates of jars to
                         include
     on the driver and executor classpaths. Will search the local
        maven repo, then maven central and any additional remote
        repositories given by --repositories. The format for the
           coordinates should be groupId:artifactId:version.
   --exclude-packages Comma-separated list of groupId:artifactId, to
                      exclude while
      resolving the dependencies provided in --packages to avoid
                   dependency conflicts.
   --repositories Comma-separated list of additional remote repositories
                            to
        search for the maven coordinates given with --packages.
   --py-files PY_FILES Comma-separated list of .zip, .egg, or .py files
                       to place
```

on the PYTHONPATH for Python apps.
--files FILES Comma-separated list of files to be placed in the working
directory of each executor.

--conf PROP=VALUE Arbitrary Spark configuration property.
--properties-file FILE Path to a file from which to load extra properties. If not
specified, this will look for conf/spark-defaults.conf.

--**driver-memory** MEM Memory for driver (e.g. 1000M, 2G) (Default: 1024M).
--driver-Java-options Extra Java options to pass to the driver.
--driver-library-path Extra library path entries to pass to the driver.
--driver-class-path Extra class path entries to pass to the driver. Note that
jars added with --jars are automatically included in the classpath.

--**executor-memory** MEM Memory per executor (e.g. 1000M, 2G) (Default: 1G).

--proxy-user NAME User to impersonate when submitting the application.
This argument does not work with --principal / --keytab.

--help, -h Show this help message and exit.
--verbose, -v Print additional debug output.
--version, Print the version of current Spark.

Spark standalone with cluster deploy mode only:
--driver-cores NUM Cores for driver (Default: 1).

Spark standalone or Mesos with cluster deploy mode only:
--supervise If given, restarts the driver on failure.
--kill SUBMISSION_ID If given, kills the driver specified.
--status SUBMISSION_ID If given, requests the status of the driver specified.

Spark standalone and Mesos only:
--**total-executor-cores** NUM Total cores for all executors.

Spark standalone and YARN only:
--**executor-cores** NUM Number of cores per executor. (Default: 1 in YARN mode,
or all available cores on the worker in standalone mode)

```
                        YARN-only:
       --driver-cores NUM Number of cores used by the driver, only in
                          cluster mode
                          (Default: 1).
       --queue QUEUE_NAME The YARN queue to submit to (Default: "default").
        --num-executors NUM Number of executors to launch (Default: 2).
           If dynamic allocation is enabled, the initial number of
                    executors will be at least NUM.
       --archives ARCHIVES Comma separated list of archives to be extracted
                          into the
                    working directory of each executor.
         --principal PRINCIPAL Principal to be used to login to KDC, while
                          running on
                          secure HDFS.
         --keytab KEYTAB The full path to the file that contains the keytab
                          for the
            principal specified above. This keytab will be copied to
             the node running the Application Master via the Secure
           Distributed Cache, for renewing the login tickets and the
                    delegation tokens periodically.
```

You can also submit Spark code in the form of executable Java jars so that the job is executed in a cluster. Usually, you do this once you have reached a workable solution using the shell.

Use `./bin/spark-submit` when submitting a Spark job to a cluster (local, YARN, and Mesos).

The following are Shell Commands (the most important ones are in bold):

```
scala> :help
All commands can be abbreviated, e.g., :he instead of :help.
:edit <id>|<line> edit history
:help [command] print this summary or command-specific help
:history [num] show the history (optional num is commands to show)
:h? <string> search the history
:imports [name name ...] show import history, identifying sources of
names
:implicits [-v] show the implicits in scope
:javap <path|class> disassemble a file or class name
:line <id>|<line> place line(s) at the end of history
:load <path> interpret lines in a file
:paste [-raw] [path] enter paste mode or paste a file
:power enable power user mode
:quit exit the interpreter
```

```
:replay [options] reset the repl and replay all previous commands
:require <path> add a jar to the classpath
:reset [options] reset the repl to its initial state, forgetting all
session entries
:save <path> save replayable session to a file
:sh <command line> run a shell command (result is implicitly =>
List[String])
:settings <options> update compiler options, if possible; see reset
:silent disable/enable automatic printing of results
:type [-v] <expr> display the type of an expression without evaluating
it
:kind [-v] <expr> display the kind of expression's type
:warnings show the suppressed warnings from the most recent line which
had any
```

Using the spark-shell, we will now load some data as an RDD:

```
scala> val rdd_one = sc.parallelize(Seq(1,2,3))
rdd_one: org.apache.spark.rdd.RDD[Int] = ParallelCollectionRDD[0] at
parallelize at <console>:24

scala> rdd_one.take(10)
res0: Array[Int] = Array(1, 2, 3)
```

As you see, we are running the commands one by one. Alternately, we can also paste
the commands:

```
scala> :paste
// Entering paste mode (ctrl-D to finish)

val rdd_one = sc.parallelize(Seq(1,2,3))
rdd_one.take(10)

// Exiting paste mode, now interpreting.
rdd_one: org.apache.spark.rdd.RDD[Int] = ParallelCollectionRDD[10] at
parallelize at <console>:26
res10: Array[Int] = Array(1, 2, 3)
```

In the next section, we will go deeper into the operations.

Actions and Transformations

RDDs are immutable and every operation creates a new RDD. Now, the two main operations that you can perform on an RDD are **Transformations** and **Actions**.

Transformations change the elements in the RDD such as splitting the input element, filtering out elements, and performing calculations of some sort. Several transformations can be performed in a sequence; however no execution takes place during the planning.

 For transformations, Spark adds them to a DAG of computation and, only when driver requests some data, does this DAG actually gets executed. This is called *lazy* evaluation.

The reasoning behind the lazy evaluation is that Spark can look at all the transformations and plan the execution, making use of the understanding the Driver has of all the operations. For instance, if a filter transformation is applied immediately after some other transformation, Spark will optimize the execution so that each Executor performs the transformations on each partition of data efficiently. Now, this is possible only when Spark is waiting until something needs to be executed.

Actions are operations, which actually trigger the computations. Until an action operation is encountered, the execution plan within the spark program is created in the form of a DAG and does nothing. Clearly, there could be several transformations of all sorts within the execution plan, but nothing happens until you perform an action.

The following is a depiction of the various operations on some arbitrary data where we just wanted to remove all pens and bikes and just count cars. Each print statement is an action which triggers the execution of all the transformation steps in the DAG based execution plan until that point as shown in the following diagram:

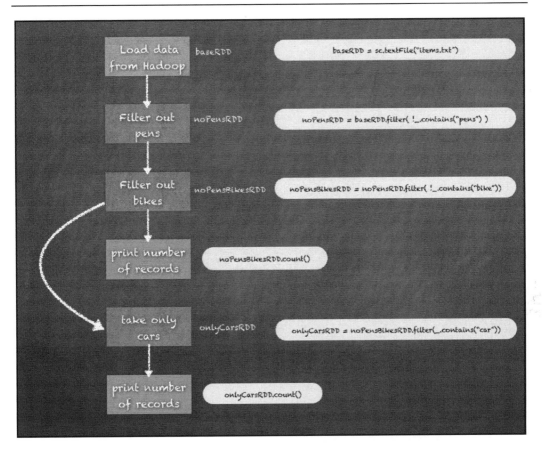

For example, an action count on a directed acyclic graph of transformations triggers the execution of the transformation all the way up to the base RDD. If there is another action performed, then there is a new chain of executions that could take place. This is a clear case of why any caching that could be done at different stages in the directed acyclic graph will greatly speed up the next execution of the program. Another way that the execution is optimized is through the reuse of the shuffle files from the previous execution.

Another example is the collect action that collects or pulls all the data from all the nodes to the driver. You could use a partial function when invoking collect to selectively pull the data.

Transformations

Transformations creates a new RDD from an existing RDD by applying transformation logic to each of the elements in the existing RDD. Some of the transformation functions involve splitting the element, filtering out elements, and performing calculations of some sort. Several transformations can be performed in a sequence. However, no execution takes place during the planning.

Transformations can be divided into four categories, as follows.

General transformations

General transformations are transformation functions that handle most of the general purpose use cases, applying the transformational logic to existing RDDs and generating a new RDD. The common operations of aggregation, filters and so on are all known as general transformations.

Examples of general transformation functions are:

- `map`
- `filter`
- `flatMap`
- `groupByKey`
- `sortByKey`
- `combineByKey`

Math/Statistical transformations

Mathematical or statistical transformations are transformation functions which handle some statistical functionality, and which usually apply some mathematical or statistical operation on existing RDDs, generating a new RDD. Sampling is a great example of this and is used often in Spark programs.

Examples of such transformations are:

- `sampleByKey`
- `randomSplit`

Set theory/relational transformations

Set theory/relational transformations are transformation functions, which handle transformations like Joins of datasets and other relational algebraic functionality such as `cogroup`. These functions work by applying the transformational logic to existing RDDs and generating a new RDD.

Examples of such transformations are:

- `cogroup`
- `join`
- `subtractByKey`
- `fullOuterJoin`
- `leftOuterJoin`
- `rightOuterJoin`

Data structure-based transformations

Data structure-based transformations are transformation functions which operate on the underlying data structures of the RDD, the partitions in the RDD. In these functions, you can directly work on partitions without directly touching the elements/data inside the RDD. These are essential in any Spark program beyond the simple programs where you need more control of the partitions and distribution of partitions in the cluster. Typically, performance improvements can be realized by redistributing the data partitions according to the cluster state and the size of the data, and the exact use case requirements.

Examples of such transformations are:

- `partitionBy`
- `repartition`
- `zipwithIndex`
- `coalesce`

The following is the list of transformation functions as available in the latest Spark 2.1.1:

Transformation	Meaning
map(func)	Return a new distributed dataset formed by passing each element of the source through a function func.
filter(func)	Return a new dataset formed by selecting those elements of the source on which func returns true.
flatMap(func)	Similar to map, but each input item can be mapped to 0 or more output items (so func should return a Seq rather than a single item).
mapPartitions(func)	Similar to map, but runs separately on each partition (block) of the RDD, so func must be of type Iterator<T> => Iterator<U> when running on an RDD of type T.
mapPartitionsWithIndex(func)	Similar to mapPartitions, but also provides func with an integer value representing the index of the partition, so func must be of type (Int, Iterator<T>) => Iterator<U> when running on an RDD of type T.
sample(withReplacement, fraction, seed)	Sample a fraction fraction of the data, with or without replacement, using a given random number generator seed.

`union(otherDataset)`	Return a new dataset that contains the union of the elements in the source dataset and the argument.
`intersection(otherDataset)`	Return a new RDD that contains the intersection of elements in the source dataset and the argument.
`distinct([numTasks]))`	Return a new dataset that contains the distinct elements of the source dataset.
`groupByKey([numTasks])`	When called on a dataset of `(K, V)` pairs, returns a dataset of `(K, Iterable<V>)` pairs. Note: If you are grouping in order to perform an aggregation (such as a sum or average) over each key, using `reduceByKey` or `aggregateByKey` will yield much better performance. Note: By default, the level of parallelism in the output depends on the number of partitions of the parent RDD. You can pass an optional `numTasks` argument to set a different number of tasks.

reduceByKey(func, [numTasks])	When called on a dataset of (K, V) pairs, returns a dataset of (K, V) pairs where the values for each key are aggregated using the given reduce function func, which must be of type (V, V) => V. As in groupByKey, the number of reduce tasks is configurable through an optional second argument.
aggregateByKey(zeroValue)(seqOp, combOp, [numTasks])	When called on a dataset of (K, V) pairs, returns a dataset of (K, U) pairs where the values for each key are aggregated using the given combine functions and a neutral *zero* value. Allows an aggregated value type that is different than the input value type, while avoiding unnecessary allocations. As in groupByKey, the number of reduce tasks is configurable through an optional second argument.
sortByKey([ascending], [numTasks])	When called on a dataset of (K, V) pairs where K implements ordered, returns a dataset of (K, V) pairs sorted by keys in ascending or descending order, as specified in the boolean ascending argument.

`join(otherDataset, [numTasks])`	When called on datasets of type `(K, V)` and `(K, W)`, returns a dataset of `(K, (V, W))` pairs with all pairs of elements for each key. Outer joins are supported through `leftOuterJoin`, `rightOuterJoin`, and `fullOuterJoin`.
`cogroup(otherDataset, [numTasks])`	When called on datasets of type `(K, V)` and `(K, W)`, returns a dataset of `(K, (Iterable<V>, Iterable<W>))` tuples. This operation is also called `groupWith`.
`cartesian(otherDataset)`	When called on datasets of types `T` and `U`, returns a dataset of `(T, U)` pairs (all pairs of elements).
`pipe(command, [envVars])`	Pipe each partition of the RDD through a shell command, for example, a Perl or bash script. RDD elements are written to the process's `stdin`, and lines output to its `stdout` are returned as an RDD of strings.
`coalesce(numPartitions)`	Decrease the number of partitions in the RDD to `numPartitions`. Useful for running operations more efficiently after filtering down a large dataset.
`repartition(numPartitions)`	Reshuffle the data in the RDD randomly to create either more or fewer partitions and balance it across them. This always shuffles all data over the network.

	Repartition the RDD according to the given partitioner and, within each resulting partition, sort records by their keys. This is more efficient than calling `repartition` and then sorting within each partition because it can push the sorting down into the shuffle machinery.
`repartitionAndSortWithinPartitions(partitioner)`	

We will illustrate the most common transformations:

map function

`map` applies transformation function to input partitions to generate output partitions in the output RDD.

As shown in the following snippet, this is how we can map an RDD of a text file to an RDD with lengths of the lines of text:

```
scala> val rdd_two = sc.textFile("wiki1.txt")
rdd_two: org.apache.spark.rdd.RDD[String] = wiki1.txt
MapPartitionsRDD[8] at textFile at <console>:24

scala> rdd_two.count
res6: Long = 9

scala> rdd_two.first
res7: String = Apache Spark provides programmers with an application
programming interface centered on a data structure called the
resilient distributed dataset (RDD), a read-only multiset of data
items distributed over a cluster of machines, that is maintained in a
fault-tolerant way.

scala> val rdd_three = rdd_two.map(line => line.length)
res12: org.apache.spark.rdd.RDD[Int] = MapPartitionsRDD[11] at map at
<console>:2

scala> rdd_three.take(10)
res13: Array[Int] = Array(271, 165, 146, 138, 231, 159, 159, 410, 281)
```

The following diagram explains of how map() works. You can see that each partition of the RDD results in a new partition in a new RDD essentially applying the transformation to all elements of the RDD:

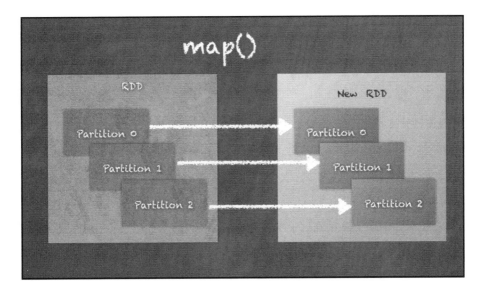

flatMap function

flatMap() applies transformation function to input partitions to generate output partitions in the output RDD just like map() function. However, flatMap() also flattens any collection in the input RDD elements.

As shown in the following snippet, we can use flatMap() on a RDD of a text file to convert the lines in the text to a RDD containing the individual words. We also show map() called on the same RDD before flatMap() is called just to show the difference in behavior:

```
scala> val rdd_two = sc.textFile("wiki1.txt")
rdd_two: org.apache.spark.rdd.RDD[String] = wiki1.txt
MapPartitionsRDD[8] at textFile at <console>:24

scala> rdd_two.count
res6: Long = 9

scala> rdd_two.first
res7: String = Apache Spark provides programmers with an application
programming interface centered on a data structure called the
resilient distributed dataset (RDD), a read-only multiset of data
```

items distributed over a cluster of machines, that is maintained in a fault-tolerant way.

```scala
scala> val rdd_three = rdd_two.map(line => line.split(" "))
rdd_three: org.apache.spark.rdd.RDD[Array[String]] =
MapPartitionsRDD[16] at map at <console>:26
```

```scala
scala> rdd_three.take(1)
res18: Array[Array[String]] = Array(Array(Apache, Spark, provides,
programmers, with, an, application, programming, interface, centered,
on, a, data, structure, called, the, resilient, distributed, dataset,
(RDD),, a, read-only, multiset, of, data, items, distributed, over, a,
cluster, of, machines,, that, is, maintained, in, a, fault-tolerant,
way.)
```

```scala
scala> val rdd_three = rdd_two.flatMap(line => line.split(" "))
rdd_three: org.apache.spark.rdd.RDD[String] = MapPartitionsRDD[17] at
flatMap at <console>:26
```

```scala
scala> rdd_three.take(10)
res19: Array[String] = Array(Apache, Spark, provides, programmers,
with, an, application, programming, interface, centered)
```

The following diagram explains how flatMap() works. You can see that each partition of the RDD results in a new partition in a new RDD, essentially applying the transformation to all elements of the RDD:

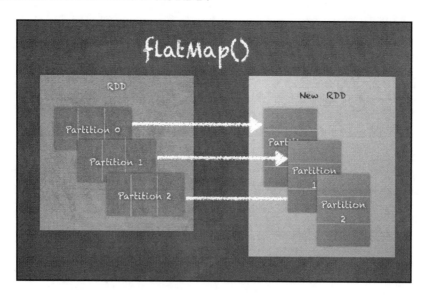

filter function

`filter` applies transformation function to input partitions to generate filtered output partitions in the output RDD.

The following snippet shows how we can filter an RDD of a text file to an RDD with only lines containing the word `Spark`:

```
scala> val rdd_two = sc.textFile("wiki1.txt")
rdd_two: org.apache.spark.rdd.RDD[String] = wiki1.txt
MapPartitionsRDD[8] at textFile at <console>:24

scala> rdd_two.count
res6: Long = 9

scala> rdd_two.first
res7: String = Apache Spark provides programmers with an application
programming interface centered on a data structure called the
resilient distributed dataset (RDD), a read-only multiset of data
items distributed over a cluster of machines, that is maintained in a
fault-tolerant way.

scala> val rdd_three = rdd_two.filter(line => line.contains("Spark"))
rdd_three: org.apache.spark.rdd.RDD[String] = MapPartitionsRDD[20] at
filter at <console>:26

scala>rdd_three.count
res20: Long = 5
```

The following diagram explains how `filter` works. You can see that each partition of the RDD results in a new partition in a new RDD, essentially applying the filter transformation on all elements of the RDD.

Note that the partitions do not change, and some partitions could be empty too, when applying filter

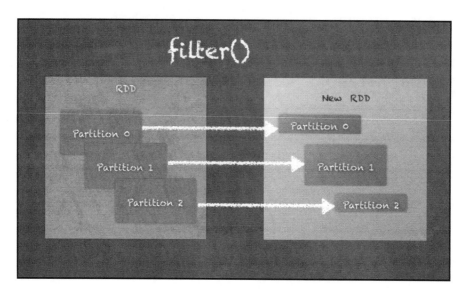

coalesce

coalesce applies a transformation function to input partitions to combine the input partitions into fewer partitions in the output RDD.

As shown in the following code snippet, this is how we can combine all partitions to a single partition:

```
scala> val rdd_two = sc.textFile("wiki1.txt")
rdd_two: org.apache.spark.rdd.RDD[String] = wiki1.txt
MapPartitionsRDD[8] at textFile at <console>:24

scala> rdd_two.partitions.length
res21: Int = 2

scala> val rdd_three = rdd_two.coalesce(1)
rdd_three: org.apache.spark.rdd.RDD[String] = CoalescedRDD[21] at
coalesce at <console>:26

scala> rdd_three.partitions.length
res22: Int = 1
```

The following diagram explains how `coalesce` works. You can see that a new RDD is created from the original RDD essentially reducing the number of partitions by combining them as needed:

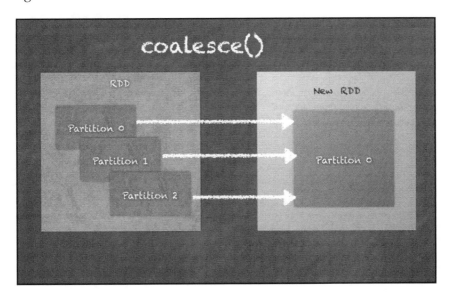

repartition

`repartition` applies a `transformation` function to input partitions to `repartition` the input into fewer or more output partitions in the output RDD.

As shown in the following code snippet, this is how we can map an RDD of a text file to an RDD with more partitions:

```
scala> val rdd_two = sc.textFile("wiki1.txt")
rdd_two: org.apache.spark.rdd.RDD[String] = wiki1.txt
MapPartitionsRDD[8] at textFile at <console>:24

scala> rdd_two.partitions.length
res21: Int = 2

scala> val rdd_three = rdd_two.repartition(5)
rdd_three: org.apache.spark.rdd.RDD[String] = MapPartitionsRDD[25] at
repartition at <console>:26

scala> rdd_three.partitions.length
res23: Int = 5
```

The following diagram explains how `repartition` works. You can see that a new RDD is created from the original RDD, essentially redistributing the partitions by combining/splitting them as needed:

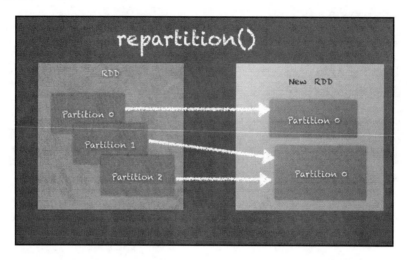

Actions

Action triggers the entire **DAG (Directed Acyclic Graph)** of transformations built so far to be materialized by running the code blocks and functions. All operations are now executed as the DAG specifies.

There are two kinds of action operations:

- **Driver**: One kind of action is the driver action such as collect count, count by key, and so on. Each such action performs some calculations on the remote executor and pulls the data back into the driver.

 Driver-based action has the problem that actions on large datasets can easily overwhelm the memory available on the driver taking down the application, so you should use the driver involved actions judiciously

- **Distributed**: Another kind of action is a distributed action, which is executed on the nodes in the cluster. An example of such a distributed action is `saveAsTextfile`. This is the most common action operation due to the desirable distributed nature of the operation.

The following is the list of action functions as available in the latest Spark 2.1.1:

Action	Meaning
`reduce(func)`	Aggregate the elements of the dataset using a function `func` (which takes two arguments and returns one). The function should be commutative and associative so that it can be computed correctly in parallel.
`collect()`	Return all the elements of the dataset as an array at the driver program. This is usually useful after a filter or other operation that returns a sufficiently small subset of the data.
`count()`	Return the number of elements in the dataset.
`first()`	Return the first element of the dataset (similar to `take(1)`).
`take(n)`	Return an array with the first n elements of the dataset.
`takeSample(withReplacement, num, [seed])`	Return an array with a random sample of num elements of the dataset, with or without replacement, optionally pre-specifying a random number generator seed.
`takeOrdered(n, [ordering])`	Return the first n elements of the RDD using either their natural order or a custom comparator.
`saveAsTextFile(path)`	Write the elements of the dataset as a text file (or set of text files) in a given directory in the local filesystem, HDFS or any other Hadoop-supported file system. Spark will call `toString` on each element to convert it to a line of text in the file.
`saveAsSequenceFile(path)` (Java and Scala)	Write the elements of the dataset as a Hadoop SequenceFile in a given path in the local filesystem, HDFS, or any other Hadoop-supported file system. This is available on RDDs of key-value pairs that implement Hadoop's `Writable` interface. In Scala, it is also available on types that are implicitly convertible to `Writable` (Spark includes conversions for basic types like `Int`, `Double`, `String`, and so on).
`saveAsObjectFile(path)` (Java and Scala)	Write the elements of the dataset in a simple format using Java serialization, which can then be loaded using `SparkContext.objectFile()`.
`countByKey()`	Only available on RDDs of type (`K`, `V`). Returns a hashmap of (`K`, `Int`) pairs with the count of each key.

	Run a function `func` on each element of the dataset. This is usually done for side effects such as updating an accumulator (`http://spark.apache.org/docs/latest/programming-guide.html#accumulators`) or interacting with external storage systems.
`foreach(func)`	Note: modifying variables other than accumulators outside of the `foreach()` may result in undefined behavior. See understanding closures (`http://spark.apache.org/docs/latest/programming-guide.html#understanding-closures-a-nameclosureslinka`) for more details.

reduce

`reduce()` applies the reduce function to all the elements in the RDD and sends it to the Driver.

The following is example code to illustrate this. You can use `SparkContext` and the parallelize function to create an RDD from a sequence of integers. Then you can add up all the numbers of the RDD using the `reduce` function on the RDD.

 Since this is an action, the results are printed as soon as you run the `reduce` function.

Shown below is the code to build a simple RDD from a small array of numbers and then perform a reduce operation on the RDD:

```scala
scala> val rdd_one = sc.parallelize(Seq(1,2,3,4,5,6))
rdd_one: org.apache.spark.rdd.RDD[Int] = ParallelCollectionRDD[26] at
parallelize at <console>:24

scala> rdd_one.take(10)
res28: Array[Int] = Array(1, 2, 3, 4, 5, 6)

scala> rdd_one.reduce((a,b) => a +b)
res29: Int = 21
```

The following diagram is an illustration of `reduce()`. Driver runs the reduce function on the executors and collects the results in the end.

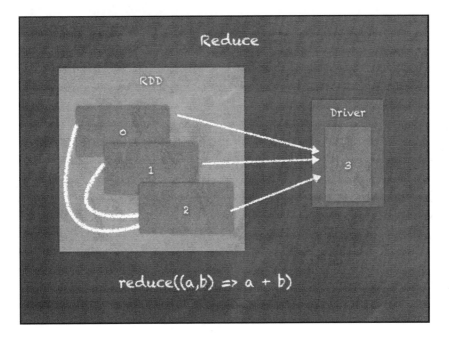

count

`count()` simply counts the number of elements in the RDD and sends it to the Driver.

The following is an example of this function. We created an RDD from a Sequence of integers using SparkContext and parallelize function and then called count on the RDD to print the number of elements in the RDD.

```
scala> val rdd_one = sc.parallelize(Seq(1,2,3,4,5,6))
rdd_one: org.apache.spark.rdd.RDD[Int] = ParallelCollectionRDD[26] at
parallelize at <console>:24

scala> rdd_one.count
res24: Long = 6
```

The following is an illustration of count (). The Driver asks each of the executor/task to count the number of elements in the partition being handled by the task and then adds up the counts from all the tasks together at the Driver level.

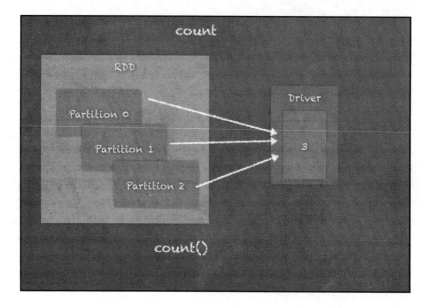

collect

collect () simply collects all elements in the RDD and sends it to the Driver.

Shown here is an example showing what collect function essentially does. When you call collect on an RDD, the Driver collects all the elements of the RDD by pulling them into the Driver.

Calling collect on large RDDs will cause out-of-memory issues on the Driver.

Shown below is the code to collect the content of the RDD and display it:

```scala
scala> rdd_two.collect
res25: Array[String] = Array(Apache Spark provides programmers with an
application programming interface centered on a data structure called
the resilient distributed dataset (RDD), a read-only multiset of data
items distributed over a cluster of machines, that is maintained in a
fault-tolerant way., It was developed in response to limitations in
```

the MapReduce cluster computing paradigm, which forces a particular
linear dataflow structure on distributed programs., "MapReduce
programs read input data from disk, map a function across the data,
reduce the results of the map, and store reduction results on disk. ",
Spark's RDDs function as a working set for distributed programs that
offers a (deliberately) restricted form of distributed shared memory.,
The availability of RDDs facilitates t...

The following is an illustration of collect(). Using collect, the Driver is pulling all
the elements of the RDD from all partitions.

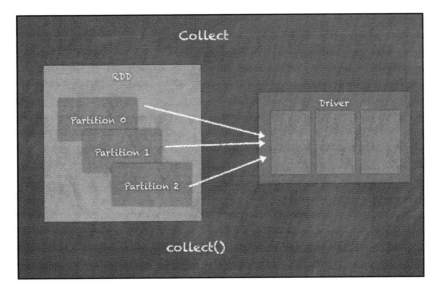

Caching

Caching enables Spark to persist data across computations and operations. In fact,
this is one of the most important technique in Spark to speed up computations,
particularly when dealing with iterative computations.

Caching works by storing the RDD as much as possible in the memory. If there is not
enough memory then the current data in storage is evicted, as per LRU policy. If the
data being asked to cache is larger than the memory available, the performance will
come down because Disk will be used instead of memory.

You can mark an RDD as cached using either persist() or cache()

cache() is simply a synonym for persist(MEMORY_ONLY)

persist can use memory or disk or both:

persist(newLevel: StorageLevel)

The following are the possible values for Storage level:

Storage Level	Meaning
MEMORY_ONLY	Stores RDD as deserialized Java objects in the JVM. If the RDD does not fit in memory, some partitions will not be cached and will be recomputed on the fly each time they're needed. This is the default level.
MEMORY_AND_DISK	Stores RDD as deserialized Java objects in the JVM. If the RDD does not fit in memory, store the partitions that don't fit on disk, and read them from there when they're needed.
MEMORY_ONLY_SER (Java and Scala)	Stores RDD as serialized Java objects (one byte array per partition). This is generally more space-efficient than deserialized objects, especially when using a fast serializer, but more CPU-intensive to read.
MEMORY_AND_DISK_SER (Java and Scala)	Similar to MEMORY_ONLY_SER, but spill partitions that don't fit in memory to disk instead of recomputing them on the fly each time they're needed.
DISK_ONLY	Store the RDD partitions only on disk.
MEMORY_ONLY_2, MEMORY_AND_DISK_2, and so on.	Same as the preceding levels, but replicate each partition on two cluster nodes.
OFF_HEAP (experimental)	Similar to MEMORY_ONLY_SER, but store the data in off-heap memory. This requires off-heap memory to be enabled.

Storage level to choose depends on the situation

- If RDDs fit into memory, use MEMORY_ONLY as that's the fastest option for execution performance
- Try MEMORY_ONLY_SER is there are serializable objects being used in order to make the objects smaller
- DISK should not be used unless your computations are expensive.
- Use replicated storage for best fault tolerance if you can spare the additional memory needed. This will prevent recomputation of lost partitions for best availability.

unpersist() simply frees up the cached content.

The following are examples of how to call persist() function using different types of storage (memory or disk):

```scala
scala> import org.apache.spark.storage.StorageLevel
import org.apache.spark.storage.StorageLevel

scala> rdd_one.persist(StorageLevel.MEMORY_ONLY)
res37: rdd_one.type = ParallelCollectionRDD[26] at parallelize at
<console>:24

scala> rdd_one.unpersist()
res39: rdd_one.type = ParallelCollectionRDD[26] at parallelize at
<console>:24

scala> rdd_one.persist(StorageLevel.DISK_ONLY)
res40: rdd_one.type = ParallelCollectionRDD[26] at parallelize at
<console>:24

scala> rdd_one.unpersist()
res41: rdd_one.type = ParallelCollectionRDD[26] at parallelize at
<console>:24
```

The following is an illustration of the performance improvement we get by caching.

First, we will run the code:

```scala
scala> val rdd_one = sc.parallelize(Seq(1,2,3,4,5,6))
rdd_one: org.apache.spark.rdd.RDD[Int] = ParallelCollectionRDD[0] at
parallelize at <console>:24
```

```
scala> rdd_one.count
res0: Long = 6

scala> rdd_one.cache
res1: rdd_one.type = ParallelCollectionRDD[0] at parallelize at
<console>:24

scala> rdd_one.count
res2: Long = 6
```

You can use the WebUI to look at the improvement achieved as shown in the following screenshots:

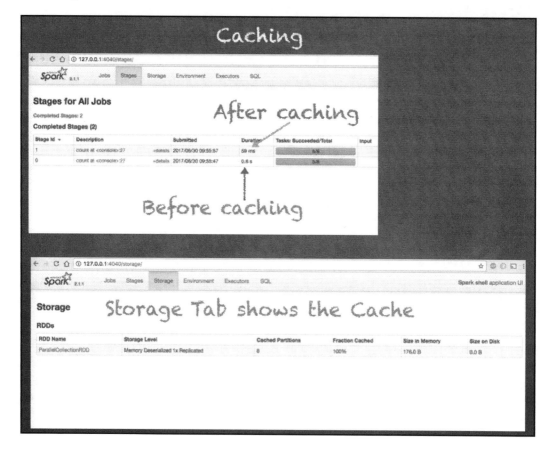

Loading and saving data

Loading data into an RDD and Saving an RDD onto an output system both support several different methods. We will cover the most common ones in this section.

Loading data

Loading data into an RDD can be done by using `SparkContext`. Some of the most common methods are:.

- `textFile`
- `wholeTextFiles`
- `load` from a JDBC datasource

textFile

`textFile()` can be used to load textFiles into an RDD and each line becomes an element in the RDD.

```
sc.textFile(name, minPartitions=None, use_unicode=True)
```

The following is an example of loading a `textfile` into an RDD using `textFile()`:

```
scala> val rdd_two = sc.textFile("wiki1.txt")
rdd_two: org.apache.spark.rdd.RDD[String] = wiki1.txt
MapPartitionsRDD[8] at textFile at <console>:24

scala> rdd_two.count
res6: Long = 9
```

wholeTextFiles

`wholeTextFiles()` can be used to load multiple text files into a paired RDD containing pairs `<filename, textOfFile>` representing the filename and the entire content of the file. This is useful when loading multiple small text files and is different from `textFile` API because when whole `TextFiles()` is used, the entire content of the file is loaded as a single record:

```
sc.wholeTextFiles(path, minPartitions=None, use_unicode=True)
```

The following is an example of loading a `textfile` into an RDD using
`wholeTextFiles()`:

```
scala> val rdd_whole = sc.wholeTextFiles("wiki1.txt")
rdd_whole: org.apache.spark.rdd.RDD[(String, String)] = wiki1.txt
MapPartitionsRDD[37] at wholeTextFiles at <console>:25
```

```
scala> rdd_whole.take(10)
res56: Array[(String, String)] =
Array((file:/Users/salla/spark-2.1.1-bin-hadoop2.7/wiki1.txt,Apache
Spark provides programmers with an application programming interface
centered on a data structure called the resilient distributed dataset
(RDD), a read-only multiset of data
```

Load from a JDBC Datasource

You can load data from an external data source which supports **Java Database Connectivity (JDBC)**. Using a JDBC driver, you can connect to a relational database such as Mysql and load the content of a table into Spark as shown in in the following code snippet:

```
sqlContext.load(path=None, source=None, schema=None, **options)
```

The following is an example of loading from a JDBC datasource:

```
val dbContent = sqlContext.load(source="jdbc",
url="jdbc:mysql://localhost:3306/test",  dbtable="test",
partitionColumn="id")
```

Saving RDD

Saving data from an RDD into a file system can be done by either:

- `saveAsTextFile`
- `saveAsObjectFile`

The following is an example of saving an RDD to a text file

```
scala> rdd_one.saveAsTextFile("out.txt")
```

There are many more ways of loading and saving data, particularly when integrating with HBase, Cassandra and so on.

Summary

In this chapter, we discussed the internals of Apache Spark, what RDDs are, DAGs and lineages of RDDs, Transformations, and Actions. We also looked at various deployment modes of Apache Spark using standalone, YARN, and Mesos deployments. We also did a local install on our local machine and then looked at Spark shell and how it can be used to interact with Spark.

In addition, we also looked at loading data into RDDs and saving RDDs to external systems as well as the secret sauce of Spark's phenomenal performance, the caching functionality, and how we can use memory and/or disk to optimize the performance.

In the next chapter, we will dig deeper into RDD API and how it all works in `Chapter 7`, *Special RDD Operations*.

7
Special RDD Operations

"It's supposed to be automatic, but actually you have to push this button."

- John Brunner

In this chapter, you learn how RDDs can be tailored to different needs, and how these RDDs provide new functionalities (and dangers!) Moreover, we investigate other useful objects that Spark provides, such as broadcast variables and accumulators. In a nutshell, the following topics will be covered throughout this chapter:

- Types of RDDs
- Aggregations
- Partitioning and shuffling
- Broadcast variables
- Accumulators

Types of RDDs

Resilient Distributed Datasets (RDDs) are the fundamental object used in Apache Spark. RDDs are immutable collections representing datasets and have the inbuilt capability of reliability and failure recovery. By nature, RDDs create new RDDs upon any operation such as transformation or action. They also store the lineage, which is used to recover from failures. We have also seen in the previous chapter some details about how RDDs can be created and what kind of operations can be applied to RDDs.

The following is a simply example of the RDD lineage:

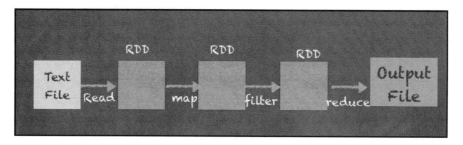

Let's start looking at the simplest RDD again by creating a RDD from a sequence of numbers:

```
scala> val rdd_one = sc.parallelize(Seq(1,2,3,4,5,6))
rdd_one: org.apache.spark.rdd.RDD[Int] = ParallelCollectionRDD[28] at
parallelize at <console>:25

scala> rdd_one.take(100)
res45: Array[Int] = Array(1, 2, 3, 4, 5, 6)
```

The preceding example shows RDD of integers and any operation done on the RDD results in another RDD. For example, if we multiply each element by 3, the result is shown in the following snippet:

```
scala> val rdd_two = rdd_one.map(i => i * 3)
rdd_two: org.apache.spark.rdd.RDD[Int] = MapPartitionsRDD[29] at map
at <console>:27

scala> rdd_two.take(10)
res46: Array[Int] = Array(3, 6, 9, 12, 15, 18)
```

Let's do one more operation, adding 2 to each element and also print all three RDDs:

```
scala> val rdd_three = rdd_two.map(i => i+2)
rdd_three: org.apache.spark.rdd.RDD[Int] = MapPartitionsRDD[30] at map
at <console>:29

scala> rdd_three.take(10)
res47: Array[Int] = Array(5, 8, 11, 14, 17, 20)
```

An interesting thing to look at is the lineage of each RDD using the `toDebugString` function:

```scala
scala> rdd_one.toDebugString
res48: String = (8) ParallelCollectionRDD[28] at parallelize at
<console>:25 []

scala> rdd_two.toDebugString
res49: String = (8) MapPartitionsRDD[29] at map at <console>:27 []
 | ParallelCollectionRDD[28] at parallelize at <console>:25 []

scala> rdd_three.toDebugString
res50: String = (8) MapPartitionsRDD[30] at map at <console>:29 []
 | MapPartitionsRDD[29] at map at <console>:27 []
 | ParallelCollectionRDD[28] at parallelize at <console>:25 []
```

The following is the lineage shown in the Spark web UI:

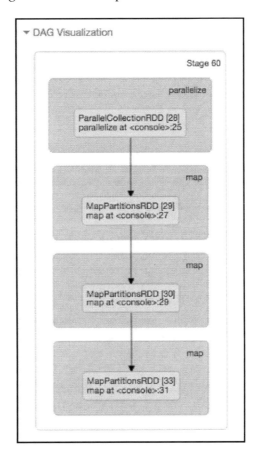

RDD does not need to be the same datatype as the first RDD (integer). The following is a RDD which writes a different datatype of a tuple of (string, integer).

```scala
scala> val rdd_four = rdd_three.map(i => ("str"+(i+2).toString, i-2))
rdd_four: org.apache.spark.rdd.RDD[(String, Int)] =
MapPartitionsRDD[33] at map at <console>:31

scala> rdd_four.take(10)
res53: Array[(String, Int)] = Array((str7,3), (str10,6), (str13,9),
(str16,12), (str19,15), (str22,18))
```

The following is a RDD of the `StatePopulation` file where each record is converted to `upperCase`.

```scala
scala> val upperCaseRDD = statesPopulationRDD.map(_.toUpperCase)
upperCaseRDD: org.apache.spark.rdd.RDD[String] = MapPartitionsRDD[69]
at map at <console>:27

scala> upperCaseRDD.take(10)
res86: Array[String] = Array(STATE,YEAR,POPULATION,
ALABAMA,2010,4785492, ALASKA,2010,714031, ARIZONA,2010,6408312,
ARKANSAS,2010,2921995, CALIFORNIA,2010,37332685,
COLORADO,2010,5048644, DELAWARE,2010,899816, DISTRICT OF
COLUMBIA,2010,605183, FLORIDA,2010,18849098)
```

The following is a diagram of the preceding transformation:

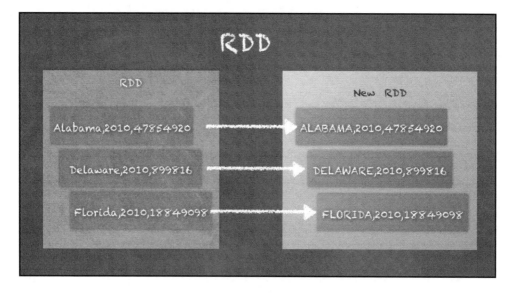

Pair RDD

Pair RDDs are RDDs consisting of key-value tuples which suits many use cases such as aggregation, sorting, and joining data. The keys and values can be simple types such as integers and strings or more complex types such as case classes, arrays, lists, and other types of collections. The key-value based extensible data model offers many advantages and is the fundamental concept behind the MapReduce paradigm.

Creating a `PairRDD` can be done easily by applying transformation to any RDD to convert the RDD to an RDD of key-value pairs.

Let's read the `statesPopulation.csv` into an RDD using the `SparkContext`, which is available as `sc`.

The following is an example of a basic RDD of the state population and how `PairRDD` looks like for the same RDD splitting the records into tuples (pairs) of state and population:

```scala
scala> val statesPopulationRDD = sc.textFile("statesPopulation.csv")
statesPopulationRDD: org.apache.spark.rdd.RDD[String] =
statesPopulation.csv MapPartitionsRDD[47] at textFile at <console>:25

scala> statesPopulationRDD.first
res4: String = State,Year,Population

scala> statesPopulationRDD.take(5)
res5: Array[String] = Array(State,Year,Population,
Alabama,2010,4785492, Alaska,2010,714031, Arizona,2010,6408312,
Arkansas,2010,2921995)

scala> val pairRDD = statesPopulationRDD.map(record =>
(record.split(",")(0), record.split(",")(2)))
pairRDD: org.apache.spark.rdd.RDD[(String, String)] =
MapPartitionsRDD[48] at map at <console>:27

scala> pairRDD.take(10)
res59: Array[(String, String)] = Array((Alabama,4785492),
(Alaska,714031), (Arizona,6408312), (Arkansas,2921995),
(California,37332685), (Colorado,5048644), (Delaware,899816),
(District of Columbia,605183), (Florida,18849098))
```

The following is a diagram of the preceding example showing how the RDD elements are converted to (key - value) pairs:

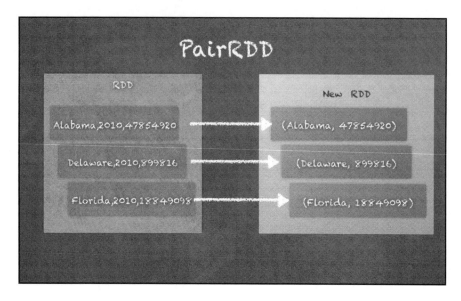

DoubleRDD

DoubleRDD is an RDD consisting of a collection of double values. Due to this property, many statistical functions are available to use with the DoubleRDD.

The following are examples of DoubleRDD where we create an RDD from a sequence of double numbers:

```scala
scala> val rdd_one = sc.parallelize(Seq(1.0,2.0,3.0))
rdd_one: org.apache.spark.rdd.RDD[Double] = ParallelCollectionRDD[52]
at parallelize at <console>:25

scala> rdd_one.mean
res62: Double = 2.0

scala> rdd_one.min
res63: Double = 1.0

scala> rdd_one.max
res64: Double = 3.0

scala> rdd_one.stdev
res65: Double = 0.816496580927726
```

The following is a diagram of the DoubleRDD and how you can run a `sum()` function on the DoubleRDD:

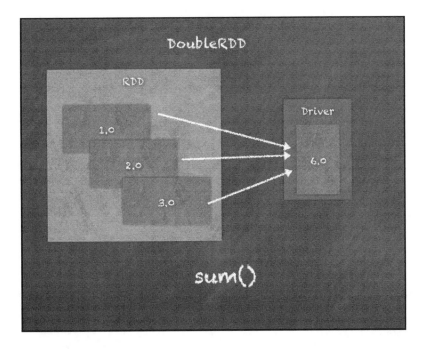

SequenceFileRDD

`SequenceFileRDD` is created from a `SequenceFile` which is a format of files in the Hadoop File System. The `SequenceFile` can be compressed or uncompressed.

Map Reduce processes can use SequenceFiles, which are pairs of Keys and Values. Key and Value are of Hadoop writable datatypes, such as Text, IntWritable, and so on.

The following is an example of a `SequenceFileRDD`, which shows how we can write and read `SequenceFile`:

```
scala> val pairRDD = statesPopulationRDD.map(record =>
(record.split(",")(0), record.split(",")(2)))
pairRDD: org.apache.spark.rdd.RDD[(String, String)] =
MapPartitionsRDD[60] at map at <console>:27

scala> pairRDD.saveAsSequenceFile("seqfile")

scala> val seqRDD = sc.sequenceFile[String, String]("seqfile")
seqRDD: org.apache.spark.rdd.RDD[(String, String)] =
MapPartitionsRDD[62] at sequenceFile at <console>:25

scala> seqRDD.take(10)
res76: Array[(String, String)] = Array((State,Population),
(Alabama,4785492), (Alaska,714031), (Arizona,6408312),
(Arkansas,2921995), (California,37332685), (Colorado,5048644),
(Delaware,899816), (District of Columbia,605183), (Florida,18849098))
```

The following is a diagram of **SequenceFileRDD** as seen in the preceding example:

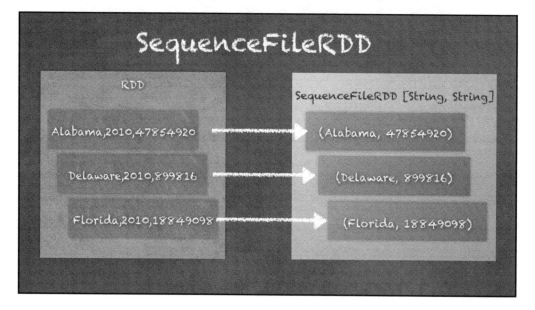

CoGroupedRDD

CoGroupedRDD is an RDD that cogroups its parents. Both parent RDDs have to be pairRDDs for this to work, as a cogroup essentially generates a pairRDD consisting of the common key and list of values from both parent RDDs. Take a look at the following code snippet:

```
class CoGroupedRDD[K] extends RDD[(K, Array[Iterable[_]])]
```

The following is an example of a CoGroupedRDD where we create a cogroup of two pairRDDs, one having pairs of State, Population and the other having pairs of State, Year:

```
scala> val pairRDD = statesPopulationRDD.map(record =>
(record.split(",")(0), record.split(",")(2)))
pairRDD: org.apache.spark.rdd.RDD[(String, String)] =
MapPartitionsRDD[60] at map at <console>:27

scala> val pairRDD2 = statesPopulationRDD.map(record =>
(record.split(",")(0), record.split(",")(1)))
pairRDD2: org.apache.spark.rdd.RDD[(String, String)] =
MapPartitionsRDD[66] at map at <console>:27

scala> val cogroupRDD = pairRDD.cogroup(pairRDD2)
cogroupRDD: org.apache.spark.rdd.RDD[(String, (Iterable[String],
Iterable[String]))] = MapPartitionsRDD[68] at cogroup at <console>:31

scala> cogroupRDD.take(10)
res82: Array[(String, (Iterable[String], Iterable[String]))] =
Array((Montana,(CompactBuffer(990641, 997821, 1005196, 1014314,
1022867, 1032073, 1042520),CompactBuffer(2010, 2011, 2012, 2013, 2014,
2015, 2016))), (California,(CompactBuffer(37332685, 37676861,
38011074, 38335203, 38680810, 38993940, 39250017),CompactBuffer(2010,
2011, 2012, 2013, 2014, 2015, 2016))),
```

The following is a diagram of the cogroup of **pairRDD** and **pairRDD2** by creating pairs of values for each key:

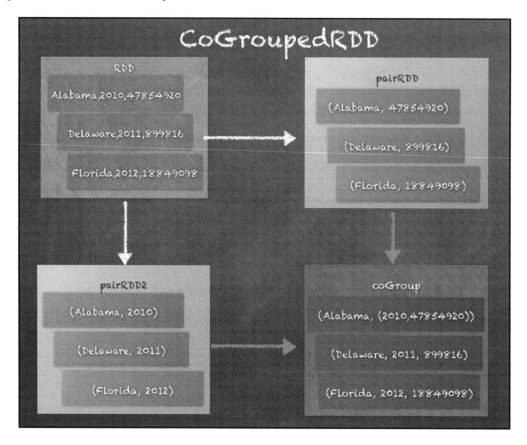

ShuffledRDD

ShuffledRDD shuffles the RDD elements by key so as to accumulate values for the same key on the same executor to allow an aggregation or combining logic. A very good example is to look at what happens when reduceByKey() is called on a PairRDD:

```
class ShuffledRDD[K, V, C] extends RDD[(K, C)]
```

The following is a `reduceByKey` operation on the `pairRDD` to aggregate the records by the State:

```scala
scala> val pairRDD = statesPopulationRDD.map(record =>
(record.split(",")(0), 1))
pairRDD: org.apache.spark.rdd.RDD[(String, Int)] =
MapPartitionsRDD[82] at map at <console>:27

scala> pairRDD.take(5)
res101: Array[(String, Int)] = Array((State,1), (Alabama,1),
(Alaska,1), (Arizona,1), (Arkansas,1))

scala> val shuffledRDD = pairRDD.reduceByKey(_+_)
shuffledRDD: org.apache.spark.rdd.RDD[(String, Int)] = ShuffledRDD[83]
at reduceByKey at <console>:29

scala> shuffledRDD.take(5)
res102: Array[(String, Int)] = Array((Montana,7), (California,7),
(Washington,7), (Massachusetts,7), (Kentucky,7))
```

The following diagram, is an illustration of the shuffling by Key to send the records of the same Key(State) to the same partitions:

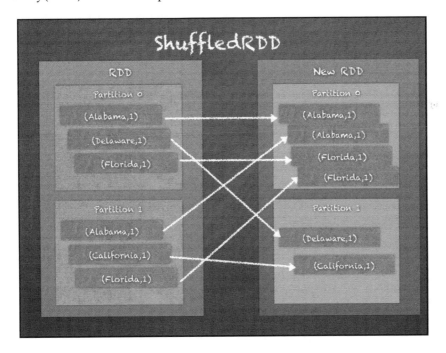

UnionRDD

UnionRDD is the result of a union operation of two RDDs. Union simply creates an RDD with elements from both RDDs as shown in the following code snippet:

```
class UnionRDD[T: ClassTag]( sc: SparkContext, var rdds: Seq[RDD[T]])
extends RDD[T](sc, Nil)
```

The following code snippet is the API call to create a UnionRDD by combining the elements of the two RDDs:

```
scala> val rdd_one = sc.parallelize(Seq(1,2,3))
rdd_one: org.apache.spark.rdd.RDD[Int] = ParallelCollectionRDD[85] at
parallelize at <console>:25

scala> val rdd_two = sc.parallelize(Seq(4,5,6))
rdd_two: org.apache.spark.rdd.RDD[Int] = ParallelCollectionRDD[86] at
parallelize at <console>:25

scala> val rdd_one = sc.parallelize(Seq(1,2,3))
rdd_one: org.apache.spark.rdd.RDD[Int] = ParallelCollectionRDD[87] at
parallelize at <console>:25

scala> rdd_one.take(10)
res103: Array[Int] = Array(1, 2, 3)

scala> val rdd_two = sc.parallelize(Seq(4,5,6))
rdd_two: org.apache.spark.rdd.RDD[Int] = ParallelCollectionRDD[88] at
parallelize at <console>:25

scala> rdd_two.take(10)
res104: Array[Int] = Array(4, 5, 6)

scala> val unionRDD = rdd_one.union(rdd_two)
unionRDD: org.apache.spark.rdd.RDD[Int] = UnionRDD[89] at union at
<console>:29

scala> unionRDD.take(10)
res105: Array[Int] = Array(1, 2, 3, 4, 5, 6)
```

The following diagram is an illustration of a union of two RDDs where the elements from both **RDD 1** and **RDD 2** are combined into a new RDD **UnionRDD**:

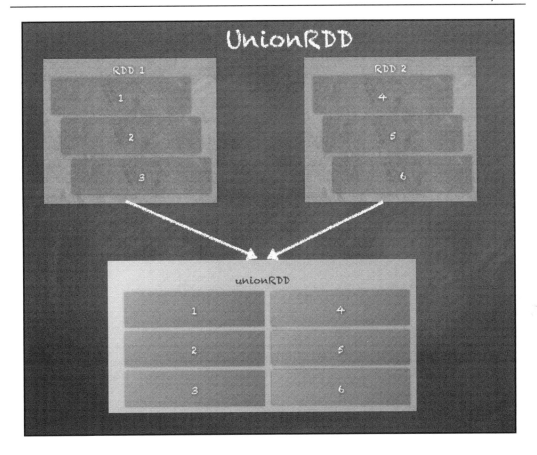

HadoopRDD

HadoopRDD provides core functionality for reading data stored in HDFS using the MapReduce API from the Hadoop 1.x libraries. HadoopRDD is the default used and can be seen when loading data from any file system into an RDD:

```
class HadoopRDD[K, V] extends RDD[(K, V)]
```

When loading the state population records from the CSV, the underlying base RDD is actually HadoopRDD as in the following code snippet:

```
scala> val statesPopulationRDD = sc.textFile("statesPopulation.csv")
statesPopulationRDD: org.apache.spark.rdd.RDD[String] =
statesPopulation.csv MapPartitionsRDD[93] at textFile at <console>:25

scala> statesPopulationRDD.toDebugString
```

```
res110: String =
(2) statesPopulation.csv MapPartitionsRDD[93] at textFile at
<console>:25 []
  | statesPopulation.csv HadoopRDD[92] at textFile at <console>:25 []
```

The following diagram is an illustration of a **HadoopRDD** created by loading a textfile from the file system into an RDD:

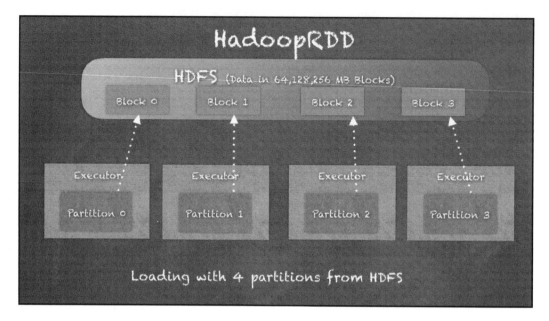

NewHadoopRDD

NewHadoopRDD provides core functionality for reading data stored in HDFS, HBase tables, Amazon S3 using the new MapReduce API from Hadoop 2.x libraries. NewHadoopRDD can read from many different formats thus is used to interact with several external systems.

 Prior to NewHadoopRDD, HadoopRDD was the only available option which used the old MapReduce API from Hadoop 1.x

```
class NewHadoopRDD[K, V](
  sc : SparkContext,
  inputFormatClass: Class[_ <: InputFormat[K, V]],
```

```
    keyClass: Class[K],
    valueClass: Class[V],
    @transient private val _conf: Configuration)
extends RDD[(K, V)]
```

As seen in the preceding code snippet, `NewHadoopRDD` takes an input format class, a key class, and a value class. Let's look at examples of `NewHadoopRDD`.

The simplest example is to use SparkContext's `wholeTextFiles` function to create `WholeTextFileRDD`. Now, `WholeTextFileRDD` actually extends `NewHadoopRDD` as shown in the following code snippet:

```
scala> val rdd_whole = sc.wholeTextFiles("wiki1.txt")
rdd_whole: org.apache.spark.rdd.RDD[(String, String)] = wiki1.txt
MapPartitionsRDD[3] at wholeTextFiles at <console>:31

scala> rdd_whole.toDebugString
res9: String =
(1) wiki1.txt MapPartitionsRDD[3] at wholeTextFiles at <console>:31 []
 | WholeTextFileRDD[2] at wholeTextFiles at <console>:31 []
```

Let's look at another example where we will use the function `newAPIHadoopFile` using the `SparkContext`:

```
import org.apache.hadoop.mapreduce.lib.input.KeyValueTextInputFormat

import org.apache.hadoop.io.Text

val newHadoopRDD = sc.newAPIHadoopFile("statesPopulation.csv",
classOf[KeyValueTextInputFormat], classOf[Text],classOf[Text])
```

Aggregations

Aggregation techniques allow you to combine the elements in the RDD in arbitrary ways to perform some computation. In fact, aggregation is the most important part of big data analytics. Without aggregation, we would not have any way to generate reports and analysis like *Top States by Population*, which seems to be a logical question asked when given a dataset of all State populations for the past 200 years. Another simpler example is that of a need to just count the number of elements in the RDD, which asks the executors to count the number of elements in each partition and send to the Driver, which then adds the subsets to compute the total number of elements in the RDD.

In this section, our primary focus is on the aggregation functions used to collect and combine data by key. As seen earlier in this chapter, a PairRDD is an RDD of (key - value) pairs where key and value are arbitrary and can be customized as per the use case.

In our example of state populations, a PairRDD could be the pairs of <State, <Population, Year>> which means State is taken as the key and the tuple <Population, Year> is considered the value. This way of breaking down the key and value can generate aggregations such as *Top Years by Population per State*. On the contrary, in case our aggregations are done around Year say *Top States by Population per Year*, we can use a pairRDD of pairs of <Year, <State, Population>>.

The following is the sample code to generate a pairRDD from the StatePopulation dataset both with State as the key as well as the Year as the key:

```scala
scala> val statesPopulationRDD = sc.textFile("statesPopulation.csv")
statesPopulationRDD: org.apache.spark.rdd.RDD[String] =
statesPopulation.csv MapPartitionsRDD[157] at textFile at <console>:26

scala> statesPopulationRDD.take(5)
res226: Array[String] = Array(State,Year,Population,
Alabama,2010,4785492, Alaska,2010,714031, Arizona,2010,6408312,
Arkansas,2010,2921995)
```

Next, we can generate a pairRDD using State as the key and a tuple of <Year, Population> as the value as shown in the following code snippet:

```scala
scala> val pairRDD = statesPopulationRDD.map(record =>
record.split(",")).map(t => (t(0), (t(1), t(2))))
pairRDD: org.apache.spark.rdd.RDD[(String, (String, String))] =
MapPartitionsRDD[160] at map at <console>:28

scala> pairRDD.take(5)
res228: Array[(String, (String, String))] =
Array((State,(Year,Population)), (Alabama,(2010,4785492)),
(Alaska,(2010,714031)), (Arizona,(2010,6408312)),
(Arkansas,(2010,2921995)))
```

As mentioned earlier, we can also generate a PairRDD using Year as the key and a tuple of <State, Population> as the value as shown in the following code snippet:

```scala
scala> val pairRDD = statesPopulationRDD.map(record =>
record.split(",")).map(t => (t(1), (t(0), t(2))))
pairRDD: org.apache.spark.rdd.RDD[(String, (String, String))] =
MapPartitionsRDD[162] at map at <console>:28
```

```scala
scala> pairRDD.take(5)
res229: Array[(String, (String, String))] =
Array((Year,(State,Population)), (2010,(Alabama,4785492)),
(2010,(Alaska,714031)), (2010,(Arizona,6408312)),
(2010,(Arkansas,2921995)))
```

We will now look into how we can use the common aggregation functions on the `pairRDD` of `<State, <Year, Population>>`:

- `groupByKey`
- `reduceByKey`
- `aggregateByKey`
- `combineByKey`

groupByKey

`groupByKey` groups the values for each key in the RDD into a single sequence. `groupByKey` also allows controlling the partitioning of the resulting key-value pair RDD by passing a partitioner. By default, a `HashPartitioner` is used but a custom partitioner can be given as an argument. The ordering of elements within each group is not guaranteed, and may even differ each time the resulting RDD is evaluated.

> `groupByKey` is an expensive operation due to all the data shuffling needed. `reduceByKey` or `aggregateByKey` provide much better performance. We will look at this later in this section.

`groupByKey` can be invoked either using a custom partitioner or just using the default `HashPartitioner` as shown in the following code snippet:

```scala
def groupByKey(partitioner: Partitioner): RDD[(K, Iterable[V])]
```

```scala
def groupByKey(numPartitions: Int): RDD[(K, Iterable[V])]
```

> As currently implemented, `groupByKey` must be able to hold all the key-value pairs for any key in memory. If a key has too many values, it can result in an `OutOfMemoryError`.

`groupByKey` works by sending all elements of the partitions to the partition based on the partitioner so that all pairs of (key - value) for the same key are collected in the same partition. Once this is done, the aggregation operation can be done easily.

Shown here is an illustration of what happens when `groupByKey` is called:

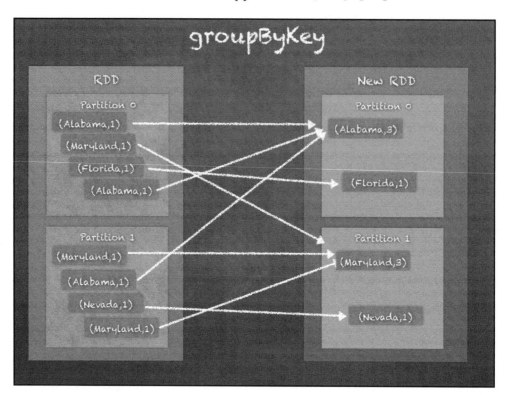

reduceByKey

`groupByKey` involves a lot of shuffling and `reduceByKey` tends to improve the performance by not sending all elements of the `PairRDD` using shuffles, rather using a local combiner to first do some basic aggregations locally and then send the resultant elements as in `groupByKey`. This greatly reduces the data transferred, as we don't need to send everything over. `reduceBykey` works by merging the values for each key using an associative and commutative reduce function. Of course, first, this will
also perform the merging locally on each mapper before sending results to a reducer.

If you are familiar with Hadoop MapReduce, this is very similar to a combiner in MapReduce programming.

`reduceByKey` can be invoked either using a custom partitioner or just using the default HashPartitioner as shown in the following code snippet:

```
def reduceByKey(partitioner: Partitioner, func: (V, V) => V): RDD[(K,
V)]

def reduceByKey(func: (V, V) => V, numPartitions: Int): RDD[(K, V)]

def reduceByKey(func: (V, V) => V): RDD[(K, V)]
```

`reduceByKey` works by sending all elements of the partitions to the partition based on the `partitioner` so that all pairs of (key - value) for the same Key are collected in the same partition. But before the shuffle, local aggregation is also done reducing the data to be shuffled. Once this is done, the aggregation operation can be done easily in the final partition.

The following diagram is an illustration of what happens when `reduceBykey` is called:

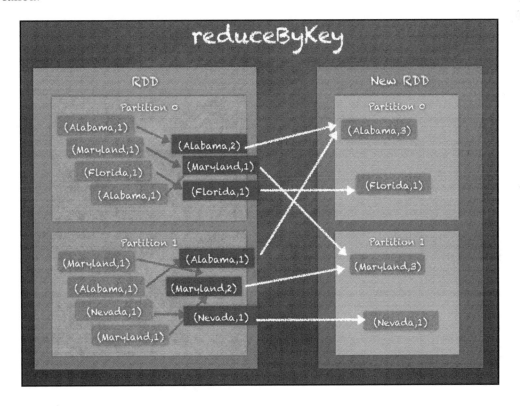

aggregateByKey

aggregateByKey is quite similar to reduceByKey, except that aggregateByKey allows more flexibility and customization of how to aggregate within partitions and between partitions to allow much more sophisticated use cases such as generating a list of all <Year, Population> pairs as well as total population for each State in one function call.

aggregateByKey works by aggregating the values of each key, using given combine functions and a neutral initial/zero value.
This function can return a different result type, U, than the type of the values in this RDD V, which is the biggest difference. Thus, we need one operation for merging a V into a U and one operation for merging two U's. The former operation is used for merging values within a partition, and the latter is used for merging values between partitions. To avoid memory allocation, both of these functions are allowed to modify and return their first argument instead of creating a new U:

```
def aggregateByKey[U: ClassTag](zeroValue: U, partitioner:
Partitioner)(seqOp: (U, V) => U,
 combOp: (U, U) => U): RDD[(K, U)]

def aggregateByKey[U: ClassTag](zeroValue: U, numPartitions:
Int)(seqOp: (U, V) => U,
 combOp: (U, U) => U): RDD[(K, U)]

def aggregateByKey[U: ClassTag](zeroValue: U)(seqOp: (U, V) => U,
 combOp: (U, U) => U): RDD[(K, U)]
```

aggregateByKey works by performing an aggregation within the partition operating on all elements of each partition and then applies another aggregation logic when combining the partitions themselves. Ultimately, all pairs of (key - value) for the same Key are collected in the same partition; however, the aggregation as to how it is done and the output generated is not fixed as in groupByKey and reduceByKey, but is more flexible and customizable when using aggregateByKey.

The following diagram is an illustration of what happens when `aggregateByKey` is called. Instead of adding up the counts as in `groupByKey` and `reduceByKey`, here we are generating lists of values for each Key:

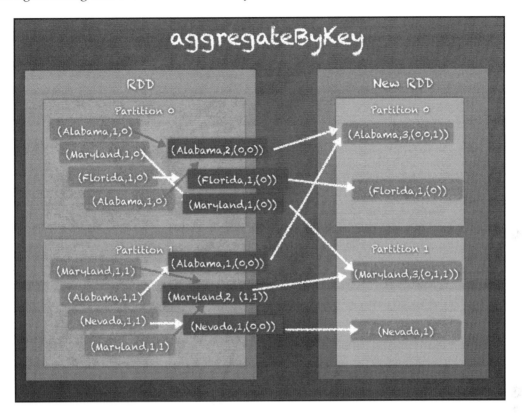

combineByKey

`combineByKey` is very similar to `aggregateByKey`; in fact, `combineByKey` internally invokes `combineByKeyWithClassTag`, which is also invoked by `aggregateByKey`. As in `aggregateByKey`, the `combineByKey` also works by applying an operation within each partition and then between combiners.

combineByKey turns an RDD[K,V] into an RDD[K,C], where C is a list of Vs collected or combined under the name key K.

There are three functions expected when you call combineByKey.

- createCombiner, which turns a V into C, which is a one element list
- mergeValue to merge a V into a C by appending the V to the end of the list
- mergeCombiners to combine two Cs into one

> In aggregateByKey, the first argument is simply a zero value but in combineByKey, we provide the initial function which takes the current value as a parameter.

combineByKey can be invoked either using a custom partitioner or just using the default HashPartitioner as shown in the following code snippet:

```
def combineByKey[C](createCombiner: V => C, mergeValue: (C, V) => C,
mergeCombiners: (C, C) => C, numPartitions: Int): RDD[(K, C)]

def combineByKey[C](createCombiner: V => C, mergeValue: (C, V) => C,
mergeCombiners: (C, C) => C, partitioner: Partitioner, mapSideCombine:
Boolean = true, serializer: Serializer = null): RDD[(K, C)]
```

combineByKey works by performing an aggregation within the partition operating on all elements of each partition and then applies another aggregation logic when combining the partitions themselves. Ultimately, all pairs of (key - value) for the same Key are collected in the same partition however the aggregation as to how it is done and the output generated is not fixed as in groupByKey and reduceByKey, but is more flexible and customizable when using combineByKey.

The following diagram is an illustration of what happens when `combineBykey` is called:

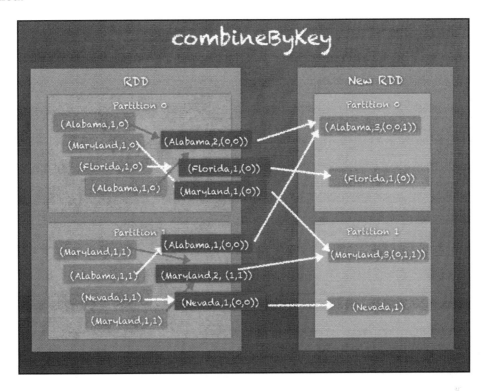

Comparison of groupByKey, reduceByKey, combineByKey, and aggregateByKey

Let's consider the example of StatePopulation RDD generating a `pairRDD` of `<State, <Year, Population>>`.

`groupByKey` as seen in the preceding section will do `HashPartitioning` of the `PairRDD` by generating a hashcode of the keys and then shuffling the data to collect the values for each key in the same partition. This obviously results in too much shuffling.

`reduceByKey` improves upon `groupByKey` using a local combiner logic to minimize the data sent in a shuffle phase. The result will be the same as `groupByKey`, but will be much more performant.

aggregateByKey is very similar to reduceByKey in how it works but with one big difference, which makes it the most powerful one among the three. aggregateBykey does not need to operate on the same datatype and can do different aggregation within the partition and do a different aggregation between partitions.

combineByKey is very similar in performance to aggregateByKey except for the initial function to create the combiner.

The function to use depends on your use case but when in doubt just refer to this section on *Aggregation* to choose the right function for your use case. Also, pay close attention to the next section as *Partitioning and shuffling* are covered in that section.

The following is the code showing all four ways of calculating total population by state.

Step 1. Initialize the RDD:

```scala
scala> val statesPopulationRDD =
sc.textFile("statesPopulation.csv").filter(_.split(",")(0) != "State")
statesPopulationRDD: org.apache.spark.rdd.RDD[String] =
statesPopulation.csv MapPartitionsRDD[1] at textFile at <console>:24

scala> statesPopulationRDD.take(10)
res27: Array[String] = Array(Alabama,2010,4785492, Alaska,2010,714031,
Arizona,2010,6408312, Arkansas,2010,2921995, California,2010,37332685,
Colorado,2010,5048644, Delaware,2010,899816, District of
Columbia,2010,605183, Florida,2010,18849098, Georgia,2010,9713521)
```

Step 2. Convert to pair RDD:

```scala
scala> val pairRDD = statesPopulationRDD.map(record =>
record.split(",")).map(t => (t(0), (t(1).toInt, t(2).toInt)))
pairRDD: org.apache.spark.rdd.RDD[(String, (Int, Int))] =
MapPartitionsRDD[26] at map at <console>:26

scala> pairRDD.take(10)
res15: Array[(String, (Int, Int))] = Array((Alabama,(2010,4785492)),
(Alaska,(2010,714031)), (Arizona,(2010,6408312)),
(Arkansas,(2010,2921995)), (California,(2010,37332685)),
(Colorado,(2010,5048644)), (Delaware,(2010,899816)), (District of
Columbia,(2010,605183)), (Florida,(2010,18849098)),
(Georgia,(2010,9713521)))
```

Step 3. groupByKey - Grouping the values and then adding up populations:

```
scala> val groupedRDD = pairRDD.groupByKey.map(x => {var sum=0;
x._2.foreach(sum += _._2); (x._1, sum)})
groupedRDD: org.apache.spark.rdd.RDD[(String, Int)] =
MapPartitionsRDD[38] at map at <console>:28

scala> groupedRDD.take(10)
res19: Array[(String, Int)] = Array((Montana,7105432),
(California,268280590), (Washington,48931464),
(Massachusetts,46888171), (Kentucky,30777934),
(Pennsylvania,89376524), (Georgia,70021737), (Tennessee,45494345),
(North Carolina,68914016), (Utah,20333580))
```

Step 4. reduceByKey - Reduce the values by key simply adding the populations:

```
scala> val reduceRDD = pairRDD.reduceByKey((x, y) => (x._1,
x._2+y._2)).map(x => (x._1, x._2._2))
reduceRDD: org.apache.spark.rdd.RDD[(String, Int)] =
MapPartitionsRDD[46] at map at <console>:28

scala> reduceRDD.take(10)
res26: Array[(String, Int)] = Array((Montana,7105432),
(California,268280590), (Washington,48931464),
(Massachusetts,46888171), (Kentucky,30777934),
(Pennsylvania,89376524), (Georgia,70021737), (Tennessee,45494345),
(North Carolina,68914016), (Utah,20333580))
```

Step 5. aggregateBykey - aggregate the populations under each key and adds them up:

```
Initialize the array
scala> val initialSet = 0
initialSet: Int = 0

provide function to add the populations within a partition
scala> val addToSet = (s: Int, v: (Int, Int)) => s+ v._2
addToSet: (Int, (Int, Int)) => Int = <function2>

provide funtion to add populations between partitions
scala> val mergePartitionSets = (p1: Int, p2: Int) => p1 + p2
mergePartitionSets: (Int, Int) => Int = <function2>

scala> val aggregatedRDD =
pairRDD.aggregateByKey(initialSet)(addToSet, mergePartitionSets)
aggregatedRDD: org.apache.spark.rdd.RDD[(String, Int)] =
ShuffledRDD[41] at aggregateByKey at <console>:34
```

```
scala> aggregatedRDD.take(10)
res24: Array[(String, Int)] = Array((Montana,7105432),
(California,268280590), (Washington,48931464),
(Massachusetts,46888171), (Kentucky,30777934),
(Pennsylvania,89376524), (Georgia,70021737), (Tennessee,45494345),
(North Carolina,68914016), (Utah,20333580))
```

Step 6. combineByKey - combine within partitions and then merging combiners:

```
createcombiner function
scala> val createCombiner = (x:(Int,Int)) => x._2
createCombiner: ((Int, Int)) => Int = <function1>


function to add within partition
scala> val mergeValues = (c:Int, x:(Int, Int)) => c +x._2
mergeValues: (Int, (Int, Int)) => Int = <function2>


function to merge combiners
scala> val mergeCombiners = (c1:Int, c2:Int) => c1 + c2
mergeCombiners: (Int, Int) => Int = <function2>


scala> val combinedRDD = pairRDD.combineByKey(createCombiner,
mergeValues, mergeCombiners)
combinedRDD: org.apache.spark.rdd.RDD[(String, Int)] = ShuffledRDD[42]
at combineByKey at <console>:34


scala> combinedRDD.take(10)
res25: Array[(String, Int)] = Array((Montana,7105432),
(California,268280590), (Washington,48931464),
(Massachusetts,46888171), (Kentucky,30777934),
(Pennsylvania,89376524), (Georgia,70021737), (Tennessee,45494345),
(North Carolina,68914016), (Utah,20333580))
```

As you see, all four aggregations result in the same output. It's just how they work that is different.

Partitioning and shuffling

We have seen how Apache Spark can handle distributed computing much better than Hadoop. We also saw the inner workings, mainly the fundamental data structure known as **Resilient Distributed Dataset (RDD)**. RDDs are immutable collections representing datasets and have the inbuilt capability of reliability and failure recovery. RDDs operate on data not as a single blob of data, rather RDDs manage and operate data in partitions spread across the cluster. Hence, the concept of data partitioning is critical to the proper functioning of Apache Spark Jobs and can have a big effect on the performance as well as how the resources are utilized.

RDD consists of partitions of data and all operations are performed on the partitions of data in the RDD. Several operations like transformations are functions executed by an executor on the specific partition of data being operated on. However, not all operations can be done by just performing isolated operations on the partitions of data by the respective executors. Operations like aggregations (seen in the preceding section) require data to be moved across the cluster in a phase known as **shuffling**. In this section, we will look deeper into the concepts of partitioning and shuffling.

Let's start looking at a simple RDD of integers by executing the following code. Spark Context's `parallelize` function creates an RDD from the Sequence of integers. Then, using the `getNumPartitions()` function, we can get the number of partitions of this RDD.

```
scala> val rdd_one = sc.parallelize(Seq(1,2,3))
rdd_one: org.apache.spark.rdd.RDD[Int] = ParallelCollectionRDD[120] at
parallelize at <console>:25

scala> rdd_one.getNumPartitions
res202: Int = 8
```

The RDD can be visualized as shown in the following diagram, which shows the 8 partitions in the RDD:

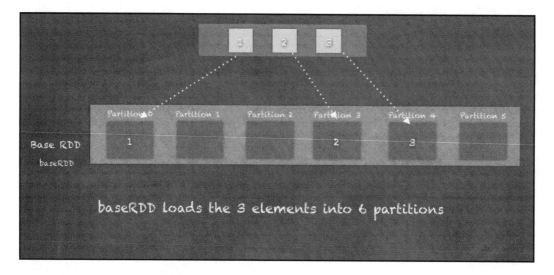

The number of partitions is important because this number directly influences the number of tasks that will be running RDD transformations. If the number of partitions is too small, then we will use only a few CPUs/cores on a lot of data thus having a slower performance and leaving the cluster underutilized. On the other hand, if the number of partitions is too large then you will use more resources than you actually need and in a multi-tenant environment could be causing starvation of resources for other Jobs being run by you or others in your team.

Partitioners

Partitioning of RDDs is done by partitioners. Partitioners assign a partition index to the elements in the RDD. All elements in the same partition will have the same partition index.

Spark comes with two partitioners the `HashPartitioner` and the `RangePartitioner`. In addition to these, you can also implement a custom partitioner.

HashPartitioner

HashPartitioner is the default partitioner in Spark and works by calculating a hash value for each key of the RDD elements. All the elements with the same hashcode end up in the same partition as shown in the following code snippet:

```
partitionIndex = hashcode(key) % numPartitions
```

The following is an example of the String hashCode() function and how we can generate partitionIndex:

```
scala> val str = "hello"
str: String = hello

scala> str.hashCode
res206: Int = 99162322

scala> val numPartitions = 8
numPartitions: Int = 8

scala> val partitionIndex = str.hashCode % numPartitions
partitionIndex: Int = 2
```

> The default number of partitions is either from the Spark configuration parameter spark.default.parallelism or the number of cores in the cluster

The following diagram is an illustration of how hash partitioning works. We have an RDD with 3 elements **a**, **b**, and **e**. Using String hashcode we get the `partitionIndex` for each element based on the number of partitions set at 6:

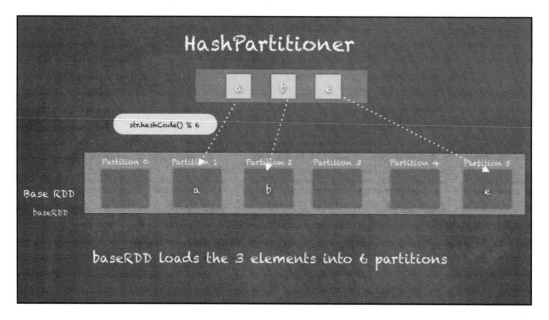

RangePartitioner

`RangePartitioner` works by partitioning the RDD into roughly equal ranges. Since the range has to know the starting and ending keys for any partition, the RDD needs to be sorted first before a `RangePartitioner` can be used.

`RangePartitioning` first needs reasonable boundaries for the partitions based on the RDD and then create a function from key K to the `partitionIndex` where the element belongs. Finally, we need to repartition the RDD, based on the `RangePartitioner` to distribute the RDD elements correctly as per the ranges we determined.

The following is an example of how we can use RangePartitioning of a PairRDD. We also can see how the partitions changed after we repartition the RDD using a RangePartitioner:

```scala
import org.apache.spark.RangePartitioner
scala> val statesPopulationRDD = sc.textFile("statesPopulation.csv")
statesPopulationRDD: org.apache.spark.rdd.RDD[String] =
statesPopulation.csv MapPartitionsRDD[135] at textFile at <console>:26

scala> val pairRDD = statesPopulationRDD.map(record =>
(record.split(",")(0), 1))
pairRDD: org.apache.spark.rdd.RDD[(String, Int)] =
MapPartitionsRDD[136] at map at <console>:28

scala> val rangePartitioner = new RangePartitioner(5, pairRDD)
rangePartitioner: org.apache.spark.RangePartitioner[String,Int] =
org.apache.spark.RangePartitioner@c0839f25

scala> val rangePartitionedRDD = pairRDD.partitionBy(rangePartitioner)
rangePartitionedRDD: org.apache.spark.rdd.RDD[(String, Int)] =
ShuffledRDD[130] at partitionBy at <console>:32

scala> pairRDD.mapPartitionsWithIndex((i,x) => Iterator(""+i +
":"+x.length)).take(10)
res215: Array[String] = Array(0:177, 1:174)

scala> rangePartitionedRDD.mapPartitionsWithIndex((i,x) =>
Iterator(""+i + ":"+x.length)).take(10)
res216: Array[String] = Array(0:70, 1:77, 2:70, 3:63, 4:71)
```

The following diagram is an illustration of the `RangePartitioner` as seen in the preceding example:

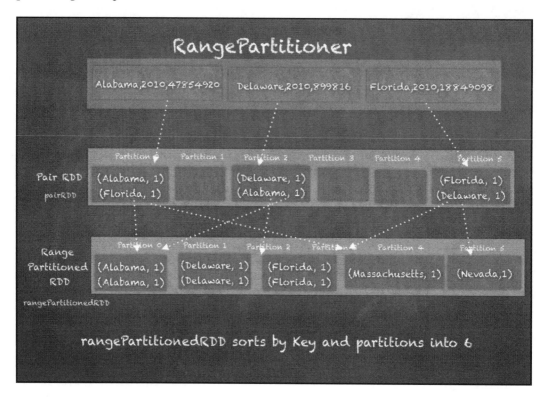

Shuffling

Whatever the partitioner used, many operations will cause a repartitioning of data across the partitions of an RDD. New partitions can be created or several partitions can be collapsed/coalesced. All the data movement necessary for the repartitioning is called **shuffling,** and this is an important concept to understand when writing a Spark Job. The shuffling can cause a lot of performance lag as the computations are no longer in memory on the same executor but rather the executors are exchanging data over the wire.

A good example is the example of `groupByKey()`, we saw earlier in the *Aggregations* section. Obviously, lot of data was flowing between executors to make sure all values for a key are collected onto the same executor to perform the `groupBy` operation.

Shuffling also determines the Spark Job execution process and influences how the Job is split into Stages. As we have seen in this chapter and the previous chapter, Spark holds a DAG of RDDs, which represent the lineage of the RDDs such that not only does Spark use the lineage to plan the execution of the job but also any loss of executors can be recovered from. When an RDD is undergoing a transformation, an attempt is made to make sure the operations are performed on the same node as the data. However, often we use join operations, reduce, group, or aggregate operations among others, which cause repartitioning intentionally or unintentionally. This shuffling in turn determines where a particular stage in the processing has ended and a new stage has begun.

The following diagram is an illustration of how a Spark Job is split into stages. This example shows a `pairRDD` being filtered, transformed using map before invoking `groupByKey` followed by one last transformation using `map()`:

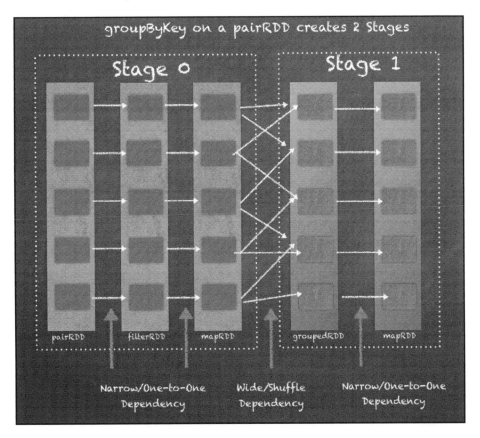

The more shuffling we have, the more stages occur in the job execution affecting the performance. There are two key aspects which are used by Spark Driver to determine the stages. This is done by defining two types of dependencies of the RDDs, the narrow dependencies and the wide dependencies.

Narrow Dependencies

When an RDD can be derived from another RDD using a simple one-to-one transformation such as a `filter()` function, `map()` function, `flatMap()` function, and so on, then the child RDD is said to depend on the parent RDD on a one-to-one basis. This dependency is known as narrow dependency as the data can be transformed on the same node as the one containing the original RDD/parent RDD partition without requiring any data transfer over the wire between other executors.

 Narrow dependencies are in the same stage of the job execution.

The following diagram is an illustration of how a narrow dependency transforms one RDD to another RDD, applying one-to-one transformation on the RDD elements:

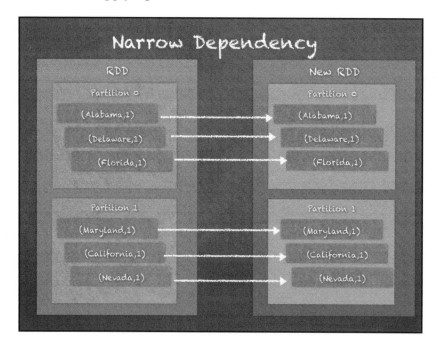

Wide Dependencies

When an RDD can be derived from one or more RDDs by transferring data over the wire or exchanging data to repartition or redistribute the data using functions, such as `aggregateByKey`, `reduceByKey` and so on, then the child RDD is said to depend on the parent RDDs participating in a shuffle operation. This dependency is known as a Wide dependency as the data cannot be transformed on the same node as the one containing the original RDD/parent RDD partition thus requiring data transfer over the wire between other executors.

> Wide dependencies introduce new stages in the job execution.

The following diagram is an illustration of how wide dependency transforms one RDD to another RDD shuffling data between executors:

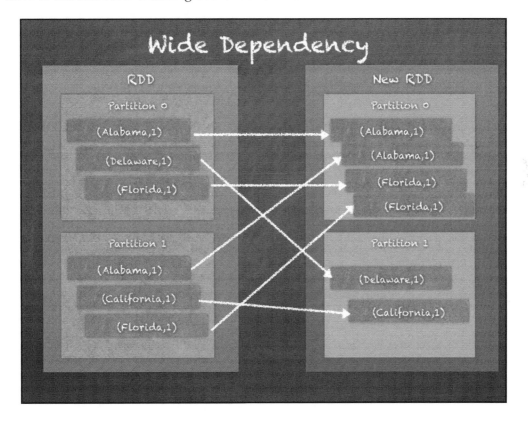

Broadcast variables

Broadcast variables are shared variables across all executors. Broadcast variables are created once in the Driver and then are read only on executors. While it is simple to understand simple datatypes broadcasted, such as an `Integer`, broadcast is much bigger than simple variables conceptually. Entire datasets can be broadcasted in a Spark cluster so that executors have access to the broadcasted data. All the tasks running within an executor all have access to the broadcast variables.

Broadcast uses various optimized methods to make the broadcasted data accessible to all executors. This is an important challenge to solve as if the size of the datasets broadcasted is significant, you cannot expect 100s or 1000s of executors to connect to the Driver and pull the dataset. Rather, the executors pull the data via HTTP connection and the more recent addition which is similar to BitTorrent where the dataset itself is distributed like a torrent amongst the cluster. This enables a much more scalable method to distribute the broadcasted variables to all executors rather than having each executor pull the data from the Driver one by one which can cause failures on the Driver when you have a lot of executors.

The driver can only broadcast the data it has and you cannot broadcast RDDs by using references. This is because only Driver knows how to interpret RDDs and executors only know the particular partitions of data they are handling.

If you look deeper into how broadcast works, you will see that the mechanism works by first having the Driver divide the serialized object into small chunks and then stores those chunks in the BlockManager of the driver. When the code is serialized to be run on the executors, then each executor first attempts to fetch the object from its own internal BlockManager. If the broadcast variable was fetched before, it will find it and use it. However, if it does not exist, the executor then uses remote fetches to fetch the small chunks from the driver and/or other executors if available. Once it gets the chunks, it puts the chunks in its own BlockManager, ready for any other executors to fetch from. This prevents the driver from being the bottleneck in sending out multiple copies of the broadcast data (one per executor).

The following diagram is an illustration of how broadcast works in a Spark cluster:

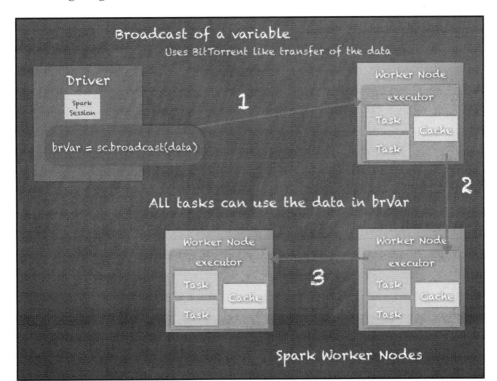

Broadcast variables can be both created and destroyed too. We will look into the creation and destruction of broadcast variables. There is also a way to remove broadcasted variables from memory which we will also look at.

Creating broadcast variables

Creating a broadcast variable can be done using the Spark Context's `broadcast()` function on any data of any data type provided that the data/variable is serializable.

Let's look at how we can broadcast an Integer variable and then use the broadcast variable inside a transformation operation executed on the executors:

```scala
scala> val rdd_one = sc.parallelize(Seq(1,2,3))
rdd_one: org.apache.spark.rdd.RDD[Int] = ParallelCollectionRDD[101] at
parallelize at <console>:25

scala> val i = 5
```

```
i: Int = 5

scala> val bi = sc.broadcast(i)
bi: org.apache.spark.broadcast.Broadcast[Int] = Broadcast(147)

scala> bi.value
res166: Int = 5

scala> rdd_one.take(5)
res164: Array[Int] = Array(1, 2, 3)

scala> rdd_one.map(j => j + bi.value).take(5)
res165: Array[Int] = Array(6, 7, 8)
```

Broadcast variables can also be created on more than just primitive data types as shown in the next example where we will broadcast a HashMap from the Driver.

The following is a simple transformation of an integer RDD by multiplying each element with another integer by looking up the HashMap. The RDD of 1,2,3 is transformed to 1 X 2 , 2 X 3, 3 X 4 = 2,6,12 :

```
scala> val rdd_one = sc.parallelize(Seq(1,2,3))
rdd_one: org.apache.spark.rdd.RDD[Int] = ParallelCollectionRDD[109] at
parallelize at <console>:25

scala> val m = scala.collection.mutable.HashMap(1 -> 2, 2 -> 3, 3 ->
4)
m: scala.collection.mutable.HashMap[Int,Int] = Map(2 -> 3, 1 -> 2, 3
-> 4)

scala> val bm = sc.broadcast(m)
bm:
org.apache.spark.broadcast.Broadcast[scala.collection.mutable.HashMap[
Int,Int]] = Broadcast(178)

scala> rdd_one.map(j => j * bm.value(j)).take(5)
res191: Array[Int] = Array(2, 6, 12)
```

Cleaning broadcast variables

Broadcast variables do occupy memory on all executors and depending on the size of the data contained in the broadcasted variable, this could cause resource issues at some point. There is a way to remove broadcasted variables from the memory of all executors.

Calling `unpersist()` on a broadcast variable removed the data of the broadcast variable from the memory cache of all executors to free up resources. If the variable is used again, then the data is retransmitted to the executors in order for it to be used again. The Driver, however, holds onto the memory as if the Driver does not have the data, then broadcast variable is no longer valid.

We look at destroying broadcast variables next.

The following is an example of how `unpersist()` can be invoked on a broadcast variable. After calling `unpersist` if we access the broadcast variable again, it works as usual but behind the scenes, the executors are pulling the data for the variable again.

```scala
scala> val rdd_one = sc.parallelize(Seq(1,2,3))
rdd_one: org.apache.spark.rdd.RDD[Int] = ParallelCollectionRDD[101] at
parallelize at <console>:25

scala> val k = 5
k: Int = 5

scala> val bk = sc.broadcast(k)
bk: org.apache.spark.broadcast.Broadcast[Int] = Broadcast(163)

scala> rdd_one.map(j => j + bk.value).take(5)
res184: Array[Int] = Array(6, 7, 8)

scala> bk.unpersist

scala> rdd_one.map(j => j + bk.value).take(5)
res186: Array[Int] = Array(6, 7, 8)
```

Destroying broadcast variables

You can also destroy broadcast variables, completely removing them from all executors and the Driver too making them inaccessible. This can be quite helpful in managing the resources optimally across the cluster.

Calling `destroy()` on a broadcast variable destroys all data and metadata related to the specified broadcast variable. Once a broadcast variable has been destroyed, it cannot be used again and will have to be recreated all over again.

The following is an example of destroying broadcast variables:

```
scala> val rdd_one = sc.parallelize(Seq(1,2,3))
rdd_one: org.apache.spark.rdd.RDD[Int] = ParallelCollectionRDD[101] at
parallelize at <console>:25

scala> val k = 5
k: Int = 5

scala> val bk = sc.broadcast(k)
bk: org.apache.spark.broadcast.Broadcast[Int] = Broadcast(163)

scala> rdd_one.map(j => j + bk.value).take(5)
res184: Array[Int] = Array(6, 7, 8)

scala> bk.destroy
```

If an attempt is made to use a destroyed broadcast variable, an exception is thrown

The following is an example of an attempt to reuse a destroyed broadcast variable:

```
scala> rdd_one.map(j => j + bk.value).take(5)
17/05/27 14:07:28 ERROR Utils: Exception encountered
org.apache.spark.SparkException: Attempted to use Broadcast(163) after
it was destroyed (destroy at <console>:30)
 at
org.apache.spark.broadcast.Broadcast.assertValid(Broadcast.scala:144)
 at
org.apache.spark.broadcast.TorrentBroadcast$$anonfun$writeObject$1.app
ly$mcV$sp(TorrentBroadcast.scala:202)
 at org.apache.spark.broadcast.TorrentBroadcast$$anonfun$wri
```

Thus, broadcast functionality can be use to greatly improve the flexibility and performance of Spark jobs.

Accumulators

Accumulators are shared variables across executors typically used to add counters to your Spark program. If you have a Spark program and would like to know errors or total records processed or both, you can do it in two ways. One way is to add extra logic to just count errors or total records, which becomes complicated when handling all possible computations. The other way is to leave the logic and code flow fairly intact and add Accumulators.

Accumulators can only be updated by adding to the value.

The following is an example of creating and using a long Accumulator using Spark Context and the `longAccumulator` function to initialize a newly created accumulator variable to zero. As the accumulator is used inside the map transformation, the Accumulator is incremented. At the end of the operation, the Accumulator holds a value of 351.

```scala
scala> val acc1 = sc.longAccumulator("acc1")
acc1: org.apache.spark.util.LongAccumulator = LongAccumulator(id:
10355, name: Some(acc1), value: 0)

scala> val someRDD = statesPopulationRDD.map(x => {acc1.add(1); x})
someRDD: org.apache.spark.rdd.RDD[String] = MapPartitionsRDD[99] at
map at <console>:29

scala> acc1.value
res156: Long = 0   /*there has been no action on the RDD so accumulator
did not get incremented*/

scala> someRDD.count
res157: Long = 351

scala> acc1.value
res158: Long = 351

scala> acc1
res145: org.apache.spark.util.LongAccumulator = LongAccumulator(id:
10355, name: Some(acc1), value: 351)
```

There are inbuilt accumulators which can be used for many use cases:

- `LongAccumulator`: for computing sum, count, and average of 64-bit integers
- `DoubleAccumulator`: for computing sum, count, and averages for double precision floating numbers.
- `CollectionAccumulator[T]` : for collecting a list of elements

All the preceding Accumulators are built on top of the `AccumulatorV2` class. By following the same logic, we can potentially build very complex and customized Accumulators to use in our project.

We can build a custom accumulator by extending the `AccumulatorV2` class. The following is an example showing the necessary functions to implement. `AccumulatorV2[Int, Int]` shown in the following code means that the Input and Output are both of Integer type:

```
class MyAccumulator extends AccumulatorV2[Int, Int] {
    //simple boolean check
    override def isZero: Boolean = ???

    //function to copy one Accumulator and create another one
    override def copy(): AccumulatorV2[Int, Int] = ???

    //to reset the value
    override def reset(): Unit = ???

    //function to add a value to the accumulator
    override def add(v: Int): Unit = ???

    //logic to merge two accumulators
    override def merge(other: AccumulatorV2[Int, Int]): Unit = ???

    //the function which returns the value of the accumulator
    override def value: Int = ???
}
```

Next, we will look at a practical example of a custom accumulator. Again, we shall use the `statesPopulation` CSV file for this. Our goal is to accumulate the sum of year and sum of population in a custom accumulator.

Step 1. Import the package containing the AccumulatorV2 class:

```
import org.apache.spark.util.AccumulatorV2
```

Step 2. Case class to contain the Year and Population:

```
case class YearPopulation(year: Int, population: Long)
```

Step 3. StateAccumulator class extends AccumulatorV2:

```
class StateAccumulator extends AccumulatorV2[YearPopulation,
YearPopulation] {
    //declare the two variables one Int for year and Long for
population
    private var year = 0
    private var population:Long = 0L

    //return iszero if year and population are zero
    override def isZero: Boolean = year == 0 && population == 0L

    //copy accumulator and return a new accumulator
    override def copy(): StateAccumulator = {
        val newAcc = new StateAccumulator
        newAcc.year =      this.year
        newAcc.population = this.population
        newAcc
    }

    //reset the year and population to zero
    override def reset(): Unit = { year = 0 ; population = 0L }

    //add a value to the accumulator
    override def add(v: YearPopulation): Unit = {
        year += v.year
        population += v.population
    }

    //merge two accumulators
    override def merge(other: AccumulatorV2[YearPopulation,
YearPopulation]): Unit = {
        other match {
            case o: StateAccumulator => {
                year += o.year
                population += o.population
            }
            case _ =>
        }
    }

    //function called by Spark to access the value of accumulator
    override def value: YearPopulation = YearPopulation(year,
```

```
population)
}
```

Step 4. Create a new StateAccumulator and register the same with SparkContext:

```
val statePopAcc = new StateAccumulator

sc.register(statePopAcc, "statePopAcc")
```

Step 5. Read the statesPopulation.csv as an RDD:

```
val statesPopulationRDD =
sc.textFile("statesPopulation.csv").filter(_.split(",")(0) != "State")
```

```
scala> statesPopulationRDD.take(10)
res1: Array[String] = Array(Alabama,2010,4785492, Alaska,2010,714031,
Arizona,2010,6408312, Arkansas,2010,2921995, California,2010,37332685,
Colorado,2010,5048644, Delaware,2010,899816, District of
Columbia,2010,605183, Florida,2010,18849098, Georgia,2010,9713521)
```

Step 6. Use the StateAccumulator:

```
statesPopulationRDD.map(x => {
    val toks = x.split(",")
    val year = toks(1).toInt
    val pop = toks(2).toLong
    statePopAcc.add(YearPopulation(year, pop))
    x
}).count
```

Step 7. Now, we can examine the value of the StateAccumulator:

```
scala> statePopAcc
res2: StateAccumulator = StateAccumulator(id: 0, name:
Some(statePopAcc), value: YearPopulation(704550,2188669780))
```

In this section, we examined accumulators and how to build a custom accumulator. Thus, using the preceding illustrated example, you can create complex accumulators to meet your needs.

Summary

In this chapter, we discussed the many types of RDDs, such as `shuffledRDD`, `pairRDD`, `sequenceFileRDD`, `HadoopRDD`, and so on. We also looked at the three main types of aggregations, `groupByKey`, `reduceByKey`, and `aggregateByKey`. We looked into how partitioning works and why it is important to have a proper plan around partitioning to increase the performance. We also looked at shuffling and the concepts of narrow and wide dependencies which are basic tenets of how Spark jobs are broken into stages. Finally, we looked at the important concepts of broadcast variables and accumulators.

The true power of the flexibility of RDDs makes it easy to adapt to most use cases and perform the necessary operations to accomplish the goal.

In the next chapter, we will switch gears to the higher layer of abstraction added to the RDDs as part of the Tungsten initiative known as DataFrames and Spark SQL and how it all comes together in the `Chapter 8`, *Introduce a Little Structure – Spark SQL*.

8
Introduce a Little Structure - Spark SQL

"One machine can do the work of fifty ordinary men. No machine can do the work of one extraordinary man."

- Elbert Hubbard

In this chapter, you will learn how to use Spark for the analysis of structured data (unstructured data, such as a document containing arbitrary text or some other format has to be transformed into a structured form); we will see how DataFrames/datasets are the corner stone here, and how Spark SQL's APIs make querying structured data simple yet robust. Moreover, we introduce datasets and see the difference between datasets, DataFrames, and RDDs. In a nutshell, the following topics will be covered in this chapter:

- Spark SQL and DataFrames
- DataFrame and SQL API
- DataFrame schema
- datasets and encoders
- Loading and saving data
- Aggregations
- Joins

Spark SQL and DataFrames

Before Apache Spark, Apache Hive was the go-to technology whenever anyone wanted to run an SQL-like query on a large amount of data. Apache Hive essentially translated SQL queries into MapReduce-like, like logic, automatically making it very easy to perform many kinds of analytics on big data without actually learning to write complex code in Java and Scala.

With the advent of Apache Spark, there was a paradigm shift in how we can perform analysis on big data scale. Spark SQL provides an easy-to-use SQL-like layer on top of Apache Spark's distributed computation abilities. In fact, Spark SQL can be used as an online analytical processing database.

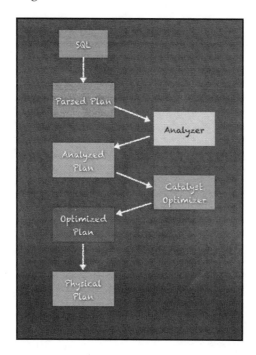

Spark SQL works by parsing the SQL-like statement into an **Abstract Syntax Tree (AST)**, subsequently converting that plan to a logical plan and then optimizing the logical plan into a physical plan that can be executed. The final execution uses the underlying DataFrame API, making it very easy for anyone to use DataFrame APIs by simply using an SQL-like interface rather than learning all the internals. Since this book dives into technical details of various APIs, we will primarily cover the DataFrame APIs, showing Spark SQL API in some places to contrast the different ways of using the APIs.

Thus, DataFrame API is the underlying layer beneath Spark SQL. In this chapter, we will show you how to create DataFrames using various techniques, including SQL queries and performing operations on the DataFrames.

A DataFrame is an abstraction of the **Resilient Distributed dataset (RDD)**, dealing with higher level functions optimized using catalyst optimizer and also highly performant via the Tungsten Initiative. You can think of a dataset as an efficient table of an RDD with heavily optimized binary representation of the data. The binary representation is achieved using encoders, which serializes the various objects into a binary structure for much better performance than RDD representation. Since DataFrames uses the RDD internally anyway, a DataFrame/dataset is also distributed exactly like an RDD, and thus is also a distributed dataset. Obviously, this also means datasets are immutable.

The following is an illustration of the binary representation of data:

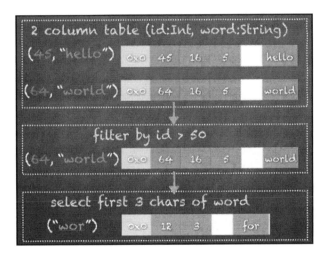

datasets were added in Spark 1.6 and provide the benefits of strong typing on top of DataFrames. In fact, since Spark 2.0, the DataFrame is simply an alias of a dataset.

 `org.apache.spark.sql` defines type `DataFrame` as a `dataset[Row]`, which means that most of the APIs will work well with both datasets and `DataFrames`
type DataFrame = dataset[Row]

A DataFrame is conceptually similar to a table in a Relational Database. Hence, a DataFrame contains rows of data, with each row comprised of several columns.

One of the first things we need to keep in mind is that, just like RDDs, DataFrames are immutable. This property of DataFrames being immutable means every transformation or action creates a new DataFrame.

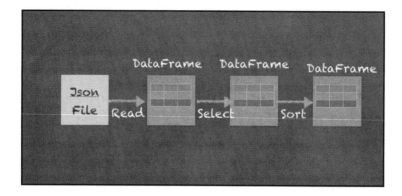

Let's start looking more into DataFrames and how they are different from RDDs. RDD's, as seen before, represent a low-level API of data manipulation in Apache Spark. The DataFrames were created on top of RDDs to abstract the low-level inner workings of RDDs and expose high-level APIs, which are easier to use and provide a lot of functionality out-of-the-box. DataFrame was created by following similar concepts found in the Python pandas package, R language, Julia language, and so on.

As we mentioned before, DataFrames translate the SQL code and domain specific language expressions into optimized execution plans to be run on top of Spark Core APIs in order for the SQL statements to perform a wide variety of operations. DataFrames support many different types of input data sources and many types of operations. These includes all types of SQL operations, such as joins, group by, aggregations, and window functions, as most of the databases. Spark SQL is also quite similar to the Hive query language, and since Spark provides a natural adapter to Apache Hive, users who have been working in Apache Hive can easily transfer their knowledge, applying it to Spark SQL, thus minimizing the transition time.

DataFrames essentially depend on the concept of a table, as seen previously. The table can be operated on very similar to how Apache Hive works. In fact, many of the operations on the tables in Apache Spark are similar to how Apache Hive handles tables and operates on those tables. Once you have a table that is the DataFrame, the DataFrame can be registered as a table and you can operate on the data using Spark SQL statements in lieu of DataFrame APIs.

DataFrames depend on the catalyst optimizer and the Tungsten performance improvements, so let's briefly examine how catalyst optimizer works. A catalyst optimizer creates a parsed logical plan from the input SQL and then analyzes the logical plan by looking at all the various attributes and columns used in the SQL statement. Once the analyzed logical plan is created, catalyst optimizer further tries to optimize the plan by combining several operations and also rearranging the logic to get better performance.

In order to understand the catalyst optimizer, think about it as a common sense logic Optimizer which can reorder operations such as filters and transformations, sometimes grouping several operations into one so as to minimize the amount of data that is shuffled across the worker nodes. For example, catalyst optimizer may decide to broadcast the smaller datasets when performing joint operations between different datasets. Use explain to look at the execution plan of any data frame. The catalyst optimizer also computes statistics of the DataFrame's columns and partitions, improving the speed of execution.

For example, if there are transformations and filters on the data partitions, then the order in which we filter data and apply transformations matters a lot to the overall performance of the operations. As a result of all the optimizations, the optimized logical plan is generated, which is then converted into a physical plan. Obviously, several physical plans are possibilities to execute the same SQL statement and generate the same result. The cost optimization logic determines and picks a good physical plan, based on cost optimizations and estimations.

Tungsten performance improvements are another key ingredient in the secret sauce behind the phenomenal performance improvements offered by Spark 2.x compared to the previous releases, such as Spark 1.6 and older. Tungsten implements a complete overhaul of memory management and other performance improvements. Most important memory management improvements use binary encoding of the objects and referencing them in both off-heap and on-heap memory. Thus, Tungsten allows the usage of office heap memory using the binary encoding mechanism to encode all the objects. Binary encoded objects take up much less memory. Project Tungsten also improves shuffle performance.

The data is typically loaded into DataFrames through the `DataFrameReader`, and data is saved from DataFrames through `DataFrameWriter`.

DataFrame API and SQL API

The creation of a DataFrame can be done in several ways:

- By executing SQL queries
- Loading external data such as Parquet, JSON, CSV, text, Hive, JDBC, and so on
- Converting RDDs to data frames

A DataFrame can be created by loading a CSV file. We will look at a CSV `statesPopulation.csv`, which is being loaded as a DataFrame.

The CSV has the following format of US states populations from years 2010 to 2016.

State	Year	Population
Alabama	2010	4785492
Alaska	2010	714031
Arizona	2010	6408312
Arkansas	2010	2921995
California	2010	37332685

Since this CSV has a header, we can use it to quickly load into a DataFrame with an implicit schema detection.

```scala
scala> val statesDF = spark.read.option("header",
"true").option("inferschema", "true").option("sep",
",").csv("statesPopulation.csv")
statesDF: org.apache.spark.sql.DataFrame = [State: string, Year: int
... 1 more field]
```

Once the DataFrame is loaded, it can be examined for the schema:

```scala
scala> statesDF.printSchema
root
 |-- State: string (nullable = true)
 |-- Year: integer (nullable = true)
 |-- Population: integer (nullable = true)
```

option("header", "true").option("inferschema", "true").option("sep", ",") tells Spark that the CSV has a header; a comma separator is used to separate the fields/columns and also that schema can be inferred implicitly.

DataFrame works by parsing the logical plan, analyzing the logical plan, optimizing the plan, and then finally executing the physical plan of execution.

Using explain on DataFrame shows the plan of execution:

```scala
scala> statesDF.explain(true)
== Parsed Logical Plan ==
Relation[State#0,Year#1,Population#2] csv
== Analyzed Logical Plan ==
State: string, Year: int, Population: int
Relation[State#0,Year#1,Population#2] csv
== Optimized Logical Plan ==
Relation[State#0,Year#1,Population#2] csv
== Physical Plan ==
*FileScan csv [State#0,Year#1,Population#2] Batched: false, Format:
CSV, Location: InMemoryFileIndex[file:/Users/salla/states.csv],
PartitionFilters: [], PushedFilters: [], ReadSchema:
struct<State:string,Year:int,Population:int>
```

A DataFrame can also be registered as a table name (shown as follows), which will then allow you to type SQL statements like a relational Database.

```scala
scala> statesDF.createOrReplaceTempView("states")
```

Once we have the DataFrame as a structured DataFrame or a table, we can run commands to operate on the data:

```scala
scala> statesDF.show(5)
scala> spark.sql("select * from states limit 5").show
+----------+----+----------+
|     State|Year|Population|
+----------+----+----------+
|   Alabama|2010|   4785492|
|    Alaska|2010|    714031|
|   Arizona|2010|   6408312|
|  Arkansas|2010|   2921995|
|California|2010|  37332685|
+----------+----+----------+
```

If you see in the preceding piece of code, we have written an SQL-like statement and executed it using `spark.sql` API.

Note that the Spark SQL is simply converted to the DataFrame API for execution and the SQL is only a DSL for ease of use.

Using the `sort` operation on the DataFrame, you can order the rows in the DataFrame by any column. We see the effect of descending `sort` using the `Population` column as follows. The rows are ordered by the Population in a descending order.

```
scala> statesDF.sort(col("Population").desc).show(5)
scala> spark.sql("select * from states order by Population desc limit
5").show
+----------+----+----------+
| State|Year|Population|
+----------+----+----------+
|California|2016| 39250017|
|California|2015| 38993940|
|California|2014| 38680810|
|California|2013| 38335203|
|California|2012| 38011074|
+----------+----+----------+
```

Using `groupBy` we can group the DataFrame by any column. The following is the code to group the rows by `State` and then add up the `Population` counts for each `State`.

```
scala> statesDF.groupBy("State").sum("Population").show(5)
scala> spark.sql("select State, sum(Population) from states group by
State limit 5").show
+---------+---------------+
| State|sum(Population)|
+---------+---------------+
| Utah| 20333580|
| Hawaii| 9810173|
|Minnesota| 37914011|
| Ohio| 81020539|
| Arkansas| 20703849|
+---------+---------------+
```

Using the `agg` operation, you can perform many different operations on columns of the DataFrame, such as finding the `min`, `max`, and `avg` of a column. You can also perform the operation and rename the column at the same time to suit your use case.

```
scala>
statesDF.groupBy("State").agg(sum("Population").alias("Total")).show(5
)
scala> spark.sql("select State, sum(Population) as Total from states
group by State limit 5").show
+---------+--------+
| State| Total|
+---------+--------+
```

```
|   Utah|20333580|
| Hawaii| 9810173|
|Minnesota|37914011|
|   Ohio|81020539|
| Arkansas|20703849|
+--------+--------+
```

Naturally, the more complicated the logic gets, the execution plan also gets more complicated. Let's look at the plan for the preceding operation of `groupBy` and `agg` API invocations to better understand what is really going on under the hood. The following is the code showing the execution plan of the group by and summation of population per `State`:

```scala
scala>
statesDF.groupBy("State").agg(sum("Population").alias("Total")).explai
n(true)

== Parsed Logical Plan ==
'Aggregate [State#0], [State#0, sum('Population) AS Total#31886]
+- Relation[State#0,Year#1,Population#2] csv

== Analyzed Logical Plan ==
State: string, Total: bigint
Aggregate [State#0], [State#0, sum(cast(Population#2 as bigint)) AS
Total#31886L]
+- Relation[State#0,Year#1,Population#2] csv

== Optimized Logical Plan ==
Aggregate [State#0], [State#0, sum(cast(Population#2 as bigint)) AS
Total#31886L]
+- Project [State#0, Population#2]
  +- Relation[State#0,Year#1,Population#2] csv

== Physical Plan ==
*HashAggregate(keys=[State#0], functions=[sum(cast(Population#2 as
bigint))], output=[State#0, Total#31886L])
+- Exchange hashpartitioning(State#0, 200)
  +- *HashAggregate(keys=[State#0],
functions=[partial_sum(cast(Population#2 as bigint))],
output=[State#0, sum#31892L])
  +- *FileScan csv [State#0,Population#2] Batched: false, Format: CSV,
Location: InMemoryFileIndex[file:/Users/salla/states.csv],
PartitionFilters: [], PushedFilters: [], ReadSchema:
struct<State:string,Population:int>
```

DataFrame operations can be chained together very well so that the execution takes advantage of the cost optimization (Tungsten performance improvements and catalyst optimizer working together).

We can also chain the operations together in a single statement, as shown as follows, where we not only group the data by State column and then sum the Population value, but also sort the DataFrame by the summation column:

```
scala>
statesDF.groupBy("State").agg(sum("Population").alias("Total")).sort(c
ol("Total").desc).show(5)
scala> spark.sql("select State, sum(Population) as Total from states
group by State order by Total desc limit 5").show
+----------+---------+
|    State|   Total|
+----------+---------+
|California|268280590|
|    Texas|185672865|
|  Florida|137618322|
| New York|137409471|
| Illinois| 89960023|
+----------+---------+
```

The preceding chained operation consists of multiple transformations and actions, which can be visualized using the following diagram:

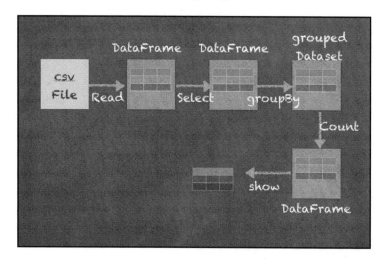

It's also possible to create multiple aggregations at the same time, as follows:

```scala
scala> statesDF.groupBy("State").agg(
          min("Population").alias("minTotal"),
          max("Population").alias("maxTotal"),
          avg("Population").alias("avgTotal"))
        .sort(col("minTotal").desc).show(5)

scala> spark.sql("select State, min(Population) as minTotal,
max(Population) as maxTotal, avg(Population) as avgTotal from states
group by State order by minTotal desc limit 5").show
+----------+--------+--------+-------------------+
|     State|minTotal|maxTotal|           avgTotal|
+----------+--------+--------+-------------------+
|California|37332685|39250017|3.8325798571428575E7|
|     Texas|25244310|27862596|  2.6524695E7|
|  New York|19402640|19747183|  1.962992442857143E7|
|   Florida|18849098|20612439|1.9659760285714287E7|
|  Illinois|12801539|12879505|1.2851431857142856E7|
+----------+--------+--------+-------------------+
```

Pivots

Pivoting is a great way of transforming the table to create a different view, more suitable to doing many summarizations and aggregations. This is accomplished by taking the values of a column and making each of the values an actual column.

To understand this better, let's pivot the rows of the DataFrame by `Year` and examine the result, which shows that, now, the column `Year` created several new columns by converting each unique value into an actual column. The end result of this is that, now, instead of just looking at year columns, we can use the per year columns created to summarize and aggregate by `Year`.

```scala
scala>
statesDF.groupBy("State").pivot("Year").sum("Population").show(5)
+---------+--------+--------+--------+--------+--------+--------+--------+
|    State|    2010|    2011|    2012|    2013|    2014|    2015|    2016|
+---------+--------+--------+--------+--------+--------+--------+--------+
|     Utah| 2775326| 2816124| 2855782| 2902663| 2941836| 2990632| 3051217|
|   Hawaii| 1363945| 1377864| 1391820| 1406481| 1416349| 1425157|
1428557|
|Minnesota| 5311147| 5348562| 5380285| 5418521| 5453109| 5482435|
5519952|
```

```
| Ohio|11540983|11544824|11550839|11570022|11594408|11605090|11614373|
| Arkansas| 2921995| 2939493| 2950685| 2958663| 2966912| 2977853|
2988248|
+---------+--------+--------+--------+--------+--------+--------+-----
---+
```

Filters

DataFrame also supports Filters, which can be used to quickly filter the DataFrame rows to generate new DataFrames. The Filters enable very important transformations of the data to narrow down the DataFrame to our use case. For example, if all you want is to analyze the state of California, then using `filter` API performs the elimination of non-matching rows on every partition of data, thus improving the performance of the operations.

Let's look at the execution plan for the filtering of the DataFrame to only consider the state of California.

```
scala> statesDF.filter("State == 'California'").explain(true)

== Parsed Logical Plan ==
'Filter ('State = California)
+- Relation[State#0,Year#1,Population#2] csv

== Analyzed Logical Plan ==
State: string, Year: int, Population: int
Filter (State#0 = California)
+- Relation[State#0,Year#1,Population#2] csv

== Optimized Logical Plan ==
Filter (isnotnull(State#0) && (State#0 = California))
+- Relation[State#0,Year#1,Population#2] csv

== Physical Plan ==
*Project [State#0, Year#1, Population#2]
+- *Filter (isnotnull(State#0) && (State#0 = California))
 +- *FileScan csv [State#0,Year#1,Population#2] Batched: false,
Format: CSV, Location:
InMemoryFileIndex[file:/Users/salla/states.csv], PartitionFilters: [],
PushedFilters: [IsNotNull(State), EqualTo(State,California)],
ReadSchema: struct<State:string,Year:int,Population:int>
```

Now that we can seen the execution plan, let's now execute the `filter` command, as follows:

```
scala> statesDF.filter("State == 'California'").show
+----------+----+----------+
|     State|Year|Population|
+----------+----+----------+
|California|2010|  37332685|
|California|2011|  37676861|
|California|2012|  38011074|
|California|2013|  38335203|
|California|2014|  38680810|
|California|2015|  38993940|
|California|2016|  39250017|
+----------+----+----------+
```

User-Defined Functions (UDFs)

UDFs define new column-based functions that extend the functionality of Spark SQL. Often, the inbuilt functions provided in Spark do not handle the exact need we have. In such cases, Apache Spark supports the creation of UDFs, which can be used.

 `udf()` internally calls a case class User-Defined Function, which itself calls ScalaUDF internally.

Let's go through an example of an UDF which simply converts State column values to uppercase.

First, we create the function we need in Scala.

```
import org.apache.spark.sql.functions._

scala> val toUpper: String => String = _.toUpperCase
toUpper: String => String = <function1>
```

Then, we have to encapsulate the created function inside the `udf` to create the UDF.

```
scala> val toUpperUDF = udf(toUpper)
toUpperUDF: org.apache.spark.sql.expressions.UserDefinedFunction =
UserDefinedFunction(<function1>,StringType,Some(List(StringType)))
```

Now that we have created the `udf`, we can use it to convert the State column to uppercase.

```
scala> statesDF.withColumn("StateUpperCase",
toUpperUDF(col("State"))).show(5)
+----------+----+----------+--------------+
|     State|Year|Population|StateUpperCase|
+----------+----+----------+--------------+
|   Alabama|2010|   4785492|       ALABAMA|
|    Alaska|2010|    714031|        ALASKA|
|   Arizona|2010|   6408312|       ARIZONA|
|  Arkansas|2010|   2921995|      ARKANSAS|
|California|2010|  37332685|    CALIFORNIA|
+----------+----+----------+--------------+
```

Schema structure of data

A schema is the description of the structure of your data and can be either Implicit or Explicit.

Since the DataFrames are internally based on the RDD, there are two main methods of converting existing RDDs into datasets. An RDD can be converted into a dataset by using reflection to infer the schema of the RDD. A second method for creating datasets is through a programmatic interface, using which you can take an existing RDD and provide a schema to convert the RDD into a dataset with schema.

In order to create a DataFrame from an RDD by inferring the schema using reflection, the Scala API for Spark provides case classes which can be used to define the schema of the table. The DataFrame is created programmatically from the RDD, because the case classes are not easy to use in all cases. For instance, creating a case classes on a 1000 column table is time consuming.

Implicit schema

Let us look at an example of loading a **CSV** (**comma-separated Values**) file into a DataFrame. Whenever a text file contains a header, read API can infer the schema by reading the header line. We also have the option to specify the separator to be used to split the text file lines.

We read the `csv` inferring the schema from the header line and uses comma (,) as the separator. We also show use of `schema` command and `printSchema` command to verify the schema of the input file.

```scala
scala> val statesDF = spark.read.option("header", "true")
                               .option("inferschema", "true")
                               .option("sep", ",")
                               .csv("statesPopulation.csv")
statesDF: org.apache.spark.sql.DataFrame = [State: string, Year: int
... 1 more field]

scala> statesDF.schema
res92: org.apache.spark.sql.types.StructType = StructType(
StructField(State,StringType,true),
StructField(Year,IntegerType,true),
StructField(Population,IntegerType,true))

scala> statesDF.printSchema
root
 |-- State: string (nullable = true)
 |-- Year: integer (nullable = true)
 |-- Population: integer (nullable = true)
```

Explicit schema

A schema is described using `StructType`, which is a collection of `StructField` objects.

> `StructType` and `StructField` belong to the `org.apache.spark.sql.types` package.
> DataTypes such as `IntegerType`, `StringType` also belong to the `org.apache.spark.sql.types` package.

Using these imports, we can define a custom explicit schema.

First, import the necessary classes:

```scala
scala> import org.apache.spark.sql.types.{StructType, IntegerType, StringType}
import org.apache.spark.sql.types.{StructType, IntegerType, StringType}
```

Define a schema with two columns/fields-an `Integer` followed by a `String`:

```
scala> val schema = new StructType().add("i", IntegerType).add("s",
StringType)
schema: org.apache.spark.sql.types.StructType =
StructType(StructField(i,IntegerType,true),
StructField(s,StringType,true))
```

It's easy to print the newly created `schema`:

```
scala> schema.printTreeString
root
 |-- i: integer (nullable = true)
 |-- s: string (nullable = true)
```

There is also an option to print JSON, which is as follows, using `prettyJson` function:

```
scala> schema.prettyJson
res85: String =
{
 "type" : "struct",
 "fields" : [ {
 "name" : "i",
 "type" : "integer",
 "nullable" : true,
 "metadata" : { }
 }, {
 "name" : "s",
 "type" : "string",
 "nullable" : true,
 "metadata" : { }
 } ]
}
```

All the data types of Spark SQL are located in the package `org.apache.spark.sql.types`. You can access them by doing:

```
import org.apache.spark.sql.types._
```

Encoders

Spark 2.x supports a different way of defining schema for complex data types. First, let's look at a simple example.

Encoders must be imported using the import statement in order for you to use Encoders:

```
import org.apache.spark.sql.Encoders
```

Let's look at a simple example of defining a tuple as a data type to be used in the dataset APIs:

```
scala> Encoders.product[(Integer, String)].schema.printTreeString
root
 |-- _1: integer (nullable = true)
 |-- _2: string (nullable = true)
```

The preceding code looks complicated to use all the time, so we can also define a case class for our need and then use it. We can define a case class Record with two fields-an Integer and a String:

```
scala> case class Record(i: Integer, s: String)
defined class Record
```

Using Encoders , we can easily create a schema on top of the case class, thus allowing us to use the various APIs with ease:

```
scala> Encoders.product[Record].schema.printTreeString
root
 |-- i: integer (nullable = true)
 |-- s: string (nullable = true)
```

All the data types of Spark SQL are located in the package org.apache.spark.sql.types. You can access them by doing:

```
import org.apache.spark.sql.types._
```

You should use the DataTypes object in your code to create complex Spark SQL types such as arrays or maps, as follows:

```
scala> import org.apache.spark.sql.types.DataTypes
import org.apache.spark.sql.types.DataTypes

scala> val arrayType = DataTypes.createArrayType(IntegerType)
arrayType: org.apache.spark.sql.types.ArrayType =
ArrayType(IntegerType,true)
```

The following are the data types supported in Spark SQL APIs:

Data type	Value type in Scala	API to access or create a data type
ByteType	Byte	ByteType
ShortType	Short	ShortType
IntegerType	Int	IntegerType
LongType	Long	LongType
FloatType	Float	FloatType
DoubleType	Double	DoubleType
DecimalType	java.math.BigDecimal	DecimalType
StringType	String	StringType
BinaryType	Array[Byte]	BinaryType
BooleanType	Boolean	BooleanType
TimestampType	java.sql.Timestamp	TimestampType
DateType	java.sql.Date	DateType
ArrayType	scala.collection.Seq	ArrayType(elementType, [containsNull])
MapType	scala.collection.Map	MapType(keyType, valueType, [valueContainsNull]) Note: The default value of valueContainsNull is true.
StructType	org.apache.spark.sql.Row	StructType(fields) Note: fields is a Seq of StructFields. Also, two fields with the same name are not allowed.

Loading and saving datasets

We need to have data read into the cluster as input and output or results written back to the storage to do anything practical with our code. Input data can be read from a variety of datasets and sources such as Files, Amazon S3 storage, Databases, NoSQLs, and Hive, and the output can similarly also be saved to Files, S3, Databases, Hive, and so on.

Several systems have support for Spark via a connector, and this number is growing day by day as more systems are latching onto the Spark processing framework.

Loading datasets

Spark SQL can read data from external storage systems such as files, Hive tables, and JDBC databases through the `DataFrameReader` interface.

The format of the API call is `spark.read.inputtype`

- Parquet
- CSV
- Hive Table
- JDBC
- ORC
- Text
- JSON

Let's look at a couple of simple examples of reading CSV files into DataFrames:

```
scala> val statesPopulationDF = spark.read.option("header",
"true").option("inferschema", "true").option("sep",
",").csv("statesPopulation.csv")
statesPopulationDF: org.apache.spark.sql.DataFrame = [State: string,
Year: int ... 1 more field]

scala> val statesTaxRatesDF = spark.read.option("header",
"true").option("inferschema", "true").option("sep",
",").csv("statesTaxRates.csv")
statesTaxRatesDF: org.apache.spark.sql.DataFrame = [State: string,
TaxRate: double]
```

Saving datasets

Spark SQL can save data to external storage systems such as files, Hive tables and JDBC databases through `DataFrameWriter` interface.

The format of the API call is `dataframe.write.outputtype`

- Parquet
- ORC
- Text
- Hive table

- JSON
- CSV
- JDBC

Let's look at a couple of examples of writing or saving a DataFrame to a CSV file:

```scala
scala> statesPopulationDF.write.option("header",
"true").csv("statesPopulation_dup.csv")

scala> statesTaxRatesDF.write.option("header",
"true").csv("statesTaxRates_dup.csv")
```

Aggregations

Aggregation is the method of collecting data based on a condition and performing analytics on the data. Aggregation is very important to make sense of data of all sizes, as just having raw records of data is not that useful for most use cases.

For example, if you look at the following table and then the aggregated view, it is obvious that just raw records do not help you understand the data.

Imagine a table containing one temperature measurement per day for every city in the world for five years.

Shown in the following is a table containing records of average temperature per day per city:

City	Date	Temperature
Boston	12/23/2016	32
New York	12/24/2016	36
Boston	12/24/2016	30
Philadelphia	12/25/2016	34
Boston	12/25/2016	28

If we want to compute the average temperature per city for all the days we have measurements for in the above table, we can see results which look similar to the following table:

City	Average Temperature
Boston	30 - (32 + 30 + 28)/3
New York	36
Philadelphia	34

Aggregate functions

Most aggregations can be done using functions that can be found in the `org.apache.spark.sql.functions` package. In addition, custom aggregation functions can also be created, also known as **User Defined Aggregation Functions (UDAF)**.

> Each grouping operation returns a `RelationalGroupeddataset`, on which you can specify aggregations.

We will load the sample data to illustrate all the different types of aggregate functions in this section:

```
val statesPopulationDF = spark.read.option("header",
"true").option("inferschema", "true").option("sep",
",").csv("statesPopulation.csv")
```

Count

Count is the most basic aggregate function, which simply counts the number of rows for the column specified. An extension is the `countDistinct`, which also eliminates duplicates.

The `count` API has several implementations, as follows. The exact API used depends on the specific use case:

```
def count(columnName: String): TypedColumn[Any, Long]
    Aggregate function: returns the number of items in a group.

def count(e: Column): Column
    Aggregate function: returns the number of items in a group.
```

```
def countDistinct(columnName: String, columnNames: String*): Column
Aggregate function: returns the number of distinct items in a group.

def countDistinct(expr: Column, exprs: Column*): Column
Aggregate function: returns the number of distinct items in a group.
```

Let's look at examples of invoking count and countDistinct on the DataFrame to print the row counts:

```
import org.apache.spark.sql.functions._
scala> statesPopulationDF.select(col("*")).agg(count("State")).show
scala> statesPopulationDF.select(count("State")).show
+-----------+
|count(State)|
+-----------+
|        350|
+-----------+

scala>
statesPopulationDF.select(col("*")).agg(countDistinct("State")).show
scala> statesPopulationDF.select(countDistinct("State")).show
+--------------------+
|count(DISTINCT State)|
+--------------------+
|                  50|
+--------------------+
```

First

Gets the first record in the RelationalGroupeddataset.

The first API has several implementations, as follows. The exact API used depends on the specific use case:

```
def first(columnName: String): Column
Aggregate function: returns the first value of a column in a group.

def first(e: Column): Column
Aggregate function: returns the first value in a group.

def first(columnName: String, ignoreNulls: Boolean): Column
Aggregate function: returns the first value of a column in a group.

def first(e: Column, ignoreNulls: Boolean): Column
Aggregate function: returns the first value in a group.
```

Let's look at an example of invoking `first` on the DataFrame to output the first row:

```
import org.apache.spark.sql.functions._
scala> statesPopulationDF.select(first("State")).show
+------------------+
|first(State, false)|
+------------------+
|           Alabama|
+------------------+
```

Last

Gets the last record in the `RelationalGroupeddataset`.

The `last` API has several implementations, as follows. The exact API used depends on the specific use case:

```
def last(columnName: String): Column
Aggregate function: returns the last value of the column in a group.


def last(e: Column): Column
Aggregate function: returns the last value in a group.


def last(columnName: String, ignoreNulls: Boolean): Column
Aggregate function: returns the last value of the column in a group.


def last(e: Column, ignoreNulls: Boolean): Column
Aggregate function: returns the last value in a group.
```

Let's look at an example of invoking `last` on the DataFrame to output the last row.

```
import org.apache.spark.sql.functions._
scala> statesPopulationDF.select(last("State")).show
+------------------+
|last(State, false)|
+------------------+
|           Wyoming|
+------------------+
```

approx_count_distinct

Approximate distinct count is much faster at approximately counting the distinct records rather than doing an exact count, which usually needs a lot of shuffles and other operations. While the approximate count is not 100% accurate, many use cases can perform equally well even without an exact count.

The `approx_count_distinct` API has several implementations, as follows. The exact API used depends on the specific use case.

```
def approx_count_distinct(columnName: String, rsd: Double): Column
Aggregate function: returns the approximate number of distinct items
in a group.

def approx_count_distinct(e: Column, rsd: Double): Column
Aggregate function: returns the approximate number of distinct items
in a group.

def approx_count_distinct(columnName: String): Column
Aggregate function: returns the approximate number of distinct items
in a group.

def approx_count_distinct(e: Column): Column
Aggregate function: returns the approximate number of distinct items
in a group.
```

Let's look at an example of invoking `approx_count_distinct` on the DataFrame to print the approximate count of the DataFrame:

```
import org.apache.spark.sql.functions._
scala>
statesPopulationDF.select(col("*")).agg(approx_count_distinct("State")
).show
+---------------------------+
|approx_count_distinct(State)|
+---------------------------+
|  48|
+---------------------------+

scala> statesPopulationDF.select(approx_count_distinct("State",
0.2)).show
+---------------------------+
|approx_count_distinct(State)|
+---------------------------+
|  49|
+---------------------------+
```

Min

The minimum of the column value of one of the columns in the DataFrame. An example is if you want to find the minimum temperature of a city.

The `min` API has several implementations, as follows. The exact API used depends on the specific use case:

```
def min(columnName: String): Column
Aggregate function: returns the minimum value of the column in a
group.
```

```
def min(e: Column): Column
Aggregate function: returns the minimum value of the expression in a
group.
```

Let's look at an example of invoking `min` on the DataFrame to print the minimum Population:

```
import org.apache.spark.sql.functions._
scala> statesPopulationDF.select(min("Population")).show
+---------------+
|min(Population)|
+---------------+
|         564513|
+---------------+
```

Max

The maximum of the column value of one of the columns in the DataFrame. An example is if you want to find the maximum temperature of a city.

The `max` API has several implementations, as follows. The exact API used depends on the specific use case.

```
def max(columnName: String): Column
Aggregate function: returns the maximum value of the column in a
group.
```

```
def max(e: Column): Column
Aggregate function: returns the maximum value of the expression in a
group.
```

Let's look at an example of invoking `max` on the DataFrame to print the maximum Population:

```
import org.apache.spark.sql.functions._
scala> statesPopulationDF.select(max("Population")).show
+--------------+
|max(Population)|
+--------------+
|      39250017|
+--------------+
```

Average

The average of the values is calculated by adding the values and dividing by the number of values.

 Average of 1,2,3 is $(1 + 2 + 3) / 3 = 6/3 = 2$

The `avg` API has several implementations, as follows. The exact API used depends on the specific use case:

```
def avg(columnName: String): Column
Aggregate function: returns the average of the values in a group.

def avg(e: Column): Column
Aggregate function: returns the average of the values in a group.
```

Let's look at an example of invoking `avg` on the DataFrame to print the average population:

```
import org.apache.spark.sql.functions._
scala> statesPopulationDF.select(avg("Population")).show
+----------------+
| avg(Population)|
+----------------+
|6253399.371428572|
+----------------+
```

Sum

Computes the sum of the values of the column. Optionally, `sumDistinct` can be used to only add up distinct values.

The `sum` API has several implementations, as follows. The exact API used depends on the specific use case:

```
def sum(columnName: String): Column
Aggregate function: returns the sum of all values in the given column.

def sum(e: Column): Column
Aggregate function: returns the sum of all values in the expression.

def sumDistinct(columnName: String): Column
Aggregate function: returns the sum of distinct values in the
expression

def sumDistinct(e: Column): Column
Aggregate function: returns the sum of distinct values in the
expression.
```

Let's look at an example of invoking `sum` on the DataFrame to print the summation (total) `Population`.

```
import org.apache.spark.sql.functions._
scala> statesPopulationDF.select(sum("Population")).show
+---------------+
|sum(Population)|
+---------------+
|    2188689780|
+---------------+
```

Kurtosis

Kurtosis is a way of quantifying differences in the shape of distributions, which may look very similar in terms of means and variances, yet are actually different. In such cases, kurtosis becomes a good measure of the weight of the distribution at the tail of the distribution, as compared to the middle of the distribution.

The `kurtosis` API has several implementations, as follows. The exact API used depends on the specific use case.

```
def kurtosis(columnName: String): Column
Aggregate function: returns the kurtosis of the values in a group.

def kurtosis(e: Column): Column
Aggregate function: returns the kurtosis of the values in a group.
```

Let's look at an example of invoking `kurtosis` on the DataFrame on the `Population` column:

```
import org.apache.spark.sql.functions._
scala> statesPopulationDF.select(kurtosis("Population")).show
+--------------------+
|kurtosis(Population)|
+--------------------+
|   7.727421920829375|
+--------------------+
```

Skewness

Skewness measures the asymmetry of the values in your data around the average or mean.

The `skewness` API has several implementations, as follows. The exact API used depends on the specific use case.

```
def skewness(columnName: String): Column
Aggregate function: returns the skewness of the values in a group.

def skewness(e: Column): Column
Aggregate function: returns the skewness of the values in a group.
```

Let's look at an example of invoking `skewness` on the DataFrame on the Population column:

```
import org.apache.spark.sql.functions._
scala> statesPopulationDF.select(skewness("Population")).show
+--------------------+
|skewness(Population)|
+--------------------+
|   2.5675329049100024|
+--------------------+
```

Variance

Variance is the average of the squared differences of each of the values from the mean.

The `var` API has several implementations, as follows. The exact API used depends on the specific use case:

```
def var_pop(columnName: String): Column
Aggregate function: returns the population variance of the values in a
group.

def var_pop(e: Column): Column
Aggregate function: returns the population variance of the values in a
group.

def var_samp(columnName: String): Column
Aggregate function: returns the unbiased variance of the values in a
group.

def var_samp(e: Column): Column
Aggregate function: returns the unbiased variance of the values in a
group.
```

Now, let's look at an example of invoking `var_pop` on the DataFrame measuring variance of `Population`:

```
import org.apache.spark.sql.functions._
scala> statesPopulationDF.select(var_pop("Population")).show
+--------------------+
|  var_pop(Population)|
+--------------------+
|4.948359064356177E13|
+--------------------+
```

Standard deviation

Standard deviation is the square root of the variance (see previously).

The `stddev` API has several implementations, as follows. The exact API used depends on the specific use case:

```
def stddev(columnName: String): Column
Aggregate function: alias for stddev_samp.

def stddev(e: Column): Column
```

```
Aggregate function: alias for stddev_samp.

def stddev_pop(columnName: String): Column
Aggregate function: returns the population standard deviation of the
expression in a group.

def stddev_pop(e: Column): Column
Aggregate function: returns the population standard deviation of the
expression in a group.

def stddev_samp(columnName: String): Column
Aggregate function: returns the sample standard deviation of the
expression in a group.

def stddev_samp(e: Column): Column
Aggregate function: returns the sample standard deviation of the
expression in a group.
```

Let's look at an example of invoking stddev on the DataFrame printing the standard deviation of Population:

```
import org.apache.spark.sql.functions._
scala> statesPopulationDF.select(stddev("Population")).show
+---------------------+
|stddev_samp(Population)|
+---------------------+
|   7044528.191173398|
+---------------------+
```

Covariance

Covariance is a measure of the joint variability of two random variables. If the greater values of one variable mainly corresponds with the greater values of the other variable, and the same holds for the lesser values, then the variables tend to show similar behavior and the covariance is positive. If the opposite is true, and the greater values of one variable correspond with the lesser values of the other variable, then the covariance is negative.

The covar API has several implementations, as follows. The exact API used depends on the specific use case.

```
def covar_pop(columnName1: String, columnName2: String): Column
Aggregate function: returns the population covariance for two columns.

def covar_pop(column1: Column, column2: Column): Column
Aggregate function: returns the population covariance for two columns.
```

```
def covar_samp(columnName1: String, columnName2: String): Column
Aggregate function: returns the sample covariance for two columns.

def covar_samp(column1: Column, column2: Column): Column
Aggregate function: returns the sample covariance for two columns.
```

Let's look at an example of invoking `covar_pop` on the DataFrame to calculate the covariance between the year and population columns:

```
import org.apache.spark.sql.functions._
scala> statesPopulationDF.select(covar_pop("Year", "Population")).show
+-------------------------+
|covar_pop(Year, Population)|
+-------------------------+
|     183977.56000006935|
+-------------------------+
```

groupBy

A common task seen in data analysis is to group the data into grouped categories and then perform calculations on the resultant groups of data.

A quick way to understand grouping is to imagine being asked to assess what supplies you need for your office very quickly. You could start looking around you and just group different types of items, such as pens, paper, staplers, and analyze what you have and what you need.

Let's run `groupBy` function on the `DataFrame` to print aggregate counts of each State:

```
scala> statesPopulationDF.groupBy("State").count.show(5)
+---------+-----+
|    State|count|
+---------+-----+
|     Utah|    7|
|   Hawaii|    7|
|Minnesota|    7|
|     Ohio|    7|
| Arkansas|    7|
+---------+-----+
```

You can also `groupBy` and then apply any of the aggregate functions seen previously, such as `min`, `max`, `avg`, `stddev`, and so on:

```
import org.apache.spark.sql.functions._
scala> statesPopulationDF.groupBy("State").agg(min("Population"),
avg("Population")).show(5)
+---------+---------------+--------------------+
| State|min(Population)| avg(Population)|
+---------+---------------+--------------------+
| Utah| 2775326| 2904797.1428571427|
| Hawaii| 1363945| 1401453.2857142857|
|Minnesota| 5311147| 5416287.285714285|
| Ohio| 11540983|1.1574362714285715E7|
| Arkansas| 2921995| 2957692.714285714|
+---------+---------------+--------------------+
```

Rollup

Rollup is a multi-dimensional aggregation used to perform hierarchical or nested calculations. For example, if we want to show the number of records for each State+Year group, as well as for each State (aggregating over all years to give a grand total for each `State` irrespective of the `Year`), we can use `rollup` as follows:

```
scala> statesPopulationDF.rollup("State", "Year").count.show(5)
+------------+----+-----+
| State|Year|count|
+------------+----+-----+
|South Dakota|2010| 1|
| New York|2012| 1|
| California|2014| 1|
| Wyoming|2014| 1|
| Hawaii|null| 7|
+------------+----+-----+
```

The `rollup` calculates the count for state and year, such as California+2014, as well as California state (adding up all years).

Cube

Cube is a multi-dimensional aggregation used to perform hierarchical or nested calculations just like rollup, but with the difference that cube does the same operation for all dimensions. For example, if we want to show the number of records for each State and Year group, as well as for each State (aggregating over all Years to give a grand total for each State irrespective of the Year), we can use rollup as follows. In addition, cube also shows a grand total for each Year (irrespective of the State):

```scala
scala> statesPopulationDF.cube("State", "Year").count.show(5)
+------------+----+-----+
|       State|Year|count|
+------------+----+-----+
|South Dakota|2010|    1|
|    New York|2012|    1|
|        null|2014|   50|
|     Wyoming|2014|    1|
|      Hawaii|null|    7|
+------------+----+-----+
```

Window functions

Window functions allow you to perform aggregations over a window of data rather than entire data or some filtered data. The use cases of such window functions are:

- Cumulative sum
- Delta from previous value for same key
- Weighted moving average

The best way to understand window functions is to imagine a sliding window over the larger dataset universe. You can specify a window looking at three rows T-1, T, and T+1, and by performing a simple calculation. You can also specify a window of latest/most recent ten values:

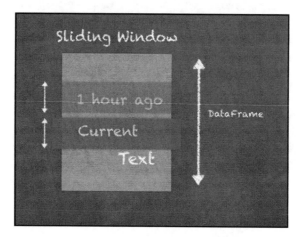

The API for the window specification requires three properties, the `partitionBy()`, `orderBy()`, and the `rowsBetween()`. The `partitionBy` chunks the data into the partitions/groups as specified by `partitionBy()`. `orderBy()` is used to order the data within each partition of data.

The `rowsBetween()` specifies the window frame or the span of the sliding window to perform the calculations.

To try out the windows function, there are certain packages that are needed. You can import the necessary packages using import directives, as follows:

```
import org.apache.spark.sql.expressions.Window
import org.apache.spark.sql.functions.col
import org.apache.spark.sql.functions.max
```

Now, you are ready to write some code to learn about the window functions. Let's create a window specification for the partitions sorted by `Population` and partitioned by `State`. Also, specify that we want to consider all rows until the current row as part of the `Window`.

```
val windowSpec = Window
.partitionBy("State")
.orderBy(col("Population").desc)
.rowsBetween(Window.unboundedPreceding, Window.currentRow)
```

Compute the `rank` over the window specification. The result will be a rank (row number) added to each row, as long as it falls within the `Window` specified. In this example, we chose to partition by `State` and then order the rows of each `State` further by descending order. Hence, all State rows have their own rank numbers assigned.

```
import org.apache.spark.sql.functions._
scala> statesPopulationDF.select(col("State"), col("Year"),
max("Population").over(windowSpec),
rank().over(windowSpec)).sort("State", "Year").show(10)
+-------+----+----------------------------------------------------
----------------------------------------------------------------
+-------+----------------------------------------------------
------------------------------------------------------+
| State|Year|max(Population) OVER (PARTITION BY State ORDER BY
Population DESC NULLS LAST ROWS BETWEEN UNBOUNDED PRECEDING AND
CURRENT ROW)|RANK() OVER (PARTITION BY State ORDER BY Population DESC
NULLS LAST ROWS BETWEEN UNBOUNDED PRECEDING AND CURRENT ROW)|
+-------+----+----------------------------------------------------
----------------------------------------------------------------
+-------+----------------------------------------------------
------------------------------------------------------+
|Alabama|2010|  4863300|  6|
|Alabama|2011|  4863300|  7|
|Alabama|2012|  4863300|  5|
|Alabama|2013|  4863300|  4|
|Alabama|2014|  4863300|  3|
```

ntiles

The ntiles is a popular aggregation over a window and is commonly used to divide input dataset into n parts. For example, in predictive analytics, deciles (10 parts) are often used to first group the data and then divide it into 10 parts to get a fair distribution of data. This is a natural function of the window function approach, hence ntiles is a good example of how window functions can help.

For example, if we want to partition the `statesPopulationDF` by `State` (window specification was shown previously), order by population, and then divide into two portions, we can use `ntile` over the `windowspec`:

```scala
import org.apache.spark.sql.functions._
scala> statesPopulationDF.select(col("State"), col("Year"),
ntile(2).over(windowSpec), rank().over(windowSpec)).sort("State",
"Year").show(10)
+-------+----+--------------------------------------------------------
----------------------------------------------------------+------
-----------------------------------------------------------------
----------------------------------------+
| State|Year|ntile(2) OVER (PARTITION BY State ORDER BY Population
DESC NULLS LAST ROWS BETWEEN UNBOUNDED PRECEDING AND CURRENT
ROW)|RANK() OVER (PARTITION BY State ORDER BY Population DESC NULLS
LAST ROWS BETWEEN UNBOUNDED PRECEDING AND CURRENT ROW)|
+-------+----+--------------------------------------------------------
----------------------------------------------------------+------
-----------------------------------------------------------------
----------------------------------------+
|Alabama|2010|   2|   6|
|Alabama|2011|   2|   7|
|Alabama|2012|   2|   5|
|Alabama|2013|   1|   4|
|Alabama|2014|   1|   3|
|Alabama|2015|   1|   2|
|Alabama|2016|   1|   1|
| Alaska|2010|   2|   7|
| Alaska|2011|   2|   6|
| Alaska|2012|   2|   5|
+-------+----+--------------------------------------------------------
----------------------------------------------------------+------
-----------------------------------------------------------------
--
```

As shown previously, we have used `Window` function and `ntile()` together to divide the rows of each `State` into two equal portions.

A popular use of this function is to compute deciles used in data science Models.

Joins

In traditional databases, joins are used to join one transaction table with another lookup table to generate a more complete view. For example, if you have a table of online transactions by customer ID and another table containing the customer city and customer ID, you can use join to generate reports on the transactions by city.

Transactions table: The following table has three columns, the **CustomerID**, the **Purchased item**, and how much the customer paid for the item:

CustomerID	Purchased item	Price paid
1	Headphone	25.00
2	Watch	100.00
3	Keyboard	20.00
1	Mouse	10.00
4	Cable	10.00
3	Headphone	30.00

Customer Info table: The following table has two columns, the **CustomerID** and the **City** the customer lives in:

CustomerID	City
1	Boston
2	New York
3	Philadelphia
4	Boston

Joining the transaction table with the customer info table will generate a view as follows:

CustomerID	Purchased item	Price paid	City
1	Headphone	25.00	Boston
2	Watch	100.00	New York
3	Keyboard	20.00	Philadelphia
1	Mouse	10.00	Boston
4	Cable	10.00	Boston
3	Headphone	30.00	Philadelphia

Now, we can use this joined view to generate a report of **Total sale price** by **City**:

City	#Items	Total sale price
Boston	3	45.00
Philadelphia	2	50.00
New York	1	100.00

Joins are an important function of Spark SQL, as they enable you to bring two datasets together, as seen previously. Spark, of course, is not only meant to generate reports, but is used to process data on a petabyte scale to handle real-time streaming use cases, machine learning algorithms, or plain analytics. In order to accomplish these goals, Spark provides the API functions needed.

A typical join between two datasets takes place using one or more keys of the left and right datasets and then evaluates a conditional expression on the sets of keys as a Boolean expression. If the result of the Boolean expression returns true, then the join is successful, else the joined DataFrame will not contain the corresponding join.

The join API has 6 different implementations:

```
join(right: dataset[_]): DataFrame
Condition-less inner join

join(right: dataset[_], usingColumn: String): DataFrame
Inner join with a single column

join(right: dataset[_], usingColumns: Seq[String]): DataFrame
Inner join with multiple columns

join(right: dataset[_], usingColumns: Seq[String], joinType: String):
DataFrame
Join with multiple columns and a join type (inner, outer,....)
```

```
join(right: dataset[_], joinExprs: Column): DataFrame
Inner Join using a join expression

join(right: dataset[_], joinExprs: Column, joinType: String):
DataFrame
Join using a Join expression and a join type (inner, outer, ...)
```

We will use one of the APIs to understand how to use join APIs ; however, you can choose to use other APIs depending on the use case:

```
def  join(right: dataset[_], joinExprs: Column, joinType: String):
DataFrame
Join with another DataFrame using the given join expression

right: Right side of the join.
joinExprs: Join expression.
joinType : Type of join to perform. Default is inner join

// Scala:
import org.apache.spark.sql.functions._
import spark.implicits._
df1.join(df2, $"df1Key" === $"df2Key", "outer")
```

Note that joins will be covered in detail in the next few sections.

Inner workings of join

Join works by operating on the partitions of a DataFrame using the multiple executors. However, the actual operations and the subsequent performance depends on the type of `join` and the nature of the datasets being joined. In the next section, we will look at the types of joins.

Shuffle join

Join between two big datasets involves shuffle join where partitions of both left and right datasets are spread across the executors. Shuffles are expensive and it's important to analyze the logic to make sure the distribution of partitions and shuffles is done optimally. The following is an illustration of how shuffle join works internally:

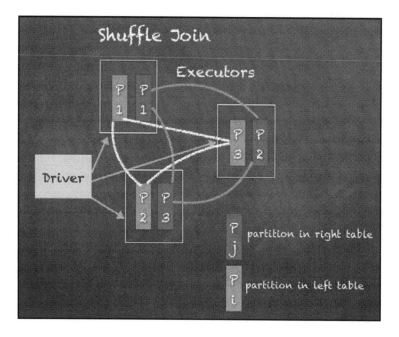

Broadcast join

A join between one large dataset and a smaller dataset can be done by broadcasting the smaller dataset to all executors where a partition from the left dataset exists. The following is an illustration of how a broadcast join works internally:

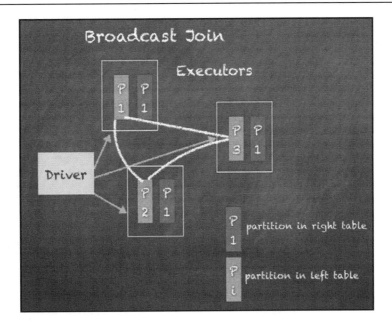

Join types

The following is a table of the different types of joins. This is important, as the choice made when joining two datasets makes all the difference in the output, and also the performance.

Join type	Description
inner	The inner join compares each row from *left* to rows from *right* and combines matched pair of rows from *left* and *right* datasets only when both have non-NULL values.
cross	The cross join matches every row from *left* with every row from *right* generating a Cartesian cross product.
outer, full, fullouter	The full outer Join gives all rows in *left* and *right* filling in NULL if only in *right* or *left*.
leftanti	The leftanti Join gives only rows in *left* based on non-existence on *right* side.
left, leftouter	The leftouter Join gives all rows in *left* plus common rows of *left* and *right* (inner join). Fills in NULL if not in *right*.
leftsemi	The leftsemi Join gives only rows in *left* based on existence on *right* side. The does not include *right*-side values.
right, rightouter	The rightouter Join gives all rows in *right* plus common rows of *left* and *right* (inner join). Fills in NULL if not in *left*.

We will examine how the different join types work by using the sample datasets.

```scala
scala> val statesPopulationDF = spark.read.option("header",
"true").option("inferschema", "true").option("sep",
",").csv("statesPopulation.csv")
statesPopulationDF: org.apache.spark.sql.DataFrame = [State: string,
Year: int ... 1 more field]

scala> val statesTaxRatesDF = spark.read.option("header",
"true").option("inferschema", "true").option("sep",
",").csv("statesTaxRates.csv")
statesTaxRatesDF: org.apache.spark.sql.DataFrame = [State: string,
TaxRate: double]

scala> statesPopulationDF.count
res21: Long = 357

scala> statesTaxRatesDF.count
res32: Long = 47

%sql
statesPopulationDF.createOrReplaceTempView("statesPopulationDF")
statesTaxRatesDF.createOrReplaceTempView("statesTaxRatesDF")
```

Inner join

Inner join results in rows from both `statesPopulationDF` and `statesTaxRatesDF` when state is non-NULL in both datasets.

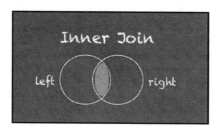

Join the two datasets by the state column as follows:

```
val joinDF = statesPopulationDF.join(statesTaxRatesDF,
statesPopulationDF("State") === statesTaxRatesDF("State"), "inner")

%sql
val joinDF = spark.sql("SELECT * FROM statesPopulationDF INNER JOIN
statesTaxRatesDF ON statesPopulationDF.State =
statesTaxRatesDF.State")

scala> joinDF.count
res22: Long = 329

scala> joinDF.show
+--------------------+----+----------+--------------------+-------+
| State|Year|Population| State|TaxRate|
+--------------------+----+----------+--------------------+-------+
| Alabama|2010| 4785492| Alabama| 4.0|
| Arizona|2010| 6408312| Arizona| 5.6|
| Arkansas|2010| 2921995| Arkansas| 6.5|
| California|2010| 37332685| California| 7.5|
| Colorado|2010| 5048644| Colorado| 2.9|
| Connecticut|2010| 3579899| Connecticut| 6.35|
```

You can run the explain() on the joinDF to look at the execution plan:

```
scala> joinDF.explain
== Physical Plan ==
*BroadcastHashJoin [State#570], [State#577], Inner, BuildRight
:- *Project [State#570, Year#571, Population#572]
: +- *Filter isnotnull(State#570)
: +- *FileScan csv [State#570,Year#571,Population#572] Batched: false,
Format: CSV, Location:
InMemoryFileIndex[file:/Users/salla/spark-2.1.0-bin-
hadoop2.7/statesPopulation.csv], PartitionFilters: [], PushedFilters:
[IsNotNull(State)], ReadSchema:
struct<State:string,Year:int,Population:int>
+- BroadcastExchange HashedRelationBroadcastMode(List(input[0, string,
true]))
  +- *Project [State#577, TaxRate#578]
  +- *Filter isnotnull(State#577)
  +- *FileScan csv [State#577,TaxRate#578] Batched: false, Format: CSV,
Location: InMemoryFileIndex[file:/Users/salla/spark-2.1.0-bin-
hadoop2.7/statesTaxRates.csv], PartitionFilters: [], PushedFilters:
[IsNotNull(State)], ReadSchema: struct<State:string,TaxRate:double>
```

Left outer join

Left outer join results in all rows from `statesPopulationDF`, including any common in `statesPopulationDF` and `statesTaxRatesDF`.

Join the two datasets by the state column, shown as follows:

```
val joinDF = statesPopulationDF.join(statesTaxRatesDF,
statesPopulationDF("State") === statesTaxRatesDF("State"),
"leftouter")

%sql
val joinDF = spark.sql("SELECT * FROM statesPopulationDF LEFT OUTER
JOIN statesTaxRatesDF ON statesPopulationDF.State =
statesTaxRatesDF.State")

scala> joinDF.count
res22: Long = 357

scala> joinDF.show(5)
+----------+----+----------+----------+-------+
|     State|Year|Population|     State|TaxRate|
+----------+----+----------+----------+-------+
|   Alabama|2010|   4785492|   Alabama|    4.0|
|    Alaska|2010|    714031|      null|   null|
|   Arizona|2010|   6408312|   Arizona|    5.6|
|  Arkansas|2010|   2921995|  Arkansas|    6.5|
|California|2010|  37332685|California|    7.5|
+----------+----+----------+----------+-------+
```

Right outer join

Right outer join results in all rows from `statesTaxRatesDF`, including any common in `statesPopulationDF` and `statesTaxRatesDF`.

Join the two datasets by the `State` column as follows:

```
val joinDF = statesPopulationDF.join(statesTaxRatesDF,
statesPopulationDF("State") === statesTaxRatesDF("State"),
"rightouter")

%sql
val joinDF = spark.sql("SELECT * FROM statesPopulationDF RIGHT OUTER
JOIN statesTaxRatesDF ON statesPopulationDF.State =
statesTaxRatesDF.State")

scala> joinDF.count
res22: Long = 323

scala> joinDF.show
+--------------------+----+----------+--------------------+-------+
| State|Year|Population| State|TaxRate|
+--------------------+----+----------+--------------------+-------+
| Colorado|2011| 5118360| Colorado| 2.9|
| Colorado|2010| 5048644| Colorado| 2.9|
| null|null| null|Connecticut| 6.35|
| Florida|2016| 20612439| Florida| 6.0|
| Florida|2015| 20244914| Florida| 6.0|
| Florida|2014| 19888741| Florida| 6.0|
```

Outer join

Outer join results in all rows from statesPopulationDF and statesTaxRatesDF.

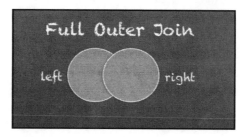

Join the two datasets by the State column as follows:

```
val joinDF = statesPopulationDF.join(statesTaxRatesDF,
statesPopulationDF("State") === statesTaxRatesDF("State"),
"fullouter")

%sql
val joinDF = spark.sql("SELECT * FROM statesPopulationDF FULL OUTER
JOIN statesTaxRatesDF ON statesPopulationDF.State =
statesTaxRatesDF.State")

scala> joinDF.count
res22: Long = 351

scala> joinDF.show
+--------------------+----+----------+--------------------+-------+
| State|Year|Population| State|TaxRate|
+--------------------+----+----------+--------------------+-------+
| Delaware|2010| 899816| null| null|
| Delaware|2011| 907924| null| null|
| West Virginia|2010| 1854230| West Virginia| 6.0|
| West Virginia|2011| 1854972| West Virginia| 6.0|
| Missouri|2010| 5996118| Missouri| 4.225|
| null|null| null| Connecticut| 6.35|
```

Left anti join

Left anti join results in rows from only statesPopulationDF if, and only if, there is NO corresponding row in statesTaxRatesDF.

Join the two datasets by the `State` column as follows:

```
val joinDF = statesPopulationDF.join(statesTaxRatesDF,
statesPopulationDF("State") === statesTaxRatesDF("State"), "leftanti")

%sql
val joinDF = spark.sql("SELECT * FROM statesPopulationDF LEFT ANTI
JOIN statesTaxRatesDF ON statesPopulationDF.State =
statesTaxRatesDF.State")

scala> joinDF.count
res22: Long = 28

scala> joinDF.show(5)
+--------+----+----------+
|   State|Year|Population|
+--------+----+----------+
|  Alaska|2010|    714031|
|Delaware|2010|    899816|
| Montana|2010|    990641|
|  Oregon|2010|   3838048|
|  Alaska|2011|    722713|
+--------+----+----------+
```

Left semi join

Left semi join results in rows from only `statesPopulationDF` if, and only if, there is a corresponding row in `statesTaxRatesDF`.

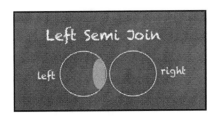

Join the two datasets by the state column as follows:

```
val joinDF = statesPopulationDF.join(statesTaxRatesDF,
statesPopulationDF("State") === statesTaxRatesDF("State"), "leftsemi")

%sql
val joinDF = spark.sql("SELECT * FROM statesPopulationDF LEFT SEMI
JOIN statesTaxRatesDF ON statesPopulationDF.State =
statesTaxRatesDF.State")

scala> joinDF.count
res22: Long = 322

scala> joinDF.show(5)
+----------+----+----------+
|   State|Year|Population|
+----------+----+----------+
|  Alabama|2010|  4785492|
|  Arizona|2010|  6408312|
| Arkansas|2010|  2921995|
|California|2010| 37332685|
| Colorado|2010|  5048644|
+----------+----+----------+
```

Cross join

Cross join matches every row from *left* with every row from *right,* generating a Cartesian cross product.

Join the two datasets by the `State` column as follows:

```scala
scala> val joinDF=statesPopulationDF.crossJoin(statesTaxRatesDF)
joinDF: org.apache.spark.sql.DataFrame = [State: string, Year: int ...
3 more fields]

%sql
val joinDF = spark.sql("SELECT * FROM statesPopulationDF CROSS JOIN
statesTaxRatesDF")

scala> joinDF.count
res46: Long = 16450

scala> joinDF.show(10)
+-------+----+----------+-----------+-------+
| State|Year|Population|      State|TaxRate|
+-------+----+----------+-----------+-------+
|Alabama|2010|   4785492|    Alabama|    4.0|
|Alabama|2010|   4785492|    Arizona|    5.6|
|Alabama|2010|   4785492|   Arkansas|    6.5|
|Alabama|2010|   4785492| California|    7.5|
|Alabama|2010|   4785492|   Colorado|    2.9|
|Alabama|2010|   4785492|Connecticut|   6.35|
|Alabama|2010|   4785492|    Florida|    6.0|
|Alabama|2010|   4785492|    Georgia|    4.0|
|Alabama|2010|   4785492|     Hawaii|    4.0|
|Alabama|2010|   4785492|      Idaho|    6.0|
+-------+----+----------+-----------+-------+
```

You can also use join with cross jointype instead of calling the cross join API. `statesPopulationDF.join(statesTaxRatesDF, statesPopulationDF("State").isNotNull, "cross").count`.

Performance implications of join

The join type chosen directly impacts the performance of the join. This is because joins require the shuffling of data between executors to execute the tasks, hence different joins, and even the order of the joins, need to be considered when using join.

The following is a table you could use to refer to when writing `Join` code:

Join type	Performance considerations and tips
inner	Inner join requires the left and right tables to have the same column. If you have duplicate or multiple copies of the keys on either the left or right side, the join will quickly blow up into a sort of a Cartesian join, taking a lot longer to complete than if designed correctly to minimize the multiple keys.
cross	Cross Join matches every row from *left* with every row from *right*, generating a Cartesian cross product. This is to be used with caution, as this is the worst performant join, to be used in specific use cases only.
outer, full, fullouter	Fullouter Join gives all rows in *left* and *right* filling in NULL if only in *right* or *left*. If used on tables with little in common, can result in very large results and thus slow performance.
leftanti	Leftanti Join gives only rows in *left* based on non-existence on *right* side. Very good performance, as only one table is fully considered and the other is only checked for the join condition.
left, leftouter	Leftouter Join gives all rows in *left* plus common rows of *left* and *right* (inner join). Fills in NULL if not in *right*. If used on tables with little in common, can result in very large results and thus slow performance.
leftsemi	Leftsemi Join gives only rows in *left* based on existence on *right* side. Does not include *right* side values. Very good performance, as only one table is fully considered and other is only checked for the join condition.
right, rightouter	Rightouter Join gives all rows in *right* plus common rows of *left* and *right* (inner join). Fills in NULL if not in *left*. Performance is similar to the leftouter join mentioned previously in this table.

Summary

In this chapter, we discussed the origin of DataFrames and how Spark SQL provides the SQL interface on top of DataFrames. The power of DataFrames is such that execution times have decreased manyfold over original RDD-based computations. Having such a powerful layer with a simple SQL-like interface makes them all the more powerful. We also looked at various APIs to create, and manipulate DataFrames, as well as digging deeper into the sophisticated features of aggregations, including `groupBy`, `Window`, `rollup`, and `cubes`. Finally, we also looked at the concept of joining datasets and the various types of joins possible, such as inner, outer, cross, and so on.

In the next chapter, we will explore the exciting world of real-time data processing and analytics in the `Chapter 9`, *Stream Me Up, Scotty - Spark Streaming*.

Stream Me Up, Scotty - Spark Streaming

9

"I really like streaming services. It's a great way for people to find your music"

- Kygo

In this chapter, we will learn about Spark Streaming and find out how we can take advantage of it to process streams of data using the Spark API. Moreover, in this chapter, we will learn various ways of processing real-time streams of data using a practical example to consume and process tweets from Twitter. In a nutshell, the following topics will be covered throughout this chapter:

- A brief introduction to streaming
- Spark Streaming
- Discretized streams
- Stateful/stateless transformations
- Checkpointing
- Interoperability with streaming platforms (Apache Kafka)
- Structured streaming

A Brief introduction to streaming

In today's world of interconnected devices and services, it is hard to even spend a few hours a day without our smartphone to check Facebook, or order an Uber ride, or tweet something about the burger you just bought, or check the latest news or sports updates on your favorite team. We depend on our phones and Internet, for a lot of things, whether it is to get work done, or just browse, or e-mail your friend. There is simply no way around this phenomenon, and the number and variety of applications and services will only grow over time.

As a result, the smart devices are everywhere, and they generate a lot of data all the time. This phenomenon, also broadly referred to as the Internet of Things, has changed the dynamics of data processing forever. Whenever you use any of the services or apps on your iPhone, or Droid or Windows phone, in some shape or form, real-time data processing is at work. Since so much is depending on the quality and value of the apps, there is a lot of emphasis on how the various startups and established companies are tackling the complex challenges of **SLAs (Service Level Agreements)**, and usefulness and also the timeliness of the data.

One of the paradigms being researched and adopted by organisations and service providers is the building of very scalable, near real-time or real-time processing frameworks on a very cutting-edge platform or infrastructure. Everything must be fast and also reactive to changes and failures. You would not like it if your Facebook updated once every hour or if you received email only once a day; so, it is imperative that data flow, processing, and the usage are all as close to real time as possible. Many of the systems we are interested in monitoring or implementing generate a lot of data as an indefinite continuous stream of events.

As in any other data processing system, we have the same fundamental challenges of a collection of data, storage, and processing of data. However, the additional complexity is due to the real-time needs of the platform. In order to collect such indefinite streams of events and then subsequently process all such events in order to generate actionable insights, we need to use highly scalable specialized architectures to deal with tremendous rates of events. As such, many systems have been built over the decades starting from AMQ, RabbitMQ, Storm, Kafka, Spark, Flink, Gearpump, Apex, and so on.

Modern systems built to deal with such large amounts of streaming data come with very flexible and scalable technologies that are not only very efficient but also help realize the business goals much better than before. Using such technologies, it is possible to consume data from a variety of data sources and then use it in a variety of use cases almost immediately or at a later time as needed.

Let us talk about what happens when you take out your smartphone and book an Uber ride to go to the airport. With a few touches on the smartphone screen, you're able to select a point, choose the credit card, make the payment, and book the ride. Once you're done with your transaction, you then get to monitor the progress of your car real-time on a map on your phone. As the car is making its way toward you, you're able to monitor exactly where the car is and you can also make a decision to pick up coffee at the local Starbucks while you're waiting for the car to pick you up.

You could also make informed decisions regarding the car and the subsequent trip to the airport by looking at the expected time of arrival of the car. If it looks like the car is going to take quite a bit of time picking you up, and if this poses a risk to the flight you are about to catch, you could cancel the ride and hop in a taxi that just happens to be nearby. Alternatively, if it so happens that the traffic situation is not going to let you reach the airport on time, thus posing a risk to the flight you are due to catch, then you also get to make a decision regarding rescheduling or canceling your flight.

Now in order to understand how such real-time streaming architectures work to provide such invaluable information, we need to understand the basic tenets of streaming architectures. On the one hand, it is very important for a real-time streaming architecture to be able to consume extreme amounts of data at very high rates while , on the other hand, also ensuring reasonable guarantees that the data that is getting ingested is also processed.

The following images diagram shows a generic stream processing system with a producer putting events into a messaging system while a consumer is reading from the messaging system:

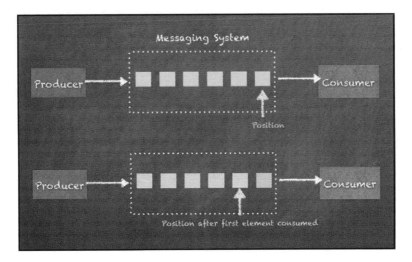

Processing of real-time streaming data can be categorized into the following three essential paradigms:

- At least once processing
- At most once processing
- Exactly once processing

Let's look at what these three stream processing paradigms mean to our business use cases.

While exactly once processing of real-time events is the ultimate nirvana for us, it is very difficult to always achieve this goal in different scenarios. We have to compromise on the property of exactly once processing in cases where the benefit of such a guarantee is outweighed by the complexity of the implementation.

At least once processing

The at least once processing paradigm involves a mechanism to save the position of the last event received **only after** the event is actually processed and results persisted somewhere so that, if there is a failure and the consumer restarts, the consumer will read the old events again and process them. However, since there is no guarantee that the received events were not processed at all or partially processed, this causes a potential duplication of events as they are fetched again. This results in the behavior that events ate processed at least once.

At least once is ideally suitable for any application that involves updating some instantaneous ticker or gauge to show current values. Any cumulative sum, counter, or dependency on the accuracy of aggregations (`sum`, `groupBy`, and so on) does not fit the use case for such processing simply because duplicate events will cause incorrect results.

The sequence of operations for the consumer are as follows:

1. Save results
2. Save offsets

Shown in the following is an illustration of what happens if there are a failure and **consumer** restarts. Since the events have already been processed but the offsets have not saved, the consumer will read from the previous offsets saved, thus causing duplicates. Event 0 is processed twice in the following figure:

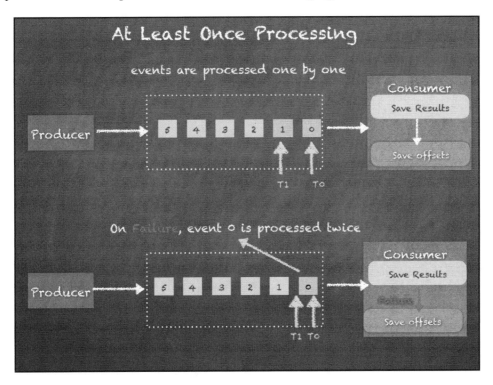

At most once processing

The At most once processing paradigm involves a mechanism to save the position of the last event received before the event is actually processed and results persisted somewhere so that, if there is a failure and the consumer restarts, the consumer will not try to read the old events again. However, since there is no guarantee that the received events were all processed, this causes potential loss of events as they are never fetched again. This results in the behavior that the events are processed at most once or not processed at all.

At most once is ideally suitable for any application that involves updating some instantaneous ticker or gauge to show current values, as well as any cumulative sum, counter, or other aggregation, provided accuracy is not mandatory or the application needs absolutely all events. Any events lost will cause incorrect results or missing results.

The sequence of operations for the consumer are as follows:

1. Save offsets
2. Save results

Shown in the following is an illustration of what happens if there are a failure and the **consumer** restarts. Since the events have not been processed but offsets are saved, the consumer will read from the saved offsets, causing a gap in events consumed. Event 0 is never processed in the following figure:

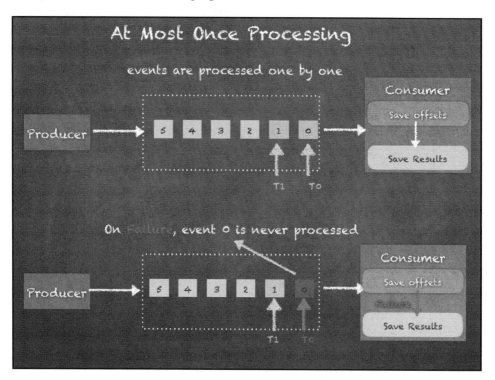

Exactly once processing

The Exactly once processing paradigm is similar to the at least once paradigm, and involves a mechanism to save the position of the last event received only after the event has actually been processed and the results persisted somewhere so that, if there is a failure and the consumer restarts, the consumer will read the old events again and process them. However, since there is no guarantee that the received events were not processed at all or were partially processed, this causes a potential duplication of events as they are fetched again. However, unlike the at least once paradigm, the duplicate events are not processed and are dropped, thus resulting in the exactly once paradigm.

Exactly once processing paradigm is suitable for any application that involves accurate counters, aggregations, or which in general needs every event processed only once and also definitely once (without loss).

The sequence of operations for the consumer are as follows:

1. Save results
2. Save offsets

The following is illustration shows what happens if there are a failure and the **consumer** restarts. Since the events have already been processed but offsets have not saved, the consumer will read from the previous offsets saved, thus causing duplicates. Event 0 is processed only once in the following figure because the **consumer** drops the duplicate event 0:

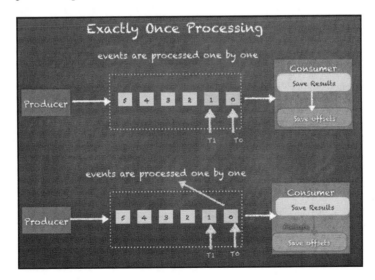

How does the Exactly once paradigm drop duplicates? There are two techniques which can help here:

1. Idempotent updates
2. Transactional updates

 Spark Streaming also implements structured streaming in Spark 2.0+, which support Exactly once processing out of the box. We will look at structured streaming later in this chapter.

Idempotent updates involve saving results based on some unique ID/key generated so that, if there is a duplicate, the generated unique ID/key will already be in the results (for instance, a database) so that the consumer can drop the duplicate without updating the results. This is complicated as it's not always possible or easy to generate unique keys. It also requires additional processing on the consumer end. Another point is that the database can be separate for results and offsets.

Transactional updates save results in batches that have a transaction beginning and a transaction commit phase within so that, when the commit occurs, we know that the events were processed successfully. Hence, when duplicate events are received, they can be dropped without updating results. This technique is much more complicated than the idempotent updates as now we need some transactional data store. Another point is that the database must be the same for results and offsets.

 You should look into the use case you're trying to build and see if at least once processing, or At most once processing, can be reasonably wide and still achieve an acceptable level of performance and accuracy.

We will be looking at the paradigms closely when we learn about Spark Streaming and how to use Spark Streaming and consume events from Apache Kafka in the following sections.

Spark Streaming

Spark Streaming is not the first streaming architecture to come into existence. Several technologies have existed over time to deal with the real-time processing needs of various business use cases. Twitter Storm was one of the first popular stream processing technologies out there and was in used by many organizations fulfilling the needs of many businesses.

Apache Spark comes with a streaming library, which has rapidly evolved to be the most widely used technology. Spark Streaming has some distinct advantages over the other technologies, the first and foremost being the tight integration between Spark Streaming APIs and the Spark core APIs making building a dual purpose real-time and batch analytical platform feasible and efficient than otherwise. Spark Streaming also integrates with Spark ML and Spark SQL, as well as GraphX, making it the most powerful stream processing technology that can serve many unique and complex use cases. In this section, we will look deeper into what Spark Streaming is all about.

For more information on Spark Streaming, you can refer to `https://spark.apache.org/docs/2.1.0/streaming-programming-guide.html`.

Spark Streaming supports several input sources and can write results to several sinks.

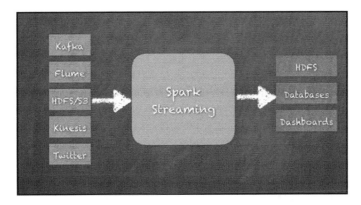

While Flink, Heron (successor to Twitter Storm), Samza, and so on all handle events as they are collected with minimal latency, Spark Streaming consumes continuous streams of data and then processes the collected data in the form of micro-batches. The size of the micro-batch can be as low as 500 milliseconds but usually cannot go lower than that.

Apache Apex, Gear pump, Flink, Samza, Heron, or other upcoming technologies compete with Spark Streaming in some use cases. If you need true event-by-event processing, then Spark Streaming is not the right fit for your use case.

The way streaming works are by creating batches of events at regular time intervals as per configuration and delivering the micro-batches of data at every specified interval for further processing.

Just like `SparkContext`, Spark Streaming has a `StreamingContext`, which is the main entry point for the streaming job/application. `StreamingContext` is dependent on `SparkContext`. In fact, the `SparkContext` can be directly used in the streaming job. The `StreamingContext` is similar to the `SparkContext`, except that `StreamingContext` also requires the program to specify the time interval or duration of the batching interval, which can be in milliseconds or minutes.

Remember that `SparkContext` is the main point of entry, and the task scheduling and resource management is part of `SparkContext`, so `StreamingContext` reuses the logic.

StreamingContext

`StreamingContext` is the main entry point for streaming and essentially takes care of the streaming application, including checkpointing, transformations, and actions on DStreams of RDDs.

Creating StreamingContext

A new StreamingContext can be created in two ways:

1. Create a `StreamingContext` using an existing `SparkContext` as follows:

```scala
StreamingContext(sparkContext: SparkContext, batchDuration:
Duration)
    scala> val ssc = new StreamingContext(sc, Seconds(10))
```

2. Create a `StreamingContext` by providing the configuration necessary for a new `SparkContext` as follows:

```
StreamingContext(conf: SparkConf, batchDuration: Duration)
scala> val conf = new SparkConf().setMaster("local[1]")
                                 .setAppName("TextStreams")
scala> val ssc = new StreamingContext(conf, Seconds(10))
```

3. A third method is to use `getOrCreate()`, which is used to either recreate a `StreamingContext` from checkpoint data or to create a new `StreamingContext`. If checkpoint data exists in the provided `checkpointPath`, then `StreamingContext` will be recreated from the checkpoint data. If the data does not exist, then the `StreamingContext` will be created by calling the provided `creatingFunc`:

```
def getOrCreate(
  checkpointPath: String,
  creatingFunc: () => StreamingContext,
  hadoopConf: Configuration = SparkHadoopUtil.get.conf,
  createOnError: Boolean = false
): StreamingContext
```

Starting StreamingContext

The `start()` method starts the execution of the streams defined using the `StreamingContext`. This essentially starts the entire streaming application:

```
def start(): Unit
scala> ssc.start()
```

Stopping StreamingContext

Stopping the `StreamingContext` stops all processing and you will have to recreate a new `StreamingContext` and invoke `start()` on it to restart the application. There are two APIs useful to stop a stream processing application.

Stop the execution of the streams immediately (do not wait for all received data to be processed):

```
def stop(stopSparkContext: Boolean)
scala> ssc.stop(false)
```

Stop the execution of the streams, with the option of ensuring that all received data has been processed:

```
def stop(stopSparkContext: Boolean, stopGracefully: Boolean)
scala> ssc.stop(true, true)
```

Input streams

There are several types of input streams such as `receiverStream` and `fileStream` that can be created using the `StreamingContext` as shown in the following subsections:

receiverStream

Create an input stream with any arbitrary user implemented receiver. It can be customized to meet the use cases.

Find more details at `http://spark.apache.org/docs/latest/` `streaming-custom-receivers.html`.

Following is the API declaration for the `receiverStream`:

```
def receiverStream[T: ClassTag](receiver: Receiver[T]):
ReceiverInputDStream[T
```

socketTextStream

This creates an input stream from TCP source `hostname:port`. Data is received using a TCP socket and the received bytes are interpreted as UTF8 encoded \n delimited lines:

```
def socketTextStream(hostname: String, port: Int,
      storageLevel: StorageLevel =
StorageLevel.MEMORY_AND_DISK_SER_2):
    ReceiverInputDStream[String]
```

rawSocketStream

Create an input stream from network source `hostname:port`, where data is received as serialized blocks (serialized using the Spark's serializer) that can be directly pushed into the block manager without deserializing them. This is the most efficient way to receive data.

```
def rawSocketStream[T: ClassTag](hostname: String, port: Int,
    storageLevel: StorageLevel =
StorageLevel.MEMORY_AND_DISK_SER_2):
    ReceiverInputDStream[T]
```

fileStream

Create an input stream that monitors a Hadoop-compatible filesystem for new files and reads them using the given key-value types and input format. Files must be written to the monitored directory by moving them from another location within the same filesystem. File names starting with a dot (.) are ignored, so this is an obvious choice for the moved file names in the monitored directory. Using an atomic file rename function call, the filename which starts with . can be now renamed to an actual usable filename so that `fileStream` can pick it up and let us process the file content:

```
def fileStream[K: ClassTag, V: ClassTag, F <: NewInputFormat[K, V]:
ClassTag] (directory: String): InputDStream[(K, V)]
```

textFileStream

Create an input stream that monitors a Hadoop-compatible filesystem for new files and reads them as text files (using a key as `LongWritable`, value as Text, and input format as `TextInputFormat`). Files must be written to the monitored directory by moving them from another location within the same filesystem. File names starting with . are ignored:

```
def textFileStream(directory: String): DStream[String]
```

binaryRecordsStream

Create an input stream that monitors a Hadoop-compatible filesystem for new files and reads them as flat binary files, assuming a fixed length per record, generating one byte array per record. Files must be written to the monitored directory by moving them from another location within the same filesystem. File names starting with . are ignored:

```
def binaryRecordsStream(directory: String, recordLength: Int):
DStream[Array[Byte]]
```

queueStream

Create an input stream from a queue of RDDs. In each batch, it will process either one or all of the RDDs returned by the queue:

```
def queueStream[T: ClassTag](queue: Queue[RDD[T]], oneAtATime: Boolean
= true): InputDStream[T]
```

textFileStream example

Shown in the following is a simple example of Spark Streaming using `textFileStream`. In this example, we create a `StreamingContext` from the spark-shell `SparkContext` (`sc`) and an interval of 10 seconds. This starts the `textFileStream`, which monitors the directory named **streamfiles** and processes any new file found in the directory. In this example, we are simply printing the number of elements in the RDD:

```
scala> import org.apache.spark._
scala> import org.apache.spark.streaming._

scala> val ssc = new StreamingContext(sc, Seconds(10))
scala> val filestream = ssc.textFileStream("streamfiles")
scala> filestream.foreachRDD(rdd => {println(rdd.count())})
scala> ssc.start
```

twitterStream example

Let us look at another example of how we can process tweets from Twitter using Spark Streaming:

1. First, open a terminal and change the directory to `spark-2.1.1-bin-hadoop2.7`.

2. Create a folder `streamouts` under the `spark-2.1.1-bin-hadoop2.7` folder where you have spark installed. When the application runs, `streamouts` folder will have collected tweets to text files.

3. Download the following jars into the directory:
   - `http://central.maven.org/maven2/org/apache/bahir/spark-streaming-twitter_2.11/2.1.0/spark-streaming-twitter_2.11-2.1.0.jar`
   - `http://central.maven.org/maven2/org/twitter4j/twitter4j-core/4.0.6/twitter4j-core-4.0.6.jar`
   - `http://central.maven.org/maven2/org/twitter4j/twitter4j-stream/4.0.6/twitter4j-stream-4.0.6.jar`

4. Launch spark-shell with the jars needed for Twitter integration specified:

   ```
   ./bin/spark-shell --jars twitter4j-stream-4.0.6.jar,
                            twitter4j-core-4.0.6.jar,
                            spark-streaming-twitter_2.11-2.1.0.jar
   ```

5. Now, we can write a sample code. Shown in the following is the code to test Twitter event processing:

   ```
   import org.apache.spark._
   import org.apache.spark.streaming._
   import org.apache.spark.streaming.Twitter._
   import twitter4j.auth.OAuthAuthorization
   import twitter4j.conf.ConfigurationBuilder

   //you can replace the next 4 settings with your own Twitter
        account settings.
   System.setProperty("twitter4j.oauth.consumerKey",
                  "8wVysSpBc0LGzbwKMRh8hldSm")
   System.setProperty("twitter4j.oauth.consumerSecret",
   "FpV5MUDWliR6sInqIYIdkKMQEKaAUHdGJkEb4MVhDkh7dXtXPZ")
   System.setProperty("twitter4j.oauth.accessToken",
             "817207925756358656-
   yR0JR92VBdA2rBbgJaF7PYREbiV8VZq")
   System.setProperty("twitter4j.oauth.accessTokenSecret",
             "JsiVkUItwWCGyOLQEtnRpEhbXyZS9jNSzcMtycn68aBaS")
   ```

```
val ssc = new StreamingContext(sc, Seconds(10))

val twitterStream = TwitterUtils.createStream(ssc, None)

twitterStream.saveAsTextFiles("streamouts/tweets", "txt")
ssc.start()

//wait for 30 seconds

ss.stop(false)
```

You will see the `streamouts` folder contains several `tweets` output in text files. You can now open the directory `streamouts` and check that the files contain `tweets`.

Discretized streams

Spark Streaming is built on an abstraction called **Discretized Streams** referred, to as **DStreams**. A DStream is represented as a sequence of RDDs, with each RDD created at each time interval. The DStream can be processed in a similar fashion to regular RDDs using similar concepts such as a directed cyclic graph-based execution plan (Directed Acyclic Graph). Just like a regular RDD processing, the transformations and actions that are part of the execution plan are handled for the DStreams.

DStream essentially divides a never ending stream of data into smaller chunks known as micro-batches based on a time interval, materializing each individual micro-batch as a RDD which can then processed as a regular RDD. Each such micro-batch is processed independently and no state is maintained between micro-batches thus making the processing stateless by nature. Let's say the batch interval is 5 seconds, then while events are being consumed, real-time and a micro-batch are created at every 5-second interval and the micro-batch is handed over for further processing as an RDD. One of the main advantages of Spark Streaming is that the API calls used to process the micro-batch of events are very tightly integrated into the spark for APIs to provide seamless integration with the rest of the architecture. When a micro-batch is created, it gets turned into an RDD, which makes it a seamless process using spark APIs.

The `DStream` class looks like the following in the source code showing the most important variable, a `HashMap[Time, RDD]` pairs:

```
class DStream[T: ClassTag] (var ssc: StreamingContext)

//hashmap of RDDs in the DStream
var generatedRDDs = new HashMap[Time, RDD[T]]()
```

Shown in the following is an illustration of a DStream comprising an RDD created every **T** seconds:

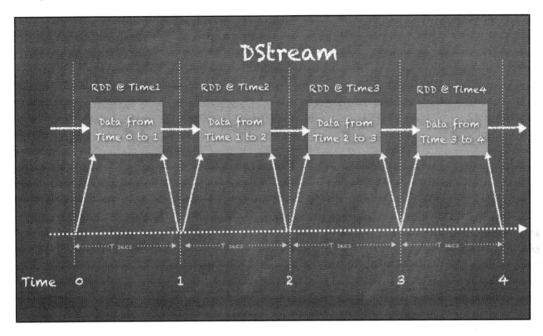

In the following example, a streaming context is created to create micro-batches every 5 seconds and to create an RDD, which is just like a Spark core API RDD. The RDDs in the DStream can be processed just like any other RDD.

The steps involved in building a streaming application are as follows:

1. Create a `StreamingContext` from the `SparkContext`.
2. Create a `DStream` from `StreamingContext`.
3. Provide transformations and actions that can be applied to each RDD.
4. Finally, the streaming application is started by calling `start()` on the `StreamingContext`. This starts the entire process of consuming and processing real-time events.

Once the Spark Streaming application has started, no further operations can be added. A stopped context cannot be restarted and you have to create a new streaming context if such a need arises.

Shown in the following is an example of how to create a simple streaming job accessing Twitter:

1. Create a `StreamingContext` from the `SparkContext`:

```
scala> val ssc = new StreamingContext(sc, Seconds(5))
ssc: org.apache.spark.streaming.StreamingContext =
   org.apache.spark.streaming.StreamingContext@8ea5756
```

2. Create a `DStream` from `StreamingContext`:

```
scala> val twitterStream = TwitterUtils.createStream(ssc, None)
twitterStream: org.apache.spark.streaming.dstream
.ReceiverInputDStream[twitter4j.Status] =
org.apache.spark.streaming.Twitter.TwitterInputDStream@46219d14
```

3. Provide transformations and actions that can be applied to each RDD:

```
val aggStream = twitterStream
    .flatMap(x => x.getText.split(" ")).filter(_.startsWith("#"))
    .map(x => (x, 1))
    .reduceByKey(_ + _)
```

4. Finally, the streaming application is started by calling `start()` on the `StreamingContext`. This starts the entire process of consuming and processing real-time events:

```
ssc.start()
//to stop just call stop on the StreamingContext
ssc.stop(false)
```

5. Created a `DStream` of type `ReceiverInputDStream`, which is defined as an abstract class for defining any `InputDStream` that has to start a receiver on worker nodes to receive external data. Here, we are receiving from Twitter stream:

```
class InputDStream[T: ClassTag](_ssc: StreamingContext)
extends
                                    DStream[T](_ssc)

class ReceiverInputDStream[T: ClassTag](_ssc:
StreamingContext)
                             extends InputDStream[T](_ssc)
```

6. If you run a transformation `flatMap()` on the `twitterStream`, you get a `FlatMappedDStream`, as shown in the following:

```
scala> val wordStream = twitterStream.flatMap(x => x.getText()
                                            .split(" "))
wordStream: org.apache.spark.streaming.dstream.DStream[String] =
org.apache.spark.streaming.dstream.FlatMappedDStream@1ed2dbd5
```

Transformations

Transformations on a DStream are similar to the transformations applicable to a Spark core RDD. Since DStream consists of RDDs, a transformation also applies to each RDD to generate a transformed RDD for the RDD, and then a transformed DStream is created. Every transformation creates a specific `DStream` derived class.

The following diagram shows the hierarchy of DStream classes starting from the parent DStream class. We can also see the different classes inheriting from the parent class:

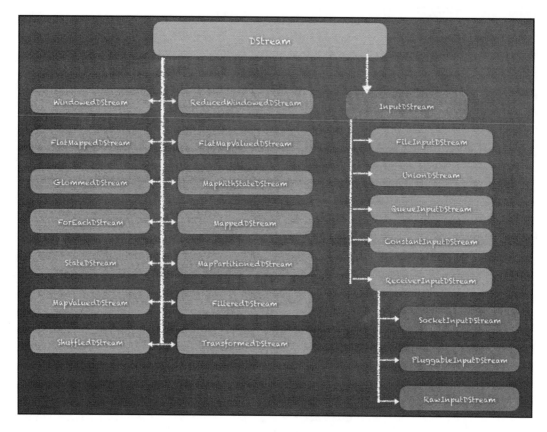

There are a lot of DStream classes purposely built for the functionality. Map transformations, window functions, reduce actions, and different types of input streams are all implemented using different class derived from DStream class.

Shown in the following is an illustration of a transformation on a base DStream to generate a filtered DStream. Similarly, any transformation is applicable to a DStream:

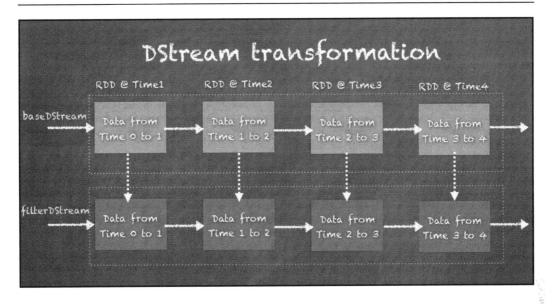

Refer to the following table for the types of transformations possible.

Transformation	Meaning
map(func)	This applies the transformation function to each element of the DStream and returns a new DStream.
flatMap(func)	This is similar to map; however, just like RDD's flatMap versus map, using flatMap operates on each element and applies flatMap, producing multiple output items per each input.
filter(func)	This filters out the records of the DStream to return a new DStream.
repartition(numPartitions)	This creates more or fewer partitions to redistribute the data to change the parallelism.
union(otherStream)	This combines the elements in two source DStreams and returns a new DStream.
count()	This returns a new DStream by counting the number of elements in each RDD of the source DStream.
reduce(func)	This returns a new DStream by applying the reduce function on each element of the source DStream.
countByValue()	This computes the frequency of each key and returns a new DStream of (key, long) pairs.

`reduceByKey(func, [numTasks])`	This aggregates the data by key in the source DStream's RDDs and returns a new DStream of (key, value) pairs.
`join(otherStream, [numTasks])`	This joins two DStreams of *(K, V)* and *(K, W)* pairs and returns a new DStream of *(K, (V, W))* pairs combining the values from both DStreams.
`cogroup(otherStream, [numTasks])`	`cogroup()`, when called on a DStream of *(K, V)* and *(K, W)* pairs, will return a new DStream of *(K, Seq[V], Seq[W])* tuples.
`transform(func)`	This applies a transformation function on each RDD of the source DStream and returns a new DStream.
`updateStateByKey(func)`	This updates the state for each key by applying the given function on the previous state of the key and the new values for the key. Typically, it used to maintain a state machine.

Window operations

Spark Streaming provides windowed processing, which allows you to apply transformations over a sliding window of events. The sliding window is created over an interval specified. Every time the window slides over a source DStream, the source RDDs, which fall within the window specification, are combined and operated upon to generate the windowed DStream. There are two parameters that need to be specified for the window:

- **Window length**: This specifies the length in interval considered as the window
- **Sliding interval**: This is the interval at which the window is created

The window length and the sliding interval must both be a multiple of the block interval.

Shown in the following is an illustration shows a DStream with a sliding window operation showing how the old window (dotted line rectangle) slides by one interval to the right into the new window (solid line rectangle):

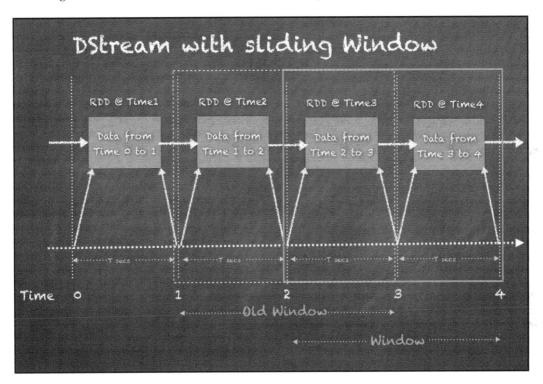

Some of the common window operation are as follows.

Transformation	Meaning
`window(windowLength, slideInterval)`	This creates a window on the source DStream and returns the same as a new DStream.
`countByWindow(windowLength, slideInterval)`	This returns count of elements in the DStream by applying a sliding window.
`reduceByWindow(func, windowLength, slideInterval)`	This returns a new DStream by applying the reduce function on each element of the source DStream after creating a sliding window of length `windowLength`.
`reduceByKeyAndWindow(func, windowLength, slideInterval, [numTasks])`	This aggregates the data by key in the window applied to the source DStream's RDDs and returns a new DStream of (key, value) pairs. The computation is provided by function `func`.
`reduceByKeyAndWindow(func, invFunc, windowLength, slideInterval, [numTasks])`	This aggregates the data by key in the window applied to the source DStream's RDDs and returns a new DStream of (key, value) pairs. The key difference between the preceding function and this one is the `invFunc`, which provides the computation to be done at the beginning of the sliding window.
`countByValueAndWindow(windowLength, slideInterval, [numTasks])`	This computes the frequency of each key and returns a new DStream of (key, long) pairs within the sliding window as specified.

Let us look at the Twitter stream example in more detail. Our goal is to print the top five words used in tweets streamed every five seconds, using a window of length 15 seconds, sliding every 10 seconds. Hence, we can get the top five words in 15 seconds.

To run this code, follow these steps:

1. First, open a terminal and change directory to `spark-2.1.1-bin-hadoop2.7`.

2. Create a folder `streamouts` under the `spark-2.1.1-bin-hadoop2.7` folder where you have spark installed. When the application runs, the `streamouts` folder will have collected tweets to text files.

3. Download the following jars into the directory:

   - `http://central.maven.org/maven2/org/apache/bahir/spark-streaming-twitter_2.11/2.1.0/spark-streaming-twitter_2.11-2.1.0.jar`

   - `http://central.maven.org/maven2/org/twitter4j/twitter4j-core/4.0.6/twitter4j-core-4.0.6.jar`

   - `http://central.maven.org/maven2/org/twitter4j/twitter4j-stream/4.0.6/twitter4j-stream-4.0.6.jar`

4. Launch spark-shell with the jars needed for Twitter integration specified:

   ```
   ./bin/spark-shell --jars twitter4j-stream-4.0.6.jar,
                           twitter4j-core-4.0.6.jar,
                           spark-streaming-twitter_2.11-2.1.0.jar
   ```

5. Now, we can write the code. Shown in the following is the code used to test Twitter event processing:

   ```
   import org.apache.log4j.Logger
   import org.apache.log4j.Level
   Logger.getLogger("org").setLevel(Level.OFF)

   import java.util.Date
   import org.apache.spark._
   import org.apache.spark.streaming._
   import org.apache.spark.streaming.Twitter._
   import twitter4j.auth.OAuthAuthorization
   import twitter4j.conf.ConfigurationBuilder

   System.setProperty("twitter4j.oauth.consumerKey",
                    "8wVysSpBc0LGzbwKMRh8hldSm")
   System.setProperty("twitter4j.oauth.consumerSecret",
   "FpV5MUDWliR6sInqIYIdkKMQEKaAUHdGJkEb4MVhDkh7dXtXPZ")
   System.setProperty("twitter4j.oauth.accessToken",
   ```

```
          "817207925756358656-
yR0JR92VBdA2rBbgJaF7PYREbiV8VZq")
       System.setProperty("twitter4j.oauth.accessTokenSecret",
             "JsiVkUItwWCGyOLQEtnRpEhbXyZS9jNSzcMtycn68aBaS")

   val ssc = new StreamingContext(sc, Seconds(5))

   val twitterStream = TwitterUtils.createStream(ssc, None)

   val aggStream = twitterStream
        .flatMap(x => x.getText.split(" "))
        .filter(_.startsWith("#"))
        .map(x => (x, 1))
        .reduceByKeyAndWindow(_ + _, _ - _, Seconds(15),
                          Seconds(10), 5)

   ssc.checkpoint("checkpoints")
   aggStream.checkpoint(Seconds(10))

   aggStream.foreachRDD((rdd, time) => {
     val count = rdd.count()

     if (count > 0) {
       val dt = new Date(time.milliseconds)
       println(s"\n\n$dt rddCount = $count\nTop 5 words\n")
       val top5 = rdd.sortBy(_._2, ascending = false).take(5)
       top5.foreach {
         case (word, count) =>
         println(s"[$word] - $count")
       }
     }
   })

   ssc.start

   //wait 60 seconds
   ss.stop(false)
```

6. The output is displayed on the console every 15 seconds and looks something like the following:

```
Mon May 29 02:44:50 EDT 2017 rddCount = 1453
Top 5 words

[#RT] - 64
[#de] - 24
[#a] - 15
[#to] - 15
```

```
[#the] - 13


Mon May 29 02:45:00 EDT 2017 rddCount = 3312
Top 5 words

[#RT] - 161
[#df] - 47
[#a] - 35
[#the] - 29
[#to] - 29
```

Stateful/stateless transformations

As seen previously, Spark Streaming uses a concept of DStreams, which are essentially micro-batches of data created as RDDs. We also saw types of transformations that are possible on DStreams. The transformations on DStreams can be grouped into two types: **Stateless transformations** and **Stateful transformations.**

In Stateless transformations, the processing of each micro-batch of data does not depend on the previous batches of data. Thus, this is a stateless transformation, with each batch doing its own processing independently of anything that occurred prior to this batch.

In Stateful transformations, the processing of each micro-batch of data depends on the previous batches of data either fully or partially. Thus, this is a stateful transformation, with each batch considering what happened prior to this batch and then using the information while computing the data in this batch.

Stateless transformations

Stateless transformations transform one DStream to another by applying transformations to each of the RDDs within the DStream. Transformations such as map(), flatMap(), union(), join(), and reduceByKey are all examples of stateless transformations.

Shown in the following is an illustration showing a `map()` transformation on `inputDStream` to generate a new `mapDstream`:

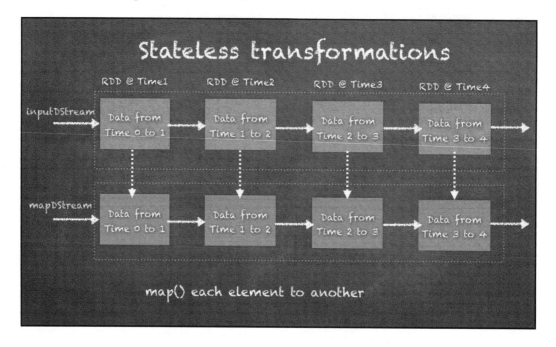

Stateful transformations

Stateful transformations operate on a DStream, but the computations depend on the previous state of processing. Operations such as `countByValueAndWindow`, `reduceByKeyAndWindow`, `mapWithState`, and `updateStateByKey` are all examples of stateful transformations. In fact, all window-based transformations are all stateful because, by the definition of window operations, we need to keep track of the window length and sliding interval of DStream.

Checkpointing

Real-time streaming applications are meant to be long running and resilient to failures of all sorts. Spark Streaming implements a checkpointing mechanism that maintains enough information to recover from failures.

There are two types of data that needs to be checkpointed:

- Metadata checkpointing
- Data checkpointing

Checkpointing can be enabled by calling `checkpoint()` function on the `StreamingContext` as follows:

```
def checkpoint(directory: String)
```

Specifies the directory where the checkpoint data will be reliably stored.

 Note that this must be a fault-tolerant file system like HDFS.

Once checkpoint directory is set, any DStream can be checkpointed into the directory based on a specified interval. Looking at the Twitter example, we can checkpoint each DStream every 10 seconds into the directory `checkpoints`:

```
val ssc = new StreamingContext(sc, Seconds(5))

val twitterStream = TwitterUtils.createStream(ssc, None)

val wordStream = twitterStream.flatMap(x => x.getText().split(" "))

val aggStream = twitterStream
 .flatMap(x => x.getText.split(" ")).filter(_.startsWith("#"))
 .map(x => (x, 1))
 .reduceByKeyAndWindow(_ + _, _ - _, Seconds(15), Seconds(10), 5)

ssc.checkpoint("checkpoints")

aggStream.checkpoint(Seconds(10))

wordStream.checkpoint(Seconds(10))
```

The `checkpoints` directory looks something like the following after few seconds, showing the metadata as well as the RDDs and the `logfiles` are maintained as part of the checkpointing:

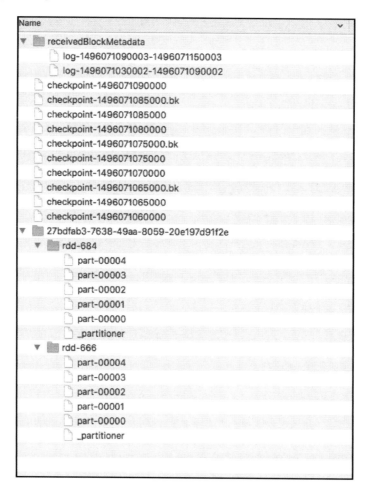

Metadata checkpointing

Metadata checkpointing saves information defining the streaming operations, which are represented by a **Directed Acyclic Graph (DAG)** to the HDFS. This can be used to recover the DAG, if there is a failure and the application is restarted. The driver restarts and reads the metadata from HDFS, and rebuilds the DAG and recovers all the operational state before the crash.

Metadata includes the following:

- **Configuration**: the configuration that was used to create the streaming application
- **DStream operations**: the set of DStream operations that define the streaming application
- **Incomplete batches**: batches whose jobs are queued but have not completed yet

Data checkpointing

Data checkpointing saves the actual RDDs to HDFS so that, if there is a failure of the Streaming application, the application can recover the checkpointed RDDs and continue from where it left off. While streaming application recovery is a good use case for the data checkpointing, checkpointing also helps in achieving better performance whenever some RDDs are lost because of cache cleanup or loss of an executor by instantiating the generated RDDs without a need to wait for all the parent RDDs in the lineage (DAG) to be recomputed.

Checkpointing must be enabled for applications with any of the following requirements:

- **Usage of stateful transformations**: If either `updateStateByKey` or `reduceByKeyAndWindow` (with inverse function) is used in the application, then the checkpoint directory must be provided to allow for periodic RDD checkpointing.
- **Recovering from failures of the driver running the application**: Metadata checkpoints are used to recover with progress information.

If your streaming application does not have the stateful transformations, then the application can be run without enabling checkpointing.

There might be loss of data received but not processed yet in your streaming application.

Note that checkpointing of RDDs incurs the cost of saving each RDD to storage. This may cause an increase in the processing time of those batches where RDDs get checkpointed. Hence, the interval of checkpointing needs to be set carefully so as not to cause performance issues. At tiny batch sizes (say 1 second), checkpointing too frequently every tiny batch may significantly reduce operation throughput. Conversely, checkpointing too infrequently causes the lineage and task sizes to grow, which may cause processing delays as the amount of data to be persisted is large.

For stateful transformations that require RDD checkpointing, the default interval is a multiple of the batch interval that is at least 10 seconds.

A checkpoint interval of 5 to 10 sliding intervals of a DStream is a good setting to start with.

Driver failure recovery

Driver failure recovery can be accomplished by using `StreamingContext.getOrCreate()` to either initialize `StreamingContext` from an existing checkpoint or to create a new StreamingContext.

The two conditions for a streaming application when started are as follows:

- When the program is being started for the first time, it needs to create a new `StreamingContext`, set up all the streams, and then call `start()`
- When the program is being restarted after failure, it needs to initialize a `StreamingContext` from the checkpoint data in the checkpoint directory and then call `start()`

We will implement a function `createStreamContext()`, which creates the `StreamingContext` and sets up the various DStreams to parse the tweets and generate the top five tweet hashtags every 15 seconds using a window. But instead of calling `createStreamContext()` and then calling `ssc.start()`, we will call `getOrCreate()` so that if the `checkpointDirectory` exists, then the context will be recreated from the checkpoint data. If the directory does not exist (the application is running for the first time), then the function `createStreamContext()` will be called to create a new context and set up the DStreams:

```
val ssc = StreamingContext.getOrCreate(checkpointDirectory,
                                       createStreamContext _)
```

Shown in the following is the code showing the definition of the function and how `getOrCreate()` can be called:

```
val checkpointDirectory = "checkpoints"

// Function to create and setup a new StreamingContext
def createStreamContext(): StreamingContext = {
  val ssc = new StreamingContext(sc, Seconds(5))

  val twitterStream = TwitterUtils.createStream(ssc, None)

  val wordStream = twitterStream.flatMap(x => x.getText().split(" "))

  val aggStream = twitterStream
    .flatMap(x => x.getText.split(" ")).filter(_.startsWith("#"))
    .map(x => (x, 1))
    .reduceByKeyAndWindow(_ + _, _ - _, Seconds(15), Seconds(10), 5)

  ssc.checkpoint(checkpointDirectory)

  aggStream.checkpoint(Seconds(10))

  wordStream.checkpoint(Seconds(10))

  aggStream.foreachRDD((rdd, time) => {
    val count = rdd.count()

    if (count > 0) {
      val dt = new Date(time.milliseconds)
      println(s"\n\n$dt rddCount = $count\nTop 5 words\n")
      val top10 = rdd.sortBy(_._2, ascending = false).take(5)
      top10.foreach {
        case (word, count) => println(s"[$word] - $count")
      }
    }
  })
  ssc
}

// Get StreamingContext from checkpoint data or create a new one
val ssc = StreamingContext.getOrCreate(checkpointDirectory,
createStreamContext _)
```

Interoperability with streaming platforms (Apache Kafka)

Spark Streaming has very good integration with Apache Kafka, which is the most popular messaging platform currently. Kafka integration has several approaches, and the mechanism has evolved over time to improve the performance and reliability.

There are three main approaches for integrating Spark Streaming with Kafka:

- Receiver-based approach
- Direct stream approach
- Structured streaming

Receiver-based approach

The receiver-based approach was the first integration between Spark and Kafka. In this approach, the driver starts receivers on the executors that pull data using high-level APIs, from Kafka brokers. Since receivers are pulling events from Kafka brokers, receivers update the offsets into Zookeeper, which is also used by Kafka cluster. The key aspect is the usage of a **WAL** (**Write Ahead Log**), which the receiver keeps writing to as it consumes data from Kafka. So, when there is a problem and executors or receivers are lost or restarted, the WAL can be used to recover the events and process them. Hence, this log-based design provides both durability and consistency.

Each receiver creates an input DStream of events from a Kafka topic while querying Zookeeper for the Kafka topics, brokers, offsets, and so on. After this, the discussion we had about DStreams in previous sections comes into play.

Long-running receivers make parallelism complicated as the workload is not going to be properly distributed as we scale the application. Dependence on HDFS is also a problem along with the duplication of write operations. As for the reliability needed for exactly once paradigm of processing, only the idempotent approach will work. The reason why a transactional approach, will not work in the receiver-based approach is that there is no way to access the offset ranges from the HDFS location or Zookeeper.

 The receiver-based approach works with any messaging system, so it's more general purpose.

You can create a receiver-based stream by invoking the `createStream()` API as follows:

```
def createStream(
  ssc: StreamingContext, // StreamingContext object
  zkQuorum: String, //Zookeeper quorum
(hostname:port,hostname:port,..)
  groupId: String, //The group id for this consumer
  topics: Map[String, Int], //Map of (topic_name to numPartitions) to
                   consume. Each partition is consumed in its own
thread
  storageLevel: StorageLevel = StorageLevel.MEMORY_AND_DISK_SER_2
  Storage level to use for storing the received objects
  (default: StorageLevel.MEMORY_AND_DISK_SER_2)
): ReceiverInputDStream[(String, String)] //DStream of (Kafka message
key, Kafka message value)
```

Shown in the following is an example of creating a receiver-based stream that pulls messages from Kafka brokers:

```
val topicMap = topics.split(",").map((_, numThreads.toInt)).toMap
val lines = KafkaUtils.createStream(ssc, zkQuorum, group,
                             topicMap).map(_._2)
```

Shown in the following is an illustration of how the driver launches receivers on executors to pull data from Kafka using the high-level API. The receivers pull the topic offset ranges from the Kafka Zookeeper cluster and then also update Zookeeper as they pull events from the brokers:

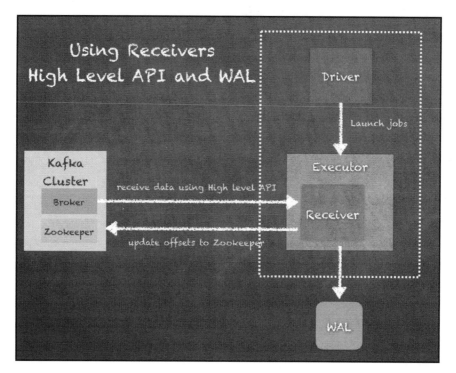

Direct stream

The direct stream based approach is the newer approach with respect to Kafka integration and works by using the driver to connect to the brokers directly and pull events. The key aspect is that using direct stream API, Spark tasks work on a 1:1 ratio when looking at spark partition to Kafka topic/partition. No dependency on HDFS or WAL makes it flexible. Also, since now we can have direct access to offsets, we can use idempotent or transactional approach for exactly once processing.

Create an input stream that directly pulls messages from Kafka brokers without using any receiver. This stream can guarantee that each message from Kafka is included in transformations exactly once.

Properties of a direct stream are as follows:

- **No receivers**: This stream does not use any receiver, but rather directly queries Kafka.
- **Offsets**: This does not use Zookeeper to store offsets, and the consumed offsets are tracked by the stream itself. You can access the offsets used in each batch from the generated RDDs.
- **Failure recovery**: To recover from driver failures, you have to enable checkpointing in the `StreamingContext`.
- **End-to-end semantics**: This stream ensures that every record is effectively received and transformed exactly once, but gives no guarantees on whether the transformed data are outputted exactly once.

You can create a direct stream by using KafkaUtils, `createDirectStream()` API as follows:

```
def createDirectStream[
  K: ClassTag, //K type of Kafka message key
  V: ClassTag, //V type of Kafka message value
  KD <: Decoder[K]: ClassTag, //KD type of Kafka message key decoder
  VD <: Decoder[V]: ClassTag, //VD type of Kafka message value decoder
  R: ClassTag //R type returned by messageHandler
](
  ssc: StreamingContext, //StreamingContext object
  KafkaParams: Map[String, String],
  /*
  KafkaParams Kafka <a
href="http://Kafka.apache.org/documentation.html#configuration">
  configuration parameters</a>. Requires "metadata.broker.list" or
"bootstrap.servers"
to be set with Kafka broker(s) (NOT zookeeper servers) specified in
  host1:port1,host2:port2 form.
  */
  fromOffsets: Map[TopicAndPartition, Long], //fromOffsets Per-
topic/partition Kafka offsets defining the (inclusive) starting point
of the stream
  messageHandler: MessageAndMetadata[K, V] => R //messageHandler
Function for translating each message and metadata into the desired
type
): InputDStream[R] //DStream of R
```

Shown in the following is an example of a direct stream created to pull data from Kafka topics and create a DStream:

```
val topicsSet = topics.split(",").toSet
val KafkaParams : Map[String, String] =
        Map("metadata.broker.list" -> brokers,
            "group.id" -> groupid )

val rawDstream = KafkaUtils.createDirectStream[String, String,
StringDecoder, StringDecoder](ssc, KafkaParams, topicsSet)
```

The direct stream API can only be used with Kafka, so this is not a general purpose approach.

Shown in the following is an illustration of how the driver pulls offset information from Zookeeper and directs the executors to launch tasks to pull events from brokers based on the offset ranges prescribed by the driver:

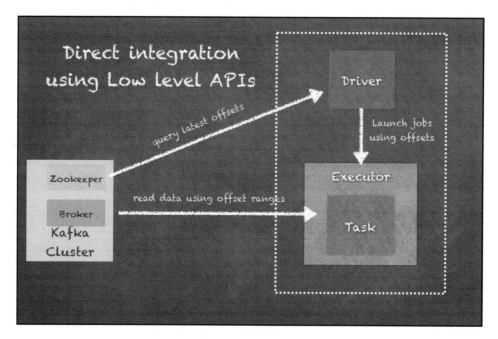

Structured streaming

Structured streaming is new in Apache Spark 2.0+ and is now in GA from Spark 2.2 release. You will see details in the next section along with examples of how to use structured streaming.

> For more details on the Kafka integration in structured streaming, refer to https://spark.apache.org/docs/latest/structured-streaming-kafka-integration.html.

An example of how to use Kafka source stream in structured streaming is as follows:

```
val ds1 = spark
 .readStream
 .format("Kafka")
 .option("Kafka.bootstrap.servers", "host1:port1,host2:port2")
 .option("subscribe", "topic1")
 .load()

ds1.selectExpr("CAST(key AS STRING)", "CAST(value AS STRING)")
 .as[(String, String)]
```

An example of how to use Kafka source instead of source stream (in case you want more batch analytics approach) is as follows:

```
val ds1 = spark
 .read
 .format("Kafka")
 .option("Kafka.bootstrap.servers", "host1:port1,host2:port2")
 .option("subscribe", "topic1")
 .load()

ds1.selectExpr("CAST(key AS STRING)", "CAST(value AS STRING)")
 .as[(String, String)]
```

Structured streaming

Structured streaming is a scalable and fault-tolerant stream processing engine built on top of Spark SQL engine. This brings stream processing and computations closer to batch processing, rather than the DStream paradigm and challenges involved with Spark streaming APIs at this time. The structured streaming engine takes care of several challenges like exactly-once stream processing, incremental updates to results of processing, aggregations, and so on.

The structured streaming API also provides the means to tackle a big challenge of Spark streaming, that is, Spark streaming processes incoming data in micro-batches and uses the received time as a means of splitting the data, thus not considering the actual event time of the data. The structured streaming allows you to specify such an event time in the data being received so that any late coming data is automatically handled.

 The structured streaming is GA in Spark 2.2, and the APIs are marked GA. Refer to `https://spark.apache.org/docs/latest/structured-streaming-programming-guide.html`.

The key idea behind structured streaming is to treat a live data stream as an unbounded table being appended to continuously as events are processed from the stream. You can then run computations and SQL queries on this unbounded table as you normally do on batch data. A Spark SQL query for instance will process the unbounded table:

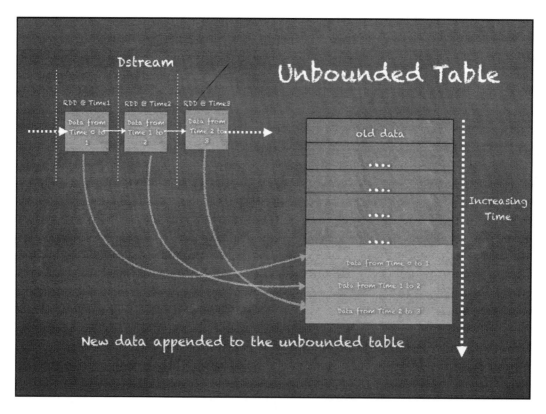

As the DStream keeps changing with time, more and more data will be processed to generate the results. Hence, the unbounded input table is used to generate a result table. The output or results table can be written to an external sink known as **Output**.

The **Output** is what gets written out and can be defined in a different mode:

- **Complete mode**: The entire updated result table will be written to the external storage. It is up to the storage connector to decide how to handle the writing of the entire table.
- **Append mode**: Only any new rows appended to the result table since the last trigger will be written to the external storage. This is applicable only on the queries where existing rows in the result table are not expected to change.
- **Update mode**: Only the rows that were updated in the result table since the last trigger will be written to the external storage. Note that this is different from the complete mode in that this mode only outputs the rows that have changed since the last trigger. If the query doesn't contain aggregations, it will be equivalent to Append mode.

Shown in the following is an illustration of the output from the unbounded table:

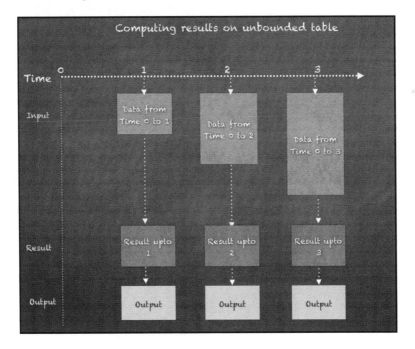

We will show an example of creating a Structured streaming query by listening to input on localhost port 9999.

 If using a Linux or Mac, it's easy to start a simple server on port 9999: nc -lk 9999.

Shown in the following is an example where we start by creating an `inputStream` calling SparkSession's `readStream` API and then extracting the words from the lines. Then we group the words and count the occurrences before finally writing the results to the output stream:

```
//create stream reading from localhost 9999
val inputLines = spark.readStream
  .format("socket")
  .option("host", "localhost")
  .option("port", 9999)
  .load()
inputLines: org.apache.spark.sql.DataFrame = [value: string]

// Split the inputLines into words
val words = inputLines.as[String].flatMap(_.split(" "))
words: org.apache.spark.sql.Dataset[String] = [value: string]

// Generate running word count
val wordCounts = words.groupBy("value").count()
wordCounts: org.apache.spark.sql.DataFrame = [value: string, count:
bigint]

val query = wordCounts.writeStream
  .outputMode("complete")
  .format("console")
query:
org.apache.spark.sql.streaming.DataStreamWriter[org.apache.spark.sql.R
ow] = org.apache.spark.sql.streaming.DataStreamWriter@4823f4d0

query.start()
```

As you keep typing words in the terminal, the query keeps updating and generating results which are printed on the console:

```
scala> -------------------------------------------
Batch: 0
-------------------------------------------
+-----+-----+
|value|count|
```

```
+-----+-----+
| dog|  1|
+-----+-----+


-------------------------------------------
Batch: 1
-------------------------------------------
+-----+-----+
|value|count|
+-----+-----+
| dog|  1|
| cat|  1|
+-----+-----+

scala> -------------------------------------------
Batch: 2
-------------------------------------------

+-----+-----+
|value|count|
+-----+-----+
| dog|  2|
| cat|  1|
+-----+-----+
```

Handling Event-time and late data

Event time is the time inside the data itself. Traditional Spark Streaming only handled time as the received time for the DStream purposes, but this is not enough for many applications where we need the event time. For example, if you want to get the number of times hashtag appears in a tweet every minute, then you should want to use the time when the data was generated, not when Spark receives the event. To get event time into the mix, it is very easy to do so in structured streaming by considering the event time as a column in the row/event. This allows window-based aggregations to be run using the event time rather than the received time. Furthermore, this model naturally handles data that has arrived later than expected based on its event time. Since Spark is updating the result table, it has full control over updating old aggregates when there is late data as well as cleaning up old aggregates to limit the size of intermediate state data. There is also support for watermarking event streams, which allows the user to specify the threshold of late data and allows the engine to accordingly clean up the old state.

Watermarks enable the engine to track the current event times and determine whether the event needs to be processed or has been already processed by checking the threshold of how late data can be received. For instance, if the event time is denoted by `eventTime` and the threshold interval of late arriving data is `lateThreshold`, then by checking the difference between the `max(eventTime)` − `lateThreshold` and comparing with the specific window starting at time T, the engine can determine if the event can be considered for processing in this window or not.

Shown in the following is an extension of the preceding example on structured streaming listening on port 9999. Here we are enabling `Timestamp` as part of the input data so that we can do Window operations on the unbounded table to generate results:

```
import java.sql.Timestamp
import org.apache.spark.sql.SparkSession
import org.apache.spark.sql.functions._

// Create DataFrame representing the stream of input lines from
connection to host:port
val inputLines = spark.readStream
 .format("socket")
 .option("host", "localhost")
 .option("port", 9999)
 .option("includeTimestamp", true)
 .load()

// Split the lines into words, retaining timestamps
val words = inputLines.as[(String, Timestamp)].flatMap(line =>
 line._1.split(" ").map(word => (word, line._2))
).toDF("word", "timestamp")

// Group the data by window and word and compute the count of each
group
val windowedCounts = words.withWatermark("timestamp", "10 seconds")
 .groupBy(
 window($"timestamp", "10 seconds", "10 seconds"), $"word"
).count().orderBy("window")

// Start running the query that prints the windowed word counts to the
console
val query = windowedCounts.writeStream
 .outputMode("complete")
 .format("console")
 .option("truncate", "false")
```

```
query.start()
query.awaitTermination()
```

Fault tolerance semantics

Delivering **end-to-end exactly once semantics** was one of the key goals behind the design of Structured streaming, which implements the Structured streaming sources, the output sinks, and the execution engine to reliably track the exact progress of the processing so that it can handle any kind of failure by restarting and/or reprocessing. Every streaming source is assumed to have offsets (similar to Kafka offsets) to track the read position in the stream. The engine uses checkpointing and write ahead logs to record the offset range of the data being processed in each trigger. The streaming sinks are designed to be idempotent for handling reprocessing. Together, using replayable sources and idempotent sinks, Structured streaming can ensure end-to-end exactly once semantics under any failure.

 Remember that exactly once the paradigm is more complicated in traditional streaming using some external database or store to maintain the offsets.

The structured streaming is still evolving and has several challenges to overcome before it can be widely used. Some of them are as follows:

- Multiple streaming aggregations are not yet supported on streaming datasets
- Limiting and taking first N rows is not supported on streaming datasets
- Distinct operations on streaming datasets are not supported
- Sorting operations are supported on streaming datasets only after an aggregation step is performed and that too exclusively when in complete output mode
- Any kind of join operations between two streaming datasets are not yet supported
- Only a few types of sinks - file sink and for each sink are supported

Summary

In this chapter, we discussed the concepts of the stream processing systems, Spark streaming, DStreams of Apache Spark, what DStreams are, DAGs and lineages of DStreams, Transformations, and Actions. We also looked at window concept of stream processing. We also looked at a practical examples of consuming tweets from Twitter using Spark Streaming.

In addition, we looked at receiver-based and direct stream approaches of consuming data from Kafka. In the end, we also looked at the new structured streaming, which promises to solve many of the challenges such as fault tolerance and exactly once semantics on the stream. We also discussed how structured streaming also simplifies the integration with messaging systems such as Kafka or other messaging systems.

In the next chapter, we will look at graph processing and how it all works.

10
Everything is Connected - GraphX

"Technology made large populations possible; large populations now make technology indispensable."

- Joseph Wood Krutch

In this chapter, we'll learn how many real-world problems can be modeled (and resolved) using graphs. We see that Apache Spark comes with its own graph library, and what you learned about RDDs can be used here too (this time as vertex and edge RDDs).

In a nutshell, the following topics will be covered in this chapter:

- A brief introduction to graph theory
- GraphX
- VertexRDD and EdgeRDD
- Graph operators
- Pregel API
- PageRank

A brief introduction to graph theory

To better understand graphs, let's look at Facebook and how you typically use Facebook. Every day you use your smart phone to post messages on your friend's wall or update your status. Your friends are all posting messages and photos and videos of their own.

You have friends, your friends have friends, who have friends, and so on. Facebook has settings that let you make new friends or remove friends from your friend list. Facebook also has permissions, which allow granular control on who sees what and who can communicate with who.

Now, when you consider that there are a billion Facebook users, the friends and friend's friends list for all users gets quite large and complicated. It is hard to even comprehend and manage all the different relationships or friendships.

So, if someone wants to find out if you and another person *X* are related at all, they can simply start by looking at all your friends and all your friends' friends, and so on, and try to get to the person *X*. If person *X* is a friend of a friend, then you and person *X* are indirectly connected.

 Search for a celebrity or two in your Facebook account and see if someone is a friend of your friend. Maybe you can try to add them as a friend.

We need to build the storage and retrieval of such data about people and their friends so as to allow us to answer questions such as:

- Is X a friend of Y?
- Are X and Y connected directly or within two steps?
- How many friends does X have?

We can start by trying out a simple data structure such as an array such that every person has an array of friends. So now, it's easy to just take the length of the array to answer 3. We can also just scan the array and quickly answer 1. Now, question 2 will need little more work, take the array of friends of *X* and for each such friend scan the array of friends.

We have sort of solved the problem by having a specialized data structure as shown in the following example where we create a case class `Person` and then add friends to build a relationship like this john | ken | mary | dan:

```scala
case class Person(name: String) {
  val friends = scala.collection.mutable.ArrayBuffer[Person]()

  def numberOfFriends() = friends.length

  def isFriend(other: Person) = friends.find(_.name == other.name)
```

```scala
def isConnectedWithin2Steps(other: Person) = {
  for {f <- friends} yield {f.name == other.name ||
                           f.isFriend(other).isDefined}
}.find(_ == true).isDefined
}
```

```scala
scala> val john = Person("John")
john: Person = Person(John)

scala> val ken = Person("Ken")
ken: Person = Person(Ken)

scala> val mary = Person("Mary")
mary: Person = Person(Mary)

scala> val dan = Person("Dan")
dan: Person = Person(Dan)

scala> john.numberOfFriends
res33: Int = 0

scala> john.friends += ken
res34: john.friends.type = ArrayBuffer(Person(Ken))      //john -> ken

scala> john.numberOfFriends
res35: Int = 1

scala> ken.friends += mary
res36: ken.friends.type = ArrayBuffer(Person(Mary))      //john -> ken
-> mary

scala> ken.numberOfFriends
res37: Int = 1

scala> mary.friends += dan
res38: mary.friends.type = ArrayBuffer(Person(Dan))    //john -> ken ->
mary -> dan

scala> mary.numberOfFriends
res39: Int = 1

scala> john.isFriend(ken)
res40: Option[Person] = Some(Person(Ken))         //Yes, ken is a
friend of john

scala> john.isFriend(mary)
res41: Option[Person] = None        //No, mary is a friend of ken not
john
```

```
scala> john.isFriend(dan)
res42: Option[Person] = None        //No, dan is a friend of mary not
john

scala> john.isConnectedWithin2Steps(ken)
res43: Boolean = true       //Yes, ken is a friend of john

scala> john.isConnectedWithin2Steps(mary)
res44: Boolean = true       //Yes, mary is a friend of ken who is a
friend of john

scala> john.isConnectedWithin2Steps(dan)
res45: Boolean = false      //No, dan is a friend of mary who is a
friend of ken who is a friend of john
```

If we build out the Person() instances for all Facebook users and add the friends to the arrays as the preceding code shows, then eventually, we will be able to perform lots of the queries on who is a friend and what is the relationship between any two persons.

The following diagram shows the data structures' Person() instances and how they are related to each other logically:

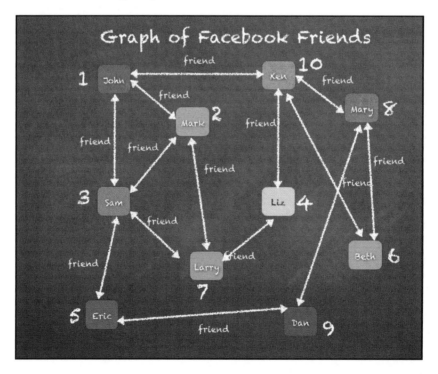

If you want to use the preceding graph and just find out **John**'s friends, **John**'s friend's friends and so on so that we can quickly find out direct friends, indirect friends (friends level 2), and level 3 (friends' friends' friends), you will see something like the following diagram:

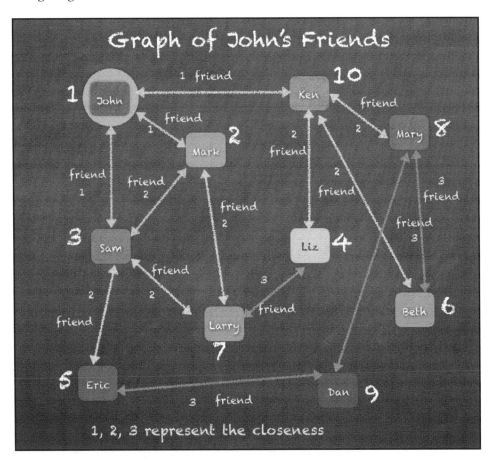

We can easily extend the `Person()` class and provide more and more functionality to answer different questions. That is not the point here, what we want to look at is the preceding diagram showing `Person` and friends of the `Person` and how drawing all the friends of each `Person` yields in a mesh of relationships between persons.

We now introduce the graph theory, which stems from the field of Mathematics. Graph theory defines a graph as a structure made up of vertices, nodes, or points, which are connected by edges, arcs, and lines. If you consider a set of `Vertices` as V and a set of `Edges` as E, then a `Graph G` can be defined as an ordered pair of V and E.

```
Graph G = (V, E)
V - set of Vertices
E - set of Edges
```

In our example of the Facebook friends drawing, we can simply consider each of the persons as a vertex in the set of vertices and then each link between any two persons can be considered as an edge in the set of edges.

By this logic, we can list the **Vertices** and **Edges** as shown in the following diagram:

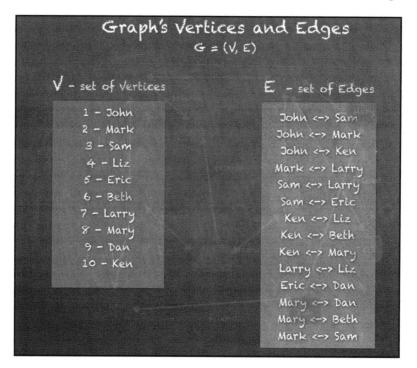

This depiction as a mathematical graph yields to various methodologies of traversing and querying the Graph using mathematical techniques. When the techniques are applied to computer science as a way to develop programmatical methods to perform the math necessary, the formal approach is, of course, to develop algorithms to implement the mathematical rules at a scalable efficient level.

We have already attempted to implement a simple graph-like program using the case class `Person`, but this is just the simplest use case, which should make it obvious that there are a lot of sophisticated extensions possible, such as the following questions to be answered:

- What's the best way from X to Y? An example of such a question can be your car GPS telling you the best way to go to the grocery store.
- Recognize the critical edges, which can cause partitions of the graph? An example of such a question is to determine the critical links connecting the internet services/water pipes/power lines of various cities in the state. A critical edge breaks connectivity and produces two subgraphs of well-connected cities, but there will not be any communication between the two subgraphs.

Answering the preceding questions yields to several algorithms such as minimum spanning tree, shortest path , page rank, **ALS (alternating least squares)**, and max-cut min-flow algorithms, and so on, which are applicable to a broad set of use cases.

The other examples are LinkedIn profiles and connections, Twitter followers, Google page rank, airline scheduling, GPS in your car, and so on, where you can clearly see a graph of vertices and edges. Using graph algorithms, the graph seen earlier in the Facebook, LinkedIn, Google examples can be analyzed using various algorithms to yield different business use cases.

Shown below are illustration of some real-life use cases of graphs which show the use of graphs and graph algorithms in some real-life use cases such as:

- help determine flight routes between airports
- plan how to layout water pipelines to all the households in the locality
- make your car GPS to plan the route to drive to the grocery

- design how the internet traffic is routed from city to city, state to state and country to country

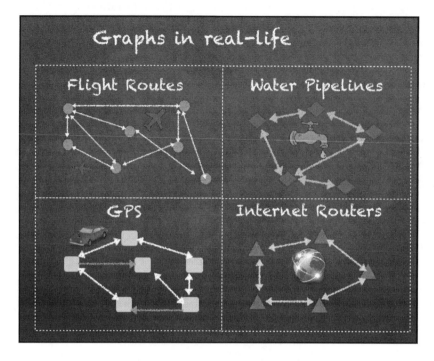

Let's now start digging deeper into how we can use Spark GraphX.

GraphX

As shown in the preceding section, we can model many real-life use cases as Graphs with a set of vertices and a set of edges linking the vertices. We also wrote simple code trying to implement some basic graph operations and queries such as, *Is X a friend of Y* ? However, as we explored further, the algorithms only get more complicated along with use cases and also the size of graphs is much much larger than can be handled on one machine.

 It is not possible to fit one billion Facebook users along with all their friendship relations into one machine or even a few machines.

What we need to do is to look beyond the one machine and few machines thrown together and rather start considering highly scalable architectures to implement the complex graph algorithms, which can handle the volume of data and complex interconnections of the data elements. We have already seen an introduction to Spark, how Spark solves some challenges of distributed computing and big data analytics. We also saw real-time stream processing and Spark SQL along with DataFrames and RDDs. Can we also solve the challenges of graph algorithms? The answer to this is GraphX, which comes with Apache Spark and just like other libraries, sits on top of Spark Core.

GraphX extends the spark RDD by providing a graph abstraction on top of the RDD concept. Graphs in GraphX are created using the concept of vertices or nodes to represent the objects and edges or links to describe the relation between objects and GraphX provides the means to realize many use cases, which suit the graph processing paradigm. In this section, we will learn about GraphX, how to create vertices, edges, and graphs comprising vertices and edges. We will also write code to learn by example some techniques surrounding graph algorithms and processing.

To get started , you will need to import some packages as listed here:

```
import org.apache.spark._
import org.apache.spark.graphx._
import org.apache.spark.rdd.RDD

import org.apache.spark.graphx.GraphLoader
import org.apache.spark.graphx.GraphOps
```

The fundamental data structure of GraphX is a graph, which abstractly represents a graph with arbitrary objects associated with vertices and edges. The graph provides basic operations to access and manipulate the data associated with vertices and edges as well as the underlying structure. Like Spark RDDs, the graph is a functional data structure in which mutating operations return new graphs. This immutable nature of the Graph object makes it possible to do large-scale parallel computations without the risk of running into synchronization problems.

 Concurrent updates or modification of objects is the primary reason for complex multithreading programming done in many programs.

The graph defines the basic data structure and there is a helper class GraphOps, which contains additional convenience operations and graph algorithms.

A graph is defined as follows as a class template with two attributes specifying the data type of the two pieces, which make up the graph, namely, the vertices and the edges:

```
class Graph[VD: ClassTag, ED: ClassTag]
```

A graph consists of vertices and edges as we already discussed. The set of vertices is in a special data structure known as VertexRDD. Similarly, the set of edges is in a special data structure known as EdgeRDD. Together the vertices and edges form the graph and all the subsequent operations can be done using the two data structures.

So, the declaration of the class Graph looks like this:

```
class Graph[VD, ED] {
    //A RDD containing the vertices and their associated attributes.
    val vertices: VertexRDD[VD]

    //A RDD containing the edges and their associated attributes.
      The entries in the RDD contain just the source id and target id
      along with the edge data.
    val edges: EdgeRDD[ED]

    //A RDD containing the edge triplets, which are edges along with the
      vertex data associated with the adjacent vertices.
    val triplets: RDD[EdgeTriplet[VD, ED]]
}
```

Now, let's look at the two main components of the Graph class, the VertexRDD, and the EdgeRDD.

VertexRDD and EdgeRDD

A VertexRDD contains the set of vertices or nodes in a special data structure and an EdgeRDD contains the set of edges or links between the nodes/vertices again in a special data structure. Both the VertexRDD and the EdgeRDD are based on RDDs and the VertexRDD deals with every single node in the graph while the EdgeRDD contains all links between all nodes. In this section, we will look at how to create VertexRDD and EdgeRDD and then use these objects in building a graph.

VertexRDD

As seen earlier, the `VertexRDD` is an RDD containing the vertices and their associated attributes. Each element in the RDD represents a vertex or node in the graph. In order to maintain the uniqueness of the vertex, we need to have a way of assigning a unique ID to each of the vertexes. For this purpose, GraphX defines a very important identifier known as `VertexId`.

 `VertexId` is defined as a 64-bit vertex identifier that uniquely identifies a vertex within a graph. It does not need to follow any ordering or any constraints other than uniqueness.

The declaration of `VertexId` is as follows as simply an alias for a 64-bit `Long` number:

```
type VertexId = Long
```

The `VertexRDD` extends an RDD of a pair of VertexID and vertex attributes represented by `RDD[(VertexId, VD)]`. It also ensures that there is only one entry for each vertex and by preindexing the entries for fast, efficient joins. Two VertexRDDs with the same index can be joined efficiently.

```
class VertexRDD[VD]() extends RDD[(VertexId, VD)]
```

`VertexRDD` also implements many functions, which provide important functionality related to graph operations. Each function typically accepts inputs of vertices represented by `VertexRDD`.

Let's load vertices into a `VertexRDD` of users. For this, we shall first declare a case class `User` as shown here:

```
case class User(name: String, occupation: String)
```

Now, using the file `users.txt`, create the `VertexRDD`:

VertexID	Name	Occupation
1	John	Accountant
2	Mark	Doctor
3	Sam	Lawyer
4	Liz	Doctor
5	Eric	Accountant
6	Beth	Accountant

7	Larry	Engineer
8	Marry	Cashier
9	Dan	Doctor
10	Ken	Librarian

Each line of the file `users.txt` contains **VertexId**, the **Name**, and the **Occupation**, so we can use the `String` split function here:

```scala
scala> val users = sc.textFile("users.txt").map{ line =>
  val fields = line.split(",")
  (fields(0).toLong, User(fields(1), fields(2)))
}
users: org.apache.spark.rdd.RDD[(Long, User)] = MapPartitionsRDD[2645]
at map at <console>:127

scala> users.take(10)
res103: Array[(Long, User)] = Array((1,User(John,Accountant)),
(2,User(Mark,Doctor)), (3,User(Sam,Lawyer)), (4,User(Liz,Doctor)),
(5,User(Eric,Accountant)), (6,User(Beth,Accountant)),
(7,User(Larry,Engineer)), (8,User(Mary,Cashier)),
(9,User(Dan,Doctor)), (10,User(Ken,Librarian)))
```

EdgeRDD

The `EdgeRDD` represents the set of Edges between the vertices and is a member of the Graph class as seen earlier. `EdgeRDD`, just like `VertexRDD`, extends from RDD and takes both Edge attributes and Vertex attributes.

`EdgeRDD[ED, VD]` extends `RDD[Edge[ED]]` by storing the edges in columnar format on each partition for performance. It may additionally store the vertex attributes associated with each edge to provide the triplet view:

```scala
class EdgeRDD[ED]() extends RDD[Edge[ED]]
```

EdgeRDD also implements many functions, which provide important functionality related to graph operations. Each function typically accepts inputs of edges represented by EdgeRDD. Each Edge consists of a source vertexId, destination vertexId and edge attributes such as a `String`, `Integer`, or any case class. In the following example, we use a `String` friend as the attribute. Later in this chapter, we use the distance in miles (`Integer`) as the attribute.

We can create EdgeRDD by reading a file of pairs of vertexIds:

Source Vertex ID	Target/Destination Vertex ID	Distance in Miles
1	3	5
3	1	5
1	2	1
2	1	1
4	10	5
10	4	5
1	10	5
10	1	5
2	7	6
7	2	6
7	4	3
4	7	3
2	3	2

Each line of the `friends.txt` file contains the source `vertexId` and destination `vertexId`, so we can use the `String` split function here:

```scala
scala> val friends = sc.textFile("friends.txt").map{ line =>
  val fields = line.split(",")
  Edge(fields(0).toLong, fields(1).toLong, "friend")
}
friends:
org.apache.spark.rdd.RDD[org.apache.spark.graphx.Edge[String]] =
MapPartitionsRDD[2648] at map at <console>:125

scala> friends.take(10)
res109: Array[org.apache.spark.graphx.Edge[String]] =
Array(Edge(1,3,friend), Edge(3,1,friend), Edge(1,2,friend),
Edge(2,1,friend), Edge(4,10,friend), Edge(10,4,friend),
Edge(1,10,friend), Edge(10,1,friend), Edge(2,7,friend),
Edge(7,2,friend))
```

We now have vertices and edges, so it is time to put everything together and explore how we can build a `Graph` from the lists of vertices and edges:

```scala
scala> val graph = Graph(users, friends)
graph: org.apache.spark.graphx.Graph[User,String] =
org.apache.spark.graphx.impl.GraphImpl@327b69c8

scala> graph.vertices
res113: org.apache.spark.graphx.VertexRDD[User] = VertexRDDImpl[2658]
at RDD at VertexRDD.scala:57

scala> graph.edges
res114: org.apache.spark.graphx.EdgeRDD[String] = EdgeRDDImpl[2660] at
RDD at EdgeRDD.scala:41
```

Using the `Graph` object, we can look at the vertices and edges using the `collect()` function, which will show all vertices and edges. Each vertex is of the form (`VertexId`, `User`) and each edge is of the form (`srcVertexId`, `dstVertexId`, `edgeAttribute`).

```scala
scala> graph.vertices.collect
res111: Array[(org.apache.spark.graphx.VertexId, User)] =
Array((4,User(Liz,Doctor)), (6,User(Beth,Accountant)),
(8,User(Mary,Cashier)), (10,User(Ken,Librarian)),
(2,User(Mark,Doctor)), (1,User(John,Accountant)),
(3,User(Sam,Lawyer)), (7,User(Larry,Engineer)), (9,User(Dan,Doctor)),
(5,User(Eric,Accountant)))

scala> graph.edges.collect
res112: Array[org.apache.spark.graphx.Edge[String]] =
Array(Edge(1,2,friend), Edge(1,3,friend), Edge(1,10,friend),
Edge(2,1,friend), Edge(2,3,friend), Edge(2,7,friend),
Edge(3,1,friend), Edge(3,2,friend), Edge(3,10,friend),
Edge(4,7,friend), Edge(4,10,friend), Edge(7,2,friend),
Edge(7,4,friend), Edge(10,1,friend), Edge(10,4,friend),
Edge(3,5,friend), Edge(5,3,friend), Edge(5,9,friend),
Edge(6,8,friend), Edge(6,10,friend), Edge(8,6,friend),
Edge(8,9,friend), Edge(8,10,friend), Edge(9,5,friend),
Edge(9,8,friend), Edge(10,6,friend), Edge(10,8,friend))
```

Now that we have a graph created, we will look at various operations in the next section.

Graph operators

Let's start with the operations we can directly perform using `Graph` object, such as filtering the vertices and edges of the graph to filter out based on some attribute of the object. We will also see an example of `mapValues()`, which can transform the graph to yield a custom RDD.

First, let's examine the vertices and the edges using the `Graph` object we created in the previous section and then look at some graph operators.

```
scala> graph.vertices.collect
res111: Array[(org.apache.spark.graphx.VertexId, User)] =
Array((4,User(Liz,Doctor)), (6,User(Beth,Accountant)),
(8,User(Mary,Cashier)), (10,User(Ken,Librarian)),
(2,User(Mark,Doctor)), (1,User(John,Accountant)),
(3,User(Sam,Lawyer)), (7,User(Larry,Engineer)), (9,User(Dan,Doctor)),
(5,User(Eric,Accountant)))
```

```
scala> graph.edges.collect
res112: Array[org.apache.spark.graphx.Edge[String]] =
Array(Edge(1,2,friend), Edge(1,3,friend), Edge(1,10,friend),
Edge(2,1,friend), Edge(2,3,friend), Edge(2,7,friend),
Edge(3,1,friend), Edge(3,2,friend), Edge(3,10,friend),
Edge(4,7,friend), Edge(4,10,friend), Edge(7,2,friend),
Edge(7,4,friend), Edge(10,1,friend), Edge(10,4,friend),
Edge(3,5,friend), Edge(5,3,friend), Edge(5,9,friend),
Edge(6,8,friend), Edge(6,10,friend), Edge(8,6,friend),
Edge(8,9,friend), Edge(8,10,friend), Edge(9,5,friend),
Edge(9,8,friend), Edge(10,6,friend), Edge(10,8,friend))
```

Filter

A function call to `filter()` restricts the vertex set to the set of vertices satisfying the given predicate. This operation preserves the index for efficient joins with the original RDD, and it sets bits in the bitmask rather than allocating new memory:

```
def filter(pred: Tuple2[VertexId, VD] => Boolean): VertexRDD[VD]
```

Using `filter`, we can filter out everything but the vertex for user `Mark`, which can be done either using the vertexId or the `User.name` attribute. We can also filter for the `User.occupation` attribute.

The following is the code to accomplish the same:

```scala
scala> graph.vertices.filter(x => x._1 == 2).take(10)
res118: Array[(org.apache.spark.graphx.VertexId, User)] =
Array((2,User(Mark,Doctor)))

scala> graph.vertices.filter(x => x._2.name == "Mark").take(10)
res119: Array[(org.apache.spark.graphx.VertexId, User)] =
Array((2,User(Mark,Doctor)))

scala> graph.vertices.filter(x => x._2.occupation ==
"Doctor").take(10)
res120: Array[(org.apache.spark.graphx.VertexId, User)] =
Array((4,User(Liz,Doctor)), (2,User(Mark,Doctor)),
(9,User(Dan,Doctor)))
```

We can also perform `filter` on the edges too, using either the source vertexId or the destination vertexId. So we can filter out the edges to show only the edges, which originate from `John` (vertexId = 1):

```scala
scala> graph.edges.filter(x => x.srcId == 1)
res123: org.apache.spark.rdd.RDD[org.apache.spark.graphx.Edge[String]]
= MapPartitionsRDD[2672] at filter at <console>:134

scala> graph.edges.filter(x => x.srcId == 1).take(10)
res124: Array[org.apache.spark.graphx.Edge[String]] =
Array(Edge(1,2,friend), Edge(1,3,friend), Edge(1,10,friend))
```

MapValues

`mapValues()` maps each vertex attribute, preserving the index so as not to change the vertexId. Changing the vertexId would have changed the index so much that subsequent operations would fail and the vertices will not be reachable anymore. Hence, it is important to not change the vertexIds.

The declaration of this function is shown here:

```scala
def mapValues[VD2: ClassTag](f: VD => VD2): VertexRDD[VD2]
//A variant of the mapValues() function accepts a vertexId in addition
  to the vertices.
def mapValues[VD2: ClassTag](f: (VertexId, VD) => VD2): VertexRDD[VD2]
```

`mapValues()` can also operate on the edges and maps the values in an edge partitioning preserving the structure but changing the values:

```scala
def mapValues[ED2: ClassTag](f: Edge[ED] => ED2): EdgeRDD[ED2]
```

The following is the example code invoking `mapValues()` in the vertices and edges. MapValues on vertices transforms the vertices to list of pairs of (`vertexId`, `User.name`). MapValues on edges transforms the edges to triplets of (`srcId`, `dstId`, `string`):

```
scala> graph.vertices.mapValues{(id, u) => u.name}.take(10)
res142: Array[(org.apache.spark.graphx.VertexId, String)] =
Array((4,Liz), (6,Beth), (8,Mary), (10,Ken), (2,Mark), (1,John),
(3,Sam), (7,Larry), (9,Dan), (5,Eric))
```

```
scala> graph.edges.mapValues(x => s"${x.srcId} ->
${x.dstId}").take(10)
7), Edge(3,1,3 -> 1), Edge(3,2,3 -> 2), Edge(3,10,3 -> 10), Edge(4,7,4
-> 7))
```

aggregateMessages

The core aggregation operation in GraphX is `aggregateMessages`, which applies a user-defined `sendMsg` function to each edge triplet in the graph and then uses the `mergeMsg` function to aggregate these messages at their destination vertex. `aggregateMessages` is used in many graph algorithms, where we have to exchange information between vertices.

The following is the signature for this API:

```
def aggregateMessages[Msg: ClassTag] (
  sendMsg: EdgeContext[VD, ED, Msg] => Unit,
  mergeMsg: (Msg, Msg) => Msg,
  tripletFields: TripletFields = TripletFields.All)
  : VertexRDD[Msg]
```

The key functions are the `sendMsg` and `mergeMsg`, which determine what gets sent either to source vertex or destination vertex of an edge. Then, `mergeMsg` processes the messages received from all the Edges and performs a computation or aggregation.

The following is a simple example of calling `aggregateMessages` on the Graph graph, where we send a message to all destination vertices. The merge strategy at each vertex is to just add all the messages being received:

```
scala> graph.aggregateMessages[Int](_.sendToDst(1), _ + _).collect
res207: Array[(org.apache.spark.graphx.VertexId, Int)] = Array((4,2),
(6,2), (8,3), (10,4), (2,3), (1,3), (3,3), (7,2), (9,2), (5,2))
```

TriangleCounting

A triangle is created if two neighbors of a vertex are connected by an edge. In other words, a user will create a triangle with the two friends who are friends with each other.

Graph has a function `triangleCount()`, which computes the triangles in the graph.

The following is the code used to count the triangles in the graph by first invoking the `triangleCount` function and then by joining the triangles with the vertices (users) to generate the output of each user and the triangle the user belongs to:

```
scala> val triangleCounts = graph.triangleCount.vertices
triangleCounts: org.apache.spark.graphx.VertexRDD[Int] =
VertexRDDImpl[3365] at RDD at VertexRDD.scala:57

scala> triangleCounts.take(10)
res171: Array[(org.apache.spark.graphx.VertexId, Int)] = Array((4,0),
(6,1), (8,1), (10,1), (2,1), (1,1), (3,1), (7,0), (9,0), (5,0))

scala> val triangleCountsPerUser = users.join(triangleCounts).map {
case(id, (User(x,y), k)) => ((x,y), k) }
triangleCountsPerUser: org.apache.spark.rdd.RDD[((String, String),
Int)] = MapPartitionsRDD[3371] at map at <console>:153

scala> triangleCountsPerUser.collect.mkString("\n")
res170: String =
((Liz,Doctor),0)
((Beth,Accountant),1)   //1 count means this User is part of 1 triangle
((Mary,Cashier),1)   //1 count means this User is part of 1 triangle
((Ken,Librarian),1)   //1 count means this User is part of 1 triangle
((Mark,Doctor),1)   //1 count means this User is part of 1 triangle
((John,Accountant),1)   //1 count means this User is part of 1 triangle
((Sam,Lawyer),1)   //1 count means this User is part of 1 triangle
((Larry,Engineer),0)
((Dan,Doctor),0)
((Eric,Accountant),0)
```

The diagram of the two triangles we just computed in the preceding code shows the two triangles, (**John**, **Mark**, **Sam**) and (**Ken**, **Mary**, **Beth**):

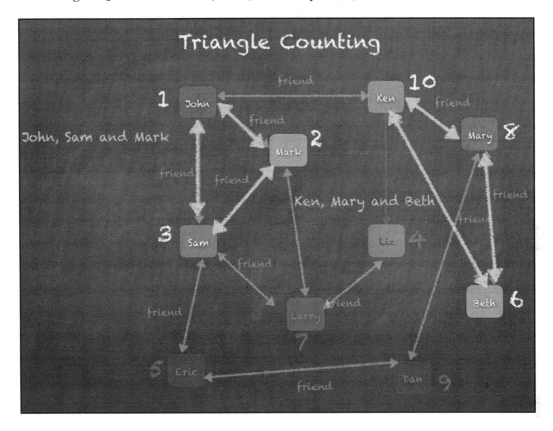

Pregel API

Graphs are inherently recursive data structures as properties of vertices depend on properties of their neighbors, which in turn depend on properties of their own neighbors. As a consequence, many important graph algorithms iteratively recompute the properties of each vertex until a fixed-point condition is reached. A range of graph-parallel abstractions have been proposed to express these iterative algorithms. GraphX exposes a variant of the Pregel API.

At a high level, the Pregel operator in GraphX is a bulk-synchronous parallel messaging abstraction constrained to the topology of the graph. The Pregel operator executes in a series of steps in which vertices receive the sum of their inbound messages from the previous super step, compute a new value for the vertex property, and then send messages to neighboring vertices in the next super step. Using Pregel, messages are computed in parallel as a function of the edge triplet and the message computation has access to both the source and destination vertex attributes. Vertices that do not receive a message are skipped within a super step. The Pregel operators terminate iteration and return the final graph when there are no messages remaining.

Some algorithms which come built-in using Pregel API are as follows:

- ConnectedComponents
- ShortestPaths
- Traveling salesman
- PageRank (covered in the next section)

The Pregel API signature is shown in the following code, which shows the various arguments needed. The exact usage will be shown in the subsequent sections, so you can refer to this signature for clarification:

```
def pregel[A]
 (initialMsg: A,    // the initial message to all vertices
 maxIter: Int = Int.MaxValue,   // number of iterations
 activeDir: EdgeDirection = EdgeDirection.Out)
 // incoming or outgoing edges
 (vprog: (VertexId, VD, A) => VD,
 sendMsg: EdgeTriplet[VD, ED] => Iterator[(VertexId, A)],
 //send message function
 mergeMsg: (A, A) => A) //merge strategy
 : Graph[VD, ED]
```

ConnectedComponents

Connected components are essentially subgraphs within a graph, where the vertices are connected to each other in some way. This means that every vertex in the same component has an edge to/from some other vertex in the component. Whenever no other edge exists to connect a vertex to a component, a new component is created with that specific vertex. This continues until all vertices are in some component.

The graph object provides a `connectComponents()` function to compute the connected components. This uses the Pregel API underneath to calculate the component a vertex belongs to. The following is the code to calculate connected components in the graph. Obviously, in this example, we had only one connected component, so it shows one as the component number for all users:

```
scala> graph.connectedComponents.vertices.collect
res198: Array[(org.apache.spark.graphx.VertexId,
org.apache.spark.graphx.VertexId)] = Array((4,1), (6,1), (8,1),
(10,1), (2,1), (1,1), (3,1), (7,1), (9,1), (5,1))

scala> graph.connectedComponents.vertices.join(users).take(10)
res197: Array[(org.apache.spark.graphx.VertexId,
(org.apache.spark.graphx.VertexId, User))] =
Array((4,(1,User(Liz,Doctor))), (6,(1,User(Beth,Accountant))),
(8,(1,User(Mary,Cashier))), (10,(1,User(Ken,Librarian))),
(2,(1,User(Mark,Doctor))), (1,(1,User(John,Accountant))),
(3,(1,User(Sam,Lawyer))), (7,(1,User(Larry,Engineer))),
(9,(1,User(Dan,Doctor))), (5,(1,User(Eric,Accountant))))
```

Traveling salesman problem

Traveling salesman problem tried to find the shortest path through an undirected graph traversing every vertex, for example, user, John, wants to drive to every other user minimizing the total distance driven. As the number of vertices and edges increase, the number of permutations also increases polynomially to cover all the possible paths from vertex to vertex. The time complexity increases polynomially to a point that the problem can take a very long time to solve. Rather than solve it completely and accurately, an approach known as a **greedy** algorithm is used to solve the problem as optimally as possible.

To solve the traveling salesman problem, the greedy approach is to quickly choose the shortest edge, knowing that this could be a nonoptimal selection if we traverse further depth-wise.

A diagram of the greedy algorithm on the graph of users and friends is as follows, where we see the traversal picking the shortest weighted edge at each vertex. Also note that the vertices **Larry** (7) and **Liz** (4) are never visited:

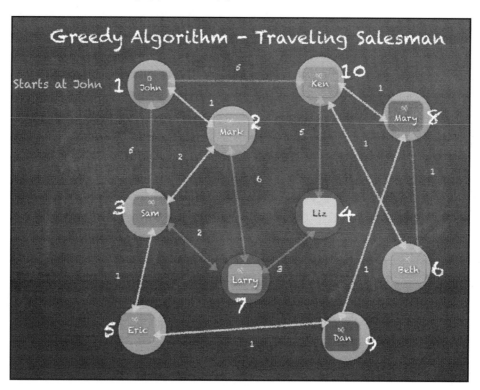

ShortestPaths

Shortest paths algorithm finds the path between two vertices by starting at the source Vertex and then traversing the edges connecting the vertices to other vertices until it reaches the target vertex. The shortest paths algorithm works by exchanging messages between various vertices. Also this shortest paths algorithm is not directly a part of the `Graph` or `GraphOps` objects, rather must be invoked using `lib.ShortestPaths()`:

```scala
scala>
lib.ShortestPaths.run(graph,Array(1)).vertices.join(users).take(10)

res204: Array[(org.apache.spark.graphx.VertexId,
(org.apache.spark.graphx.lib.ShortestPaths.SPMap, User))] =
```

```
Array((4,(Map(1 -> 2),User(Liz,Doctor))), (6,(Map(1 ->
2),User(Beth,Accountant))), (8,(Map(1 -> 2),User(Mary,Cashier))),
(10,(Map(1 -> 1),User(Ken,Librarian))), (2,(Map(1 ->
1),User(Mark,Doctor))), (1,(Map(1 -> 0),User(John,Accountant))),
(3,(Map(1 -> 1),User(Sam,Lawyer))), (7,(Map(1 ->
2),User(Larry,Engineer))), (9,(Map(1 -> 3),User(Dan,Doctor))),
(5,(Map(1 -> 2),User(Eric,Accountant))))
```

`ShortestPaths` picks the shortest paths in terms of number of hops between the two vertices. The following diagram shows three ways **John** can reach **Larry** and two of the paths are of length 2 and one of length 3. From the results of the preceding code, it clearly shows that the path chosen from **Larry** to John is of length 2.

The same is shown in the output in above code block as a vector containing the length of the path and the nodes (7,(Map(1 -> 2),User(Larry,Engineer))):

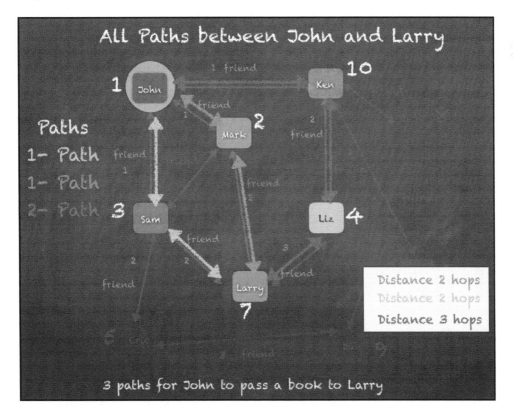

We can also compute the shortest path using weighted edges, which means every edge connecting users is not the same. For example, if we can consider the edge value/weight/attribute as the distance between where each user lives, we get a weighted graph. In this case, the shortest path is calculated by the distance between two users in miles:

```scala
scala> val srcId = 1 //vertex ID 1 is the user John
srcId: Int = 1

scala> val initGraph = graph.mapVertices((id, x) => if(id == srcId)
0.0 else Double.PositiveInfinity)
initGraph: org.apache.spark.graphx.Graph[Double,Long] =
org.apache.spark.graphx.impl.GraphImpl@2b9b8608

scala> val weightedShortestPath =
initGraph.pregel(Double.PositiveInfinity, 5)(
 | (id, dist, newDist) => math.min(dist, newDist),
 | triplet => {
 | if (triplet.srcAttr + triplet.attr < triplet.dstAttr) {
 | Iterator((triplet.dstId, triplet.srcAttr + triplet.attr))
 | }
 | else {
 | Iterator.empty
 | }
 | },
 | (a, b) => math.min(a, b)
 | )
weightedShortestPath: org.apache.spark.graphx.Graph[Double,Long] =
org.apache.spark.graphx.impl.GraphImpl@1f87fdd3

scala> weightedShortestPath.vertices.take(10).mkString("\n")
res247: String =
(4,10.0)
(6,6.0)
(8,6.0)
(10,5.0)
(2,1.0)
(1,0.0)
(3,3.0)
(7,7.0)
(9,5.0)
(5,4.0)
```

The following is a diagram that uses Pregel API to compute the **Single Source Shortest Path** from **John** to **Larry** starting from initialization and iteration by iteration until we reach the best paths.

Initialization of the graph is done by setting the value of vertex representing **John** to zero and all other vertices to positive infinity:

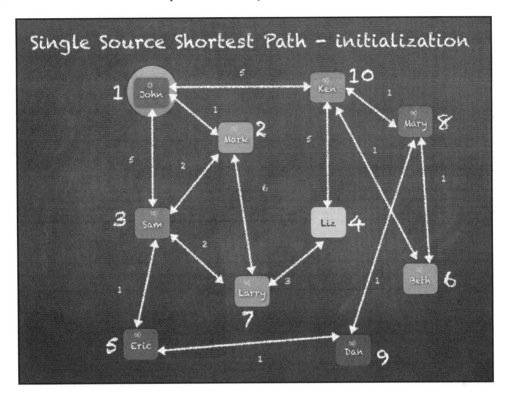

Once the initialization is complete, we will use Pregel for four iterations of recomputing the vertex values. In each iteration, we go through all the vertices and, at each vertex, check whether there is a better path from a source vertex to a destination vertex. If there is such an edge/path, then the vertex value is updated.

Let's define two functions *distance(v)* and *distance(s, t)*, where *distance(v)* gives the value of a vertex and *distance(s,t)* gives the value of the edge connecting s to t.

In Iteration 1, every user except John is set to infinity and John is at 0, since he is the source vertex. Now, we use Pregel to loop through the vertices and check whether there is anything better than infinity. Using Ken as an example, we will check if *distance("John") + distance("John", "Ken") < distance("Ken")*.

This is equivalent to checking whether *0 + 5 < Infinity*, which is `true`; so we update Ken's distance to 5.

Similarly, we check for Mary, *distance("Ken") + distance("Ken", "Mary") < distance("Mary")*, which turns out to be `false`, since at that time Ken is still at infinity. Hence, in iteration 1, we could only update the users who are connected to John.

In the next iteration, Mary, Liz, Eric and so on, are all updated since now we have updated values for Ken, Mark, and Sam from iteration 1. This continues for a number of iterations specified in the Pregel API call.

Shown below are the illustrations of the various iterations when computing single source shortest path on the graph:

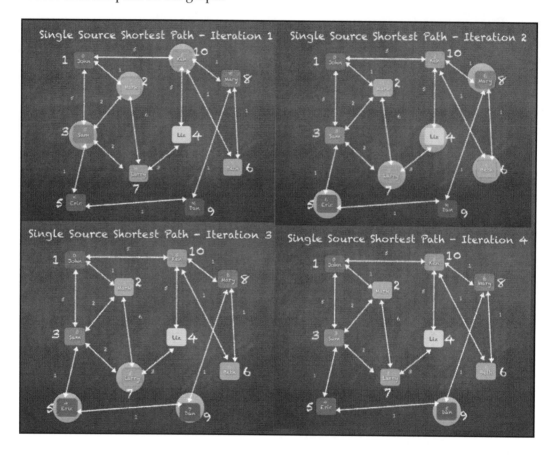

The shortest paths from **John** to **Larry** after four iterations shows that the shortest path is five miles. The path from **John** to **Larry** can be seen if you follow the path **John | Mark | Sam | Larry**:

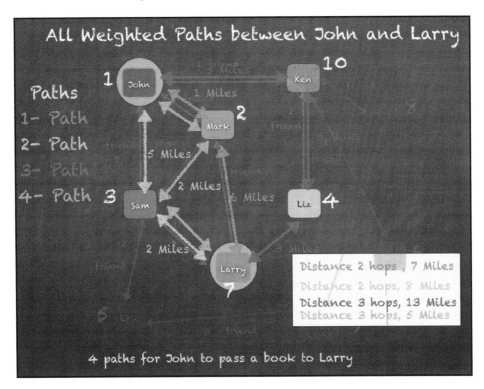

PageRank

PageRank is one of the most important algorithms in the graph processing space. Originating at Google, the algorithm named after Larry page, the founder of Google, has evolved into many types of use cases based on the concept of ranking vertices or nodes based on relationships or edges.

Google PageRank works by counting the number and quality of links to a page to determine a rough estimate of how important the website is. The underlying assumption is that more important websites are likely to receive more links from other websites. For more information, you can read the description at `https://en.wikipedia.org/wiki/PageRank`

Using Google PageRank as an example, you can improve the relative importance of a web page on your company website or maybe your blog by promoting the web page among other popular websites and technical blogs. Using this approach, your blog website may appear in Google search results about some article higher than other similar web pages, if there are a lot of third-party websites, which show your blog website and the content.

 Search Engine Optimization (SEO) is one of the biggest industries in the marketing world, where pretty much every website out there is investing into this technology. SEO involves various techniques and strategies essentially to improve how far up your website appears in any search engine results when anyone searches for some relevant words. This is based on Google PageRank-like concept.

If you consider web pages as nodes/vertices and the hyperlinks between the web pages as edges, we essentially created a graph. Now, if you can count the rank of a web page as the number of hyperlinks/edges pointed into such as your `myblog.com` site having links on `cnn.com` or `msnbc.com` so that a user can click on the link and come to your `myblog.com` page. This can be a factor representing the importance of the `myblog.com` vertex. If we apply this simple logic recursively, we eventually end up with a rank assigned to each vertex calculated using the number of incoming edges and PageRank based on the ranks of the source vertices. A page that is linked to by many pages with high PageRank receives a high rank itself. Let's look at how to solve the PageRank problem at a big data scale using Spark GraphX. As we have seen, PageRank measures the importance of each vertex in a graph, assuming an edge from **a** to **b** represents the value of **b** boosted by **a**. For example, if a Twitter user is followed by many others, the user will be ranked highly.

GraphX comes with static and dynamic implementations of PageRank as methods on the `pageRank` object. Static PageRank runs for a fixed number of iterations, while dynamic PageRank runs until the ranks converge. `GraphOps` allows calling these algorithms directly as methods on the graph:

```scala
scala> val prVertices = graph.pageRank(0.0001).vertices
prVertices: org.apache.spark.graphx.VertexRDD[Double] =
VertexRDDImpl[8245] at RDD at VertexRDD.scala:57

scala> prVertices.join(users).sortBy(_._2._1, false).take(10)
res190: Array[(org.apache.spark.graphx.VertexId, (Double, User))] =
Array((10,(1.4600029149839906,User(Ken,Librarian))),
(8,(1.1424200609462447,User(Mary,Cashier))),
(3,(1.1279748817993318,User(Sam,Lawyer))),
(2,(1.1253662371576425,User(Mark,Doctor))),
(1,(1.0986118723393328,User(John,Accountant))),
```

```
(9,(0.8215535923013982,User(Dan,Doctor))),
(5,(0.8186673059832846,User(Eric,Accountant))),
(7,(0.8107902215195832,User(Larry,Engineer))),
(4,(0.8047583729877394,User(Liz,Doctor))),
(6,(0.783902117150218,User(Beth,Accountant))))
```

The diagram of the PageRank algorithm on the graph is as follows:

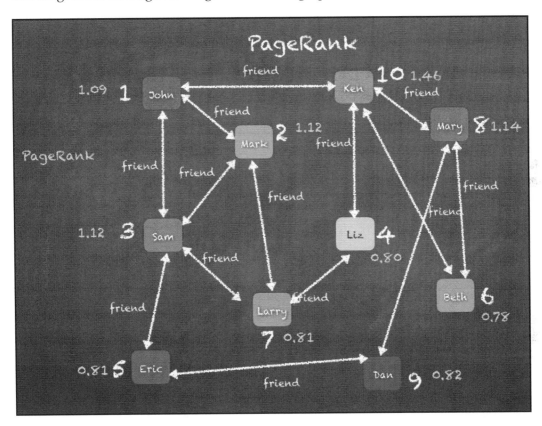

Summary

In this chapter, we have introduced graph theory using Facebook as an example; Apache Spark's graph processing library GraphX, `VertexRDD`, and EdgeRDDs; graph operators, `aggregateMessages`, `TriangleCounting`, and the Pregel API; and use cases such as the PageRank algorithm. We have also seen the traveling salesman problem and connected components and so on. We have seen how the GraphX API can be used to develop graph processing algorithms at scale.

In Chapter 11, *Learning Machine Learning - Spark MLlib and ML*, we will explore the exciting world of Apache Spark's Machine Learning library.

11
Learning Machine Learning - Spark MLlib and Spark ML

"Each of us, actually every animal, is a data scientist. We collect data from our sensors, and then we process the data to get abstract rules to perceive our environment and control our actions in that environment to minimize pain and/or maximize pleasure. We have memory to store those rules in our brains, and then we recall and use them when needed. Learning is lifelong; we forget rules when they no longer apply or revise them when the environment changes."

- Ethem Alpaydin, Machine Learning: The New AI

The purpose of this chapter is to provide a conceptual introduction to statistical machine learning (ML) techniques for those who might not normally be exposed to such approaches during their typical required statistical training. This chapter also aims to take a newcomer from having minimal knowledge of machine learning all the way to being a knowledgeable practitioner in a few steps. We will focus on Spark's machine learning APIs, called Spark MLlib and ML, in theoretical and practical ways. Furthermore, we will provide some examples covering feature extraction and transformation, dimensionality reduction, regression, and classification analysis. In a nutshell, we will cover the following topics in this chapter:

- Introduction to machine learning
- Spark machine learning APIs
- Feature extractor and transformation
- Dimensionality reduction using PCA for regression
- Binary and multiclass classification

Introduction to machine learning

In this section, we will try to define machine learning from computer science, statistics, and data analytical perspectives. **Machine learning (ML)** is the branch of computer science that provides the computers the ability to learn without being explicitly programmed (Arthur Samuel in 1959). This field of study being evolved from the study of pattern recognition and computational learning theory in artificial intelligence.

More specifically, ML explores the study and construction of algorithms that can learn from heuristics and make predictions on data. This kind of algorithms overcome the strictly static program instructions by making data-driven predictions or decisions, through building a model from sample inputs. Now let's more explicit and versatile definition from Prof. Tom M. Mitchell, who explained what machine learning really means from the computer science perspective:

> *A computer program is said to learn from experience E with respect to some class of tasks T and performance measure P, if its performance at tasks in T, as measured by P, improves with experience E.*

Based on that definition, we can conclude that a computer program or machine can:

- Learn from data and histories
- Be improved with experience
- Interactively enhance a model that can be used to predict the outcomes of questions

Typical machine learning tasks are concept learning, predictive modeling, clustering, and finding useful patterns. The ultimate goal is to improve learning in such a way that it becomes automatic so that no human interactions are needed anymore, or to reduce the level of human interaction as much as possible. Although machine learning is sometimes conflated with **Knowledge Discovery and Data Mining (KDDM)**, but KDDM, focuses more on exploratory data analysis and is known as unsupervised learning. Typical machine learning applications can be classified into scientific knowledge discovery and more commercial applications, ranging from Robotics or **Human-Computer Interaction (HCI)** to anti-spam filtering and recommender systems.

Typical machine learning workflow

A typical machine learning application involves several steps ranging from the input, processing, to output, which forms a scientific workflow, as shown in *Figure 1*. The following steps are involved in a typical machine learning application:

1. Load the sample data.
2. Parse the data into the input format for the algorithm.
3. Preprocess the data and handle the missing values.
4. Split the data into two sets: one for building the model (training dataset) and one for testing the model (validation dataset).
5. Run the algorithm to build or train your ML model.
6. Make predictions with the training data and observe the results.
7. Test and evaluate the model with the test data or, alternatively, validate the model using a cross-validator technique using the third dataset, called the validation dataset.
8. Tune the model for better performance and accuracy.
9. Scale up the model so that it will be able to handle massive datasets in future.
10. Deploy the ML model in commercialization.

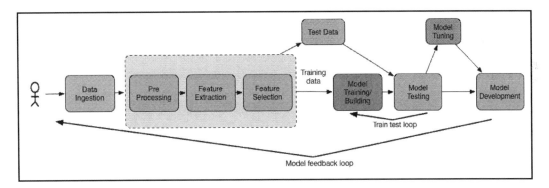

Figure 1: Machine learning workflow

Often, the machine learning algorithms have some ways to handle skewness in the datasets. That skewness is sometimes immense though. In step 4, the experimental dataset is randomly split, often into a training set and a test set, which is called sampling. The training dataset is used to train the model, whereas the test dataset is used to evaluate the performance of the best model at the very end.

The better practice is to use the training dataset as much as you can to increase generalization performance. On the other hand, it is recommended to use the test dataset only once, to avoid the overfitting problem while computing the prediction error and the related metrics.

Machine learning tasks

depending on the nature of the learning feedback available to a learning system, ML tasks or process are typically classified into three broad categories: supervised learning, unsupervised learning, and reinforcements learning shown in figure 2. Furthermore, there are other machine learning tasks as well, for example, dimensionality reduction, recommendation system, frequent pattern mining, and so on.

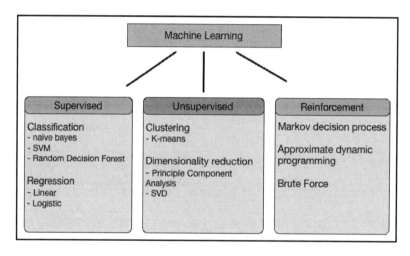

Figure 2: Machine learning tasks

Supervised learning

A supervised learning application makes predictions based on a set of examples, and the goal is to learn general rules that map inputs to outputs aligning with the real world. For example, a dataset for spam filtering usually contains spam messages as well as non-spam messages. Therefore, we are able to know whether messages in the training set are spam or ham. Nevertheless, we might have the opportunity to use this information to train our model in order to classify new unseen messages.

The following figure shows the schematic diagram of supervised learning. After the algorithm has found the required patterns, those patterns can be used to make predictions for unlabeled test data. This is the most popular and useful type of machine learning task, that is not an exception for Spark as well, where most of the algorithms are supervised learning techniques:

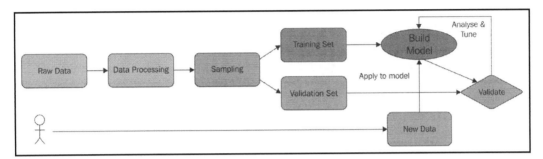

Figure 3: Supervised learning in action

Examples include classification and regression for solving supervised learning problems. We will provide several examples of supervised learning, such as logistic regression, random forest, decision trees, Naive Bayes, One-vs-the-Rest, and so on in this book. However, to make the discussion concrete, only logistic regression and the random forest will be discussed, and other algorithms will be discussed in Chapter 12, *Advanced Machine Learning Best Practices*, with some practical examples. On the other hand, linear regression will be discussed for the regression analysis.

Unsupervised learning

In unsupervised learning, data points have no labels related with them. Therefore, we need to put labels on it algorithmically, as shown in the following figure. In other words, the correct classes of the training dataset in unsupervised learning are unknown. Consequently, classes have to be inferred from the unstructured datasets, which imply that the goal of an unsupervised learning algorithm is to preprocess the data in some structured ways by describing its structure.

To overcome this obstacle in unsupervised learning, clustering techniques are commonly used to group the unlabeled samples based on certain similarity measures. Therefore, this task also involves mining hidden patterns toward feature learning. Clustering is the process of intelligently categorizing the items in your dataset. The overall idea is that two items in the same cluster are "closer" to each other than items that belong to separate clusters. That is the general definition, leaving the interpretation of "closeness" open.

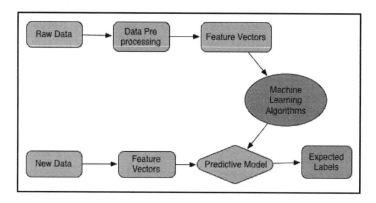

Figure 4: Unsupervised learning

Examples include clustering, frequent pattern mining, and dimensionality reduction for solving unsupervised learning problems (it can be applied to supervised learning problems too). We will provide several examples of unsupervised learning, such as k-means, bisecting k-means, Gaussian mixture model, **Latent dirichlet allocation (LDA)**, and so on, in this book. We will also show how to use a dimensionality reduction algorithm such as **Principal Component Analysis (PCA)** or **Singular Value Decomposition (SVD)** in supervised learning through regression analysis.

Dimensionality reduction (DR): Dimensionality reduction is a technique used to reduce the number of random variables under certain considerations. This technique is used for both supervised and unsupervised learning. Typical advantages of using DR techniques are as follows:

- It reduces the time and storage space required in machine learning tasks
- It helps remove multicollinearity and improves the performance of the machine learning model
- Data visualization becomes easier when reduced to very low dimensions such as 2D or 3D

Reinforcement learning

As a human being, you and we also learn from past experiences. We haven't got so charming by accident. Years of positive compliments as well as negative criticism have all helped shape us who we are today. You learn what makes people happy by interacting with friends, family, or even strangers, and you figure out how to ride a bike by trying out different muscle movements until it just clicks. When you perform actions, you're sometimes rewarded immediately. For example, finding a shopping mall nearby might yield instant gratification. Other times, the reward doesn't appear right away, such as traveling a long distance to find an exceptional place to eat. These are all about Reinforcement Learning (RL).

Thus RL is a technique, where the model itself learns from a series of actions or behaviors. The complexity of the dataset, or sample complexity, is very important in the reinforcement learning needed for the algorithms to learn a target function successfully. Moreover, in response to each data point for achieving the ultimate goal, maximization of the reward function should be ensured while interacting with an external environment, as demonstrated in the following figure:

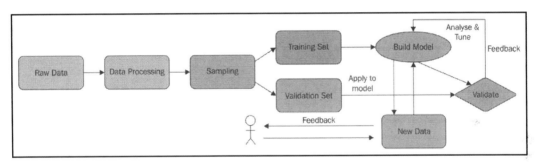

Figure 5: Reinforcement learning

Reinforcement learning techniques are being used in many areas. Here's a very short list includes the following:

- Advertising helps in learning rank, using one-shot learning for emerging items, and new users will bring more money
- Teaching robots new tasks, while retaining prior knowledge
- Deriving complex hierarchical schemes, from chess gambits to trading strategies

- Routing problems, for example, management of a shipping fleet, which trucks/truckers to assign to which cargo
- In robotics, the algorithm must choose the robot's next action based on a set of sensor readings
- It is also a natural fit for **Internet of Things (IoT)** applications, where a computer program interacts with a dynamic environment in which it must perform a certain goal without an explicit mentor
- One of the simplest RL problems is called n-armed bandits. The thing is there are n-many slot machines but each has different fixed pay-out probability. The goal is to maximize the profit by always choosing the machine with the best payout

- An emerging area for applying is the stock market trading. Where a trader acts like a reinforcement agent since buying and selling (i.e. action) particular stock changes the state of the trader by generating profit or loss i.e. reward.

Recommender system

A recommender system is a subclass of an information filtering system that looks to predict the rating or preference that users usually provide for an item. The concept of recommender systems has become very common in recent years subsequently being applied in different applications.

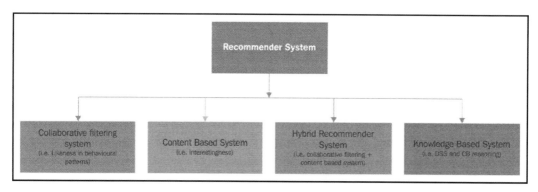

Figure 6: Different recommender system

The most popular ones are probably products (for example, movies, music, books, research articles, news, search queries, social tags, and so on). Recommender systems can be classified into the following four categories typically:

- Collaborative filtering, also referred to as social filtering that filters information by using the recommendations of other people. The thing is people who agreed in their evaluation of certain items in the past are likely to agree again in the future. Therefore, a person who wants to see a movie for example, might ask for recommendations from his/her friends. Now once he received the recommendations from some of his/her friends who have similar interests, are trusted more than recommendations from others. This information is used in the decision on which movie to see.

- Content-based filtering (also known as cognitive filtering), which recommends items based on a comparison between the content of the items and a user profile. The content of each item is represented as a set of descriptors or terms, typically the words that occur in a document. The user profile is represented with the same terms and built up by analyzing the content of items that have been seen by the user. However, while implementing these types of recommendation systems, some issues that need to be considered are as follows:
    - First, terms can be assigned automatically or manually. For automatic assignment, a method has to be chosen so that these items can be extracted from the item list. Second, terms have to be represented in a way so that both the user profile and the items can be compared in a meaningful way. The learning algorithm itself has to be chosen wisely so that it's going to be able to learn a user profile based on already observer (that is, seen) items and makes appropriate recommendations based on this user profile. Content-based filtering systems are mostly used with text documents, where term parsers are used to select single words from the documents. The vector space model and latent semantic indexing are two methods that use these terms to represent documents as vectors in a multidimensional space. Furthermore, it is also used in relevance feedback, genetic algorithms, neural networks, and the Bayesian classifier for learning a user profile.

- A hybrid recommender system is a recent research and hybrid approach (that is, combining collaborative filtering and content-based filtering). Netflix is a good example of such a recommendation system that uses the **Restricted Boltzmann Machines** (**RBM**) and a form of the matrix factorization algorithm for large movie database like IMDb (see more at `https://pdfs.semanticscholar.org/789a/d4218d1e2e920b4d192023f840fe8246d746.pdf`). This recommendation which simply recommends movies, dramas, or streaming by comparing the watching and searching habits of similar users, is called rating prediction.
- Knowledge-based systems, where knowledge about users and products is used to reason what fulfills a user's requirements, using perception tree, decision support systems, and case-based reasoning.

In this chapter, we will discuss the collaborative filtering based recommender system for the movie recommendations.

Semisupervised learning

Between supervised and unsupervised learning, there is a small place for semi-supervised learning. In this case, the ML model usually receives an incomplete training signal. More statistically, the ML model receives a training set with some of the target outputs missing. Semi-supervised learning is more or less assumption based and often uses three kinds of assumption algorithms as the learning algorithm for the unlabeled datasets. The following assumptions are used: smoothness, cluster, and manifold. In other words, semi-supervised learning can furthermore be denoted as weakly supervised or a bootstrapping technique for using the hidden wealth of unlabeled examples to enhance the learning from a small amount of labeled data.

As already mentioned that the acquisition of labeled data for a learning problem often requires a skilled human agent. Therefore, the cost associated with the labeling process thus may render a fully labeled training set infeasible, whereas acquisition of unlabeled data is relatively inexpensive.

For example: to transcribe an audio segment, in determining the 3D structure of a protein or determining whether there is oil at a particular location, expectation minimization and human cognition, and transitive. The In such situations, semi-supervised learning can be of great practical value.

Spark machine learning APIs

In this section, we will describe two key concepts introduced by the Spark machine learning libraries (Spark MLlib and Spark ML) and the most widely used implemented algorithms that align with the supervised and unsupervised learning techniques we discussed in the previous sections.

Spark machine learning libraries

As already stated, in the pre-Spark era, big data modelers typically used to build their ML models using statistical languages such as R, STATA, and SAS. However, this kind of workflow (that is, the execution flow of these ML algorithms) lacks efficiency, scalability, and throughput, as well as accuracy, with, of course, extended execution times.

Then, data engineers used to reimplement the same model in Java, for example, to deploy on Hadoop. Using Spark, the same ML model can be rebuilt, adopted, and deployed, making the whole workflow much more efficient, robust, and faster, allowing you to provide hands-on insight to increase the performance. Moreover, implementing these algorithms in Hadoop means that these algorithms can run in parallel that cannot be run on R, STATA and SAS and so on. The Spark machine learning library is divided into two packages: Spark MLlib (`spark.mllib`) and Spark ML (`spark.ml`).

Spark MLlib

MLlib is Spark's scalable machine learning library and is an extension of the Spark Core API which provides a library of easy-to-use machine learning algorithms. Spark algorithms are implemented in Scala and then expose the API for Java, Scala, Python, and R. Spark provides support of local vectors and matrix data types stored on a single machine, as well as distributed matrices backed by one or multiple RDDs. The beauties of Spark MLlib are numerous. For example, algorithms are highly scalable and leverage Spark's ability to work with a massive amounts of data.

- They are fast foward designed for parallel computing with an in-memory based operation that is 100 times faster compared to MapReduce data processing (they also support disk-based operation, which is 10 times faster compared to what MapReduce has as normal data processing).

- They are diverse, since they cover common machine learning algorithms for regression analysis, classification, clustering, recommender systems, text analytics, and frequent pattern mining, and obviously cover all the steps required to build a scalable machine learning application.

Spark ML

Spark ML adds a new set of machine learning APIs to let users quickly assemble and configure practical machine learning pipelines on top of datasets. Spark ML aims to offer a uniform set of high-level APIs built on top of DataFrames rather than RDDs that help users create and tune practical machine learning pipelines. Spark ML API standardizes machine learning algorithms to make the learning tasks easier to combine multiple algorithms into a single pipeline or data workflow for data scientists. The Spark ML uses the concepts of DataFrame and Datasets, which are much newer concepts introduced (as experimental) in Spark 1.6 and then used in Spark 2.0+.

 In Scala and Java, DataFrame and Dataset have been unified, that is, DataFrame is just a type alias for a dataset of row. In Python and R, given the lack of type safety, DataFrame is the main programming interface.

The datasets hold diverse data types such as columns storing text, feature vectors, and true labels for the data. In addition to this, Spark ML also uses the transformer to transform one DataFrame into another or vice-versa, where the concept of the estimator is used to fit on a DataFrame to produce a new transformer. The pipeline API, on the other hand, can restrain multiple transformers and estimators together to specify an ML data workflow. The concept of the parameter was introduced to specify all the transformers and estimators to share a common API under an umbrella during the development of an ML application.

Spark MLlib or Spark ML?

Spark ML provides a higher-level API built on top of DataFrames for constructing ML pipelines. Basically, Spark ML provides you with a toolset to create pipelines of different machine learning related transformations on your data. It makes it easy to, for example, chain feature extraction, dimensionality reduction, and the training of a classifier into one model, which as a whole can be later used for classification. MLlib, however, is older and has been in development longer, it has more features because of this. Therefore, using Spark ML is recommended because, the API is more versatile and flexible with DataFrames.

Feature extraction and transformation

Suppose you are going to build a machine learning model that will predict whether a credit card transaction is fraudulent or not. Now, based on the available background knowledge and data analysis, you might decide which data fields (aka features) are important for training your model. For example, amount, customer name, buying company name, and the address of the credit card owners are worth to providing for the overall learning process. These are important to consider since, if you just provide a randomly generated transaction ID, that will not carry any information so would not be useful at all. Thus, once you have decided which features to include in your training set, you then need to transform those features to train the model for better learning. The feature transformations help you add additional background information to the training data. The information enables the machine learning model to benefit from this experience eventually. To make the preceding discussion more concrete, suppose you have the following address of one of the customers represented in the string:

```
"123 Main Street, Seattle, WA 98101"
```

If you see the preceding address, the address lacks proper semantics. In other words, the string has limited expressive power. This address will be useful only for learning address patterns associated with that exact address in a database, for example. However, breaking it up into fundamental parts can provide additional features such as the following:

- "Address" (123 Main Street)
- "City" (Seattle)
- "State" (WA)
- "Zip" (98101)

If you see the preceding patterns, your ML algorithm can now group more different transactions together and discover broader patterns. This is normal, since some customer's zip codes contribute to more fraudulent activity than others. Spark provides several algorithms implemented for the feature extractions and to make transformation easier. For example, the current version provides the following algorithms for feature extractions:

- TF-IDF
- Word2vec
- CountVectorizer

On the other hand, a feature transformer is an abstraction that includes feature transformers and learned models. Technically, a transformer implements a method named `transform()`, which converts one DataFrame into another, generally by appending one or more columns. Spark supports the following transformers to RDD or DataFrame:

- Tokenizer
- StopWordsRemover
- n-gram
- Binarizer
- PCA
- PolynomialExpansion
- Discrete cosine transform (DCT)
- StringIndexer
- IndexToString
- OneHotEncoder
- VectorIndexer
- Interaction
- Normalizer
- StandardScaler
- MinMaxScaler
- MaxAbsScaler
- Bucketizer
- ElementwiseProduct
- SQLTransformer
- VectorAssembler
- QuantileDiscretizer

Due to page limitations, we cannot describe all of them. But we will discuss some widely used algorithms such as `CountVectorizer`, `Tokenizer`, `StringIndexer`, `StopWordsRemover`, `OneHotEncoder`, and so on. PCA, which is commonly used in dimensionality reduction, will be discussed in the next section.

CountVectorizer

CountVectorizer and CountVectorizerModel aim to help convert a collection of text documents to vectors of token counts. When the prior dictionary is not available, CountVectorizer can be used as an estimator to extract the vocabulary and generates a CountVectorizerModel. The model produces sparse representations for the documents over the vocabulary, which can then be passed to other algorithms such LDA.

Suppose we have the text corpus as follows:

```
+---+----------------+
|id |name            |
+---+----------------+
|0  |[Jason, David]  |
|1  |[David, Martin] |
|2  |[Martin, Jason] |
|3  |[Jason, Daiel]  |
|4  |[Daiel, Martin] |
|5  |[Moahmed, Jason]|
|6  |[David, David]  |
|7  |[Jason, Martin] |
+---+----------------+
```

Figure 7: Text corpus containing name only

Now, if we want to convert the preceding collection of texts to vectors of token counts, Spark provides the CountVectorizer () API for doing so. First, let's create a simple DataFrame for the earlier table, as follows:

```
val df = spark.createDataFrame(
Seq((0, Array("Jason", "David")),
(1, Array("David", "Martin")),
(2, Array("Martin", "Jason")),
(3, Array("Jason", "Daiel")),
(4, Array("Daiel", "Martin")),
(5, Array("Moahmed", "Jason")),
(6, Array("David", "David")),
(7, Array("Jason", "Martin")))).toDF("id", "name")
df.show(false)
```

In many cases, you can set the input column with setInputCol. Let's look at an example of it and let's fit a CountVectorizerModel object from the corpus, as follows:

```
val cvModel: CountVectorizerModel = new CountVectorizer()
                    .setInputCol("name")
                    .setOutputCol("features")
```

```
.setVocabSize(3)
.setMinDF(2)
.fit(df)
```

Now let's downstream the vectorizer using the extractor, as follows:

```
val feature = cvModel.transform(df)
spark.stop()
```

Now let's check to make sure it works properly:

```
feature.show(false)
```

The preceding line of code produces the following output:

```
+---+---------------+--------------------+
|id |name           |features            |
+---+---------------+--------------------+
|0  |[Jason, David] |(3,[0,1],[1.0,1.0]) |
|1  |[David, Martin]|(3,[1,2],[1.0,1.0]) |
|2  |[Martin, Jason]|(3,[0,2],[1.0,1.0]) |
|3  |[Jason, Daiel] |(3,[0],[1.0])       |
|4  |[Daiel, Martin]|(3,[2],[1.0])       |
|5  |[Moahmed, Jason]|(3,[0],[1.0])      |
|6  |[David, David] |(3,[1],[2.0])       |
|7  |[Jason, Martin]|(3,[0,2],[1.0,1.0]) |
+---+---------------+--------------------+
```

Figure 8: Name text corpus has been featurized

Now let's move to the feature transformers. One of the most important transformers is the tokenizer, which is frequently used in the machine learning task for handling categorical data. We will see how to work with this transformer in the next section.

Tokenizer

Tokenization is the process of enchanting important components from raw text, such as words, and sentences, and breaking the raw texts into individual terms (also called words). If you want to have more advanced tokenization on regular expression matching, RegexTokenizer is a good option for doing so. By default, the parameter *pattern* (regex, default: s+) is used as delimiters to split the input text. Otherwise, you can also set parameter *gaps* to false, indicating the regex *pattern* denotes *tokens* rather than splitting gaps. This way, you can find all matching occurrences as the tokenization result.

Suppose you have the following sentences:

- Tokenization,is the process of enchanting words,from the raw text.
- If you want,to have more advance tokenization, `RegexTokenizer`,is a good option.
- Here,will provide a sample example on how to tokenize sentences.
- This way, you can find all matching occurrences.

Now, you want to tokenize each meaningful word from the preceding four sentences. Let's create a DataFrame from the earlier sentences, as follows:

```
val sentence = spark.createDataFrame(Seq(
  (0, "Tokenization,is the process of enchanting words,from the raw
text"),
  (1, " If you want,to have more advance tokenization,RegexTokenizer,
      is a good option"),
  (2, " Here,will provide a sample example on how to tockenize
sentences"),
  (3, "This way,you can find all matching occurrences"))).toDF("id",
                                                       "sentence")
```

Now let's create a tokenizer by instantiating the `Tokenizer ()` API, as follows:

```
val tokenizer = new
Tokenizer().setInputCol("sentence").setOutputCol("words")
```

Now, count the number of tokens in each sentence using a UDF, as follows: `import org.apache.spark.sql.functions._`

```
val countTokens = udf { (words: Seq[String]) => words.length }
```

Now tokenize words form each sentence, as follows:

```
val tokenized = tokenizer.transform(sentence)
```

Finally, show each token against each raw sentence, as follows:

```
tokenized.select("sentence", "words")
.withColumn("tokens", countTokens(col("words")))
.show(false)
```

The preceding line of code prints a snap from the tokenized DataFrame containing the raw sentence, bag of words, and number of tokens:

```
+--------------------------------------------------------+--------------------------------------------------------------------------------+------+
|sentence                                                |words                                                                           |tokens|
+--------------------------------------------------------+--------------------------------------------------------------------------------+------+
|Tokenization,is the process of enchanting words,from the raw text|[tokenization,is, the, process, of, enchanting, words,from, the, raw, text]      |9     |
| If you want,to have more advance tokenization,RegexTokenizer,is a good option|[, if, you, want,to, have, more, advance, tokenization,regextokenizer,is, a, good, option]|11    |
| Here,will provide a sample example on how to tockenize sentences|[, here,will, provide, a, sample, example, on, how, to, tockenize, sentences]    |11    |
|This way,you can find all matching occurrences           |[this, way,you, can, find, all, matching, occurrences]                          |7     |
+--------------------------------------------------------+--------------------------------------------------------------------------------+------+
```

Figure 9: Tokenized words from the raw texts

However, if you use `RegexTokenizer` API, you will get better results. This goes as follows:

Create a regex tokenizer by instantiating the `RegexTokenizer ()` API:

```
val regexTokenizer = new RegexTokenizer()
                    .setInputCol("sentence")
                    .setOutputCol("words")
                    .setPattern("\\W+")
                    .setGaps(true)
```

Now tokenize words from each sentence, as follows:

```
val regexTokenized = regexTokenizer.transform(sentence)
regexTokenized.select("sentence", "words")
                .withColumn("tokens", countTokens(col("words")))
                .show(false)
```

The preceding line of code prints a snap from the tokenized DataFrame using RegexTokenizer containing the raw sentence, bag of words, and number of tokens:

```
+--------------------------------------------------------+--------------------------------------------------------------------------------+------+
|sentence                                                |words                                                                           |tokens|
+--------------------------------------------------------+--------------------------------------------------------------------------------+------+
|Tokenization,is the process of enchanting words,from the raw text|[tokenization, is, the, process, of, enchanting, words, from, the, raw, text]    |11    |
| If you want,to have more advance tokenization,RegexTokenizer,is a good option|[if, you, want, to, have, more, advance, tokenization, regextokenizer, is, a, good, option]|13    |
| Here,will provide a sample example on how to tockenize sentences|[here, will, provide, a, sample, example, on, how, to, tockenize, sentences]     |11    |
|This way,you can find all matching occurrences           |[this, way, you, can, find, all, matching, occurrences]                         |8     |
+--------------------------------------------------------+--------------------------------------------------------------------------------+------+
```

Figure 10: Better tokenization using RegexTokenizer

StopWordsRemover

Stop words are words that should be excluded from the input, typically because the words appear frequently and don't carry as much meaning. Spark's StopWordsRemover takes as input a sequence of strings, which is tokenized by Tokenizer or RegexTokenizer. Then, it removes all the stop words from the input sequences. The list of stop words is specified by the stopWords parameter. The current implementation for the StopWordsRemover API provides the options for the Danish, Dutch, Finnish, French, German, Hungarian, Italian, Norwegian, Portuguese, Russian, Spanish, Swedish, Turkish, and English languages. To provide an example, we can simply extend the preceding Tokenizer example in the previous section, since they are already tokenized. For this example, however, we will use the RegexTokenizer API.

At first, create a stop word remover instance from the StopWordsRemover () API, as follows:

```
val remover = new StopWordsRemover()
            .setInputCol("words")
            .setOutputCol("filtered")
```

Now, let's remove all the stop words and print the results as follows:

```
val newDF = remover.transform(regexTokenized)
  newDF.select("id", "filtered").show(false)
```

The preceding line of code prints a snap from the filtered DataFrame excluding the stop words:

```
+---+------------------------------------------------------------+
|id |filtered                                                    |
+---+------------------------------------------------------------+
|0  |[tokenization, process, enchanting, words, raw, text]       |
|1  |[want, advance, tokenization, regextokenizer, good, option]|
|2  |[provide, sample, example, tockenize, sentences]            |
|3  |[way, find, matching, occurrences]                          |
+---+------------------------------------------------------------+
```

Figure 11: Filtered (that is. without stop words) tokens

StringIndexer

StringIndexer encodes a string column of labels to a column of label indices. The indices are in [0, numLabels), ordered by label frequencies, so the most frequent label gets index 0. If the input column is numeric, we cast it to string and index the string values. When downstream pipeline components such as estimator or transformer make use of this string-indexed label, you must set the input column of the component to this string-indexed column name. In many cases, you can set the input column with setInputCol. Suppose you have some categorical data in the following format:

```
+---+-------+-----------+
|id |name   |address    |
+---+-------+-----------+
|0  |Jason  |Germany    |
|1  |David  |France     |
|2  |Martin |Spain      |
|3  |Jason  |USA        |
|4  |Daiel  |UK         |
|5  |Moahmed|Bangladesh |
|6  |David  |Ireland    |
|7  |Jason  |Netherlands|
+---+-------+-----------+
```

Figure 12: DataFrame for applying String Indexer

Now, we want to index the name column so that the most frequent name (that is, Jason in our case) gets index 0. To make this, Spark provides StringIndexer API for doing so. For our example, this can be done, as follows:

At first, let's create a simple DataFrame for the preceding table:

```
val df = spark.createDataFrame(
  Seq((0, "Jason", "Germany"),
  (1, "David", "France"),
  (2, "Martin", "Spain"),
  (3, "Jason", "USA"),
  (4, "Daiel", "UK"),
  (5, "Moahmed", "Bangladesh"),
  (6, "David", "Ireland"),
  (7, "Jason", "Netherlands"))).toDF("id", "name", "address")
```

Now let's index the name column, as follows:

```
val indexer = new StringIndexer()
  .setInputCol("name")
  .setOutputCol("label")
  .fit(df)
```

Now let's downstream the indexer using the transformer, as follows:

```
val indexed = indexer.transform(df)
```

Now let's check to make sure if it works properly:

```
indexed.show(false)
```

```
+---+-------+-----------+-----+
|id |name   |address    |label|
+---+-------+-----------+-----+
|0  |Jason  |Germany    |0.0  |
|1  |David  |France     |1.0  |
|2  |Martin |Spain      |3.0  |
|3  |Jason  |USA        |0.0  |
|4  |Daiel  |UK         |4.0  |
|5  |Moahmed|Bangladesh |2.0  |
|6  |David  |Ireland    |1.0  |
|7  |Jason  |Netherlands|0.0  |
+---+-------+-----------+-----+
```

Figure 13: Label creation using StringIndexer

Another important transformer is the OneHotEncoder, which is frequently used in machine learning tasks for handling categorical data. We will see how to work with this transformer in the next section.

OneHotEncoder

A one-hot encoding maps a column of label indices to a column of binary vectors, with at most a single value. This encoding allows algorithms that expect continuous features, such as Logistic Regression, to use categorical features. Suppose you have some categorical data in the following format (the same that we used for describing the StringIndexer in the previous section):

```
+---+-------+-----------+
|id |name   |address    |
+---+-------+-----------+
|0  |Jason  |Germany    |
|1  |David  |France     |
|2  |Martin |Spain      |
|3  |Jason  |USA        |
|4  |Daiel  |UK         |
|5  |Moahmed|Bangladesh |
|6  |David  |Ireland    |
|7  |Jason  |Netherlands|
+---+-------+-----------+
```

Figure 14: DataFrame for applying OneHotEncoder

Now, we want to index the name column so that the most frequent name in the dataset (that is, **Jason** in our case) gets index **0**. However, what's the use of just indexing them? In other words, you can further vectorize them and then you can feed the DataFrame to any ML models easily. Since we have already seen how to create a DataFrame in the previous section, here, we will just show how to encode them toward Vectors:

```
val indexer = new StringIndexer()
                .setInputCol("name")
                .setOutputCol("categoryIndex")
                .fit(df)
val indexed = indexer.transform(df)
val encoder = new OneHotEncoder()
                .setInputCol("categoryIndex")
                .setOutputCol("categoryVec")
```

Now let's transform it into a vector using `Transformer` and then see the contents, as follows:

```
val encoded = encoder.transform(indexed)
encoded.show()
```

The resulting DataFrame containing a snap is as follows:

```
+---+-------+-----------+-------------+-------------+
| id|   name|    address|categoryIndex|  categoryVec|
+---+-------+-----------+-------------+-------------+
|  0|  Jason|    Germany|          0.0|(4,[0],[1.0])|
|  1|  David|     France|          1.0|(4,[1],[1.0])|
|  2| Martin|      Spain|          3.0|(4,[3],[1.0])|
|  3|  Jason|        USA|          0.0|(4,[0],[1.0])|
|  4|  Daiel|         UK|          4.0|    (4,[],[])|
|  5|Moahmed| Bangladesh|          2.0|(4,[2],[1.0])|
|  6|  David|    Ireland|          1.0|(4,[1],[1.0])|
|  7|  Jason|Netherlands|          0.0|(4,[0],[1.0])|
+---+-------+-----------+-------------+-------------+
```

Figure 15: Creating category index and vector using OneHotEncoder

Now you can see that a new column containing feature vectors has been added in the resulting DataFrame.

Spark ML pipelines

MLlib's goal is to make practical machine learning (ML) scalable and easy. Spark introduced the pipeline API for the easy creation and tuning of practical ML pipelines. As discussed previously, extracting meaningful knowledge through feature engineering in an ML pipeline creation involves a sequence of data collection, preprocessing, feature extraction, feature selection, model fitting, validation, and model evaluation stages. For example, classifying the text documents might involve text segmentation and cleaning, extracting features, and training a classification model with cross-validation toward tuning. Most ML libraries are not designed for distributed computation or they do not provide native support for pipeline creation and tuning.

Dataset abstraction

When running SQL queries from another programming language (for example, Java), the result is returned as a DataFrame. A DataFrame is a distributed collection of data organized into named columns. A dataset, on the other hand, is an interface that tries to provide the benefits of RDDs out of the Spark SQL. A dataset can be constructed from some JVM objects such as primitive types (for example, `String`, `Integer`, and `Long`), Scala case classes, and Java Beans. An ML pipeline involves a number of the sequences of dataset transformations and models. Each transformation takes an input dataset and outputs the transformed dataset, which becomes the input to the next stage. Consequently, the data import and export are the start and end points of an ML pipeline. To make these easier, Spark MLlib and Spark ML provide import and export utilities of a dataset, DataFrame, RDD, and model for several application-specific types, including:

- LabeledPoint for classification and regression
- LabeledDocument for cross-validation and Latent Dirichlet Allocation (LDA)
- Rating and ranking for collaborative filtering

However, real datasets usually contain numerous types, such as user ID, item IDs, labels, timestamps, and raw records. Unfortunately, the current utilities of Spark implementation cannot easily handle datasets consisting of these types, especially time-series datasets. The feature transformation usually forms the majority of a practical ML pipeline. A feature transformation can be viewed as appending or dropping a new column created from existing columns.

In the following figure, you will see that the text tokenizer breaks a document into a bag of words. After that, the TF-IDF algorithm converts a bag of words into a feature vector. During the transformations, the labels need to be preserved for the model-fitting stage:

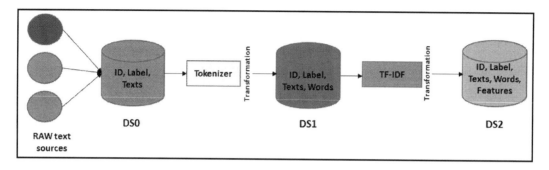

Figure 16: Text processing for machine learning model (DS indicates data sources)

Here, the ID, text, and words are conceded during the transformations steps. They are useful in making predictions and model inspection. However, they are actually unnecessary for model fitting to state. These also don't provide much information if the prediction dataset contains only the predicted labels. Consequently, if you want to inspect the prediction metrics, such as the accuracy, precision, recall, weighted true positives, and weighted false positives, it is quite useful to look at the predicted labels along with the raw input text and tokenized words. The same recommendation also applies to other machine learning applications using Spark ML and Spark MLlib.

Therefore, an easy conversion between RDDs, dataset, and DataFrames has been made possible for in-memory, disk, or external data sources such as Hive and Avro. Although creating new columns from existing columns is easy with user-defined functions, the manifestation of dataset is a lazy operation. In contrast, the dataset supports only some standard data types. However, to increase the usability and to make a better fit for the machine learning model, Spark has also added the support for the `Vector` type as a user-defined type that supports both dense and sparse feature vectors under `mllib.linalg.DenseVector` and `mllib.linalg.Vector`.

Complete DataFrame, dataset, and RDD examples in Java, Scala, and Python can be found in the `examples/src/main/` folder under the Spark distribution. Interested readers can refer to Spark SQL's user guide at `http://spark.apache.org/docs/latest/sql-programming-guide.html` to learn more about DataFrame, dataset, and the operations they support.

Creating a simple pipeline

Spark provides pipeline APIs under Spark ML. A pipeline comprises a sequence of stages consisting of transformers and estimators. There are two basic types of pipeline stages, called transformer and estimator:

- A transformer takes a dataset as an input and produces an augmented dataset as the output so that the output can be fed to the next step. For example, **Tokenizer** and **HashingTF** are two transformers. Tokenizer transforms a dataset with text into a dataset with tokenized words. A HashingTF, on the other hand, produces the term frequencies. The concept of tokenization and HashingTF is commonly used in text mining and text analytics.
- On the contrary, an estimator must be the first on the input dataset to produce a model. In this case, the model itself will be used as the transformer for transforming the input dataset into the augmented output dataset. For example, a **Logistic Regression** or linear regression can be used as an estimator after fitting the training dataset with corresponding labels and features.

After that, it produces a logistic or linear regression model, which implies that developing a pipeline is easy and simple. Well, all you need to do is to declare required stages, then configure the related stage's parameters; finally, chain them in a pipeline object, as shown in the following figure:

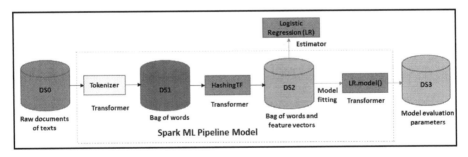

Figure 17: Spark ML pipeline model using logistic regression estimator (DS indicates data store. and the steps inside the dashed line only happen during pipeline fitting)

If you look at *Figure 17*, the fitted model consists of a Tokenizer, a HashingTF feature extractor, and a fitted logistic regression model. The fitted pipeline model acts as a transformer that can be used for prediction, model validation, model inspection, and, finally, model deployment. However, to increase the performance in terms of prediction accuracy, the model itself needs to be tuned.

Now we know about the available algorithms in Spark MLlib and ML, now it's time to get prepared before starting to use them in a formal way for solving supervised and unsupervised learning problems. In the next section, we will start on feature extraction and transformation.

Unsupervised machine learning

In this section, to make the discussion concrete, only the dimensionality reduction using PCA and the LDA for topic modeling will be discussed for text clustering. Other algorithms for unsupervised learning will be discussed in Chapter 13, *My Name is Bayes, Naive Bayes* with some practical examples.

Dimensionality reduction

Dimensionality reduction is the process of reducing the number of variables under consideration. It can be used to extract latent features from raw and noisy features or to compress data while maintaining the structure. Spark MLlib provides support for dimensionality reduction on the RowMatrix class. The most commonly used algorithms for reducing the dimensionality of data are PCA and SVD. However, in this section, we will discuss PCA only to make the discussion more concrete.

PCA

PCA is a statistical procedure that uses an orthogonal transformation to convert a set of observations of possibly correlated variables into a set of values of linearly uncorrelated variables called principal components. A PCA algorithm can be used to project vectors to a low-dimensional space using PCA. Then, based on the reduced feature vectors, an ML model can be trained. The following example shows how to project 6D feature vectors into four-dimensional principal components. Suppose, you have a feature vector as follows:

```
val data = Array(
 Vectors.dense(3.5, 2.0, 5.0, 6.3, 5.60, 2.4),
 Vectors.dense(4.40, 0.10, 3.0, 9.0, 7.0, 8.75),
 Vectors.dense(3.20, 2.40, 0.0, 6.0, 7.4, 3.34) )
```

Now let's create a DataFrame from it, as follows:

```
val df =
spark.createDataFrame(data.map(Tuple1.apply)).toDF("features")
df.show(false)
```

The preceding code produces a feature DataFrame having 6D feature vector for the PCA:

```
+-------------------------+
|features                 |
+-------------------------+
|[3.5,2.0,5.0,6.3,5.6,2.4] |
|[4.4,0.1,3.0,9.0,7.0,8.75]|
|[3.2,2.4,0.0,6.0,7.4,3.34]|
+-------------------------+
```

Figure 18: Creating a feature DataFrame (6-dimensional feature vectors) for PCA

Now let's instantiate the PCA model by setting necessary parameters as follows:

```
val pca = new PCA()
  .setInputCol("features")
  .setOutputCol("pcaFeatures")
  .setK(4)
  .fit(df)
```

Now, to make a difference, we set the output column as pcaFeatures using the setOutputCol() method. Then, we set the dimension of the PCA. Finally, we fit the DataFrame to make the transformation. Note that the PCA model includes an explainedVariance member. A model can be loaded from such older data but will have an empty vector for explainedVariance. Now let's show the resulting features:

```
val result = pca.transform(df).select("pcaFeatures")
result.show(false)
```

The preceding code produces a feature DataFrame having 4D feature vectors as principal components using the PCA:

```
+-------------------------------------------------------------------------------------+
|pcaFeatures                                                                           |
+-------------------------------------------------------------------------------------+
|[-5.149253129088702,3.2157431427730385,-6.828533673828153,5.774261462142295]         |
|[-12.372614091904445,0.804196667817684,-6.828533673828154,5.774261462142296]         |
|[-5.649682494292658,-2.189177804885822,-6.828533673828155,5.7742614621422925]        |
+-------------------------------------------------------------------------------------+
```

Figure 19: Four-dimensional principal components (PCA features)

Using PCA

PCA, which is used widely in dimensionality reduction, is a statistical method that helps to find the rotation matrix. For example, if we want to check if the first coordinate has the largest variance possible. Also it helps to check if there is any succeeding coordinate that will turn the largest variance possible.

Eventually, the PCA model calculates such parameters and returns them as a rotation matrix. The columns of the rotation matrix are called principal components. Spark MLlib supports PCA for tall and skinny matrices stored in a row-oriented format and any vectors.

Regression Analysis - a practical use of PCA

In this section, we will first explore the **MSD (Million Song Dataset)** that will be used for the regression analysis. Then we will show how to use PCA to reduce the dimensions of the dataset. Finally, we will evaluate the linear regression model for the regression quality.

Dataset collection and exploration

In this section, we will describe the very famous MNIST dataset. This dataset will be used throughout this chapter. The MNIST database of handwritten digits (downloaded from `https://www.csie.ntu.edu.tw/~cjlin/libsvmtools/datasets/multiclass.html`) has a training set of 60,000 examples and a test set of 10,000 examples. It is a subset of a larger set available from NIST. The digits have been size-normalized and centered in a fixed-size image. Consequently, this is a very good example dataset for those who are trying to learn techniques and pattern recognition methods on real-world data while spending minimal efforts on preprocessing and formatting. The original black and white (bi-level) images from NIST were size-normalized to fit in a 20 x 20 pixel box while preserving their aspect ratio.

The MNIST database was constructed from NIST's special database 3 and special database 1, which contain binary images of handwritten digits. A sample of the dataset is given in the following:

```
+-----+--------------------+
|label|            features|
+-----+--------------------+
|  5.0|(780,[152,153,154...|
|  0.0|(780,[127,128,129...|
|  4.0|(780,[160,161,162...|
|  1.0|(780,[158,159,160...|
|  9.0|(780,[208,209,210...|
|  2.0|(780,[155,156,157...|
|  1.0|(780,[124,125,126...|
|  3.0|(780,[151,152,153...|
|  1.0|(780,[152,153,154...|
|  4.0|(780,[134,135,161...|
|  3.0|(780,[123,124,125...|
|  5.0|(780,[216,217,218...|
|  3.0|(780,[143,144,145...|
|  6.0|(780,[72,73,74,99...|
|  1.0|(780,[151,152,153...|
|  7.0|(780,[211,212,213...|
|  2.0|(780,[151,152,153...|
|  8.0|(780,[159,160,161...|
|  6.0|(780,[100,101,102...|
|  9.0|(780,[209,210,211...|
|  4.0|(780,[129,130,131...|
|  0.0|(780,[129,130,131...|
|  9.0|(780,[183,184,185...|
|  1.0|(780,[158,159,160...|
|  1.0|(780,[99,100,101,...|
|  2.0|(780,[124,125,126...|
|  4.0|(780,[185,186,187...|
|  3.0|(780,[150,151,152...|
|  2.0|(780,[145,146,147...|
|  7.0|(780,[240,241,242...|
+-----+--------------------+
only showing top 30 rows
```

Figure 20: A snap of the MNIST dataset

You can see that there are 780 features altogether. Consequently, sometimes, many machine learning algorithms will fail due to the high-dimensional nature of your dataset. Therefore, to address this issue, in the next section, we will show you how to reduce the dimensions without sacrificing the qualities machine learning tasks, such as classification. However, before diving into the problem, let's get some background knowledge on regression analysis first.

What is regression analysis?

Linear regression belongs to the family of regression algorithms. The goal of regression is to find relationships and dependencies between variables. It is modeling the relationship between a continuous scalar dependent variable y (also, label or target in machine learning terminology) and one or more (a D-dimensional vector) explanatory variables (also, independent variables, input variables, features, observed data, observations, attributes, dimensions, data point, and so on) denoted x using a linear function. In regression analysis, the goal is to predict a continuous target variable, as shown in the following figure:

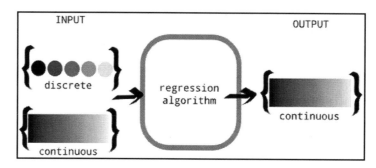

Figure 21: A regression algorithm is meant to produce continuous output. The input is allowed to be either discrete or continuous (source: Nishant Shukla. Machine Learning with TensorFlow. Manning Publications co. 2017)

Now, you might have some confusion in your mind about what the basic difference between a classification and a regression problem is. The following information box will make it clearer:

Regression versus classification: On the other hand, another area, called classification, is about predicting a label from a finite set but with discrete values. This distinction is important to know because discrete-valued output is handled better by classification, which will be discussed in upcoming sections.

The model for a multiple regression that involves a linear combination of input variables takes the following form:

$$y = ss_0 + ss_1x_1 + ss_2x_2 + ss_3x_3 + ... + e$$

Figure 22 shows an example of simple linear regression with one independent variable (*x* axis). The model (red line) is calculated using training data (blue points), where each point has a known label (*y* axis) to fit the points as accurately as possible by minimizing the value of a chosen loss function. We can then use the model to predict unknown labels (we only know *x* value and want to predict *y* value).

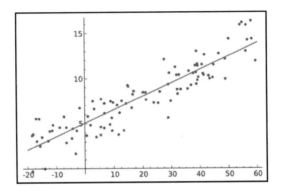

Figure 22: Regression graph that separates data points (the dots [.] refer to data points in the graph and the red line refers to the regression)

Spark provides an RDD-based implementation of the linear regression algorithm. You can train a linear regression model with no regularization using stochastic gradient descent. This solves the least squares regression formulation $f(weights) = 1/n \ ||A\ weights-y||^2$ (which is the mean squared error). Here, the data matrix has n rows, and the input RDD holds the set of rows of A, each with its corresponding right-hand side label y. For more information, refer to `https://github.com/apache/spark/blob/master/mllib/src/main/scala/org/apache/spark/mllib/regression/LinearRegression.scala`.

Step 1. Load the dataset and create RDD

For loading the MNIST dataset in LIBSVM format, here we used the built-in API called MLUtils from Spark MLlib:

```
val data = MLUtils.loadLibSVMFile(spark.sparkContext,
"data/mnist.bz2")
```

Step 2. Compute the number of features to make the dimensionality reduction easier:

```
val featureSize = data.first().features.size
println("Feature Size: " + featureSize)
```

This will result in the following output:

```
Feature Size: 780
```

So the dataset has 780 columns -i.e. features so this can be considered as high-dimensional one (features). Therefore, sometimes it is worth reducing the dimensions of the dataset.

Step 3. Now prepare the training and test set as follows:

The thing is that we will train the `LinearRegressionwithSGD` model twice. First, we will use the normal dataset with the original dimensions of the features, secondly, using half of the features. With the original one, the training and test set preparation go as follows:

```
val splits = data.randomSplit(Array(0.75, 0.25), seed = 12345L)
val (training, test) = (splits(0), splits(1))
```

Now, for the reduced features, the training goes as follows:

```
val pca = new PCA(featureSize/2).fit(data.map(_.features))
val training_pca = training.map(p => p.copy(features =
pca.transform(p.features)))
val test_pca = test.map(p => p.copy(features =
pca.transform(p.features)))
```

Step 4. Training the linear regression model
Now iterate 20 times and train the `LinearRegressionWithSGD` for the normal features and reduced features, respectively, as follows:

```
val numIterations = 20
val stepSize = 0.0001
val model = LinearRegressionWithSGD.train(training, numIterations)
val model_pca = LinearRegressionWithSGD.train(training_pca,
numIterations)
```

Beware! Sometimes, `LinearRegressionWithSGD()` returns NaN. In my opinion, there are two reasons for this happening:

- If the `stepSize` is big. In that case, you should use something smaller, such as 0.0001, 0.001, 0.01, 0.03, 0.1, 0.3, 1.0, and so on.
- Your train data has NaN. If so, the result will likely be NaN. So, it is recommended to remove the null values prior to training the model.

Step 5. Evaluating both models

Before we evaluate the classification model, first, let's prepare for computing the MSE for the normal to see the effects of dimensionality reduction on the original predictions. Obviously, if you want a formal way to quantify the accuracy of the model and potentially increase the precision and avoid overfitting. Nevertheless, you can do from residual analysis. Also it would be worth to analyse the selection of the training and test set to be used for the model building and then the evaluation. Finally, selection techniques help you to describe the various attributes of a model:

```
val valuesAndPreds = test.map { point =>
                    val score = model.predict(point.features)
                    (score, point.label)
                }
```

Now compute the prediction sets for the PCA one as follows:

```
val valuesAndPreds_pca = test_pca.map { point =>
                    val score = model_pca.predict(point.features)
                    (score, point.label)
                }
```

Now compute the MSE and print them for each case as follows:

```
val MSE = valuesAndPreds.map { case (v, p) => math.pow(v - p 2)
}.mean()
val MSE_pca = valuesAndPreds_pca.map { case (v, p) => math.pow(v - p,
2) }.mean()
println("Mean Squared Error = " + MSE)
println("PCA Mean Squared Error = " + MSE_pca)
```

You will get the following output:

```
Mean Squared Error = 2.9164359135973043E78
PCA Mean Squared Error = 2.9156682256149184E78
```

Note that the MSE is actually calculated using the following formula:

$$\text{RMSD} = \sqrt{\frac{\sum_{t=1}^{n}(\hat{y}_t - y_t)^2}{n}}.$$

Step 6. Observing the model coefficient for both models

Compute the model coefficient as follows:

```
println("Model coefficients:"+ model.toString())
println("Model with PCA coefficients:"+ model_pca.toString())
```

Now you should observer the following output on your terminal/console:

```
Model coefficients: intercept = 0.0, numFeatures = 780
Model with PCA coefficients: intercept = 0.0, numFeatures = 390
```

Binary and multiclass classification

Binary classifiers are used to separate the elements of a given dataset into one of two possible groups (for example, fraud or not fraud) and are a special case of multiclass classification. Most binary classification metrics can be generalized to multiclass classification metrics. A multiclass classification describes a classification problem, where there are *M>2* possible labels for each data point (the case where *M=2* is the binary classification problem).

For multiclass metrics, the notion of positives and negatives is slightly different. Predictions and labels can still be positive or negative, but they must be considered in the context of a particular class. Each label and prediction takes on the value of one of the multiple classes and so they are said to be positive for their particular class and negative for all other classes. So, a true positive occurs whenever the prediction and the label match, while a true negative occurs when neither the prediction nor the label takes on the value of a given class. By this convention, there can be multiple true negatives for a given data sample. The extension of false negatives and false positives from the former definitions of positive and negative labels is straightforward.

Performance metrics

While there are many different types of classification algorithms, evaluation metrics more or less shares similar principles. In a supervised classification problem, there exists a true output and a model-generated predicted output for each data point. For this reason, the results for each data point can be assigned to one of four categories:

- **True positive** (TP): Label is positive and prediction is also positive.
- **True negative** (TN): Label is negative and prediction is also negative.
- **False positive** (FP): Label is negative but prediction is positive.
- **False negative** (FN): Label is positive but prediction is negative.

Now, to get a clearer idea about these parameters, refer to the following figure:

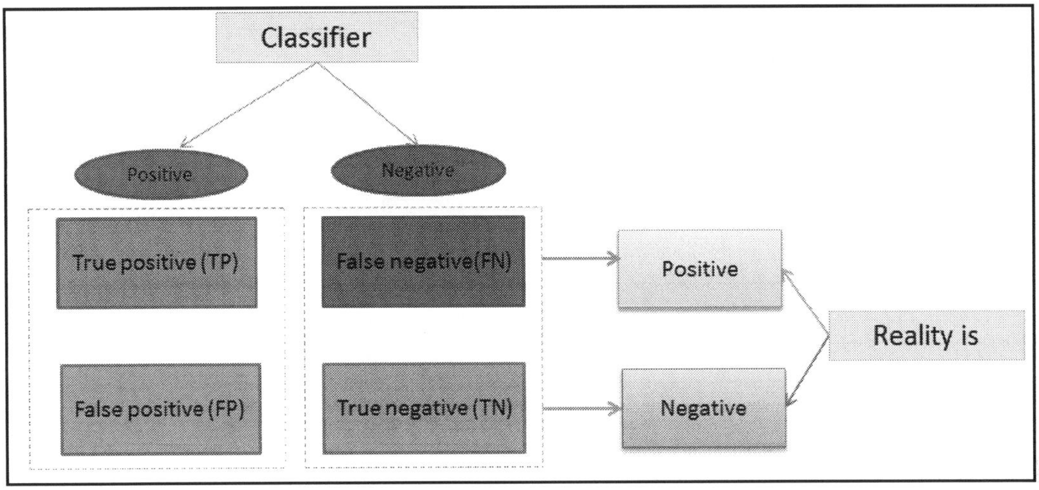

Figure 23: Prediction classifier (that is. confusion matrix)

The TP, FP, TN, FN are the building blocks for most classifier evaluation metrics. A fundamental point when considering classifier evaluation is that pure accuracy (that is, was the prediction correct or incorrect) is not generally a good metric. The reason for this is that a dataset may be highly unbalanced. For example, if a model is designed to predict fraud from a dataset where 95% of the data points are not fraud and 5% of the data points are fraud. Then suppose a naive classifier predicts not fraud (regardless of input) will be 95% accurate. For this reason, metrics such as precision and recall are typically used because they take into account the type of error. In most applications, there is some desired balance between precision and recall, which can be captured by combining the two into a single metric, called the **F-measure**.

Precision signifies how many of the positively classified were relevant. On the other hand, recall signifies how good a test is at detecting the positives? In binary classification, recall is called sensitivity. It is important to note that the the precision may not decrease with recall. The relationship between recall and precision can be observed in the stair step area of the plot:

- Receiver operating characteristic (ROC)
- Area under ROC curve
- Area under precision-recall curve

These curves are typically used in binary classification to study the output of a classifier. However, sometimes it is good to combine precision and recall to choose between two models. In contrast, using precision and recall with multiple-number evaluation metrics makes it harder to compare algorithms. Suppose you have two algorithms that perform as follows:

Classifier	Precision	Recall
X	96%	89%
Y	99%	84%

Here, neither classifier is obviously superior, so it doesn't immediately guide you toward picking the optimal one. But using F1 score, which is a measure that combines precision and recall (that is, the harmonic mean of precision and recall), balanced the F1 score. Let's calculate it and place it in the table:

Classifier	Precision	Recall	F1 score
X	96%	89%	92.36%
Y	99%	84%	90.885%

Therefore, having F1-score helps make a decision for selecting from a large number of classifiers. It gives a clear preference ranking among all of them and therefore a clear direction for progress, that is, classifier **X**.

For the binary classification, the preceding performance metrics can be calculated as follows:

Metric	Definition
Precision (Positive Predictive Value)	$PPV = \frac{TP}{TP+FP}$
Recall (True Positive Rate)	$TPR = \frac{TP}{P} = \frac{TP}{TP+FN}$
F-measure	$F(\beta) = (1+\beta^2) \cdot \left(\frac{PPV \cdot TPR}{\beta^2 \cdot PPV + TPR} \right)$
Receiver Operating Characteristic (ROC)	$FPR(T) = \int_T^\infty P_0(T)\,dT$ $TPR(T) = \int_T^\infty P_1(T)\,dT$
Area Under ROC Curve	$AUROC = \int_0^1 \frac{TP}{P} d\left(\frac{FP}{N}\right)$
Area Under Precision-Recall Curve	$AUPRC = \int_0^1 \frac{TP}{TP+FP} d\left(\frac{TP}{P}\right)$

Figure 24: Mathematical formula for computing performance metrics for binary classifiers (source: `https://spark.apache.org/ docs/2.1.0/mllib-evaluation-metrics.html`)

However, in multiclass classification problems where more than two predicted labels are associated, computing the earlier metrics is more complex but can be computed using the following mathematical equations:

Metric	Definition
Confusion Matrix	$C_{ij} = \sum_{k=0}^{N-1} \hat{\delta}(\mathbf{y}_k - \ell_i) \cdot \hat{\delta}(\hat{\mathbf{y}}_k - \ell_j)$ $\begin{pmatrix} \sum_{k=0}^{N-1} \hat{\delta}(\mathbf{y}_k - \ell_1) \cdot \hat{\delta}(\hat{\mathbf{y}}_k - \ell_1) & \cdots & \sum_{k=0}^{N-1} \hat{\delta}(\mathbf{y}_k - \ell_1) \cdot \hat{\delta}(\hat{\mathbf{y}}_k - \ell_N) \\ \vdots & \ddots & \vdots \\ \sum_{k=0}^{N-1} \hat{\delta}(\mathbf{y}_k - \ell_N) \cdot \hat{\delta}(\hat{\mathbf{y}}_k - \ell_1) & \cdots & \sum_{k=0}^{N-1} \hat{\delta}(\mathbf{y}_k - \ell_N) \cdot \hat{\delta}(\hat{\mathbf{y}}_k - \ell_N) \end{pmatrix}$
Accuracy	$ACC = \frac{TP}{TP+FP} = \frac{1}{N} \sum_{i=0}^{N-1} \hat{\delta}(\hat{\mathbf{y}}_i - \mathbf{y}_i)$
Precision by label	$PPV(\ell) = \frac{TP}{TP+FP} = \frac{\sum_{i=0}^{N-1} \hat{\delta}(\hat{\mathbf{y}}_i - \ell) \cdot \hat{\delta}(\mathbf{y}_i - \ell)}{\sum_{i=0}^{N-1} \hat{\delta}(\hat{\mathbf{y}}_i - \ell)}$
Recall by label	$TPR(\ell) = \frac{TP}{P} = \frac{\sum_{i=0}^{N-1} \hat{\delta}(\hat{\mathbf{y}}_i - \ell) \cdot \hat{\delta}(\mathbf{y}_i - \ell)}{\sum_{i=0}^{N-1} \hat{\delta}(\mathbf{y}_i - \ell)}$
F-measure by label	$F(\beta, \ell) = (1 + \beta^2) \cdot \left(\frac{PPV(\ell) \cdot TPR(\ell)}{\beta^2 \cdot PPV(\ell) + TPR(\ell)} \right)$
Weighted precision	$PPV_w = \frac{1}{N} \sum_{\ell \in L} PPV(\ell) \cdot \sum_{i=0}^{N-1} \hat{\delta}(\mathbf{y}_i - \ell)$
Weighted recall	$TPR_w = \frac{1}{N} \sum_{\ell \in L} TPR(\ell) \cdot \sum_{i=0}^{N-1} \hat{\delta}(\mathbf{y}_i - \ell)$
Weighted F-measure	$F_w(\beta) = \frac{1}{N} \sum_{\ell \in L} F(\beta, \ell) \cdot \sum_{i=0}^{N-1} \hat{\delta}(\mathbf{y}_i - \ell)$

Figure 25: Mathematical formula for computing performance metrics for multiclass classifiers

Where $\delta^{\wedge}(x)$ is called modified delta function and that can be defined as follows (source: https://spark.apache.org/docs/2.1.0/mllib-evaluation-metrics.html):

$$\hat{\delta}(x) = \begin{cases} 1 & \text{if } x = 0, \\ 0 & \text{otherwise} \end{cases}$$

Binary classification using logistic regression

Logistic regression is widely used to predict a binary response. This is a linear method that can be written mathematically as follows:

$$L(\mathbf{w}; \mathbf{x}, y) := \log\left(1 + \exp\left(-y\mathbf{w}^T\mathbf{x}\right)\right)$$

In the preceding equation, *L(w; x, y)* is the loss function is called logistic loss.

For binary classification problems, the algorithm will output a binary logistic regression model. Given a new data point, denoted by *x*, the model makes predictions by applying the logistic function:

$$f(z) = 1/(1 + e - z)$$

Where $z = w^T x$, and by default, if $f(w^T x) > 0.5$, the outcome is positive, or negative otherwise, though unlike linear SVMs, the raw output of the logistic regression model, *f(z)*, has a probabilistic interpretation (that is, the probability that *x* is positive).

Linear SVM is the newest extremely fast machine learning (data mining) algorithm for solving multiclass classification problems from ultralarge datasets that implements an original proprietary version of a cutting plane algorithm for designing a linear support vector machine (source: www.linearsvm.com/).

Breast cancer prediction using logistic regression of Spark ML

In this section, we will look at how to develop a cancer diagnosis pipeline with Spark ML. A real dataset will be used to predict the probability of breast cancer. To be more specific, Wisconsin Breast Cancer Dataset will be used.

Dataset collection

Here, we have used simpler datasets that are structured and manually curated for machine learning application development, and, of course, many of them show good classification accuracy. The Wisconsin Breast Cancer Dataset from the UCI machine learning repository (`https://archive.ics.uci.edu/ml/datasets/Breast+Cancer+Wisconsin+(Original)`, contains data that was donated by researchers at the University of Wisconsin and includes measurements from digitized images of fine-needle aspirations of breast masses. The values represent characteristics of the cell nuclei present in the digital images described in the following subsection:

```
0.  Sample code number id number
1.  Clump Thickness 1 - 10
2.  Uniformity of Cell Size 1 - 10
3.  Uniformity of Cell Shape 1 - 10
4.  Marginal Adhesion 1 - 10
5.  Single Epithelial Cell Size 1 - 10
6.  Bare Nuclei 1 - 10
7.  Bland Chromatin 1 - 10
8.  Normal Nucleoli 1 - 10
9.  Mitoses 1 - 10
10. Class: (2 for benign, 4 for malignant)
```

To read more about the Wisconsin Breast Cancer Dataset, refer to the authors' publication: *Nuclear feature extraction for breast tumor diagnosis, IS&T/SPIE 1993 International Symposium on Electronic Imaging: Science and Technology*, volume 1905, pp 861-870 by *W.N. Street, W.H. Wolberg*, and *O.L. Mangasarian, 1993*.

Developing the pipeline using Spark ML

Now we will show you how to predict the possibility of breast cancer with step-by-step example:

Step 1: Load and parse the data

```
val rdd = spark.sparkContext.textFile("data/wbcd.csv")
val cancerRDD = parseRDD(rdd).map(parseCancer)
```

The `parseRDD()` method goes as follows:

```
def parseRDD(rdd: RDD[String]): RDD[Array[Double]] = {
  rdd.map(_.split(",")).filter(_(6) !=
"?").map(_.drop(1)).map(_.map(_.toDouble))
}
```

The `parseCancer()` method is as follows:

```
def parseCancer(line: Array[Double]): Cancer = {
  Cancer(if (line(9) == 4.0) 1 else 0, line(0), line(1), line(2),
line(3), line(4), line(5), line(6), line(7), line(8))
}
```

Note that here we have simplified the dataset. For the value 4.0, we have converted them to 1.0, and 0.0 otherwise. The `Cancer` class is a case class that can be defined as follows:

```
case class Cancer(cancer_class: Double, thickness: Double, size:
Double, shape: Double, madh: Double, epsize: Double, bnuc: Double,
bchrom: Double, nNuc: Double, mit: Double)
```

Step 2: Convert RDD to DataFrame for the ML pipeline

```
import spark.sqlContext.implicits._
val cancerDF = cancerRDD.toDF().cache()
cancerDF.show()
```

The DataFrame looks like the following:

```
+------------+---------+----+-----+----+------+----+------+----+---+
|cancer_class|thickness|size|shape|madh|epsize|bnuc|bchrom|nNuc|mit|
+------------+---------+----+-----+----+------+----+------+----+---+
|         0.0|      5.0| 1.0|  1.0| 1.0|   2.0| 1.0|   3.0| 1.0|1.0|
|         0.0|      5.0| 4.0|  4.0| 5.0|   7.0|10.0|   3.0| 2.0|1.0|
|         0.0|      3.0| 1.0|  1.0| 1.0|   2.0| 2.0|   3.0| 1.0|1.0|
|         0.0|      6.0| 8.0|  8.0| 1.0|   3.0| 4.0|   3.0| 7.0|1.0|
|         0.0|      4.0| 1.0|  1.0| 3.0|   2.0| 1.0|   3.0| 1.0|1.0|
|         1.0|      8.0|10.0| 10.0| 8.0|   7.0|10.0|   9.0| 7.0|1.0|
|         0.0|      1.0| 1.0|  1.0| 1.0|   2.0|10.0|   3.0| 1.0|1.0|
|         0.0|      2.0| 1.0|  2.0| 1.0|   2.0| 1.0|   3.0| 1.0|1.0|
|         0.0|      2.0| 1.0|  1.0| 1.0|   2.0| 1.0|   1.0| 1.0|5.0|
|         0.0|      4.0| 2.0|  1.0| 1.0|   2.0| 1.0|   2.0| 1.0|1.0|
|         0.0|      1.0| 1.0|  1.0| 1.0|   1.0| 1.0|   3.0| 1.0|1.0|
|         0.0|      2.0| 1.0|  1.0| 1.0|   2.0| 1.0|   2.0| 1.0|1.0|
|         1.0|      5.0| 3.0|  3.0| 3.0|   2.0| 3.0|   4.0| 4.0|1.0|
|         0.0|      1.0| 1.0|  1.0| 1.0|   2.0| 3.0|   3.0| 1.0|1.0|
|         1.0|      8.0| 7.0|  5.0|10.0|   7.0| 9.0|   5.0| 5.0|4.0|
|         1.0|      7.0| 4.0|  6.0| 4.0|   6.0| 1.0|   4.0| 3.0|1.0|
|         0.0|      4.0| 1.0|  1.0| 1.0|   2.0| 1.0|   2.0| 1.0|1.0|
|         0.0|      4.0| 1.0|  1.0| 1.0|   2.0| 1.0|   3.0| 1.0|1.0|
|         1.0|     10.0| 7.0|  7.0| 6.0|   4.0|10.0|   4.0| 1.0|2.0|
|         0.0|      6.0| 1.0|  1.0| 1.0|   2.0| 1.0|   3.0| 1.0|1.0|
+------------+---------+----+-----+----+------+----+------+----+---+
only showing top 20 rows
```

Figure 26: A snap of the cancer dataset

Step 3: Feature extraction and transformation

At first, let's select the feature column, as follows:

```
val featureCols = Array("thickness", "size", "shape", "madh",
"epsize", "bnuc", "bchrom", "nNuc", "mit")
```

Now let's assemble them into a feature vector, as follows:

```
val assembler = new
VectorAssembler().setInputCols(featureCols).setOutputCol("features")
```

Now transform them into a DataFrame, as follows:

```
val df2 = assembler.transform(cancerDF)
```

Let's see the structure of the transformed DataFrame:

```
df2.show()
```

Now you should observe a DataFrame containing the features calculated based on the columns on the left:

```
+------------+---------+----+-----+----+------+----+------+----+---+--------------------+
|cancer_class|thickness|size|shape|madh|epsize|bnuc|bchrom|nNuc|mit|            features|
+------------+---------+----+-----+----+------+----+------+----+---+--------------------+
|         0.0|      5.0| 1.0|  1.0| 1.0|   2.0| 1.0|   3.0| 1.0|1.0|[5.0,1.0,1.0,1.0,...|
|         0.0|      5.0| 4.0|  4.0| 5.0|   7.0|10.0|   3.0| 2.0|1.0|[5.0,4.0,4.0,5.0,...|
|         0.0|      3.0| 1.0|  1.0| 1.0|   2.0| 2.0|   3.0| 1.0|1.0|[3.0,1.0,1.0,1.0,...|
|         0.0|      6.0| 8.0|  8.0| 1.0|   3.0| 4.0|   3.0| 7.0|1.0|[6.0,8.0,8.0,1.0,...|
|         0.0|      4.0| 1.0|  1.0| 3.0|   2.0| 1.0|   3.0| 1.0|1.0|[4.0,1.0,1.0,3.0,...|
|         1.0|      8.0|10.0| 10.0| 8.0|   7.0|10.0|   9.0| 7.0|1.0|[8.0,10.0,10.0,8....|
|         0.0|      1.0| 1.0|  1.0| 1.0|   2.0|10.0|   3.0| 1.0|1.0|[1.0,1.0,1.0,1.0,...|
|         0.0|      2.0| 1.0|  2.0| 1.0|   2.0| 1.0|   3.0| 1.0|1.0|[2.0,1.0,2.0,1.0,...|
|         0.0|      2.0| 1.0|  1.0| 1.0|   2.0| 1.0|   1.0| 1.0|5.0|[2.0,1.0,1.0,1.0,...|
|         0.0|      4.0| 2.0|  1.0| 1.0|   2.0| 1.0|   2.0| 1.0|1.0|[4.0,2.0,1.0,1.0,...|
|         0.0|      1.0| 1.0|  1.0| 1.0|   1.0| 1.0|   3.0| 1.0|1.0|[1.0,1.0,1.0,1.0,...|
|         0.0|      2.0| 1.0|  1.0| 1.0|   2.0| 1.0|   2.0| 1.0|1.0|[2.0,1.0,1.0,1.0,...|
|         1.0|      5.0| 3.0|  3.0| 3.0|   2.0| 3.0|   4.0| 4.0|1.0|[5.0,3.0,3.0,3.0,...|
|         0.0|      1.0| 1.0|  1.0| 1.0|   2.0| 3.0|   3.0| 1.0|1.0|[1.0,1.0,1.0,1.0,...|
|         1.0|      8.0| 7.0|  5.0|10.0|   7.0| 9.0|   5.0| 5.0|4.0|[8.0,7.0,5.0,10.0...|
|         1.0|      7.0| 4.0|  6.0| 4.0|   6.0| 1.0|   4.0| 3.0|1.0|[7.0,4.0,6.0,4.0,...|
|         0.0|      4.0| 1.0|  1.0| 1.0|   2.0| 1.0|   2.0| 1.0|1.0|[4.0,1.0,1.0,1.0,...|
|         0.0|      4.0| 1.0|  1.0| 1.0|   2.0| 1.0|   3.0| 1.0|1.0|[4.0,1.0,1.0,1.0,...|
|         1.0|     10.0| 7.0|  7.0| 6.0|   4.0|10.0|   4.0| 1.0|2.0|[10.0,7.0,7.0,6.0...|
|         0.0|      6.0| 1.0|  1.0| 1.0|   2.0| 1.0|   3.0| 1.0|1.0|[6.0,1.0,1.0,1.0,...|
+------------+---------+----+-----+----+------+----+------+----+---+--------------------+
only showing top 20 rows
```

Figure 27: New DataFrame containing features

Finally, let's use the `StringIndexer` and create the label for the training dataset, as follows:

```
val labelIndexer = new
StringIndexer().setInputCol("cancer_class").setOutputCol("label")
val df3 = labelIndexer.fit(df2).transform(df2)
df3.show()
```

Now you should observe a DataFrame containing the features and labels calculated based on the columns in the left:

```
+------------+---------+----+-----+----+------+----+------+----+---+--------------------+-----+
|cancer_class|thickness|size|shape|madh|epsize|bnuc|bchrom|nNuc|mit|            features|label|
+------------+---------+----+-----+----+------+----+------+----+---+--------------------+-----+
|         0.0|      5.0| 1.0|  1.0| 1.0|   2.0| 1.0|   3.0| 1.0|1.0|[5.0,1.0,1.0,1.0,...|  0.0|
|         0.0|      5.0| 4.0|  4.0| 5.0|   7.0|10.0|   3.0| 2.0|1.0|[5.0,4.0,4.0,5.0,...|  0.0|
|         0.0|      3.0| 1.0|  1.0| 1.0|   2.0| 2.0|   3.0| 1.0|1.0|[3.0,1.0,1.0,1.0,...|  0.0|
|         0.0|      6.0| 8.0|  8.0| 1.0|   3.0| 4.0|   3.0| 7.0|1.0|[6.0,8.0,8.0,1.0,...|  0.0|
|         0.0|      4.0| 1.0|  1.0| 3.0|   2.0| 1.0|   3.0| 1.0|1.0|[4.0,1.0,1.0,3.0,...|  0.0|
|         1.0|      8.0|10.0| 10.0| 8.0|   7.0|10.0|   9.0| 7.0|1.0|[8.0,10.0,10.0,8....|  1.0|
|         0.0|      1.0| 1.0|  1.0| 1.0|   2.0|10.0|   3.0| 1.0|1.0|[1.0,1.0,1.0,1.0,...|  0.0|
|         0.0|      2.0| 1.0|  2.0| 1.0|   2.0| 1.0|   3.0| 1.0|1.0|[2.0,1.0,2.0,1.0,...|  0.0|
|         0.0|      2.0| 1.0|  1.0| 1.0|   2.0| 1.0|   1.0| 1.0|5.0|[2.0,1.0,1.0,1.0,...|  0.0|
|         0.0|      4.0| 2.0|  1.0| 1.0|   2.0| 1.0|   2.0| 1.0|1.0|[4.0,2.0,1.0,1.0,...|  0.0|
|         0.0|      1.0| 1.0|  1.0| 1.0|   1.0| 1.0|   3.0| 1.0|1.0|[1.0,1.0,1.0,1.0,...|  0.0|
|         0.0|      2.0| 1.0|  1.0| 1.0|   2.0| 1.0|   2.0| 1.0|1.0|[2.0,1.0,1.0,1.0,...|  0.0|
|         1.0|      5.0| 3.0|  3.0| 3.0|   2.0| 3.0|   4.0| 4.0|1.0|[5.0,3.0,3.0,3.0,...|  1.0|
|         0.0|      1.0| 1.0|  1.0| 1.0|   2.0| 3.0|   3.0| 1.0|1.0|[1.0,1.0,1.0,1.0,...|  0.0|
|         1.0|      8.0| 7.0|  5.0|10.0|   7.0| 9.0|   5.0| 5.0|4.0|[8.0,7.0,5.0,10.0...|  1.0|
|         1.0|      7.0| 4.0|  6.0| 4.0|   6.0| 1.0|   4.0| 3.0|1.0|[7.0,4.0,6.0,4.0,...|  1.0|
|         0.0|      4.0| 1.0|  1.0| 1.0|   2.0| 1.0|   2.0| 1.0|1.0|[4.0,1.0,1.0,1.0,...|  0.0|
|         0.0|      4.0| 1.0|  1.0| 1.0|   2.0| 1.0|   3.0| 1.0|1.0|[4.0,1.0,1.0,1.0,...|  0.0|
|         1.0|     10.0| 7.0|  7.0| 6.0|   4.0|10.0|   4.0| 1.0|2.0|[10.0,7.0,7.0,6.0...|  1.0|
|         0.0|      6.0| 1.0|  1.0| 1.0|   2.0| 1.0|   3.0| 1.0|1.0|[6.0,1.0,1.0,1.0,...|  0.0|
+------------+---------+----+-----+----+------+----+------+----+---+--------------------+-----+
only showing top 20 rows
```

Figure 28: New DataFrame containing features and labels to training the ML models

Step 4: Create test and training set

```
val splitSeed = 1234567
val Array(trainingData, testData) = df3.randomSplit(Array(0.7, 0.3),
splitSeed)
```

Step 5: Creating an estimator using the training sets

Let's create an estimator for the pipeline using the logistic regression with `elasticNetParam`. We also specify the max iteration and regression parameter, as follows:

```
val lr = new
```

```
LogisticRegression().setMaxIter(50).setRegParam(0.01).setElasticNetPar
am(0.01)
val model = lr.fit(trainingData)
```

Step 6: Getting raw prediction, probability, and prediction for the test set

Transform the model using the test set to get raw prediction, probability, and prediction for the test set:

```
val predictions = model.transform(testData)
predictions.show()
```

The resulting DataFrame is as follows:

cancer_class	thickness	size	shape	madh	epsize	bnuc	bchrom	nNuc	mit	features	label	rawPrediction	probability	prediction
0.0	1.0	1.0	1.0	1.0	1.0	1.0	2.0	1.0	1.0	[1.0,1.0,1.0,1.0,...	0.0	[5.15956430979038...	[0.99428860556932...	0.0
0.0	1.0	1.0	1.0	1.0	1.0	1.0	2.0	1.0	1.0	[1.0,1.0,1.0,1.0,...	0.0	[5.15956430979038...	[0.99428860556932...	0.0
0.0	1.0	1.0	1.0	1.0	1.0	1.0	3.0	1.0	1.0	[1.0,1.0,1.0,1.0,...	0.0	[4.88229871718381...	[0.99247744702488...	0.0
0.0	1.0	1.0	1.0	1.0	1.0	1.0	3.0	1.0	1.0	[1.0,1.0,1.0,1.0,...	0.0	[4.88229871718381...	[0.99247744702488...	0.0
0.0	1.0	1.0	1.0	1.0	2.0	1.0	1.0	1.0	1.0	[1.0,1.0,1.0,1.0,...	0.0	[5.26929960916807...	[0.99487914377217...	0.0
0.0	1.0	1.0	1.0	1.0	2.0	1.0	1.0	1.0	1.0	[1.0,1.0,1.0,1.0,...	0.0	[5.26929960916807...	[0.99487914377217...	0.0
0.0	1.0	1.0	1.0	1.0	2.0	1.0	1.0	1.0	1.0	[1.0,1.0,1.0,1.0,...	0.0	[5.26929960916807...	[0.99487914377217...	0.0
0.0	1.0	1.0	1.0	1.0	2.0	1.0	1.0	1.0	1.0	[1.0,1.0,1.0,1.0,...	0.0	[5.26929960916807...	[0.99487914377217...	0.0
0.0	1.0	1.0	1.0	1.0	2.0	1.0	1.0	1.0	1.0	[1.0,1.0,1.0,1.0,...	0.0	[5.26929960916807...	[0.99487914377217...	0.0
0.0	1.0	1.0	1.0	1.0	2.0	1.0	1.0	1.0	1.0	[1.0,1.0,1.0,1.0,...	0.0	[5.26929960916807...	[0.99487914377217...	0.0
0.0	1.0	1.0	1.0	1.0	2.0	1.0	2.0	1.0	1.0	[1.0,1.0,1.0,1.0,...	0.0	[4.99203401656150...	[0.99325398211858...	0.0
0.0	1.0	1.0	1.0	1.0	2.0	1.0	2.0	1.0	1.0	[1.0,1.0,1.0,1.0,...	0.0	[4.99203401656150...	[0.99325398211858...	0.0
0.0	1.0	1.0	1.0	1.0	2.0	1.0	2.0	3.0	1.0	[1.0,1.0,1.0,1.0,...	0.0	[4.74802132478210...	[0.99140567173413...	0.0
0.0	1.0	1.0	1.0	1.0	2.0	1.0	3.0	1.0	1.0	[1.0,1.0,1.0,1.0,...	0.0	[4.71476842395493...	[0.99111766179519...	0.0
0.0	1.0	1.0	1.0	1.0	2.0	1.0	3.0	1.0	1.0	[1.0,1.0,1.0,1.0,...	0.0	[4.71476842395493...	[0.99111766179519...	0.0
0.0	1.0	1.0	1.0	1.0	2.0	1.0	3.0	1.0	1.0	[1.0,1.0,1.0,1.0,...	0.0	[4.71476842395493...	[0.99111766179519...	0.0
0.0	1.0	1.0	1.0	1.0	2.0	1.0	3.0	1.0	1.0	[1.0,1.0,1.0,1.0,...	0.0	[4.71476842395493...	[0.99111766179519...	0.0
0.0	1.0	1.0	1.0	1.0	2.0	1.0	3.0	2.0	1.0	[1.0,1.0,1.0,1.0,...	0.0	[4.59276207806523...	[0.98997663106901...	0.0
0.0	1.0	1.0	1.0	1.0	2.0	5.0	1.0	1.0	1.0	[1.0,1.0,1.0,1.0,...	0.0	[4.10129026316119...	[0.98371817931939...	0.0
0.0	1.0	1.0	1.0	1.0	4.0	3.0	1.0	1.0	1.0	[1.0,1.0,1.0,1.0,...	0.0	[4.35023434970686...	[0.98726059831436...	0.0

only showing top 20 rows

Figure 29: New DataFrame with raw prediction and actual prediction against each row

Step 7: Generating objective history of training

Let's generate the objective history of the model in each iteration, as follows:

```
val trainingSummary = model.summary
val objectiveHistory = trainingSummary.objectiveHistory
objectiveHistory.foreach(loss => println(loss))
```

The preceding code segment produces the following output in terms of training loss:

```
0.6562291876496595
0.6087867761081431
0.538972588904556
0.4928455913405332
0.46269258074999386
0.3527914819973198
0.20206901337404978
```

```
0.16459454874996993
0.13783437051276512
0.11478053164710095
0.11420433621438157
0.11138884788059378
0.11041889032338036
0.10849477236373875
0.10818880537879513
0.10682868640074723
0.10641395229253267
0.10555411704574749
0.10505186414044905
0.10470425580130915
0.10376219754747162
0.10331139609033112
0.10276173290225406
0.10245982201904923
0.10198833366394071
0.10168248313103552
0.10163242551955443
0.10162826209311404
0.10162119367292953
0.10161235376791203
0.1016114803209495
0.10161090505556039
0.1016107261254795
0.10161056082112738
0.10161050381332608
0.10161048515341387
0.10161043900301985
0.10161042057436288
0.10161040971267737
0.10161040846923354
0.10161040625542347
0.10161040595207525
0.10161040575664354
0.10161040565870835
0.10161040519559975
0.10161040489834573
0.10161040445215266
0.1016104043469577
0.1016104042793553
0.1016104042606048
0.10161040423579716
```

As you can see, the loss gradually reduces in later iterations.

Step 8: Evaluating the model

First, we will have to make sure that the classifier that we used comes from the binary logistic regression summary:

```
val binarySummary =
trainingSummary.asInstanceOf[BinaryLogisticRegressionSummary]
```

Now let's obtain the ROC as a `DataFrame` and `areaUnderROC`. A value approximate to 1.0 is better:

```
val roc = binarySummary.roc
roc.show()
println("Area Under ROC: " + binarySummary.areaUnderROC)
```

The preceding lines prints the value of `areaUnderROC`, as follows:

```
Area Under ROC: 0.9959095884623509
```

This is excellent! Now let's compute other metrics, such as true positive rate, false positive rate, false negative rate, and total count, and a number of instances correctly and wrongly predicted, as follows:

```
import org.apache.spark.sql.functions._

// Calculate the performance metrics
val lp = predictions.select("label", "prediction")
val counttotal = predictions.count()
val correct = lp.filter($"label" === $"prediction").count()
val wrong = lp.filter(not($"label" === $"prediction")).count()
val truep = lp.filter($"prediction" === 0.0).filter($"label" ===
$"prediction").count()
val falseN = lp.filter($"prediction" === 0.0).filter(not($"label" ===
$"prediction")).count()
val falseP = lp.filter($"prediction" === 1.0).filter(not($"label" ===
$"prediction")).count()
val ratioWrong = wrong.toDouble / counttotal.toDouble
val ratioCorrect = correct.toDouble / counttotal.toDouble

println("Total Count: " + counttotal)
println("Correctly Predicted: " + correct)
println("Wrongly Identified: " + wrong)
println("True Positive: " + truep)
println("False Negative: " + falseN)
println("False Positive: " + falseP)
println("ratioWrong: " + ratioWrong)
println("ratioCorrect: " + ratioCorrect)
```

Now you should observe an output from the preceding code as follows:

Total Count: 209
Correctly Predicted: 202
Wrongly Identified: 7
True Positive: 140
False Negative: 4
False Positive: 3
ratioWrong: 0.03349282296650718
ratioCorrect: 0.9665071770334929

Finally, let's judge the accuracy of the model. However, first, we need to set the model threshold to maximize fMeasure:

```
val fMeasure = binarySummary.fMeasureByThreshold
val fm = fMeasure.col("F-Measure")
val maxFMeasure = fMeasure.select(max("F-
Measure")).head().getDouble(0)
val bestThreshold = fMeasure.where($"F-Measure" ===
maxFMeasure).select("threshold").head().getDouble(0)
model.setThreshold(bestThreshold)
```

Now let's compute the accuracy, as follows:

```
val evaluator = new
BinaryClassificationEvaluator().setLabelCol("label")
val accuracy = evaluator.evaluate(predictions)
println("Accuracy: " + accuracy)
```

The preceding code produces the following output, which is almost 99.64%:

```
Accuracy:  0.9963975418520874
```

Multiclass classification using logistic regression

A binary logistic regression can be generalized into multinomial logistic regression to train and predict multiclass classification problems. For example, for *K* possible outcomes, one of the outcomes can be chosen as a pivot, and the other *K−1* outcomes can be separately regressed against the pivot outcome. In spark.mllib, the first class 0 is chosen as the pivot class.

For multiclass classification problems, the algorithm will output a multinomial logistic regression model, which contains $k-1 binary$ logistic regression models regressed against the first class. Given a new data point, $k-1 models$ will be run, and the class with the largest probability will be chosen as the predicted class. In this section, we will show you an example of a classification using the logistic regression with L-BFGS for faster convergence.

Step 1. Load and parse the MNIST dataset in LIVSVM format

```
// Load training data in LIBSVM format.
 val data = MLUtils.loadLibSVMFile(spark.sparkContext,
"data/mnist.bz2")
```

Step 2. Prepare the training and test sets

Split data into training (75%) and test (25%), as follows:

```
val splits = data.randomSplit(Array(0.75, 0.25), seed = 12345L)
val training = splits(0).cache()
val test = splits(1)
```

Step 3. Run the training algorithm to build the model

Run the training algorithm to build the model by setting a number of classes (10 for this dataset). For better classification accuracy, you can also specify intercept and validate the dataset using the Boolean true value, as follows:

```
val model = new LogisticRegressionWithLBFGS()
                .setNumClasses(10)
                .setIntercept(true)
                .setValidateData(true)
                .run(training)
```

Set intercept as true if the algorithm should add an intercept using `setIntercept()`. If you want the algorithm to validate the training set before the model building itself, you should set the value as true using the `setValidateData()` method.

Step 4. Clear the default threshold

Clear the default threshold so that the training does not occur with the default setting, as follows:

```
model.clearThreshold()
```

Step 5. Compute raw scores on the test set

Compute raw scores on the test set so that we can evaluate the model using the aforementioned performance metrics, as follows:

```
val scoreAndLabels = test.map { point =>
  val score = model.predict(point.features)
  (score, point.label)
}
```

Step 6. Instantiate a multiclass metrics for the evaluation

```
val metrics = new MulticlassMetrics(scoreAndLabels)
```

Step 7. Constructing the confusion matrix

```
println("Confusion matrix:")
println(metrics.confusionMatrix)
```

In a confusion matrix, each column of the matrix represents the instances in a predicted class, while each row represents the instances in an actual class (or vice versa). The name stems from the fact that it makes it easy to see if the system is confusing two classes. For more, refer to matrix (https://en.wikipedia.org/wiki/Confusion_matrix.Confusion):

```
1466.0  1.0     4.0     2.0     3.0     11.0    18.0    1.0     11.0    4.0
0.0     1709.0  11.0    3.0     2.0     6.0     1.0     5.0     15.0    4.0
10.0    17.0    1316.0  24.0    22.0    8.0     20.0    17.0    26.0    8.0
3.0     9.0     38.0    1423.0  1.0     52.0    9.0     11.0    31.0    15.0
3.0     4.0     23.0    1.0     1363.0  4.0     10.0    7.0     5.0     43.0
19.0    7.0     11.0    50.0    12.0    1170.0  23.0    6.0     32.0    11.0
6.0     2.0     15.0    3.0     10.0    19.0    1411.0  2.0     8.0     2.0
4.0     7.0     10.0    7.0     14.0    4.0     2.0     1519.0  8.0     48.0
9.0     22.0    26.0    43.0    11.0    46.0    16.0    5.0     1268.0  8.0
6.0     3.0     5.0     23.0    39.0    8.0     0.0     60.0    14.0    1327.0
```

Figure 30: Confusion matrix generated by the logistic regression classifier

Step 8. Overall statistics

Now let's compute the overall statistics to judge the performance of the model:

```
val accuracy = metrics.accuracy
println("Summary Statistics")
println(s"Accuracy = $accuracy")
// Precision by label
val labels = metrics.labels
labels.foreach { l =>
  println(s"Precision($l) = " + metrics.precision(l))
```

```
}
// Recall by label
labels.foreach { l =>
  println(s"Recall($l) = " + metrics.recall(l))
}
// False positive rate by label
labels.foreach { l =>
  println(s"FPR($l) = " + metrics.falsePositiveRate(l))
}
// F-measure by label
labels.foreach { l =>
  println(s"F1-Score($l) = " + metrics.fMeasure(l))
}
```

The preceding code segment produces the following output, containing some performance metrics, such as accuracy, precision, recall, true positive rate , false positive rate, and f1 score:

```
Summary Statistics
----------------------
Accuracy = 0.9203609775377116
Precision(0.0) = 0.9606815203145478
Precision(1.0) = 0.9595732734418866
  .
  .
  .
Precision(8.0) = 0.8942172073342737
Precision(9.0) = 0.9027210884353741

Recall(0.0) = 0.9638395792241946
Recall(1.0) = 0.9732346241457859
  .
  .
  .
Recall(8.0) = 0.8720770288858322
Recall(9.0) = 0.8936026936026936

FPR(0.0) = 0.004392386530014641
FPR(1.0) = 0.005363128491620112
  .
  .
  .
FPR(8.0) = 0.010927369417935456
FPR(9.0) = 0.010441004672897197

F1-Score(0.0) = 0.9622579586478502
F1-Score(1.0) = 0.966355668645745
  .
  .
  .
F1-Score(9.0) = 0.8981387478849409
```

Now let's compute the overall, that is, summary statistics:

```
println(s"Weighted precision: ${metrics.weightedPrecision}")
println(s"Weighted recall: ${metrics.weightedRecall}")
println(s"Weighted F1 score: ${metrics.weightedFMeasure}")
println(s"Weighted false positive rate:
${metrics.weightedFalsePositiveRate}")
```

The preceding code segment prints the following output containing weighted precision, recall, f1 score, and false positive rate:

```
Weighted precision: 0.920104303076327
Weighted recall: 0.9203609775377117
Weighted F1 score: 0.9201934861645358
Weighted false positive rate: 0.008752250453215607
```

The overall statistics say that the accuracy of the model is more than 92%. However, we can still improve it using a better algorithm such as **random forest** (**RF**). In the next section, we will look at the random forest implementation to classify the same model.

Improving classification accuracy using random forests

Random forests (also sometimes called random decision forests) are ensembles of decision trees. Random forests are one of the most successful machine learning models for classification and regression. They combine many decision trees in order to reduce the risk of overfitting. Like decision trees, random forests handle categorical features, extend to the multiclass classification setting, do not require feature scaling, and are able to capture nonlinearities and feature interactions. There are numerous advantageous RFs. They can overcome the overfitting problem across their training dataset by combining many decision trees.

A forest in the RF or RDF usually consists of hundreds of thousands of trees. These trees are actually trained on different parts of the same training set. More technically, an individual tree that has grown very deep tends to learn from highly unpredictable patterns. This kind of nature of the trees creates overfitting problems on the training sets. Moreover, low biases make the classifier a low performer even if your dataset quality is good in terms of features presented. On the other hand, an RF helps to average multiple decision trees together with the goal of reducing the variance to ensure consistency by computing proximities between pairs of cases.

However, this increases a small bias or some loss of the interpretability of the results. But, eventually, the performance of the final model is increased dramatically. While using the RF as a classifier, here goes the parameter setting:

- If the number of trees is 1, then no bootstrapping is used at all; however, if the number of trees is > *1*, then bootstrapping is accomplished. The supported values are `auto`, `all`, `sqrt`, `log2`, and `onethird`.
- The supported numerical values are *(0.0-1.0]* and *[1-n]*. However, if `featureSubsetStrategy` is chosen as `auto`, the algorithm chooses the best feature subset strategy automatically.
- If `numTrees == 1`, the `featureSubsetStrategy` is set to be `all`. However, if `numTrees > 1` (that is, forest), `featureSubsetStrategy` is set to be `sqrt` for classification.
- Moreover, if a real value *n* is set in the range of *(0, 1.0]*, `n*number_of_features` will be used. However, if an integer value say *n* is in the `range (1, the number of features)`, only n features are used alternatively.
- The `categoricalFeaturesInfo` parameter , which is a map, is used for storing arbitrary categorical features. An entry *(n -> k)* indicates that feature *n* is categorical with *k* categories indexed from *0: {0, 1,...,k-1}*.
- The impurity criterion is used only for the information gain calculation. The supported values are *gini* and *variance* for classification and regression, respectively.
- The `maxDepth` is the maximum depth of the tree (for example, depth 0 means 1 leaf node, depth 1 means 1 internal node + 2 leaf nodes, and so on).
- The `maxBins` signifies the maximum number of bins used for splitting the features, where the suggested value is 100 to get better results.
- Finally, the random seed is used for bootstrapping and choosing feature subsets to avoid the random nature of the results.

As already mentioned, since RF is fast and scalable enough for the large-scale dataset, Spark is a suitable technology to implement the RF to take the massive scalability. However, if the proximities are calculated, storage requirements also grow exponentially.

Classifying MNIST dataset using random forest

In this section, we will show an example of a classification using the random forest. We will break down the code step-by-step so that you can understand the solution easily.

Step 1. Load and parse the MNIST dataset in LIVSVM format

```
// Load training data in LIBSVM format.
 val data = MLUtils.loadLibSVMFile(spark.sparkContext,
"data/mnist.bz2")
```

Step 2. Prepare the training and test sets

Split data into training (75%) and test (25%) and also set the seed for the reproducibility, as follows:

```
val splits = data.randomSplit(Array(0.75, 0.25), seed = 12345L)
val training = splits(0).cache()
val test = splits(1)
```

Step 3. Run the training algorithm to build the model

Train a random forest model with an empty `categoricalFeaturesInfo`. This required since all the features are continuous in the dataset:

```
val numClasses = 10 //number of classes in the MNIST dataset
val categoricalFeaturesInfo = Map[Int, Int]()
val numTrees = 50 // Use more in practice.More is better
val featureSubsetStrategy = "auto" // Let the algorithm choose.
val impurity = "gini" // see above notes on RandomForest for
explanation
val maxDepth = 30 // More is better in practice
val maxBins = 32 // More is better in practice
val model = RandomForest.trainClassifier(training, numClasses,
categoricalFeaturesInfo, numTrees, featureSubsetStrategy, impurity,
maxDepth, maxBins)
```

Note that training a random forest model is very resource extensive. Consequently, it will take more memory, so beware of OOM. I would say increase the Java heap space prior to running this code.

Step 4. Compute raw scores on the test set

Compute raw scores on the test set so that we can evaluate the model using the aforementioned performance metrics, as follows:

```
val scoreAndLabels = test.map { point =>
  val score = model.predict(point.features)
  (score, point.label)
}
```

Step 5. Instantiate a multiclass metrics for the evaluation

```
val metrics = new MulticlassMetrics(scoreAndLabels)
```

Step 6. Constructing the confusion matrix

```
println("Confusion matrix:")
println(metrics.confusionMatrix)
```

The preceding code prints the following confusion matrix for our classification:

```
1500.0  0.0     8.0     1.0     3.0     6.0     6.0     3.0     2.0     5.0
0.0     1737.0  1.0     3.0     0.0     3.0     1.0     1.0     7.0     2.0
3.0     6.0     1416.0  19.0    5.0     3.0     1.0     9.0     6.0     4.0
0.0     1.0     5.0     1509.0  0.0     21.0    0.0     3.0     18.0    18.0
1.0     3.0     9.0     1.0     1415.0  3.0     2.0     7.0     4.0     17.0
2.0     2.0     0.0     20.0    0.0     1275.0  12.0    0.0     8.0     7.0
4.0     2.0     3.0     2.0     2.0     13.0    1453.0  0.0     8.0     0.0
0.0     3.0     10.0    8.0     4.0     3.0     0.0     1572.0  0.0     11.0
10.0    0.0     11.0    19.0    6.0     12.0    3.0     7.0     1388.0  14.0
1.0     2.0     5.0     10.0    28.0    2.0     0.0     21.0    13.0    1407.0
```

Figure 31: Confusion matrix generated by the random forest classifier

Step 7. Overall statistics

Now let's compute the overall statistics to judge the performance of the model:

```
val accuracy = metrics.accuracy
println("Summary Statistics")
println(s"Accuracy = $accuracy")
// Precision by label
val labels = metrics.labels
labels.foreach { l =>
  println(s"Precision($l) = " + metrics.precision(l))
}
// Recall by label
labels.foreach { l =>
  println(s"Recall($l) = " + metrics.recall(l))
```

```
}
// False positive rate by label
labels.foreach { l =>
  println(s"FPR($l) = " + metrics.falsePositiveRate(l))
}
// F-measure by label
labels.foreach { l =>
  println(s"F1-Score($l) = " + metrics.fMeasure(l))
}
```

The preceding code segment produces the following output, containing some performance metrics, such as accuracy, precision, recall, true positive rate , false positive rate, and F1 score:

```
Summary Statistics:
----------------------------
Precision(0.0) = 0.9861932938856016
Precision(1.0) = 0.9891799544419134
.

.
Precision(8.0) = 0.9546079779917469
Precision(9.0) = 0.9474747474747475

Recall(0.0) = 0.9778357235984355
Recall(1.0) = 0.9897435897435898
.

.
Recall(8.0) = 0.9442176870748299
Recall(9.0) = 0.9449294828744124

FPR(0.0) = 0.0015387997362057595
FPR(1.0) = 0.0014151646059883808
.

.
FPR(8.0) = 0.0048136532710962
FPR(9.0) = 0.0056967572304995615

F1-Score(0.0) = 0.9819967266775778
F1-Score(1.0) = 0.9894616918256907
.

.
F1-Score(8.0) = 0.9493844049247605
F1-Score(9.0) = 0.9462004034969739
```

Now let's compute the overall statistics, as follows:

```
println(s"Weighted precision: ${metrics.weightedPrecision}")
println(s"Weighted recall: ${metrics.weightedRecall}")
```

```
println(s"Weighted F1 score: ${metrics.weightedFMeasure}")
println(s"Weighted false positive rate:
${metrics.weightedFalsePositiveRate}")
val testErr = labelAndPreds.filter(r => r._1 != r._2).count.toDouble /
test.count()
println("Accuracy = " + (1-testErr) * 100 + " %")
```

The preceding code segment prints the following output, containing weighted precision, recall, F1 score, and false positive rate:

```
Overall statistics
--------------------------
Weighted precision: 0.966513107682512
Weighted recall: 0.9664712469534286
Weighted F1 score: 0.9664794711607312
Weighted false positive rate: 0.003675328222679072
Accuracy = 96.64712469534287 %
```

The overall statistics say that the accuracy of the model is more than 96%, which is better than that of logistic regression. However, we can still improve it using better model tuning.

Summary

In this chapter, we had a brief introduction to the topic and got a grasp of simple, yet powerful and common ML techniques. Finally, you saw how to build your own predictive model using Spark. You learned how to build a classification model, how to use the model to make predictions, and finally, how to use common ML techniques such as dimensionality reduction and One-Hot Encoding.

In the later sections, you saw how to apply the regression technique to high-dimensional datasets. Then, you saw how to apply a binary and multiclass classification algorithm for predictive analytics. Finally, you saw how to achieve outstanding classification accuracy using a random forest algorithm. However, we have other topics in machine learning that need to be covered too, for example, recommendation systems and model tuning for even more stable performance before you finally deploy the models.

In the next chapter, we will cover some advanced topics of Spark. We will provide examples of machine learning model tuning for better performance, and we will also cover two examples for movie recommendation and text clustering, respectively.

My Name is Bayes, Naive Bayes

12

"Prediction is very difficult, especially if it's about the future"

-Niels Bohr

Machine learning (ML) in combination with big data is a radical combination that has created some great impacts in the field of research in Academia and Industry. Moreover, many research areas are also entering into big data since datasets are being generated and produced in an unprecedented way from diverse sources and technologies, commonly referred as the **Data Deluge**. This imposes great challenges on ML, data analytics tools, and algorithms to find the real **VALUE** out of big data criteria such as volume, velocity, and variety. However, making predictions from these huge dataset has never been easy.

Considering this challenge, in this chapter we will dig deeper into ML and find out how to use a simple yet powerful method to build a scalable classification model and even more. In a nutshell, the following topics will be covered throughout this chapter:

- Multinomial classification
- Bayesian inference
- Naive Bayes
- Decision trees
- Naive Bayes versus decision trees

Multinomial classification

In ML, **multinomial** (also known as multiclass) classification is the task of classifying data objects or instances into more than two classes, that is, having more than two labels or classes. Classifying data objects or instances into two classes is called **binary classification**. More technically, in multinomial classification, each training instance belongs to one of N different classes subject to N >=2. The goal is then to construct a model that correctly predicts the classes to which the new instances belong. There may be numerous scenarios having multiple categories in which the data points belong. However, if a given point belongs to multiple categories, this problem decomposes trivially into a set of unlinked binary problems, which can be solved naturally using a binary classification algorithm.

Readers are suggested not be confused distinguishing the multiclass classification with multilabel classification, where multiple labels are to be predicted for each instance. For more on Spark-based implementation for the multilabel classification, interested readers should refer to https://spark.apache.org/docs/latest/mllib-evaluation-metrics.html#multilabel-classification.

Multiclass classification techniques can be divided into several categories as follows:

- Transformation to binary
- Extension from binary
- Hierarchical classification

Transformation to binary

Using the transformation to binary technique, a multiclass classification problem can be transformed into an equivalent strategy for multiple binary classification problems. In other words, this technique can be referred to as a *problem transformation techniques*. A detailed discussion from the theoretical and practical perspectives is out of the scope of this chapter. Therefore, here we will discuss only one example of the problem transformation technique called **One-Vs-The-Rest (OVTR)** algorithm as the representative of this category.

Classification using One-Vs-The-Rest approach

In this subsection, we will describe an example of performing multiclass classification using the OVTR algorithm by converting the problem into equivalent multiple binary classification problems. The OVTR strategy breaks down the problem and trains each binary classifier per class. In other words, the OVTR classifier strategy consists of fitting one binary classifier per class. It then treats all the samples of the current class as positive samples, and consequently other samples of other classifiers are treated as negatives samples.

This is a modular machine learning technique no doubt. However, on the downside, this strategy requires a base classifier from the multiclass family. The reason is that the classifier must produce a real value also called *confidence scores* instead of a prediction of the actual labels. The second disadvantage of this strategy is that if the dataset (aka training set) contains discrete class labels, these eventually lead to vague prediction results. In that case, multiple classes can be predicted for a single sample. To make the preceding discussion clearer, now let's see an example as follows.

Suppose that we have a set of 50 observations divided into three classes. Thus, we will use the same logic as before for selecting the negative examples too. For the training phase, let's have the following setting:

- **Classifier 1** has 30 positive examples and 20 negative examples
- **Classifier 2** has 36 positive examples and 14 negative examples
- **Classifier 3** has 14 positive examples and 24 negative examples

On the other hand, for the testing phase, suppose I have a new instance that need to be classified into one of the previous classes. Each of the three classifiers, of course, produces a probability with respect to the estimation This is an estimation of how low an instance belongs to the negative or positive examples in the classifier? In this case, we should always compare the probabilities of positive class in one versus the rest. Now that for N classes, we will have N probability estimates of the positive class for one test sample. Compare them, and whichever probability is the maximum of N probabilities belongs to that particular class. Spark provides multiclass to binary reduction with the OVTR algorithm, where the **Logistic Regression** algorithm is used as the base classifier.

Now let's see another example of a real dataset to demonstrate how Spark classifies all the features using OVTR algorithm. The OVTR classifier eventually predicts handwritten characters from the **Optical Character Reader (OCR)** dataset. However, before diving into the demonstration, let's explore the OCR dataset first to get the exploratory nature of the data. It is to be noted that when OCR software first processes a document, it divides the paper or any object into a matrix such that each cell in the grid contains a single glyph (also known different graphical shapes), which is just an elaborate way of referring to a letter, symbol, or number or any contextual information from the paper or the object.

To demonstrate the OCR pipeline, let's assume that the document contains only alpha characters in English that match glyphs to one of the 26 capital letters, that is, *A* to *Z*. We will use the OCR letter dataset from the *UCI Machine Learning Data Repository*. The dataset was denoted by W. *Frey* and *D. J. Slate*. While exploring the dataset, you should observe 20,000 examples of 26 English capital letters. Letter written in capital letters are available as printed using 20 different, randomly reshaped and distorted black and white fonts as glyphs of different shapes. In short, predicting all the characters from 26 alphabets turns the problem itself into a multiclass classification problem with 26 classes. Consequently, a binary classifier will not be able to serve our purpose.

Figure 1: Some of the printed glyphs (Source: Letter recognition using Holland-style adaptive classifiers. ML. V. 6. p. 161-182. by W. Frey and D.J. Slate [1991])

The preceding figure shows the images that I explained earlier.*The dataset* provides an example of some of the printed glyphs distorted in this way; therefore, the letters are computationally challenging for a computer to identify. Yet, these glyphs are easily recognized by a human being. The following figure shows the statistical attributes of the top 20 rows:

letter	xbox	ybox	width	height	onpix	xbar	ybar	x2bar	y2bar	xybar	x2ybar	xy2bar	xedge	xedgey	yedge	yedgex
T	2	8	3	5	1	8	13	0	6	6	10	8	0	8	0	8
I	5	12	3	7	2	10	5	5	4	13	3	9	2	8	4	10
D	4	11	6	8	6	10	6	2	6	10	3	7	3	7	3	9
N	7	11	6	6	3	5	9	4	6	4	4	10	6	10	2	8
G	2	1	3	1	1	8	6	6	6	6	5	9	1	7	5	10
S	4	11	5	8	3	8	8	6	9	5	6	6	0	8	9	7
B	4	2	5	4	4	8	7	6	6	7	6	6	2	8	7	10
A	1	1	3	2	1	8	2	2	2	8	2	8	1	6	2	7
J	2	2	4	4	2	10	6	2	6	12	4	8	1	6	1	7
M	11	15	13	9	7	13	2	6	2	12	1	9	8	1	1	8
X	3	9	5	7	4	8	7	3	8	5	6	8	2	8	6	7
O	6	13	4	7	4	6	7	6	3	10	7	9	5	9	5	8
G	4	9	6	7	6	7	8	6	2	6	5	11	4	8	7	8
M	6	9	8	6	9	7	8	6	5	7	5	8	8	9	8	6
R	5	9	5	7	6	6	11	7	3	7	3	9	2	7	5	11
F	6	9	5	4	3	10	6	3	5	10	5	7	3	9	6	9
O	3	4	4	3	2	8	7	7	5	7	6	8	2	8	3	8
C	7	10	5	5	2	6	8	6	8	11	7	11	2	8	5	9
T	6	11	6	8	5	6	11	5	6	11	9	4	3	12	2	4
J	2	2	3	3	1	10	6	3	6	12	4	9	0	7	1	7

only showing top 20 rows

Figure 2: The snapshot of the dataset shown as the data frame

Exploration and preparation of the OCR dataset

According to the dataset description, glyphs are scanned using an OCR reader on to the computer then they are automatically converted into pixels. Consequently, all the 16 statistical attributes (in **figure 2**) are recorded to the computer too. The the concentration of black pixels across various areas of the box provide a way to differentiate 26 letters using OCR or a machine learning algorithm to be trained.

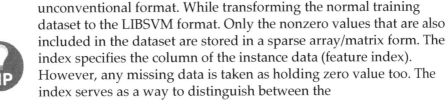

Recall that **support vector machines (SVM)**, Logistic Regression, Naive Bayesian-based classifier, or any other classifier algorithms (along with their associated learners) require all the features to be numeric. LIBSVM allows you to use a sparse training dataset in an unconventional format. While transforming the normal training dataset to the LIBSVM format. Only the nonzero values that are also included in the dataset are stored in a sparse array/matrix form. The index specifies the column of the instance data (feature index). However, any missing data is taken as holding zero value too. The index serves as a way to distinguish between the features/parameters. For example, for three features, indices 1, 2, and 3 would correspond to the x, y, and z coordinates, respectively. The correspondence between the same index values of different data instances is merely mathematical when constructing the hyperplane; these serve as coordinates. If you skip any index in between, it should be assigned a default value of zero.

In most practical cases, we might need to normalize the data against all the features points. In short, we need to convert the current tab-separated OCR data into LIBSVM format to make the training step easier. Thus, I'm assuming you have downloaded the data and converted into LIBSVM format using their own script. The resulting dataset that is transformed into LIBSVM format consisting of labels and features is shown in the following figure:

```
+-----+------------------+
|label|          features|
+-----+------------------+
|  8.0|(17,[0,1,2,3,4,5,...|
| 10.0|(17,[0,1,2,3,4,5,...|
|  9.0|(17,[0,1,2,3,4,5,...|
|  8.0|(17,[0,1,2,3,4,5,...|
| 10.0|(17,[0,1,2,3,4,5,...|
|  8.0|(17,[0,1,2,3,4,5,...|
|  5.0|(17,[0,1,2,3,4,5,...|
|  6.0|(17,[0,1,2,3,4,5,...|
|  8.0|(17,[0,1,2,3,4,5,...|
|  7.0|(17,[0,1,2,3,4,5,...|
|  6.0|(17,[0,1,2,3,4,5,...|
|  8.0|(17,[0,1,2,3,4,5,...|
|  8.0|(17,[0,1,2,3,4,5,...|
|  9.0|(17,[0,1,2,3,4,5,...|
|  4.0|(17,[0,1,2,3,4,5,...|
|  7.0|(17,[0,1,2,3,4,5,...|
|  7.0|(17,[0,1,2,3,4,5,...|
|  8.0|(17,[0,1,2,3,4,5,...|
|  8.0|(17,[0,1,2,3,4,5,...|
+-----+------------------+
only showing top 20 rows
```

Figure 3: A snapshot of 20 rows of the OCR dataset in LIBSVM format

Interested readers can refer to the following research article for gaining in-depth knowledge: *Chih-Chung Chang* and *Chih-Jen Lin, LIBSVM: a library for support vector machines, ACM Transactions on Intelligent Systems and Technology,* 2:27:1--27:27, 2011. You can also refer to a public script provided on my GitHub repository at https://github.com/rezacsedu/RandomForestSpark/ that directly converts the OCR data in CSV into LIBSVM format. I read the data about all the letters and assigned a unique numeric value to each. All you need is to show the input and output file path and run the script.

Now let's dive into the example. The example that I will be demonstrating has 11 steps including data parsing, Spark session creation, model building, and model evaluation.

Step 1. Creating Spark session - Create a Spark session by specifying master URL, Spark SQL warehouse, and application name as follows:

```
val spark = SparkSession.builder
                    .master("local[*]") //change acordingly
                    .config("spark.sql.warehouse.dir", "/home/exp/")
                    .appName("OneVsRestExample")
                    .getOrCreate()
```

Step 2. Loading, parsing, and creating the data frame - Load the data file from the HDFS or local disk and create a data frame, and finally show the data frame structure as follows:

```
val inputData = spark.read.format("libsvm")
                    .load("data/Letterdata_libsvm.data")
inputData.show()
```

Step 3. Generating training and test set to train the model - Let's generate the training and test set by splitting 70% for training and 30% for the test:

```
val Array(train, test) = inputData.randomSplit(Array(0.7, 0.3))
```

Step 4. Instantiate the base classifier - Here the base classifier acts as the multiclass classifier. For this case, it is the Logistic Regression algorithm that can be instantiated by specifying parameters such as the number of max iterations, tolerance, regression parameter, and Elastic Net parameters.

Note that Logistic Regression is an appropriate regression analysis to conduct when the dependent variable is dichotomous (binary). Like all regression analyses, Logistic Regression is a predictive analysis. Logistic regression is used to describe data and to explain the relationship between one dependent binary variable and one or more nominal, ordinal, interval, or ratio level independent variables.

For a a Spark-based implementation of the Logistic Regression algorithm, interested readers can refer to `https://spark.apache.org/docs/latest/mllib-linear-methods.html#logistic-regression`.

In brief, the following parameters are used to training a Logistic Regression classifier:

- `MaxIter`: This specifies the number of maximum iterations. In general, more is better.
- `Tol`: This is the tolerance for the stopping criteria. In general, less is better, which helps the model to be trained more intensively. The default value is 1E-4.
- `FirIntercept`: This signifies if you want to intercept the decision function while generating the probabilistic interpretation.
- `Standardization`: This signifies a Boolean value depending upon if would like to standardize the training or not.
- `AggregationDepth`: More is better.
- `RegParam`: This signifies the regression params. Less is better for most cases.
- `ElasticNetParam`: This signifies more advanced regression params. Less is better for most cases.

Nevertheless, you can specify the fitting intercept as a `Boolean` value as true or false depending upon your problem type and dataset properties:

```
val classifier = new LogisticRegression()
                      .setMaxIter(500)
                      .setTol(1E-4)
                      .setFitIntercept(true)
                      .setStandardization(true)
                      .setAggregationDepth(50)
                      .setRegParam(0.0001)
                      .setElasticNetParam(0.01)
```

Step 5. Instantiate the OVTR classifier - Now instantiate an OVTR classifier to convert the multiclass classification problem into multiple binary classifications as follows:

```
val ovr = new OneVsRest().setClassifier(classifier)
```

Here `classifier` is the Logistic Regression estimator. Now it's time to train the model.

Step 6. Train the multiclass model - Let's train the model using the training set as follows:

```
val ovrModel = ovr.fit(train)
```

Step 7. Score the model on the test set - We can score the model on test data using the transformer (that is, `ovrModel`) as follows:

```
val predictions = ovrModel.transform(test)
```

Step 8. Evaluate the model - In this step, we will predict the labels for the characters in the first column. But before that we need instantiate an `evaluator` to compute the classification performance metrics such as accuracy, precision, recall, and `f1` measure as follows:

```
val evaluator = new MulticlassClassificationEvaluator()
                        .setLabelCol("label")
                        .setPredictionCol("prediction")
val evaluator1 = evaluator.setMetricName("accuracy")
val evaluator2 = evaluator.setMetricName("weightedPrecision")
val evaluator3 = evaluator.setMetricName("weightedRecall")
val evaluator4 = evaluator.setMetricName("f1")
```

Step 9. Compute performance metrics - Compute the classification accuracy, precision, recall, `f1` measure, and error on test data as follows:

```
val accuracy = evaluator1.evaluate(predictions)
val precision = evaluator2.evaluate(predictions)
val recall = evaluator3.evaluate(predictions)
val f1 = evaluator4.evaluate(predictions)
```

Step 10. Print the performance metrics:

```
println("Accuracy = " + accuracy)
println("Precision = " + precision)
println("Recall = " + recall)
println("F1 = " + f1)
println(s"Test Error = ${1 - accuracy}")
```

You should observe the value as follows:

```
Accuracy = 0.5217246545696688
Precision = 0.488360500637862
Recall = 0.5217246545696688
F1 = 0.4695649096879411
Test Error = 0.47827534543033123
```

Step 11. Stop the Spark session:

```
spark.stop() // Stop Spark session
```

This way, we can convert a multinomial classification problem into multiple binary classifications problem without sacrificing the problem types. However, from step 10, we can observe that the classification accuracy is not good at all. It might be because of several reasons such as the nature of the dataset we used to train the model. Also even more importantly, we did not tune the hyperparameters while training the Logistic Regression model. Moreover, while performing the transformation, the OVTR had to sacrifice some accuracy.

Hierarchical classification

In a hierarchical classification task, the classification problem can be resolved by dividing the output space into a tree. In that tree, parent nodes are divided into multiple child nodes. The process persists until each child node depicts a single class. Several methods have been proposed based on the hierarchical classification technique. Computer vision is an example of such areas where recognizing pictures or written text are something that use hierarchical processing does. An extensive discussion on this classifier is out of the scope of this chapter.

Extension from binary

This is a technique for extending existing binary classifiers to solve multiclass classification problems. To address multiclass classification problems, several algorithms have been proposed and developed based on neural networks, DTs, Random forest, k-nearest neighbors, Naive Bayes, and SVM. In the following sections, we will discuss the Naive Bayes and the DT algorithm as two representatives of this category.

Now, before starting to solve multiclass classification problems using Naive Bayes algorithms, let's have a brief overview of Bayesian inference in the next section.

Bayesian inference

In this section, we will briefly discuss **Bayesian inference** (**BI**) and its underlying theory. Readers will be familiar with this concept from the theoretical and computational viewpoints.

An overview of Bayesian inference

Bayesian inference is a statistical method based on Bayes theorem. It is used to update the probability of a hypothesis (as a strong statistical proof) so that statistical models can repeatedly update towards more accurate learning. In other words, all types of uncertainty are revealed in terms of statistical probability in the Bayesian inference approach. This is an important technique in theoretical as well as mathematical statistics. We will discuss the Bayes theorem broadly in a later section.

Furthermore, Bayesian updating is predominantly foremost in the incremental learning and dynamic analysis of the sequence of the dataset. For example time series analysis, genome sequencing in biomedical data analytics, science, engineering, philosophy, and law are some example where Bayesian inference is used widely. From the philosophical perspective and decision theory, Bayesian inference is strongly correlated to predictive probability. This theory, however, is more formally known as the **Bayesian probability**.

What is inference?

Inference or model evaluation is the process of updating probabilities of the denouement derived from the model at the end. As a result, all the probabilistic evidence is eventually known against the observation at hand so that observations can be updated while using the Bayesian model for classification analysis. Later on, this information is fetched to the Bayesian model by instantiating the consistency against all the observations in the dataset. The rules that are fetched to the model are referred to as prior probabilities where a probability is assessed before making reference to certain relevant observations, especially subjectively or on the assumption that all possible outcomes be given the same probability. Then beliefs are computed when all the evidence is known as posterior probabilities. These posterior probabilities reflect the levels of hypothesis computed based on updated evidence.

The Bayes theorem is used to compute the posterior probabilities that signify a consequence of two antecedents. Based on these antecedents, a prior probability and a likelihood function are derived from a statistical model for the new data for model adaptability. We will further discuss the Bayes theorem in a later section.

How does it work?

Here we discuss a general setup for a statistical inference problem. At the first place, from the data, we estimate the desired quantity and there might be unknown quantities too that we would like to estimate. It could be simply a response variable or predicted variable, a class, a label, or simply a number. If you are familiar with the *frequentist* approach, you might know that in this approach the unknown quantity say θ is assumed to be a fixed (nonrandom) quantity that is to be estimated by the observed data.

However, in the Bayesian framework, an unknown quantity say θ is treated as a random variable. More specifically, it is assumed that we have an initial guess about the distribution of θ, which is commonly referred to as the **prior distribution**. Now, after observing some data, the distribution of θ is updated. This step is usually performed using Bayes' rule (for more details, refer to the next section). This is why this approach is called the Bayesian approach. However, in short, from the prior distribution, we can compute predictive distributions for future observations.

This unpretentious process can be justified as the appropriate methodology to uncertain inference with the help of numerous arguments. However, the consistency is maintained with the clear principles of the rationality of these arguments. In spite of this strong mathematical evidence, many machine learning practitioners are uncomfortable with, and a bit reluctant of, using the Bayesian approach. The reason behind this is that often they view the selection of a posterior probability or prior as being arbitrary and subjective; however, in reality, this is subjective but not arbitrary.

Inappropriately, many Bayesians don't really think in true Bayesian terms. One can, therefore, find many pseudo-Bayesian procedures in the literature, in which models and priors are used that cannot be taken seriously as expressions of prior belief. There may also be computational difficulties with the Bayesian approach. Many of these can be addressed using **Markov chain Monte Carlo** methods, which are another main focus of my research. The details of this approach will be clearer as you go through this chapter.

Naive Bayes

In ML, **Naive Bayes** (**NB**) is an example of the probabilistic classifier based on the well-known Bayes' theorem with strong independence assumptions between the features. We will discuss Naive Bayes in detail in this section.

An overview of Bayes' theorem

In probability theory, **Bayes' theorem** describes the probability of an event based on a prior knowledge of conditions that is related to that certain event. This is a theorem of probability originally stated by the Reverend Thomas Bayes. In other words, it can be seen as a way of understanding how the probability theory is true and affected by a new piece of information. For example, if cancer is related to age, the information about *age* can be used to assess the probability that a person might have cancer more accurately.

Bayes' theorem is stated mathematically as the following equation:

$$P(A \mid B) = \frac{P(B \mid A)\, P(A)}{P(B)},$$

In the preceding equation, A and B are events with $P(B) \neq 0$, and the other terms can be described as follows:

- $P(A)$ and $P(B)$ are the probabilities of observing A and B without regard to each other (that is, independence)
- $P(A \mid B)$ is the conditional probability of observing event A given that B is true
- $P(B \mid A)$ is the conditional probability of observing event B given that A is true

As you probably know, a well-known Harvard study shows that only 10% of happy people are rich. However, you might think that this statistic is very compelling but you might be somewhat interested in knowing the percentage of rich people are also really happy. Bayes' theorem helps you out on how to calculate this reserving statistic using two additional clues:

1. The percentage of people overall who are happy, that is, *P(A)*.
2. The percentage of people overall who are rich, that is *P(B)*.

The key idea behind Bayes' theorem is reversing the statistic considering the overall rates. Suppose that the following pieces of information are available as a prior:

1. 40% of people are happy and => *P(A)*.
2. 5% of people are rich => *P(B)*.

Now let's consider that the Harvard study is correct, that is, *P(B|A) = 10%*. Now the fraction of rich people who are happy, that is, *P(A | B)*, can be calculated as follows:

P(A | B) = {P(A)* P(B | A)}/ P(B) = (40%*10%)/5% = 80%

Consequently, a majority of the people are also happy! Nice. To make it clearer, now let's assume the population of the whole world is 1,000 for simplicity. Then, according to our calculation, there are two facts that exist:

- Fact 1: This tells us 400 people are happy, and the Harvard study tells us that 40 of these happy people are also rich.
- Fact 2: There are 50 rich people altogether, and so the fraction who are happy is 40/50 = 80%.

This proves the Bayes theorem and its effectiveness. However, more comprehensive examples can be found at `https://onlinecourses.science.psu.edu/stat414/node/43`.

My name is Bayes, Naive Bayes

I'm Bayes, Naive Bayes (NB). I'm a successful classifier based upon the principle of **maximum a posteriori** (**MAP**). As a classifier, I am highly scalable, requiring a number of parameters linear in the number of variables (features/predictors) in a learning problem. I have several properties, for example, I am computationally faster, if you can hire me to classify something I'm simple to implement, and I can work well with high-dimensional datasets. Moreover, I can handle missing values in your dataset. Nevertheless, I'm adaptable since the model can be modified with new training data without rebuilding the model.

In Bayesian statistics, a MAP estimate is an estimate of an unknown quantity that equals the mode of the posterior distribution. The MAP estimate can be used to obtain a point estimate of an unobserved quantity on the basis of empirical data.

Sounds something similar to James Bond movies? Well, you/we can think a classifer as agent 007, right? Just kidding. I believe I am not as the parameters of the Naive Bayes classifier such as priori and conditional probabilities are learned or rather determined using a deterministic set of steps: this involves two very trivial operations that can be blindingly fast on modern computers, that is, counting and dividing. There is no *iteration*. There is no *epoch*. There is *no optimization of a cost equation* (which can be complex, of cubic order on an average or at least of square order complexity).

There is no *error back-propagation*. There is no operation(s) involving *solving a matrix equation*. These make Naive Bayes and its overall training faster.

However, before hiring this agent, you/we can discover his pros and cons so that we can use this agent like a trump card by utilizing it's best only. Well, here's table summarizing the pros and cons of this agent:

Agent	Pros	Cons	Better at
Naive Bayes (NB)	- Computationally fast - Simple to implement - Works well with high dimensions - Can handle missing values - Requires a small amount of data to train the model - It is scalable - Is adaptable since the model can be modified with new training data without rebuilding the model	- Relies on independence assumptions and so performs badly if the assumption does not meet - Relatively low accuracy - If you have no occurrences of a class label and a certain attribute value together then the frequency-based probability estimate will be zero	- When data has lots of missing values - When dependencies of features from each other are similar between features - Spam filtering and classification - Classifying a news article about technology, politics, sports, and so on. - Text mining

Table 1: Pros and the cons of the Naive Bayes algorithm

Building a scalable classifier with NB

In this section, we will see a step-by-step example using **Naive Bayes** (**NB**) algorithm. As already stated, NB is highly scalable, requiring a number of parameters linear in the number of variables (features/predictors) in a learning problem. This scalability has enabled the Spark community to make predictive analytics on large-scale datasets using this algorithm. The current implementation of NB in Spark MLlib supports both the multinomial NB and Bernoulli NB.

Bernoulli NB is useful if the feature vectors are binary. One application would be text classification with a bag of words (BOW) approach. On the other hand, multinomial NB is typically used for discrete counts. For example, if we have a text classification problem, we can take the idea of Bernoulli trials one step further and instead of BOW in a document we can use the frequency count in a document.

In this section, we will see how to predict the digits from the **Pen-Based Recognition of Handwritten Digits** dataset by incorporating Spark machine learning APIs including Spark MLlib, Spark ML, and Spark SQL:

Step 1. Data collection, preprocessing, and exploration - The Pen-based recognition of handwritten digits dataset was downloaded from the UCI Machine Learning Repository at https://www.csie.ntu.edu.tw/~cjlin/libsvmtools/datasets/ multiclass/pendigits. This dataset was generated after collecting around 250 digit samples each from 44 writers, correlated to the location of the pen at fixed time intervals of 100 milliseconds. Each digit was then written inside a 500 x 500 pixel box. Finally, those images were scaled to an integer value between 0 and 100 to create consistent scaling between each observation. A well-known spatial resampling technique was used to obtain 3 and 8 regularly spaced points on an arc trajectory. A sample image along with the lines from point to point can be visualized by plotting the 3 or 8 sampled points based on their (x, y) coordinates; it looks like what is shown in the following table:

Set	'0'	'1'	'2'	'3'	'4'	'5'	'6'	'7'	'8'	'9'	Total
Training	780	779	780	719	780	720	720	778	718	719	7493
Test	363	364	364	336	364	335	336	364	335	336	3497

Table 2: Number of digits used for the training and the test set

As shown in the preceding table, the training set consists of samples written by 30 writers and the testing set consists of samples written by 14 writers.

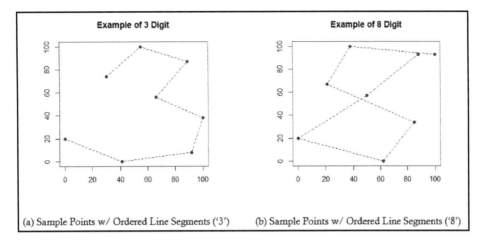

Figure 4: Example of digit 3 and 8 respectively

More on this dataset can be found at `http://archive.ics.uci.edu/ml/machine-learning-databases/pendigits/pendigits-orig.names`. A digital representation of a sample snapshot of the dataset is shown in the following figure:

```
+-----+--------------------+
|label|            features|
+-----+--------------------+
|  8.0|(16,[0,1,2,3,4,5,...|
|  2.0|(16,[1,2,3,4,5,6,...|
|  1.0|(16,[1,2,3,4,5,6,...|
|  4.0|(16,[1,2,3,4,5,6,...|
|  1.0|(16,[1,2,3,4,5,6,...|
|  6.0|(16,[0,1,2,3,4,5,...|
|  4.0|(16,[1,2,3,4,5,6,...|
|  0.0|(16,[1,2,3,4,5,6,...|
|  5.0|(16,[0,1,2,3,4,5,...|
|  0.0|(16,[0,1,2,3,5,6,...|
|  9.0|(16,[0,1,2,3,5,6,...|
|  8.0|(16,[0,1,2,3,4,5,...|
|  5.0|(16,[0,1,2,3,4,5,...|
|  9.0|(16,[0,1,2,3,5,6,...|
|  7.0|(16,[1,2,3,4,5,6,...|
|  3.0|(16,[0,1,2,3,4,5,...|
|  3.0|(16,[0,1,2,3,4,5,...|
|  9.0|(16,[0,1,2,3,4,5,...|
|  2.0|(16,[0,1,2,3,4,5,...|
|  2.0|(16,[1,2,3,4,5,6,...|
+-----+--------------------+
only showing top 20 rows
```

Figure 5: A snap of the 20 rows of the hand-written digit dataset

Now to predict the dependent variable (that is, label) using the independent variables (that is, features), we need to train a multiclass classifier since, as shown previously, the dataset now has nine classes, that is, nine handwritten digits. For the prediction, we will use the Naive Bayes classifier and evaluate the model's performance.

Step 2. Load the required library and packages:

```
import org.apache.spark.ml.classification.NaiveBayes
import org.apache.spark.ml.evaluation
                        .MulticlassClassificationEvaluator
import org.apache.spark.sql.SparkSession
```

Step 3. Create an active Spark session:

```
val spark = SparkSession
            .builder
            .master("local[*]")
            .config("spark.sql.warehouse.dir", "/home/exp/")
            .appName(s"NaiveBayes")
            .getOrCreate()
```

Note that here the master URL has been set as `local[*]`, which means all the cores of your machine will be used for processing the Spark job. You should set SQL warehouse accordingly and other configuration parameter based on the requirements.

Step 4. Create the DataFrame - Load the data stored in LIBSVM format as a DataFrame:

```
val data = spark.read.format("libsvm")
                .load("data/pendigits.data")
```

For digits classification, the input feature vectors are usually sparse, and sparse vectors should be supplied as input to take advantage of sparsity. Since the training data is only used once, and moreover the size of the dataset is relatively smaller (that is, few MBs), we can cache it if you use the DataFrame more than once.

Step 5. Prepare the training and test set - Split the data into training and test sets (25% held out for testing):

```
val Array(trainingData, testData) = data
                .randomSplit(Array(0.75, 0.25), seed = 12345L)
```

Step 6. Train the Naive Bayes model - Train a Naive Bayes model using the training set as follows:

```
val nb = new NaiveBayes()
val model = nb.fit(trainingData)
```

Step 7. Calculate the prediction on the test set - Calculate the prediction using the model transformer and finally show the prediction against each label as follows:

```
val predictions = model.transform(testData)
predictions.show()
```

```
+-----+--------------------+--------------------+--------------------+----------+
|label|            features|       rawPrediction|         probability|prediction|
+-----+--------------------+--------------------+--------------------+----------+
|  0.0|(16,[0,1,2,3,4,5,...|[-2439.0893277449...|[1.32132340702018...|       4.0|
|  0.0|(16,[0,1,2,3,4,5,...|[-1941.7868705353...|[1.0,1.5395790656...|       0.0|
|  0.0|(16,[0,1,2,3,4,5,...|[-2024.4356335162...|[1.0,1.6764090944...|       0.0|
|  0.0|(16,[0,1,2,3,4,5,...|[-1989.5775697073...|[1.0,2.2647494021...|       0.0|
|  0.0|(16,[0,1,2,3,4,5,...|[-1706.6857288506...|[1.0,5.1940219699...|       0.0|
|  0.0|(16,[0,1,2,3,4,5,...|[-1838.2628605334...|[1.0,7.2364926581...|       0.0|
|  0.0|(16,[0,1,2,3,4,5,...|[-2168.4931444350...|[1.0,6.8428584454...|       0.0|
|  0.0|(16,[0,1,2,3,4,5,...|[-2068.2067411172...|[1.0,1.1943331620...|       0.0|
|  0.0|(16,[0,1,2,3,4,5,...|[-2132.6929489447...|[1.0,1.9943684266...|       0.0|
|  0.0|(16,[0,1,2,3,4,5,...|[-1983.0451148771...|[1.0,4.9959906892...|       0.0|
|  0.0|(16,[0,1,2,3,4,5,...|[-2049.2850893323...|[1.0,1.3644883115...|       0.0|
|  0.0|(16,[0,1,2,3,4,5,...|[-1971.1755138520...|[1.0,1.6415723270...|       0.0|
|  0.0|(16,[0,1,2,3,4,5,...|[-2216.9188759036...|[1.0,1.3805417667...|       0.0|
|  0.0|(16,[0,1,2,3,4,5,...|[-2216.0583349043...|[1.0,7.7430733808...|       0.0|
|  0.0|(16,[0,1,2,3,4,5,...|[-2290.1517462265...|[1.0,1.3312677171...|       0.0|
|  0.0|(16,[0,1,2,3,4,5,...|[-2268.9492946577...|[0.01491770995335...|       6.0|
|  0.0|(16,[0,1,2,3,4,5,...|[-2377.8867352336...|[1.27336913041488...|       8.0|
|  0.0|(16,[0,1,2,3,4,5,...|[-2206.2037445466...|[1.20068275169939...|       6.0|
|  0.0|(16,[0,1,2,3,4,5,...|[-2290.1662968738...|[2.82560057752915...|       8.0|
|  0.0|(16,[0,1,2,3,4,5,...|[-2662.3029788480...|[2.38039426503477...|       8.0|
+-----+--------------------+--------------------+--------------------+----------+
only showing top 20 rows
```

Figure 6: Prediction against each label (that is, each digit)

As you can see in the preceding figure, some labels were predicted accurately and some of them were wrongly. Again we need to know the weighted accuracy, precision, recall and f1 measures without evaluating the model naively.

Step 8. Evaluate the model - Select the prediction and the true label to compute test error and classification performance metrics such as accuracy, precision, recall, and f1 measure as follows:

```
val evaluator = new MulticlassClassificationEvaluator()
                        .setLabelCol("label")
                        .setPredictionCol("prediction")
val evaluator1 = evaluator.setMetricName("accuracy")
val evaluator2 = evaluator.setMetricName("weightedPrecision")
val evaluator3 = evaluator.setMetricName("weightedRecall")
val evaluator4 = evaluator.setMetricName("f1")
```

Step 9. Compute the performance metrics - Compute the classification accuracy, precision, recall, f1 measure, and error on test data as follows:

```
val accuracy = evaluator1.evaluate(predictions)
val precision = evaluator2.evaluate(predictions)
val recall = evaluator3.evaluate(predictions)
val f1 = evaluator4.evaluate(predictions)
```

Step 10. Print the performance metrics:

```
println("Accuracy = " + accuracy)
println("Precision = " + precision)
println("Recall = " + recall)
println("F1 = " + f1)
println(s"Test Error = ${1 - accuracy}")
```

You should observe values as follows:

```
Accuracy = 0.8284365162644282
Precision = 0.8361211320692463
Recall = 0.828436516264428
F1 = 0.8271828540349192
Test Error = 0.17156348373557184
```

The performance is not that bad. However, you can still increase the classification accuracy by performing hyperparameter tuning. There are further opportunities to improve the prediction accuracy by selecting appropriate algorithms (that is, classifier or regressor) through cross-validation and train split, which will be discussed in the following section.

Tune me up!

You already know my pros and cons, I have a con that is, my classification accuracy is relatively low. However, if you tune me up, I can perform much better. Well, should we trust Naive Bayes? If so, shouldn't we look at how to increase the prediction performance of this guy? Let's say using the WebSpam dataset. At first, we should observe the performance of the NB model, and after that we will see how to increase the performance using the cross-validation technique.

The WebSpam dataset that downloaded from `http://www.csie.ntu.edu.tw/~cjlin/libsvmtools/datasets/binary/webspam_wc_normalized_trigram.svm.bz2` contains features and corresponding labels, that is, spam or ham. Therefore, this is a supervised machine learning problem, and the task here is to predict whether a given message is spam or ham (that is, not spam). The original dataset size is 23.5 GB, where the classes are labeled as +1 or -1 (that is, a binary classification problem). Later on, we replaced -1 with 0.0 and +1 with 1.0 since Naive Bayes does not permit using signed integers. The modified dataset is shown in the following figure:

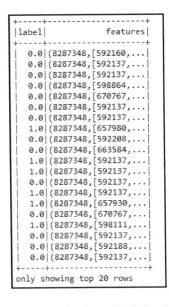

Figure 7: A snapshot of the 20 rows of the WebSpam dataset

At first, we need to import necessary packages as follows:

```
import org.apache.spark.ml.classification.NaiveBayes
import
org.apache.spark.ml.evaluation.MulticlassClassificationEvaluator
import org.apache.spark.sql.SparkSession
import org.apache.spark.ml.Pipeline;
import org.apache.spark.ml.PipelineStage;
import org.apache.spark.ml.classification.LogisticRegression
import org.apache.spark.ml.evaluation.BinaryClassificationEvaluator
import org.apache.spark.ml.feature.{HashingTF, Tokenizer}
import org.apache.spark.ml.linalg.Vector
import org.apache.spark.ml.tuning.{CrossValidator, ParamGridBuilder}
```

Now create the Spark Session as the entry point to the code as follows:

```
val spark = SparkSession
      .builder
      .master("local[*]")
      .config("spark.sql.warehouse.dir", "/home/exp/")
      .appName("Tuned NaiveBayes")
      .getOrCreate()
```

Let's load the WebSpam dataset and prepare the training set to train the Naive Bayes model as follows:

```
// Load the data stored in LIBSVM format as a DataFrame.
 val data = spark.read.format("libsvm").load("hdfs://data/
webspam_wc_normalized_trigram.svm")
 // Split the data into training and test sets (30% held out for
testing)
 val Array(trainingData, testData) = data.randomSplit(Array(0.75,
0.25), seed = 12345L)
 // Train a NaiveBayes model with using the training set
 val nb = new NaiveBayes().setSmoothing(0.00001)
 val model = nb.fit(trainingData)
```

In the preceding code, setting the seed is required for reproducibility. Now let's make the prediction on the validation set as follows:

```
val predictions = model.transform(testData)
predictions.show()
```

Now let's obtain `evaluator` and compute the classification performance metrics like accuracy, precision, recall, and `f1` measure as follows:

```
val evaluator = new MulticlassClassificationEvaluator()
                     .setLabelCol("label")
                     .setPredictionCol("prediction")
val evaluator1 = evaluator.setMetricName("accuracy")
val evaluator2 = evaluator.setMetricName("weightedPrecision")
val evaluator3 = evaluator.setMetricName("weightedRecall")
val evaluator4 = evaluator.setMetricName("f1")
```

Now let's compute and print the performance metrics:

```
val accuracy = evaluator1.evaluate(predictions)
val precision = evaluator2.evaluate(predictions)
val recall = evaluator3.evaluate(predictions)
val f1 = evaluator4.evaluate(predictions)
// Print the performance metrics
println("Accuracy = " + accuracy)
println("Precision = " + precision)
println("Recall = " + recall)
println("F1 = " + f1)
println(s"Test Error = ${1 - accuracy}")
```

You should receive the following output:

```
Accuracy = 0.8839357429715676
Precision = 0.86393574297188752
Recall = 0.8739357429718876
F1 = 0.8739357429718876
Test Error = 0.11606425702843237
```

Although the accuracy is at a satisfactory level, we can further improve it by applying the cross-validation technique. The technique goes as follows:

- Create a pipeline by chaining an NB estimator as the only stage of the pipeline
- Now prepare the param grid for tuning
- Perform the 10-fold cross-validation
- Now fit the model using the training set
- Compute the prediction on the validation set

The first step in model tuning techniques such as cross-validation is pipeline creation. A pipeline can be created by chaining a transformer, an estimator, and related parameters.

Step 1. Pipeline creation - Let's create a Naive Bayes estimator (nb is an estimator in the following case) and create a pipeline by chaining the estimator as follows:

```
val nb = new NaiveBayes().setSmoothing(00001)
val pipeline = new Pipeline().setStages(Array(nb))
```

A pipeline can be considered as the data workflow system for training and prediction using the model. ML pipelines provide a uniform set of high-level APIs built on top of DataFrames that help users create and tune practical machine learning pipelines. DataFrame, transformer, estimator, pipeline, and parameter are the five most important components in Pipeline creation. For more on Pipeline, interested readers should refer to https://spark.apache.org/docs/latest/ml-pipeline.html

In the earlier case, the only stage in our pipeline is an estimator that is an algorithm for fitting on a DataFrame to produce a transformer to make sure the training is carried out successfully.

Step 2. Creating grid parameters - Let's use ParamGridBuilder to construct a grid of parameters to search over:

```
val paramGrid = new ParamGridBuilder()
                .addGrid(nb.smoothing, Array(0.001, 0.0001))
                .build()
```

Step 3. Performing 10-fold cross-validation - We now treat the pipeline as an estimator, wrapping it in a cross-validator instance. This will allow us to jointly choose parameters for all Pipeline stages. A CrossValidator requires an estimator, a set of estimator ParamMaps, and an evaluator. Note that the evaluator here is a BinaryClassificationEvaluator, and its default metric is areaUnderROC. However, if you use the evaluator as MultiClassClassificationEvaluator, you will be able to use the other performance metrics as well:

```
val cv = new CrossValidator()
            .setEstimator(pipeline)
            .setEvaluator(new BinaryClassificationEvaluator)
            .setEstimatorParamMaps(paramGrid)
            .setNumFolds(10)  // Use 3+ in practice
```

Step 4. Fit the cross-validation model with the training set as follows:

```
val model = cv.fit(trainingData)
```

Step 5. Compute performance as follows:

```
val predictions = model.transform(validationData)
predictions.show()
```

Step 6. Obtain the evaluator, compute the performance metrics, and display the results. Now let's obtain `evaluator` and compute the classification performance metrics such as accuracy, precision, recall, and f1 measure. Here `MultiClassClassificationEvaluator` will be used for accuracy, precision, recall, and f1 measure:

```
val evaluator = new MulticlassClassificationEvaluator()
                        .setLabelCol("label")
                        .setPredictionCol("prediction")
val evaluator1 = evaluator.setMetricName("accuracy")
val evaluator2 = evaluator.setMetricName("weightedPrecision")
val evaluator3 = evaluator.setMetricName("weightedRecall")
val evaluator4 = evaluator.setMetricName("f1")
```

Now compute the classification accuracy, precision, recall, f1 measure, and error on test data as follows:

```
val accuracy = evaluator1.evaluate(predictions)
val precision = evaluator2.evaluate(predictions)
val recall = evaluator3.evaluate(predictions)
val f1 = evaluator4.evaluate(predictions)
```

Now let's print the performance metrics:

```
println("Accuracy = " + accuracy)
println("Precision = " + precision)
println("Recall = " + recall)
println("F1 = " + f1)
println(s"Test Error = ${1 - accuracy}")
```

You should now receive the results as follows:

```
Accuracy = 0.9678714859437751
Precision = 0.9686742518830365
Recall = 0.9678714859437751
F1 = 0.9676697179934564
Test Error = 0.032128514056224855
```

Now this is much better compared to the previous one, right? Please note that you might receive a slightly different result due to the random split of the dataset and your platform.

The decision trees

In this section, we will discuss the DT algorithm in detail. A comparative analysis of Naive Bayes and DT will be discussed too. DTs are commonly considered as a supervised learning technique used for solving classification and regression tasks. A DT is simply a decision support tool that uses a tree-like graph (or a model of decisions) and their possible consequences, including chance event outcomes, resource costs, and utility. More technically, each branch in a DT represents a possible decision, occurrence, or reaction in terms of statistical probability.

Compared to Naive Bayes, DT is a far more robust classification technique. The reason is that at first DT splits the features into training and test set. Then it produces a good generalization to infer the predicted labels or classes. Most interestingly, DT algorithm can handle both binary and multiclass classification problems.

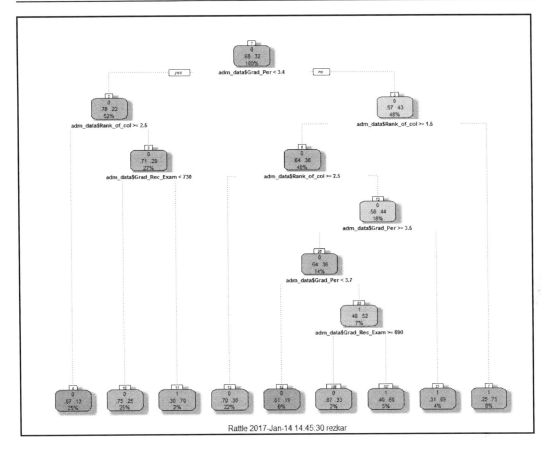

Figure 8: A sample decision tree on the admission test dataset using the Rattle package of R

For instance, in the preceding example figure, DTs learn from the admission data to approximate a sine curve with a set of `if...else` decision rules. The dataset contains the record of each student who applied for admission, say to an American university. Each record contains the graduate record exam score, CGPA score, and the rank of the column. Now we will have to predict who is competent based on these three features (variables). DTs can be used to solve this kind of problem after training the DT model and pruning unwanted branches of the tree. In general, a deeper tree signifies more complex decision rules and a better fitted model. Therefore, the deeper the tree, the more complex the decision rules and the more fitted the model.

If you would like to draw the preceding figure, just run my R script, execute it on RStudio, and feed the admission dataset. The script and the dataset can be found in my GitHub repository at `https://github.com/rezacsedu/AdmissionUsingDecisionTree`.

Advantages and disadvantages of using DTs

Before hiring me, you can discover my pros and cons and when I work best from Table 3 so that you don't have any late regrets!

Agent	Pros	Cons	Better at
Decision trees (DTs)	-Simple to implement, train, and interpret -Trees can be visualized -Requires little data preparation -Less model building and prediction time -Can handle both numeric and categorical data -Possible of validating the model using the statistical tests -Robust against noise and missing values -High accuracy	-Interpretation is hard with large and complex trees -Duplication may occur within the same subtree -Possible issues with diagonal decision boundaries -DT learners can create overcomplex trees that do not generalize data well -Sometimes DTs can be unstable because of small variants in the data -Learning the DTs itself an NP-complete problem (aka. nondeterministic polynomial time -complete problem) -DTs learners create biased trees if some classes dominate	-Targeting highly accurate classification -Medical diagnosis and prognosis -Credit risk analytics

Table 3: Pros and cons of the decision tree

Decision tree versus Naive Bayes

As stated in the preceding table, DTs are very easy to understand and debug because of their flexibility for training datasets. They will work with both classification as well as regression problems.

If you are trying to predict values out of categorical or continuous values, DTs will handle both problems. Consequently, if you just have tabular data, feed it to the DT and it will build the model toward classifying your data without any additional requirement for upfront or manual interventions. In summary, DTs are very simple to implement, train, and interpret. With very little data preparation, DTs can build the model with much less prediction time. As said earlier, they can handle both numeric and categorical data and are very robust against noise and missing values. They are very easy to validate the model using statistical tests. More interestingly, the constructed trees can be visualized. Overall, they provide very high accuracy.

However, on the downside, DTs sometimes tend to the overfitting problem for the training data. This means that you generally have to prune the tree and find an optimal one for better classification or regression accuracy. Moreover, duplication may occur within the same subtree. Sometimes it also creates issues with diagonal decision boundaries towards overfitting and underfitting. Furthermore, DT learners can create over-complex trees that do not generalize the data well this makes overall interpretation hard. DTs can be unstable because of small variants in the data, and as a result learning DT is itself an NP-complete problem. Finally, DT learners create biased trees if some classes dominate over others.

 Readers are suggested to refer to *Tables 1* and *3* to get a comparative summary between Naive Bayes and DTs.

On the other hand, there is a saying while using Naive Bayes: *NB requires you build a classification by hand*. There's no way to feed a bunch of tabular data to it, and it picks the best features for the classification. In this case, however, choosing the right features and features that matter is up to the user, that is, you. On the other hand, DTs will pick the best features from tabular data. Given this fact, you probably need to combine Naive Bayes with other statistical techniques to help toward best feature extraction and classify them later on. Alternatively, use DTs to get better accuracy in terms of precision, recall, and f1 measure. Another positive thing about Naive Bayes is that it will answer as a continuous classifier. However, the downside is that they are harder to debug and understand. Naive Bayes does quite well when the training data doesn't have good features with low amounts of data.

In summary, if you are trying to choose the better classifier from these two often times it is best to test each one to solve a problem. My recommendation would be to build a DT as well as a Naive Bayes classifier using the training data you have and then compare the performance using available performance metrics and then decide which one best solves your problem subject to the dataset nature.

Building a scalable classifier with DT algorithm

As you have already seen, using the OVTR classifier we observed the following values of the performance metrics on the OCR dataset:

```
Accuracy = 0.5217246545696688
Precision = 0.488360500637862
Recall = 0.5217246545696688
F1 = 0.4695649096879411
Test Error = 0.47827534543033123
```

This signifies that the accuracy of the model on that dataset is very low. In this section, we will see how we could improve the performance using the DT classifier. An example with Spark 2.1.0 will be shown using the same OCR dataset. The example will have several steps including data loading, parsing, model training, and, finally, model evaluation.

Since we will be using the same dataset, to avoid redundancy, we will escape the dataset exploration step and will enter into the example:

Step 1. Load the required library and packages as follows:

```
import org.apache.spark.ml.Pipeline // for Pipeline creation
import org.apache.spark.ml.classification
                        .DecisionTreeClassificationModel
import org.apache.spark.ml.classification.DecisionTreeClassifier
import org.apache.spark.ml.evaluation
                        .MulticlassClassificationEvaluator
import org.apache.spark.ml.feature
                        .{IndexToString, StringIndexer,
VectorIndexer}
import org.apache.spark.sql.SparkSession //For a Spark session
```

Step 2. Create an active Spark session as follows:

```
val spark = SparkSession
              .builder
              .master("local[*]")
              .config("spark.sql.warehouse.dir", "/home/exp/")
              .appName("DecisionTreeClassifier")
              .getOrCreate()
```

Note that here the master URL has been set as `local[*]`, which means all the cores of your machine will be used for processing the Spark job. You should set SQL warehouse accordingly and other configuration parameter based on requirements.

Step 3. Create the DataFrame - Load the data stored in LIBSVM format as a DataFrame as follows:

```
val data = spark.read.format("libsvm").load("datab
                        /Letterdata_libsvm.data")
```

For the classification of digits, the input feature vectors are usually sparse, and sparse vectors should be supplied as input to take advantage of the sparsity. Since the training data is only used once, and moreover the size of the dataset is relatively small (that is, a few MBs), we can cache it if you use the DataFrame more than once.

Step 4. Label indexing - Index the labels, adding metadata to the label column. Then let's fit on the whole dataset to include all labels in the index:

```
val labelIndexer = new StringIndexer()
              .setInputCol("label")
              .setOutputCol("indexedLabel")
              .fit(data)
```

Step 5. Identifying categorical features - The following code segment automatically identifies categorical features and indexes them:

```
val featureIndexer = new VectorIndexer()
              .setInputCol("features")
              .setOutputCol("indexedFeatures")
              .setMaxCategories(4)
              .fit(data)
```

For this case, if the number of features is more than four distinct values, they will be treated as continuous.

Step 6. Prepare the training and test sets - Split the data into training and test sets (25% held out for testing):

```
val Array(trainingData, testData) = data.randomSplit
                                (Array(0.75, 0.25), 12345L)
```

Step 7. Train the DT model as follows:

```
val dt = new DecisionTreeClassifier()
                .setLabelCol("indexedLabel")
                .setFeaturesCol("indexedFeatures")
```

Step 8. Convert the indexed labels back to original labels as follows:

```
val labelConverter = new IndexToString()
                .setInputCol("prediction")
                .setOutputCol("predictedLabel")
                .setLabels(labelIndexer.labels)
```

Step 9. Create a DT pipeline - Let's create a DT pipeline by changing the indexers, label converter and tree together:

```
val pipeline = new Pipeline().setStages(Array(labelIndexer,
                        featureIndexer, dt, labelconverter))
```

Step 10. Running the indexers - Train the model using the transformer and run the indexers:

```
val model = pipeline.fit(trainingData)
```

Step 11. Calculate the prediction on the test set - Calculate the prediction using the model transformer and finally show the prediction against each label as follows:

```
val predictions = model.transform(testData)
predictions.show()
```

```
+-----+------------------+------------+------------------+------------------+------------------+----------+---------------+
|label|          features|indexedLabel|    indexedFeatures|    rawPrediction|       probability|prediction|predictedLabel|
+-----+------------------+------------+------------------+------------------+------------------+----------+---------------+
| 1.0|(17,[0,1,2,3,4,5,...|        12.0|(17,[0,1,2,3,4,5,...|[0.0,0.0,0.0,0.0,...|[0.0,0.0,0.0,0.0,...|       9.0|            3.0|
| 1.0|(17,[0,1,2,3,4,5,...|        12.0|(17,[0,1,2,3,4,5,...|[0.0,0.0,0.0,0.0,...|[0.0,0.0,0.0,0.0,...|       9.0|            3.0|
| 1.0|(17,[0,1,2,3,4,5,...|        12.0|(17,[0,1,2,3,4,5,...|[0.0,0.0,0.0,0.0,...|[0.0,0.0,0.0,0.0,...|       9.0|            3.0|
| 1.0|(17,[0,1,2,3,4,5,...|        12.0|(17,[0,1,2,3,4,5,...|[0.0,0.0,0.0,0.0,...|[0.0,0.0,0.0,0.0,...|       9.0|            3.0|
| 1.0|(17,[0,1,2,3,4,5,...|        12.0|(17,[0,1,2,3,4,5,...|[0.0,0.0,0.0,0.0,...|[0.0,0.0,0.0,0.0,...|       9.0|            3.0|
| 1.0|(17,[0,1,2,3,4,5,...|        12.0|(17,[0,1,2,3,4,5,...|[0.0,0.0,0.0,0.0,...|[0.0,0.0,0.0,0.0,...|       9.0|            3.0|
| 2.0|(17,[0,1,2,3,4,5,...|        11.0|(17,[0,1,2,3,4,5,...|[0.0,0.0,0.0,0.0,...|[0.0,0.0,0.0,0.0,...|       9.0|            3.0|
| 2.0|(17,[0,1,2,3,4,5,...|        11.0|(17,[0,1,2,3,4,5,...|[0.0,0.0,0.0,0.0,...|[0.0,0.0,0.0,0.0,...|       9.0|            3.0|
| 2.0|(17,[0,1,2,3,4,5,...|        11.0|(17,[0,1,2,3,4,5,...|[0.0,0.0,0.0,0.0,...|[0.0,0.0,0.0,0.0,...|       9.0|            3.0|
| 3.0|(17,[0,1,2,3,4,5,...|         9.0|(17,[0,1,2,3,4,5,...|[0.0,0.0,0.0,0.0,...|[0.0,0.0,0.0,0.0,...|       9.0|            3.0|
| 3.0|(17,[0,1,2,3,4,5,...|         9.0|(17,[0,1,2,3,4,5,...|[0.0,0.0,0.0,0.0,...|[0.0,0.0,0.0,0.0,...|       9.0|            3.0|
| 3.0|(17,[0,1,2,3,4,5,...|         9.0|(17,[0,1,2,3,4,5,...|[0.0,0.0,0.0,0.0,...|[0.0,0.0,0.0,0.0,...|       9.0|            3.0|
| 3.0|(17,[0,1,2,3,4,5,...|         9.0|(17,[0,1,2,3,4,5,...|[0.0,0.0,0.0,0.0,...|[0.0,0.0,0.0,0.0,...|       9.0|            3.0|
| 3.0|(17,[0,1,2,3,4,5,...|         9.0|(17,[0,1,2,3,4,5,...|[0.0,0.0,0.0,0.0,...|[0.0,0.0,0.0,0.0,...|       9.0|            3.0|
| 3.0|(17,[0,1,2,3,4,5,...|         9.0|(17,[0,1,2,3,4,5,...|[0.0,0.0,0.0,0.0,...|[0.0,0.0,0.0,0.0,...|       9.0|            3.0|
| 3.0|(17,[0,1,2,3,4,5,...|         9.0|(17,[0,1,2,3,4,5,...|[0.0,0.0,0.0,0.0,...|[0.0,0.0,0.0,0.0,...|       9.0|            3.0|
| 3.0|(17,[0,1,2,3,4,5,...|         9.0|(17,[0,1,2,3,4,5,...|[0.0,0.0,0.0,0.0,...|[0.0,0.0,0.0,0.0,...|       9.0|            3.0|
| 3.0|(17,[0,1,2,3,4,5,...|         9.0|(17,[0,1,2,3,4,5,...|[0.0,0.0,0.0,0.0,...|[0.0,0.0,0.0,0.0,...|       9.0|            3.0|
| 3.0|(17,[0,1,2,3,4,5,...|         9.0|(17,[0,1,2,3,4,5,...|[0.0,0.0,0.0,0.0,...|[0.0,0.0,0.0,0.0,...|       9.0|            3.0|
| 3.0|(17,[0,1,2,3,4,5,...|         9.0|(17,[0,1,2,3,4,5,...|[0.0,0.0,0.0,0.0,...|[0.0,0.0,0.0,0.0,...|       9.0|            3.0|
+-----+------------------+------------+------------------+------------------+------------------+----------+---------------+
only showing top 20 rows
```

Figure 9: Prediction against each label (that is, each letter)

As you can see from the preceding figure, some labels were predicted accurately and some of them were predicted wrongly. However, we know the weighted accuracy, precision, recall, and f1 measures, but we need to evaluate the model first.

Step 12. Evaluate the model - Select the prediction and the true label to compute test error and classification performance metrics such as accuracy, precision, recall, and f1 measure as follows:

```
val evaluator = new MulticlassClassificationEvaluator()
                        .setLabelCol("label")
                        .setPredictionCol("prediction")
val evaluator1 = evaluator.setMetricName("accuracy")
val evaluator2 = evaluator.setMetricName("weightedPrecision")
val evaluator3 = evaluator.setMetricName("weightedRecall")
val evaluator4 = evaluator.setMetricName("f1")
```

Step 13. Compute the performance metrics - Compute the classification accuracy, precision, recall, f1 measure, and error on test data as follows:

```
val accuracy = evaluator1.evaluate(predictions)
val precision = evaluator2.evaluate(predictions)
val recall = evaluator3.evaluate(predictions)
val f1 = evaluator4.evaluate(predictions)

println("Accuracy = " + accuracy)
println("Precision = " + precision)
println("Recall = " + recall)
println("F1 = " + f1)
println(s"Test Error = ${1 - accuracy}")
```

You should observe values as follows:

```
Accuracy = 0.994277821625888
Precision = 0.9904583933020722
Recall = 0.994277821625888
F1 = 0.9919966504321712
Test Error = 0.005722178374112041
```

Now the performance is excellent, right? However, you can still increase the classification accuracy by performing hyperparameter tuning. There are further opportunities to improve the prediction accuracy by selecting appropriate algorithms (that is, classifier or regressor) through cross-validation and train split.

Step 15. Print the DT nodes:

```
val treeModel = model.stages(2).asInstanceOf
                            [DecisionTreeClassificationModel]
println("Learned classification tree model:\n" + treeModel
              .toDebugString)
```

Finally, we will print a few nodes in the DT, as shown in the following figure:

```
Learned classification tree model:
DecisionTreeClassificationModel (uid=dtc_fbc6a27aa70b) of depth 5 with 19 nodes
  If (feature 16 <= 7.0)
   If (feature 16 <= 6.0)
    If (feature 16 <= 5.0)
     If (feature 16 <= 4.0)
      If (feature 16 <= 3.0)
       Predict: 9.0
      Else (feature 16 > 3.0)
       Predict: 7.0
     Else (feature 16 > 4.0)
      Predict: 5.0
    Else (feature 16 > 5.0)
     Predict: 3.0
   Else (feature 16 > 6.0)
    Predict: 1.0
  Else (feature 16 > 7.0)
   If (feature 16 <= 8.0)
    Predict: 0.0
   Else (feature 16 > 8.0)
    If (feature 16 <= 9.0)
     Predict: 2.0
    Else (feature 16 > 9.0)
     If (feature 16 <= 10.0)
      Predict: 4.0
     Else (feature 16 > 10.0)
      If (feature 16 <= 11.0)
       Predict: 6.0
      Else (feature 16 > 11.0)
       Predict: 8.0
```

Figure 10: A few decision tree nodes that were generated during the model building

Summary

In this chapter, we discussed some advanced algorithms in ML and found out how to use a simple yet powerful method of Bayesian inference to build another kind of classification model, multinomial classification algorithms. Moreover, the Naive Bayes algorithm was discussed broadly from the theoretical and technical perspectives. At the last pace, a comparative analysis between the DT and Naive Bayes algorithms was discussed and a few guidelines were provided.

In the next chapter, we will dig even deeper into ML and find out how we can take advantage of ML to cluster records belonging to a dataset of unsupervised observations.

13
Time to Put Some Order - Cluster Your Data with Spark MLlib

"If you take a galaxy and try to make it bigger, it becomes a cluster of galaxies, not a galaxy. If you try to make it smaller than that, it seems to blow itself apart"

- Jeremiah P. Ostriker

In this chapter, we will delve deeper into machine learning and find out how we can take advantage of it to cluster records belonging to a certain group or class for a dataset of unsupervised observations. In a nutshell, the following topics will be covered in this chapter:

- Unsupervised learning
- Clustering techniques
- Hierarchical clustering (HC)
- Centroid-based clustering (CC)
- Distribution-based clustering (DC)
- Determining number of clusters
- A comparative analysis between clustering algorithms
- Submitting jobs on computing clusters

Unsupervised learning

In this section, we will provide a brief introduction to unsupervised machine learning technique with appropriate examples. Let's start the discussion with a practical example. Suppose you have a large collection of not-pirated-totally-legal mp3s in a crowded and massive folder on your hard drive. Now, what if you can build a predictive model that helps automatically group together similar songs and organize them into your favorite categories such as country, rap, rock, and so on. This act of assigning an item to a group such that a mp3 to is added to the respective playlist in an unsupervised way. In the previous chapters, we assumed you're given a training dataset of correctly labeled data. Unfortunately, we don't always have that extravagance when we collect data in the real-world. For example, suppose we would like to divide up a large amount of music into interesting playlists. How could we possibly group together songs if we don't have direct access to their metadata? One possible approach could be a mixture of various machine learning techniques, but clustering is often at the heart of the solution.

In short, iIn unsupervised machine learning problem, correct classes of the training dataset are not available or unknown. Thus, classes have to be deduced from the structured or unstructured datasets as shown in *Figure 1*. This essentially implies that the goal of this type of algorithm is to preprocess the data in some structured ways. In other words, the main objective of the unsupervised learning algorithms is to explore the unknown/hidden patterns in the input data that are unlabeled. Unsupervised learning, however, also comprehends other techniques to explain the key features of the data in an exploratory way toward finding the hidden patterns. To overcome this challenge, clustering techniques are used widely to group unlabeled data points based on certain similarity measures in an unsupervised way.

For an in-depth theoretical knowledge of how unsupervised algorithms work, please refer to the following three books: *Bousquet, O.; von Luxburg, U.; Raetsch, G., eds* (2004). *Advanced Lectures on Machine Learning. Springer-Verlag.* ISBN 978-3540231226. Or *Duda, Richard O.; Hart, Peter E.; Stork, David G.* (2001). *Unsupervised Learning and Clustering. Pattern classification* (2nd Ed.). *Wiley.* ISBN 0-471-05669-3 and *Jordan, Michael I.; Bishop, Christopher M.* (2004) *Neural Networks.* In *Allen B. Tucker Computer Science Handbook, Second Edition* (Section VII: Intelligent Systems). *Boca Raton*, FL: Chapman and Hall/CRC Press LLC. ISBN 1-58488-360-X.

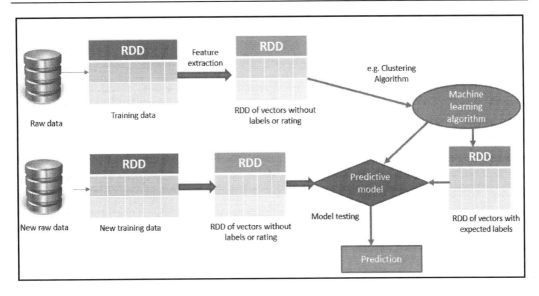

Figure 1: Unsupervised learning with Spark

Unsupervised learning example

In clustering tasks, an algorithm groups related features into categories by analyzing similarities between input examples where similar features are clustered and marked using circles around. Clustering uses include but are not limited to the following: search result grouping such as grouping customers, anomaly detection for suspicious pattern finding, text categorization for finding useful pattern in tests, social network analysis for finding coherent groups, data center computing clusters for finding a way to put related computers together, astronomic data analysis for galaxy formation, and real estate data analysis to identify neighborhoods based on similar features. We will show a Spark MLlib-based solution for the last use cases.

Clustering techniques

In this section, we will discuss clustering techniques along with challenges and suitable examples. A brief overview of hierarchical clustering, centroid-based clustering, and distribution-based clustering will be provided too.

Unsupervised learning and the clustering

Clustering analysis is about dividing data samples or data points and putting them into corresponding homogeneous classes or clusters. Thus a trivial definition of clustering can be thought as the process of organizing objects into groups whose members are similar in some way.

A *cluster* is, therefore, a collection of objects that are *similar* between them and are *dissimilar* to the objects belonging to other clusters. As shown in *Figure 2*, if a collection of objects is given, clustering algorithms put those objects into a group based on similarity. A clustering algorithm such as K-means has then located the centroid of the group of data points. However, to make the clustering accurate and effective, the algorithm evaluates the distance between each point from the centroid of the cluster. Eventually, the goal of clustering is to determine the intrinsic grouping in a set of unlabeled data.

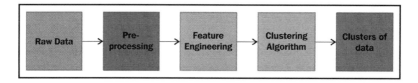

Figure 2: Clustering raw data

Spark supports many clustering algorithms such as **K-means**, **Gaussian mixture**, **power iteration clustering (PIC)**, **latent dirichlet allocation (LDA)**, **bisecting K-means**, and **Streaming K-means**. LDA is used for document classification and clustering commonly used in text mining. PIC is used for clustering vertices of a graph consisting of pairwise similarities as edge properties. However, to keep the objective of this chapter clearer and focused, we will confine our discussion to the K-means, bisecting K-means, and Gaussian mixture algorithms.

Hierarchical clustering

The hierarchical clustering technique is based on the fundamental idea of objects or features that are more related to those nearby than others far away. Bisecting K-means is an example of such hierarchical clustering algorithm that connects data objects to form clusters based on their corresponding distance.

In the hierarchical clustering technique, a cluster can be described trivially by the maximum distance needed to connect parts of the cluster. As a result, different clusters will be formed at different distances. Graphically, these clusters can be represented using a dendrogram. Interestingly, the common name hierarchical clustering evolves from the concept of the dendrogram.

Centroid-based clustering

In centroid-based clustering technique, clusters are represented by a central vector. However, the vector itself may not necessarily be a member of the data points. In this type of learning, a number of the probable clusters must be provided prior to training the model. K-means is a very famous example of this learning type, where, if you set the number of clusters to a fixed integer to say K, the K-means algorithm provides a formal definition as an optimization problem, which is a separate problem to be resolved to find the K cluster centers and assign the data objects the nearest cluster center. In short, this is an optimization problem where the objective is to minimize the squared distances from the clusters.

Distribution-based clustestering

Distribution-based clustering algorithms are based on statistical distribution models that provide more convenient ways to cluster related data objects to the same distribution. Although the theoretical foundations of these algorithms are very robust, they mostly suffer from overfitting. However, this limitation can be overcome by putting constraints on the model complexity.

Centroid-based clustering (CC)

In this section, we discuss the centroid-based clustering technique and its computational challenges. An example of using K-means with Spark MLlib will be shown for a better understanding of the centroid-based clustering.

Challenges in CC algorithm

As discussed previously, in a centroid-based clustering algorithm like K-means, setting the optimal value of the number of clusters K is an optimization problem. This problem can be described as NP-hard (that is non-deterministic polynomial-time hard) featuring high algorithmic complexities, and thus the common approach is trying to achieve only an approximate solution. Consequently, solving these optimization problems imposes an extra burden and consequently nontrivial drawbacks. Furthermore, the K-means algorithm expects that each cluster has approximately similar size. In other words, data points in each cluster have to be uniform to get better clustering performance.

Another major drawback of this algorithm is that this algorithm tries to optimize the cluster centers but not cluster borders, and this often tends to inappropriately cut the borders in between the clusters. However, sometimes, we can have the advantage of visual inspection, which is often not available for data on hyperplanes or multidimensional data. Nonetheless, a complete section on how to find the optimal value of K will be discussed later in this chapter.

How does K-means algorithm work?

Suppose we have n data points x_i, $i=1...n$ that need to be partitioned into k clusters. Now that the target here is to assign a cluster to each data point. K-means then aims to find the positions $\mu_i, i=1...k$ of the clusters that minimize the distance from the data points to the cluster. Mathematically, the K-means algorithm tries to achieve the goal by solving the following equation, that is, an optimization problem:

$$\underset{\mathbf{c}}{\arg\min} \sum_{i=1}^{k} \sum_{\mathbf{x} \in c_i} d(\mathbf{x}, \mu_i) = \underset{\mathbf{c}}{\arg\min} \sum_{i=1}^{k} \sum_{\mathbf{x} \in c_i} \|\mathbf{x} - \mu_i\|_2^2$$

In the preceding equation, c_i is the set of data points assigned to cluster i, and $d(x, \mu_i)$ $= ||x - \mu_i||_2^2$ is the Euclidean distance to be calculated (we will explain why we should use this distance measurement shortly). Therefore, we can understand that the overall clustering operation using K-means is not a trivial one but an NP-hard optimization problem. This also means that the K-means algorithm not only tries to find the global minima but also often gets stuck in different solutions.

Now, let's see how we could formulate the algorithm before we can feed the data to the K-means model. At first, we need to decide the number of tentative clusters, k priory. Then, typically, you need to follow these steps:

1. Initialize the center of the clusters	$\mu_i =$ some value $, i = 1, \ldots, k$
2. Attribute the closest cluster to each data point	$\mathbf{c}_i = \{ j : d(\mathbf{x}_j, \mu_i) \leq d(\mathbf{x}_j, \mu_l), l \neq i, j = 1, \ldots, n \}$
3. Set the position of each cluster to the mean of all data points belonging to that cluster	$\mu_i = \frac{1}{|c_i|} \sum_{j \in c_i} \mathbf{x}_j, \forall i$
4. Repeat steps 2-3 until convergence	

Clustering using the K-means algorithm begins by initializing all the coordinates to centroids. With every pass of the algorithm, each point is assigned to its nearest centroid based on some distance metric, usually *Euclidean distance*.

Distance calculation: Note that there are other ways to calculate the distance too, for example:
Chebyshev distance can be used to measure the distance by considering only the most notable dimensions.
The *Hamming distance* algorithm can identify the difference between two strings. On the other hand, to make the distance metric scale-undeviating, *Mahalanobis distance* can be used to normalize the covariance matrix. The *Manhattan distance* is used to measure the distance by considering only axis-aligned directions. The *Minkowski distance* algorithm is used to make the Euclidean distance, Manhattan distance, and Chebyshev distance. The *Haversine distance* is used to measure the great-circle distances between two points on a sphere from the location, that is, longitudes and latitudes.

Considering these distance-measuring algorithms, it is clear that the Euclidean distance algorithm would be the most appropriate to solve our purpose of distance calculation in the K-means algorithm. The centroids are then updated to be the centers of all the points assigned to it in that iteration. This repeats until there is a minimal change in the centers. In short, the K-means algorithm is an iterative algorithm and works in two steps:

- **Cluster assignment step**: K-means goes through each of the m data points in the dataset which is assigned to a cluster that is represented by the closest of the k centroids. For each point, the distances to each centroid is then calculated and simply pick the least distant one.

- **Update step**: For each cluster, a new centroid is calculated as the mean of all points in the cluster. From the previous step, we have a set of points which are assigned to a cluster. Now, for each such set, we calculate a mean that we declare a new centroid of the cluster.

An example of clustering using K-means of Spark MLlib

To further demonstrate the clustering example, we will use the *Saratoga NY Homes* dataset downloaded from `http://course1.winona.edu/bdeppa/Stat%20425/Datasets.html` as an unsupervised learning technique using Spark MLlib. The dataset contains several features of houses located in the suburb of the New York City. For example, price, lot size, waterfront, age, land value, new construct, central air, fuel type, heat type, sewer type, living area, pct.college, bedrooms, fireplaces, bathrooms, and the number of rooms. However, only a few features have been shown in the following table:

Price	Lot Size	Water Front	Age	Land Value	Rooms
132,500	0.09	0	42	5,000	5
181,115	0.92	0	0	22,300	6
109,000	0.19	0	133	7,300	8
155,000	0.41	0	13	18,700	5
86,060	0.11	0	0	15,000	3
120,000	0.68	0	31	14,000	8
153,000	0.4	0	33	23,300	8
170,000	1.21	0	23	146,000	9
90,000	0.83	0	36	222,000	8
122,900	1.94	0	4	212,000	6
325,000	2.29	0	123	126,000	12

Table 1: Sample data from the Saratoga NY Homes dataset

The target of this clustering technique here is to show an exploratory analysis based on the features of each house in the city for finding possible neighborhoods for the house located in the same area. Before performing feature extraction, we need to load and parse the Saratoga NY Homes dataset. This step also includes loading packages and related dependencies, reading the dataset as RDD, model training, prediction, collecting the local parsed data, and clustering comparing.

Step 1. Import-related packages:

```
package com.chapter13.Clustering
import org.apache.spark.{SparkConf, SparkContext}
import org.apache.spark.mllib.clustering.{KMeans, KMeansModel}
import org.apache.spark.mllib.linalg.Vectors
import org.apache.spark._
import org.apache.spark.rdd.RDD
import org.apache.spark.sql.functions._
import org.apache.spark.sql.types._
import org.apache.spark.sql._
import org.apache.spark.sql.SQLContext
```

Step 2. Create a Spark session - the entry point - Here we at first set the Spark configuration by setting the application name and master URL. For simplicity, it's standalone with all the cores on your machine:

```
val spark = SparkSession
                .builder
                .master("local[*]")
                .config("spark.sql.warehouse.dir", "E:/Exp/")
                .appName("KMeans")
                .getOrCreate()
```

Step 3. Load and parse the dataset - Read, parse, and create RDDs from the dataset as follows:

```
//Start parsing the dataset
val start = System.currentTimeMillis()
val dataPath = "data/Saratoga NY Homes.txt"
//val dataPath = args(0)
val landDF = parseRDD(spark.sparkContext.textFile(dataPath))
                        .map(parseLand).toDF().cache()
landDF.show()
```

Note that, to make the preceding code work, you should import the following package:

```
import spark.sqlContext.implicits._
```

You will get the following output:

Price	LotSize	Waterfront	Age	LandValue	NewConstruct	CentralAir	FuelType	HeatType	SewerType	LivingArea	PctCollege	Bedrooms	Fireplaces	Bathrooms	rooms
132500.0	0.09	0.0	42.0	50000.0	0.0	0.0	3.0	4.0	2.0	906.0	35.0	2.0	1.0	1.0	5.0
181115.0	0.92	0.0	0.0	22300.0	0.0	0.0	2.0	3.0	2.0	1953.0	51.0	3.0	0.0	2.5	6.0
109000.0	0.19	0.0	133.0	7300.0	0.0	0.0	2.0	3.0	3.0	1944.0	51.0	4.0	1.0	1.0	8.0
155000.0	0.41	0.0	13.0	18700.0	0.0	0.0	2.0	2.0	2.0	1944.0	51.0	3.0	1.0	1.5	5.0
86060.0	0.11	0.0	0.0	15000.0	1.0	1.0	2.0	2.0	3.0	840.0	51.0	2.0	0.0	1.0	3.0
120000.0	0.68	0.0	31.0	14000.0	0.0	0.0	2.0	2.0	2.0	1152.0	22.0	4.0	1.0	1.0	8.0
153000.0	0.4	0.0	33.0	23300.0	0.0	0.0	4.0	3.0	2.0	2752.0	51.0	4.0	1.0	1.5	8.0
170000.0	1.21	0.0	23.0	14600.0	0.0	0.0	4.0	2.0	2.0	1662.0	35.0	4.0	1.0	1.5	9.0
90000.0	0.83	0.0	36.0	22200.0	0.0	0.0	3.0	4.0	2.0	1632.0	51.0	3.0	0.0	1.5	8.0
122900.0	1.94	0.0	4.0	21200.0	0.0	0.0	2.0	2.0	1.0	1416.0	44.0	3.0	0.0	1.5	6.0
325000.0	2.29	0.0	123.0	12600.0	0.0	0.0	4.0	2.0	2.0	2894.0	51.0	7.0	0.0	1.0	12.0
120000.0	0.92	0.0	1.0	22300.0	0.0	0.0	2.0	2.0	2.0	1624.0	51.0	3.0	0.0	2.0	6.0
85860.0	8.97	0.0	13.0	4800.0	0.0	0.0	3.0	4.0	2.0	704.0	41.0	2.0	0.0	1.0	4.0
97000.0	0.11	0.0	153.0	3100.0	0.0	0.0	2.0	3.0	3.0	1383.0	57.0	3.0	0.0	2.0	5.0
127000.0	0.14	0.0	9.0	300.0	0.0	0.0	4.0	2.0	2.0	1300.0	41.0	3.0	0.0	1.5	8.0
89900.0	0.0	0.0	88.0	2500.0	0.0	0.0	2.0	3.0	3.0	936.0	57.0	3.0	0.0	1.0	4.0
155000.0	0.13	0.0	9.0	300.0	0.0	0.0	4.0	2.0	2.0	1300.0	41.0	3.0	0.0	1.5	7.0
253750.0	2.0	0.0	0.0	49800.0	0.0	1.0	2.0	2.0	1.0	2816.0	71.0	4.0	1.0	2.5	12.0
60000.0	0.21	0.0	82.0	8500.0	0.0	0.0	4.0	3.0	2.0	924.0	35.0	2.0	0.0	1.0	6.0
87500.0	0.88	0.0	17.0	19400.0	0.0	0.0	4.0	2.0	2.0	1092.0	35.0	3.0	0.0	1.0	6.0

only showing top 20 rows

Figure 3: A snapshot of the Saratoga NY Homes dataset

The following is the `parseLand` method that is used to create a `Land` class from an array of `Double` as follows:

```
// function to create a  Land class from an Array of Double
def parseLand(line: Array[Double]): Land = {
  Land(line(0), line(1), line(2), line(3), line(4), line(5),
    line(6), line(7), line(8), line(9), line(10),
    line(11), line(12), line(13), line(14), line(15)
  )
}
```

And the `Land` class that reads all the features as a double is as follows:

```
case class Land(
    Price: Double, LotSize: Double, Waterfront: Double, Age: Double,
    LandValue: Double, NewConstruct: Double, CentralAir: Double,
    FuelType: Double, HeatType: Double, SewerType: Double,
    LivingArea: Double, PctCollege: Double, Bedrooms: Double,
    Fireplaces: Double, Bathrooms: Double, rooms: Double
)
```

As you already know, to train the K-means model, we need to ensure all the data points and features to be numeric. Therefore, we further need to convert all the data points to double as follows:

```
// method to transform an RDD of Strings into an RDD of Double
def parseRDD(rdd: RDD[String]): RDD[Array[Double]] = {
  rdd.map(_.split(",")).map(_.map(_.toDouble))
}
```

Step 4. Preparing the training set - At first, we need to convert the data frame (that is, `landDF`) to an RDD of doubles and cache the data to create a new data frame to link the cluster numbers as follows:

```
val rowsRDD = landDF.rdd.map(r => (
  r.getDouble(0), r.getDouble(1), r.getDouble(2),
  r.getDouble(3), r.getDouble(4), r.getDouble(5),
  r.getDouble(6), r.getDouble(7), r.getDouble(8),
  r.getDouble(9), r.getDouble(10), r.getDouble(11),
  r.getDouble(12), r.getDouble(13), r.getDouble(14),
  r.getDouble(15))
)
rowsRDD.cache()
```

Now that we need to convert the preceding RDD of doubles into an RDD of dense vectors as follows:

```
// Get the prediction from the model with the ID so we can
   link them back to other information
val predictions = rowsRDD.map{r => (
  r._1, model.predict(Vectors.dense(
    r._2, r._3, r._4, r._5, r._6, r._7, r._8, r._9,
    r._10, r._11, r._12, r._13, r._14, r._15, r._16
  )
))}
```

Step 5. Train the K-means model - Train the model by specifying 10 clusters, 20 iterations, and 10 runs as follows:

```
val numClusters = 5
val numIterations = 20
val run = 10
val model = KMeans.train(numericHome, numClusters,numIterations, run,
                   KMeans.K_MEANS_PARALLEL)
```

The Spark-based implementation of K-means starts working by initializing a set of cluster centers using the K-means algorithm by *Bahmani et al., Scalable K-Means++, VLDB 2012*. This is a variant of K-means++ that tries to find dissimilar cluster centers by starting with a random center and then doing passes where more centers are chosen with a probability proportional to their squared distance to the current cluster set. It results in a provable approximation to an optimal clustering. The original paper can be found at `http://theory.stanford.edu/~sergei/papers/vldb12-kmpar.pdf`.

Step 6. Evaluate the model error rate - The standard K-means algorithm aims at minimizing the sum of squares of the distance between the points of each set, that is, the squared Euclidean distance, which is the WSSSE's objective. The K-means algorithm aims at minimizing the sum of squares of the distance between the points of each set (that is, the cluster center). However, if you really wanted to minimize the sum of squares of the distance between the points of each set, you would end up with a model where each cluster is its own cluster center; in that case, that measure would be 0.

Therefore, once you have trained your model by specifying the parameters, you can evaluate the result by using **Within Set Sum of Squared Errors (WSSE)**. Technically, it is something like the sum of the distances of each observation in each K cluster that can be computed as follows:

```
// Evaluate clustering by computing Within Set Sum of Squared Errors
val WCSSS = model.computeCost(landRDD)
println("Within-Cluster Sum of Squares = " + WCSSS)
```

The preceding model training set produces the value of WCSSS:

```
Within-Cluster Sum of Squares = 1.455560123603583E12
```

Step 7. Compute and print the cluster centers - At first, we get the prediction from the model with the ID so that we can link them back to other information related to each house. Note that we will use an RDD of rows that we prepared in step 4:

```
// Get the prediction from the model with the ID so we can link them
   back to other information
val predictions = rowsRDD.map{r => (
  r._1, model.predict(Vectors.dense(
     r._2, r._3, r._4, r._5, r._6, r._7, r._8, r._9, r._10,
     r._11, r._12, r._13, r._14, r._15, r._16
  )
))}
```

However, it should be provided when a prediction is requested about the price. This should be done as follows:

```
val predictions = rowsRDD.map{r => (
  r._1, model.predict(Vectors.dense(
    r._1, r._2, r._3, r._4, r._5, r._6, r._7, r._8, r._9, r._10,
    r._11, r._12, r._13, r._14, r._15, r._16
  )
)) }
```

For better visibility and an exploratory analysis, convert the RDD to a DataFrame as follows:

```
import spark.sqlContext.implicits._
val predCluster = predictions.toDF("Price", "CLUSTER")
predCluster.show()
```

This should produce the output shown in the following figure:

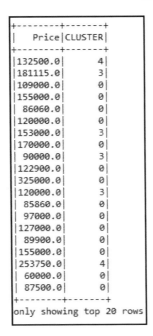

Figure 4: A snapshot of the clusters predicted

Since there's no distinguishable ID in the dataset, we represented the `Price` field to make the linking. From the preceding figure, you can understand where does a house having a certain price falls, that is, in which cluster. Now for better visibility, let's join the prediction DataFrame with the original DataFrame to know the individual cluster number for each house:

```
val newDF = landDF.join(predCluster, "Price")
newDF.show()
```

You should observe the output in the following figure:

Price	LotSize	Waterfront	Age	LandValue	NewConstruct	CentralAir	FuelType	HeatType	SewerType	LivingArea	PctCollege	Bedrooms	Fireplaces	Bathrooms	rooms	CLUSTER
132500.0	0.21	0.0	77.0	3500.0	0.0	0.0	2.0	2.0	3.0	1379.0	36.0	3.0	0.0	1.0	7.0	4
132500.0	0.37	0.0	19.0	13000.0	0.0	0.0	3.0	4.0	3.0	1988.0	63.0	2.0	0.0	1.0	5.0	4
132500.0	0.37	0.0	19.0	13000.0	0.0	0.0	3.0	4.0	3.0	1988.0	63.0	2.0	0.0	1.0	4.0	4
132500.0	0.09	0.0	42.0	50000.0	0.0	0.0	3.0	4.0	2.0	906.0	35.0	2.0	1.0	1.0	5.0	4
253750.0	2.0	0.0	0.0	49800.0	0.0	1.0	2.0	2.0	1.0	2816.0	71.0	4.0	1.0	2.5	12.0	4
290000.0	0.66	0.0	15.0	31200.0	0.0	1.0	2.0	2.0	2.0	2305.0	51.0	4.0	1.0	2.5	11.0	4
290000.0	0.46	0.0	22.0	48000.0	0.0	1.0	2.0	2.0	3.0	2030.0	64.0	4.0	1.0	2.5	10.0	4
290000.0	0.61	0.0	34.0	32300.0	0.0	0.0	2.0	3.0	3.0	2728.0	64.0	4.0	1.0	2.5	10.0	4
290000.0	0.12	0.0	3.0	108300.0	0.0	1.0	2.0	2.0	3.0	1620.0	57.0	3.0	1.0	2.5	7.0	4
290000.0	1.0	1.0	33.0	21700.0	0.0	0.0	4.0	2.0	2.0	944.0	27.0	1.0	1.0	1.0	4.0	4
290000.0	0.15	0.0	13.0	400.0	0.0	1.0	2.0	2.0	3.0	1750.0	47.0	2.0	1.0	2.5	6.0	4
290000.0	0.51	0.0	7.0	39100.0	0.0	0.0	2.0	2.0	3.0	2362.0	64.0	4.0	1.0	2.5	6.0	4
290000.0	0.71	1.0	73.0	61800.0	0.0	0.0	4.0	2.0	2.0	1838.0	71.0	4.0	0.0	2.0	8.0	4
205980.0	0.14	0.0	1.0	45200.0	1.0	1.0	2.0	2.0	3.0	1983.0	64.0	3.0	1.0	2.5	5.0	4
275000.0	0.54	0.0	19.0	30200.0	0.0	0.0	2.0	3.0	3.0	2175.0	64.0	4.0	1.0	2.5	10.0	4
275000.0	0.47	0.0	35.0	27000.0	0.0	0.0	2.0	3.0	3.0	2588.0	64.0	4.0	1.0	2.5	8.0	4
275000.0	0.37	0.0	14.0	31200.0	0.0	1.0	2.0	2.0	2.0	2011.0	40.0	4.0	1.0	2.5	8.0	4
275000.0	0.61	0.0	21.0	16100.0	0.0	1.0	2.0	2.0	2.0	2486.0	62.0	4.0	1.0	2.5	8.0	4
275000.0	0.46	0.0	7.0	18400.0	0.0	0.0	2.0	2.0	3.0	1865.0	57.0	3.0	0.0	2.5	8.0	4
275000.0	0.03	0.0	16.0	27000.0	0.0	1.0	2.0	2.0	3.0	1812.0	57.0	2.0	1.0	2.5	7.0	4

only showing top 20 rows

Figure 5: A snapshot of the clusters predicted across each house

To make the analysis, we dumped the output in RStudio and generated the clusters shown in *Figure 6*. The R script can be found on my GitHub repositories at `https://github.com/rezacsedu/ScalaAndSparkForBigDataAnalytics`. Alternatively, you can write your own script and do the visualization accordingly.

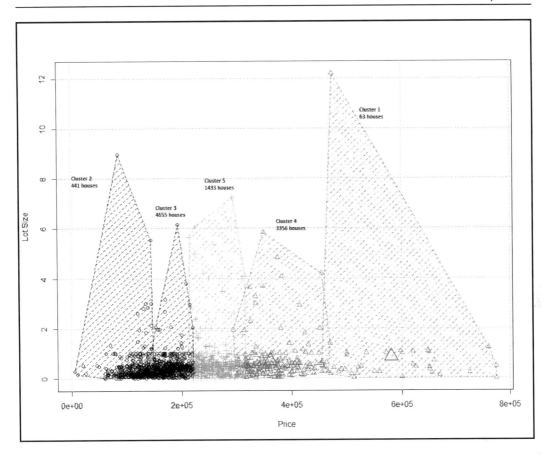

Figure 6: Clusters of the neighborhoods

Now, for more extensive analysis and visibility, we can observe related statistics for each cluster. For example, below I printed thestatistics related to cluster 3 and 4 in *Figure 8* and *Figure 9*, respectively:

```
newDF.filter("CLUSTER = 0").show()
newDF.filter("CLUSTER = 1").show()
newDF.filter("CLUSTER = 2").show()
newDF.filter("CLUSTER = 3").show()
newDF.filter("CLUSTER = 4").show()
```

Now get the descriptive statistics for each cluster as follows:

```
newDF.filter("CLUSTER = 0").describe().show()
newDF.filter("CLUSTER = 1").describe().show()
newDF.filter("CLUSTER = 2").describe().show()
newDF.filter("CLUSTER = 3").describe().show()
newDF.filter("CLUSTER = 4").describe().show()
```

At first, let's observe the related statistics of cluster 3 in the following figure:

summary	Price	LotSize	Waterfront	CLUSTER
count	4655	4655	4655	4655
mean	162537.34135338347	0.4691321160042959	0.003007518796992	0.0
stddev	51449.17174680274	0.6264212879059081	0.05476420278337016	0.0
min	10300.0	0.0	0.0	0
max	600000.0	8.97	1.0	0

Figure 7: Statistics on cluster 3

Now let's observe the related statistics of cluster 4 in the following figure:

summary	Price	LotSize	Waterfront	CLUSTER
count	3356	3356	3356	3356
mean	208313.6853396901	0.5529678188319437	0.006555423122765197	0.0
stddev	55025.18531388466	0.6481204374941402	0.08071177527503304	0.0
min	5000.0	0.01	0.0	0
max	600000.0	7.24	1.0	0

Figure 8: Statistics on cluster 4

Note that, since the original screenshot was too large to fit in this page, the original images were modified and the column containing other variables of the houses were removed.

Due to the random nature of this algorithm, you might receive different results for each successful iteration. However, you can lock the random nature of this algorithm by setting the seed as follows:

```
val numClusters = 5
val numIterations = 20
val seed = 12345
val model = KMeans.train(landRDD, numClusters, numIterations, seed)
```

Step 8. Stop the Spark session - Finally, stop the Spark session using the stop method as follows:

```
spark.stop()
```

In the preceding example, we dealt with a very small set of features; common-sense and visual inspection would also lead us to the same conclusions. From the above example using the K-means algorithm, we can understand that there are some limitations for this algorithm. For example, it's really difficult to predict the K-value, and with a global cluster it does not work well. Moreover, different initial partitions can result in different final clusters, and, finally, it does not work well with clusters of different sizes and densities.

 To overcome these limitations, we have some more robust algorithms in this book like MCMC (Markov Chain Monte Carlo; see also at `https://en.wikipedia.org/wiki/Markov_chain_Monte_Carlo`) presented in the book: *Tribble, Seth D.*, **Markov chain Monte Carlo** algorithms using completely uniformly distributed driving sequences, Diss. Stanford University, 2007.

Hierarchical clustering (HC)

In this section, we discuss the hierarchical clustering technique and its computational challenges. An example of using the bisecting K-means algorithm of hierarchical clustering with Spark MLlib will be shown too for a better understanding of hierarchical clustering.

An overview of HC algorithm and challenges

A hierarchical clustering technique is computationally different from the centroid-based clustering in the way the distances are computed. This is one of the most popular and widely used clustering analysis technique that looks to build a hierarchy of clusters. Since a cluster usually consists of multiple objects, there will be other candidates to compute the distance too. Therefore, with the exception of the usual choice of distance functions, you also need to decide on the linkage criterion to be used. In short, there are two types of strategies in hierarchical clustering:

- **Bottom-up approach**: In this approach, each observation starts within its own cluster. After that, the pairs of clusters are merged together and one moves up the hierarchy.

- **Top-down approach**: In this approach, all observations start in one cluster, splits are performed recursively, and one moves down the hierarchy.

These bottom-up or top-down approaches are based on the **single-linkage clustering (SLINK)** technique, which considers the minimum object distances, the **complete linkage clustering (CLINK)**, which considers the maximum of object distances, and the **unweighted pair group method with arithmetic mean (UPGMA)**. The latter is also known as **average-linkage clustering**. Technically, these methods will not produce unique partitions out of the dataset (that is, different clusters).

 A comparative analysis on these three approaches can be found at `https://nlp.stanford.edu/IR-book/completelink.html`.

However, the user still needs to choose appropriate clusters from the hierarchy for better cluster prediction and assignment. Although algorithms of this class like bisecting K-means are computationally faster than the K-means algorithm, there are three disadvantages to this type of algorithm:

- First, these methods are not very robust toward outliers or datasets containing noise or missing values. This disadvantage either imposes additional clusters or even causes other clusters to merge. This problem is commonly referred to as the chaining phenomenon, especially for single-linkage clustering.
- Second, from the algorithmic analysis, the complexity is for agglomerative clustering and for divisive clustering, which makes them too slow for large data sets.
- Third, SLINK and CLINK were previously used widely in data mining tasks as theoretical foundations of cluster analysis, but nowadays they are considered obsolete.

Bisecting K-means with Spark MLlib

Bisecting K-means can often be much faster than regular K-means, but it will generally produce a different clustering. A bisecting K-means algorithm is based on the paper, *A comparison of document clustering* techniques by *Steinbach, Karypis*, and *Kumar*, with modification to fit with Spark MLlib.

Bisecting K-means is a kind of divisive algorithm that starts from a single cluster that contains all the data points. Iteratively, it then finds all the divisible clusters on the bottom level and bisects each of them using K-means until there are K leaf clusters in total or no leaf clusters divisible. After that, clusters on the same level are grouped together to increase the parallelism. In other words, bisecting K-means is computationally faster than the regular K-means algorithm. Note that if bisecting all the divisible clusters on the bottom level results in more than K leaf clusters, larger clusters will always get higher priority.

Note that if the bisecting of all the divisible clusters on the bottom level results in more than K leaf clusters, larger clusters will always get higher priority. The following parameters are used in the Spark MLlib implementation:

- **K**: This is the desired number of leaf clusters. However, the actual number could be smaller if there are no divisible leaf clusters left during the computation. The default value is 4.
- **MaxIterations**: This is the max number of K-means iterations to split the clusters. The default value is 20.
- **MinDivisibleClusterSize**: This is the minimum number of points. The default value is set as 1.
- **Seed**: This is a random seed that disallows random clustering and tries to provide almost similar result in each iteration. However, it is recommended to use a long seed value like 12345 and so on.

Bisecting K-means clustering of the neighborhood using Spark MLlib

In the previous section, we saw how to cluster similar houses together to determine the neighborhood. The bisecting K-means is also similar to regular K-means except that the model training that takes different training parameters as follows:

```
// Cluster the data into two classes using KMeans
val bkm = new BisectingKMeans()
                .setK(5) // Number of clusters of the similar houses
                .setMaxIterations(20)// Number of max iteration
                .setSeed(12345) // Setting seed to disallow
randomness
val model = bkm.run(landRDD)
```

You should refer to the previous example and just reuse the previous steps to get the trained data. Now let's evaluate clustering by computing WSSSE as follows:

```
val WCSSS = model.computeCost(landRDD)
println("Within-Cluster Sum of Squares = " + WCSSS) // Less is better
```

Distribution-based clustering (DC)

In this section, we will discuss the distribution-based clustering technique and its computational challenges. An example of using **Gaussian mixture models (GMMs)** with Spark MLlib will be shown for a better understanding of distribution-based clustering.

Challenges in DC algorithm

A distribution-based clustering algorithm like GMM is an expectation-maximization algorithm. To avoid the overfitting problem, GMM usually models the dataset with a fixed number of Gaussian distributions. The distributions are initialized randomly, and the related parameters are iteratively optimized too to fit the model better to the training dataset. This is the most robust feature of GMM and helps the model to be converged toward the local optimum. However, multiple runs of this algorithm may produce different results.

In other words, unlike the bisecting K-means algorithm and soft clustering, GMM is optimized for hard clustering, and in order to obtain of that type, objects are often assigned to the Gaussian distribution. Another advantageous feature of GMM is that it produces complex models of clusters by capturing all the required correlations and dependence between data points and attributes.

On the down-side, GMM has some assumptions about the format and shape of the data, and this puts an extra burden on us (that is, users). More specifically, if the following two criteria do not meet, performance decreases drastically:

- Non-Gaussian dataset: The GMM algorithm assumes that the dataset has an underlying Gaussian, which is generative distribution. However, many practical datasets do not satisfy this assumption that is subject to provide low clustering performance.
- If the clusters do not have even sizes, there is a high chance that small clusters will be dominated by larger ones.

How does a Gaussian mixture model work?

Using GMM is a popular technique of soft clustering. GMM tries to model all the data points as a finite mixture of Gaussian distributions; the probability that each point belongs to each cluster is computed along with the cluster related statistics and represents an amalgamate distribution: where all the points are derived from one of K Gaussian subdistributions having own probability. In short, the functionality of GMM can be described in a three-steps pseudocode:

1. **Objective function:** Compute and maximize the log-likelihood using expectation–maximization (EM) as a framework
2. **EM algorithm:**
   - **E step:** Compute the posterior probability of membership -i.e. nearer data points
   - **M step:** Optimize the parameters.
3. **Assignment:** Perform soft assignment during step E.

Technically, when a statistical model is given, parameters of that model (that is, when applied to a data set) are estimated using the **maximum-likelihood estimation (MLE)**. On the other hand, **EM** algorithm is an iterative process of finding maximum likelihood.

 Since the GMM is an unsupervised algorithm, GMM model depends on the inferred variables. Then EM iteration rotates toward performing the expectation (E) and maximization (M) step.

The Spark MLlib implementation uses the expectation-maximization algorithm to induce the maximum-likelihood model from a given a set of data points. The current implementation uses the following parameters:

- **K** is the number of desired clusters to cluster your data points
- **ConvergenceTol** is the maximum change in log-likelihood at which we consider convergence achieved.
- **MaxIterations** is the maximum number of iterations to perform without reaching the convergence point.
- **InitialModel** is an optional starting point from which to start the EM algorithm. If this parameter is omitted, a random starting point will be constructed from the data.

An example of clustering using GMM with Spark MLlib

In the previous sections, we saw how to cluster the similar houses together to determine the neighborhood. Using GMM, it is also possible to cluster the houses toward finding the neighborhood except the model training that takes different training parameters as follows:

```
val K = 5
val maxIteration = 20
val model = new GaussianMixture()
                .setK(K)// Number of desired clusters
                .setMaxIterations(maxIteration)//Maximum iterations
                .setConvergenceTol(0.05) // Convergence tolerance.
                .setSeed(12345) // setting seed to disallow randomness
                .run(landRDD) // fit the model using the training set
```

You should refer to the previous example and just reuse the previous steps of getting the trained data. Now to evaluate the model's performance, GMM does not provide any performance metrics like WCSS as a cost function. However, GMM provides some performance metrics like mu, sigma, and weight. These parameters signify the maximum likelihood among different clusters (five clusters in our case). This can be demonstrated as follows:

```
// output parameters of max-likelihood model
for (i <- 0 until model.K) {
  println("Cluster " + i)
  println("Weight=%f\nMU=%s\nSigma=\n%s\n" format(model.weights(i),
          model.gaussians(i).mu, model.gaussians(i).sigma))
}
```

You should observe the following output:

Cluster 1:

Weight=0.062914

MU=[0.7808989073647417,0.027594804693120447,43.592594389644596,46431.34374059474,0.15006962027130458,0.2976156919639882,2.89886101554574,2.3996120048708147,2.4470830298894057,1887.577268849958,52.2947838682471,3.261785551442653,0.5617365219634057,1.884482686574011,7.445246170818636]

Sigma=

1.3102878656532657   -0.008781556531403927 ... (15 total)

-0.008781556531403927 0.026833331447068984 ...

-7.778315613332572   -0.22791269559972674 ...

-1994.3759086646505   953.5473866305449   ...

-0.047375946352474545 -0.004141141861757399...

0.037134027030446944 -8.540323116658249E-4...

0.18951000788031888   0.006470217824087922 ...

0.09271897737610613   0.0036900139379503023...

-0.18856936310448533 0.002380060277798572 ...

68.41825719674146   -4.1514710237897745 ...

0.03436783576161607   -0.1939395215895821 ...

-0.013693506665595243 -0.020101496691984813...

0.07766511419505753   -7.837804459298127E-4...

0.05849863330847962   -4.91629596665423E-4 ...

0.21074653933320067   -0.03620197853953523 ...

Figure 9: Cluster 1

Cluster 2:

Weight=0.062916

MU=[0.7808963058537262,0.027594300109707637,43.59271302953474,46430.948520786165,0.1500671062662067,0.297611147
4897629,2.898874780088942,2.3996095379912377,2.4470782768357395,1887.5686676601638,52.29480896675908,3.2617797
716636363,0.5617320485051086,1.8844738211391,7.445223617464369]

Sigma=

1.310268484362083   -0.008781324169799203 ... (15 total)

-0.008781324169799203 0.026832854711163028   ...

-7.778307903368862   -0.22791180189966537 ...

-1994.312293144824   953.5408564069132   ...

-0.047374773188269   -0.004140996766905095...

0.03713394906123063   -8.538912936897718E-4...

0.18950712664774483   0.006469719690237634 ...

0.09271774632030978   0.003690014536237195 ...

-0.18856667725951917   0.002380147914518987 ...

68.41855307532745   -4.151157768413957   ...

0.03435556638123301   -0.19393666789368957 ...

-0.013692860075417968 -0.020100969638081837...

0.07766539257767785   -7.836426721759263E-4...

0.058499301884249254 -4.913759714689525E-4...

0.21074627737377502   -0.03620069422593031 ...

Figure 10: Cluster 2

Cluster 3:

Weight=0.062915

MU=[0.7808981865995427,0.02759468347830766,43.59262858361646,46431.26749714549,0.1500691630940002,0.29761477506046585,2.8988635085309786,2.399611526771179,2.4470822675213055,1887.5755390299287,52.294789589124775,3.2617844704782777,0.5617355795036949,1.8844808976383316,7.445241787598352]

Sigma=

1.310283325188202   −0.008781498067640526 ... (15 total)

−0.008781498067640526 0.02683321692203967   ...

−7.778318179295566   −0.2279126380278217   ...

−1994.3651943924194   953.5453019313146   ...

−0.04737570401219658   −0.004141111055433465...

0.037134001244643104   −8.540032585036882E−4...

0.18950953750130048   0.006470120609376332 ...

0.09271869144891273   0.0036900109219803134...

−0.18856885182984973   0.002380070860293689 ...

68.41831257137832   −4.1514050538828   ...

0.03436459261474013   −0.19393882754318761 ...

−0.01369338064977525   −0.020101378563885663...

0.07766520283662945   −7.837509961456534E−4...

0.05849877693251591   −4.915780719425822E−4...

0.21074640369183104   −0.03620169856259542 ...

Figure 11: Cluster 3

Cluster 4:

Weight=0.062914

MU=[0.7808992393728132,0.027594857592962586,43.592578423292814,46431.373286351896,0.1500697901951163,0.29761605 64124643,2.898860089904809,2.3996121902034595,2.4470832872542676,1887.5779548277749,52.29478143593403,3.2617859 602083223,0.5617369056497247,1.8844833973712003,7.445247871566899]

Sigma=

1.3102898209522704   -0.008781582527563107 ... (15 total)

-0.008781582527563107 0.026833381427386702 ...

-7.778313620309155   -0.2279126919235134   ...

-1994.3796587358433   953.5483992884145   ...

-0.04737604387775983   -0.004141154489440008...

0.037134040114905426   -8.540440057795036E-4...

0.18951016842223162   0.006470255770598361 ...

0.0927190997773798   0.003690015897543276 ...

-0.18856955926488908   0.0023800577384774702...

68.41823645079883   -4.151497911732236   ...

0.03436931403004916   -0.1939398262567097   ...

-0.013693555188677108 -0.020101546506840207...

0.07766507105646259   -7.83792536234814,6E-4...

0.05849857421583572   -4.916501535027908E-4...

0.21074661417458015   -0.036202094871478796...

Figure 12: Cluster 4

Cluster 5:

Weight=0.748341

MU=[0.4058231162813968,0.0023199464802859684,22.644237040865264,30564.074445916867,0.012172001781884387,0.3909
70832200064,2.27538815618734,2.570878771841545,2.778403168061976,1710.3840312560203,56.668355015374146,3.118440132
412651,0.6153426261265736,1.9054511351698555,6.905949369774216]

Sigma=

0.17589935013824443   1.318739954100798E-4   ... (15 totals)

1.318739954100798E-4   0.0023145643286145772   ...

0.1927311852469183   0.029438024228507845   ...

1108.2263125353527   116.97771555806634   ...

7.447161249472683E-4   -2.8238392691917215E-5...

-0.007840809295101704   -2.8837901025969534E-4...

0.023475650829693853   0.0019903868910481287   ...

-0.007865077010407383   -8.710340648340969E-5   ...

-0.064056665959152722   -5.685489003490323E-4   ...

54.81575059498132   0.06205695119789516   ...

0.08164968346291952   -0.02645130673658966   ...

0.07800513455809353   -0.001357416457442531   ...

0.023165924984143067   -1.9025716915325663E-4...

0.03441444210703747   -8.997788887508309E-5   ...

0.17565249306476233   -0.0017924278494132312...

Figure 13: Cluster 5

The weight of clusters 1 to 4 signifies that these clusters are homogeneous and
significantly different compared with cluster 5.

Determining number of clusters

The beauty of clustering algorithms like K-means algorithm is that it does the clustering on the data with an unlimited number of features. It is a great tool to use when you have a raw data and would like to know the patterns in that data. However, deciding the number of clusters prior to doing the experiment might not be successful but may sometimes lead to an overfitting or underfitting problem. On the other hand, one common thing to all three algorithms (that is, K-means, bisecting K-means, and Gaussian mixture) is that the number of clusters must be determined in advance and supplied to the algorithm as a parameter. Hence, informally, determining the number of clusters is a separate optimization problem to be solved.

In this section, we will use a heuristic approach based on the Elbow method. We start from K = 2 clusters, and then we ran the K-means algorithm for the same data set by increasing K and observing the value of cost function **Within-Cluster Sum of Squares (WCSS)**. At some point, a big drop in cost function can be observed, but then the improvement became marginal with the increasing value of K. As suggested in cluster analysis literature, we can pick the K after the last big drop of WCSS as an optimal one.

By analysing below parameters, you can find out the performance of K-means:

- **Betweenness:** This is the between sum of squares also called as *intracluster similarity*.
- **Withiness:** This is the within sum of square also called *intercluster similarity*.
- **Totwithinss:** This is the sum of all the withiness of all the clusters also called *total intracluster similarity*.

It is to be noted that a robust and accurate clustering model will have a lower value of withiness and a higher value of betweenness. However, these values depend on the number of clusters, that is, K that is chosen before building the model.

Now let us discuss how to take advantage of the Elbow method to determine the number of clusters. As shown in the following, we calculated the cost function WCSS as a function of a number of clusters for the K-means algorithm applied to home data based on all the features. It can be observed that a big drop occurs when K = 5. Therefore, we chose the number of clusters as 5, as shown in *Figure 10*. Basically, this is the one after the last big drop.

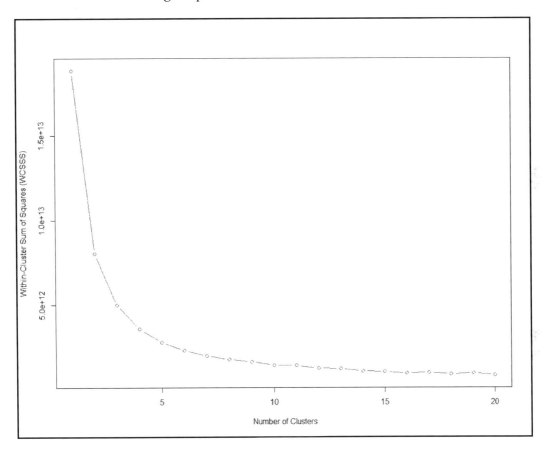

Figure 14: Number of clusters as a function of WCSS

A comparative analysis between clustering algorithms

Gaussian mixture is used mainly for expectation minimization, which is an example of an optimization algorithm. Bisecting K-means, which is faster than regular K-means, also produces slightly different clustering results. Below we try to compare these three algorithms. We will show a performance comparison in terms of model building time and the computional cost for each algorithm. As shown in the following code, we can compute the cost in terms of WCSS. The following lines of code can be used to compute the WCSS for the K-means and bisecting algorithms:

```
val WCSSS = model.computeCost(landRDD) // land RDD is the training set
println("Within-Cluster Sum of Squares = " + WCSSS) // Less is better
```

For the dataset we used throughout this chapter, we got the following values of WCSS:

```
Within-Cluster Sum of Squares of Bisecting K-means =
2.096980212594632E11
Within-Cluster Sum of Squares of K-means = 1.455560123603583E12
```

This means that K-means shows slightly better performance in terms of the compute cost. Unfortunately, we don't have any metrics like WCSS for the GMM algorithm. Now let's observe the model building time for these three algorithms. We can start the system clock before starting model training and stop it immediately after the training has been finished as follows (for K-means):

```
val start = System.currentTimeMillis()
val numClusters = 5
val numIterations = 20
val seed = 12345
val runs = 50
val model = KMeans.train(landRDD, numClusters, numIterations, seed)
val end = System.currentTimeMillis()
println("Model building and prediction time: "+ {end - start} + "ms")
```

For the training set we used throughout this chapter, we got the following values of model building time:

```
Model building and prediction time for Bisecting K-means: 2680ms
Model building and prediction time for Gaussian Mixture: 2193ms
Model building and prediction time for K-means: 3741ms
```

In different research articles, it has been found that the bisecting K-means algorithm has been shown to result in better cluster assignment for data points. Moreover, compared to K-means, bisecting K-means, alos converges well towards global minima. K-means on the other hand, gets stuck in local minima. In other words, using bisecting K-means algorithm, we can avoid the local minima that K-means can suffer from.

Note that you might observe different values of the preceding parameters depending upon your machine's hardware configuration and the random nature of the dataset.

 More details analysis is up to the readers from the theoretical views. Interested readers should also refer to Spark MLlib-based clustering techniques at `https://spark.apache.org/docs/latest/mllib-clustering.html` to get more insights.

Submitting Spark job for cluster analysis

The examples shown in this chapter can be made scalable for the even larger dataset to serve different purposes. You can package all three clustering algorithms with all the required dependencies and submit them as a Spark job in the cluster. Now use the following lines of code to submit your Spark job of K-means clustering, for example (use similar syntax for other classes), for the Saratoga NY Homes dataset:

```
# Run application as standalone mode on 8 cores
SPARK_HOME/bin/spark-submit \
--class org.apache.spark.examples.KMeansDemo \
--master local[8] \
KMeansDemo-0.1-SNAPSHOT-jar-with-dependencies.jar \
Saratoga_NY_Homes.txt

# Run on a YARN cluster
export HADOOP_CONF_DIR=XXX
SPARK_HOME/bin/spark-submit \
--class org.apache.spark.examples.KMeansDemo \
--master yarn \
--deploy-mode cluster \  # can be client for client mode
--executor-memory 20G \
--num-executors 50 \
KMeansDemo-0.1-SNAPSHOT-jar-with-dependencies.jar \
Saratoga_NY_Homes.txt

# Run on a Mesos cluster in cluster deploy mode with supervising
SPARK_HOME/bin/spark-submit \
--class org.apache.spark.examples.KMeansDemo \
```

```
--master mesos://207.184.161.138:7077 \ # Use your IP aadress
--deploy-mode cluster \
--supervise \
--executor-memory 20G \
--total-executor-cores 100 \
KMeansDemo-0.1-SNAPSHOT-jar-with-dependencies.jar \
Saratoga_NY_Homes.txt
```

Summary

In this chapter, we delved even deeper into machine learning and found out how we can take advantage of machine learning to cluster records belonging to a dataset of unsupervised observations. Consequently, you learnt the practical know-how needed to quickly and powerfully apply supervised and unsupervised techniques on available data to new problems through some widely used examples based on the understandings from the previous chapters. The examples we are talking about will be demonstrated from the Spark perspective. For any of the K-means, bisecting K-means, and Gaussian mixture algorithms, it is not guaranteed that the algorithm will produce the same clusters if run multiple times. For example, we observed that running the K-means algorithm multiple times with the same parameters generated slightly different results at each run.

For a performance comparison between K-means and Gaussian mixture, see *Jung. et. al and cluster analysis* lecture notes. In addition to K-means, bisecting K-means, and Gaussian mixture, MLlib provides implementations of three other clustering algorithms, namely, PIC, LDA, and streaming K-means. One thing is also worth mentioning is that to fine tune clustering analysis, often we need to remove unwanted data objects called outlier or anomaly. But using distance based clustering it's really difficult to identify such data pints. Therefore, other distance metrics other than Euclidean can be used. Nevertheless, these links would be a good resource to start with:

1. https://mapr.com/ebooks/spark/08-unsupervised-anomaly-detection-apache-spark.html
2. https://github.com/keiraqz/anomaly-detection
3. http://www.dcc.fc.up.pt/~ltorgo/Papers/ODCM.pdf

In the next chapter, we will dig even deeper into tuning Spark applications for better performance. We will see some best practice to optimize the performance of Spark applications.

14
Text Analytics Using Spark ML

"Programs must be written for people to read, and only incidentally for machines to execute."

- Harold Abelson

In this chapter, we will discuss the wonderful field of text analytics using Spark ML. Text analytics is a wide area in machine learning and is useful in many use cases, such as sentiment analysis, chat bots, email spam detection, and natural language processing. We will learn how to use Spark for text analysis with a focus on use cases of text classification using a 10,000 sample set of Twitter data.

In a nutshell, the following topics will be covered in this chapter:

- Understanding text analytics
- Transformers and Estimators
- Tokenizer
- StopWordsRemover
- NGrams
- TF-IDF
- Word2Vec
- CountVectorizer
- Topic modeling using LDA
- Implementing text classification

Understanding text analytics

We have explored the world of machine learning and Apache Spark's support for machine learning in the last few chapters. As we discussed, machine learning has a workflow, which is explained in the following steps:

1. Loading or ingesting data.
2. Cleansing the data.
3. Extracting features from the data.
4. Training a model on the data to generate desired outcomes based on features.
5. Evaluate or predict some outcome based on the data.

A simplified view of a typical pipeline is as shown in the following diagram:

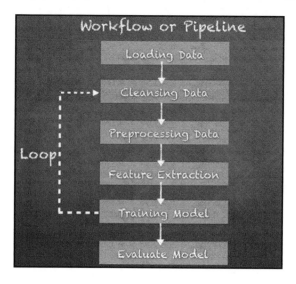

Hence, there are several stages of transformation of data possible before the model is trained and then subsequently deployed. Moreover, we should expect refinement of the features and model attributes. We could even explore a completely different algorithm repeating the entire sequence of tasks as part of a new workflow.

A pipeline of steps can be created using several steps of transformation, and for this purpose, we use a **domain specific language (DSL)** to define the nodes (data transformation steps) to create a **DAG (Directed Acyclic Graph)** of nodes. Hence, the ML pipeline is a sequence of Transformers and Estimators to fit a Pipeline model to an input dataset. Each stage in the pipeline is known as *Pipeline stage*, which are listed as follows:

- Estimator
- Model
- Pipeline
- Transformer
- Predictor

When you look at a line of text, we see sentences, phrases, words, nouns, verbs, punctuation, and so on, which when put together, have a meaning and purpose. Humans are very good at understanding sentences, words, and slangs and annotations or contexts extremely well. This comes from years of practice and learning how to read/write, proper grammar, punctuation, exclamations, and so on. So, how can we write a computer program to try to replicate this kind of capability?

Text analytics

Text analytics is the way to unlock the meaning from a collection of text. By using various techniques and algorithms to process and analyze the text data, we can uncover patterns and themes in the data. The goal of all this is to make sense of the unstructured text in order to derive contextual meaning and relationships.

Text analytics utilizes several broad categories of techniques, which we will cover next.

Sentiment analysis

Analyzing the political opinions of people on Facebook, Twitter, and other social media is a good example of sentiment analysis. Similarly, analyzing the reviews of restaurants on Yelp is also another great example of sentiment analysis.

Natural Language Processing (NLP) frameworks and libraries, such as OpenNLP and Stanford NLP, are typically used to implement sentiment analysis.

Topic modeling

Topic modeling is a useful technique for detecting the topics or themes in a corpus of documents. This is an unsupervised algorithm, which can find themes in a set of documents. An example is to detect topics covered in a news article. Another example is to detect the ideas in a patent application.

The **latent dirichlet allocation (LDA)** is a popular clustering model using unsupervised algorithm, while **latent semantic analysis (LSA)** uses a probabilistic model on co-occurrence data.

TF-IDF (term frequency - inverse document frequency)

TF-IDF measures how frequently words appear in documents and the relative frequency across the set of documents. This information can be used in building classifiers and predictive models. The examples are spam classification, chat conversations, and so on.

Named entity recognition (NER)

Named entity recognition detects the usage of words and nouns in sentences to extract information about persons, organizations, locations, and so on. This gives important contextual information on the actual content of the documents rather than just treating words as the primary entities.

Stanford NLP and OpenNLP have implementation for NER algorithms.

Event extraction

Event extraction expands on the NER establishing relationships around the entities detected. This can be used to make inferences on the relationship between two entities. Hence, there is an additional layer of semantic understanding to make sense of the document content.

Transformers and Estimators

Transformer is a function object that transforms one dataset to another by applying the transformation logic (function) to the input dataset yielding an output dataset. There are two types of Transformers the standard Transformer and the Estimator Transformer.

Standard Transformer

A standard Transformer transforms the input dataset into the output dataset, explicitly applying transformation function to the input data. There is no dependency on the input data other than reading the input column and generating the output column.

Such Transformers are invoked as shown next:

```
outputDF = transfomer.transform(inputDF)
```

Examples of standard Transformers are as follows and will be explained in detail in the subsequent sections:

- `Tokenizer`: This splits sentences into words using space as the delimiter
- `RegexTokenizer`: This splits sentences into words using regular expressions to split
- `StopWordsRemover`: This removes commonly used stop words from the list of words
- `Binarizer`: This converts the strings to binary numbers 0/1
- `NGram`: This creates N word phrases from the sentences
- `HashingTF`: This creates Term frequency counts using hash table to index the words
- `SQLTransformer`: This implements the transformations, which are defined by SQL statements
- `VectorAssembler`: This combines a given list of columns into a single vector column

The diagram of a standard Transformer is as follows, where the input column from an input dataset is transformed into an output column generating the output dataset:

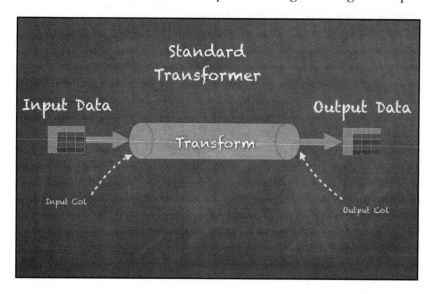

Estimator Transformer

An Estimator Transformer transforms the input dataset into the output dataset by first generating a Transformer based on the input dataset. Then the Transformer processes the input data, reading the input column and generating the output column in the output dataset.

Such Transformers are invoked as shown next:

```
transformer = estimator.fit(inputDF)
outputDF = transformer.transform(inputDF)
```

The examples of Estimator Transformers are as follows:

- IDF
- LDA
- Word2Vec

The diagram of an Estimator Transformer is as follows, where the input column from an input dataset is transformed into an output column generating the output dataset:

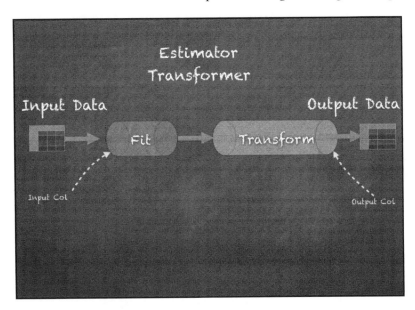

In the next few sections, we will look deeper into text analytics using a simple example dataset, which consists of lines of text (sentences), as shown in the following screenshot:

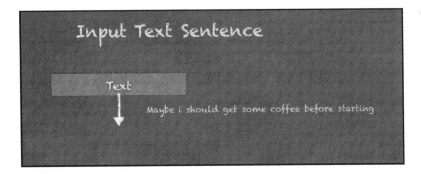

The upcoming code is used to load the text data into the input dataset.

Initialize a sequence of sentences called lines using a sequence of pairs of ID and text as shown next.

```
val lines = Seq(
 | (1, "Hello there, how do you like the book so far?"),
```

```
|  (2,  "I am new to Machine Learning"),
|  (3,  "Maybe i should get some coffee before starting"),
|  (4,  "Coffee is best when you drink it hot"),
|  (5,  "Book stores have coffee too so i should go to a book store")
|  )
lines: Seq[(Int, String)] = List((1,Hello there, how do you like the
book so far?), (2,I am new to Machine Learning), (3,Maybe i should get
some coffee before starting), (4,Coffee is best when you drink it
hot), (5,Book stores have coffee too so i should go to a book store))
```

Next, invoke the `createDataFrame()` function to create a DataFrame from the sequence of sentences we saw earlier.

```
scala> val sentenceDF = spark.createDataFrame(lines).toDF("id",
"sentence")
sentenceDF: org.apache.spark.sql.DataFrame = [id: int, sentence:
string]
```

Now you can see the newly created dataset, which shows the Sentence DataFrame containing two column IDs and sentences.

```
scala> sentenceDF.show(false)
|id|sentence |
|1 |Hello there, how do you like the book so far? |
|2 |I am new to Machine Learning |
|3 |Maybe i should get some coffee before starting |
|4 |Coffee is best when you drink it hot |
|5 |Book stores have coffee too so i should go to a book store|
```

Tokenization

Tokenizer converts the input string into lowercase and then splits the string with whitespaces into individual tokens. A given sentence is split into words either using the default space delimiter or using a customer regular expression based Tokenizer. In either case, the input column is transformed into an output column. In particular, the input column is usually a String and the output column is a Sequence of Words.

Tokenizers are available by importing two packages shown next, the `Tokenizer` and the `RegexTokenize`:

```
import org.apache.spark.ml.feature.Tokenizer
import org.apache.spark.ml.feature.RegexTokenizer
```

First, you need to initialize a `Tokenizer` specifying the input column and the output column:

```
scala> val tokenizer = new
Tokenizer().setInputCol("sentence").setOutputCol("words")
tokenizer: org.apache.spark.ml.feature.Tokenizer = tok_942c8332b9d8
```

Next, invoking the `transform()` function on the input dataset yields an output dataset:

```
scala> val wordsDF = tokenizer.transform(sentenceDF)
wordsDF: org.apache.spark.sql.DataFrame = [id: int, sentence: string
... 1 more field]
```

The following is the output dataset showing the input column IDs, sentence, and the output column words, which contain the sequence of words:

```
scala> wordsDF.show(false)
|id|sentence |words |
|1 |Hello there, how do you like the book so far? |[hello, there,,
how, do, you, like, the, book, so, far?] |
|2 |I am new to Machine Learning |[i, am, new, to, machine, learning]
|
|3 |Maybe i should get some coffee before starting |[maybe, i, should,
get, some, coffee, before, starting] |
|4 |Coffee is best when you drink it hot |[coffee, is, best, when,
you, drink, it, hot] |
|5 |Book stores have coffee too so i should go to a book store|[book,
stores, have, coffee, too, so, i, should, go, to, a, book, store]|
```

On the other hand, if you wanted to set up a regular expression based `Tokenizer`, you have to use the `RegexTokenizer` instead of `Tokenizer`. For this, you need to initialize a `RegexTokenizer` specifying the input column and the output column along with the regex pattern to be used:

```
scala> val regexTokenizer = new
RegexTokenizer().setInputCol("sentence").setOutputCol("regexWords").se
tPattern("\\W")
regexTokenizer: org.apache.spark.ml.feature.RegexTokenizer =
regexTok_15045df8ce41
```

Next, invoking the `transform()` function on the input dataset yields an output dataset:

```
scala> val regexWordsDF = regexTokenizer.transform(sentenceDF)
regexWordsDF: org.apache.spark.sql.DataFrame = [id: int, sentence:
string ... 1 more field]
```

The following is the output dataset showing the input column IDs, sentence, and the output column `regexWordsDF`, which contain the sequence of words:

```
scala> regexWordsDF.show(false)
|id|sentence |regexWords |
|1 |Hello there, how do you like the book so far? |[hello, there, how,
do, you, like, the, book, so, far] |
|2 |I am new to Machine Learning |[i, am, new, to, machine, learning]
|
|3 |Maybe i should get some coffee before starting |[maybe, i, should,
get, some, coffee, before, starting] |
|4 |Coffee is best when you drink it hot |[coffee, is, best, when,
you, drink, it, hot] |
|5 |Book stores have coffee too so i should go to a book store|[book,
stores, have, coffee, too, so, i, should, go, to, a, book, store]|
```

The diagram of a `Tokenizer` is as follows, wherein the sentence from the input text is split into words using the space delimiter:

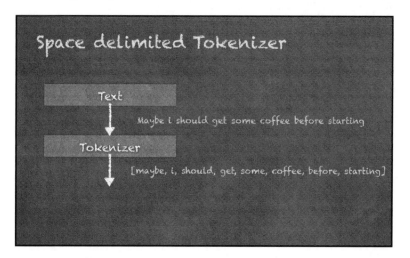

StopWordsRemover

`StopWordsRemover` is a Transformer that takes a `String` array of words and returns a `String` array after removing all the defined stop words. Some examples of stop words are I, you, my, and, or, and so on which are fairly commonly used in the English language. You can override or extend the set of stop words to suit the purpose of the use case. Without this cleansing process, the subsequent algorithms might be biased because of the common words.

In order to invoke `StopWordsRemover`, you need to import the following package:

```
import org.apache.spark.ml.feature.StopWordsRemover
```

First, you need to initialize a `StopWordsRemover`, specifying the input column and the output column. Here, we are choosing the words column created by the `Tokenizer` and generate an output column for the filtered words after removal of stop words:

```
scala> val remover = new
StopWordsRemover().setInputCol("words").setOutputCol("filteredWords")
remover: org.apache.spark.ml.feature.StopWordsRemover =
stopWords_48d2cecd3011
```

Next, invoking the `transform()` function on the input dataset yields an output dataset:

```
scala> val noStopWordsDF = remover.transform(wordsDF)
noStopWordsDF: org.apache.spark.sql.DataFrame = [id: int, sentence:
string ... 2 more fields]
```

The following is the output dataset showing the input column IDs, sentence, and the output column `filteredWords`, which contains the sequence of words:

```
scala> noStopWordsDF.show(false)
|id|sentence |words |filteredWords |
|1 |Hello there, how do you like the book so far? |[hello, there,,
how, do, you, like, the, book, so, far?] |[hello, there,, like, book,
far?] |
|2 |I am new to Machine Learning |[i, am, new, to, machine, learning]
|[new, machine, learning] |
|3 |Maybe i should get some coffee before starting |[maybe, i, should,
get, some, coffee, before, starting] |[maybe, get, coffee, starting] |
|4 |Coffee is best when you drink it hot |[coffee, is, best, when,
you, drink, it, hot] |[coffee, best, drink, hot] |
|5 |Book stores have coffee too so i should go to a book store|[book,
stores, have, coffee, too, so, i, should, go, to, a, book,
store]|[book, stores, coffee, go, book, store]|
```

The following is the output dataset showing just the sentence and the `filteredWords`, which contains the sequence of filtered words:

```
scala> noStopWordsDF.select("sentence", "filteredWords").show(5,false)
|sentence |filteredWords |
|Hello there, how do you like the book so far? |[hello, there,, like,
book, far?] |
```

```
|I am new to Machine Learning |[new, machine, learning] |
|Maybe i should get some coffee before starting |[maybe, get, coffee,
starting] |
|Coffee is best when you drink it hot ||coffee, best, drink, hot] |
|Book stores have coffee too so i should go to a book store|[book,
stores, coffee, go, book, store]|
```

The diagram of the `StopWordsRemover` is as follows, which shows the words filtered to remove stop words such as I, should, some, and before:

Stop words are set by default, but can be overridden or amended very easily, as shown in the following code snippet, where we will remove hello from the filtered words considering hello as a stop word:

```
scala> val noHello = Array("hello") ++ remover.getStopWords
noHello: Array[String] = Array(hello, i, me, my, myself, we, our,
ours, ourselves, you, your, yours, yourself, yourselves, he, him, his,
himself, she, her, hers, herself, it, its, itself, they, them, their,
theirs, themselves, what, which, who, whom, this, that, these, those,
am, is, are, was, were ...
scala>

//create new transfomer using the amended Stop Words list
scala> val removerCustom = new
StopWordsRemover().setInputCol("words").setOutputCol("filteredWords").
setStopWords(noHello)
removerCustom: org.apache.spark.ml.feature.StopWordsRemover =
stopWords_908b488ac87f
```

```
//invoke transform function
scala> val noStopWordsDFCustom = removerCustom.transform(wordsDF)
noStopWordsDFCustom: org.apache.spark.sql.DataFrame = [id: int,
sentence: string ... 2 more fields]

//output dataset showing only sentence and filtered words - now will
not show hello
scala> noStopWordsDFCustom.select("sentence",
"filteredWords").show(5,false)
+----------------------------------------------------------+----------
----------------------------+
|sentence |filteredWords |
+----------------------------------------------------------+----------
----------------------------+
|Hello there, how do you like the book so far? |[there,, like, book,
far?] |
|I am new to Machine Learning |[new, machine, learning] |
|Maybe i should get some coffee before starting |[maybe, get, coffee,
starting] |
|Coffee is best when you drink it hot |[coffee, best, drink, hot] |
|Book stores have coffee too so i should go to a book store|[book,
stores, coffee, go, book, store]|
+----------------------------------------------------------+----------
----------------------------+
```

NGrams

NGrams are word combinations created as sequences of words. N stands for the number of words in the sequence. For example, 2-gram is two words together, 3-gram is three words together. setN() is used to specify the value of N.

In order to generate NGrams, you need to import the package:

```
import org.apache.spark.ml.feature.NGram
```

First, you need to initialize an NGram generator specifying the input column and the output column. Here, we are choosing the filtered words column created by the StopWordsRemover and generating an output column for the filtered words after removal of stop words:

```
scala> val ngram = new
NGram().setN(2).setInputCol("filteredWords").setOutputCol("ngrams")
ngram: org.apache.spark.ml.feature.NGram = ngram_e7a3d3ab6115
```

Next, invoking the `transform()` function on the input dataset yields an output dataset:

```scala
scala> val nGramDF = ngram.transform(noStopWordsDF)
nGramDF: org.apache.spark.sql.DataFrame = [id: int, sentence: string
... 3 more fields]
```

The following is the output dataset showing the input column ID, sentence, and the output column `ngram`, which contain the sequence of n-grams:

```scala
scala> nGramDF.show(false)
|id|sentence |words |filteredWords |ngrams |
|1 |Hello there, how do you like the book so far? |[hello, there,,
how, do, you, like, the, book, so, far?] |[hello, there,, like, book,
far?] |[hello there,, there, like, like book, book far?] |
|2 |I am new to Machine Learning |[i, am, new, to, machine, learning]
|[new, machine, learning] |[new machine, machine learning] |
|3 |Maybe i should get some coffee before starting |[maybe, i, should,
get, some, coffee, before, starting] |[maybe, get, coffee, starting]
|[maybe get, get coffee, coffee starting] |
|4 |Coffee is best when you drink it hot |[coffee, is, best, when,
you, drink, it, hot] |[coffee, best, drink, hot] |[coffee best, best
drink, drink hot] |
|5 |Book stores have coffee too so i should go to a book store|[book,
stores, have, coffee, too, so, i, should, go, to, a, book,
store]|[book, stores, coffee, go, book, store]|[book stores, stores
coffee, coffee go, go book, book store]|
```

The following is the output dataset showing the sentence and 2-grams:

```scala
scala> nGramDF.select("sentence", "ngrams").show(5,false)
|sentence |ngrams |
|Hello there, how do you like the book so far? |[hello there,, there,
like, like book, book far?] |
|I am new to Machine Learning |[new machine, machine learning] |
|Maybe i should get some coffee before starting |[maybe get, get
coffee, coffee starting] |
|Coffee is best when you drink it hot |[coffee best, best drink, drink
hot] |
|Book stores have coffee too so i should go to a book store|[book
stores, stores coffee, coffee go, go book, book store]|
```

The diagram of an NGram is as follows, which shows 2-grams generated from the sentence after tokenizing and removing stop words:

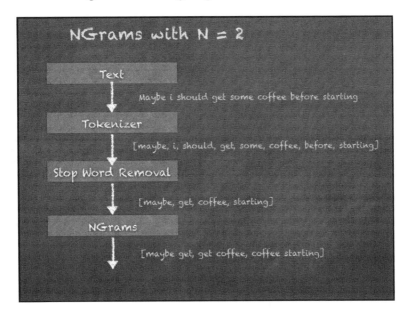

TF-IDF

TF-IDF stands for term frequency-inverse document frequency, which measures how important a word is to a document in a collection of documents. It is used extensively in informational retrieval and reflects the weightage of the word in the document. The TF-IDF value increases in proportion to the number of occurrences of the words otherwise known as frequency of the word/term and consists of two key elements, the term frequency and the inverse document frequency.

TF is the term frequency, which is the frequency of a word/term in the document. For a term *t*, *tf* measures the number of times term *t* occurs in document *d*. *tf* is implemented in Spark using hashing where a term is mapped into an index by applying a hash function.

IDF is the inverse document frequency, which represents the information a term provides about the tendency of the term to appear in documents. IDF is a log-scaled inverse function of documents containing the term:

IDF = TotalDocuments/Documents containing Term

Once we have *TF* and *IDF*, we can compute the *TF-IDF* value by multiplying the *TF* and *IDF*:

TF-IDF = TF * IDF

We will now look at how we can generate *TF* using the HashingTF Transformer in Spark ML.

HashingTF

HashingTF is a Transformer, which takes a set of terms and converts them into vectors of fixed length by hashing each term using a hash function to generate an index for each term. Then, term frequencies are generated using the indices of the hash table.

In Spark, the HashingTF uses the **MurmurHash3** algorithm to hash terms.

In order to use `HashingTF`, you need to import the following package:

```
import org.apache.spark.ml.feature.HashingTF
```

First, you need to initialize a `HashingTF` specifying the input column and the output column. Here, we choose the filtered words column created by the `StopWordsRemover` Transformer and generate an output column `rawFeaturesDF`. We also choose the number of features as 100:

```
scala> val hashingTF = new
HashingTF().setInputCol("filteredWords").setOutputCol("rawFeatures").s
etNumFeatures(100)
hashingTF: org.apache.spark.ml.feature.HashingTF =
hashingTF_b05954cb9375
```

Next, invoking the `transform()` function on the input dataset yields an output dataset:

```
scala> val rawFeaturesDF = hashingTF.transform(noStopWordsDF)
rawFeaturesDF: org.apache.spark.sql.DataFrame = [id: int, sentence:
string ... 3 more fields]
```

The following is the output dataset showing the input column IDs, sentence, and the output column `rawFeaturesDF`, which contains the features represented by a vector:

```
scala> rawFeaturesDF.show(false)
|id |sentence |words |filteredWords |rawFeatures |
|1 |Hello there, how do you like the book so far? |[hello, there,,
how, do, you, like, the, book, so, far?] |[hello, there,, like, book,
far?] |(100,[30,48,70,93],[2.0,1.0,1.0,1.0]) |
|2 |I am new to Machine Learning |[i, am, new, to, machine, learning]
|[new, machine, learning] |(100,[25,52,72],[1.0,1.0,1.0]) |
|3 |Maybe i should get some coffee before starting |[maybe, i, should,
get, some, coffee, before, starting] |[maybe, get, coffee, starting]
|(100,[16,51,59,99],[1.0,1.0,1.0,1.0]) |
|4 |Coffee is best when you drink it hot |[coffee, is, best, when,
you, drink, it, hot] |[coffee, best, drink, hot]
|(100,[31,51,63,72],[1.0,1.0,1.0,1.0]) |
|5 |Book stores have coffee too so i should go to a book store|[book,
stores, have, coffee, too, so, i, should, go, to, a, book,
store]|[book, stores, coffee, go, book,
store]|(100,[43,48,51,77,93],[1.0,1.0,1.0,1.0,2.0])|
```

Let's look at the preceding output to have a better understanding. If you just look at columns `filteredWords` and `rawFeatures` alone, you can see that,

1. The array of words [hello, there, like, book, and far] is transformed to raw feature vector (100,[30,48,70,93],[2.0,1.0,1.0,1.0]).

2. The array of words (book, stores, coffee, go, book, and store) is transformed to raw feature vector (100,[43,48,51,77,93],[1.0,1.0,1.0,1.0,2.0]).

So, what does the vector represent here? The underlying logic is that each word is hashed into an integer and counted for the number of occurrences in the word array.

Spark internally uses a `hashMap` for this mutable.HashMap.empty[Int, Double], which stores the hash value of each word as Integer key and the number of occurrences as double value. Double is used so that we can use it in conjunction with IDF (we'll talk about it in the next section). Using this map, the array [book, stores, coffee, go, book, store] can be seen as [hashFunc(book), hashFunc(stores), hashFunc(coffee), hashFunc(go), hashFunc(book), hashFunc(store)], which is equal to [43,48,51,77,93]. Then, if you count the number of occurrences too, that is, book-2, coffee-1,go-1,store-1,stores-1.

Combining the preceding information, we can generate a vector (numFeatures, hashValues, Frequencies), which in this case will be (100, [43, 48, 51, 77, 93], [1.0, 1.0, 1.0, 1.0, 2.0]).

Inverse Document Frequency (IDF)

Inverse Document Frequency (**IDF**) is an estimator, which is fit onto a dataset and then generates features by scaling the input features. Hence, IDF works on output of a HashingTF Transformer.

In order to invoke IDF, you need to import the package:

```
import org.apache.spark.ml.feature.IDF
```

First, you need to initialize an IDF specifying the input column and the output column. Here, we are choosing the words column rawFeatures created by the HashingTF and generate an output column feature:

```
scala> val idf = new
IDF().setInputCol("rawFeatures").setOutputCol("features")
idf: org.apache.spark.ml.feature.IDF = idf_d8f9ab7e398e
```

Next, invoking the fit() function on the input dataset yields an output Transformer:

```
scala> val idfModel = idf.fit(rawFeaturesDF)
idfModel: org.apache.spark.ml.feature.IDFModel = idf_d8f9ab7e398e
```

Further, invoking the transform() function on the input dataset yields an output dataset:

```
scala> val featuresDF = idfModel.transform(rawFeaturesDF)
featuresDF: org.apache.spark.sql.DataFrame = [id: int, sentence:
string ... 4 more fields]
```

The following is the output dataset showing the input column ID and the output column features, which contain the vector of scaled features produced by HashingTF in the previous transformation:

```
scala> featuresDF.select("id", "features").show(5, false)
|id|features |
|1
|(20,[8,10,13],[0.6931471805599453,3.295836866004329,0.693147180559945
3]) |
|2 |(20,[5,12],[1.0986122886681098,1.3862943611198906]) |
|3
```

```
|(20,[11,16,19],[0.4054651081081644,1.0986122886681098,2.1972245773362
196])|
|4
|(20,[3,11,12],[0.6931471805599453,0.8109302162163288,0.69314718055994
53])|
|5
|(20,[3,8,11,13,17],[0.6931471805599453,0.6931471805599453,0.405465108
1081644,1.3862943611198906,1.0986122886681098])|
```

The following is the output dataset showing the input column IDs, sentence, rawFeatures, and the output column features, which contain the vector of scaled features produced by HashingTF in the previous transformation:

```
scala> featuresDF.show(false)
|id|sentence |words |filteredWords |rawFeatures |features |
|1 |Hello there, how do you like the book so far? |[hello, there,,
how, do, you, like, the, book, so, far?] |[hello, there,, like, book,
far?] |(20,[8,10,13],[1.0,3.0,1.0])
|(20,[8,10,13],[0.6931471805599453,3.295836866004329,0.693147180559945
3])|
|2 |I am new to Machine Learning |[i, am, new, to, machine, learning]
|[new, machine, learning] |(20,[5,12],[1.0,2.0])
|(20,[5,12],[1.0986122886681098,1.3862943611198906])|
|3 |Maybe i should get some coffee before starting |[maybe, i, should,
get, some, coffee, before, starting] |[maybe, get, coffee, starting]
|(20,[11,16,19],[1.0,1.0,2.0])
|(20,[11,16,19],[0.4054651081081644,1.0986122886681098,2.1972245773362
196])|
|4 |Coffee is best when you drink it hot |[coffee, is, best, when,
you, drink, it, hot] |[coffee, best, drink, hot]
|(20,[3,11,12],[1.0,2.0,1.0])
|(20,[3,11,12],[0.6931471805599453,0.8109302162163288,0.69314718055994
53])|
|5 |Book stores have coffee too so i should go to a book store|[book,
stores, have, coffee, too, so, i, should, go, to, a, book,
store]|[book, stores, coffee, go, book,
store]|(20,[3,8,11,13,17],[1.0,1.0,1.0,2.0,1.0])|(20,[3,8,11,13,17],[0
.6931471805599453,0.6931471805599453,0.4054651081081644,1.386294361119
8906,1.0986122886681098])|
```

The diagram of the TF-IDF is as follows, which shows the generation of **TF-IDF Features**:

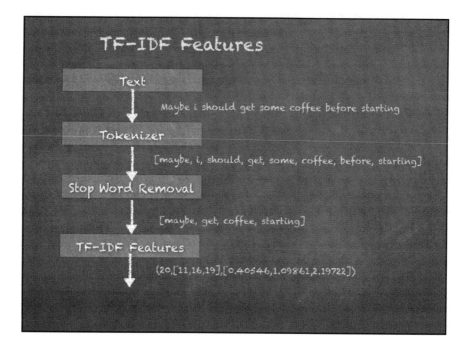

Word2Vec

Word2Vec is a sophisticated neural network style natural language processing tool and uses a technique called **skip-grams** to convert a sentence of words into an embedded vector representation. Let's look at an example of how this can be used by looking at a collection of sentences about animals:

- A dog was barking
- Some cows were grazing the grass
- Dogs usually bark randomly
- The cow likes grass

Using neural network with a hidden layer (machine learning algorithm used in many unsupervised learning applications), we can learn (with enough examples) that *dog* and *barking* are related, *cow* and *grass* are related in the sense that they appear close to each other a lot, which is measured by probabilities. The output of Word2vec is a vector of Double features.

In order to invoke Word2vec, you need to import the package:

```
import org.apache.spark.ml.feature.Word2Vec
```

First, you need to initialize a Word2vec Transformer specifying the input column and the output column. Here, we are choosing the words column created by the Tokenizer and generate an output column for the word vector of size 3:

```
scala> val word2Vec = new
Word2Vec().setInputCol("words").setOutputCol("wordvector").setVectorSi
ze(3).setMinCount(0)
word2Vec: org.apache.spark.ml.feature.Word2Vec = w2v_fe9d488fdb69
```

Next, invoking the fit() function on the input dataset yields an output Transformer:

```
scala> val word2VecModel = word2Vec.fit(noStopWordsDF)
word2VecModel: org.apache.spark.ml.feature.Word2VecModel =
w2v_fe9d488fdb69
```

Further, invoking the transform() function on the input dataset yields an output dataset:

```
scala> val word2VecDF = word2VecModel.transform(noStopWordsDF)
word2VecDF: org.apache.spark.sql.DataFrame = [id: int, sentence:
string ... 3 more fields]
```

The following is the output dataset showing the input column IDs, sentence, and the output column wordvector:

```
scala> word2VecDF.show(false)
|id|sentence |words |filteredWords |wordvector |
|1 |Hello there, how do you like the book so far? |[hello, there,,
how, do, you, like, the, book, so, far?] |[hello, there,, like, book,
far?]
|[0.006875938177108765,-0.0081967521458642,0.0040686681866645815]|
|2 |I am new to Machine Learning |[i, am, new, to, machine, learning]
|[new, machine, learning]
|[0.026012470324834187,0.023195965060343344,-0.10863214979569116] |
|3 |Maybe i should get some coffee before starting |[maybe, i, should,
get, some, coffee, before, starting] |[maybe, get, coffee, starting]
|[-0.004304863978177309,-0.004591284319758415,0.02117823390290141]|
```

```
|4 |Coffee is best when you drink it hot |[coffee, is, best, when,
you, drink, it, hot] |[coffee, best, drink, hot]
|[0.054064739029854536,-0.003801364451646805,0.06522738828789443] |
|5 |Book stores have coffee too so i should go to a book store|[book,
stores, have, coffee, too, so, i, should, go, to, a, book,
store]|[book, stores, coffee, go, book,
store]|[-0.05887459063281615,-0.07891856770341595,0.07510609552264214]
|
```

The diagram of the **Word2Vec Features** is as follows, which shows the words being converted into a vector:

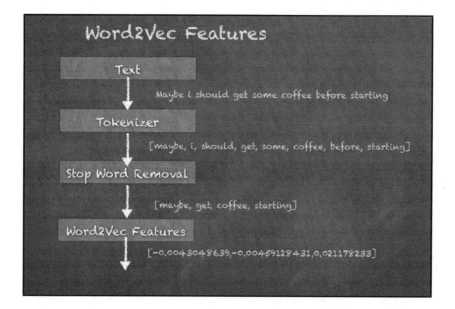

CountVectorizer

CountVectorizer is used to convert a collection of text documents to vectors of token counts essentially producing sparse representations for the documents over the vocabulary. The end result is a vector of features, which can then be passed to other algorithms. Later on, we will see how to use the output from the CountVectorizer in LDA algorithm to perform topic detection.

In order to invoke CountVectorizer, you need to import the package:

```
import org.apache.spark.ml.feature.CountVectorizer
```

First, you need to initialize a CountVectorizer Transformer specifying the input column and the output column. Here, we are choosing the filteredWords column created by the StopWordRemover and generate output column features:

```scala
scala> val countVectorizer = new
CountVectorizer().setInputCol("filteredWords").setOutputCol("features"
)
countVectorizer: org.apache.spark.ml.feature.CountVectorizer =
cntVec_555716178088
```

Next, invoking the fit() function on the input dataset yields an output Transformer:

```scala
scala> val countVectorizerModel = countVectorizer.fit(noStopWordsDF)
countVectorizerModel: org.apache.spark.ml.feature.CountVectorizerModel
= cntVec_555716178088
```

Further, invoking the transform() function on the input dataset yields an output dataset.

```scala
scala> val countVectorizerDF =
countVectorizerModel.transform(noStopWordsDF)
countVectorizerDF: org.apache.spark.sql.DataFrame = [id: int,
sentence: string ... 3 more fields]
```

The following is the output dataset showing the input column IDs, sentence, and the output column features:

```scala
scala> countVectorizerDF.show(false)
|id |sentence |words |filteredWords |features |
|1 |Hello there, how do you like the book so far? |[hello, there,,
how, do, you, like, the, book, so, far?] |[hello, there,, like, book,
far?] |(18,[1,4,5,13,15],[1.0,1.0,1.0,1.0,1.0])|
|2 |I am new to Machine Learning |[i, am, new, to, machine, learning]
|[new, machine, learning] |(18,[6,7,16],[1.0,1.0,1.0]) |
|3 |Maybe i should get some coffee before starting |[maybe, i, should,
get, some, coffee, before, starting] |[maybe, get, coffee, starting]
|(18,[0,8,9,14],[1.0,1.0,1.0,1.0]) |
|4 |Coffee is best when you drink it hot |[coffee, is, best, when,
you, drink, it, hot] |[coffee, best, drink, hot]
|(18,[0,3,10,12],[1.0,1.0,1.0,1.0]) |
|5 |Book stores have coffee too so i should go to a book store|[book,
stores, have, coffee, too, so, i, should, go, to, a, book,
store]|[book, stores, coffee, go, book,
store]|(18,[0,1,2,11,17],[1.0,2.0,1.0,1.0,1.0])|
```

The diagram of a `CountVectorizer` is as follows, which shows the features generated from `StopWordsRemover` transformation:

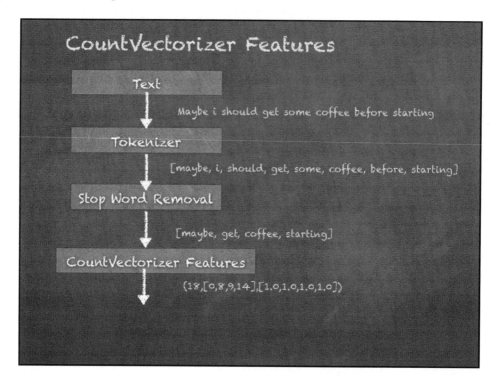

Topic modeling using LDA

LDA is a topic model, which infers topics from a collection of text documents. LDA can be thought of as an unsupervised clustering algorithm as follows:

- Topics correspond to cluster centers and documents correspond to rows in a dataset
- Topics and documents both exist in a feature space, where feature vectors are vectors of word counts
- Rather than estimating a clustering using a traditional distance, LDA uses a function based on a statistical model of how text documents are generated

In order to invoke LDA, you need to import the package:

```
import org.apache.spark.ml.clustering.LDA
```

Step 1. First, you need to initialize an LDA model setting 10 topics and 10 iterations of clustering:

```
scala> val lda = new LDA().setK(10).setMaxIter(10)
lda: org.apache.spark.ml.clustering.LDA = lda_18f248b08480
```

Step 2. Next invoking the `fit()` function on the input dataset yields an output transformer:

```
scala> val ldaModel = lda.fit(countVectorizerDF)
ldaModel: org.apache.spark.ml.clustering.LDAModel = lda_18f248b08480
```

Step 3. Extract `logLikelihood`, which calculates a lower bound on the provided documents given the inferred topic:

```
scala> val ll = ldaModel.logLikelihood(countVectorizerDF)
ll: Double = -275.3298948279124
```

Step 4. Extract `logPerplexity`, which calculates an upper bound on the perplexity of the provided documents given the inferred topics:

```
scala> val lp = ldaModel.logPerplexity(countVectorizerDF)
lp: Double = 12.512670220189033
```

Step 5. Now, we can use `describeTopics()` to get the topics generated by LDA:

```
scala> val topics = ldaModel.describeTopics(10)
topics: org.apache.spark.sql.DataFrame = [topic: int, termIndices:
array<int> ... 1 more field]
```

Step 6. The following is the output dataset showing the `topic`, `termIndices`, and `termWeights` computed by LDA model:

```
scala> topics.show(10, false)
|topic|termIndices    |termWeights    |
|0  |[2, 5, 7, 12, 17, 9, 13, 16, 4, 11]  |[0.06403877783050851,
0.0638177222807826, 0.06296749987731722, 0.06129482302538905,
0.05906095287220612, 0.0583855194291998, 0.05794181263149175,
0.057342702589298085, 0.05638654243412251, 0.05601913313272188]  |
|1  |[15, 5, 13, 8, 1, 6, 9, 16, 2, 14]  |[0.06889315890755099,
0.06415969116685549, 0.058990446579892136, 0.05840283223031986,
0.05676844625413551, 0.0566842803396241, 0.05633554021408156,
0.05580861561950114, 0.05511658232053423, 0.05471754535803045]  |
|2  |[17, 14, 1, 5, 12, 2, 4, 8, 11, 16]  |[0.06230542516700517,
```

```
0.06207673834677118, 0.06089143673912089, 0.060721809302399316,
0.06020894045877178, 0.05953822260375286, 0.05897033457363252,
0.057504989644756616, 0.05586725037894327, 0.05562088924566989] |
|3 |[15, 2, 11, 16, 1, 7, 17, 8, 10, 3] |[0.06995373276880751,
0.06249041124300946, 0.06196061278107645, 0.05879695651399876,
0.05816564815895558, 0.05798721645705949, 0.05724374708387087,
0.056034215734402475, 0.05474217418082123, 0.05443850583761207] |
|4 |[16, 9, 5, 7, 1, 12, 14, 10, 13, 4] |[0.06739359010780331,
0.06716438619386095, 0.06391509491709904, 0.062049068666162915,
0.06050715515506004, 0.05925113958472128, 0.057946856127790804,
0.05594837087703049, 0.055000929117413805, 0.053537418286233956]|
|5 |[5, 15, 6, 17, 7, 8, 16, 11, 10, 2] |[0.061611492476326836,
0.06131944264846151, 0.06092975441932787, 0.059812552365763404,
0.05959889552537741, 0.05929123338151455, 0.05899808901872648,
0.05892061664356089, 0.05706951425713708, 0.05636134431063274] |
|6 |[15, 0, 4, 14, 2, 10, 13, 7, 6, 8] |[0.06669864676186414,
0.0613859230159798, 0.05902091745149218, 0.058507882633921676,
0.058373998449322555, 0.05740944364508325, 0.057039150886628136,
0.057021822698594314, 0.05677330199892444, 0.056741558062814376]|
|7 |[12, 9, 8, 15, 16, 4, 7, 13, 17, 10]|[0.06770789917351365,
0.06320078344027158, 0.06225712567900613, 0.058773135159638154,
0.05832535181576588, 0.057727684814461444, 0.056683575112703555,
0.05651178333610803, 0.056202395617563274, 0.05538103218174723]|
|8 |[14, 11, 10, 7, 12, 9, 13, 16, 5, 1]|[0.06757347958335463,
0.06362319365053591, 0.063359294927315, 0.06319462709331332,
0.05969320243218982, 0.058380063437908046, 0.057412693576813126,
0.056710451222381435, 0.056254581639201336, 0.054737785085167814] |
|9 |[3, 16, 5, 7, 0, 2, 10, 15, 1, 13] |[0.06603941595604573,
0.06312775362528278, 0.06248795574460503, 0.06240547032037694,
0.0613859713404773, 0.06017781222489122, 0.05945655694365531,
0.05910351349013983, 0.05751269894725456, 0.05605239791764803] |
```

The diagram of an LDA is as follows, which shows the topics created from the features of TF-IDF:

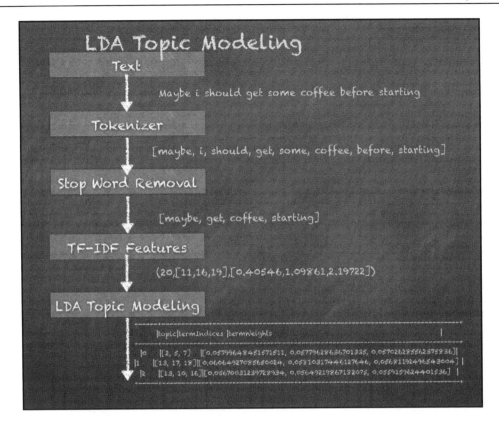

Implementing text classification

Text classification is one of the most widely used paradigms in the field of machine learning and is useful in use cases such as spam detection and email classification and just like any other machine learning algorithm, the workflow is built of Transformers and algorithms. In the field of text processing, preprocessing steps such as stop-word removal, stemming, tokenizing, n-gram extraction, TF-IDF feature weighting come into play. Once the desired processing is complete, the models are trained to classify the documents into two or more classes.

Binary classification is the classification of inputting two output classes such as spam/not spam and a given credit card transaction is fraudulent or not. Multiclass classification can generate multiple output classes such as hot, cold, freezing, and rainy. There is another technique called Multilabel classification, which can generate multiple labels such as speed, safety, and fuel efficiency can be produced from descriptions of car features.

For this purpose, we will using a 10k sample dataset of tweets and we will use the preceding techniques on this dataset. Then, we will tokenize the text lines into words, remove stop words, and then use `CountVectorizer` to build a vector of the words (features).

Then we will split the data into training (80%)-testing (20%) and train a Logistic Regression model. Finally, we will evaluate against the test data and look at how it is performed.

The steps in the workflow are shown in the following diagram:

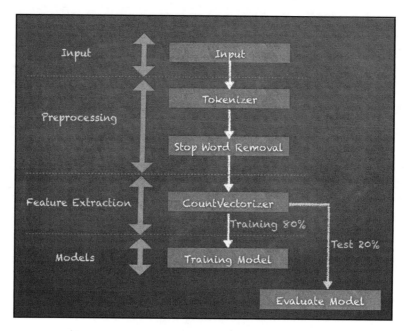

Step 1. Load the input text data containing 10k tweets along with label and ID:

```
scala> val inputText =
sc.textFile("Sentiment_Analysis_Dataset10k.csv")
inputText: org.apache.spark.rdd.RDD[String] =
Sentiment_Analysis_Dataset10k.csv MapPartitionsRDD[1722] at textFile
at <console>:77
```

Step 2. Convert the input lines to a DataFrame:

```
scala> val sentenceDF = inputText.map(x => (x.split(",")(0),
x.split(",")(1), x.split(",")(2))).toDF("id", "label", "sentence")
sentenceDF: org.apache.spark.sql.DataFrame = [id: string, label:
string ... 1 more field]
```

Step 3. Transform the data into words using a `Tokenizer` with white space delimiter:

```scala
scala> import org.apache.spark.ml.feature.Tokenizer
import org.apache.spark.ml.feature.Tokenizer

scala> val tokenizer = new
Tokenizer().setInputCol("sentence").setOutputCol("words")
tokenizer: org.apache.spark.ml.feature.Tokenizer = tok_ebd4c89f166e

scala> val wordsDF = tokenizer.transform(sentenceDF)
wordsDF: org.apache.spark.sql.DataFrame = [id: string, label: string
... 2 more fields]

scala> wordsDF.show(5, true)
| id|label| sentence| words|
| 1| 0|is so sad for my ...|[is, so, sad, for...|
| 2| 0|I missed the New ...|[i, missed, the, ...|
| 3| 1| omg its already ...|[, omg, its, alre...|
| 4| 0| .. Omgaga. Im s...|[, , .., omgaga.,...|
| 5| 0|i think mi bf is ...|[i, think, mi, bf...|
```

Step 4. Remove stop words and create a new DataFrame with the filtered words:

```scala
scala> import org.apache.spark.ml.feature.StopWordsRemover
import org.apache.spark.ml.feature.StopWordsRemover

scala> val remover = new
StopWordsRemover().setInputCol("words").setOutputCol("filteredWords")
remover: org.apache.spark.ml.feature.StopWordsRemover =
stopWords_d8dd48c9cdd0

scala> val noStopWordsDF = remover.transform(wordsDF)
noStopWordsDF: org.apache.spark.sql.DataFrame = [id: string, label:
string ... 3 more fields]

scala> noStopWordsDF.show(5, true)
| id|label| sentence| words| filteredWords|
| 1| 0|is so sad for my ...|[is, so, sad, for...|[sad, apl, friend...|
| 2| 0|I missed the New ...|[i, missed, the, ...|[missed, new, moo...|
| 3| 1| omg its already ...|[, omg, its, alre...|[, omg, already, ...|
| 4| 0| .. Omgaga. Im s...|[, , .., omgaga.,...|[, , .., omgaga.,...|
| 5| 0|i think mi bf is ...|[i, think, mi, bf...|[think, mi, bf, c...|
```

Step 5. Create a feature vector from the filtered words:

```
scala> import org.apache.spark.ml.feature.CountVectorizer
import org.apache.spark.ml.feature.CountVectorizer

scala> val countVectorizer = new
CountVectorizer().setInputCol("filteredWords").setOutputCol("features"
)
countVectorizer: org.apache.spark.ml.feature.CountVectorizer =
cntVec_fdf1512dfcbd

scala> val countVectorizerModel = countVectorizer.fit(noStopWordsDF)
countVectorizerModel: org.apache.spark.ml.feature.CountVectorizerModel
= cntVec_fdf1512dfcbd

scala> val countVectorizerDF =
countVectorizerModel.transform(noStopWordsDF)
countVectorizerDF: org.apache.spark.sql.DataFrame = [id: string,
label: string ... 4 more fields]

scala> countVectorizerDF.show(5,true)
| id|label| sentence| words| filteredWords| features|
| 1| 0|is so sad for my ...|[is, so, sad, for...|[sad, apl,
friend...|(23481,[35,9315,2...|
| 2| 0|I missed the New ...|[i, missed, the, ...|[missed, new,
moo...|(23481,[23,175,97...|
| 3| 1| omg its already ...|[, omg, its, alre...|[, omg, already,
...|(23481,[0,143,686...|
| 4| 0| .. Omgaga. Im s...|[, , .., omgaga.,...|[, , ..,
omgaga.,...|(23481,[0,4,13,27...|
| 5| 0|i think mi bf is ...|[i, think, mi, bf...|[think, mi, bf,
c...|(23481,[0,33,731,...|
```

Step 6. Create the `inputData` DataFrame with just a label and the features:

```
scala> val inputData=countVectorizerDF.select("label",
"features").withColumn("label", col("label").cast("double"))
inputData: org.apache.spark.sql.DataFrame = [label: double, features:
vector]
```

Step 7. Split the data using a random split into 80% training and 20% testing datasets:

```
scala> val Array(trainingData, testData) =
inputData.randomSplit(Array(0.8, 0.2))
trainingData: org.apache.spark.sql.Dataset[org.apache.spark.sql.Row] =
[label: double, features: vector]
testData: org.apache.spark.sql.Dataset[org.apache.spark.sql.Row] =
[label: double, features: vector]
```

Step 8. Create a Logistic Regression model:

```scala
scala> import org.apache.spark.ml.classification.LogisticRegression
import org.apache.spark.ml.classification.LogisticRegression

scala> val lr = new LogisticRegression()
lr: org.apache.spark.ml.classification.LogisticRegression =
logreg_a56accef5728
```

Step 9. Create a Logistic Regression model by fitting the `trainingData`:

```scala
scala> var lrModel = lr.fit(trainingData)
lrModel: org.apache.spark.ml.classification.LogisticRegressionModel =
logreg_a56accef5728

scala> lrModel.coefficients
res160: org.apache.spark.ml.linalg.Vector =
[7.499178040193577,8.794520490564185,4.837543313917086,-5.995818019393
418,1.1754740390468577,3.2104594489397584,1.7840290776286476,-1.839192
3375331787,1.3427471762591,6.963032309971087,-6.92725055841986,-10.781
468845891563,3.9752.836891070557657,3.8758544006087523,-11.76089493557
6934,-6.252988307540...

scala> lrModel.intercept
res161: Double = -5.397920610780994
```

Step 10. Examine the model summary especially `areaUnderROC`, which should be > *0.90* for a good model:

```scala
scala> import
org.apache.spark.ml.classification.BinaryLogisticRegressionSummary
import
org.apache.spark.ml.classification.BinaryLogisticRegressionSummary

scala> val summary = lrModel.summary
summary:
org.apache.spark.ml.classification.LogisticRegressionTrainingSummary =
org.apache.spark.ml.classification.BinaryLogisticRegressionTrainingSum
mary@1dce712c

scala> val bSummary =
summary.asInstanceOf[BinaryLogisticRegressionSummary]
bSummary:
org.apache.spark.ml.classification.BinaryLogisticRegressionSummary =
org.apache.spark.ml.classification.BinaryLogisticRegressionTrainingSum
mary@1dce712c

scala> bSummary.areaUnderROC
```

```
res166: Double = 0.9999231930196596

scala> bSummary.roc
res167: org.apache.spark.sql.DataFrame = [FPR: double, TPR: double]

scala> bSummary.pr.show()
| recall|precision|
| 0.0| 1.0|
| 0.2306543172990738| 1.0|
| 0.2596354944726621| 1.0|
| 0.2832387212429041| 1.0|
|0.30504929787869733| 1.0|
| 0.3304451747833881| 1.0|
|0.35255452644158947| 1.0|
| 0.3740663280549746| 1.0|
| 0.3952793546459516| 1.0|
```

Step 11. Transform both training and testing datasets using the trained model:

```
scala> val training = lrModel.transform(trainingData)
training: org.apache.spark.sql.DataFrame = [label: double, features:
vector ... 3 more fields]

scala> val test = lrModel.transform(testData)
test: org.apache.spark.sql.DataFrame = [label: double, features:
vector ... 3 more fields]
```

Step 12. Count the number of records with matching label and prediction columns. They should match for correct model evaluation else they will mismatch:

```
scala> training.filter("label == prediction").count
res162: Long = 8029

scala> training.filter("label != prediction").count
res163: Long = 19

scala> test.filter("label == prediction").count
res164: Long = 1334

scala> test.filter("label != prediction").count
res165: Long = 617
```

The results can be put into a table as shown next:

Dataset	Total	label = prediction	label != prediction
Training	8048	8029 (99.76%)	19 (0.24%)
Testing	1951	1334 (68.35%)	617 (31.65%)

While training data produced excellent matches, the testing data only had 68.35% match. Hence, there is room for improvement which can be done by exploring the model parameters.

Logistic regression is an easy-to-understand method for predicting a binary outcome using a linear combination of inputs and randomized noise in the form of a logistic random variable. Hence, Logistic Regression model can be tuned using several parameters. (The full set of parameters and how to tune such a Logistic Regression model is out of scope for this chapter.)

Some parameters that can be used to tune the model are:

- Model hyperparameters include the following parameters:
    - `elasticNetParam`: This parameter specifies how you would like to mix L1 and L2 regularization
    - `regParam`: This parameter determines how the inputs should be regularized before being passed in the model
- Training parameters include the following parameters:
    - `maxIter`: This is total number of interactions before stopping
    - `weightCol`: This is the name of the weight column to weigh certain rows more than others
- Prediction parameters include the following parameter:
    - `threshold`: This is the probability threshold for binary prediction. This determines the minimum probability for a given class to be predicted.

We have now seen how to build a simple classification model, so any new tweet can be labeled based on the training set. Logistic Regression is only one of the models that can be used.

Other models which can be used in place of Logistic Regression are as follows:

- Decision trees
- Random Forest
- Gradient Boosted Trees
- Multilayer Perceptron

Summary

In this chapter, we have introduced the world of text analytics using Spark ML with emphasis on text classification. We have learned about Transformers and Estimators. We have seen how Tokenizers can be used to break sentences into words, how to remove stop words, and generate n-grams. We also saw how to implement `HashingTF` and `IDF` to generate TF-IDF-based features. We also looked at `Word2Vec` to convert sequences of words into vectors.

Then, we also looked at LDA, a popular technique used to generate topics from documents without knowing much about the actual text. Finally, we implemented text classification on the set of 10k tweets from the Twitter dataset to see how it all comes together using Transformers, Estimators, and the Logistic Regression model to perform binary classification.

In the next chapter, we will dig even deeper toward tuning Spark applications for better performance.

15
Spark Tuning

"Harpists spend 90 percent of their lives tuning their harps and 10 percent playing out of tune."

- Igor Stravinsky

In this chapter, we will dig deeper into Apache Spark internals and see that while Spark is great in making us feel like we are using just another Scala collection, we don't have to forget that Spark actually runs in a distributed system. Therefore, some extra care should be taken. In a nutshell, the following topics will be covered in this chapter:

- Monitoring Spark jobs
- Spark configuration
- Common mistakes in Spark app development
- Optimization techniques

Monitoring Spark jobs

Spark provides web UI for monitoring all the jobs running or completed on computing nodes (drivers or executors). In this section, we will discuss in brief how to monitor Spark jobs using Spark web UI with appropriate examples. We will see how to monitor the progress of jobs (including submitted, queued, and running jobs). All the tabs in the Spark web UI will be discussed briefly. Finally, we will discuss the logging procedure in Spark for better tuning.

Spark web interface

The web UI (also known as Spark UI) is the web interface for running Spark applications to monitor the execution of jobs on a web browser such as Firefox or Google Chrome. When a SparkContext launches, a web UI that displays useful information about the application gets started on port 4040 in standalone mode. The Spark web UI is available in different ways depending on whether the application is still running or has finished its execution.

Also, you can use the web UI after the application has finished its execution by persisting all the events using `EventLoggingListener`. The `EventLoggingListener`, however, cannot work alone, and the incorporation of the Spark history server is required. Combining these two features, the following facilities can be achieved:

- A list of scheduler stages and tasks
- A summary of RDD sizes
- Memory usage
- Environmental information
- Information about the running executors

You can access the UI at `http://<driver-node>:4040` in a web browser. For example, a Spark job submitted and running as a standalone mode can be accessed at `http://localhost:4040`.

 Note that if multiple SparkContexts are running on the same host, they will bind to successive ports beginning with 4040, 4041, 4042, and so on. By default, this information will be available for the duration of your Spark application only. This means that when your Spark job finishes its execution, the binding will no longer be valid or accessible.

As long as the job is running, stages can be observed on Spark UI. However, to view the web UI after the job has finished the execution, you could try setting `spark.eventLog.enabled` as true before submitting your Spark jobs. This forces Spark to log all the events to be displayed in the UI that are already persisted on storage such as local filesystem or HDFS.

In the previous chapter, we saw how to submit a Spark job to a cluster. Let's reuse one of the commands for submitting the k-means clustering, as follows:

```
# Run application as standalone mode on 8 cores
```

```
SPARK_HOME/bin/spark-submit \
  --class org.apache.spark.examples.KMeansDemo \
  --master local[8] \
  KMeansDemo-0.1-SNAPSHOT-jar-with-dependencies.jar \
  Saratoga_NY_Homes.txt
```

If you submit the job using the preceding command, you will not be able to see the status of the jobs that have finished the execution, so to make the changes permanent, use the following two options:

```
spark.eventLog.enabled=true
spark.eventLog.dir=file:///home/username/log"
```

By setting the preceding two configuration variables, we asked the Spark driver to make the event logging enabled to be saved at `file:///home/username/log`.

In summary, with the following changes, your submitting command will be as follows:

```
# Run application as standalone mode on 8 cores
SPARK_HOME/bin/spark-submit \
  --conf "spark.eventLog.enabled=true" \
  --conf "spark.eventLog.dir=file:///tmp/test" \
  --class org.apache.spark.examples.KMeansDemo \
  --master local[8] \
  KMeansDemo-0.1-SNAPSHOT-jar-with-dependencies.jar \
  Saratoga_NY_Homes.txt
```

Figure 1: Spark web UI

As shown in the preceding screenshot, Spark web UI provides the following tabs:

- **Jobs**
- **Stages**
- **Storage**
- **Environment**
- **Executors**
- **SQL**

It is to be noted that all the features may not be visible at once as they are lazily created on demand, for example, while running a streaming job.

Jobs

Depending upon the SparkContext, the **Jobs** tab shows the status of all the Spark jobs in a Spark application. When you access the **Jobs** tab on the Spark UI using a web browser at `http://localhost:4040` (for standalone mode), you should observe the following options:

- **User**: This shows the active user who has submitted the Spark job
- **Total Uptime**: This shows the total uptime for the jobs
- **Scheduling Mode**: In most cases, it is first-in-first-out (aka FIFO)
- **Active Jobs**: This shows the number of active jobs
- **Completed Jobs**: This shows the number of completed jobs
- **Event Timeline**: This shows the timeline of a job that has completed its execution

Internally, the **Jobs** tab is represented by the `JobsTab` class, which is a custom **SparkUI** tab with the jobs prefix. The **Jobs** tab uses `JobProgressListener` to access statistics about the Spark jobs to display the above information on the page. Take a look at the following screenshot:

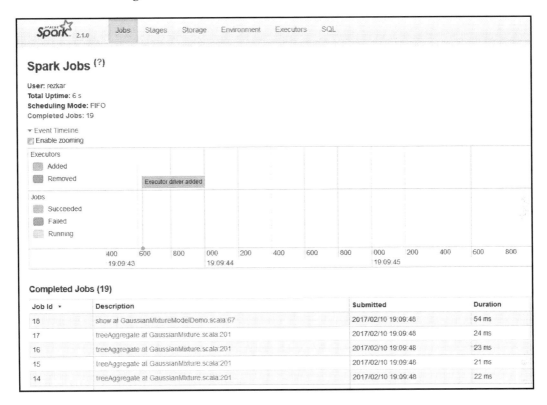

Figure 2: The jobs tab in the Spark web UI

If you further expand the **Active Jobs** option in the **Jobs** tab, you will be able to see the execution plan, status, number of completed stages, and the job ID of that particular job as **DAG Visualization,** as shown in the following:

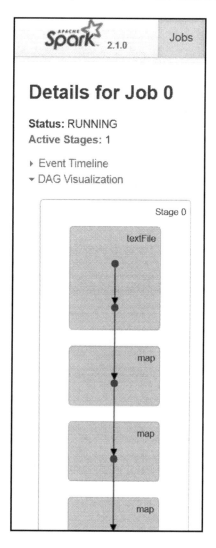

Figure 3: The DAG visualization for task in the Spark web UI (abridged)

When a user enters the code in the Spark console (for example, Spark shell or using Spark submit), Spark Core creates an operator graph. This is basically what happens when a user executes an action (for example, reduce, collect, count, first, take, countByKey, saveAsTextFile) or transformation (for example, map, flatMap, filter, mapPartitions, sample, union, intersection, distinct) on an RDD (which are immutable objects) at a particular node.

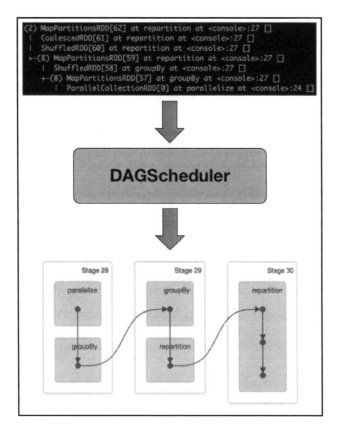

Figure 4: DAG scheduler transforming RDD lineage into stage DAG

During the transformation or action, **Directed Acyclic Graph** (**DAG**) information is used to restore the node to last transformation and actions (refer to *Figure 4* and *Figure 5* for a clearer picture) to maintain the data resiliency. Finally, the graph is submitted to a DAG scheduler.

How does Spark compute the DAG from the RDD and subsequently execute the task?

At a high level, when any action is called on the RDD, Spark creates the DAG and submits it to the DAG scheduler. The DAG scheduler divides operators into stages of tasks. A stage comprises tasks based on partitions of the input data. The DAG scheduler pipelines operators together. For example, many map operators can be scheduled in a single stage. The final result of a DAG scheduler is a set of stages. The stages are passed on to the task scheduler. The task scheduler launches tasks through the cluster manager (Spark Standalone/YARN/Mesos). The task scheduler doesn't know about the dependencies of the stages. The worker executes the tasks on the stage.

The DAG scheduler then keeps track of which RDDs the stage outputs materialized from. It then finds a minimal schedule to run jobs and divides the related operators into stages of tasks. Based on partitions of the input data, a stage comprises multiple tasks. Then, operators are pipelined together with the DAG scheduler. Practically, more than one map or reduce operator (for example) can be scheduled in a single stage.

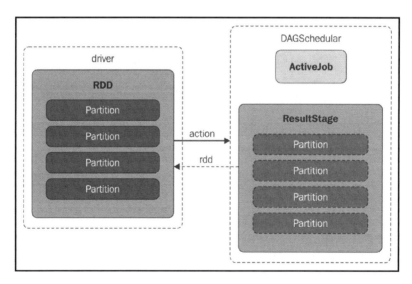

Figure 5: Executing action leads to new ResultStage and ActiveJob in DAGScheduler

Two fundamental concepts in DAG scheduler are jobs and stages. Thus, it has to track them through internal registries and counters. Technically speaking, DAG scheduler is a part of SparkContext's initialization that works exclusively on the driver (immediately after the task scheduler and scheduler backend are ready). DAG scheduler is responsible for three major tasks in Spark execution. It computes an execution DAG, that is, DAG of stages, for a job. It determines the preferred node to run each task on and handles failures due to shuffle output files being lost.

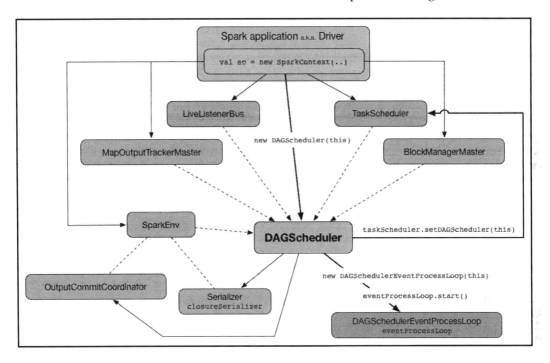

Figure 6: DAGScheduler as created by SparkContext with other services

The final result of a DAG scheduler is a set of stages. Therefore, most of the statistics and the status of the job can be seen using this visualization, for example, execution plan, status, number of completed stages, and the job ID of that particular job.

Stages

The **Stages** tab in Spark UI shows the current status of all stages of all jobs in a Spark application, including two optional pages for the tasks and statistics for a stage and pool details. Note that this information is available only when the application works in a fair scheduling mode. You should be able to access the **Stages** tab at `http://localhost:4040/stages`. Note that when there are no jobs submitted, the tab shows nothing but the title. The Stages tab shows the stages in a Spark application. The following stages can be seen in this tab:

- **Active Stages**
- **Pending Stages**
- **Completed Stages**

For example, when you submit a Spark job locally, you should be able to see the following status:

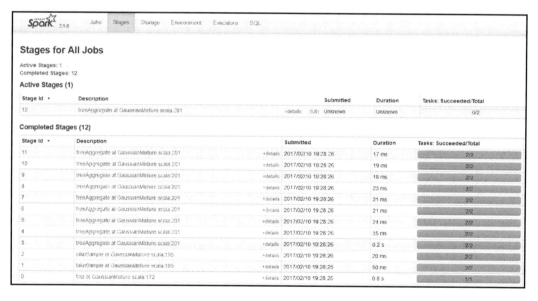

Figure 7: The stages for all jobs in the Spark web UI

In this case, there's only one stage that is an active stage. However, in the upcoming chapters, we will be able to observe other stages when we will submit our Spark jobs to AWS EC2 clusters.

To further dig down to the summary of the completed jobs, click on any link contained in the **Description** column and you should find the related statistics on execution time as metrics. An approximate time of min, median, 25th percentile, 75th percentile, and max for the metrics can also be seen in the following figure:

Summary Metrics for 2 Completed Tasks

Metric	Min	25th percentile	Median
Duration	0.2 s	0.2 s	0.2 s
GC Time	0 ms	0 ms	0 ms
Input Size / Records	27.6 KB / 1	27.6 KB / 1	28.6 KB / 1

▾ Aggregated Metrics by Executor

Executor ID ▴	Address	Task Time	Total Tasks	Failed Tasks	Killed Tasks
driver	10.2.17.13:53512	0.5 s	2	0	0

Tasks (2)

Index ▴	ID	Attempt	Status	Locality Level	Executor ID / Host	Launch Time
0	4	0	SUCCESS	PROCESS_LOCAL	driver / localhost	2017/02/04 12:57:01
1	5	0	SUCCESS	PROCESS_LOCAL	driver / localhost	2017/02/04 12:57:01

Figure 8: The summary for completed jobs on the Spark web UI

Your case might be different as I have executed and submitted only two jobs for demonstration purposes during the writing of this book. You can see other statistics on the executors as well. For my case, I submitted these jobs in the standalone mode by utilizing 8 cores and 32 GB of RAM. In addition to these, information related to the executor, such as ID, IP address with the associated port number, task completion time, number of tasks (including number of failed tasks, killed tasks, and succeeded tasks), and input size of the dataset per records are shown.

The other section in the image shows other information related to these two tasks, for example, index, ID, attempts, status, locality level, host information, launch time, duration, **Garbage Collection (GC)** time, and so on.

Storage

The **Storage** tab shows the size and memory use for each RDD, DataFrame, or Dataset. You should be able to see the storage-related information of RDDs, DataFrames, or Datasets. The following figure shows storage metadata such as RDD name, storage level, the number of cache partitions, the percentage of a fraction of the data that was cached, and the size of the RDD in the main memory:

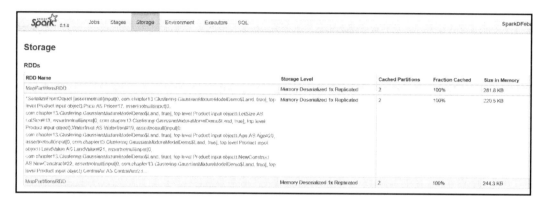

Figure 9: Storage tab shows space consumed by an RDD in disk

Note that if the RDD cannot be cached in the main memory, disk space will be used instead. A more detailed discussion will be carried out in a later section of this chapter.

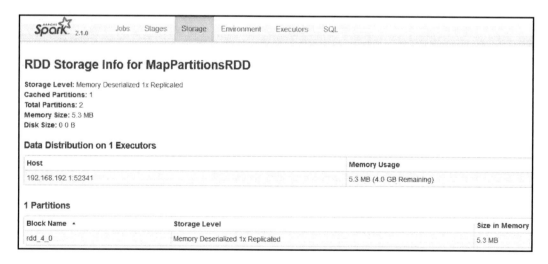

Figure 10: Data distribution and the storage used by the RDD in disk

Environment

The **Environment** tab shows the environmental variables that are currently set on your machine (that is, driver). More specifically, runtime information such as **Java Home**, **Java Version**, and **Scala Version** can be seen under **Runtime Information**. Spark properties such as Spark application ID, app name, and driver host information, driver port, executor ID, master URL, and the schedule mode can be seen. Furthermore, other system-related properties and job properties such as AWT toolkit version, file encoding type (for example, UTF-8), and file encoding package information (for example, sun.io) can be seen under **System Properties**.

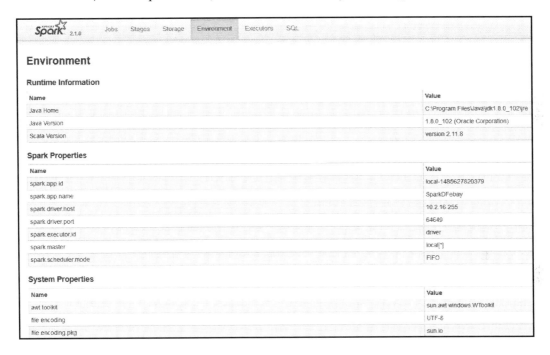

Figure 11: Environment tab on Spark web UI

Executors

The **Executors** tab uses `ExecutorsListener` to collect information about executors for a Spark application. An executor is a distributed agent that is responsible for executing tasks. Executors are instantiated in different ways. For example, they can be instantiated when `CoarseGrainedExecutorBackend` receives `RegisteredExecutor` message for Spark Standalone and YARN. The second case is when a Spark job is submitted to Mesos. The Mesos's `MesosExecutorBackend` gets registered. The third case is when you run your Spark jobs locally, that is, `LocalEndpoint` is created. An executor typically runs for the entire lifetime of a Spark application, which is called static allocation of executors, although you can also opt in for dynamic allocation. The executor backends exclusively manage all the executors in a computing node or clusters. An executor reports heartbeat and partial metrics for active tasks to the **HeartbeatReceiver** RPC endpoint on the driver periodically and the results are sent to the driver. They also provide in-memory storage for RDDs that are cached by user programs through block manager. Refer to the following figure for a clearer idea on this:

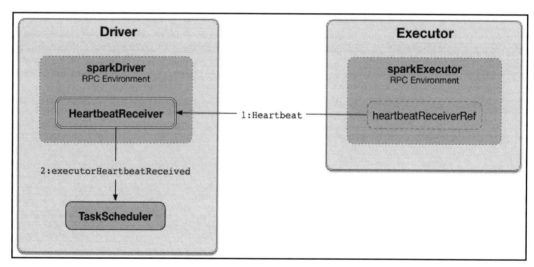

Figure 12: Spark driver instantiates an executor that is responsible for HeartbeatReceiver's Heartbeat message handler

When an executor starts, it first registers with the driver and communicates directly to execute tasks, as shown in the following figure:

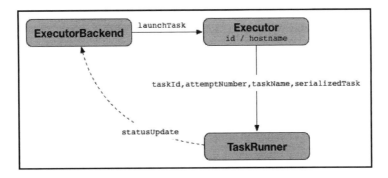

Figure 13: Launching tasks on executor using TaskRunners

You should be able to access the **Executors** tab at
`http://localhost:4040/executors`.

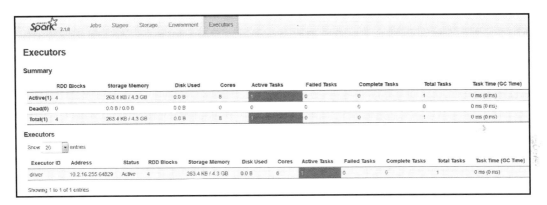

Figure 14: Executor tab on Spark web UI

As shown in the preceding figure, **Executor ID**, **Address**, **Status**, RDD Blocks, **Storage Memory**, **Disk Used**, **Cores**, **Active Tasks**, **Failed Tasks**, **Complete Tasks**, **Total Tasks**, **Task Time (GC Time)**, **Input**, **Shuffle Read**, **Shuffle Write**, and **Thread Dump** about the executor can be seen.

SQL

The **SQL** tab in the Spark UI displays all the accumulator values per operator. You should be able to access the SQL tab at `http://localhost:4040/SQL/`. It displays all the SQL query executions and underlying information by default. However, the SQL tab displays the details of the SQL query execution only after a query has been selected.

A detailed discussion on SQL is out of the scope of this chapter. Interested readers should refer to `http://spark.apache.org/docs/latest/sql-programming-guide.html#sql` for more on how to submit an SQL query and see its result output.

Visualizing Spark application using web UI

When a Spark job is submitted for execution, a web application UI is launched that displays useful information about the application. An event timeline displays the relative ordering and interleaving of application events. The timeline view is available on three levels: across all jobs, within one job, and within one stage. The timeline also shows executor allocation and deallocation.

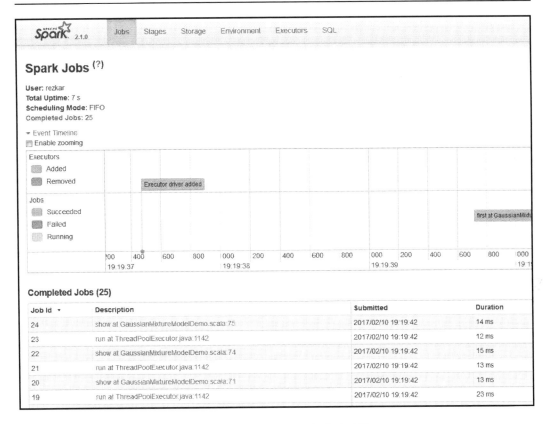

Figure 15: Spark jobs executed as DAG on Spark web UI

Observing the running and completed Spark jobs

To access and observe the running and the completed Spark jobs, open `http://spark_driver_host:4040` in a web browser. Note that you will have to replace `spark_driver_host` with an IP address or hostname accordingly.

Note that if multiple SparkContexts are running on the same host, they will bind to successive ports beginning with 4040, 4041, 4042, and so on. By default, this information will be available for the duration of your Spark application only. This means that when your Spark job finishes its execution, the binding will no longer be valid or accessible.

Now, to access the active jobs that are still executing, click on the **Active Jobs** link and you will see the related information of those jobs. On the other hand, to access the status of the completed jobs, click on **Completed Jobs** and you will see the information as DAG style as discussed in the preceding section.

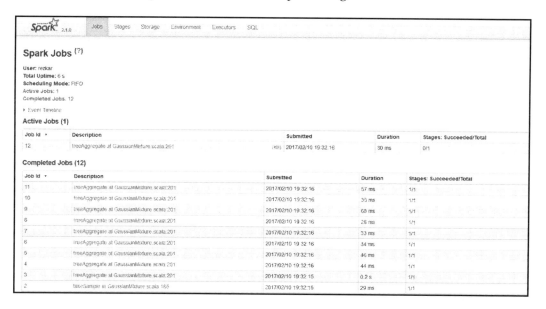

Figure 16: Observing the running and completed Spark jobs

You can achieve these by clicking on the job description link under the **Active Jobs** or **Completed Jobs**.

Debugging Spark applications using logs

Seeing the information about all running Spark applications depends on which cluster manager you are using. You should follow these instructions while debugging your Spark application:

- **Spark Standalone**: Go to the Spark master UI at `http://master:18080`. The master and each worker show cluster and the related job statistics. In addition, a detailed log output for each job is also written to the working directory of each worker. We will discuss how to enable the logging manually using the `log4j` with Spark.

- **YARN**: If your cluster manager is YARN, and suppose that you are running your Spark jobs on the Cloudera (or any other YARN-based platform), then go to the YARN applications page in the Cloudera Manager Admin Console. Now, to debug Spark applications running on YARN, view the logs for the Node Manager role. To make this happen, open the log event viewer and then filter the event stream to choose a time window and log level and to display the Node Manager source. You can access logs through the command as well. The format of the command is as follows:

```
yarn logs -applicationId <application ID> [OPTIONS]
```

For example, the following are the valid commands for these IDs:

```
yarn logs -applicationId application_561453090098_0005
yarn logs -applicationId application_561453090070_0005 userid
```

Note that the user IDs are different. However, this is only true if `yarn.log-aggregation-enable` is true in `yarn-site.xml` and the application has already finished the execution.

Logging with log4j with Spark

Spark uses `log4j` for its own logging. All the operations that happen backend get logged to the Spark shell console (which is already configured to the underlying storage). Spark provides a template of `log4j` as a property file, and we can extend and modify that file for logging in Spark. Move to the `SPARK_HOME/conf` directory and you should see the `log4j.properties.template` file. This could help us as the starting point for our own logging system.

Now, let's create our own custom logging system while running a Spark job. When you are done, rename the file as `log4j.properties` and put it under the same directory (that is, project tree). A sample snapshot of the file can be seen as follows:

```
# Set everything to be logged to the console
log4j.rootCategory=INFO, console
log4j.appender.console=org.apache.log4j.ConsoleAppender
log4j.appender.console.target=System.err
log4j.appender.console.layout=org.apache.log4j.PatternLayout
log4j.appender.console.layout.ConversionPattern=%d{yy/MM/dd HH:mm:ss} %p %c{1}: %m%n

# Set the default spark-shell log level to WARN. When running the spark-shell, the
# log level for this class is used to overwrite the root logger's log level, so that
# the user can have different defaults for the shell and regular Spark apps.
log4j.logger.org.apache.spark.repl.Main=WARN

# Settings to quiet third party logs that are too verbose
log4j.logger.org.spark_project.jetty=WARN
log4j.logger.org.spark_project.jetty.util.component.AbstractLifeCycle=ERROR
log4j.logger.org.apache.spark.repl.SparkIMain$exprTyper=INFO
log4j.logger.org.apache.spark.repl.SparkILoop$SparkILoopInterpreter=INFO
log4j.logger.org.apache.parquet=ERROR
log4j.logger.parquet=ERROR

# SPARK-9183: Settings to avoid annoying messages when looking up nonexistent UDFs in SparkSQL with Hive support
log4j.logger.org.apache.hadoop.hive.metastore.RetryingHMSHandler=FATAL
log4j.logger.org.apache.hadoop.hive.ql.exec.FunctionRegistry=ERROR
```

Figure 17: A snap of the log4j.properties file

By default, everything goes to console and file. However, if you want to bypass all the noiser logs to a system file located at, say, `/var/log/sparkU.log`, then you can set these properties in the `log4j.properties` file as follows:

```
log4j.logger.spark.storage=INFO, RollingAppender
log4j.additivity.spark.storage=false
log4j.logger.spark.scheduler=INFO, RollingAppender
log4j.additivity.spark.scheduler=false
log4j.logger.spark.CacheTracker=INFO, RollingAppender
log4j.additivity.spark.CacheTracker=false
log4j.logger.spark.CacheTrackerActor=INFO, RollingAppender
log4j.additivity.spark.CacheTrackerActor=false
log4j.logger.spark.MapOutputTrackerActor=INFO, RollingAppender
log4j.additivity.spark.MapOutputTrackerActor=false
log4j.logger.spark.MapOutputTracker=INFO, RollingAppender
log4j.additivty.spark.MapOutputTracker=false
```

Basically, we want to hide all logs Spark generates so that we don't have to deal with them in the shell. We redirect them to be logged in the filesystem. On the other hand, we want our own logs to be logged in the shell and a separate file so that they don't get mixed up with the ones from Spark. From here, we will point Splunk to the files where our own logs are, which in this particular case is `/var/log/sparkU.log`.

Then the log4j.properties file is picked up by Spark when the application starts, so we don't have to do anything aside from placing it in the mentioned location.

Now let's see how we can create our own logging system. Look at the following code and try to understand what is happening here:

```
import org.apache.spark.{SparkConf, SparkContext}
import org.apache.log4j.LogManager
import org.apache.log4j.Level
import org.apache.log4j.Logger

object MyLog {
 def main(args: Array[String]):Unit= {
   // Stting logger level as WARN
   val log = LogManager.getRootLogger
   log.setLevel(Level.WARN)

   // Creating Spark Context
   val conf = new SparkConf().setAppName("My
App").setMaster("local[*]")
   val sc = new SparkContext(conf)

   //Started the computation and printing the logging information
   log.warn("Started")
   val data = sc.parallelize(1 to 100000)
   log.warn("Finished")
 }
}
```

The preceding code conceptually logs only the warning message. It first prints the warning message and then creates an RDD by parallelizing numbers from 1 to 100,000. Once the RDD job is finished, it prints another warning log. However, there is a problem we haven't noticed yet with the earlier code segment.

One drawback of the org.apache.log4j.Logger class is that it is not serializable (refer to the optimization technique section for more details), which implies that we cannot use it inside a *closure* while doing operations on some parts of the Spark API. For example, if you try to execute the following code, you should experience an exception that says Task not serializable:

```
object MyLog {
   def main(args: Array[String]):Unit= {
     // Stting logger level as WARN
     val log = LogManager.getRootLogger
     log.setLevel(Level.WARN)
     // Creating Spark Context
     val conf = new SparkConf().setAppName("My
```

```
App").setMaster("local[*]")
    val sc = new SparkContext(conf)
    //Started the computation and printing the logging information
    log.warn("Started")
    val i = 0
    val data = sc.parallelize(i to 100000)
    data.foreach(i => log.info("My number"+ i))
    log.warn("Finished")
  }
}
```

To solve this problem is also easy; just declare the Scala object with `extends Serializable` and now the code looks like the following:

```
class MyMapper(n: Int) extends Serializable{
  @transient lazy val log = org.apache.log4j.LogManager.getLogger
                            ("myLogger")
  def MyMapperDosomething(rdd: RDD[Int]): RDD[String] =
   rdd.map{ i =>
    log.warn("mapping: " + i)
    (i + n).toString
  }
}
```

So what is happening in the preceding code is that the closure can't be neatly distributed to all partitions since it can't close on the logger; hence, the whole instance of type `MyMapper` is distributed to all partitions; once this is done, each partition creates a new logger and uses it for logging.

In summary, the following is the complete code that helps us to get rid of this problem:

```
package com.example.Personal
import org.apache.log4j.{Level, LogManager, PropertyConfigurator}
import org.apache.spark._
import org.apache.spark.rdd.RDD

class MyMapper(n: Int) extends Serializable{
  @transient lazy val log = org.apache.log4j.LogManager.getLogger
                            ("myLogger")
  def MyMapperDosomething(rdd: RDD[Int]): RDD[String] =
   rdd.map{ i =>
    log.warn("Serialization of: " + i)
    (i + n).toString
  }
}
```

```
object MyMapper{
   def apply(n: Int): MyMapper = new MyMapper(n)
}

object MyLog {
   def main(args: Array[String]) {
      val log = LogManager.getRootLogger
      log.setLevel(Level.WARN)
      val conf = new SparkConf().setAppName("My
App").setMaster("local[*]")
      val sc = new SparkContext(conf)
      log.warn("Started")
      val data = sc.parallelize(1 to 100000)
      val mapper = MyMapper(1)
      val other = mapper.MyMapperDosomething(data)
      other.collect()
      log.warn("Finished")
   }
}
```

The output is as follows:

```
17/04/29 15:33:43 WARN root: Started
   .

   .
17/04/29 15:31:51 WARN myLogger: mapping: 1
17/04/29 15:31:51 WARN myLogger: mapping: 49992
17/04/29 15:31:51 WARN myLogger: mapping: 49999
17/04/29 15:31:51 WARN myLogger: mapping: 50000
   .

   .
17/04/29 15:31:51 WARN root: Finished
```

We will discuss the built-in logging of Spark in the next section.

Spark configuration

There are a number of ways to configure your Spark jobs. In this section, we will
discuss these ways. More specifically, according to Spark 2.x release, there are three
locations to configure the system:

- Spark properties
- Environmental variables
- Logging

Spark properties

As discussed previously, Spark properties control most of the application-specific parameters and can be set using a `SparkConf` object of Spark. Alternatively, these parameters can be set through the Java system properties. `SparkConf` allows you to configure some of the common properties as follows:

```
setAppName() // App name
setMaster() // Master URL
setSparkHome() // Set the location where Spark is installed on worker
nodes.
setExecutorEnv() // Set single or multiple environment variables to be
used when launching executors.
setJars() // Set JAR files to distribute to the cluster.
setAll() // Set multiple parameters together.
```

An application can be configured to use a number of available cores on your machine. For example, we could initialize an application with two threads as follows. Note that we run with `local [2]`, meaning two threads, which represents minimal parallelism and using `local [*]`, which utilizes all the available cores in your machine. Alternatively, you can specify the number of executors while submitting Spark jobs with the following spark-submit script:

```
val conf = new SparkConf()
            .setMaster("local[2]")
            .setAppName("SampleApp")
val sc = new SparkContext(conf)
```

There might be some special cases where you need to load Spark properties dynamically when required. You can do this while submitting a Spark job through the spark-submit script. More specifically, you may want to avoid hardcoding certain configurations in `SparkConf`.

Apache Spark precedence:

Spark has the following precedence on the submitted jobs: configs coming from a config file have the lowest priority. The configs coming from the actual code have higher priority with respect to configs coming from a config file, and configs coming from the CLI through the Spark-submit script have higher priority.

For instance, if you want to run your application with different masters, executors, or different amounts of memory, Spark allows you to simply create an empty configuration object, as follows:

```
val sc = new SparkContext(new SparkConf())
```

Then you can provide the configuration for your Spark job at runtime as follows:

```
SPARK_HOME/bin/spark-submit
  --name "SmapleApp" \
  --class org.apache.spark.examples.KMeansDemo \
  --master mesos://207.184.161.138:7077 \ # Use your IP address
  --conf spark.eventLog.enabled=false
  --conf "spark.executor.extraJavaOptions=-XX:+PrintGCDetails" \
  --deploy-mode cluster \
  --supervise \
  --executor-memory 20G \
  myApp.jar
```

SPARK_HOME/bin/spark-submit will also read configuration options from SPARK_HOME /conf/spark-defaults.conf, in which each line consists of a key and a value separated by whitespace. An example is as follows:

```
spark.master  spark://5.6.7.8:7077
spark.executor.memor y   4g
spark.eventLog.enabled true
spark.serializer org.apache.spark.serializer.KryoSerializer
```

Values that are specified as flags in the properties file will be passed to the application and merged with those ones specified through SparkConf. Finally, as discussed earlier, the application web UI at http://<driver>:4040 lists all the Spark properties under the **Environment** tab.

Environmental variables

Environment variables can be used to set the setting in the computing nodes or machine settings. For example, IP address can be set through the `conf/spark-env.sh` script on each computing node. The following table lists the name and the functionality of the environmental variables that need to be set:

Environment Variable	Meaning
SPARK_MASTER_HOST	Bind the master to a specific hostname or IP address, for example a public one.
SPARK_MASTER_PORT	Start the master on a different port (default: 7077).
SPARK_MASTER_WEBUI_PORT	Port for the master web UI (default: 8080).
SPARK_MASTER_OPTS	Configuration properties that apply only to the master in the form "-Dx=y" (default: none). See below for a list of possible options.
SPARK_LOCAL_DIRS	Directory to use for "scratch" space in Spark, including map output files and RDDs that get stored on disk. This should be on a fast, local disk in your system. It can also be a comma-separated list of multiple directories on different disks.
SPARK_WORKER_CORES	Total number of cores to allow Spark applications to use on the machine (default: all available cores).
SPARK_WORKER_MEMORY	Total amount of memory to allow Spark applications to use on the machine, e.g. `1000m`, `2g` (default: total memory minus 1 GB); note that each application's *individual* memory is configured using its `spark.executor.memory` property.
SPARK_WORKER_PORT	Start the Spark worker on a specific port (default: random).
SPARK_WORKER_WEBUI_PORT	Port for the worker web UI (default: 8081).
SPARK_WORKER_DIR	Directory to run applications in, which will include both logs and scratch space (default: SPARK_HOME/work).
SPARK_WORKER_OPTS	Configuration properties that apply only to the worker in the form "-Dx=y" (default: none). See below for a list of possible options.
SPARK_DAEMON_MEMORY	Memory to allocate to the Spark master and worker daemons themselves (default: 1g).
SPARK_DAEMON_JAVA_OPTS	JVM options for the Spark master and worker daemons themselves in the form "-Dx=y" (default: none).
SPARK_PUBLIC_DNS	The public DNS name of the Spark master and workers (default: none).

Figure 18: Environmental variables and their meaning

Logging

Finally, logging can be configured through the `log4j.properties` file under your Spark application tree, as discussed in the preceding section. Spark uses log4j for logging. There are several valid logging levels supported by log4j with Spark; they are as follows:

Log Level	Usages
OFF	This is the most specific, which allows no logging at all
FATAL	This is the most specific one that shows fatal errors with little data
ERROR	This shows only the general errors
WARN	This shows warnings that are recommended to be fixed but not mandatory
INFO	This shows information required for your Spark job
DEBUG	While debugging, those logs will be printed
TRACE	This provides the least specific error trace with a lot of data
ALL	Least specific message with all data

Table 1: Log level with log4j and Spark

You can set up the default logging for Spark shell in `conf/log4j.properties`. In standalone Spark applications or while in a Spark Shell session, use `conf/log4j.properties.template` as a starting point. In an earlier section of this chapter, we suggested you put the `log4j.properties` file under your project directory while working on an IDE-based environment like Eclipse. However, to disable logging completely, you should use the following `conf/log4j.properties.template` as `log4j.properties`. Just set the `log4j.logger.org` flags as OFF, as follows:

```
log4j.logger.org=OFF
```

In the next section, we will discuss some common mistakes made by the developer or programmer while developing and submitting Spark jobs.

Common mistakes in Spark app development

Common mistakes that happen often are application failure, a slow job that gets stuck due to numerous factors, mistakes in the aggregation, actions or transformations, an exception in the main thread and, of course, **Out Of Memory (OOM)**.

Application failure

Most of the time, application failure happens because one or more stages fail eventually. As discussed earlier in this chapter, Spark jobs comprise several stages. Stages aren't executed independently: for instance, a processing stage can't take place before the relevant input-reading stage. So, suppose that stage 1 executes successfully but stage 2 fails to execute, the whole application fails eventually. This can be shown as follows:

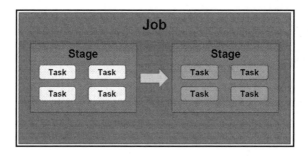

Figure 19: Two stages in a typical Spark job

To show an example, suppose you have the following three RDD operations as stages. The same can be visualized as shown in *Figure 20*, *Figure 21*, and *Figure 22*:

```
val rdd1 = sc.textFile("hdfs://data/data.csv")
                    .map(someMethod)
                    .filter(filterMethod)
```

Figure 20: Stage 1 for rdd1

```
val rdd2 = sc.hadoopFile("hdfs://data/data2.csv")
                    .groupByKey()
                    .map(secondMapMethod)
```

Conceptually, this can be shown in *Figure 21*, which first parses the data using the `hadoopFile()` method, groups it using the `groupByKey()` method, and finally, maps it:

Figure 21: Stage 2 for rdd2

```
val rdd3 = rdd1.join(rdd2).map(thirdMapMethod)
```

Conceptually, this can be shown in *Figure 22*, which first parses the data, joins it, and finally, maps it:

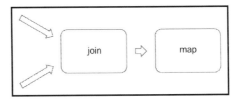

Figure 22: Stage 3 for rdd3

Now you can perform an aggregation function, for example, collect, as follows:

```
rdd3.collect()
```

Well! You have developed a Spark job consisting of three stages. Conceptually, this can be shown as follows:

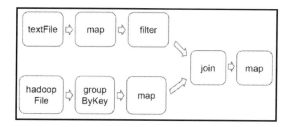

Figure 23: three stages for the rdd3.collect() operation

Now, if one of the stages fails, your job will fail eventually. As a result, the final `rdd3.collect()` statement will throw an exception about stage failure. Moreover, you may have issues with the following four factors:

- Mistakes in the aggregation operation
- Exceptions in the main thread
- OOP
- Class not found exception while submitting jobs using the `spark-submit` script
- Misconception about some API/methods in Spark core library

To get rid of the aforementioned issues, our general suggestion is to ensure that you have not made any mistakes while performing any map, flatMap, or aggregate operations. Second, ensure that there are no flaws in the main method while developing your application with Java or Scala. Sometimes you don't see any syntax error in your code, but it's important that you have developed some small test cases for your application. Most common exceptions that occur in the main method are as follows:

- `java.lang.noclassdeffounderror`
- `java.lang.nullpointerexception`
- `java.lang.arrayindexoutofboundsexception`
- `java.lang.stackoverflowerror`
- `java.lang.classnotfoundexception`
- `java.util.inputmismatchexception`

These exceptions can be avoided with the careful coding of your Spark application. Alternatively, use Eclipse's (or any other IDEs) code debugging features extensively to get rid of the semantic error to avoid the exception. For the third problem, that is, OOM, it's a very common problem. It is to be noted that Spark requires at least 8 GB of main memory, with sufficient disk space available for the standalone mode. On the other hand, to get the full cluster computing facilities, this requirement is often high.

> Preparing a JAR file including all the dependencies to execute Spark jobs is of paramount importance. Many practitioners use Google's Guava; it is included in most distributions, yet it doesn't guarantee backward compatibility. This means that sometimes your Spark job won't find a Guava class even if you explicitly provided it; this happens because one of the two versions of the Guava libraries takes precedence over the other, and this version might not include a required class. In order to overcome this issue, you usually resort to shading.

Make sure that you have set the Java heap space with –Xmx parameter with a sufficiently large value if you're coding using IntelliJ, Vim, Eclipse, Notepad, and so on. While working with cluster mode, you should specify the executor memory while submitting Spark jobs using the Spark-submit script. Suppose you have a CSV to be parsed and do some predictive analytics using a random forest classifier, you might need to specify the right amount of memory, say 20 GB, as follows:

```
--executor-memory 20G
```

Even if you receive the OOM error, you can increase this amount to, say, 32 GB or more. Since random forest is computationally intensive, requiring larger memory, this is just an example of random forest. You might experience similar issues while just parsing your data. Even a particular stage may fail due to this OOM error. Therefore, make sure that you are aware of this error.

For the `class not found exception`, make sure that you have included your main class in the resulting JAR file. The JAR file should be prepared with all the dependencies to execute your Spark job on the cluster nodes. We will provide a step-by-step JAR preparation guideline in `Chapter 17`, *Time to Go to ClusterLand - Deploying Spark on a Cluster.*

For the last issue, we can provide some examples of some misconceptions about Spark Core library. For example, when you use the `wholeTextFiles` method to prepare RDDs or DataFrames from multiple files, Spark does not run in parallel; in cluster mode for YARN, it may run out of memory sometimes.

Once, I experienced an issue where, at first, I copied six files in my S3 storage to HDFS. Then, I tried to create an RDD, as follows:

```
sc.wholeTextFiles("/mnt/temp") // note the location of the data files
is /mnt/temp/
```

Then, I tried to process those files line by line using a UDF. When I looked at my computing nodes, I saw that only one executor was running per file. However, I then got an error message saying that YARN had run out of memory. Why so? The reasons are as follows:

- The goal of `wholeTextFiles` is to have only one executor for each file to be processed
- If you use `.gz` files, for example, you will have only one executor per file, maximum

Slow jobs or unresponsiveness

Sometimes, if the SparkContext cannot connect to a Spark standalone master, then the driver may display errors such as the following:

```
02/05/17 12:44:45 ERROR AppClient$ClientActor: All masters are
unresponsive! Giving up.
02/05/17 12:45:31 ERROR SparkDeploySchedulerBackend: Application has
been killed. Reason: All masters are unresponsive! Giving up.
02/05/17 12:45:35 ERROR TaskSchedulerImpl: Exiting due to error from
cluster scheduler: Spark cluster looks down
```

At other times, the driver is able to connect to the master node but the master is unable to communicate back to the driver. Then, multiple attempts to connect are made even though the driver will report that it could not connect to the Master's log directory.

Furthermore, you might often experience very slow performance and progress in your Spark jobs. This happens because your driver program is not that fast to compute your jobs. As discussed earlier, sometimes a particular stage may take a longer time than usual because there might be a shuffle, map, join, or aggregation operation involved. Even if the computer is running out of disk storage or main memory, you may experience these issues. For example, if your master node does not respond or you experience unresponsiveness from the computing nodes for a certain period of time, you might think that your Spark job has halted and become stagnant at a certain stage:

```
/11/20 17:20:58 INFO TaskSchedulerImpl: Removed TaskSet 1.0, whose tasks have all completed, from pool
/11/20 17:20:58 INFO TaskSchedulerImpl: Removed TaskSet 2.0, whose tasks have all completed, from pool
/11/20 17:20:58 INFO DAGScheduler: Failed to run collect at ReceiverTracker.scala:270
/11/20 17:20:58 INFO TaskSchedulerImpl: Cancelling stage 1
Exception in thread "Thread-53" org.apache.spark.SparkException: Job aborted due to stage failure: All masters are unresponsive!
Giving up.
        at org.apache.spark.scheduler.DAGScheduler.org$apache$spark$scheduler$DAGScheduler$$failJobAndIndependentStages
(DAGScheduler.scala:1033)
        at org.apache.spark.scheduler.DAGScheduler$$anonfun$abortStage$1.apply(DAGScheduler.scala:1017)
        at org.apache.spark.scheduler.DAGScheduler$$anonfun$abortStage$1.apply(DAGScheduler.scala:1015)
        at scala.collection.mutable.ResizableArray$class.foreach(ResizableArray.scala:59)
        at scala.collection.mutable.ArrayBuffer.foreach(ArrayBuffer.scala:47)
        at org.apache.spark.scheduler.DAGScheduler.abortStage(DAGScheduler.scala:1015)
        at org.apache.spark.scheduler.DAGScheduler$$anonfun$handleTaskSetFailed$1.apply(DAGScheduler.scala:633)
        at org.apache.spark.scheduler.DAGScheduler$$anonfun$handleTaskSetFailed$1.apply(DAGScheduler.scala:633)
        at scala.Option.foreach(Option.scala:236)
        at org.apache.spark.scheduler.DAGScheduler.handleTaskSetFailed(DAGScheduler.scala:633)
        at org.apache.spark.scheduler.DAGSchedulerEventProcessActor$$anonfun$receive$2.applyOrElse(DAGScheduler.scala:1207)
        at akka.actor.ActorCell.receiveMessage(ActorCell.scala:498)
        at akka.actor.ActorCell.invoke(ActorCell.scala:456)
        at akka.dispatch.Mailbox.processMailbox(Mailbox.scala:237)
        at akka.dispatch.Mailbox.run(Mailbox.scala:219)
        at akka.dispatch.ForkJoinExecutorConfigurator$AkkaForkJoinTask.exec(AbstractDispatcher.scala:386)
        at scala.concurrent.forkjoin.ForkJoinTask.doExec(ForkJoinTask.java:260)
        at scala.concurrent.forkjoin.ForkJoinPool$WorkQueue.runTask(ForkJoinPool.java:1339)
        at scala.concurrent.forkjoin.ForkJoinPool.runWorker(ForkJoinPool.java:1979)
        at scala.concurrent.forkjoin.ForkJoinWorkerThread.run(ForkJoinWorkerThread.java:107)
/11/20 17:20:58 INFO DAGScheduler: Failed to run take at DStream.scala:593
/11/20 17:20:58 INFO TaskSchedulerImpl: Cancelling stage 2
/11/20 17:20:58 INFO JobScheduler: Starting job streaming job 1416484202000 ms.0 from job set of time 1416484202000 ms
/11/20 17:20:58 INFO SparkContext: Starting job: take at DStream.scala:593
/11/20 17:20:58 ERROR JobScheduler: Error running job streaming job 1416484200000 ms.0
org.apache.spark.SparkException: Job aborted due to stage failure: All masters are unresponsive! Giving up.
        at org.apache.spark.scheduler.DAGScheduler.org$apache$spark$scheduler$DAGScheduler$$failJobAndIndependentStages
(DAGScheduler.scala:1033)
        at org.apache.spark.scheduler.DAGScheduler$$anonfun$abortStage$1.apply(DAGScheduler.scala:1017)
        at org.apache.spark.scheduler.DAGScheduler$$anonfun$abortStage$1.apply(DAGScheduler.scala:1015)
        at scala.collection.mutable.ResizableArray$class.foreach(ResizableArray.scala:59)
        at scala.collection.mutable.ArrayBuffer.foreach(ArrayBuffer.scala:47)
        at org.apache.spark.scheduler.DAGScheduler.abortStage(DAGScheduler.scala:1015)
```

Figure 24: An example log for executor/driver unresponsiveness

Potential solutions could be several, including the following:

1. Check to make sure that workers and drivers are correctly configured to connect to the Spark master on the exact address listed in the Spark master web UI/logs. Then, explicitly supply the Spark cluster's master URL when starting your Spark shell:

```
$ bin/spark-shell --master spark://master-ip:7077
```

2. Set SPARK_LOCAL_IP to a cluster-addressable hostname for the driver, master, and worker processes.

Sometimes, we experience some issues due to hardware failure. For example, if the filesystem in a computing node closes unexpectedly, that is, an I/O exception, your Spark job will eventually fail too. This is obvious because your Spark job cannot write the resulting RDDs or data to store to the local filesystem or HDFS. This also implies that DAG operations cannot be performed due to the stage failures.

Sometimes, this I/O exception occurs due to an underlying disk failure or other hardware failures. This often provides logs, as follows:

Job Scheduling Information	Diagnostic Info
NA	Job initialization failed: java.io.IOException: Filesystem closed at org.apache.hadoop.hdfs.DFSClient.checkOpen(DFSClient.java:241) at org.apache.hadoop.hdfs.DFSClient.access$800(DFSClient.java:74) at org.apache.hadoop.hdfs.DFSClient$DFSOutputStream.closeInternal(DFSClient.java:3667) at org.apache.hadoop.hdfs.DFSClient$DFSOutputStream.close(DFSClient.java:3626) at org.apache.hadoop.fs.FSDataOutputStream$PositionCache.close(FSDataOutputStream.java:61) at org.apache.hadoop.fs.FSDataOutputStream.close(FSDataOutputStream.java:86) at org.apache.hadoop.security.Credentials.writeTokenStorageFile(Credentials.java:171) at org.apache.hadoop.mapred.JobInProgress.generateAndStoreTokens(JobInProgress.java:3528) at org.apache.hadoop.mapred.JobInProgress.initTasks(JobInProgress.java:696) at org.apache.hadoop.mapred.JobTracker.initJob(JobTracker.java:4207) at org.apache.hadoop.mapred.FairScheduler$JobInitializer$InitJob.run(FairScheduler.java:291) at java.util.concurrent.ThreadPoolExecutor$Worker.runTask(ThreadPoolExecutor.java:886) at java.util.concurrent.ThreadPoolExecutor$Worker.run(ThreadPoolExecutor.java:908) at java.lang.Thread.run(Thread.java:662)

Figure 25: An example filesystem closed

Nevertheless, you often experience slow job computing performance because your Java GC is somewhat busy with, or cannot do, the GC fast. For example, the following figure shows that for task 0, it took 10 hours to finish the GC! I experienced this issue in 2014, when I was new to Spark. Control of these types of issues, however, is not in our hands. Therefore, our recommendation is that you should make the JVM free and try submitting the jobs again.

Task Index	Task ID	Status	Locality Level	Executor	Launch Time	Duration	GC Time
1	0	SUCCESS	NODE_LOCAL		2014/06/13 13:14:16	12.82 h	9.59 h
2	1	SUCCESS	NODE_LOCAL		2014/06/13 13:14:16	12.00 h	8.97 h
3	2	SUCCESS	NODE_LOCAL		2014/06/13 13:14:16	12.39 h	9.16 h
0	3	SUCCESS	NODE_LOCAL		2014/06/13 13:14:16	12.09 h	8.88 h
6	4	SUCCESS	NODE_LOCAL		2014/06/13 13:14:16	11.65 h	8.54 h
4	5	SUCCESS	NODE_LOCAL		2014/06/13 13:14:16	11.68 h	8.62 h
7	6	SUCCESS	NODE_LOCAL		2014/06/13 13:14:16	12.19 h	9.12 h
12	7	SUCCESS	NODE_LOCAL		2014/06/13 13:14:16	11.62 h	8.50 h
8	8	SUCCESS	NODE_LOCAL		2014/06/13 13:14:16	12.57 h	9.40 h
9	9	SUCCESS	NODE_LOCAL		2014/06/13 13:14:16	12.02 h	8.98 h
5	10	SUCCESS	NODE_LOCAL		2014/06/13 13:14:16	12.24 h	9.04 h
11	11	SUCCESS	NODE_LOCAL		2014/06/13 13:14:16	11.11 h	8.15 h
10	12	SUCCESS	NODE_LOCAL		2014/06/13 13:14:16	11.84 h	8.68 h
13	13	SUCCESS	NODE_LOCAL		2014/06/13 13:14:16	11.85 h	8.74 h
18	14	SUCCESS	NODE_LOCAL		2014/06/13 13:14:16	12.26 h	9.17 h

Figure 26: An example where GC stalled in between

The fourth factor could be the slow response or slow job performance is due to the lack of data serialization. This will be discussed in the next section. The fifth factor could be the memory leak in the code that will tend to make your application consume more memory, leaving the files or logical devices open. Therefore, make sure that there is no option that tends to be a memory leak. For example, it is a good practice to finish your Spark application by calling `sc.stop()` or `spark.stop()`. This will make sure that one SparkContext is still open and active. Otherwise, you might get unwanted exceptions or issues. The sixth issue is that we often keep too many open files, and this sometimes creates `FileNotFoundException` in the shuffle or merge stage.

Optimization techniques

There are several aspects of tuning Spark applications toward better optimization techniques. In this section, we will discuss how we can further optimize our Spark applications by applying data serialization by tuning the main memory with better memory management. We can also optimize performance by tuning the data structure in your Scala code while developing Spark applications. The storage, on the other hand, can be maintained well by utilizing serialized RDD storage.

One of the most important aspects is garbage collection, and it's tuning if you have written your Spark application using Java or Scala. We will look at how we can also tune this for optimized performance. For distributed environment- and cluster-based system, a level of parallelism and data locality has to be ensured. Moreover, performance could further be improved by using broadcast variables.

Data serialization

Serialization is an important tuning for performance improvement and optimization in any distributed computing environment. Spark is not an exception, but Spark jobs are often data and computing extensive. Therefore, if your data objects are not in a good format, then you first need to convert them into serialized data objects. This demands a large number of bytes of your memory. Eventually, the whole process will slow down the entire processing and computation drastically.

As a result, you often experience a slow response from the computing nodes. This means that we sometimes fail to make 100% utilization of the computing resources. It is true that Spark tries to keep a balance between convenience and performance. This also implies that data serialization should be the first step in Spark tuning for better performance.

Spark provides two options for data serialization: Java serialization and Kryo serialization libraries:

- **Java serialization:** Spark serializes objects using Java's `ObjectOutputStream` framework. You handle the serialization by creating any class that implements `java.io.Serializable`. Java serialization is very flexible but often quite slow, which is not suitable for large data object serialization.
- **Kryo serialization:** You can also use Kryo library to serialize your data objects more quickly. Compared to Java serialization, Kryo serialization is much faster, with 10x speedup and is compact than that of Java. However, it has one issue, that is, it does not support all the serializable types, but you need to require your classes to be registered.

You can start using Kryo by initializing your Spark job with a `SparkConf` and calling `conf.set(spark.serializer, org.apache.spark.serializer.KryoSerializer)`. To register your own custom classes with Kryo, use the `registerKryoClasses` method, as follows:

```
val conf = new SparkConf()
              .setMaster("local[*]")
              .setAppName("MyApp")
conf.registerKryoClasses(Array(classOf[MyOwnClass1],
classOf[MyOwnClass2]))
val sc = new SparkContext(conf)
```

If your objects are large, you may also need to increase the `spark.kryoserializer.buffer` config. This value needs to be large enough to hold the largest object you serialize. Finally, if you don't register your custom classes, Kryo still works; however, the full class name with each object needs to be stored, which is wasteful indeed.

For example, in the logging subsection at the end of the monitoring Spark jobs section, the logging and computing can be optimized using the `Kryo` serialization. At first, just create the `MyMapper` class as a normal class (that is, without any serialization), as follows:

```
class MyMapper(n: Int) { // without any serialization
  @transient lazy val log =
org.apache.log4j.LogManager.getLogger("myLogger")
  def MyMapperDosomething(rdd: RDD[Int]): RDD[String] = rdd.map { i =>
    log.warn("mapping: " + i)
    (i + n).toString
  }
}
```

Now, let's register this class as a `Kyro` serialization class and then set the `Kyro` serialization as follows:

```
conf.registerKryoClasses(Array(classOf[MyMapper])) // register the
class with Kyro
conf.set("spark.serializer",
"org.apache.spark.serializer.KryoSerializer") // set Kayro
serialization
```

That's all you need. The full source code of this example is given in the following. You should be able to run and observe the same output, but an optimized one as compared to the previous example:

```scala
package com.chapter14.Serilazition
import org.apache.spark._
import org.apache.spark.rdd.RDD
class MyMapper(n: Int) { // without any serilization
  @transient lazy val log = org.apache.log4j.LogManager.getLogger
                                  ("myLogger")
  def MyMapperDosomething(rdd: RDD[Int]): RDD[String] = rdd.map { i =>
    log.warn("mapping: " + i)
    (i + n).toString
  }
}
//Companion object
object MyMapper {
  def apply(n: Int): MyMapper = new MyMapper(n)
}
//Main object
object KyroRegistrationDemo {
  def main(args: Array[String]) {
    val log = LogManager.getRootLogger
    log.setLevel(Level.WARN)
    val conf = new SparkConf()
      .setAppName("My App")
      .setMaster("local[*]")
    conf.registerKryoClasses(Array(classOf[MyMapper2]))
     // register the class with Kyro
    conf.set("spark.serializer", "org.apache.spark.serializer
            .KryoSerializer") // set Kayro serilazation
    val sc = new SparkContext(conf)
    log.warn("Started")
    val data = sc.parallelize(1 to 100000)
    val mapper = MyMapper(1)
    val other = mapper.MyMapperDosomething(data)
    other.collect()
    log.warn("Finished")
  }
}
```

The output is as follows:

```
17/04/29 15:33:43 WARN root: Started
 .

 .

17/04/29 15:31:51 WARN myLogger: mapping: 1
17/04/29 15:31:51 WARN myLogger: mapping: 49992
```

```
17/04/29 15:31:51 WARN myLogger: mapping: 49999
17/04/29 15:31:51 WARN myLogger: mapping: 50000
    .
    .
    .
17/04/29 15:31:51 WARN root: Finished
```

Well done! Now let's have a quick look at how to tune the memory. We will look at some advanced strategies to make sure the efficient use of the main memory in the next section.

Memory tuning

In this section, we will discuss some advanced strategies that can be used by users like you to make sure that an efficient use of memory is carried out while executing your Spark jobs. More specifically, we will show how to calculate the memory usages of your objects. We will suggest some advanced ways to improve it by optimizing your data structures or by converting your data objects in a serialized format using Kryo or Java serializer. Finally, we will look at how to tune Spark's Java heap size, cache size, and the Java garbage collector.

There are three considerations in tuning memory usage:

- The amount of memory used by your objects: You may even want your entire dataset to fit in the memory
- The cost of accessing those objects
- The overhead of garbage collection: If you have a high turnover in terms of objects

Although Java objects are fast enough to access, they can easily consume a factor of 2 to 5x more space than the actual (aka raw) data in their original fields. For example, each distinct Java object has 16 bytes of overhead with an object header. A Java string, for example, has almost 40 bytes of extra overhead over the raw string. Furthermore, Java collection classes like Set, List, Queue, ArrayList, Vector, LinkedList, PriorityQueue, HashSet, LinkedHashSet, TreeSet, and so on, are also used. The linked data structures, on the other hand, are too complex, occupying too much extra space since there is a wrapper object for each entry in the data structure. Finally, the collections of primitive types frequently store them in the memory as boxed objects, such as java.lang.Double and java.lang.Integer.

Memory usage and management

Memory usages by your Spark application and underlying computing nodes can be categorized as execution and storage. Execution memory is used during the computation in merge, shuffles, joins, sorts, and aggregations. On the other hand, storage memory is used for caching and propagating internal data across the cluster. In short, this is due to the large amount of I/O across the network.

Technically, Spark caches network data locally. While working with Spark iteratively or interactively, caching or persistence are optimization techniques in Spark. These two help in saving interim partial results so that they can be reused in subsequent stages. Then these interim results (as RDDs) can be kept in memory (default) or more solid storage, such as disk, and/or replicated. Furthermore, RDDs can be cached using cache operations too. They can also be persisted using a persist operation. The difference between cache and persist operations is purely syntactic. The cache is a synonym of persisting or persists (MEMORY_ONLY), that is, cache is merely persisted with the default storage level MEMORY_ONLY.

If you go under the Storage tab in your Spark web UI, you should observe the memory/storage used by an RDD, DataFrame, or Dataset object, as shown in *Figure 10*. Although there are two relevant configurations for tuning memory in Spark, users do not need to readjust them. The reason is that the default values set in the configuration files are enough for your requirements and workloads.

spark.memory.fraction is the size of the unified region as a fraction of (JVM heap space - 300 MB) (default 0.6). The rest of the space (40%) is reserved for user data structures, internal metadata in Spark, and safeguarding against OOM errors in case of sparse and unusually large records. On the other hand, spark.memory.storageFraction expresses the size of R storage space as a fraction of the unified region (default is 0.5). The default value of this parameter is 50% of Java heap space, that is, 300 MB.

A more detailed discussion on memory usage and storage is given in Chapter 15, *Text Analytics Using Spark ML*.

Now, one question might arise in your mind: which storage level to choose? To answer this question, Spark storage levels provide you with different trade-offs between memory usage and CPU efficiency. If your RDDs fit comfortably with the default storage level (MEMORY_ONLY), let your Spark driver or master go with it. This is the most memory-efficient option, allowing operations on the RDDs to run as fast as possible. You should let it go with this, because this is the most memory-efficient option. This also allows numerous operations on the RDDs to be done as fast as possible.

If your RDDs do not fit the main memory, that is, if MEMORY_ONLY does not work out, you should try using MEMORY_ONLY_SER. It is strongly recommended to not spill your RDDs to disk unless your **UDF** (aka **user-defined function** that you have defined for processing your dataset) is too expensive. This also applies if your UDF filters a large amount of the data during the execution stages. In other cases, recomputing a partition, that is, repartition, may be faster for reading data objects from disk. Finally, if you want fast fault recovery, use the replicated storage levels.

In summary, there are the following StorageLevels available and supported in Spark 2.x: (number _2 in the name denotes 2 replicas):

- DISK_ONLY: This is for disk-based operation for RDDs
- DISK_ONLY_2: This is for disk-based operation for RDDs for 2 replicas
- MEMORY_ONLY: This is the default for cache operation in memory for RDDs
- MEMORY_ONLY_2: This is the default for cache operation in memory for RDDs with 2 replicas
- MEMORY_ONLY_SER: If your RDDs do not fit the main memory, that is, if MEMORY_ONLY does not work out, this option particularly helps in storing data objects in a serialized form
- MEMORY_ONLY_SER_2: If your RDDs do not fit the main memory, that is, if MEMORY_ONLY does not work out with 2 replicas, this option also helps in storing data objects in a serialized form
- MEMORY_AND_DISK: Memory and disk (aka combined) based RDD persistence
- MEMORY_AND_DISK_2: Memory and disk (aka combined) based RDD persistence with 2 replicas

- `MEMORY_AND_DISK_SER`: If `MEMORY_AND_DISK` does not work, it can be used
- `MEMORY_AND_DISK_SER_2`: If `MEMORY_AND_DISK` does not work with 2 replicas, this option can be used
- `OFF_HEAP`: Does not allow writing into Java heap space

Note that cache is a synonym of persist (`MEMORY_ONLY`). This means that cache is solely persist with the default storage level, that is, `MEMORY_ONLY`. Detailed information can be found at `https://jaceklaskowski.gitbooks.io/mastering-apache-spark/content/spark-rdd-StorageLevel.html`.

Tuning the data structures

The first way to reduce extra memory usage is to avoid some features in the Java data structure that impose extra overheads. For example, pointer-based data structures and wrapper objects contribute to nontrivial overheads. To tune your source code with a better data structure, we provide some suggestions here, which can be useful.

First, design your data structures such that you use arrays of objects and primitive types more. Thus, this also suggests using standard Java or Scala collection classes like `Set`, `List`, `Queue`, `ArrayList`, `Vector`, `LinkedList`, `PriorityQueue`, `HashSet`, `LinkedHashSet`, and `TreeSet` more frequently.

Second, when possible, avoid using nested structures with a lot of small objects and pointers so that your source code becomes more optimized and concise. Third, when possible, consider using numeric IDs and sometimes using enumeration objects rather than using strings for keys. This is recommended because, as we have already stated, a single Java string object creates an extra overhead of 40 bytes. Finally, if you have less than 32 GB of main memory (that is, RAM), set the JVM flag -`XX:+UseCompressedOops` to make pointers 4 bytes instead of 8.

The earlier option can be set in the `SPARK_HOME/conf/spark-env.sh.template`. Just rename the file as `spark-env.sh` and set the value straight away!

Serialized RDD storage

As discussed already, despite other types of memory tuning, when your objects are too large to fit in the main memory or disk efficiently, a simpler and better way of reducing memory usage is storing them in a serialized form.

> This can be done using the serialized storage levels in the RDD persistence API, such as MEMORY_ONLY_SER. For more information, refer to the previous section on memory management and start exploring available options.

If you specify using MEMORY_ONLY_SER, Spark will then store each RDD partition as one large byte array. However, the only downside of this approach is that it can slow down data access times. This is reasonable and obvious too; fairly speaking, there's no way to avoid it since each object needs to deserialize on the fly back while reusing.

> As discussed previously, we highly recommend using Kryo serialization instead of Java serialization to make data access a bit faster.

Garbage collection tuning

Although it is not a major problem in your Java or Scala programs that just read an RDD sequentially or randomly once and then execute numerous operations on it, **Java Virtual Machine (JVM)** GC can be problematic and complex if you have a large amount of data objects w.r.t RDDs stored in your driver program. When the JVM needs to remove obsolete and unused objects from the old objects to make space for the newer ones, it is mandatory to identify them and remove them from the memory eventually. However, this is a costly operation in terms of processing time and storage. You might be wondering that the cost of GC is proportional to the number of Java objects stored in your main memory. Therefore, we strongly suggest you tune your data structure. Also, having fewer objects stored in your memory is recommended.

The first step in GC tuning is collecting the related statistics on how frequently garbage collection by JVM occurs on your machine. The second statistic needed in this regard is the amount of time spent on GC by JVM on your machine or computing nodes. This can be achieved by adding `-verbose:gc -XX:+PrintGCDetails -XX:+PrintGCTimeStamps` to the Java options in your IDE, such as Eclipse, in the JVM startup arguments and specifying a name and location for our GC log file, as follows:

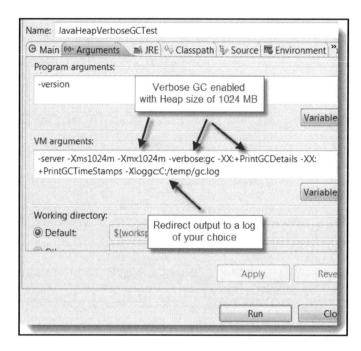

Figure 27: Setting GC verbose on Eclipse

Alternatively, you can specify `verbose:gc` while submitting your Spark jobs using the Spark-submit script, as follows:

```
--conf "spark.executor.extraJavaOptions = -verbose:gc -XX:-
PrintGCDetails -XX:+PrintGCTimeStamps"
```

In short, when specifying GC options for Spark, you must determine where you want the GC options specified, on the executors or on the driver. When you submit your jobs, specify `--driver-java-options -XX:+PrintFlagsFinal -verbose:gc` and so on. For the executor, specify `--conf spark.executor.extraJavaOptions=-XX:+PrintFlagsFinal -verbose:gc` and so on.

Now, when your Spark job is executed, you will be able to see the logs and messages printed in the worker's node at `/var/log/logs` each time a GC occurs. The downside of this approach is that these logs will not be on your driver program but on your cluster's worker nodes.

It is to be noted that `verbose:gc` only prints appropriate message or logs after each GC collection. Correspondingly, it prints details about memory. However, if you are interested in looking for more critical issues, such as a memory leak, `verbose:gc` may not be enough. In that case, you can use some visualization tools, such as jhat and VisualVM. A better way of GC tuning in your Spark application can be read at `https://databricks.com/blog/2015/05/28/tuning-java-garbage-collection-for-spark-applications.html`.

Level of parallelism

Although you can control the number of map tasks to be executed through optional parameters to the `SparkContext.text` file, Spark sets the same on each file according to its size automatically. In addition to this, for a distributed `reduce` operation such as `groupByKey` and `reduceByKey`, Spark uses the largest parent RDD's number of partitions. However, sometimes, we make one mistake, that is, not utilizing the full computing resources for your nodes in a computing cluster. As a result, the full computing resources will not be fully exploited unless you set and specify the level of parallelism for your Spark job explicitly. Therefore, you should set the level of parallelism as the second argument.

For more on this option, please refer to `https://spark.apache.org/docs/latest/api/scala/index.html#org.apache.spark.rdd.PairRDDFunctions`.

Alternatively, you can do it by setting the config property spark.default.parallelism to change the default. For operations such as parallelizing with no parent RDDs, the level of parallelism depends on the cluster manager, that is, standalone, Mesos, or YARN. For the local mode, set the level of parallelism equal to the number of cores on the local machine. For Mesos or YARN, set fine-grained mode to 8. In other cases, the total number of cores on all executor nodes or 2, whichever is larger, and in general, 2-3 tasks per CPU core in your cluster is recommended.

Broadcasting

A broadcast variable enables a Spark developer to keep a read-only copy of an instance or class variable cached on each driver program, rather than transferring a copy of its own with the dependent tasks. However, an explicit creation of a broadcast variable is useful only when tasks across multiple stages need the same data in deserialize form.

In Spark application development, using the broadcasting option of SparkContext can reduce the size of each serialized task greatly. This also helps to reduce the cost of initiating a Spark job in a cluster. If you have a certain task in your Spark job that uses large objects from the driver program, you should turn it into a broadcast variable.

To use a broadcast variable in a Spark application, you can instantiate it using `SparkContext.broadcast`. Later on, use the value method from the class to access the shared value as follows:

```
val m = 5
val bv = sc.broadcast(m)
```

Output/log: `bv: org.apache.spark.broadcast.Broadcast[Int] = Broadcast(0)`

```
bv.value()
```

Output/log: `res0: Int = 1`

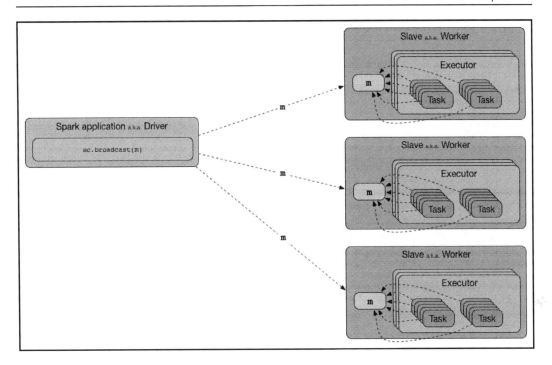

Figure 28: Broadcasting a value from driver to executors

The Broadcast feature of Spark uses the **SparkContext** to create broadcast values. After that, the **BroadcastManager** and **ContextCleaner** are used to control their life cycle, as shown in the following figure:

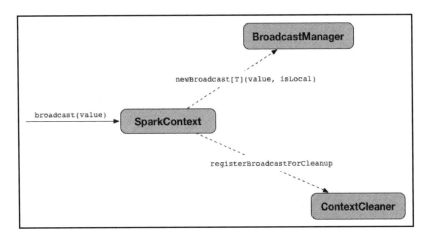

Figure 29: SparkContext broadcasts the variable/value using BroadcastManager and ContextCleaner

Spark application in the driver program automatically prints the serialized size of each task on the driver. Therefore, you can decide whether your tasks are too large to make it parallel. If your task is larger than 20 KB, it's probably worth optimizing.

Data locality

Data locality means how close the data is to the code to be processed. Technically, data locality can have a nontrivial impact on the performance of a Spark job to be executed locally or in cluster mode. As a result, if the data and the code to be processed are tied together, computation is supposed to be much faster. Usually, shipping a serialized code from a driver to an executor is much faster since the code size is much smaller than that of data.

In Spark application development and job execution, there are several levels of locality. In order from closest to farthest, the level depends on the current location of the data you have to process:

Data Locality	Meaning	Special Notes
PROCESS_LOCAL	Data and code are in the same location	Best locality possible
NODE_LOCAL	Data and the code are on the same node, for example, data stored on HDFS	A bit slower than PROCESS_LOCAL since the data has to propagate across the processes and network
NO_PREF	The data is accessed equally from somewhere else	Has no locality preference
RACK_LOCAL	The data is on the same rack of servers over the network	Suitable for large-scale data processing
ANY	The data is elsewhere on the network and not in the same rack	Not recommended unless there are no other options available

Table 2: Data locality and Spark

Spark is developed such that it prefers to schedule all tasks at the best locality level, but this is not guaranteed and not always possible either. As a result, based on the situation in the computing nodes, Spark switches to lower locality levels if available computing resources are too occupied. Moreover, if you would like to have the best data locality, there are two choices for you:

- Wait until a busy CPU gets free to start a task on your data on the same server or same node
- Immediately start a new one, which requires moving data there

Summary

In this chapter, we discussed some advanced topics of Spark toward making your Spark job's performance better. We discussed some basic techniques to tune your Spark jobs. We discussed how to monitor your jobs by accessing Spark web UI. We discussed how to set Spark configuration parameters. We also discussed some common mistakes made by Spark users and provided some recommendations. Finally, we discussed some optimization techniques that help tune Spark applications.

In the next chapter, you will see how to test Spark applications and debug to solve most common issues.

16
Time to Go to ClusterLand - Deploying Spark on a Cluster

"I see the moon like a clipped piece of silver. Like gilded bees, the stars cluster around her"

- Oscar Wilde

In the previous chapters, we have seen how to develop practical applications using different Spark APIs. However, in this chapter, we will see how Spark works in a cluster mode with its underlying architecture. Finally, we will see how to deploy a full Spark application on a cluster. In a nutshell, the following topics will be cover throughout this chapter:

- Spark architecture in a cluster
- Spark ecosystem and cluster management
- Deploying Spark on a cluster
- Deploying Spark on a standalone cluster
- Deploying Spark on a Mesos cluster
- Deploying Spark on YARN cluster
- Cloud-based deployment
- Deploying Spark on AWS

Spark architecture in a cluster

Hadoop-based **MapReduce** framework has been widely used for the last few years; however, it has some issues with I/O, algorithmic complexity, low-latency streaming jobs, and fully disk-based operation. Hadoop provides the **Hadoop Distributed File System (HDFS)** for efficient computing and storing big data cheaply, but you can only do the computations with a high-latency batch model or static data using the Hadoop-based MapReduce framework. The main big data paradigm that Spark has brought for us is the introduction of in-memory computing and caching abstraction. This makes Spark ideal for large-scale data processing and enables the computing nodes to perform multiple operations by accessing the same input data.

Spark's **Resilient Distributed Dataset (RDD)** model can do everything that the MapReduce paradigm can, and even more. Nevertheless, Spark can perform iterative computations on your dataset at scale. This option helps to execute machine learning, general purpose data processing, graph analytics, and **Structured Query Language (SQL)** algorithms much faster with or without depending upon Hadoop. Therefore, reviving the Spark ecosystem is a demand at this point.

Enough knowing about Spark's beauties and features. At this point, reviving the Spark ecosystem is your demand to know how does Spark work.

Spark ecosystem in brief

To provide you with more advanced and additional big data processing capabilities, your Spark jobs can be running on top of Hadoop-based (aka YARN) or Mesos-based clusters. On the other hand, the core APIs in Spark, which is written in Scala, enable you to develop your Spark application using several programming languages such as Java, Scala, Python, and R. Spark provides several libraries that are part of the Spark ecosystems for additional capabilities for general purpose data processing and analytics, graph processing, large-scale structured SQL, and **machine learning (ML)** areas. The Spark ecosystem consists of the following components:

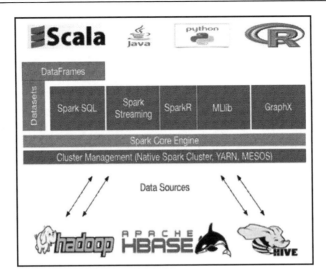

Figure 1: Spark ecosystem (up to Spark 2.1.0)

The core engine of Spark is written in Scala but supports different languages to develop your Spark application, such as R, Java, Python, and Scala. The main components/APIs in the Spark core engine are as follows:

1. **SparkSQL**: This helps in seamlessly mix SQL queries with Spark programs so that you can query structured data inside Spark programs.
2. **Spark Streaming**: This is for large-scale streaming application development that provides seamless integration of Spark with other streaming data sources such as Kafka, Flink, and Twitter.
3. **SparkMLlib** and **SparKML**: These are for RDD and dataset/DataFrame-based machine learning and pipeline creation.
4. **GraphX**: This is for large-scale graph computation and processing to make your graph data object fully connected.
5. **SparkR**: R on Spark helps in basic statistical computations and machine learning.

As we have already stated, it is very much possible to combine these APIs seamlessly to develop large-scale machine learning and data analytics applications. Moreover, Spark jobs can be submitted and executed through cluster managers such as Hadoop YARN, Mesos, and standalone, or in the cloud by accessing data storage and sources such as HDFS, Cassandra, HBase, Amazon S3, or even RDBMS. However, to the full facility of Spark, we need to deploy our Spark application on a computing cluster.

Cluster design

Apache Spark is a distributed and parallel processing system and it also provides in-memory computing capabilities. This type of computing paradigm needs an associated storage system so that you can deploy your application on top of a big data cluster. To make this happen, you will have to use distributed storage systems such as HDFS, S3, HBase, and Hive. For moving data, you will be needing other technologies such as Sqoop, Kinesis, Twitter, Flume, and Kafka.

In practice, you can configure a small Hadoop cluster very easily. You only need to have a single master and multiple worker nodes. In your Hadoop cluster, generally, a master node consists of **NameNodes**, **DataNodes**, **JobTracker**, and **TaskTracker**. A worker node, on the other hand, can be configured so that it works both as a DataNode and as a TaskTracker.

For security reasons, most of the big data cluster might set up behind a network firewall so that the complexity caused by the firewall can be overcome or at least reduced by the computing nodes. Otherwise, computing nodes cannot be accessed from outside of the network, that is, extranet. The following figure shows a simplified big data cluster that is commonly used in Spark:

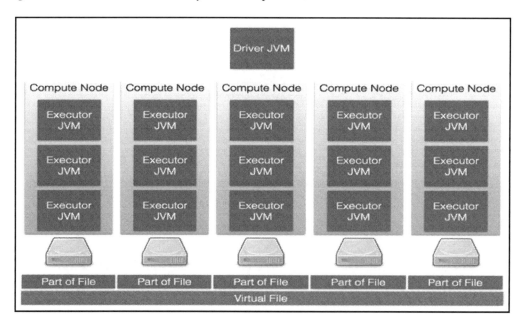

Figure 2: A general architecture for big data processing with JVM

The above picture shows a cluster consisting of five computing nodes. Here each node has a dedicated executor JVM, one per CPU core, and the Spark Driver JVM sitting outside the cluster. The disk is directly attached to the nodes using the **JBOD** (**Just a bunch of disks**) approach. Very large files are partitioned over the disks, and a virtual file system such as HDFS makes these chunks available as one large virtual file. The following simplified component model shows the driver JVM sitting outside the cluster. It talks to the cluster manager (see **Figure 4**) in order to obtain permission to schedule tasks on the worker nodes because the cluster manager keeps track on resource allocation of all processes running on the cluster.

If you have developed your Spark application using Scala or Java, it means that your job is a JVM-based process. For your JVM-based process, you can simply configure the Java heap space by specifying the following two parameters:

- **-Xmx**: This one specifies the upper limit of your Java heap space
- **-Xms**: This one is the lower limit of the Java heap space

Once you have sumitted a Spark job, heap memory need to be allocated for your Spark jobs. The following figure provides some insights on how:

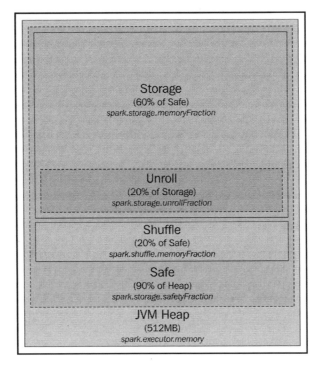

Figure 3: JVM memory management

As demonstrated in the preceding figure, Spark starts a Spark job with 512 MB of JVM heap space. However, for an uninterrupted processing of your Spark job and to avoid the **Out of Memory (OOM)** error, Spark allows the computing nodes to utilize only up to 90% of the heap (that is, ~461 MB), which is eventually increased or decreased by controlling the `spark.storage.safetyFraction` parameter in Spark environment. To be more realistic, the JVM can be seen as a concatenation of **Storage** (60% of the Java heap), 20% of the heap for execution (aka **Shuffle**), and the rest of the 20% for other storage.

Moreover, Spark is a cluster computing tool that tries to utilize both in-memory and disk-based computing and allows users to store some data in memory. In reality, Spark utilizes the main memory only for its LRU cache. For uninterrupted caching mechanism, a little amount of memory is required to be reserved for the application specific data processing. Informally, this is around 60% of the Java heap space controlled by the `spark.memory.fraction`.

Therefore, if you would like to see or calculate how much application specific data you can cache in memory in your Spark application, you can just sum up all the heap sizes usages by all the executors and multiply it by the `safetyFraction` and `spark.memory.fraction`. In practice, 54% of the total heap size (276.48 MB) you can allow Spark computing nodes to be used. Now the shuffle memory is calculated as follows:

```
Shuffle memory= Heap Size * spark.shuffle.safetyFraction *
spark.shuffle.memoryFraction
```

The default values for `spark.shuffle.safetyFraction` and `spark.shuffle.memoryFraction` are 80% and 20%, respectively. Therefore, in practical, you can use up to *0.8*0.2 = 16%* of the JVM heap for the shuffle. Finally, unroll memory is the amount of the main memory (in a computing node) that can be utilized by the unroll processes. The calculation goes as follows:

```
Unroll memory = spark.storage.unrollFraction *
spark.storage.memoryFraction * spark.storage.safetyFraction
```

The above is around 11% of the heap *(0.2*0.6*0.9 = 10.8~11%)*, that is, 56.32 MB of the Java heap space.

More detailed discussion can be found at `http://spark.apache.org/docs/latest/configuration.html`.

As we will see later, there exist a variety of different cluster managers, some of them also capable of managing other Hadoop workloads or even non-Hadoop applications in parallel to the Spark executors. Note that the executor and driver have bidirectional communication all the time, so network wise they should also be sitting close together.

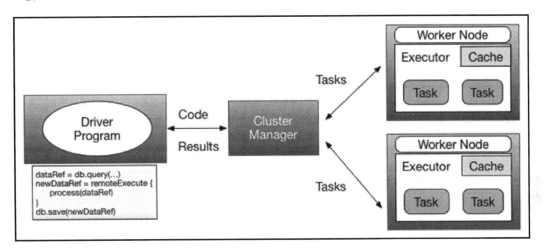

Figure 4: Driver. master. and worker architecture in Spark for cluster

Spark uses the driver (aka the driver program), master, and worker architecture (aka host, slave, or computing nodes). The driver program (or machine) talks to a single coordinator called master node. The master node actually manages all the workers (aka the slave or computing nodes) in which several executors run in parallel in a cluster. It is to be noted that the master is also a computing node having large memory, storage, OS, and underlying computing resources. Conceptually, this architecture can be shown in **Figure 4**. More details will be discussed later in this section.

In a real cluster mode, the cluster manager (aka the resource manager) manages all the resources of computing nodes in a cluster. Generally, firewalls, while adding security to the cluster, also increase the complexity. Ports between system components need to be opened up so that they can talk to each other. For instance, Zookeeper is used by many components for configuration. Apache Kafka, which is a subscribing messaging system, uses Zookeeper for configuring its topics, groups, consumers, and producers. So, client ports to Zookeeper, potentially across the firewall, need to be open.

Finally, the allocation of systems to cluster nodes needs to be considered. For instance, if Apache Spark uses Flume or Kafka, then in-memory channels will be used. Apache Spark should not be competing with other Apache components for memory usage. Depending upon your data flows and memory usage, it might be necessary to have the Spark, Hadoop, Zookeeper, Flume, and other tools on distinct cluster nodes. Alternatively, resource managers such as YARN, Mesos, or Docker, for instance, can be used to tackle this problem as well. In standard Hadoop environments, most likely YARN is there anyway.

The computing nodes that act as workers, or Spark master, will need greater resources than the cluster processing nodes within the firewall. When many Hadoop ecosystem components are deployed on the cluster, all of them will need extra memory on the master server. You should monitor worker nodes for resource usage and adjust in terms of resources and/or application location as necessary. YARN, for instance, is taking care of this.

This section has briefly set the scene for the big data cluster in terms of Apache Spark, Hadoop, and other tools. However, how might the Apache Spark cluster itself, within the big data cluster, be configured? For instance, it is possible to have many types of Spark cluster manager. The next section will examine this and describe each type of Apache Spark cluster manager.

Cluster management

The Spark context can be defined through the Spark configuration object (that is, `SparkConf`) and a Spark URL. First, the purpose of the Spark context is to connect the Spark cluster manager in which your Spark jobs will be running. The cluster or resource manager then allocates the required resources across the computing nodes for your application. The second task of the cluster manager is to allocate the executors across the cluster worker nodes so that your Spark jobs get executed. Third, the resource manager also copies the driver program (aka the application JAR file, R code, or Python script) to the computing nodes. Finally, the computing tasks are assigned to the computing nodes by the resource manager.

The following subsections describe the possible Apache Spark cluster manager options available with the current Spark version (that is, Spark 2.1.0 during the writing of this book). To know about the resource management by a resource manager (aka the cluster manager), the following shows how YARN manages all its underlying computing resources. However, this is same for any cluster manager (for example, Mesos or YARN) you use:

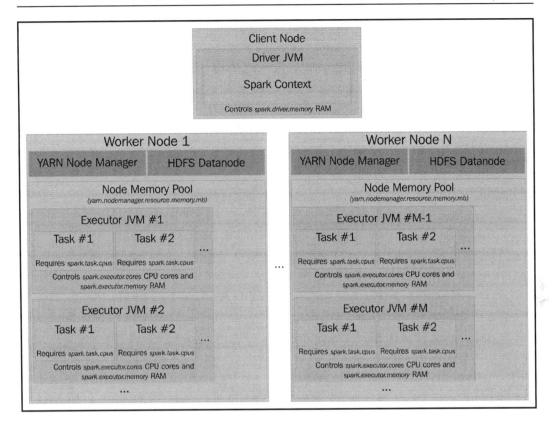

Figure 5: Resource management using YARN

A detailed discussion can be found at `http://spark.apache.org/docs/latest/cluster-overview.html#cluster-manager-types`.

Pseudocluster mode (aka Spark local)

As you already know, Spark jobs can be run in local mode. This is sometimes called pseudocluster mode of execution. This is also nondistributed and single JVM-based deployment mode where Spark issues all the execution components, for example, driver program, executor, LocalSchedulerBackend, and master, into your single JVM. This is the only mode where the driver itself is used as an executor. The following figure shows the high-level architecture of the local mode for submitting your Spark jobs:

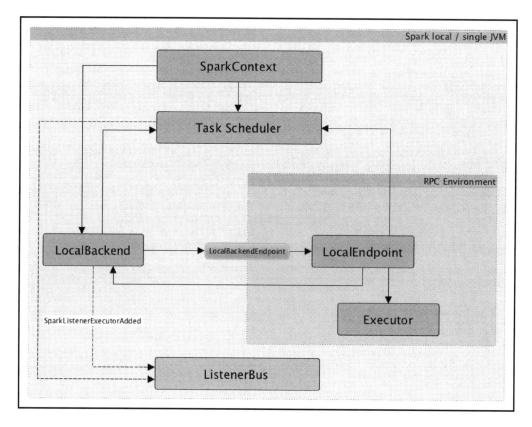

Figure 6: High-level architecture of local mode for Spark jobs (source: `https://jaceklaskowski.gitbooks.io/` `mastering-apache-spark/content/spark-local.html`)

Is it too surprising? No, I guess, since you can achieve some short of parallelism as well, where the default parallelism is the number of threads (aka Core used) as specified in the master URL, that is, local [4] for 4 cores/threads and `local [*]` for all the available threads. We will discuss this topic later in this chapter.

Standalone

By specifying a Spark configuration local URL, it is possible to have the application run locally. By specifying *local[n]*, it is possible to have Spark use *n* threads to run the application locally. This is a useful development and test option because you can also test some sort of parallelization scenarios but keep all log files on a single machine. The standalone mode uses a basic cluster manager that is supplied with Apache Spark. The spark master URL will be as follows:

```
spark://<hostname>:7077
```

Here, `<hostname>` is the name of the host on which the Spark master is running. I have specified 7077 as the port, which is the default value, but it is configurable. This simple cluster manager currently only supports **FIFO** (**first in first out**) scheduling. You can contrive to allow concurrent application scheduling by setting the resource configuration options for each application. For example, `spark.core.max` is used to share the processor cores between applications. A more detail discussion will be carried out later this chapter.

Apache YARN

If the Spark master value is set as YARN-cluster, then the application can be submitted to the cluster and then terminated. The cluster will take care of allocating resources and running tasks. However, if the application master is submitted as YARN-client, then the application stays alive during the life cycle of processing and requests resources from YARN. These are applicable at a larger scale, when integrating with Hadoop YARN. A step-by-step guideline will be provided later in this chapter to configure a single-node YARN cluster for launching your Spark jobs needing minimal resources.

Apache Mesos

Apache Mesos is an open source system for resource sharing across a cluster. It allows multiple frameworks to share a cluster by managing and scheduling resources. It is a cluster manager, which provides isolation using Linux containers, allowing multiple systems such as Hadoop, Spark, Kafka, Storm, and more to share a cluster safely. This is a master-slave based system using Zookeeper for configuration management. This way you can scalae up your Spark jobs to thousands of nodes. For a single master node Mesos cluster, the Spark master URL will be in the following form:

```
mesos://<hostname>:5050
```

The consequence of a Spark job submission by specifically using Mesos can be shown visually in the following figure:

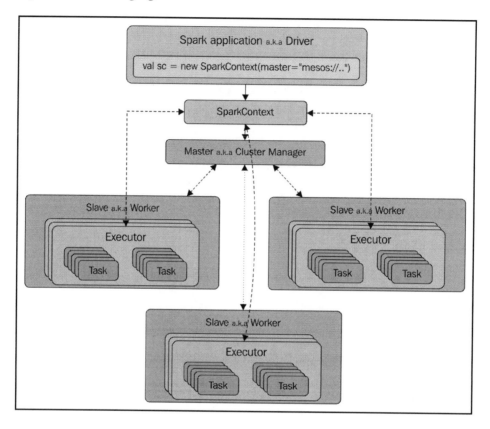

Figure 7: Mesos in action (image source: https://jaceklaskowski.gitbooks.io/mastering-apache-spark/content/spark-architecture.html)

In the preceding figure, where <hostname> is the hostname of the Mesos master server, and the port is defined as 5050, which is the default Mesos master port (this is configurable). If there are multiple Mesos master servers in a large-scale high availability Mesos cluster, then the Spark master URL would look like the following:

```
mesos://zk://<hostname>:2181
```

So, the election of the Mesos master server will be controlled by Zookeeper. The <hostname> will be the name of a host in the Zookeeper quorum. Also, the port number 2181 is the default master port for Zookeeper.

Cloud-based deployments

There are three different abstraction levels in the cloud computing paradigm:

- **Infrastructure as a Service** (aka **IaaS**)
- **Platform as a Service** (aka **PaaS**)
- **Software as a Service** (aka **SaaS**)

IaaS provides the computing infrastructure through empty virtual machines for your software running as SaaS. This is also true for the Apache Spark on OpenStack.

The advantage of OpenStack is that it can be used among multiple different cloud providers, since it is an open standard and is also based on open source. You even can use OpenStack in a local data center, and transparently and dynamically move workloads between local, dedicated, and public cloud data centers.

PaaS, in contrast, takes away from you the burden of installing and operating an Apache Spark cluster because this is provided as a Service. In other words, you can think it as a layer like what your OS does.

Sometimes, you can even Dockerize your Spark application and deploy on the cloud platform independent manner. However, there is an ongoing discussion whether Docker is IaaS or PaaS, but in our opinion, this is just a form of a lightweight preinstalled virtual machine, so more on the IaaS.

Finally, SaaS is an application layer provided and managed by cloud computing paradigm. To be frank, you won't see or have to worry about the first two layers (IaaS and PaaS).

Google Cloud, Amazon AWS, Digital Ocean, and Microsoft Azure are good examples of cloud computing services that provide these three layers as services. We will show an example of how to deploy your Spark cluster on top of Cloud using Amazon AWS later in this chapter.

Deploying the Spark application on a cluster

In this section, we will discuss how to deploy Spark jobs on a computing cluster. We will see how to deploy clusters in three deploy modes: standalone, YARN, and Mesos. The following figure summarizes terms that are needed to refer to cluster concepts in this chapter:

Term	Meaning
Application	User program built on Spark. Consists of a *driver program* and *executors* on the cluster.
Application jar	A jar containing the user's Spark application. In some cases users will want to create an "uber jar" containing their application along with its dependencies. The user's jar should never include Hadoop or Spark libraries, however, these will be added at runtime.
Driver program	The process running the main() function of the application and creating the SparkContext
Cluster manager	An external service for acquiring resources on the cluster (e.g. standalone manager, Mesos, YARN)
Deploy mode	Distinguishes where the driver process runs. In "cluster" mode, the framework launches the driver inside of the cluster. In "client" mode, the submitter launches the driver outside of the cluster.
Worker node	Any node that can run application code in the cluster
Executor	A process launched for an application on a worker node, that runs tasks and keeps data in memory or disk storage across them. Each application has its own executors.
Task	A unit of work that will be sent to one executor
Job	A parallel computation consisting of multiple tasks that gets spawned in response to a Spark action (e.g. save, collect); you'll see this term used in the driver's logs.
Stage	Each job gets divided into smaller sets of tasks called *stages* that depend on each other (similar to the map and reduce stages in MapReduce); you'll see this term used in the driver's logs.

Figure 8: Terms that are needed to refer to cluster concepts (source: http://spark.apache.org/docs/latest/cluster-overview.html#glossary)

However, before diving onto deeper, we need to know how to submit a Spark job in general.

Submitting Spark jobs

Once a Spark application is bundled as either a jar file (written in Scala or Java) or a Python file, it can be submitted using the Spark-submit script located under the bin directory in Spark distribution (aka $SPARK_HOME/bin). According to the API documentation provided in Spark website (http://spark.apache.org/docs/latest/submitting-applications.html), the script takes care of the following:

- Setting up the classpath of JAVA_HOME, SCALA_HOME with Spark
- Setting up the all the dependencies required to execute the jobs
- Managing different cluster managers
- Finally, deploying models that Spark supports

In a nutshell, Spark job submission syntax is as follows:

```
$ spark-submit [options] <app-jar | python-file> [app arguments]
```

Here, [options] can be: --conf <configuration_parameters> --class <main-class> --master <master-url> --deploy-mode <deploy-mode> ... # other options

- <main-class> is the name of the main class name. This is practically the entry point for our Spark application.
- --conf signifies all the used Spark parameters and configuration property. The format of a configuration property is a key=value format.
- <master-url> specifies the master URL for the cluster (for example, spark://HOST_NAME:PORT) for connecting to the master of the Spark standalone cluster, local for running your Spark jobs locally. By default, it allows you using only one worker thread with no parallelism. The local [k] can be used for running your Spark job locally with *K* worker threads. It is to be noted that K is the number of cores on your machine. Finally, if you specify the master with local[*] for running Spark job locally, you are giving the permission to the spark-submit script to utilize all the worker threads (logical cores) on your machine have. Finally, you can specify the master as mesos://IP_ADDRESS:PORT for connecting to the available Mesos cluster. Alternatively, you could specify using yarn to run your Spark jobs on a YARN-based cluster.

For other options on Master URL, please refer to the following figure:

Master URL	Meaning
local	Run Spark locally with one worker thread (i.e. no parallelism at all).
local[K]	Run Spark locally with K worker threads (ideally, set this to the number of cores on your machine).
local[*]	Run Spark locally with as many worker threads as logical cores on your machine.
spark://HOST:PORT	Connect to the given Spark standalone cluster master. The port must be whichever one your master is configured to use, which is 7077 by default.
mesos://HOST:PORT	Connect to the given Mesos cluster. The port must be whichever one your is configured to use, which is 5050 by default. Or, for a Mesos cluster using ZooKeeper, use mesos://zk://.... To submit with --deploy-mode cluster, the HOST:PORT should be configured to connect to the MesosClusterDispatcher.
yarn	Connect to a YARN cluster in client or cluster mode depending on the value of --deploy-mode. The cluster location will be found based on the HADOOP_CONF_DIR or YARN_CONF_DIR variable.

Figure 9: Details about the master URLs supported by Spark\

- `<deploy-mode>` you have to specify this if you want to deploy your driver on the worker nodes (cluster) or locally as an external client (client). Four (4) modes are supported: local, standalone, YARN, and Mesos.
- `<app-jar>` is the JAR file you build with with dependencies. Just pass the JAR file while submitting your jobs.
- `<python-file>` is the application main source code written using Python. Just pass the `.py` file while submitting your jobs.
- `[app-arguments]` could be input or output argument specified by an application developer.

While submitting the Spark jobs using the spark-submit script, you can specify the main jar of the Spark application (and other related JARS included) using the `--jars` option. All the JARS will then be transferred to the cluster. URLs supplied after `--jars` must be separated by commas.

However, if you specify the jar using the URLs, it is a good practice to separate the JARS using commas after `--jars`. Spark uses the following URL scheme to allow different strategies for disseminating JARS:

- **file:** Specifies the absolute paths and `file:/`
- **hdfs:, http:, https:, ftp:** JARS or any other files will be pull-down from the URLs/URIs you specified as expected
- **local:** A URI starting with `local:/` can be used to point local jar files on each computing node

It is to be noted that dependent JARs, R codes, Python scripts, or any other associated data files need to be copied or replicated to the working directory for each SparkContext on the computing nodes. This sometimes creates a significant overhead and needs a pretty large amount of disk space. The disk usages increase over time. Therefore, at a certain period of time, unused data objects or associated code files need to be cleaned up. This is, however, quite easy with YARN. YARN handles the cleanup periodically and can be handled automatically. For example, with the Spark standalone mode, automatic cleanup can be configured with the `spark.worker.cleanup.appDataTtl` property while submitting the Spark jobs.

Computationally, the Spark is designed such that during the job submission (using `spark-submit` script), default Spark config values can be loaded and propagate to Spark applications from a property file. Master node will read the specified options from the configuration file named `spark-default.conf`. The exact path is `SPARK_HOME/conf/spark-defaults.conf` in your Spark distribution directory. However, if you specify all the parameters in the command line, this will get higher priority and will be used accordingly.

Running Spark jobs locally and in standalone

The examples are shown `Chapter 13`, *My Name is Bayes, Naive Bayes*, and can be made scalable for even larger dataset to solve different purposes. You can package all these three clustering algorithms with all the required dependencies and submit them as Spark job in the cluster. If you don't know how to make a package and create jar files out of the Scala class, you can bundle your application with all the dependencies using SBT or Maven.

According to Spark documentation at `http://spark.apache.org/docs/latest/submitting-applications.html#advanced-dependency-management`, both the SBT and Maven have assembly plugins for packaging your Spark application as a fat jar. If your application is already bundled with all the dependencies, use the following lines of code to submit your Spark job of k-means clustering, for example (use similar syntax for other classes), for Saratoga NY Homes dataset. For submitting and running a Spark job locally, run the following command on 8 cores:

```
$ SPARK_HOME/bin/spark-submit
  --class com.chapter15.Clustering.KMeansDemo
  --master local[8]
  KMeans-0.0.1-SNAPSHOT-jar-with-dependencies.jar
  Saratoga_NY_Homes.txt
```

In the preceding code, `com.chapter15.KMeansDemo` is the main class file written in Scala. Local [8] is the master URL utilizing eight cores of your machine. `KMeansDemo-0.1-SNAPSHOT-jar-with-dependencies.jar` is the application JAR file we just generated by Maven project; `Saratoga_NY_Homes.txt` is the input text file for the Saratoga NY Homes dataset. If the application executed successfully, you will find the message including the output in the following figure (abridged):

```
17/02/14 12:31:02 INFO Executor: Finished task 0.0 in stage 0.0 (TID 0). 3343 bytes result sent to driver
17/02/14 12:31:02 INFO TaskSetManager: Finished task 0.0 in stage 0.0 (TID 0) in 215 ms on localhost (executor driver) (1/1)
17/02/14 12:31:02 INFO TaskSchedulerImpl: Removed TaskSet 0.0, whose tasks have all completed, from pool
17/02/14 12:31:02 INFO DAGScheduler: ResultStage 0 (show at KMeansDemo.scala:56) finished in 0.225 s
17/02/14 12:31:02 INFO DAGScheduler: Job 0 finished: show at KMeansDemo.scala:56, took 0.322031 s
17/02/14 12:31:02 INFO CodeGenerator: Code generated in 19.812394 ms
```

Price	LotSize	Waterfront	Age	LandValue	NewConstruct	CentralAir	FuelType	HeatType	SewerType	LivingArea	PctCollege	Bedrooms	Fireplaces	Bathrooms	rooms
132500.0	0.09	0.0	42.0	50000.0	0.0	0.0	3.0	4.0	2.0	906.0	35.0	2.0	1.0	1.0	5.0
181115.0	0.92	0.0	0.0	22300.0	0.0	0.0	2.0	3.0	2.0	1953.0	51.0	3.0	0.0	2.5	6.0
109000.0	0.19	0.0	133.0	7300.0	0.0	0.0	2.0	3.0	3.0	1944.0	51.0	4.0	1.0	1.0	8.0
155000.0	0.41	0.0	13.0	18700.0	0.0	0.0	2.0	2.0	2.0	1944.0	51.0	3.0	1.0	1.5	5.0
86060.0	0.11	0.0	0.0	15000.0	1.0	1.0	2.0	2.0	3.0	840.0	51.0	2.0	0.0	1.0	3.0
120000.0	0.68	0.0	31.0	14000.0	0.0	0.0	2.0	2.0	2.0	1152.0	22.0	4.0	1.0	1.0	8.0
153000.0	0.4	0.0	33.0	23300.0	0.0	0.0	4.0	3.0	2.0	2752.0	51.0	4.0	1.0	1.5	8.0
170000.0	1.21	0.0	23.0	14600.0	0.0	0.0	4.0	2.0	2.0	1662.0	35.0	4.0	1.0	1.5	9.0
90000.0	0.83	0.0	36.0	22200.0	0.0	0.0	3.0	4.0	2.0	1632.0	51.0	3.0	0.0	1.5	8.0
122900.0	1.94	0.0	4.0	21200.0	0.0	0.0	2.0	2.0	1.0	1416.0	44.0	3.0	0.0	1.5	6.0
325000.0	2.29	0.0	123.0	12600.0	0.0	0.0	4.0	2.0	2.0	2894.0	51.0	7.0	0.0	1.0	12.0
120000.0	0.92	0.0	1.0	22300.0	0.0	0.0	2.0	2.0	2.0	1624.0	51.0	3.0	0.0	2.0	6.0
85860.0	8.97	0.0	13.0	4800.0	0.0	0.0	3.0	4.0	2.0	704.0	41.0	2.0	0.0	1.0	4.0
97000.0	0.11	0.0	153.0	3100.0	0.0	0.0	2.0	3.0	3.0	1383.0	57.0	3.0	0.0	2.0	5.0
127000.0	0.14	0.0	9.0	300.0	0.0	0.0	4.0	2.0	2.0	1300.0	41.0	3.0	0.0	1.5	8.0
89900.0	0.0	0.0	88.0	2500.0	0.0	0.0	2.0	3.0	3.0	936.0	57.0	3.0	0.0	1.0	4.0
155000.0	0.13	0.0	9.0	300.0	0.0	0.0	4.0	2.0	2.0	1300.0	41.0	3.0	0.0	1.5	7.0
253750.0	2.0	0.0	0.0	49800.0	0.0	1.0	2.0	2.0	1.0	2816.0	71.0	4.0	1.0	2.5	12.0
60000.0	0.21	0.0	82.0	8500.0	0.0	0.0	4.0	3.0	2.0	924.0	35.0	2.0	0.0	1.0	6.0
87500.0	0.88	0.0	17.0	19400.0	0.0	0.0	4.0	2.0	2.0	1092.0	35.0	3.0	0.0	1.0	6.0

```
only showing top 20 rows

17/02/14 12:31:02 INFO ContextCleaner: Cleaned accumulator 3
17/02/14 12:31:03 INFO BlockManagerInfo: Removed broadcast_1_piece0 on 10.2.16.255:53581 in memory (size: 9.4 kB, free: 4.0 GB)
17/02/14 12:31:03 INFO SparkContext: Starting job: takeSample at KMeans.scala:353
17/02/14 12:31:03 INFO DAGScheduler: Got job 1 (takeSample at KMeans.scala:353) with 2 output partitions
17/02/14 12:31:03 INFO DAGScheduler: Final stage: ResultStage 1 (takeSample at KMeans.scala:353)
17/02/14 12:31:03 INFO DAGScheduler: Parents of final stage: List()
```

Figure 10: Spark job output on terminal [local mode]

Now, let's dive into the cluster setup in standalone mode. To install Spark standalone mode, you should place prebuilt versions of Spark with each release on each node on the cluster. Alternatively, you can build it yourself and use it according to the instruction at `http://spark.apache.org/docs/latest/building-spark.html`.

To configure the environment as a Spark standalone mode, you will have to provide the prebuilt versions of Spark with the desired version to each node on the cluster. Alternatively, you can build it yourself and use it according to the instruction at `http://spark.apache.org/docs/latest/building-spark.html`. Now we will see how to start a standalone cluster manually. You can start a standalone master by executing the following command:

```
$ SPARK_HOME/sbin/start-master.sh
```

Once started, you should observe the following logs on terminal:

```
Starting org.apache.spark.deploy.master.Master, logging to
<SPARK_HOME>/logs/spark-asif-org.apache.spark.deploy.master.Master-1-
ubuntu.out
```

You should be able to access Spark web UI at http://localhost:8080 by default.
Observe the following UI as shown in the following figure:

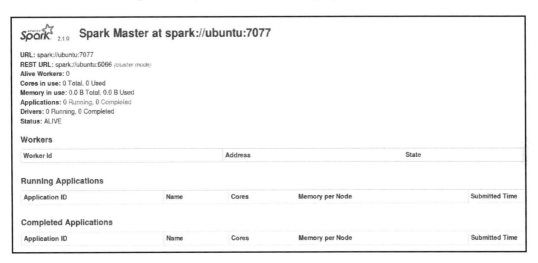

Figure 11: Spark master as standalone

You can change the port number by editing the following parameter:

```
SPARK_MASTER_WEBUI_PORT=8080
```

In the SPARK_HOME/sbin/start-master.sh, just change the port number and then
apply the following command:

```
$ sudo chmod +x SPARK_HOME/sbin/start-master.sh.
```

Alternatively, you can restart the Spark master to effect the preceding change.
However, you will have to make a similar change in the SPARK_HOME/sbin/start-
slave.sh.

As you can see here, there are no active workers associated with the master node. Now to create a slave node (aka a worker node or computing node), create workers and connect them to the master using the following command:

```
$ SPARK_HOME/sbin/start-slave.sh <master-spark-URL>
```

Upon successful completion of the preceding command, you should observe the following logs on terminal:

```
Starting org.apache.spark.deploy.worker.Worker, logging to
<SPARK_HOME>//logs/spark-asif-org.apache.spark.deploy.worker.Worker-1-
ubuntu.out
```

Once you have one of your worker nodes started, you can look at its status on the Spark web UI at http://localhost:8081. However, if you start another worker node, you can access it's status in the consecutive ports (that is, 8082, 8083, and so on). You should also see the new node listed there, along with its number of CPUs and memory, as shown in the following figure:

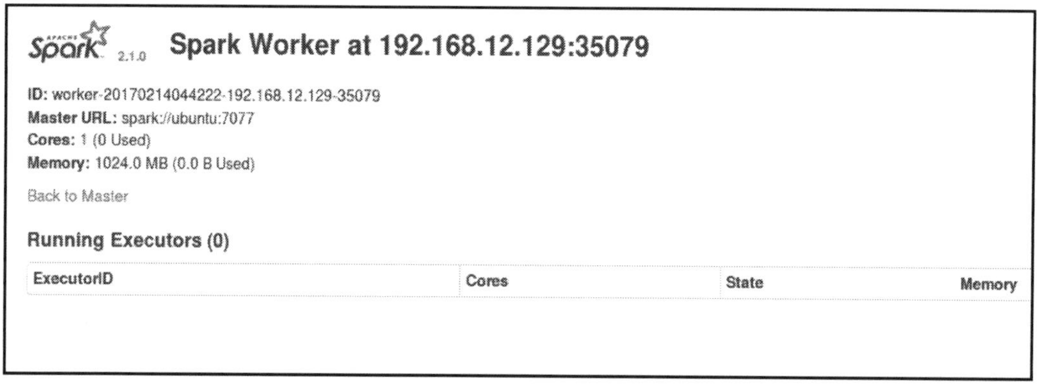

Spark Worker at 192.168.12.129:35079

ID: worker-20170214044222-192.168.12.129-35079
Master URL: spark://ubuntu:7077
Cores: 1 (0 Used)
Memory: 1024.0 MB (0.0 B Used)

Back to Master

Running Executors (0)

ExecutorID	Cores	State	Memory

Figure 12: Spark worker as standalone

Now, if you refresh `http://localhost:8080`, you should see that one worker node that is associated with your master node has been added, as shown in the following figure:

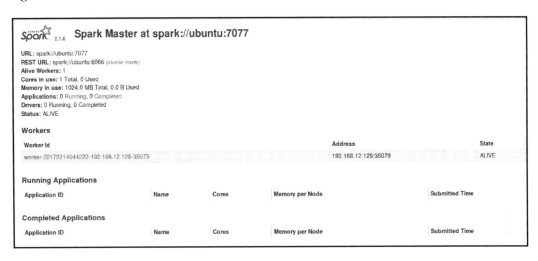

Figure 13: Spark master has now one worker node as standalone

Finally, as shown in the following figure, these are all the configuration options that can be passed to the master and worker nodes:

Argument	Meaning
-h HOST, --host HOST	Hostname to listen on
-i HOST, --ip HOST	Hostname to listen on (deprecated, use -h or --host)
-p PORT, --port PORT	Port for service to listen on (default: 7077 for master, random for worker)
--webui-port PORT	Port for web UI (default: 8080 for master, 8081 for worker)
-c CORES, --cores CORES	Total CPU cores to allow Spark applications to use on the machine (default: all available); only on worker
-m MEM, --memory MEM	Total amount of memory to allow Spark applications to use on the machine, in a format like 1000M or 2G (default: your machine's total RAM minus 1 GB); only on worker
-d DIR, --work-dir DIR	Directory to use for scratch space and job output logs (default: SPARK_HOME/work); only on worker
--properties-file FILE	Path to a custom Spark properties file to load (default: conf/spark-defaults.conf)

Figure 14: Configuration options that can be passed to the master and worker nodes (source: `http://spark.apache.org/docs/latest/spark-standalone.html#starting-a-cluster-manually`)

Now one of your master node and a worker node are reading and active. Finally, you can submit the same Spark job as standalone rather than local mode using the following commands:

```
$ SPARK_HOME/bin/spark-submit
--class "com.chapter15.Clustering.KMeansDemo"
--master spark://ubuntu:7077
KMeans-0.0.1-SNAPSHOT-jar-with-dependencies.jar
Saratoga_NY_Homes.txt
```

Once the job started, access Spark web UI at `http://localhost:80810` for master and `http://localhost:8081` for the worker, you can see the progress of your job as discussed in `Chapter 14`, *Time to Put Some Order - Cluster Your Data with Spark MLlib*.

To summarize this section, we would like to redirect you to the following image (that is, **Figure 15**) that shows the usages of the following shell scripts for launching or stopping your cluster:

* `sbin/start-master.sh` - Starts a master instance on the machine the script is executed on.
* `sbin/start-slaves.sh` - Starts a slave instance on each machine specified in the `conf/slaves` file.
* `sbin/start-slave.sh` - Starts a slave instance on the machine the script is executed on.
* `sbin/start-all.sh` - Starts both a master and a number of slaves as described above.
* `sbin/stop-master.sh` - Stops the master that was started via the `bin/start-master.sh` script.
* `sbin/stop-slaves.sh` - Stops all slave instances on the machines specified in the `conf/slaves` file.
* `sbin/stop-all.sh` - Stops both the master and the slaves as described above.

Figure 15: The usages of the shell scripts for launching or stopping your cluster\

Hadoop YARN

As already discussed, the Apache Hadoop YARN has to main components: a scheduler and an applications manager, as shown in the following figure:

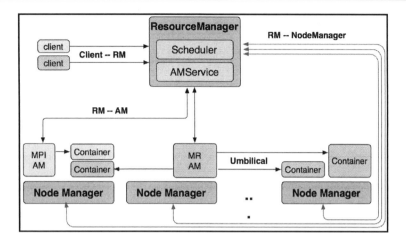

Figure 16: Apache Hadoop YARN architecture (blue: system components; yellow and pink: two applications running)

Now that using the scheduler and the applications manager, the following two deploy modes can be configured to launch your Spark jobs on a YARN-based cluster:

- **Cluster mode**: In the cluster mode, the Spark driver works within the master process of an application managed by YARN's application manager. Even the client can be terminated or disconnected away when the application has been initiated.
- **Client mode**: In this mode, the Spark driver runs inside the client process. After that, Spark master is used only for requesting computing resources for the computing nodes from YARN (YARN resource manager).

In the Spark standalone and Mesos modes, the URL of the master (that is, address) needs to be specified in the `--master` parameter. However, in the YARN mode, the address of the resource manager is read from the Hadoop configuration file in your Hadoop setting. Consequently, the `--master` parameter is `yarn`. Before submitting our Spark jobs, we, however, you need to set up your YARN cluster. The next subsection shows a step-by-step of doing so.

Configuring a single-node YARN cluster

In this subsection, we will see how to set up your YARN cluster before running your Spark jobs on YARN cluster. There are several steps so keep patience and do the following step-by-step:

Step 1: Downloading Apache Hadoop

Download the latest distribution from the Hadoop website (http://hadoop.apache.org/). I used the latest stable version 2.7.3 on Ubuntu 14.04 as follows:

```
$   cd /home
$   wget
http://mirrors.ibiblio.org/apache/hadoop/common/hadoop-2.7.3/hadoop-2.
7.3.tar.gz
```

Next, create and extract the package in /opt/yarn as follows:

```
$   mkdir -p /opt/yarn
$   cd /opt/yarn
$   tar xvzf /root/hadoop-2.7.3.tar.gz
```

Step 2: Setting the JAVA_HOME

Refer to the section of Java setup in Chapter 1, *Introduction to Scala*, for details and apply the same changes.

Step 3: Creating users and groups

The following yarn, hdfs, and mapred user accounts for hadoop group can be created as follows:

```
$   groupadd hadoop
$   useradd -g hadoop yarn
$   useradd -g hadoop hdfs
$   useradd -g hadoop mapred
```

Step 4: Creating data and log directories

To run your Spark jobs using Hadoop, it needs to have the data and the log directories with various permissions. You can use the following command:

```
$   mkdir -p /var/data/hadoop/hdfs/nn
$   mkdir -p /var/data/hadoop/hdfs/snn
$   mkdir -p /var/data/hadoop/hdfs/dn
```

```
$  chown hdfs:hadoop /var/data/hadoop/hdfs -R
$  mkdir -p /var/log/hadoop/yarn
$  chown yarn:hadoop /var/log/hadoop/yarn -R
```

Now you need to create the log directory where YARN is installed and then set the owner and group as follows:

```
$  cd /opt/yarn/hadoop-2.7.3
$  mkdir logs
$  chmod g+w logs
$  chown yarn:hadoop . -R
```

Step 5: Configuring core-site.xml

Two properties (that is, `fs.default.name` and `hadoop.http.staticuser.user`) need to be set to the `etc/hadoop/core-site.xml` file. Just copy the following lines of codes:

```
<configuration>
      <property>
            <name>fs.default.name</name>
            <value>hdfs://localhost:9000</value>
      </property>
      <property>
            <name>hadoop.http.staticuser.user</name>
            <value>hdfs</value>
      </property>
</configuration>
```

Step 6: Configuring hdfs-site.xml

Five properties (that is, `dfs.replication`, `dfs.namenode.name.dir`, `fs.checkpoint.dir`, `fs.checkpoint.edits.dir`, and `dfs.datanode.data.dir`) need to be set to the `etc/hadoop/ hdfs-site.xml` file. Just copy the following lines of codes:

```
<configuration>
 <property>
   <name>dfs.replication</name>
   <value>1</value>
 </property>
 <property>
   <name>dfs.namenode.name.dir</name>
   <value>file:/var/data/hadoop/hdfs/nn</value>
 </property>
 <property>
```

```
    <name>fs.checkpoint.dir</name>
    <value>file:/var/data/hadoop/hdfs/snn</value>
  </property>
  <property>
    <name>fs.checkpoint.edits.dir</name>
    <value>file:/var/data/hadoop/hdfs/snn</value>
  </property>
  <property>
    <name>dfs.datanode.data.dir</name>
    <value>file:/var/data/hadoop/hdfs/dn</value>
  </property>
</configuration>
```

Step 7: Configuring mapred-site.xml

One property (that is, `mapreduce.framework.name`) needs to be set to the `etc/hadoop/` `mapred-site.xml` file. First, copy and replace the original template file to the `mapred-site.xml` as follows:

```
$  cp mapred-site.xml.template mapred-site.xml
```

Now, just copy the following lines of codes:

```
<configuration>
<property>
    <name>mapreduce.framework.name</name>
    <value>yarn</value>
 </property>
</configuration>
```

Step 8: Configuring yarn-site.xml

Two properties (that is, `yarn.nodemanager.aux-services` and `yarn.nodemanager.aux-services.mapreduce.shuffle.class`) need to be set to the `etc/hadoop/yarn-site.xml` file. Just copy the following lines of codes:

```
<configuration>
<property>
    <name>yarn.nodemanager.aux-services</name>
    <value>mapreduce_shuffle</value>
 </property>
 <property>
    <name>yarn.nodemanager.aux-services.mapreduce.shuffle.class</name>
    <value>org.apache.hadoop.mapred.ShuffleHandler</value>
 </property>
</configuration>
```

Step 9: Setting Java heap space

To run your Spark job on Hadoop-based YARN cluster, you need to specify enough heap space for the JVM. You need to edit the `etc/hadoop/hadoop-env.sh` file. Enable the following properties:

```
HADOOP_HEAPSIZE="500"
HADOOP_NAMENODE_INIT_HEAPSIZE="500"
```

Now you also need to edit the `mapred-env.sh` file with the following line:

```
HADOOP_JOB_HISTORYSERVER_HEAPSIZE=250
```

Finally, make sure that you have edited `yarn-env.sh` to make the changes permanent for Hadoop YARN:

```
JAVA_HEAP_MAX=-Xmx500m
YARN_HEAPSIZE=500
```

Step 10: Formatting HDFS

If you want to start your HDFS NameNode, Hadoop needs to initialize the directory where it will store or persist its data for tracking all the metadata for your file system. The formatting will destroy everything and sets up a new file system. Then it uses the values of the parameters set on `dfs.namenode.name.dir` in `etc/hadoop/hdfs-site.xml`. For doing the format, at first, move to the `bin` directory and execute the following commands:

```
$ su - hdfs
$ cd /opt/yarn/hadoop-2.7.3/bin
$ ./hdfs namenode -format
```

If the preceding command executed successfully, you should see the following on your Ubuntu terminal:

```
INFO common.Storage: Storage directory /var/data/hadoop/hdfs/nn has
been successfully formatted
```

Step 11: Starting the HDFS

From the `bin` directory in step 10, execute the following command:

```
$ cd ../sbin
$ ./hadoop-daemon.sh start namenode
```

Upon successful execution of the preceding command, you should see the following on your terminal:

```
starting namenode, logging to /opt/yarn/hadoop-2.7.3/logs/hadoop-hdfs-
namenode-limulus.out
```

To start the `secondarynamenode` and the `datanode`, you should use the following command:

```
$ ./hadoop-daemon.sh start secondarynamenode
```

You should receive the following message on your terminal if the preceding commands succeed:

Starting secondarynamenode, logging to /opt/yarn/hadoop-2.7.3/logs/hadoop-hdfs-secondarynamenode-limulus.out

Then use the following command to start the data node:

```
$ ./hadoop-daemon.sh start datanode
```

You should receive the following message on your terminal if the preceding commands succeed:

starting datanode, logging to /opt/yarn/hadoop-2.7.3/logs/hadoop-hdfs-datanode-limulus.out

Now make sure that, you check all the services related to those nodes are running use the following command:

```
$ jps
```

You should observe something like the following:

```
35180 SecondaryNameNode
45915 NameNode
656335 Jps
75814 DataNode
```

Step 12: Starting YARN

For working with YARN, one `resourcemanager` and one node manager have to be started as the user yarn:

```
$  su - yarn
$ cd /opt/yarn/hadoop-2.7.3/sbin
$ ./yarn-daemon.sh start resourcemanager
```

You should receive the following message on your terminal if the preceding commands succeed:

> **starting resourcemanager, logging to /opt/yarn/hadoop-2.7.3/logs/yarn-yarn-resourcemanager-limulus.out**

Tehn execute the following command to start the node manager:

```
$ ./yarn-daemon.sh start nodemanager
```

You should receive the following message on your terminal if the preceding commands succeed:

```
starting nodemanager, logging to /opt/yarn/hadoop-2.7.3/logs/yarn-
yarn-nodemanager-limulus.out
```

If you want to make sure that every services in those nodes are running, you should use the `$jsp` command. Moreover, if you want to stop your resource manager or `nodemanager,` use the following g commands:

```
$ ./yarn-daemon.sh stop nodemanager
$ ./yarn-daemon.sh stop resourcemanager
```

Step 13: Verifying on the web UI

Access `http://localhost:50070` to view the status of the NameNode, and access `http://localhost:8088` for the resource manager on your browser.

The preceding steps show how to configure a Hadoop-based YARN cluster with only a few nodes. However, if you want to configure your Hadoop-based YARN clusters ranging from a few nodes to extremely large clusters with thousands of nodes, refer to `https://hadoop.apache.org/docs/current/hadoop-project-dist/hadoop-common/ClusterSetup.html`.

Submitting Spark jobs on YARN cluster

Now that our YARN cluster with the minimum requirement (for executing a small Spark job to be frank) is ready, to launch a Spark application in a cluster mode of YARN, you can use the following submit command:

```
$ SPARK_HOME/bin/spark-submit --classpath.to.your.Class --master yarn
--deploy-mode cluster [options] <app jar> [app options]
```

For running our `KMeansDemo`, it should be done like this:

```
$ SPARK_HOME/bin/spark-submit
    --class "com.chapter15.Clustering.KMeansDemo"
    --master yarn
    --deploy-mode cluster
    --driver-memory 16g
    --executor-memory 4g
    --executor-cores 4
    --queue the_queue
    KMeans-0.0.1-SNAPSHOT-jar-with-dependencies.jar
    Saratoga_NY_Homes.txt
```

The preceding `submit` command starts a YARN cluster mode with the default application master. Then `KMeansDemo` will be running as a child thread of the application master. For the status updates and for displaying them in the console, the client will periodically poll the application master. When your application (that is, `KMeansDemo` in our case) has finished its execution, the client will be exited.

 Upon submission of your job, you might want to see the progress using the Spark web UI or Spark history server. Moreover, you should refer to `Chapter 18`, *Testing and Debugging Spark*) to know how to analyze driver and executor logs.

To launch a Spark application in a client mode, you should use the earlier command, except that you will have to replace the cluster with the client. For those who want to work with Spark shell, use the following in client mode:

```
$ SPARK_HOME/bin/spark-shell --master yarn --deploy-mode client
```

Advance job submissions in a YARN cluster

If you opt for the more advanced way of submitting Spark jobs to be computed in your YARN cluster, you can specify additional parameters. For example, if you want to enable the dynamic resource allocation, make the `spark.dynamicAllocation.enabled` parameter true. However, to do so, you also need to specify `minExecutors`, `maxExecutors`, and `initialExecutors` as explained in the following. On the other hand, if you want to enable the shuffling service, set `spark.shuffle.service.enabled` as `true`. Finally, you could also try specifying how many executor instances will be running using the `spark.executor.instances` parameter.

Now, to make the preceding discussion more concrete, you can refer to the following submission command:

```
$ SPARK_HOME/bin/spark-submit
    --class "com.chapter13.Clustering.KMeansDemo"
    --master yarn
    --deploy-mode cluster
    --driver-memory 16g
    --executor-memory 4g
    --executor-cores 4
    --queue the_queue
    --conf spark.dynamicAllocation.enabled=true
    --conf spark.shuffle.service.enabled=true
    --conf spark.dynamicAllocation.minExecutors=1
    --conf spark.dynamicAllocation.maxExecutors=4
    --conf spark.dynamicAllocation.initialExecutors=4
    --conf spark.executor.instances=4
    KMeans-0.0.1-SNAPSHOT-jar-with-dependencies.jar
    Saratoga_NY_Homes.txt
```

However, the consequence of the preceding job submission script is complex and sometimes nondeterministic. From my previous experience, if you increase the number of partitions from code and the number of executors, then the app will finish faster, which is okay. But if you increase only the executor-cores, the finish time is the same. However, you might expect the time to be lower than initial time. Second, if you launch the preceding code twice, you might expect both jobs to finish in say 60 seconds, but this also might not happen. Often, both jobs might finish after 120 seconds instead. This is a bit weird, isn't it? However, here goes the explanation that would help you understand this scenario.

Suppose you have 16 cores and 8 GB memory on your machine. Now, if you use four executors with one core each, what will happen? Well, when you use an executor, Spark reserves it from YARN and YARN allocates the number of cores (for example, one in our case) and the memory required. The memory is required more than you asked for actually for faster processing. If you ask for 1 GB, it will, in fact, allocate almost 1.5 GB with 500 MB overhead. In addition, it will probably allocate an executor for the driver with probably 1024 MB memory usage (that is, 1 GB).

Sometimes, it doesn't matter how much memory your Spark job wants but how much it reserves. In the preceding example, it will not take 50 MB of the test but around 1.5 GB (including the overhead) per executor. We will discuss how to configure Spark cluster on AWS later this chapter.

Apache Mesos

The Mesos master usually replaces the Spark master as the cluster manager (aka the resource manager) when using Mesos. Now, when a driver program creates a Spark job and starts assigning the related tasks for scheduling, Mesos determines which computing nodes handle which tasks. We assume that you have already configured and installed Mesos on your machine.

 To get started, following links may be helpful to install Mesos on your machine. `http://blog.madhukaraphatak.com/mesos-single-node-setup-ubuntu/`, `https://mesos.apache.org/gettingstarted/`.

Depending upon hardware configuration, it takes a while. On my machine (Ubuntu 14.04 64-bit, with Core i7 and 32 GB of RAM), it took 1 hour to complete the build.

To submit and compute your Spark jobs by utilizing the Mesos cluster mode, make sure to check that the Spark binary packages are available in a place accessible by Mesos. Additionally, make sure that your Spark driver program can be configured in such a way that it is automatically connected to Mesos. The second option is installing Spark in the same location as the Mesos slave nodes. Then, you will have to configure the `spark.mesos.executor.home` parameter to point the location of Spark distribution. It is to be noted that the default location that could point is the `SPARK_HOME`.

When Mesos executes a Spark job on a Mesos worker node (aka computing node) for the first time, the Spark binary packages have to be available on that worker node. This will ensure that the Spark Mesos executor is running in the backend.

 The Spark binary packages can be hosted to Hadoop to make them accessible:
1. Having the URIs/URLs (including HTTP) via `http://`,
2. Using the Amazon S3 via `s3n://`,
3. Using the HDFS via `hdfs://`.
If you set the `HADOOP_CONF_DIR` environment variable, the parameter is usually set as `hdfs://...`; otherwise `file://`.

You can specify the Master URLs for Mesos as follows:

1. `mesos://host:5050` for a single-master Mesos cluster, and `mesos://zk://host1:2181,host2:2181,host3:2181/mesos` for a multimaster Mesos cluster controlled by the ZooKeeper.

For a more detailed discussion, please refer to `http://spark.apache.org/docs/latest/running-on-mesos.html`.

Client mode

In this mode, the Mesos framework works in such a way that the Spark job is launched on the client machine directly. It then waits for the computed results, also called the driver output. To interact properly with the Mesos, the driver, however, expects that there are some application-specific configurations specified in `SPARK_HOME/conf/spark-env.sh`. To make this happened, modify the `spark-env.sh.template` file at `$SPARK_HOME /conf`, and before using this client mode, in your `spark-env.sh`, set the following environment variables:

```
$ export MESOS_NATIVE_JAVA_LIBRARY=<path to libmesos.so>
```

This path is typically `/usr/local /lib/libmesos.so` on Ubuntu. On the other hand, on macOS X, the same library is called `libmesos.dylib` instead of `libmesos.so`:

```
$ export SPARK_EXECUTOR_URI=<URL of spark-2.1.0.tar.gz uploaded above>
```

Now, when submitting and starting a Spark application to be executed on the cluster, you will have to pass the Mesos `:// HOST:PORT` as the master URL. This is usually done while creating the `SparkContext` in your Spark application development as follows:

```
val conf = new SparkConf()
                .setMaster("mesos://HOST:5050")
                .setAppName("My app")
            .set("spark.executor.uri", "<path to
spark-2.1.0.tar.gz uploaded above>")
val sc = new SparkContext(conf)
```

The second option of doing so is using the `spark-submit` script and configure `spark.executor.uri` in the `SPARK_HOME/conf/spark-defaults.conf` file. When running a shell, the `spark.executor.uri` parameter is inherited from `SPARK_EXECUTOR_URI`, so it does not need to be redundantly passed in as a system property. Just use the following command to access the client mode from your Spark shell:

```
$ SPARK_HOME/bin/spark-shell --master mesos://host:5050
```

Cluster mode

Spark on Mesos also supports cluster mode. If the driver is already launched Spark job (on a cluster) and the computation is also finished, client can access the result (of driver) from the Mesos Web UI. If you have started MesosClusterDispatcher in your cluster through the SPARK_HOME/sbin/start-mesos-dispatcher.sh script, you can use the cluster mode.

Again, the condition is that you have to pass the Mesos master URL (for example, mesos://host:5050) while creating the SparkContext in your Spark application. Starting the Mesos in the cluster mode also starts the MesosClusterDispatcher as a daemon running on your host machine.

To gain a more flexible and advanced execution of your Spark jobs, you can also use the **Marathon**. The advantageous thing about using the Marathon is that you can run the MesosClusterDispatcher with Marathon. If you do that, make sure that the MesosClusterDispatcher is running in the foreground.

Marathon is a framework for Mesos that is designed to launch long-running applications, and in Mesosphere, it serves as a replacement for a traditional init system. It has many features that simplify running applications in a clustered environment, such as high-availability, node constraints, application health checks, an API for scriptability and service discovery, and an easy-to-use web user interface. It adds its scaling and self-healing capabilities to the Mesosphere feature set. Marathon can be used to start other Mesos frameworks, and it can also launch any process that can be started in the regular shell. As it is designed for long-running applications, it will ensure that applications it has launched will continue running, even if the slave node(s) they are running on fails. For more information on using Marathon with the Mesosphere, refer to the GitHub page at https://github.com/mesosphere/marathon.

To be more specific, from the client, you can submit a Spark job to your Mesos cluster by using the spark-submit script and specifying the master URL to the URL of the MesosClusterDispatcher (for example, mesos://dispatcher:7077). It goes as follows:

```
$ SPARK_HOME /bin/spark-class
org.apache.spark.deploy.mesos.MesosClusterDispatcher
```

You can view driver statuses on the Spark cluster web UI. For example, use the following job submission command for doing so:

```
$ SPARK_HOME/bin/spark-submit
--class com.chapter13.Clustering.KMeansDemo
--master mesos://207.184.161.138:7077
--deploy-mode cluster
--supervise
--executor-memory 20G
--total-executor-cores 100
KMeans-0.0.1-SNAPSHOT-jar-with-dependencies.jar
Saratoga_NY_Homes.txt
```

Note that JARS or Python files that are passed to Spark-submit should be URIs reachable by Mesos slaves, as the Spark driver doesn't automatically upload local jars. Finally, Spark can run over Mesos in two modes: *coarse-grained* (default) and *fine-grained* (deprecated). For more details, please refer to http://spark.apache.org/docs/latest/running-on-mesos.html.

In a cluster mode, the Spark driver runs on a different machine, that is, driver, master, and computing nodes are different machines. Therefore, if you try adding JARS using `SparkContext.addJar`, this will not work. To avoid this issue, make sure that the jar files on the client are also available to `SparkContext.addJar`, using the `--jars` option in the launch command:

```
$ SPARK_HOME/bin/spark-submit --class my.main.Class
    --master yarn
    --deploy-mode cluster
    --jars my-other-jar.jar, my-other-other-jar.jar
    my-main-jar.jar
    app_arg1 app_arg2
```

Deploying on AWS

In the previous section, we illustrated how to submit spark jobs in local, standalone, or deploy mode (YARN and Mesos). Here, we are going to show how to run spark application in real cluster mode on AWS EC2. To make our application running on spark cluster mode and for better scalability, we consider the **Amazon Elastic Compute Cloud (EC2)** services as IaaS or **Platform as a Service (PaaS)**. For pricing and related information, please refer to https://aws.amazon.com/ec2/pricing/.

Step 1: Key pair and access key configuration

We assume that you have EC2 accounts already created. Well! The first requirement is to create EC2 key pairs and AWS access keys. The EC2 key pair is the private key that you need when you will make a secure connection through SSH to your EC2 server or instances. For making the key, you have to go through AWS console at `http://docs.aws.amazon.com/AWSEC2/latest/UserGuide/ec2-key-pairs.html#having-ec2-create-your-key-pair`. Please refer to the following figure that shows the key-pair creation page for an EC2 account:

Figure 17: AWS key-pair generation window

Name it `aws_key_pair.pem` once you have downloaded it and save it on your local machine. Then ensure the permission by executing the following command (you should store this file in a secure location for security purpose, say `/usr/local/key`):

```
$ sudo chmod 400 /usr/local/key/aws_key_pair.pem
```

Now what you need are the AWS access keys and the credentials of your account. These are needed if you want to submit your Spark job to computing nodes from your local machine using the `spark-ec2` script. To generate and download the keys, login to your AWS IAM services at `http://docs.aws.amazon.com/IAM/latest/UserGuide/id_credentials_access-keys.html#Using_CreateAccessKey`.

Upon the completion of download (that is, `/usr/local/key`), you need to set two environment variables in your local machine. Just execute following commands:

```
$ echo "export AWS_ACCESS_KEY_ID=<access_key_id>" >> ~/.bashrc
$ echo " export AWS_SECRET_ACCESS_KEY=<secret_access_key_id>" >>
~/.bashrc
$ source ~/.bashrc
```

Step 2: Configuring Spark cluster on EC2

Up to Spark 1.6.3 release, Spark distribution (that is, `/SPARK_HOME/ec2`) provides a shell script called **spark-ec2** for launching Spark Cluster in EC2 instances from your local machine. This eventually helps in launching, managing, and shutting down the Spark Cluster that you will be using on AWS. However, since Spark 2.x, the same script was moved to AMPLab so that it would be easier to fix bugs and maintain the script itself separately.

The script can be accessed and used from the GitHub repo at `https://github.com/amplab/spark-ec2`.

Starting and using a cluster on AWS will cost money. Therefore, it is always a good practice to stop or destroy a cluster when the computation is done. Otherwise, it will incur additional cost to you. For more about AWS pricing, please refer to `https://aws.amazon.com/ec2/pricing/`.

You also need to create an IAM Instance profile for your Amazon EC2 instances (Console). For details, refer to `http://docs.aws.amazon.com/codedeploy/latest/userguide/getting-started-create-iam-instance-profile.html`. For simplicity, let's download the script and place it under a directory `ec2` in Spark home (`$SPARK_HOME/ec2`). Once you execute the following command to launch a new instance, it sets up Spark, HDFS, and other dependencies on the cluster automatically:

```
$ SPARK_HOME/spark-ec2
--key-pair=<name_of_the_key_pair>
--identity-file=<path_of_the key_pair>
--instance-type=<AWS_instance_type >
--region=<region> zone=<zone>
--slaves=<number_of_slaves>
--hadoop-major-version=<Hadoop_version>
--spark-version=<spark_version>
--instance-profile-name=<profile_name>
launch <cluster-name>
```

We believe that these parameters are self-explanatory. Alternatively, for more details, please refer to https://github.com/amplab/spark-ec2#readme.

If you already have a Hadoop cluster and want to deploy spark on it: If you are using Hadoop-YARN (or even Apache Mesos), running a spark job is relatively easier. Even if you don't use either, Spark can run in standalone mode. Spark runs a driver program, which, in turn, invokes spark executors. This means that you need to tell Spark the nodes where you want your spark daemons to run (in terms of master/slave). In your spark/conf directory, you can see a file slaves. Update it to mention all the machines you want to use. You can set up spark from source or use a binary from the website. You always should use the **Fully Qualified Domain Names (FQDN)** for all your nodes, and make sure that each of those machines are passwordless SSH accessible from your master node.

Suppose that you have already created and configured an instance profile. Now you are ready to launch the EC2 cluster. For our case, it would be something like the following:

```
$ SPARK_HOME/spark-ec2
  --key-pair=aws_key_pair
  --identity-file=/usr/local/aws_key_pair.pem
  --instance-type=m3.2xlarge
--region=eu-west-1 --zone=eu-west-1a --slaves=2
--hadoop-major-version=yarn
--spark-version=2.1.0
--instance-profile-name=rezacsedu_aws
launch ec2-spark-cluster-1
```

The following figure shows your Spark home on AWS:

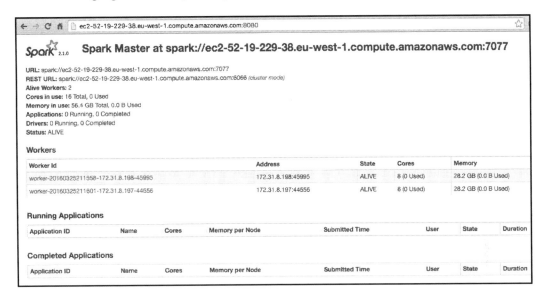

Figure 18: Cluster home on AWS

After the successful completion, spark cluster will be instantiated with two workers (slaves) nodes on your EC2 account. This task, however, sometimes might take half an hour approximately, depending on your Internet speed and hardware configuration. Therefore, you'd love to have a coffee break. Upon successful competition of the cluster setup, you will get the URL of the Spark cluster on the terminal. To make sure if the cluster is really running, check `https://<master-hostname>:8080` on your browser, where the `master-hostname` is the URL you receive on the terminal. If every think was okay, you will find your cluster running; see cluster home in **Figure 18**.

Step 3: Running Spark jobs on the AWS cluster

Now you master and worker nodes are active and running. This means that you can submit your Spark job to them for computing. However, before that, you need to log in the remote nodes using SSH. For doing so, execute the following command to SSH remote Spark cluster:

```
$ SPARK_HOME/spark-ec2
--key-pair=<name_of_the_key_pair>
--identity-file=<path_of_the _key_pair>
--region=<region>
--zone=<zone>
login <cluster-name>
```

For our case, it should be something like the following:

```
$ SPARK_HOME/spark-ec2
--key-pair=my-key-pair
--identity-file=/usr/local/key/aws-key-pair.pem
--region=eu-west-1
--zone=eu-west-1
login ec2-spark-cluster-1
```

Now copy your application, that is, JAR file (or python/R script) to the remote instance (that is, `ec2-52-48-119-121.eu-west-1.compute.amazonaws.com` in our case) by executing the following command (in a new terminal):

```
$ scp -i /usr/local/key/aws-key-pair.pem /usr/local/code/KMeans-0.0.1-
SNAPSHOT-jar-with-dependencies.jar ec2-user@ec2-52-18-252-59.eu-
west-1.compute.amazonaws.com:/home/ec2-user/
```

Then you need to copy your data (`/usr/local/data/Saratoga_NY_Homes.txt`, in our case) to the same remote instance by executing the following command:

```
$ scp -i /usr/local/key/aws-key-pair.pem
/usr/local/data/Saratoga_NY_Homes.txt ec2-user@ec2-52-18-252-59.eu-
west-1.compute.amazonaws.com:/home/ec2-user/
```

 Note that if you have already configured HDFS on your remote machine and put your code/data file, you don't need to copy the JAR and data files to the slaves; the master will do it automatically.

Well done! You are almost done! Now, finally, you will have to submit your Spark job to be computed by the slaves or worker nodes. To do so, just execute the following commands:

```
$SPARK_HOME/bin/spark-submit
  --class com.chapter13.Clustering.KMeansDemo
--master spark://ec2-52-48-119-121.eu-
west-1.compute.amazonaws.com:7077
file:///home/ec2-user/KMeans-0.0.1-SNAPSHOT-jar-with-dependencies.jar
file:///home/ec2-user/Saratoga_NY_Homes.txt
```

 Place your input file under `file:///input.txt` if HDFS is not set on your machine.

If you have already put your data on HDFS, you should issue the submit command something like following:

```
$SPARK_HOME/bin/spark-submit
  --class com.chapter13.Clustering.KMeansDemo
--master spark://ec2-52-48-119-121.eu-
west-1.compute.amazonaws.com:7077
hdfs://localhost:9000/KMeans-0.0.1-SNAPSHOT-jar-with-dependencies.jar
hdfs://localhost:9000//Saratoga_NY_Homes.txt
```

Upon successful completion of the job computation, you are supposed to see the status and related statistics of your job at port 8080.

Step 4: Pausing, restarting, and terminating the Spark cluster

When your computation is done, it is better to stop your cluster to avoid additional cost. To stop your clusters, execute the following commands from your local machine:

```
$ SPARK_HOME/ec2/spark-ec2 --region=<ec2-region> stop <cluster-name>
```

For our case, it would be the following:

```
$ SPARK_HOME/ec2/spark-ec2 --region=eu-west-1 stop ec2-spark-cluster-1
```

To restart the cluster later on, execute the following command:

```
$ SPARK_HOME/ec2/spark-ec2 -i <key-file> --region=<ec2-region> start
<cluster-name>
```

For our case, it will be something like the following:

```
$ SPARK_HOME/ec2/spark-ec2 --identity-file=/usr/local/key/-key-
pair.pem --region=eu-west-1 start ec2-spark-cluster-1
```

Finally, to terminate your Spark cluster on AWS we use the following code:

```
$ SPARK_HOME/ec2/spark-ec2 destroy <cluster-name>
```

In our case, it would be the following:

```
$ SPARK_HOME /spark-ec2 --region=eu-west-1 destroy ec2-spark-cluster-1
```

Spot instances are great for reducing AWS costs, sometimes cutting instance costs by a whole order of magnitude. A step-by-step guideline using this facility can be accessed at `http://blog.insightdatalabs.com/spark-cluster-step-by-step/`.

Sometimes, it's difficult to move large dataset, say 1 TB of raw data file. In that case, and if you want your application to scale up even more for large-scale datasets, the fastest way of doing so is loading them from Amazon S3 or EBS device to HDFS on your nodes and specifying the data file path using `hdfs://`.

The data files or any other files (data, jars, scripts, and so on) can be hosted on HDFS to make them highly accessible:
1. Having the URIs/URLs (including HTTP) via `http://`
2. Using the Amazon S3 via `s3n://`
3. Using the HDFS via `hdfs://`
If you set `HADOOP_CONF_DIR` environment variable, the parameter is usually set as `hdfs://...`; otherwise `file://`.

Summary

In this chapter, we discussed how Spark works in a cluster mode with its underlying architecture. You also saw how to deploy a full Spark application on a cluster. You saw how to deploy cluster for running Spark application in different cluster modes such as local, standalone, YARN, and Mesos. Finally, you saw how to configure Spark cluster on AWS using EC2 script. We believe that this chapter will help you to gain some good understanding of Spark. Nevertheless, due to page limitation, we could not cover many APIs and their underlying functionalities.

If you face any issues, please don't forget to report this to Spark user mailing list at `user@spark.apache.org`. Before doing so, make sure that you have subscribed to it. In the next chapter, you will see how to test and debug Spark applications.

Testing and Debugging Spark 17

"Everyone knows that debugging is twice as hard as writing a program in the first place. So if you're as clever as you can be when you write it, how will you ever debug it?"

- Brian W. Kernighan

In an ideal world, we write perfect Spark codes and everything runs perfectly all the time, right? Just kidding; in practice, we know that working with large-scale datasets is hardly ever that easy, and there are inevitably some data points that will expose any corner cases with your code.

Considering the aforementioned challenges, therefore, in this chapter, we will see how difficult it can be to test an application if it is distributed; then, we will see some ways to tackle this. In a nutshell, the following topics will be cover throughout this chapter:

- Testing in a distributed environment
- Testing Spark application
- Debugging Spark application

Testing in a distributed environment

Leslie Lamport defined the term distributed system as follows:

"A distributed system is one in which I cannot get any work done because some machine I have never heard of has crashed."

Resource sharing through **World Wide Web** (aka **WWW**), a network of connected computers (aka a cluster), is a good example of distributed systems. These distributed environments are often complex and lots of heterogeneity occurs frequently. Testing in these kinds of the heterogeneous environments is also challenging. In this section, at first, we will observe some commons issues that are often raised while working with such system.

Distributed environment

There are numerous definitions of distributed systems. Let's see some definition and then we will try to correlate the aforementioned categories afterward. Coulouris defines a distributed system as *a system in which hardware or software components located at networked computers communicate and coordinate their actions only by message passing.* On the other hand, Tanenbaum defines the term in several ways:

- *A collection of independent computers that appear to the users of the system as a single computer.*
- *A system that consists of a collection of two or more independent Computers which coordinate their processing through the exchange of synchronous or asynchronous message passing.*
- *A distributed system is a collection of autonomous computers linked by a network with software designed to produce an integrated computing facility.*

Now, based on the preceding definition, distributed systems can be categorized as follows:

- Only hardware and software are distributed:The local distributed system is connected through LAN.
- Users are distributed, but there are computing and hardware resources that are running backend, for example, WWW.
- Both users and hardware/software are distributed: Distributed computing cluster that is connected through WAN. For example, you can get these types of computing facilities while using Amazon AWS, Microsoft Azure, Google Cloud, or Digital Ocean's droplets.

Issues in a distributed system

Here we will discuss some major issues that need to be taken care of during the software and hardware testing so that Spark jobs run smoothly in cluster computing, which is essentially a distributed computing environment.

Note that all the issues are unavoidable, but we can at least tune them for betterment. You should follow the instructions and recommendations given in the previous chapter. According to *Kamal Sheel Mishra* and *Anil Kumar Tripathi, Some Issues, Challenges and Problems of Distributed Software System,* in *International Journal of Computer Science and Information Technologies*, Vol. 5 (4), 2014, 4922-4925. URL: https:/ /pdfs.semanticscholar.org/4c6d/c4d739bad13bcd0398e5180c1513f18275d8.pdf, there are several issues that need to be addressed while working with software or hardware in a distributed environment:

- Scalability
- Heterogeneous languages, platform, and architecture
- Resource management
- Security and privacy
- Transparency
- Openness
- Interoperability
- Quality of service
- Failure management
- Synchronization
- Communications
- Software architectures
- Performance analysis
- Generating test data
- Component selection for testing
- Test sequence
- Testing for system scalability and performance
- Availability of source code
- Reproducibility of events
- Deadlocks and race conditions
- Testing for fault tolerance
- Scheduling issue for distributed system
- Distributed task allocation
- Testing distributed software
- Monitoring and control mechanism from the hardware abstraction level

It's true that we cannot fully solve all of these issues, but However, using Spark, we can at least control a few of them that are related to distributed system. For example, scalability, resource management, quality of service, failure management, synchronization, communications, scheduling issue for distributed system, distributed task allocation, and monitoring and control mechanism in testing distributed software. Most of them were discussed in the previous two chapters. On the other hand, we can address some issues in the testing and software side: such as software architectures, performance analysis, generating test data, component selection for testing, test sequence, testing for system scalability and performance, and availability of source code. These will be covered explicitly or implicitly in this chapter at least.

Challenges of software testing in a distributed environment

There are some common challenges associated with the tasks in an agile software development, and those challenges become more complex while testing the software in a distributed environment before deploying them eventually. Often team members need to merge the software components in parallel after the bugs proliferating. However, based on urgency, often the merging occurs before testing phase. Sometimes, many stakeholders are distributed across teams. Therefore, there's a huge potential for misunderstanding and teams often lose in between.

For example, Cloud Foundry (`https://www.cloudfoundry.org/`) is an open source heavily distributed PaaS software system for managing deployment and scalability of applications in the Cloud. It promises different features such as scalability, reliability, and elasticity that come inherently to deployments on Cloud Foundry require the underlying distributed system to implement measures to ensure robustness, resiliency, and failover.

The process of software testing is long known to comprise *unit testing, integration testing, smoke testing, acceptance testing, scalability testing, performance testing,* and *quality of service testing*. In Cloud Foundry, the process of testing a distributed system is shown in the following figure:

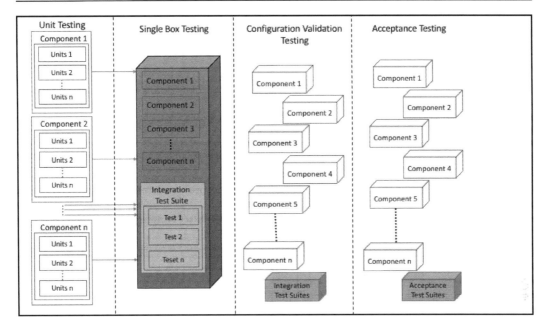

Figure 1: An example of software testing in a distributed environment like Cloud

As shown in the preceding figure (first column), the process of testing in a distributed environment like Cloud starts with running unit tests against the smallest points of contract in the system. Following successful execution of all the unit tests, integration tests are run to validate the behavior of interacting components as part of a single coherent software system (second column) running on a single box (for example, a **Virtual Machine** (**VM**) or bare metal). However, while these tests validate the overall behavior of the system as a monolith, they do not guarantee system validity in a distributed deployment. Once integration tests pass, the next step (third column) is to validate distributed deployment of the system and run the smoke tests.

As you know, that the successful configuration of the software and execution of unit tests prepares us to validate acceptability of system behavior. This verification is done by running acceptance tests (fourth column). Now, to overcome the aforementioned issues and challenges in distributed environments, there are also other hidden challenges that need to be solved by researchers and big data engineers, but those are actually out of the scope of this book.

Now that we know what real challenges are for the software testing in a distributed environment, now let's start testing our Spark code a bit. The next section is dedicated to testing Spark applications.

Testing Spark applications

There are many ways to try to test your Spark code, depending on whether it's Java (you can do basic JUnit tests to test non-Spark pieces) or ScalaTest for your Scala code. You can also do full integration tests by running Spark locally or on a small test cluster. Another awesome choice from Holden Karau is using Spark-testing base. You probably know that there is no native library for unit testing in Spark as of yet. Nevertheless, we can have the following two alternatives to use two libraries:

- ScalaTest
- Spark-testing base

However, before starting to test your Spark applications written in Scala, some background knowledge about unit testing and testing Scala methods is a mandate.

Testing Scala methods

Here, we will see some simple techniques for testing Scala methods. For Scala users, this is the most familiar unit testing framework (you can also use it for testing Java code and soon for JavaScript). ScalaTest supports a number of different testing styles, each designed to support a specific type of testing need. For details, see ScalaTest User Guide at http://www.scalatest.org/user_guide/selecting_a_style. Although ScalaTest supports many styles, one of the quickest ways to get started is to use the following ScalaTest traits and write the tests in the **TDD** (**test-driven development**) style:

1. FunSuite
2. Assertions
3. BeforeAndAfter

Feel free to browse the preceding URLs to learn more about these traits; that will make rest of this tutorial go smoothly.

It is to be noted that the TDD is a programming technique to develop software, and it states that you should start development from tests. Hence, it doesn't affect how tests are written, but when tests are written. There is no trait or testing style to enforce or encourage TDD in ScalaTest.FunSuite, Assertions, and BeforeAndAfter are only more similar to the xUnit testing frameworks.

There are three assertions available in the ScalaTest in any style trait:

- `assert`: This is used for general assertions in your Scala program.
- `assertResult`: This helps differentiate expected value from the actual values.
- `assertThrows`: This is used to ensure a bit of code throws an expected exception.

The ScalaTest's assertions are defined in the trait `Assertions`, which is further extended by `Suite`. In brief, the `Suite` trait is the super trait for all the style traits. According to the ScalaTest documentation at `http://www.scalatest.org/user_guide/using_assertions`, the `Assertions` trait also provides the following features:

- `assume` to conditionally cancel a test
- `fail` to fail a test unconditionally
- `cancel` to cancel a test unconditionally
- `succeed` to make a test succeed unconditionally
- `intercept` to ensure a bit of code throws an expected exception and then make assertions about the exception
- `assertDoesNotCompile` to ensure a bit of code does not compile
- `assertCompiles` to ensure a bit of code does compile
- `assertTypeError` to ensure a bit of code does not compile because of a type (not parse) error
- `withClue` to add more information about a failure

From the preceding list, we will show a few of them. In your Scala program, you can write assertions by calling `assert` and passing a `Boolean` expression in. You can simply start writing your simple unit test case using `Assertions`. The `Predef` is an object, where this behavior of assert is defined. Note that all the members of the `Predef` get imported into your every Scala source file. The following source code will print `Assertion success` for the following case:

```
package com.chapter16.SparkTesting
object SimpleScalaTest {
  def main(args: Array[String]):Unit= {
    val a = 5
    val b = 5
    assert(a == b)
      println("Assertion success")
  }
}
```

However, if you make a = 2 and b = 1, for example, the assertion will fail and you will experience the following output:

```
Exception in thread "main" java.lang.AssertionError: assertion failed
    at scala.Predef$.assert(Predef.scala:156)
    at com.chapter16.SparkTesting.SimpleScalaTest$.main(SimpleScalaTest.scala:7)
    at com.chapter16.SparkTesting.SimpleScalaTest.main(SimpleScalaTest.scala)
```

Figure 2: An example of assertion fail

If you pass a true expression, assert will return normally. However, assert will terminate abruptly with an Assertion Error if the supplied expression is false. Unlike the `AssertionError` and `TestFailedException` forms, the ScalaTest's assert provides more information that will tell you exactly in which line the test case failed or for which expression. Therefore, ScalaTest's assert provides better error messages than Scala's assert.

For example, for the following source code, you should experience `TestFailedException` that will tell that 5 did not equal 4:

```
package com.chapter16.SparkTesting
import org.scalatest.Assertions._
object SimpleScalaTest {
  def main(args: Array[String]):Unit= {
    val a = 5
    val b = 4
    assert(a == b)
      println("Assertion success")
  }
}
```

The following figure shows the output of the preceding Scala test:

```
Exception in thread "main" org.scalatest.exceptions.TestFailedException: 2 did not equal 1
    at org.scalatest.Assertions$class.newAssertionFailedException(Assertions.scala:500)
    at org.scalatest.Assertions$.newAssertionFailedException(Assertions.scala:1538)
    at org.scalatest.Assertions$AssertionsHelper.macroAssert(Assertions.scala:466)
    at com.chapter16.SparkTesting.SimpleScalaTest$.main(SimpleScalaTest.scala:8)
    at com.chapter16.SparkTesting.SimpleScalaTest.main(SimpleScalaTest.scala)
```

Figure 3: An example of TestFailedException

The following source code explains the use of the `assertResult` unit test to test the result of your method:

```
package com.chapter16.SparkTesting
import org.scalatest.Assertions._
object AssertResult {
  def main(args: Array[String]):Unit= {
    val x = 10
    val y = 6
    assertResult(3) {
      x - y
    }
  }
}
```

The preceding assertion will be failed and Scala will throw an exception `TestFailedException` **and prints** `Expected 3 but got 4` (*Figure 4*):

```
Exception in thread "main" org.scalatest.exceptions.TestFailedException: Expected 3, but got 4
    at org.scalatest.Assertions$class.newAssertionFailedException(Assertions.scala:495)
    at org.scalatest.Assertions$.newAssertionFailedException(Assertions.scala:1538)
    at org.scalatest.Assertions$class.assertResult(Assertions.scala:1226)
    at org.scalatest.Assertions$.assertResult(Assertions.scala:1538)
    at com.chapter16.SparkTesting.AssertResult$.main(AssertResult.scala:8)
    at com.chapter16.SparkTesting.AssertResult.main(AssertResult.scala)
```

Figure 4: Another example of TestFailedException

Now, let's see a unit testing to show expected exception:

```
package com.chapter16.SparkTesting
import org.scalatest.Assertions._
object ExpectedException {
  def main(args: Array[String]):Unit= {
    val s = "Hello world!"
    try {
      s.charAt(0)
      fail()
    } catch {
      case _: IndexOutOfBoundsException => // Expected, so continue
    }
  }
}
```

If you try to access an array element outside the index, the preceding code will tell you if you're allowed to access the first character of the preceding string `Hello world!`. If your Scala program can access the value in an index, the assertion will fail. This also means that the test case has failed. Thus, the preceding test case will fail naturally since the first index contains the character `H`, and you should experience the following error message (*Figure 5*):

```
Exception in thread "main" org.scalatest.exceptions.TestFailedException
    at org.scalatest.Assertions$class.newAssertionFailedException(Assertions.scala:493)
    at org.scalatest.Assertions$.newAssertionFailedException(Assertions.scala:1538)
    at org.scalatest.Assertions$class.fail(Assertions.scala:1313)
    at org.scalatest.Assertions$.fail(Assertions.scala:1538)
    at com.chapter16.SparkTesting.ExpectedException$.main(ExpectedException.scala:9)
    at com.chapter16.SparkTesting.ExpectedException.main(ExpectedException.scala)
```

Figure 5: Third example of TestFailedException

However, now let's try to access the index at position `-1` as follows:

```
package com.chapter16.SparkTesting
import org.scalatest.Assertions._
object ExpectedException {
  def main(args: Array[String]):Unit= {
    val s = "Hello world!"
    try {
      s.charAt(-1)
      fail()
    } catch {
      case _: IndexOutOfBoundsException => // Expected, so continue
    }
  }
}
```

Now the assertion should be true, and consequently, the test case will be passed. Finally, the code will terminate normally. Now, let's check our code snippets if it will compile or not. Very often, you may wish to ensure that a certain ordering of the code that represents emerging "user error" does not compile at all. The objective is to check the strength of the library against the error to disallow unwanted result and behavior. ScalaTest's `Assertions` trait includes the following syntax for that purpose:

```
assertDoesNotCompile("val a: String = 1")
```

If you want to ensure that a snippet of code does not compile because of a type error (as opposed to a syntax error), use the following:

```
assertTypeError("val a: String = 1")
```

A syntax error will still result on a thrown `TestFailedException`. Finally, if you want to state that a snippet of code does compile, you can make that more obvious with the following:

```
assertCompiles("val a: Int = 1")
```

A complete example is shown as follows:

```
package com.chapter16.SparkTesting
import org.scalatest.Assertions._
object CompileOrNot {
  def main(args: Array[String]):Unit= {
    assertDoesNotCompile("val a: String = 1")
    println("assertDoesNotCompile True")
    assertTypeError("val a: String = 1")
    println("assertTypeError True")
    assertCompiles("val a: Int = 1")
    println("assertCompiles True")
    assertDoesNotCompile("val a: Int = 1")
    println("assertDoesNotCompile True")
  }
}
```

The output of the preceding code is shown in the following figure:

```
AssertDoesNotCompile True
AssertTypeError True
AssertCompiles True
Exception in thread "main" org.scalatest.exceptions.TestFailedException: Expected a
compiler error, but got none for code: val a: Int = 1
    at com.chapter16.SparkTesting.CompileOrNot$.main(CompileOrNot.scala:15)
    at com.chapter16.SparkTesting.CompileOrNot.main(CompileOrNot.scala)
```

Figure 6: Multiple tests together

Now we would like to finish the Scala-based unit testing due to page limitation. However, for other unit test cases, you can refer the Scala test guideline at http:// www.scalatest.org/user_guide.

Unit testing

In software engineering, often, individual units of source code are tested to determine whether they are fit for use or not. This way of software testing method is also called the unit testing. This testing ensures that the source code developed by a software engineer or developer meets the design specifications and works as intended.

On the other hand, the goal of unit testing is to separate each part of the program (that is, in a modular way). Then try to observe if all the individual parts are working normally. There are several benefits of unit testing in any software system:

- **Find problems early:** It finds bugs or missing parts of the specification early in the development cycle.
- **Facilitates change:** It helps in refactoring and up gradation without worrying about breaking functionality.
- **Simplifies integration:** It makes integration tests easier to write.
- **Documentation:** It provides a living documentation of the system.
- **Design:** It can act as the formal design of the project.

Testing Spark applications

We have already seen how to test your Scala code using built-in `ScalaTest` package of Scala. However, in this subsection, we will see how we could test our Spark application written in Scala. The following three methods will be discussed:

- **Method 1:** Testing Spark applications using JUnit
- **Method 2:** Testing Spark applications using `ScalaTest` package
- **Method 3:** Testing Spark applications using Spark testing base

Methods 1 and 2 will be discussed here with some practical codes. However, a detailed discussion on method 3 will be provided in the next subsection. To keep the understanding easy and simple, we will use the famous word counting applications to demonstrate methods 1 and 2.

Method 1: Using Scala JUnit test

Suppose you have written an application in Scala that can tell you how many words are there in a document or text file as follows:

```scala
package com.chapter16.SparkTesting
import org.apache.spark._
import org.apache.spark.sql.SparkSession
class wordCounterTestDemo {
  val spark = SparkSession
    .builder
    .master("local[*]")
    .config("spark.sql.warehouse.dir", "E:/Exp/")
    .appName(s"OneVsRestExample")
    .getOrCreate()
  def myWordCounter(fileName: String): Long = {
    val input = spark.sparkContext.textFile(fileName)
    val counts = input.flatMap(_.split(" ")).distinct()
    val counter = counts.count()
    counter
  }
}
```

The preceding code simply parses a text file and performs a `flatMap` operation by simply splitting the words. Then, it performs another operation to take only the distinct words into consideration. Finally, the `myWordCounter` method counts how many words are there and returns the value of the counter.

Now, before proceeding into formal testing, let's check if the preceding method works well. Just add the main method and create an object as follows:

```scala
package com.chapter16.SparkTesting
import org.apache.spark._
import org.apache.spark.sql.SparkSession
object wordCounter {
  val spark = SparkSession
    .builder
    .master("local[*]")
    .config("spark.sql.warehouse.dir", "E:/Exp/")
    .appName("Testing")
    .getOrCreate()
  val fileName = "data/words.txt";
  def myWordCounter(fileName: String): Long = {
    val input = spark.sparkContext.textFile(fileName)
    val counts = input.flatMap(_.split(" ")).distinct()
    val counter = counts.count()
    counter
```

```
  }
  def main(args: Array[String]): Unit = {
    val counter = myWordCounter(fileName)
    println("Number of words: " + counter)
  }
}
```

If you execute the preceding code, you should observe the following output: `Number of words: 214`. Fantastic! It really works as a local application. Now, test the preceding test case using Scala JUnit test case.

```
package com.chapter16.SparkTesting
import org.scalatest.Assertions._
import org.junit.Test
import org.apache.spark.sql.SparkSession
class wordCountTest {
  val spark = SparkSession
    .builder
    .master("local[*]")
    .config("spark.sql.warehouse.dir", "E:/Exp/")
    .appName(s"OneVsRestExample")
    .getOrCreate()
    @Test def test() {
      val fileName = "data/words.txt"
      val obj = new wordCounterTestDemo()
      assert(obj.myWordCounter(fileName) == 214)
        }
    spark.stop()
}
```

If you see the earlier code carefully, I have used the `Test` annotation before the `test()` method. Inside the `test()` method, I invoked the `assert()` method, where the actual testing occurs. Here we tried to check if the return value of the `myWordCounter()` method is equal to 214. Now run the earlier code as a Scala Unit test as follows (*Figure 7*):

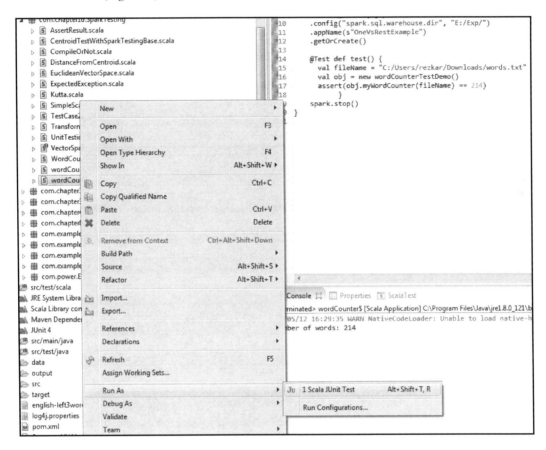

Figure 7: Running Scala code as Scala JUnit Test

Now if the test case passes, you should observe the following output on your Eclipse IDE (*Figure 8*):

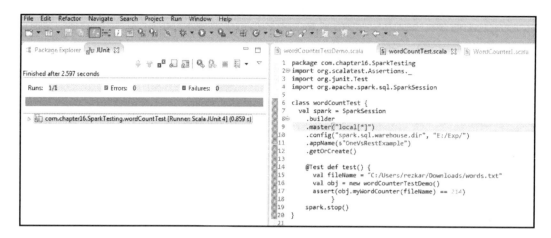

Figure 8: Word count test case passed

Now, for example, try to assert in the following way:

```
assert(obj.myWordCounter(fileName) == 210)
```

If the preceding test case fails, you should observe the following output (*Figure 9*):

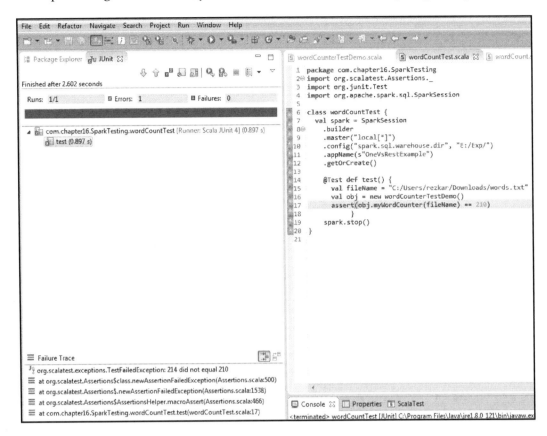

Figure 9: Test case failed

Now let's have a look at method 2 and how it helps us for the betterment.

Method 2: Testing Scala code using FunSuite

Now, let's redesign the preceding test case by returning only the RDD of the texts in the document, as follows:

```
package com.chapter16.SparkTesting
import org.apache.spark._
import org.apache.spark.rdd.RDD
import org.apache.spark.sql.SparkSession
class wordCountRDD {
  def prepareWordCountRDD(file: String, spark: SparkSession):
RDD[(String, Int)] = {
    val lines = spark.sparkContext.textFile(file)
    lines.flatMap(_.split(" ")).map((_, 1)).reduceByKey(_ + _)
  }
}
```

So, the `prepareWordCountRDD()` method in the preceding class returns an RDD of string and integer values. Now, if we want to test the `prepareWordCountRDD()` method's functionality, we can do it more explicit by extending the test class with `FunSuite` and `BeforeAndAfterAll` from the `ScalaTest` package of Scala. The testing works in the following ways:

- Extend the test class with `FunSuite` and `BeforeAndAfterAll` from the `ScalaTest` package of Scala
- Override the `beforeAll()` that creates Spark context
- Perform the test using the `test()` method and use the `assert()` method inside the `test()` method
- Override the `afterAll()` method that stops the Spark context

Based on the preceding steps, let's see a class for testing the preceding `prepareWordCountRDD()` method:

```
package com.chapter16.SparkTesting
import org.scalatest.{ BeforeAndAfterAll, FunSuite }
import org.scalatest.Assertions._
import org.apache.spark.sql.SparkSession
import org.apache.spark.rdd.RDD
class wordCountTest2 extends FunSuite with BeforeAndAfterAll {
  var spark: SparkSession = null
  def tokenize(line: RDD[String]) = {
    line.map(x => x.split(' ')).collect()
  }
  override def beforeAll() {
    spark = SparkSession
```

```
        .builder
        .master("local[*]")
        .config("spark.sql.warehouse.dir", "E:/Exp/")
        .appName(s"OneVsRestExample")
        .getOrCreate()
    }
  test("Test if two RDDs are equal") {
      val input = List("To be,", "or not to be:", "that is the question-
", "William Shakespeare")
      val expected = Array(Array("To", "be,"), Array("or", "not", "to",
"be:"), Array("that", "is", "the", "question-"), Array("William",
"Shakespeare"))
      val transformed = tokenize(spark.sparkContext.parallelize(input))
      assert(transformed === expected)
    }
  test("Test for word count RDD") {
      val fileName = "C:/Users/rezkar/Downloads/words.txt"
      val obj = new wordCountRDD
      val result = obj.prepareWordCountRDD(fileName, spark)
      assert(result.count() === 214)
    }
  override def afterAll() {
      spark.stop()
    }
  }
```

The first test says that if two RDDs materialize in two different ways, the contents should be the same. Thus, the first test should get passed. We will see this in following example. Now, for the second test, as we have seen previously, the word count of RDD is 214, but let's assume it unknown for a while. If it's 214 coincidentally, the test case should pass, which is its expected behavior.

Thus, we are expecting both tests to be passed. Now, on Eclipse, run the test suite as `ScalaTest-File`, as shown in the following figure:

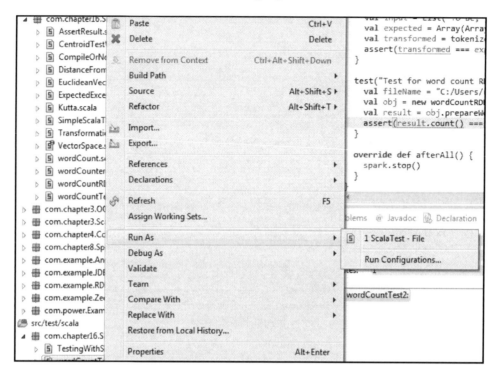

Figure 10: running the test suite as ScalaTest-File

Now you should observe the following output (*Figure 11*). The output shows how many test cases we performed and how many of them passed, failed, canceled, ignored, or were (was) in pending. It also shows the time to execute the overall test.

```
Problems @ Javadoc  Declaration  Console   ScalaTest
<terminated> wordCountTest2.scala [ScalaTest (java runner)] C:\Program Files\Java\jdk1.8.0_10
Run starting. Expected test count is: 2
wordCountTest2:
17/05/12 20:44:26 WARN NativeCodeLoader: Unable to load native-hadoop li
- Test if two RDDs are equal
- Test for word count RDD
Run completed in 2 seconds, 573 milliseconds.
Total number of tests run: 2
Suites: completed 1, aborted 0
Tests: succeeded 2, failed 0, canceled 0, ignored 0, pending 0
All tests passed.
```

Figure 11: Test result when running the two test suites as ScalaTest-file

Fantastic! The test case passed. Now, let's try changing the compare value in the assertion in the two separate tests using the `test()` method as follows:

```
test("Test for word count RDD") {
  val fileName = "data/words.txt"
  val obj = new wordCountRDD
  val result = obj.prepareWordCountRDD(fileName, spark)
  assert(result.count() === 210)
}
test("Test if two RDDs are equal") {
  val input = List("To be", "or not to be:", "that is the question-",
"William Shakespeare")
  val expected = Array(Array("To", "be,"), Array("or", "not", "to",
"be:"), Array("that", "is", "the", "question-"), Array("William",
"Shakespeare"))
  val transformed = tokenize(spark.sparkContext.parallelize(input))
  assert(transformed === expected)
}
```

Now, you should expect that the test case will be failed. Now run the earlier class as `ScalaTest-File` (*Figure 12*):

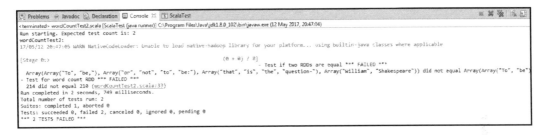

Figure 12: Test result when running the preceding two test suites as ScalaTest-File

Well done! We have learned how to perform the unit testing using Scala's FunSuite. However, if you evaluate the preceding method carefully, you should agree that there are several disadvantages. For example, you need to ensure an explicit management of `SparkContext` creation and destruction. As a developer or programmer, you have to write more lines of code for testing a sample method. Sometimes, code duplication occurs as the *Before* and the *After* step has to be repeated in all test suites. However, this is debatable since the common code could be put in a common trait.

Now the question is how could we improve our experience? My recommendation is using the Spark testing base to make life easier and more straightforward. We will discuss how we could perform the unit testing the Spark testing base.

Method 3: Making life easier with Spark testing base

Spark testing base helps you to test your most of the Spark codes with ease. So, what are the pros of this method then? There are many in fact. For example, using this the code is not verbose but we can get very succinct code. The API is itself richer than that of ScalaTest or JUnit. Multiple languages support, for example, Scala, Java, and Python. It has the support of built-in RDD comparators. You can also use it for testing streaming applications. And finally and most importantly, it supports both local and cluster mode testings. This is most important for the testing in a distributed environment.

 The GitHub repo is located at `https://github.com/holdenk/spark-testing-base`.

Before starting the unit testing with Spark testing base, you should include the following dependency in the Maven friendly `pom.xml` file in your project tree for Spark 2.x as follows:

```
<dependency>
  <groupId>com.holdenkarau</groupId>
  <artifactId>spark-testing-base_2.10</artifactId>
  <version>2.0.0_0.6.0</version>
</dependency>
```

For SBT, you can add the following dependency:

```
"com.holdenkarau" %% "spark-testing-base" % "2.0.0_0.6.0"
```

Note that it is recommended to add the preceding dependency in the `test` scope by specifying `<scope>test</scope>` for both the Maven and SBT cases. In addition to these, there are other considerations such as memory requirements and OOMs and disabling the parallel execution. The default Java options in the SBT testing are too small to support for running multiple tests. Sometimes it's harder to test Spark codes if the job is submitted in local mode! Now you can naturally understand how difficult it would be in a real cluster mode -i.e. YARN or Mesos.

To get rid of this problem, you can increase the amount of memory in your `build.sbt` file in your project tree. Just add the following parameters as follows:

```
javaOptions ++= Seq("-Xms512M", "-Xmx2048M", "-XX:MaxPermSize=2048M",
"-XX:+CMSClassUnloadingEnabled")
```

However, if you are using Surefire, you can add the following:

```
<argLine>-Xmx2048m -XX:MaxPermSize=2048m</argLine>
```

In your Maven-based build, you can make it by setting the value in the environmental variable. For more on this issue, refer to https://maven.apache.org/configure.html.

This is just an example to run spark testing base's own tests. Therefore, you might need to set bigger value. Finally, make sure that you have disabled the parallel execution in your SBT by adding the following line of code:

```
parallelExecution in Test := false
```

On the other hand, if you're using surefire, make sure that `forkCount` and `reuseForks` are set as 1 and true, respectively. Let's see an example of using Spark testing base. The following source code has three test cases. The first test case is the dummy that compares if 1 is equal to 1 or not, which obviously will be passed. The second test case counts the number of words from the sentence, say `Hello world!` `My name is Reza`, and compares if this has six words or not. The final and the last test case tries to compare two RDDs:

```
package com.chapter16.SparkTesting
import org.scalatest.Assertions._
import org.apache.spark.rdd.RDD
import com.holdenkarau.spark.testing.SharedSparkContext
import org.scalatest.FunSuite
class TransformationTestWithSparkTestingBase extends FunSuite with
SharedSparkContext {
  def tokenize(line: RDD[String]) = {
    line.map(x => x.split(' ')).collect()
  }
  test("works, obviously!") {
    assert(1 == 1)
  }
  test("Words counting") {
    assert(sc.parallelize("Hello world My name is
Reza".split("\\W")).map(_ + 1).count == 6)
  }
  test("Testing RDD transformations using a shared Spark Context") {
    val input = List("Testing", "RDD transformations", "using a
shared", "Spark Context")
    val expected = Array(Array("Testing"), Array("RDD",
"transformations"), Array("using", "a", "shared"), Array("Spark",
"Context"))
    val transformed = tokenize(sc.parallelize(input))
```

```
        assert(transformed === expected)
    }
  }
```

From the preceding source code, we can see that we can perform multiple test cases using Spark testing base. Upon successful execution, you should observe the following output (*Figure 13*):

Figure 13: A successful execution and passed test using Spark testing base

Configuring Hadoop runtime on Windows

We have already seen how to test your Spark applications written in Scala on Eclipse or IntelliJ, but there is another potential issue that should not be overlooked. Although Spark works on Windows, Spark is designed to be run on the UNIX-like operating system. Therefore, if you are working on Windows environment, then extra care needs to be taken.

While using Eclipse or IntelliJ to develop your Spark applications for solving data analytics, machine learning, data science, or deep learning applications on Windows, you might face an I/O exception error and your application might not compile successfully or may be interrupted.

Actually, the thing is that Spark expects that there is a runtime environment for Hadoop on Windows too. For example, if you run a Spark application, say `KMeansDemo.scala`, on Eclipse for the first time, you will experience an I/O exception saying the following:

> 17/02/26 13:22:00 ERROR Shell: Failed to locate the winutils binary in the hadoop binary path java.io.IOException: Could not locate executable null\bin\winutils.exe in the Hadoop binaries.

The reason is that by default, Hadoop is developed for the Linux environment, and if you are developing your Spark applications on Windows platform, a bridge is required that will provide an environment for the Hadoop runtime for Spark to be properly executed. The details of the I/O exception can be seen in the following figure:

```
17/02/26 13:22:00 ERROR Shell: Failed to locate the winutils binary in the hadoop binary path
java.io.IOException: Could not locate executable null\bin\winutils.exe in the Hadoop binaries.
        at org.apache.hadoop.util.Shell.getQualifiedBinPath(Shell.java:278)
        at org.apache.hadoop.util.Shell.getWinUtilsPath(Shell.java:300)
        at org.apache.hadoop.util.Shell.<clinit>(Shell.java:293)
        at org.apache.hadoop.util.StringUtils.<clinit>(StringUtils.java:76)
        at org.apache.hadoop.mapred.FileInputFormat.setInputPaths(FileInputFormat.java:362)
        at org.apache.spark.SparkContext$$anonfun$hadoopFile$1$$anonfun$30.apply(SparkContext.scala:1014)
        at org.apache.spark.SparkContext$$anonfun$hadoopFile$1$$anonfun$30.apply(SparkContext.scala:1014)
        at org.apache.spark.rdd.HadoopRDD$$anonfun$getJobConf$6.apply(HadoopRDD.scala:179)
        at org.apache.spark.rdd.HadoopRDD$$anonfun$getJobConf$6.apply(HadoopRDD.scala:179)
        at scala.Option.foreach(Option.scala:257)
        at org.apache.spark.rdd.HadoopRDD.getJobConf(HadoopRDD.scala:179)
        at org.apache.spark.rdd.HadoopRDD.getPartitions(HadoopRDD.scala:198)
        at org.apache.spark.rdd.RDD$$anonfun$partitions$2.apply(RDD.scala:252)
        at org.apache.spark.rdd.RDD$$anonfun$partitions$2.apply(RDD.scala:250)
        at scala.Option.getOrElse(Option.scala:121)
        at org.apache.spark.rdd.RDD.partitions(RDD.scala:250)
        at org.apache.spark.rdd.MapPartitionsRDD.getPartitions(MapPartitionsRDD.scala:35)
        at org.apache.spark.rdd.RDD$$anonfun$partitions$2.apply(RDD.scala:252)
        at org.apache.spark.rdd.RDD$$anonfun$partitions$2.apply(RDD.scala:250)
        at scala.Option.getOrElse(Option.scala:121)
        at org.apache.spark.rdd.RDD.partitions(RDD.scala:250)
        at org.apache.spark.rdd.MapPartitionsRDD.getPartitions(MapPartitionsRDD.scala:35)
        at org.apache.spark.rdd.RDD$$anonfun$partitions$2.apply(RDD.scala:252)
        at org.apache.spark.rdd.RDD$$anonfun$partitions$2.apply(RDD.scala:250)
        at scala.Option.getOrElse(Option.scala:121)
        at org.apache.spark.rdd.RDD.partitions(RDD.scala:250)
        at org.apache.spark.rdd.MapPartitionsRDD.getPartitions(MapPartitionsRDD.scala:35)
        at org.apache.spark.rdd.RDD$$anonfun$partitions$2.apply(RDD.scala:252)
        at org.apache.spark.rdd.RDD$$anonfun$partitions$2.apply(RDD.scala:250)
        at scala.Option.getOrElse(Option.scala:121)
        at org.apache.spark.rdd.RDD.partitions(RDD.scala:250)
        at org.apache.spark.rdd.MapPartitionsRDD.getPartitions(MapPartitionsRDD.scala:35)
        at org.apache.spark.rdd.RDD$$anonfun$partitions$2.apply(RDD.scala:252)
        at org.apache.spark.rdd.RDD$$anonfun$partitions$2.apply(RDD.scala:250)
        at scala.Option.getOrElse(Option.scala:121)
```

Figure 14: I/O exception occurred due to the failure of not to locate the winutils binary in the Hadoop binary path

Now, how to get rid of this problem then? The solution is straightforward. As the error message says, we need to have an executable, namely `winutils.exe`. Now download the `winutils.exe` file from `https://github.com/steveloughran/winutils/tree/master/hadoop-2.7.1/bin`, paste it in the Spark distribution directory, and configure Eclipse. More specifically, suppose your Spark distribution containing Hadoop is located at `C:/Users/spark-2.1.0-bin-hadoop2.7`. Inside the Spark distribution, there is a directory named bin. Now, paste the executable there (that is, `path = C:/Users/spark-2.1.0-binhadoop2.7/bin/`).

The second phase of the solution is going to Eclipse and then selecting the main class (that is, `KMeansDemo.scala` in this case), and then going to the **Run** menu. From the **Run** menu, go to the **Run Configurations** option and from there select the **Environment** tab, as shown in the following figure:

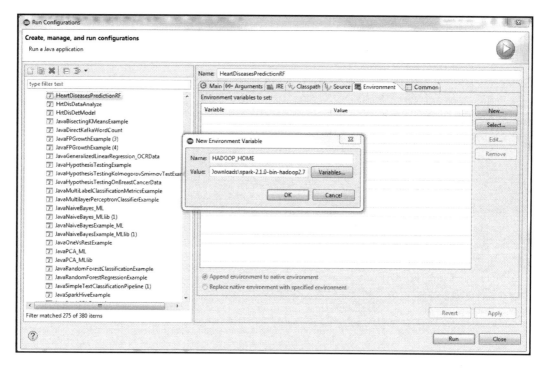

Figure 15: Solving the I/O exception occurred due to the absence of winutils binary in the Hadoop binary path

If you select the tab, you a will have the option to create a new environmental variable for Eclipse suing the JVM. Now create a new environmental variable named `HADOOP_HOME` and put the value as `C:/Users/spark-2.1.0-bin-hadoop2.7/`. Now press on **Apply** button and rerun your application, and your problem should be resolved.

It is to be noted that while working with Spark on Windows in a PySpark, the `winutils.exe` file is required too. For PySpark reference, refer to the `Chapter 19`, *PySpark and SparkR*.

Please make a note that the preceding solution is also applicable in debugging your applications. Sometimes, even if the preceding error occurs, your Spark application will run properly. However, if the size of the dataset is large, it is most likely that the preceding error will occur.

Debugging Spark applications

In this section, we will see how to debug Spark applications that are running locally (on Eclipse or IntelliJ), standalone or cluster mode in YARN or Mesos. However, before diving deeper, it is necessary to know about logging in the Spark application.

Logging with log4j with Spark recap

We have already discussed this topic in `Chapter 14`, *Time to Put Some Order - Cluster Your Data with Spark MLlib*. However, let's replay the same contents to make your brain align with the current discussion *Debugging Spark applications*. As stated earlier, Spark uses log4j for its own logging. If you configured Spark properly, Spark gets logged all the operation to the shell console.

A sample snapshot of the file can be seen from the following figure:

```
# Set everything to be logged to the console
log4j.rootCategory=INFO, console
log4j.appender.console=org.apache.log4j.ConsoleAppender
log4j.appender.console.target=System.err
log4j.appender.console.layout=org.apache.log4j.PatternLayout
log4j.appender.console.layout.ConversionPattern=%d{yy/MM/dd HH:mm:ss} %p %c{1}: %m%n

# Set the default spark-shell log level to WARN. When running the spark-shell, the
# log level for this class is used to overwrite the root logger's log level, so that
# the user can have different defaults for the shell and regular Spark apps.
log4j.logger.org.apache.spark.repl.Main=WARN

# Settings to quiet third party logs that are too verbose
log4j.logger.org.spark_project.jetty=WARN
log4j.logger.org.spark_project.jetty.util.component.AbstractLifeCycle=ERROR
log4j.logger.org.apache.spark.repl.SparkIMain$exprTyper=INFO
log4j.logger.org.apache.spark.repl.SparkILoop$SparkILoopInterpreter=INFO
log4j.logger.org.apache.parquet=ERROR
log4j.logger.parquet=ERROR

# SPARK-9183: Settings to avoid annoying messages when looking up nonexistent UDFs in SparkSQL with Hive support
log4j.logger.org.apache.hadoop.hive.metastore.RetryingHMSHandler=FATAL
log4j.logger.org.apache.hadoop.hive.ql.exec.FunctionRegistry=ERROR
```

Figure 16: A snap of the log4j.properties file

Set the default spark-shell log level to WARN. When running the spark-shell, the log level for this class is used to overwrite the root logger's log level so that the user can have different defaults for the shell and regular Spark apps. We also need to append JVM arguments when launching a job executed by an executor and managed by the driver. For this, you should edit the `conf/spark-defaults.conf`. In short, the following options can be added:

```
spark.executor.extraJavaOptions=-
Dlog4j.configuration=file:/usr/local/spark-2.1.1/conf/log4j.properties
spark.driver.extraJavaOptions=-
Dlog4j.configuration=file:/usr/local/spark-2.1.1/conf/log4j.properties
```

To make the discussion clearer, we need to hide all the logs generated by Spark. We then can redirect them to be logged in the file system. On the other hand, we want our own logs to be logged in the shell and a separate file so that they don't get mixed up with the ones from Spark. From here, we will point Spark to the files where our own logs are, which in this particular case is `/var/log/sparkU.log`. This `log4j.properties` file is then picked up by Spark when the application starts, so we don't have to do anything aside of placing it in the mentioned location:

```
package com.chapter14.Serilazition
import org.apache.log4j.LogManager
import org.apache.log4j.Level
import org.apache.spark.sql.SparkSession
```

```
object myCustomLog {
  def main(args: Array[String]): Unit = {
    val log = LogManager.getRootLogger
    //Everything is printed as INFO once the log level is set to INFO
untill you set the level to new level for example WARN.
    log.setLevel(Level.INFO)
    log.info("Let's get started!")
    // Setting logger level as WARN: after that nothing prints other
than WARN
    log.setLevel(Level.WARN)
    // Creating Spark Session
    val spark = SparkSession
      .builder
      .master("local[*]")
      .config("spark.sql.warehouse.dir", "E:/Exp/")
      .appName("Logging")
      .getOrCreate()
    // These will note be printed!
    log.info("Get prepared!")
    log.trace("Show if there is any ERROR!")
    //Started the computation and printing the logging information
    log.warn("Started")
    spark.sparkContext.parallelize(1 to 20).foreach(println)
    log.warn("Finished")
  }
}
```

In the preceding code, everything is printed as INFO once the log level is set to INFO until you set the level to new level for example WARN. However, after that no info or trace and so on, that will note be printed. In addition to that, there are several valid logging levels supported by log4j with Spark. The successful execution of the preceding code should generate the following output:

```
17/05/13 16:39:14 INFO root: Let's get started!
17/05/13 16:39:15 WARN root: Started
4
1
2
5
3
17/05/13 16:39:16 WARN root: Finished
```

You can also set up the default logging for Spark shell in `conf/log4j.properties`. Spark provides a template of the log4j as a property file, and we can extend and modify that file for logging in Spark. Move to the `SPARK_HOME/conf` directory and you should see the `log4j.properties.template` file. You should use the following `conf/log4j.properties.template` after renaming it to `log4j.properties`. While developing your Spark application, you can put the `log4j.properties` file under your project directory while working on an IDE-based environment such as Eclipse. However, to disable logging completely, just set the `log4j.logger.org` flags as `OFF` as follows:

```
log4j.logger.org=OFF
```

So far, everything is very easy. However, there is a problem we haven't noticed yet in the preceding code segment. One drawback of the `org.apache.log4j.Logger` class is that it is not serializable, which implies that we cannot use it inside a closure while doing operations on some parts of the Spark API. For example, suppose we do the following in our Spark code:

```
object myCustomLogger {
  def main(args: Array[String]):Unit= {
    // Setting logger level as WARN
    val log = LogManager.getRootLogger
    log.setLevel(Level.WARN)
    // Creating Spark Context
    val conf = new SparkConf().setAppName("My
App").setMaster("local[*]")
    val sc = new SparkContext(conf)
    //Started the computation and printing the logging information
    //log.warn("Started")
    val i = 0
    val data = sc.parallelize(i to 100000)
    data.map{number =>
      log.info("My number"+ i)
      number.toString
    }
    //log.warn("Finished")
  }
}
```

You should experience an exception that says `Task` not serializable as follows:

```
org.apache.spark.SparkException: Job aborted due to stage failure:
Task not serializable: java.io.NotSerializableException: ...
Exception in thread "main" org.apache.spark.SparkException: Task not
serializable
Caused by: java.io.NotSerializableException:
```

```
org.apache.log4j.spi.RootLogger
Serialization stack: object not serializable
```

At first, we can try to solve this problem in a naive way. What you can do is just make the Scala class (that does the actual operation) `Serializable` using `extends Serializable`. For example, the code looks as follows:

```
class MyMapper(n: Int) extends Serializable {
  @transient lazy val log =
org.apache.log4j.LogManager.getLogger("myLogger")
  def logMapper(rdd: RDD[Int]): RDD[String] =
    rdd.map { i =>
      log.warn("mapping: " + i)
      (i + n).toString
    }
}
```

This section is intended for carrying out a discussion on logging. However, we take the opportunity to make it more versatile for general purpose Spark programming and issues. In order to overcome the `task not serializable` error in a more efficient way, compiler will try to send the whole object (not only the lambda) by making it serializable and forces SPark to accept that. However, it increases shuffling significantly, especially for big objects! The other ways are making the whole class `Serializable` or by declaring the instance only within the lambda function passed in the map operation. Sometimes, keeping the not `Serializable` objects across the nodes can work. Lastly, use the `forEachPartition()` or `mapPartitions()` instead of just `map()` and create the not `Serializable` objects. In summary, these are the ways to solve the problem around:

- Serializable the class
- Declare the instance only within the lambda function passed in the map
- Make the NotSerializable object as a static and create it once per machine
- Call the `forEachPartition ()` or `mapPartitions()` instead of `map()` and create the NotSerializable object

In the preceding code, we have used the annotation `@transient lazy`, which marks the `Logger` class to be nonpersistent. On the other hand, object containing the method apply (i.e. `MyMapperObject`) that instantiate the object of the `MyMapper` class is as follows:

```
//Companion object
object MyMapper {
  def apply(n: Int): MyMapper = new MyMapper(n)
}
```

Finally, the object containing the `main()` method is as follows:

```
//Main object
object myCustomLogwithClosureSerializable {
  def main(args: Array[String]) {
    val log = LogManager.getRootLogger
    log.setLevel(Level.WARN)
    val spark = SparkSession
      .builder
      .master("local[*]")
      .config("spark.sql.warehouse.dir", "E:/Exp/")
      .appName("Testing")
      .getOrCreate()
    log.warn("Started")
    val data = spark.sparkContext.parallelize(1 to 100000)
    val mapper = MyMapper(1)
    val other = mapper.logMapper(data)
    other.collect()
    log.warn("Finished")
  }
```

Now, let's see another example that provides better insight to keep fighting the issue we are talking about. Suppose we have the following class that computes the multiplication of two integers:

```
class MultiplicaitonOfTwoNumber {
  def multiply(a: Int, b: Int): Int = {
    val product = a * b
    product
  }
}
```

Now, essentially, if you try to use this class for computing the multiplication in the lambda closure using `map()`, you will get the `Task Not Serializable` error that we described earlier. Now we simply can use `foreachPartition()` and the lambda inside as follows:

```
val myRDD = spark.sparkContext.parallelize(0 to 1000)
    myRDD.foreachPartition(s => {
        val notSerializable = new MultiplicaitonOfTwoNumber
        println(notSerializable.multiply(s.next(), s.next()))
    })
```

Now, if you compile it, it should return the desired result. For your ease, the complete code with the `main()` method is as follows:

```
package com.chapter16.SparkTesting
import org.apache.spark.sql.SparkSession
class MultiplicaitonOfTwoNumber {
  def multiply(a: Int, b: Int): Int = {
    val product = a * b
    product
  }
}
object MakingTaskSerilazible {
  def main(args: Array[String]): Unit = {
    val spark = SparkSession
      .builder
      .master("local[*]")
      .config("spark.sql.warehouse.dir", "E:/Exp/")
      .appName("MakingTaskSerilazible")
      .getOrCreate()
  val myRDD = spark.sparkContext.parallelize(0 to 1000)
    myRDD.foreachPartition(s => {
        val notSerializable = new MultiplicaitonOfTwoNumber
        println(notSerializable.multiply(s.next(), s.next()))
    })
  }
}
```

The output is as follows:

```
0
5700
1406
156
4032
7832
2550
650
```

Debugging the Spark application

In this section, we will discuss how to debug Spark applications running on locally on Eclipse or IntelliJ, as standalone or cluster mode in YARN or Mesos. Before getting started, you can also read the debugging documentation at `https://hortonworks.com/hadoop-tutorial/setting-spark-development-environment-scala/`.

Debugging Spark application on Eclipse as Scala debug

To make this happen, just configure your Eclipse to debug your Spark applications as a regular Scala code debug. To configure select **Run** | **Debug Configuration** | **Scala Application** as shown in the following figure:

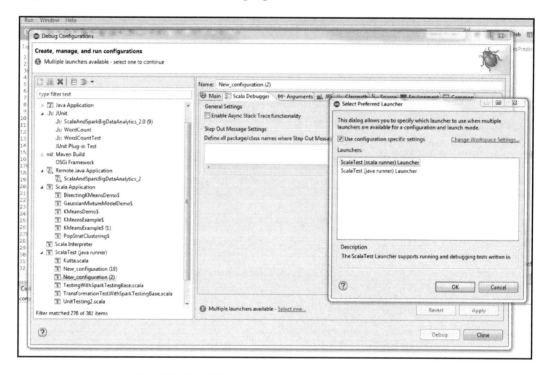

Figure 17: Configuring Eclipse to debug Spark applications as a regular Scala code debug

Suppose we want to debug our `KMeansDemo.scala` and ask Eclipse (you can have similar options on InteliJ IDE) to start the execution at line 56 and set the breakpoint in line 95. To do so, run your Scala code as debugging and you should observe the following scenario on Eclipse:

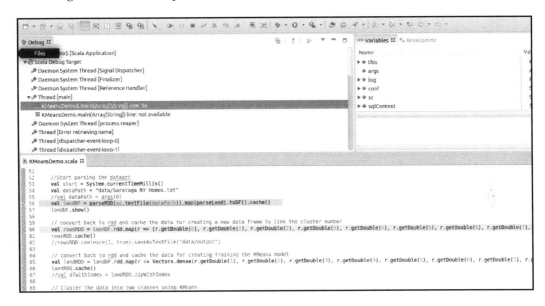

Figure 18: Debugging Spark applications on Eclipse

Then, Eclipse will pause on the line you ask it to stop the execution in line 95, as shown in the following screenshot:

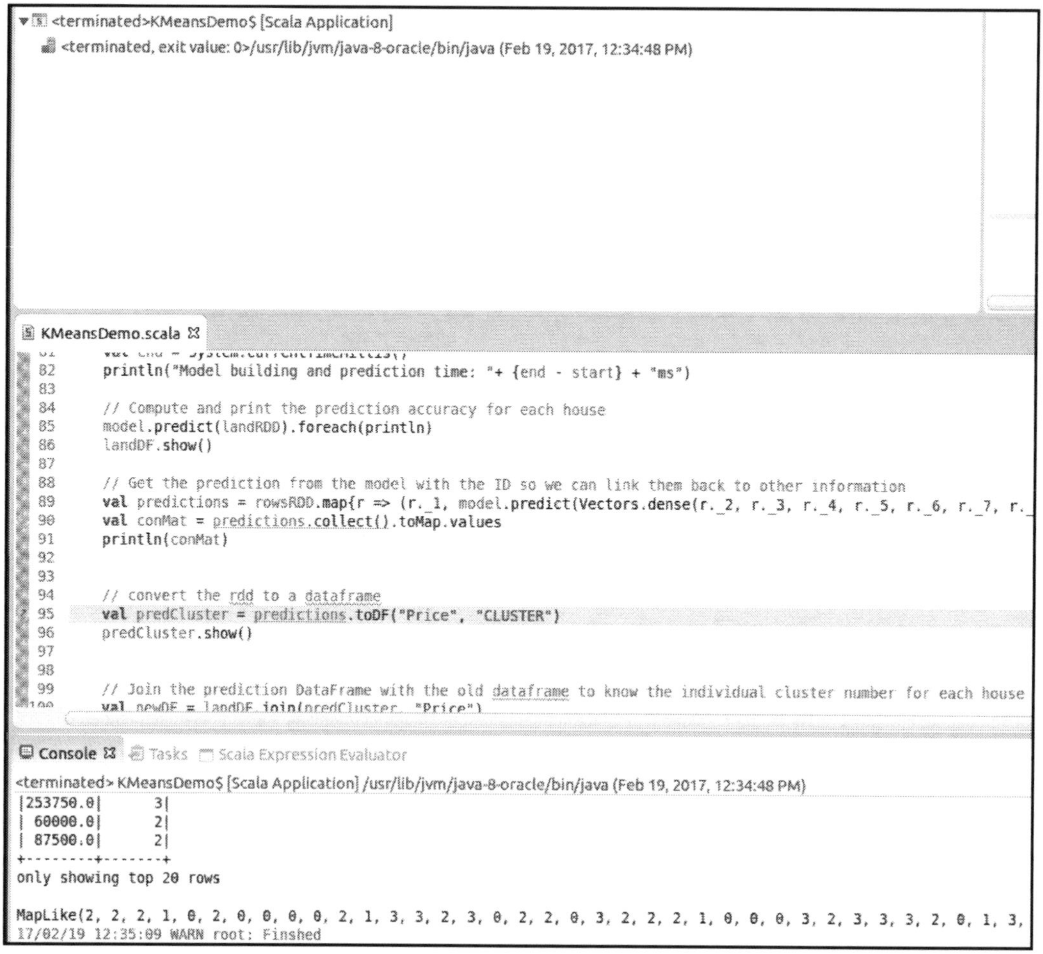

Figure 19: Debugging Spark applications on Eclipse (breakpoint)

In summary, to simplify the preceding example, if there is any error between line 56 and line 95, Eclipse will show where the error actually occurs. Otherwise, it will follow the normal workflow if not interrupted.

Debugging Spark jobs running as local and standalone mode

While debugging your Spark application locally or as standalone mode, you should know that debugging the driver program and debugging one of the executors is different since using these two types of nodes requires different submission parameters passed to `spark-submit`. Throughout this section, I'll use port 4000 as the address. For example, if you want to debug the driver program, you can add the following to your `spark-submit` command:

```
--driver-java-options -
agentlib:jdwp=transport=dt_socket,server=y,suspend=y,address=4000
```

After that, you should set your remote debugger to connect to the node where you have submitted the driver program. For the preceding case, port number 4000 was specified. However, if something (that is, other Spark jobs, other applications or services, and so on) is already running on that port, you might also need to customize that port, that is, change the port number.

On the other hand, connecting to an executor is similar to the preceding option, except for the address option. More specifically, you will have to replace the address with your local machine's address (IP address or host name with the port number). However, it is always a good practice and recommended to test that you can access your local machine from the Spark cluster where the actual computing occurs. For example, you can use the following options to make the debugging environment enable to your `spark-submit` command:

```
--num-executors 1\
--executor-cores 1 \
--conf "spark.executor.extraJavaOptions=-
agentlib:jdwp=transport=dt_socket,server=n,address=localhost:4000,susp
end=n"
```

In summary, use the following command to submit your Spark jobs (the `KMeansDemo` application in this case):

```
$ SPARK_HOME/bin/spark-submit \
--class "com.chapter13.Clustering.KMeansDemo" \
--master spark://ubuntu:7077 \
--num-executors 1\
--executor-cores 1 \
--conf "spark.executor.extraJavaOptions=-
agentlib:jdwp=transport=dt_socket,server=n,address=
```

```
host_name_to_your_computer.org:5005,suspend=n" \
--driver-java-options -
agentlib:jdwp=transport=dt_socket,server=y,suspend=y,address=4000 \
 KMeans-0.0.1-SNAPSHOT-jar-with-dependencies.jar \
Saratoga_NY_Homes.txt
```

Now, start your local debugger in a listening mode and start your Spark program. Finally, wait for the executor to attach to your debugger. You will observe the following message on your terminal:

```
Listening for transport dt_socket at address: 4000
```

It is important to know that you need to set the number of executors to 1 only. Setting multiple executors will all try to connect to your debugger and will eventually create some weird problems. It is to be noted that sometimes setting the SPARK_JAVA_OPTS helps in debugging your Spark applications that are running locally or as standalone mode. The command is as follows:

```
$ export SPARK_JAVA_OPTS=-
agentlib:jdwp=transport=dt_socket,server=y,address=4000,suspend=y,onun
caught=n
```

However, since Spark release 1.0.0, SPARK_JAVA_OPTS has been deprecated and replaced by spark-defaults.conf and command line arguments to Spark-submit or Spark-shell. It is also to be noted that setting spark.driver.extraJavaOptions and spark.executor.extraJavaOptions, which we saw in the previous section, in spark-defaults.conf is not a replacement for SPARK_JAVA_OPTS. But to be frank, SPARK_JAVA_OPTS, it still works pretty well and you can try as well.

Debugging Spark applications on YARN or Mesos cluster

When you run a Spark application on YARN, there is an option that you can enable by modifying yarn-env.sh:

```
YARN_OPTS="-
agentlib:jdwp=transport=dt_socket,server=y,suspend=n,address=4000
$YARN_OPTS"
```

Now, the remote debugging will be available through port 4000 on your Eclipse or IntelliJ IDE. The second option is by setting the SPARK_SUBMIT_OPTS. You can use either Eclipse or IntelliJ to develop your Spark applications that can be submitted to be executed on remote multinode YARN clusters. What I do is that I create a Maven project on Eclipse or IntelliJ and package my Java or Scala application as a jar file and then submit it as a Spark job. However, in order to attach your IDE such as Eclipse or IntelliJ debugger to your Spark application, you can define all the submission parameters using the SPARK_SUBMIT_OPTS environment variable as follows:

```
$ export SPARK_SUBMIT_OPTS=-
agentlib:jdwp=transport=dt_socket,server=y,suspend=y,address=4000
```

Then submit your Spark job as follows (please change the values accordingly based on your requirements and setup):

```
$ SPARK_HOME/bin/spark-submit \
--class "com.chapter13.Clustering.KMeansDemo" \
--master yarn \
--deploy-mode cluster \
--driver-memory 16g \
--executor-memory 4g \
--executor-cores 4 \
--queue the_queue \
--num-executors 1\
--executor-cores 1 \
--conf "spark.executor.extraJavaOptions=-
agentlib:jdwp=transport=dt_socket,server=n,address=
host_name_to_your_computer.org:4000,suspend=n" \
--driver-java-options -
agentlib:jdwp=transport=dt_socket,server=y,suspend=y,address=4000 \
  KMeans-0.0.1-SNAPSHOT-jar-with-dependencies.jar \
Saratoga_NY_Homes.txt
```

After running the preceding command, it will wait until you connect your debugger, as shown in the following: `Listening for transport dt_socket at address: 4000`. Now you can configure your Java remote application (Scala application will work too) on the IntelliJ debugger, as shown in the following screenshot:

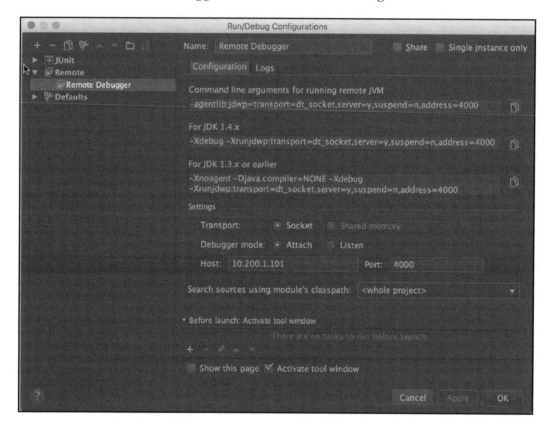

Figure 20: Configuring remote debugger on IntelliJ

For the preceding case, 10.200.1.101 is the IP address of the remote computing node where your Spark job is basically running. Finally, you will have to start the debugger by clicking on Debug under IntelliJ's Run menu. Then, if the debugger connects to your remote Spark app, you will see the logging info in the application console on IntelliJ. Now if you can set the breakpoints and the rests of them are normal debugging. The following figure shows an example how will you see on the IntelliJ when pausing a Spark job with a breakpoint:

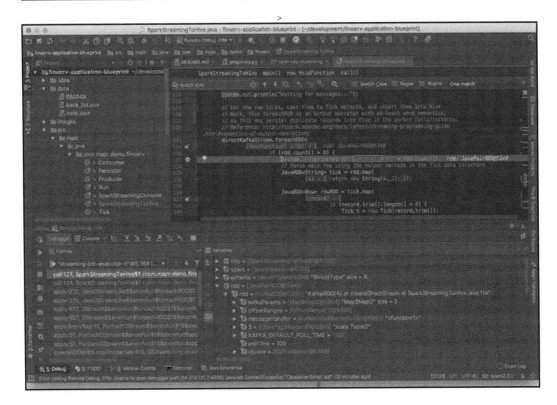

Figure 21: An example how will you see on the IntelliJ when pausing a Spark job with a breakpoint

Although it works well, but sometimes I experienced that using SPARK_JAVA_OPTS won't help you much in the debug process on Eclipse or even IntelliJ. Instead, use and export SPARK_WORKER_OPTS and SPARK_MASTER_OPTS while running your Spark jobs on a real cluster (YARN, Mesos, or AWS) as follows:

```
$ export SPARK_WORKER_OPTS="-Xdebug -
Xrunjdwp:server=y,transport=dt_socket,address=4000,suspend=n"
$ export SPARK_MASTER_OPTS="-Xdebug -
Xrunjdwp:server=y,transport=dt_socket,address=4000,suspend=n"
```

Then start your Master node as follows:

```
$ SPARKH_HOME/sbin/start-master.sh
```

Now open an SSH connection to your remote machine where the Spark job is actually running and map your localhost at 4000 (aka `localhost:4000`) to `host_name_to_your_computer.org:5000`, assuming the cluster is at `host_name_to_your_computer.org:5000` and listening on port 5000. Now that your Eclipse will consider that you're just debugging your Spark application as a local Spark application or process. However, to make this happen, you will have to configure the remote debugger on Eclipse, as shown in the following figure:

Figure 22: Connecting remote host on Eclipse for debugging Spark application

That's it! Now you can debug on your live cluster as if it were your desktop. The preceding examples are for running with the Spark Master set as YARN-client. However, it should also work when running on a Mesos cluster. If you're running using YARN-cluster mode, you may have to set the driver to attach to your debugger rather than attaching your debugger to the driver since you won't necessarily know in advance what mode the driver will be executing on.

Debugging Spark application using SBT

The preceding setting works mostly on Eclipse or IntelliJ using the Maven project. Suppose that you already have your application done and are working on your preferred IDEs such as IntelliJ or Eclipse as follows:

```
object DebugTestSBT {
  def main(args: Array[String]): Unit = {
    val spark = SparkSession
      .builder
      .master("local[*]")
      .config("spark.sql.warehouse.dir", "C:/Exp/")
      .appName("Logging")
      .getOrCreate()
    spark.sparkContext.setCheckpointDir("C:/Exp/")
    println("-------------Attach debugger now!-------------")
    Thread.sleep(8000)
    // code goes here, with breakpoints set on the lines you want to
pause
  }
}
```

Now, if you want to get this job to the local cluster (standalone), the very first step is packaging the application with all its dependencies into a fat JAR. For doing this, use the following command:

```
$ sbt assembly
```

This will generate the fat JAR. Now the task is to submit the Spark job to a local cluster. You need to have spark-submit script somewhere on your system:

```
$ export SPARK_JAVA_OPTS=-
agentlib:jdwp=transport=dt_socket,server=y,suspend=n,address=5005
```

The preceding command exports a Java argument that will be used to start Spark with the debugger:

```
$ SPARK_HOME/bin/spark-submit --class Test --master local[*] --driver-
memory 4G --executor-memory 4G /path/project-assembly-0.0.1.jar
```

In the preceding command, `--class` needs to point to a fully qualified class path to your job. Upon successful execution of this command, your Spark job will be executed without breaking at the breakpoints. Now to get the debugging facility on your IDE, say IntelliJ, you need to configure to connect to the cluster. For more details on the official IDEA documentation, refer to http://stackoverflow.com/questions/21114066/attach-intellij-idea-debugger-to-a-running-java-process.

It is to be noted that if you just create a default remote run/debug configuration and leave the default port of 5005, it should work fine. Now, when you submit the job for the next time and see the message to attach the debugger, you have eight seconds to switch to IntelliJ IDEA and trigger this run configuration. The program will then continue to execute and pause at any breakpoint you defined. You can then step through it like any normal Scala/Java program. You can even step into Spark functions to see what it's doing under the hood.

Summary

In this chapter, you saw how difficult the testing and debugging your Spark applications are. These can even be more critical in a distributed environment. We also discussed some advanced ways to tackle them altogether. In summary, you learned the way of testing in a distributed environment. Then you learned a better way of testing your Spark application. Finally, we discussed some advanced ways of debugging Spark applications.

We believe that this book will help you to gain some good understanding of Spark. Nevertheless, due to page limitation, we could not cover many APIs and their underlying functionalities. If you face any issues, please don't forget to report this to Spark user mailing list at user@spark.apache.org. Before doing so, make sure that you have subscribed to it.

This is more or less the end of our little journey with advanced topics on Spark. Now, a general suggestion from our side to you as readers or if you are relatively newer to the data science, data analytics, machine learning, Scala, or Spark is that you should at first try to understand what types of analytics you want to perform. To be more specific, for example, if your problem is a machine learning problem, try to guess what type of learning algorithms should be the best fit, that is, classification, clustering, regression, recommendation, or frequent pattern mining. Then define and formulate the problem, and after that, you should generate or download the appropriate data based on the feature engineering concept of Spark that we have discussed earlier. On the other hand, if you think that you can solve your problem using deep learning algorithms or APIs, you should use other third-party algorithms and integrate with Spark and work straight away.

Our final recommendation to the readers is to browse the Spark website (at http://spark.apache.org/) regularly to get the updates and also try to incorporate the regular Spark-provided APIs with other third-party applications or tools to get the best result of the collaboration.

18
PySpark and SparkR

In this chapter, we will discuss two other popular APIs: PySpark and SparkR for writing Spark code in Python and R programming languages respectively. The first part of this chapter will cover some technical aspects while working with Spark using PySpark. Then we will move to SparkR and see how to use it with ease. The following topics will be discussed throughout this chapter:

- Introduction to PySpark
- Installation and getting started with PySpark
- Interacting with DataFrame APIs
- UDFs with PySpark
- Data analytics using PySpark
- Introduction to SparkR
- Why SparkR?
- Installation and getting started with SparkR
- Data processing and manipulation
- Working with RDD and DataFrame using SparkR
- Data visualization using SparkR

Introduction to PySpark

Python is one of the most popular and general purpose programming languages with a number of exciting features for data processing and machine learning tasks. To use Spark from Python, PySpark was initially developed as a lightweight frontend of Python to Apache Spark and using Spark's distributed computation engine. In this chapter, we will discuss a few technical aspects of using Spark from Python IDE such as PyCharm.

Many data scientists use Python because it has a rich variety of numerical libraries with a statistical, machine learning, or optimization focus. However, processing large-scale datasets in Python is usually tedious as the runtime is single-threaded. As a result, data that fits in the main memory can only be processed. Considering this limitation and for getting the full flavor of Spark in Python, PySpark was initially developed as a lightweight frontend of Python to Apache Spark and using Spark's distributed computation engine. This way, Spark provides APIs in non-JVM languages like Python.

The purpose of this PySpark section is to provide basic distributed algorithms using PySpark. Note that PySpark is an interactive shell for basic testing and debugging and is not supposed to be used for a production environment.

Installation and configuration

There are many ways of installing and configuring PySpark on Python IDEs such as PyCharm, Spider, and so on. Alternatively, you can use PySpark if you have already installed Spark and configured the SPARK_HOME. Thirdly, you can also use PySpark from the Python shell. Below we will see how to configure PySpark for running standalone jobs.

By setting SPARK_HOME

At first, download and place the Spark distribution at your preferred place, say /home/asif/Spark. Now let's set the SPARK_HOME as follows:

```
echo "export SPARK_HOME=/home/asif/Spark" >> ~/.bashrc
```

Now let's set PYTHONPATH as follows:

```
echo "export PYTHONPATH=$SPARK_HOME/python/" >> ~/.bashrc
echo "export PYTHONPATH=$SPARK_HOME/python/lib/py4j-0.10.1-src.zip" >>
~/.bashrc
```

Now we need to add the following two paths to the environmental path:

```
echo "export PATH=$PATH:$SPARK_HOME" >> ~/.bashrc
echo "export PATH=$PATH:$PYTHONPATH" >> ~/.bashrc
```

Finally, let's refresh the current terminal so that the newly modified `PATH` variable is used:

```
source ~/.bashrc
```

PySpark depends on the `py4j` Python package. It helps the Python interpreter to dynamically access the Spark object from the JVM. This package can be installed on Ubuntu as follows:

```
$ sudo pip install py4j
```

Alternatively, the default `py4j`, which is already included in Spark (`$SPARK_HOME/python/lib`), can be used too.

Using Python shell

Like Scala interactive shell, an interactive shell is also available for Python. You can execute Python code from Spark root folder as follows:

```
$ cd $SPARK_HOME
$ ./bin/pyspark
```

If the command went fine, you should observer the following screen on Terminal (Ubuntu):

```
asif@ubuntu:~$ cd $SPARK_HOME
asif@ubuntu:~/Spark$ ./bin/pyspark
Python 2.7.6 (default, Oct 26 2016, 20:30:19)
[GCC 4.8.4] on linux2
Type "help", "copyright", "credits" or "license" for more information.
Setting default log level to "WARN".
To adjust logging level use sc.setLogLevel(newLevel). For SparkR, use setLogLevel(newLevel).
17/04/24 09:49:02 WARN NativeCodeLoader: Unable to load native-hadoop library for your platform... using
17/04/24 09:49:02 WARN Utils: Your hostname, ubuntu resolves to a loopback address: 127.0.1.1; using 19.
17/04/24 09:49:02 WARN Utils: Set SPARK_LOCAL_IP if you need to bind to another address
17/04/24 09:49:06 WARN ObjectStore: Failed to get database global_temp, returning NoSuchObjectException
Welcome to
      ____              __
     / __/__  ___ _____/ /__
    _\ \/ _ \/ _ `/ __/  '_/
   /__ / .__/\_,_/_/ /_/\_\   version 2.1.0
      /_/

Using Python version 2.7.6 (default, Oct 26 2016 20:30:19)
SparkSession available as 'spark'.
>>>
```

Figure 1: Getting started with PySpark shell

Now you can enjoy Spark using the Python interactive shell. This shell might be sufficient for experimentations and developments. However, for production level, you should use a standalone application.

PySpark should be available in the system path by now. After writing the Python code, one can simply run the code using the Python command, then it runs in local Spark instance with default configurations:

```
$ python <python_file.py>
```

Note that the current distribution of Spark is only Python 2.7+ compatible. Hence, we will have been strict on this.

Furthermore, it is better to use the `spark-submit` script if you want to pass the configuration values at runtime. The command is pretty similar to the Scala one:

```
$ cd $SPARK_HOME
$ ./bin/spark-submit  --master local[*] <python_file.py>
```

The configuration values can be passed at runtime, or alternatively, they can be changed in the `conf/spark-defaults.conf` file. After configuring the Spark config file, the changes also get reflected while running PySpark applications using a simple Python command.

However, unfortunately, at the time of this writing, there's no pip install advantage for using PySpark. But it is expected to be available in the Spark 2.2.0 release (for more, refer to `https://issues.apache.org/jira/browse/SPARK-1267`). The reason why there is no pip install for PySpark can be found in the JIRA ticket at `https://issues.apache.org/jira/browse/SPARK-1267`.

By setting PySpark on Python IDEs

We can also configure and run PySpark from Python IDEs such as PyCharm. In this section, we will show how to do it. If you're a student, you can get the free licensed copy of PyCharm once you register using your university/college/institute email address at `https://www.jetbrains.com/student/`. Moreover, there's also a community (that is, free) edition of PyCharm, so you don't need to be a student in order to use it.

Recently PySpark has been published with Spark 2.2.0 PyPI (see
`https://pypi.python.org/pypi/pyspark/`. This has been a long time coming
(previous releases included pip installable artifacts that for a variety of reasons
couldn't be published to PyPI). So if you (or your friends) want to be able to work
with PySpark locally on your laptop you've got an easier path getting started, just
execute the following command:

```
$ sudo pip install pyspark # for python 2.7
$ sudo pip3 install pyspark # for python 3.3+
```

However, if you are using Windos 7, 8 or 10, you should install pyspark manually.
For exmple using PyCharm, you can do it as follows:

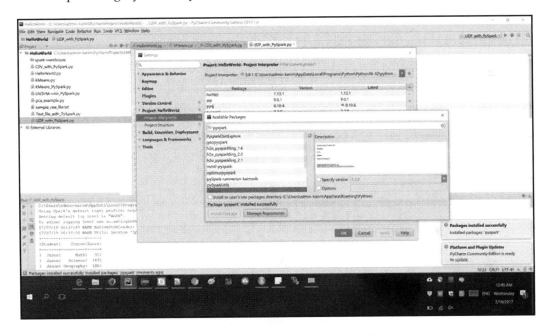

Figure 2: Installing PySpark on Pycharm IDE on Windows 10

At first, you should create a Python script with Project interpreter as Python 2.7+. Then you can import pyspark along with other required models as follows:

```
import os
import sys
import pyspark
```

Now that if you're a Windows user, Python also needs to have the Hadoop runtime; you should put the `winutils.exe` file in the `SPARK_HOME/bin` folder. Then create a environmental variable as follows:

Select your python file | **Run** | **Edit configuration** | **Create an environmental variable** whose key is `HADOOP_HOME` and the value is the `PYTHON_PATH` for example for my case it's `C:\Users\admin-karim\Downloads\spark-2.1.0-bin-hadoop2.7`. Finally, press **OK** then you're done:

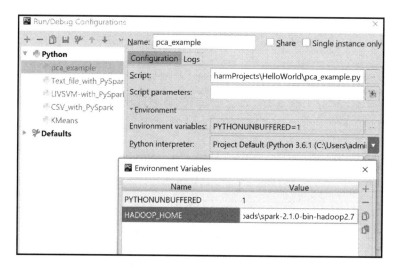

Figure 3: Setting Hadoop runtime env on Pycharm IDE on Windows 10

That's all you need. Now if you start writing Spark code, you should at first place the imports in the `try` block as follows (just for example):

```
try:
    from pyspark.ml.featureimport PCA
    from pyspark.ml.linalgimport Vectors
    from pyspark.sqlimport SparkSession
    print ("Successfully imported Spark Modules")
```

And the `catch` block can be placed as follows:

```
ExceptImportErroras e:
    print("Can not import Spark Modules", e)
    sys.exit(1)
```

Refer to the following figure that shows importing and placing Spark packages in the PySpark shell:

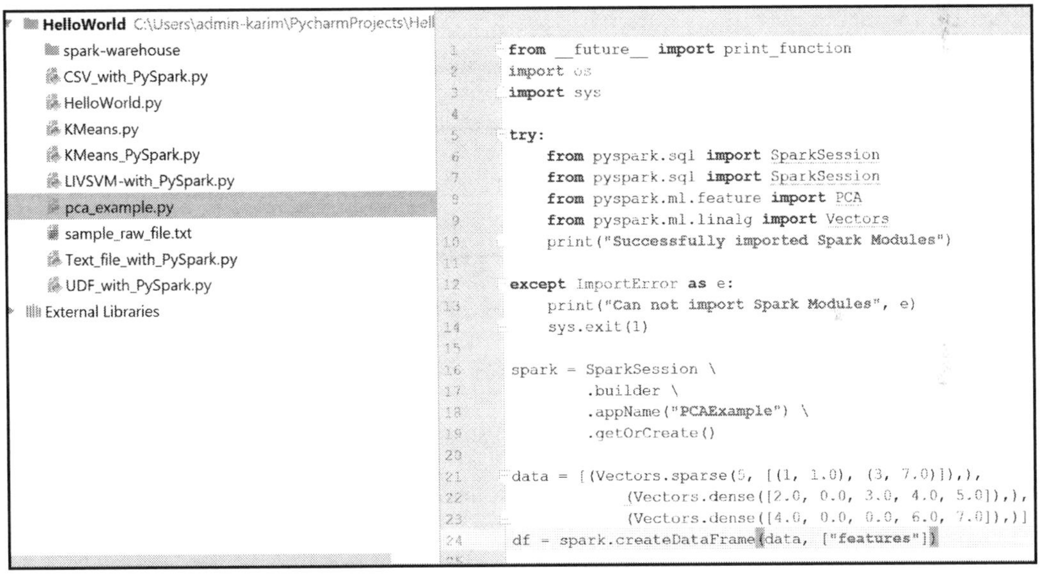

Figure 4: Importing and placing Spark packages in PySpark shell

If these blocks execute successfully, you should observe the following message on the console:

```
Run  pca_example
  C:\Users\admin-karim\AppData\Local\Programs\Python\Python36-32\python.exe C:/Users/admin-karim/PycharmProjects
  Successfully imported Spark Modules
  Using Spark's default log4j profile: org/apache/spark/log4j-defaults.properties
  Setting default log level to "WARN".
  To adjust logging level use sc.setLogLevel(newLevel). For SparkR, use setLogLevel(newLevel).
  17/07/19 17:24:57 WARN NativeCodeLoader: Unable to load native-hadoop library for your platform... using built
  [Stage 6:>                                                          (0 + 8) / 8]17/07/19 17:25:13 WARN BLAS: F
  17/07/19 17:25:13 WARN BLAS: Failed to load implementation from: com.github.fommil.netlib.NativeRefBLAS
  17/07/19 17:25:13 WARN LAPACK: Failed to load implementation from: com.github.fommil.netlib.NativeSystemLAPACK
  17/07/19 17:25:13 WARN LAPACK: Failed to load implementation from: com.github.fommil.netlib.NativeRefLAPACK
```

Figure 5: PySpark package has been imported successfully

Getting started with PySpark

Before going deeper, at first, we need to see how to create the Spark session. It can be done as follows:

```
spark = SparkSession\
        .builder\
        .appName("PCAExample")\
        .getOrCreate()
```

Now under this code block, you should place your codes, for example:

```
data = [(Vectors.sparse(5, [(1, 1.0), (3, 7.0)]),),
        (Vectors.dense([2.0, 0.0, 3.0, 4.0, 5.0]),),
        (Vectors.dense([4.0, 0.0, 0.0, 6.0, 7.0]),)]
 df = spark.createDataFrame(data, ["features"])

pca = PCA(k=3, inputCol="features", outputCol="pcaFeatures")
model = pca.fit(df)

result = model.transform(df).select("pcaFeatures")
result.show(truncate=False)
```

The preceding code demonstrates how to compute principal components on a RowMatrix and use them to project the vectors into a low-dimensional space. For a clearer picture, refer to the following code that shows how to use the PCA algorithm on PySpark:

```
import os
import sys
```

```
try:
from pyspark.sql import SparkSession
from pyspark.ml.feature import PCA
from pyspark.ml.linalg import Vectors
print ("Successfully imported Spark Modules")

except ImportErrorase:
print ("Can not import Spark Modules", e)
 sys.exit(1)

spark = SparkSession\
    .builder\
    .appName("PCAExample")\
    .getOrCreate()

data = [(Vectors.sparse(5, [(1, 1.0), (3, 7.0)]),),
    (Vectors.dense([2.0, 0.0, 3.0, 4.0, 5.0]),),
    (Vectors.dense([4.0, 0.0, 0.0, 6.0, 7.0]),)]
df = spark.createDataFrame(data, ["features"])

pca = PCA(k=3, inputCol="features", outputCol="pcaFeatures")
model = pca.fit(df)

result = model.transform(df).select("pcaFeatures")
result.show(truncate=False)

spark.stop()
```

The output is as follows:

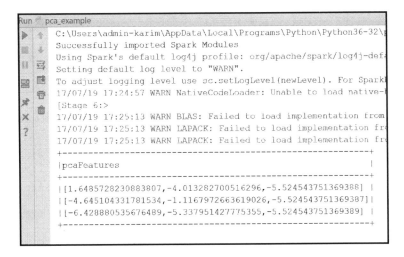

Figure 6: PCA result after successful execution of the Python script

Working with DataFrames and RDDs

SparkDataFrame is a distributed collection of rows under named columns. Less technically, it can be considered as a table in a relational database with column headers. Furthermore, PySpark DataFrame is similar to Python pandas. However, it also shares some mutual characteristics with RDD:

- **Immutable**: Just like an RDD, once a DataFrame is created, it can't be changed. We can transform a DataFrame to an RDD and vice versa after applying transformations.
- **Lazy Evaluations:** Its nature is a lazy evaluation. In other words, a task is not executed until an action is performed.
- **Distributed:** Both the RDD and DataFrame are distributed in nature.

Just like Java/Scala's DataFrames, PySpark DataFrames are designed for processing a large collection of structured data; you can even handle petabytes of data. The tabular structure helps us understand the schema of a DataFrame, which also helps optimize execution plans on SQL queries. Additionally, it has a wide range of data formats and sources.

You can create RDDs, datasets, and DataFrames in a number of ways using PySpark. In the following subsections, we will show some examples of doing that.

Reading a dataset in Libsvm format

Let's see how to read data in LIBSVM format using the read API and the `load()` method by specifying the format of the data (that is, `libsvm`) as follows:

```
# Creating DataFrame from libsvm dataset
myDF = spark.read.format("libsvm").load("C:/Exp//mnist.bz2")
```

The preceding MNIST dataset can be downloaded from https://www.csie.ntu.edu.tw/~cjlin/libsvmtools/datasets/multiclass/mnist.bz2. This will essentially return a DataFrame and the content can be seen by calling the `show()` method as follows:

```
myDF.show()
```

The output is as follows:

```
+-----+--------------------+
|label|            features|
+-----+--------------------+
|  8.0|{17,[0,1,2,3,4,5,...|
| 10.0|{17,[0,1,2,3,4,5,...|
|  9.0|{17,[0,1,2,3,4,5,...|
|  8.0|{17,[0,1,2,3,4,5,...|
| 10.0|{17,[0,1,2,3,4,5,...|
|  8.0|{17,[0,1,2,3,4,5,...|
|  5.0|{17,[0,1,2,3,4,5,...|
|  6.0|{17,[0,1,2,3,4,5,...|
|  8.0|{17,[0,1,2,3,4,5,...|
|  7.0|{17,[0,1,2,3,4,5,...|
|  6.0|{17,[0,1,2,3,4,5,...|
|  8.0|{17,[0,1,2,3,4,5,...|
|  8.0|{17,[0,1,2,3,4,5,...|
|  8.0|{17,[0,1,2,3,4,5,...|
|  9.0|{17,[0,1,2,3,4,5,...|
|  4.0|{17,[0,1,2,3,4,5,...|
|  7.0|{17,[0,1,2,3,4,5,...|
|  7.0|{17,[0,1,2,3,4,5,...|
|  8.0|{17,[0,1,2,3,4,5,...|
|  8.0|{17,[0,1,2,3,4,5,...|
+-----+--------------------+
only showing top 20 rows
```

Figure 7: A snap of the handwritten dataset in LIBSVM format

You can also specify other options such as how many features of the raw dataset you want to give to your DataFrame as follows:

```
myDF= spark.read.format("libsvm")
          .option("numFeatures", "780")
          .load("data/Letterdata_libsvm.data")
```

Now if you want to create an RDD from the same dataset, you can use the MLUtils API from `pyspark.mllib.util` as follows:

```
Creating RDD from the libsvm data file
myRDD = MLUtils.loadLibSVMFile(spark.sparkContext,
"data/Letterdata_libsvm.data")
```

Now you can save the RDD in your preferred location as follows:

```
myRDD.saveAsTextFile("data/myRDD")
```

Reading a CSV file

Let's start with loading, parsing, and viewing simple flight data. At first, download the NYC flights dataset as a CSV from `https://s3-us-west-2.amazonaws.com/sparkr-data/nycflights13.csv`. Now let's load and parse the dataset using `read.csv()` API of PySpark:

```
# Creating DataFrame from data file in CSV format
df = spark.read.format("com.databricks.spark.csv")
        .option("header", "true")
        .load("data/nycflights13.csv")
```

This is pretty similar to reading the libsvm format. Now you can see the resulting DataFrame's structure as follows:

```
df.printSchema()
```

The output is as follows:

```
root
 |-- year: string (nullable = true)
 |-- month: string (nullable = true)
 |-- day: string (nullable = true)
 |-- dep_time: string (nullable = true)
 |-- dep_delay: string (nullable = true)
 |-- arr_time: string (nullable = true)
 |-- arr_delay: string (nullable = true)
 |-- carrier: string (nullable = true)
 |-- tailnum: string (nullable = true)
 |-- flight: string (nullable = true)
 |-- origin: string (nullable = true)
 |-- dest: string (nullable = true)
 |-- air_time: string (nullable = true)
 |-- distance: string (nullable = true)
 |-- hour: string (nullable = true)
 |-- minute: string (nullable = true)
```

Figure 8: Schema of the NYC flight dataset

Now let's see a snap of the dataset using the `show()` method as follows:

```
df.show()
```

Now let's view the sample of the data as follows:

```
+----+-----+---+--------+---------+--------+---------+-------+-------+------+------+----+--------+--------+----+------+
|year|month|day|dep_time|dep_delay|arr_time|arr_delay|carrier|tailnum|flight|origin|dest|air_time|distance|hour|minute|
+----+-----+---+--------+---------+--------+---------+-------+-------+------+------+----+--------+--------+----+------+
|2013|    1|  1|     517|        2|     830|       11|     UA| N14228|  1545|   EWR| IAH|     227|    1400|   5|    17|
|2013|    1|  1|     533|        4|     850|       20|     UA| N24211|  1714|   LGA| IAH|     227|    1416|   5|    33|
|2013|    1|  1|     542|        2|     923|       33|     AA| N619AA|  1141|   JFK| MIA|     160|    1089|   5|    42|
|2013|    1|  1|     544|       -1|    1004|      -18|     B6| N804JB|   725|   JFK| BQN|     183|    1576|   5|    44|
|2013|    1|  1|     554|       -6|     812|      -25|     DL| N668DN|   461|   LGA| ATL|     116|     762|   5|    54|
|2013|    1|  1|     554|       -4|     740|       12|     UA| N39463|  1696|   EWR| ORD|     150|     719|   5|    54|
|2013|    1|  1|     555|       -5|     913|       19|     B6| N516JB|   507|   EWR| FLL|     158|    1065|   5|    55|
|2013|    1|  1|     557|       -3|     709|      -14|     EV| N829AS|  5708|   LGA| IAD|      53|     229|   5|    57|
|2013|    1|  1|     557|       -3|     838|       -8|     B6| N593JB|    79|   JFK| MCO|     140|     944|   5|    57|
|2013|    1|  1|     558|       -2|     753|        8|     AA| N3ALAA|   301|   LGA| ORD|     138|     733|   5|    58|
|2013|    1|  1|     558|       -2|     849|       -2|     B6| N793JB|    49|   JFK| PBI|     149|    1028|   5|    58|
|2013|    1|  1|     558|       -2|     853|       -3|     B6| N657JB|    71|   JFK| TPA|     158|    1005|   5|    58|
|2013|    1|  1|     558|       -2|     924|        7|     UA| N29129|   194|   JFK| LAX|     345|    2475|   5|    58|
|2013|    1|  1|     558|       -2|     923|      -14|     UA| N53441|  1124|   EWR| SFO|     361|    2565|   5|    58|
|2013|    1|  1|     559|       -1|     941|       31|     AA| N3DUAA|   707|   LGA| DFW|     257|    1389|   5|    59|
|2013|    1|  1|     559|        0|     702|       -4|     B6| N708JB|  1806|   JFK| BOS|      44|     187|   5|    59|
|2013|    1|  1|     559|       -1|     854|       -8|     UA| N76515|  1187|   EWR| LAS|     337|    2227|   5|    59|
|2013|    1|  1|     600|        0|     851|       -7|     B6| N595JB|   371|   LGA| FLL|     152|    1076|   6|     0|
|2013|    1|  1|     600|        0|     837|       12|     MQ| N542MQ|  4650|   LGA| ATL|     134|     762|   6|     0|
|2013|    1|  1|     601|        1|     844|       -6|     B6| N644JB|   343|   EWR| PBI|     147|    1023|   6|     1|
+----+-----+---+--------+---------+--------+---------+-------+-------+------+------+----+--------+--------+----+------+
only showing top 20 rows
```

Figure 9: Sample of the NYC flight dataset

Reading and manipulating raw text files

You can read a raw text data file using the `textFile()` method. Suppose you have the logs of some purchase:

```
number\tproduct_name\ttransaction_id\twebsite\tprice\tdate0\tjeans\t30
160906182001\tebay.com\t100\t12-02-20161\tcamera\t70151231120504\tamaz
on.com\t450\t09-08-20172\tlaptop\t90151231120504\tebay.ie\t1500\t07-
-5-20163\tbook\t80151231120506\tpackt.com\t45\t03-12-20164\tdrone\t887
6531120508\talibaba.com\t120\t01-05-2017
```

Now reading and creating RDD is pretty straightforward using the `textFile()` method as follows:

```
myRDD = spark.sparkContext.textFile("sample_raw_file.txt")
$cd myRDD
$ cat part-00000
number\tproduct_name\ttransaction_id\twebsite\tprice\tdate
0\tjeans\t30160906182001\tebay.com\t100\t12-02-20161\tcamera\t70151231
120504\tamazon.com\t450\t09-08-2017
```

As you can see, the structure is not that readable. So we can think of giving a better structure by converting the texts as DataFrame. At first, we need to collect the header information as follows:

```
header = myRDD.first()
```

Now filter out the header and make sure the rest looks correct as follows:

```
textRDD = myRDD.filter(lambda line: line != header)
newRDD = textRDD.map(lambda k: k.split("\\t"))
```

We still have the RDD but with a bit better structure of the data. However, converting it into DataFrame will provide a better view of the transactional data.

The following code creates a DataFrame by specifying the `header.split` is providing the names of the columns:

```
textDF = newRDD.toDF(header.split("\\t"))
textDF.show()
```

The output is as follows:

```
+------+------------+--------------+-----------+-----+----------+
|number|product_name| ransaction_id|    website|price|      date|
+------+------------+--------------+-----------+-----+----------+
|    0 |       jeans|30160906182001|   ebay.com|  100|12-02-2016|
|    1 |      camera|70151231120504| amazon.com|  450|09-08-2017|
|    2 |      laptop|90151231120504|    ebay.ie| 1500|07--5-2016|
|    3 |        book|80151231120506|  packt.com|   45|03-12-2016|
|    4 |       drone| 8876531120508|alibaba.com|  120|01-05-2017|
+------+------------+--------------+-----------+-----+----------+
```

Figure 10: Sample of the transactional data

Now you could save this DataFrame as a view and make a SQL query. Let's do a query with this DataFrame now:

```
textDF.createOrReplaceTempView("transactions")
spark.sql("SELECT * FROM transactions").show()
spark.sql("SELECT product_name, price FROM transactions WHERE price
>=500 ").show()
spark.sql("SELECT product_name, price FROM transactions ORDER BY price
DESC").show()
```

The output is as follows:

```
+------+------------+--------------+-----------+-----+----------+
|number|product_name|transaction_id|    website|price|      date|
+------+------------+--------------+-----------+-----+----------+
|     1|      camera|70151231120504| amazon.com|  450|09-08-2017|
|     3|        book|80151231120506|  packt.com|   45|03-12-2016|
|     2|      laptop|90151231120504|    ebay.ie| 1500|07--5-2016|
|     4|       drone|8876531120508|alibaba.com|  120|01-05-2017|
|     0|       jeans|30160906182001|  ebay.com|  100|12-02-2016|
+------+------------+--------------+-----------+-----+----------+

+---------+
|max_price|
+---------+
|      450|
+---------+
```

Figure 11: Query result on the transactional data using Spark SQL

Writing UDF on PySpark

Like Scala and Java, you can also work with **User Defined Functions** (aka. **UDF**) on PySpark. Let's see an example in the following. Suppose we want to see the grade distribution based on the score for some students who have taken courses at a university.

We can store them in two separate arrays as follows:

```
# Let's generate somerandom lists
students = ['Jason', 'John', 'Geroge', 'David']
courses = ['Math', 'Science', 'Geography', 'History', 'IT',
'Statistics']
```

Now let's declare an empty array for storing the data about courses and students so that later on both can be appended to this array as follows:

```
rawData = []
for (student, course) in itertools.product(students, courses):
    rawData.append((student, course, random.randint(0, 200)))
```

Note that for the preceding code to work, please import the following at the beginning of the file:

```
import itertools
import random
```

Now let's create a DataFrame from these two objects toward converting corresponding grades against each one's score. For this, we need to define an explicit schema. Let's suppose that in your planned DataFrame, there would be three columns named `Student`, `Course`, and `Score`.

At first, let's import necessary modules:

```
from pyspark.sql.types
import StructType, StructField, IntegerType, StringType
```

Now the schema can be defined as follows:

```
schema = StructType([StructField("Student", StringType(),
nullable=False),
                     StructField("Course", StringType(),
nullable=False),
                     StructField("Score", IntegerType(),
nullable=False)])
```

Now let's create an RDD from the Raw Data as follows:

```
courseRDD = spark.sparkContext.parallelize(rawData)
```

Now let's convert the RDD into the DataFrame as follows:

```
courseDF = spark.createDataFrame(courseRDD, schema)
coursedDF.show()
```

The output is as follows:

```
+-------+----------+-----+
|Student|   Course |Score|
+-------+----------+-----+
|  Jason|      Math|   87|
|  Jason|   Science|   32|
|  Jason| Geography|  126|
|  Jason|   History|   12|
|  Jason|        IT|   17|
|  Jason|Statistics|   37|
|   John|      Math|  143|
|   John|   Science|   54|
|   John| Geography|  146|
|   John|   History|   54|
|   John|        IT|   26|
|   John|Statistics|  171|
| Geroge|      Math|  102|
| Geroge|   Science|  146|
| Geroge| Geography|    5|
| Geroge|   History|  112|
| Geroge|        IT|  163|
| Geroge|Statistics|  175|
|  David|      Math|   27|
|  David|   Science|    4|
+-------+----------+-----+
only showing top 20 rows
```

Figure 12: Sample of the randomly generated score for students in subjects

Well, now we have three columns. However, we need to convert the score into grades. Say you have the following grading schema:

- *90~100=> A*
- *80~89 => B*
- *60~79 => C*
- *0~59 => D*

For this, we can create our own UDF such that this will convert the numeric score to grade. It can be done in several ways. Following is an example of doing so:

```python
# Define udf
def scoreToCategory(grade):
    if grade >= 90:
        return 'A'
    elif grade >= 80:
        return 'B'
    elif grade >= 60:
        return 'C'
    else:
        return 'D'
```

Now we can have our own UDF as follows:

```python
from pyspark.sql.functions
import udf
udfScoreToCategory = udf(scoreToCategory, StringType())
```

The second argument in the `udf()` method is the return type of the method (that is, `scoreToCategory`). Now you can call this UDF to convert the score into grade in a pretty straightforward way. Let's see an example of it:

```python
courseDF.withColumn("Grade", udfScoreToCategory("Score")).show(100)
```

The preceding line will take score as input for all entries and convert the score to a grade. Additionally, a new DataFrame with a column named `Grade` will be added.

The output is as follows:

```
+-------+----------+-----+-----+
|Student|    Course|Score|Grade|
+-------+----------+-----+-----+
|  Jason|      Math|   87|    B|
|  Jason|   Science|   32|    D|
|  Jason| Geography|  126|    A|
|  Jason|   History|   12|    D|
|  Jason|        IT|   17|    D|
|  Jason|Statistics|   37|    D|
|   John|      Math|  143|    A|
|   John|   Science|   54|    D|
|   John| Geography|  146|    A|
|   John|   History|   54|    D|
|   John|        IT|   26|    D|
|   John|Statistics|  171|    A|
| Geroge|      Math|  102|    A|
| Geroge|   Science|  146|    A|
| Geroge| Geography|    5|    D|
| Geroge|   History|  112|    A|
| Geroge|        IT|  163|    A|
| Geroge|Statistics|  175|    A|
|  David|      Math|   27|    D|
|  David|   Science|    4|    D|
|  David| Geography|    1|    D|
|  David|   History|   13|    D|
|  David|        IT|   60|    C|
|  David|Statistics|   19|    D|
+-------+----------+-----+-----+
```

Figure 13: Assigned grades

Now we can use the UDF with the SQL statement as well. However, for that, we need to register this UDF as follows:

```
spark.udf.register("udfScoreToCategory", scoreToCategory,
StringType())
```

The preceding line will register the UDF as a temporary function in the database by default. Now we need to create a team view to allow executing SQL queries:

```
courseDF.createOrReplaceTempView("score")
```

Now let's execute an SQL query on the view score as follows:

```
spark.sql("SELECT Student, Score, udfScoreToCategory(Score) as Grade
FROM score").show()
```

The output is as follows:

```
+-------+-----+-----+
|Student|Score|Grade|
+-------+-----+-----+
|  Jason|   42|    D|
|  Jason|  153|    A|
|  Jason|  120|    A|
|  Jason|   99|    A|
|  Jason|  110|    A|
|  Jason|  150|    A|
|   John|   21|    D|
|   John|   45|    D|
|   John|    1|    D|
|   John|  138|    A|
|   John|  168|    A|
|   John|   90|    A|
| Geroge|   84|    B|
| Geroge|   84|    B|
| Geroge|  192|    A|
| Geroge|  192|    A|
| Geroge|   10|    D|
| Geroge|  132|    A|
|  David|   93|    A|
|  David|  127|    A|
+-------+-----+-----+
only showing top 20 rows
```

Figure 14: Query on the students score and corresponding grades

The complete source code for this example is as follows:

```python
import os
import sys
import itertools
import random

from pyspark.sql import SparkSession
from pyspark.sql.types import StructType, StructField, IntegerType,
StringType
from pyspark.sql.functions import udf

spark = SparkSession \
        .builder \
        .appName("PCAExample") \
        .getOrCreate()

# Generate Random RDD
students = ['Jason', 'John', 'Geroge', 'David']
courses = ['Math', 'Science', 'Geography', 'History', 'IT',
'Statistics']
```

```
rawData = []
for (student, course) in itertools.product(students, courses):
    rawData.append((student, course, random.randint(0, 200)))

# Create Schema Object
schema = StructType([
    StructField("Student", StringType(), nullable=False),
    StructField("Course", StringType(), nullable=False),
    StructField("Score", IntegerType(), nullable=False)
])

courseRDD = spark.sparkContext.parallelize(rawData)
courseDF = spark.createDataFrame(courseRDD, schema)
courseDF.show()

# Define udf
def scoreToCategory(grade):
    if grade >= 90:
        return 'A'
    elif grade >= 80:
        return 'B'
    elif grade >= 60:
        return 'C'
    else:
        return 'D'

udfScoreToCategory = udf(scoreToCategory, StringType())
courseDF.withColumn("Grade", udfScoreToCategory("Score")).show(100)

spark.udf.register("udfScoreToCategory", scoreToCategory,
StringType())
courseDF.createOrReplaceTempView("score")
spark.sql("SELECT Student, Score, udfScoreToCategory(Score) as Grade
FROM score").show()

spark.stop()
```

 A more detailed discussion on using UDF can be found at `https://jaceklaskowski.gitbooks.io/mastering-apache-spark/content/spark-sql-udfs.html`.

Now let's do some analytics tasks on PySpark. In the next section, we will show an example using the k-means algorithm for a clustering task using PySpark.

Let's do some analytics with k-means clustering

Anomalous data refers to data that is unusual from normal distributions. Thus, detecting anomalies is an important task for network security, anomalous packets or requests can be flagged as errors or potential attacks.

In this example, we will use the KDD-99 dataset (can be downloaded here: http://kdd.ics.uci.edu/databases/kddcup99/kddcup99.html). A number of columns will be filtered out based on certain criteria of the data points. This will help us understand the example. Secondly, for the unsupervised task; we will have to remove the labeled data. Let's load and parse the dataset as simple texts. Then let's see how many rows there are in the dataset:

```python
INPUT = "C:/Users/rezkar/Downloads/kddcup.data"
spark = SparkSession\
        .builder\
        .appName("PCAExample")\
        .getOrCreate()

kddcup_data = spark.sparkContext.textFile(INPUT)
```

This essentially returns an RDD. Let's see how many rows in the dataset are using the count() method as follows:

```python
count = kddcup_data.count()
print(count)>>4898431
```

So, the dataset is pretty big with lots of features. Since we have parsed the dataset as simple texts, we should not expect to see the better structure of the dataset. Thus, let's work toward converting the RDD into DataFrame as follows:

```python
kdd = kddcup_data.map(lambda l: l.split(","))
from pyspark.sql import SQLContext
sqlContext = SQLContext(spark)
df = sqlContext.createDataFrame(kdd)
```

Then let's see some selected columns in the DataFrame as follows:

```
df.select("_1", "_2", "_3", "_4", "_42").show(5)
```

The output is as follows:

```
+---+---+----+---+-------+
| _1| _2|  _3| _4|    _42|
+---+---+----+---+-------+
|  0|tcp|http| SF|normal.|
|  0|tcp|http| SF|normal.|
|  0|tcp|http| SF|normal.|
|  0|tcp|http| SF|normal.|
|  0|tcp|http| SF|normal.|
+---+---+----+---+-------+
only showing top 5 rows
```

Figure 15: Sample of the KKD cup 99 dataset

Thus, this dataset is already labeled. This means that the types of malicious cyber behavior have been assigned to a row where the label is the last column (that is, _42). The first five rows off the DataFrame are labeled normal. This means that these data points are normal. Now this is the time that we need to determine the counts of the labels for the entire dataset for each type of labels:

```
#Identifying the labels for unsupervised task
labels = kddcup_data.map(lambda line: line.strip().split(",")[-1])
from time import time
start_label_count = time()
label_counts = labels.countByValue()
label_count_time = time()-start_label_count

from collections import import OrderedDict
sorted_labels = OrderedDict(sorted(label_counts.items(), key=lambda t:
t[1], reverse=True))
for label, count in sorted_labels.items():
        print label, count
```

The output is as follows:

```
smurf. 2807886
neptune. 1072017
normal. 972781
satan. 15892
ipsweep. 12481
portsweep. 10413
nmap. 2316
back. 2203
warezclient. 1020
teardrop. 979
pod. 264
guess_passwd. 53
buffer_overflow. 30
land. 21
warezmaster. 20
imap. 12
rootkit. 10
loadmodule. 9
ftp_write. 8
multihop. 7
phf. 4
perl. 3
spy. 2
```

Figure 16: Available labels (attack types) in the KDD cup dataset

We can see that there are 23 distinct labels (behavior for data objects). The most data points belong to Smurf. This is an abnormal behavior also known as DoS packet floods. The Neptune is the second highest abnormal behavior. The *normal* events are the third most occurring types of events in the dataset. However, in a real network dataset, you will not see any such labels.

Also, the normal traffic will be much higher than any anomalous traffic. As a result, identifying the anomalous attack or anomaly from the large-scale unlabeled data would be tedious. For simplicity, let's ignore the last column (that is, labels) and think that this dataset is unlabeled too. In that case, the only way to conceptualize the anomaly detection is using unsupervised learning algorithms such as k-means for clustering.

Now let's work toward clustering the data points for this. One important thing about K-means is that it only accepts numeric values for modeling. However, our dataset also contains some categorical features. Now we can assign the categorical features binary values of 1 or 0 based on whether they are *TCP* or not. This can be done as follows:

```
from numpy import array
def parse_interaction(line):
```

```
        line_split = line.split(",")
        clean_line_split = [line_split[0]]+line_split[4:-1]
        return (line_split[-1], array([float(x) for x in
clean_line_split]))

    parsed_data = kddcup_data.map(parse_interaction)
    pd_values = parsed_data.values().cache()
```

Thus, our dataset is almost ready. Now we can prepare our training and test set to training the k-means model with ease:

```
    kdd_train = pd_values.sample(False, .75, 12345)
    kdd_test = pd_values.sample(False, .25, 12345)
    print("Training set feature count: " + str(kdd_train.count()))
    print("Test set feature count: " + str(kdd_test.count()))
```

The output is as follows:

```
    Training set feature count: 3674823
    Test set feature count: 1225499
```

However, some standardization is also required since we converted some categorical features to numeric features. Standardization can improve the convergence rate during the optimization process and can also prevent features with very large variances exerting an influence during model training.

Now we will use StandardScaler, which is a feature transformer. It helps us standardize features by scaling them to unit variance. It then sets the mean to zero using column summary statistics in the training set samples:

```
    standardizer = StandardScaler(True, True)
```

Now let's compute the summary statistics by fitting the preceding transformer as follows:

```
    standardizer_model = standardizer.fit(kdd_train)
```

Now the problem is the data that we have for training the k-means does not have a normal distribution. Thus, we need to normalize each feature in the training set to have the unit standard deviation. To make this happen, we need to further transform the preceding standardizer model as follows:

```
    data_for_cluster = standardizer_model.transform(kdd_train)
```

Well done! Now the training set is finally ready to train the k-means model. As we discussed in the clustering chapter, the trickiest thing in the clustering algorithm is finding the optimal number of clusters by setting the value of K so that the data objects get clustered automatically.

One Naive approach considered a brute force is setting K=2 and observing the results and trying until you get an optimal one. However, a much better approach is the Elbow approach, where we can keep increasing the value of K and compute the **Within Set Sum of Squared Errors (WSSSE)** as the clustering cost. In short, we will be looking for the optimal K values that also minimize the WSSSE. Whenever a sharp decrease is observed, we will get to know the optimal value for K:

```
import numpy
our_k = numpy.arange(10, 31, 10)
metrics = []
def computeError(point):
 center = clusters.centers[clusters.predict(point)]
 denseCenter = DenseVector(numpy.ndarray.tolist(center))
return sqrt(sum([x**2 for x in (DenseVector(point.toArray()) -
denseCenter)]))
for k in our_k:
    clusters = KMeans.train(data_for_cluster, k, maxIterations=4,
initializationMode="random")
    WSSSE = data_for_cluster.map(lambda point:
computeError(point)).reduce(lambda x, y: x + y)
    results = (k, WSSSE)
 metrics.append(results)
print(metrics)
```

The output is as follows:

```
[(10, 3364364.5203123973), (20, 3047748.5040717563), (30,
2503185.5418753517)]
```

In this case, 30 is the best value for k. Let's check the cluster assignments for each data point when we have 30 clusters. The next test would be to run for k values of 30, 35, and 40. Three values of k are not the most you would test in a single run, but only used for this example:

```
modelk30 = KMeans.train(data_for_cluster, 30, maxIterations=4,
initializationMode="random")
 cluster_membership = data_for_cluster.map(lambda x:
modelk30.predict(x))
 cluster_idx = cluster_membership.zipWithIndex()
 cluster_idx.take(20)
 print("Final centers: " + str(modelk30.clusterCenters))
```

The output is as follows:

```
Final centers: [array([  4.10612163e+00,   6.36522840e-02,   4.85948958e-02,
        -2.21319176e-03,  -1.51849176e-02,   1.59666681e-02,
        -1.37464150e-02,   4.63552710e-03,  -2.80722691e-01,
         1.01178785e-01,   7.90818282e-02,   1.62820689e-01,
         1.08778945e-01,   3.21998554e-01,  -8.41384069e-03,
         6.05393588e-02,   0.00000000e+00,   3.30078588e-02,
        -2.46237569e-02,  -1.14832651e+00,  -1.19575475e+00,
        -3.71645499e-01,  -3.67973482e-01,   8.19357206e-01,
         8.14955084e-01,  -3.26320418e-01,   4.33755203e+00,
        -1.82859395e-01,   1.79392516e-01,  -1.71925941e+00,
        -1.75521881e+00,   6.82285609e+00,   2.23215018e-01,
        -1.16133090e-01,  -3.68177485e-01,  -3.66477378e-01,
         8.07658804e-01,   8.18438116e-01]), array([ -6.69802290e-02,  -1.36283222e-03,  -1.65369293e-03,
        -2.21319176e-03,  -1.51849176e-02,  -1.64391576e-03,
        -2.65266109e-02,  -4.38631465e-03,  -4.09296131e-01,
        -2.00370428e-03,  -8.21527723e-03,  -4.60861589e-03,
        -3.04988915e-03,  -9.62851412e-03,  -8.41384069e-03,
        -2.85810713e-02,   0.00000000e+00,  -5.21653093e-04,
        -2.88684412e-02,   6.87674624e-01,   7.54010775e-01,
        -4.65800760e-01,  -4.65512939e-01,  -2.48364764e-01,
        -2.48177638e-01,   5.39551929e-01,  -2.55781037e-01,
        -2.01125081e-01,   3.42806366e-01,   6.19909484e-01,
         5.98368428e-01,  -2.82739959e-01,   8.20664819e-01,
        -1.56479158e-01,  -4.66075407e-01,  -4.65194517e-01,
        -2.50690649e-01,  -2.49676723e-01]), array([ -6.69767578e-02,  -1.86749297e-03,  -1.65012194e-03,
        -2.21319176e-03,  -1.51849176e-02,  -1.64391576e-03,
        -2.64973873e-02,  -4.38631465e-03,  -4.09177709e-01,
        -1.99486560e-03,  -8.21527723e-03,  -4.60861589e-03,
```

Figure 17: Final cluster centers for each attack type (abridged)

Now let's compute and print the total cost for the overall clustering as follows:

```
print("Total Cost: " + str(modelk30.computeCost(data_for_cluster)))
```

The output is as follows:

```
Total Cost: 68313502.459
```

Finally, the WSSSE of our k-means model can be computed and printed as follows:

```
WSSSE = data_for_cluster.map(lambda point: computeError
(point)).reduce(lambda x, y: x + y)
 print("WSSSE: " + str(WSSSE))
```

The output is as follows:

```
WSSSE: 2503185.54188
```

Your results might be slightly different. This is due to the random placement of the centroids when we first begin the clustering algorithm. Performing this many times allows you to see how points in your data change their value of k or stay the same. The full source code for this solution is given in the following:

```
import os
import sys
import numpy as np
from collections import OrderedDict

try:
    from collections import OrderedDict
    from numpy import array
    from math import sqrt
    import numpy
    import urllib
    import pyspark
    from pyspark.sql import SparkSession
    from pyspark.mllib.feature import StandardScaler
    from pyspark.mllib.clustering import KMeans, KMeansModel
    from pyspark.mllib.linalg import DenseVector
    from pyspark.mllib.linalg import SparseVector
    from collections import OrderedDict
    from time import time
    from pyspark.sql.types import *
    from pyspark.sql import DataFrame
    from pyspark.sql import SQLContext
    from pyspark.sql import Row
    print("Successfully imported Spark Modules")

except ImportError as e:
    print ("Can not import Spark Modules", e)
    sys.exit(1)

spark = SparkSession\
        .builder\
        .appName("PCAExample")\
        .getOrCreate()

INPUT = "C:/Exp/kddcup.data.corrected"
kddcup_data = spark.sparkContext.textFile(INPUT)
count = kddcup_data.count()
print(count)
kddcup_data.take(5)
kdd = kddcup_data.map(lambda l: l.split(","))
sqlContext = SQLContext(spark)
df = sqlContext.createDataFrame(kdd)
df.select("_1", "_2", "_3", "_4", "_42").show(5)
```

```
#Identifying the leabels for unsupervised task
labels = kddcup_data.map(lambda line: line.strip().split(",")[-1])
start_label_count = time()
label_counts = labels.countByValue()
label_count_time = time()-start_label_count

sorted_labels = OrderedDict(sorted(label_counts.items(), key=lambda t:
t[1], reverse=True))
for label, count in sorted_labels.items():
    print(label, count)

def parse_interaction(line):
    line_split = line.split(",")
    clean_line_split = [line_split[0]]+line_split[4:-1]
    return (line_split[-1], array([float(x) for x in
clean_line_split]))

parsed_data = kddcup_data.map(parse_interaction)
pd_values = parsed_data.values().cache()

kdd_train = pd_values.sample(False, .75, 12345)
kdd_test = pd_values.sample(False, .25, 12345)
print("Training set feature count: " + str(kdd_train.count()))
print("Test set feature count: " + str(kdd_test.count()))

standardizer = StandardScaler(True, True)
standardizer_model = standardizer.fit(kdd_train)
data_for_cluster = standardizer_model.transform(kdd_train)

initializationMode="random"

our_k = numpy.arange(10, 31, 10)
metrics = []

def computeError(point):
    center = clusters.centers[clusters.predict(point)]
    denseCenter = DenseVector(numpy.ndarray.tolist(center))
    return sqrt(sum([x**2 for x in (DenseVector(point.toArray()) -
denseCenter)]))

for k in our_k:
    clusters = KMeans.train(data_for_cluster, k, maxIterations=4,
initializationMode="random")
    WSSSE = data_for_cluster.map(lambda point:
computeError(point)).reduce(lambda x, y: x + y)
    results = (k, WSSSE)
    metrics.append(results)
print(metrics)
```

```
modelk30 = KMeans.train(data_for_cluster, 30, maxIterations=4,
initializationMode="random")
cluster_membership = data_for_cluster.map(lambda x:
modelk30.predict(x))
cluster_idx = cluster_membership.zipWithIndex()
cluster_idx.take(20)
print("Final centers: " + str(modelk30.clusterCenters))
print("Total Cost: " + str(modelk30.computeCost(data_for_cluster)))
WSSSE = data_for_cluster.map(lambda point:
computeError(point)).reduce(lambda x, y: x + y)
print("WSSSE" + str(WSSSE))
```

 A more comprehensive discussion on this topic can be found at `https://github.com/jadianes/kdd-cup-99-spark`. Also, interested readers can refer to the main and latest documentation on PySpark APIs at `http://spark.apache.org/docs/latest/api/python/`.

Well, now it's time to move to SparkR, another Spark API to work with population statistical programming language called R.

Introduction to SparkR

R is one of the most popular statistical programming languages with a number of exciting features that support statistical computing, data processing, and machine learning tasks. However, processing large-scale datasets in R is usually tedious as the runtime is single-threaded. As a result, only datasets that fit in someone's machine memory can be processed. Considering this limitation and for getting the full flavor of Spark in R, SparkR was initially developed at the AMPLab as a lightweight frontend of R to Apache Spark and using Spark's distributed computation engine.

This way it enables the R programmer to use Spark from RStudio for large-scale data analysis from the R shell. In Spark 2.1.0, SparkR provides a distributed data frame implementation that supports operations such as selection, filtering, and aggregation. This is somewhat similar to R data frames like `dplyr` but can be scaled up for large-scale datasets.

Why SparkR?

You can write Spark codes using SparkR too that supports distributed machine learning using MLlib. In summary, SparkR inherits many benefits from being tightly integrated with Spark including the following:

- **Supports various data sources API**: SparkR can be used to read in data from a variety of sources including Hive tables, JSON files, RDBMS, and Parquet files.

- **DataFrame optimizations**: SparkR DataFrames also inherit all of the optimizations made to the computation engine in terms of code generation, memory management, and so on. From the following graph, it can be observed that the optimization engine of Spark enables SparkR competent with Scala and Python:

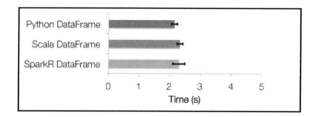

Figure 18: SparkR DataFrame versus Scala/Python DataFrame

- **Scalability:** Operations executed on SparkR DataFrames get automatically distributed across all the cores and machines available on the Spark cluster. Thus, SparkR DataFrames can be used on terabytes of data and run on clusters with thousands of machines.

Installing and getting started

The best way of using SparkR is from RStudio. Your R program can be connected to a Spark cluster from RStudio using R shell, Rescript, or other R IDEs.

Option 1. Set `SPARK_HOME` in the environment (you can check `https://stat.ethz.ch/R-manual/R-devel/library/base/html/Sys.getenv.html`), load the SparkR package, and call `sparkR.session` as follows. It will check for the Spark installation, and, if not found, it will be downloaded and cached automatically:

```
if (nchar(Sys.getenv("SPARK_HOME")) < 1) {
Sys.setenv(SPARK_HOME = "/home/spark")
}
library(SparkR, lib.loc = c(file.path(Sys.getenv("SPARK_HOME"), "R",
"lib"))))
```

Option 2. You can also manually configure SparkR on RStudio. For doing so, create an R script and execute the following lines of R code on RStudio:

```
SPARK_HOME = "spark-2.1.0-bin-hadoop2.7/R/lib"
HADOOP_HOME= "spark-2.1.0-bin-hadoop2.7/bin"
Sys.setenv(SPARK_MEM = "2g")
Sys.setenv(SPARK_HOME = "spark-2.1.0-bin-hadoop2.7")
.libPaths(c(file.path(Sys.getenv("SPARK_HOME"), "R", "lib"),
.libPaths()))
```

Now load the SparkR library as follows:

```
library(SparkR, lib.loc = SPARK_HOME)
```

Now, like Scala/Java/PySpark, the entry point to your SparkR program is the SparkR session that can be created by calling `sparkR.session` as follows:

```
sparkR.session(appName = "Hello, Spark!", master = "local[*]")
```

Furthermore, if you want, you could also specify certain Spark driver properties. Normally, these application properties and runtime environment cannot be set programmatically, as the driver JVM process would have been started; in this case, SparkR takes care of this for you. To set them, pass them as you would pass other configuration properties in the `sparkConfig` argument to `sparkR.session()` as follows:

```
sparkR.session(master = "local[*]", sparkConfig =
list(spark.driver.memory = "2g"))
```

In addition, the following Spark driver properties can be set in `sparkConfig` with `sparkR.session` from RStudio:

Property Name	Property group	spark-submit equivalent
spark.master	Application Properties	--master
spark.yarn.keytab	Application Properties	--keytab
spark.yarn.principal	Application Properties	--principal
spark.driver.memory	Application Properties	--driver-memory
spark.driver.extraClassPath	Runtime Environment	--driver-class-path
spark.driver.extraJavaOptions	Runtime Environment	--driver-java-options
spark.driver.extraLibraryPath	Runtime Environment	--driver-library-path

Figure 19: Spark driver properties can be set in `sparkConfig` with `sparkR.session` from RStudio

Getting started

Let's start with loading, parsing, and viewing simple flight data. At first, download the NY flights dataset as a CSV from `https://s3-us-west-2.amazonaws.com/sparkr-data/nycflights13.csv`. Now let's load and parse the dataset using `read.csv()` API of R:

```
#Creating R data frame
dataPath<- "C:/Exp/nycflights13.csv"
df<- read.csv(file = dataPath, header = T, sep =",")
```

Now let's view the structure of the dataset using `View()` method of R as follows:

```
View(df)
```

	year	month	day	dep_time	dep_delay	arr_time	arr_delay	carrier	tailnum	flight	origin	dest	air_time	distance	hour	minute
1	2013	1	1	517	2	830	11	UA	N14228	1545	EWR	IAH	227	1400	5	17
2	2013	1	1	533	4	850	20	UA	N24211	1714	LGA	IAH	227	1416	5	33
3	2013	1	1	542	2	923	33	AA	N619AA	1141	JFK	MIA	160	1089	5	42
4	2013	1	1	544	-1	1004	-18	B6	N804JB	725	JFK	BQN	183	1576	5	44
5	2013	1	1	554	-6	812	-25	DL	N668DN	461	LGA	ATL	116	762	5	54
6	2013	1	1	554	-4	740	12	UA	N39463	1696	EWR	ORD	150	719	5	54
7	2013	1	1	555	-5	913	19	B6	N516JB	507	EWR	FLL	158	1065	5	55
8	2013	1	1	557	-3	709	-14	EV	N829AS	5708	LGA	IAD	53	229	5	57
9	2013	1	1	557	-3	838	-8	B6	N593JB	79	JFK	MCO	140	944	5	57
10	2013	1	1	558	-2	753	8	AA	N3ALAA	301	LGA	ORD	138	733	5	58
11	2013	1	1	558	-2	849	-2	B6	N793JB	49	JFK	PBI	149	1028	5	58
12	2013	1	1	558	-2	853	-3	B6	N657JB	71	JFK	TPA	158	1005	5	58
13	2013	1	1	558	-2	924	7	UA	N29129	194	JFK	LAX	345	2475	5	58
14	2013	1	1	558	-2	923	-14	UA	N53441	1124	EWR	SFO	361	2565	5	58
15	2013	1	1	559	-1	941	31	AA	N3DUAA	707	LGA	DFW	257	1389	5	59
16	2013	1	1	559	0	702	-4	B6	N708JB	1806	JFK	BOS	44	187	5	59
17	2013	1	1	559	-1	854	-8	UA	N76515	1187	EWR	LAS	337	2227	5	59
18	2013	1	1	600	0	851	-7	B6	N595JB	371	LGA	FLL	152	1076	6	0
19	2013	1	1	600	0	837	12	MQ	N542MQ	4650	LGA	ATL	134	762	6	0
20	2013	1	1	601	1	844	-6	B6	N644JB	343	EWR	PBI	147	1023	6	1

Figure 20: A snap of the NYC flight dataset

Now let's create the Spark DataFrame from the R DataFrame as follows:

```
##Converting Spark DataFrame
flightDF<- as.DataFrame(df)
```

Let's see the structure by exploring the schema of the DataFrame:

```
printSchema(flightDF)
```

The output is as follows:

```
root
 |-- year: integer (nullable = true)
 |-- month: integer (nullable = true)
 |-- day: integer (nullable = true)
 |-- dep_time: string (nullable = true)
 |-- dep_delay: string (nullable = true)
 |-- arr_time: string (nullable = true)
 |-- arr_delay: string (nullable = true)
 |-- carrier: string (nullable = true)
 |-- tailnum: string (nullable = true)
 |-- flight: integer (nullable = true)
 |-- origin: string (nullable = true)
 |-- dest: string (nullable = true)
 |-- air_time: string (nullable = true)
 |-- distance: integer (nullable = true)
 |-- hour: string (nullable = true)
 |-- minute: string (nullable = true)
```

Figure 21: The schema of the NYC flight dataset

Now let's see the first 10 rows of the DataFrame:

```
showDF(flightDF, numRows = 10)
```

The output is as follows:

```
+----+-----+---+--------+---------+--------+---------+-------+-------+------+------+----+--------+--------+----+------+
|year|month|day|dep_time|dep_delay|arr_time|arr_delay|carrier|tailnum|flight|origin|dest|air_time|distance|hour|minute|
+----+-----+---+--------+---------+--------+---------+-------+-------+------+------+----+--------+--------+----+------+
|2013|    1|  1|     517|        2|     830|       11|     UA| N14228|  1545|   EWR| IAH|     227|    1400|   5|    17|
|2013|    1|  1|     533|        4|     850|       20|     UA| N24211|  1714|   LGA| IAH|     227|    1416|   5|    33|
|2013|    1|  1|     542|        2|     923|       33|     AA| N619AA|  1141|   JFK| MIA|     160|    1089|   5|    42|
|2013|    1|  1|     544|       -1|    1004|      -18|     B6| N804JB|   725|   JFK| BQN|     183|    1576|   5|    44|
|2013|    1|  1|     554|       -6|     812|      -25|     DL| N668DN|   461|   LGA| ATL|     116|     762|   5|    54|
|2013|    1|  1|     554|       -4|     740|       12|     UA| N39463|  1696|   EWR| ORD|     150|     719|   5|    54|
|2013|    1|  1|     555|       -5|     913|       19|     B6| N516JB|   507|   EWR| FLL|     158|    1065|   5|    55|
|2013|    1|  1|     557|       -3|     709|      -14|     EV| N829AS|  5708|   LGA| IAD|      53|     229|   5|    57|
|2013|    1|  1|     557|       -3|     838|       -8|     B6| N593JB|    79|   JFK| MCO|     140|     944|   5|    57|
|2013|    1|  1|     558|       -2|     753|        8|     AA| N3ALAA|   301|   LGA| ORD|     138|     733|   5|    58|
+----+-----+---+--------+---------+--------+---------+-------+-------+------+------+----+--------+--------+----+------+
only showing top 10 rows
```

Figure 22: The first 10 rows of the NYC flight dataset

So, you can see the same structure. However, this is not scalable since we loaded the CSV file using standard R API. To make it faster and scalable, like in Scala, we can use external data source APIs.

Using external data source APIs

As mentioned earlier, we can create DataFrame using external data source APIs as well. For the following example, we used `com.databricks.spark.csv` API as follows:

```
flightDF<- read.df(dataPath,
```

```
header='true',
source = "com.databricks.spark.csv",
inferSchema='true')
```

Let's see the structure by exploring the schema of the DataFrame:

```
printSchema(flightDF)
```

The output is as follows:

```
root
 |-- year: integer (nullable = true)
 |-- month: integer (nullable = true)
 |-- day: integer (nullable = true)
 |-- dep_time: string (nullable = true)
 |-- dep_delay: string (nullable = true)
 |-- arr_time: string (nullable = true)
 |-- arr_delay: string (nullable = true)
 |-- carrier: string (nullable = true)
 |-- tailnum: string (nullable = true)
 |-- flight: integer (nullable = true)
 |-- origin: string (nullable = true)
 |-- dest: string (nullable = true)
 |-- air_time: string (nullable = true)
 |-- distance: integer (nullable = true)
 |-- hour: string (nullable = true)
 |-- minute: string (nullable = true)
```

Figure 23: The same schema of the NYC flight dataset using external data source API

Now let's see the first 10 rows of the DataFrame:

```
showDF(flightDF, numRows = 10)
```

The output is as follows:

year	month	day	dep_time	dep_delay	arr_time	arr_delay	carrier	tailnum	flight	origin	dest	air_time	distance	hour	minute
2013	1	1	517	2	830	11	UA	N14228	1545	EWR	IAH	227	1400	5	17
2013	1	1	533	4	850	20	UA	N24211	1714	LGA	IAH	227	1416	5	33
2013	1	1	542	2	923	33	AA	N619AA	1141	JFK	MIA	160	1089	5	42
2013	1	1	544	-1	1004	-18	B6	N804JB	725	JFK	BQN	183	1576	5	44
2013	1	1	554	-6	812	-25	DL	N668DN	461	LGA	ATL	116	762	5	54
2013	1	1	554	-4	740	12	UA	N39463	1696	EWR	ORD	150	719	5	54
2013	1	1	555	-5	913	19	B6	N516JB	507	EWR	FLL	158	1065	5	55
2013	1	1	557	-3	709	-14	EV	N829AS	5708	LGA	IAD	53	229	5	57
2013	1	1	557	-3	838	-8	B6	N593JB	79	JFK	MCO	140	944	5	57
2013	1	1	558	-2	753	8	AA	N3ALAA	301	LGA	ORD	138	733	5	58

only showing top 10 rows

Figure 24: Same sample data from NYC flight dataset using external data source API

So, you can see the same structure. Well done! Now it's time to explore something more, such as data manipulation using SparkR.

Data manipulation

Show the column names in the SparkDataFrame as follows:

```
columns(flightDF)
[1] "year"    "month"    "day"    "dep_time"  "dep_delay"  "arr_time"  "arr_delay"
"carrier"  "tailnum"  "flight"  "origin"  "dest"
[13] "air_time"  "distance"  "hour"  "minute"
```

Show the number of rows in the SparkDataFrame as follows:

```
count(flightDF)
[1] 336776
```

Filter flights data whose destination is only Miami and show the first six entries as follows:

```
showDF(flightDF[flightDF$dest == "MIA", ], numRows = 10)
```

The output is as follows:

year	month	day	dep_time	dep_delay	arr_time	arr_delay	carrier	tailnum	flight	origin	dest	air_time	distance	hour	minute
2013	1	1	542	2	923	33	AA	N619AA	1141	JFK	MIA	160	1089	5	42
2013	1	1	606	-4	858	-12	AA	N633AA	1895	EWR	MIA	152	1085	6	6
2013	1	1	607	0	858	-17	UA	N53442	1077	EWR	MIA	157	1085	6	7
2013	1	1	623	13	920	5	AA	N3EMAA	1837	LGA	MIA	153	1096	6	23
2013	1	1	655	-5	1002	-18	DL	N997DL	2003	LGA	MIA	161	1096	6	55
2013	1	1	659	-1	1008	-7	AA	N3EKAA	2279	LGA	MIA	159	1096	6	59
2013	1	1	753	-2	1056	-14	AA	N3HMAA	2267	LGA	MIA	157	1096	7	53
2013	1	1	759	-1	1057	-30	DL	N955DL	1843	JFK	MIA	158	1089	7	59
2013	1	1	826	71	1136	51	AA	N3GVAA	443	JFK	MIA	160	1089	8	26
2013	1	1	856	-4	1222	-10	DL	N970DL	2143	LGA	MIA	158	1096	8	56

only showing top 10 rows

Figure 25: Flights with destination Miami only

Select specific columns. For example, let's select all the flights that are going to Iowa that are delayed. Also, include the origin airport names:

```
delay_destination_DF<- select(flightDF, "flight", "dep_delay",
"origin", "dest")
 delay_IAH_DF<- filter(delay_destination_DF, delay_destination_DF$dest
== "IAH") showDF(delay_IAH_DF, numRows = 10)
```

The output is as follows:

```
+------+---------+------+----+
|flight|dep_delay|origin|dest|
+------+---------+------+----+
|  1545|        2|   EWR| IAH|
|  1714|        4|   LGA| IAH|
|   496|       -4|   LGA| IAH|
|   473|       -4|   LGA| IAH|
|  1479|        0|   EWR| IAH|
|  1220|        0|   EWR| IAH|
|  1004|        2|   LGA| IAH|
|   455|       -1|   EWR| IAH|
|  1086|      134|   LGA| IAH|
|  1461|        5|   EWR| IAH|
+------+---------+------+----+
only showing top 10 rows
```

Figure 26: All the flights that are going to Iowa that are delayed

We can even use it to chain data frame operations. To show an example, at first, group the flights by date and then find the average daily delay. Then, finally, write the result into a SparkDataFrame as follows:

```
install.packages(c("magrittr"))
library(magrittr)
groupBy(flightDF, flightDF$day) %>% summarize(avg(flightDF$dep_delay),
avg(flightDF$arr_delay)) ->dailyDelayDF
```

Now print the computed DataFrame:

```
head(dailyDelayDF)
```

The output is as follows:

```
  day avg(dep_delay) avg(arr_delay)
1  31       9.506521       3.359225
2  28      15.743213       8.183567
3  26       9.748002       3.656098
4  27      12.083969       3.331213
5  12      15.177765      11.138973
6  22      18.712073      17.404916
```

Figure 27: Group the flights by date and then find the average daily delay

Let's see another example that aggregates average arrival delay for the entire destination airport:

```
avg_arr_delay<- collect(select(flightDF, avg(flightDF$arr_delay)))
 head(avg_arr_delay)
avg(arr_delay)
 1 6.895377
```

Even more complex aggregation can be performed. For example, the following code aggregates the average, maximum, and minimum delay per each destination airport. It also shows the number of flights that land in those airports:

```
flight_avg_arrival_delay_by_destination<- collect(agg(
  groupBy(flightDF, "dest"),
  NUM_FLIGHTS=n(flightDF$dest),
  AVG_DELAY = avg(flightDF$arr_delay),
  MAX_DELAY=max(flightDF$arr_delay),
  MIN_DELAY=min(flightDF$arr_delay)
  ))
head(flight_avg_arrival_delay_by_destination)
```

The output is as follows:

	dest	NUM_FLIGHTS	AVG_DELAY	MAX_DELAY	MIN_DELAY
1	PSE	365	7.871508	NA	-1
2	MSY	3799	6.490175	NA	-1
3	BUR	371	8.175676	NA	-1
4	SNA	825	-7.868227	NA	-1
5	GRR	765	18.189560	NA	-1
6	GSO	1606	14.112601	NA	-1

Figure 28: Maximum and minimum delay per each destination airport

Querying SparkR DataFrame

Similar to Scala, we can perform a SQL query on the DataFrame once it is saved as `TempView` using the `createOrReplaceTempView()` method. Let's see an example of that. At first, let's save the fight DataFrame (that is, `flightDF`) as follows:

```
# First, register the flights SparkDataFrame as a table
createOrReplaceTempView(flightDF, "flight")
```

Now let's select destination and destinations of all the flights with their associated carrier information as follows:

```
destDF<- sql("SELECT dest, origin, carrier FROM flight")
  showDF(destDF, numRows=10)
```

The output is as follows:

```
+----+------+-------+
|dest|origin|carrier|
+----+------+-------+
| IAH|   EWR|     UA|
| IAH|   LGA|     UA|
| MIA|   JFK|     AA|
| BQN|   JFK|     B6|
| ATL|   LGA|     DL|
| ORD|   EWR|     UA|
| FLL|   EWR|     B6|
| IAD|   LGA|     EV|
| MCO|   JFK|     B6|
| ORD|   LGA|     AA|
+----+------+-------+
only showing top 10 rows
```

Figure 29: All the flights with their associated carrier information

Now let's make the SQL a bit more complex, such as finding the destination's airport of all the flights that are at least 120 minutes delayed as follows:

```
selected_flight_SQL<- sql("SELECT dest, origin, arr_delay FROM flight
WHERE arr_delay>= 120")
showDF(selected_flight_SQL, numRows = 10)
```

The preceding code segment queries and shows the name of the airports of all the flights that are delayed by at least 2 hours:

```
+----+------+---------+
|dest|origin|arr_delay|
+----+------+---------+
| CLT|   LGA|      137|
| BWI|   JFK|      851|
| BOS|   EWR|      123|
| IAH|   LGA|      145|
| RIC|   EWR|      127|
| MCO|   EWR|      125|
| MCI|   EWR|      136|
| IAD|   JFK|      123|
| DAY|   EWR|      123|
| BNA|   LGA|      138|
+----+------+---------+
only showing top 10 rows
```

Figure 30: Destination airports of all the flights that are delayed by at least 2 hours

Now let's do a more complex query. Let's find the origins of all the flights to Iowa that are delayed by at least 2 hours. Finally, sort them by arrival delay and limit the count up to 20 as follows:

```
selected_flight_SQL_complex<- sql("SELECT origin, dest, arr_delay FROM
flight WHERE dest='IAH' AND arr_delay>= 120 ORDER BY arr_delay DESC
LIMIT 20")
showDF(selected_flight_SQL_complex, numRows=20)
```

The preceding code segment queries and shows the name of the airports of all the flights that are delayed by at least 2 hours to Iowa:

```
+------+----+---------+
|origin|dest|arr_delay|
+------+----+---------+
|   JFK| IAH|      783|
|   LGA| IAH|      435|
|   LGA| IAH|      390|
|   EWR| IAH|      374|
|   EWR| IAH|      373|
|   LGA| IAH|      370|
|   LGA| IAH|      363|
|   EWR| IAH|      338|
|   LGA| IAH|      324|
|   LGA| IAH|      321|
|   LGA| IAH|      312|
|   LGA| IAH|      309|
|   EWR| IAH|      302|
|   LGA| IAH|      301|
|   EWR| IAH|      297|
|   LGA| IAH|      294|
|   EWR| IAH|      292|
|   EWR| IAH|      288|
|   EWR| IAH|      283|
|   LGA| IAH|      278|
+------+----+---------+
```

Figure 31: Origins of all the flights that are delayed by at least 2 hours where the destination is Iowa

Visualizing your data on RStudio

In the previous section, we have seen how to load, parse, manipulate, and query the DataFrame. Now it would be great if we could show the data for better visibility. For example, what could be done for the airline carriers? I mean, is it possible to find the most frequent carriers from the plot? Let's give `ggplot2` a try. At first, load the library for the same:

```
library(ggplot2)
```

Now we already have the SparkDataFrame. What if we directly try to use our SparkSQL DataFrame class in `ggplot2`?

```
my_plot<- ggplot(data=flightDF, aes(x=factor(carrier)))
>>
ERROR: ggplot2 doesn't know how to deal with data of class
SparkDataFrame.
```

Obviously, it doesn't work that way because the `ggplot2` function doesn't know how to deal with those types of distributed data frames (the Spark ones). Instead, we need to collect the data locally and convert it back to a traditional R data frame as follows:

```
flight_local_df<- collect(select(flightDF,"carrier"))
```

Now let's have a look at what we got using the `str()` method as follows:

```
str(flight_local_df)
```

The output is as follows:

```
'data.frame':  336776 obs. of 1 variable: $ carrier: chr "UA" "UA"
"AA" "B6" ...
```

This is good because when we collect results from a SparkSQL DataFrame, we get a regular R `data.frame`. It is also very convenient since we can manipulate it as needed. And now we are ready to create the `ggplot2` object as follows:

```
my_plot<- ggplot(data=flight_local_df, aes(x=factor(carrier)))
```

Finally, let's give the plot a proper representation as a bar diagram as follows:

```
my_plot + geom_bar() + xlab("Carrier")
```

The output is as follows:

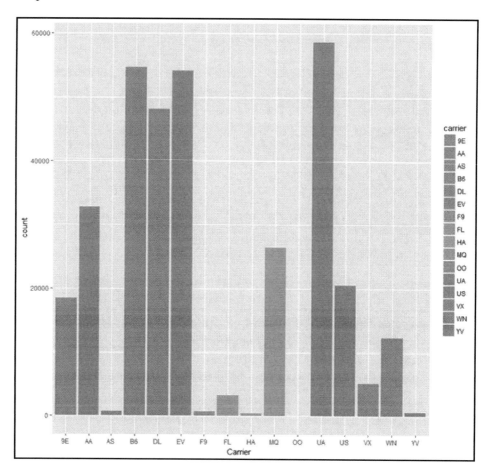

Figure 32: Most frequent carriers are UA. B6. EV. and DL

From the graph, it is clear that the most frequent carriers are UA, B6, EV, and DL. This gets clearer from the following line of code in R:

```
carrierDF = sql("SELECT carrier, COUNT(*) as cnt FROM flight GROUP BY
carrier ORDER BY cnt DESC")
showDF(carrierDF)
```

The output is as follows:

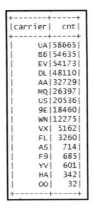

Figure 33: Most most frequent carriers are UA, B6, EV, and DL

The full source code of the preceding analysis is given in the following to understand the flow of the code:

```
#Configure SparkR
SPARK_HOME = "C:/Users/rezkar/Downloads/spark-2.1.0-bin-
hadoop2.7/R/lib"
HADOOP_HOME= "C:/Users/rezkar/Downloads/spark-2.1.0-bin-hadoop2.7/bin"
Sys.setenv(SPARK_MEM = "2g")
Sys.setenv(SPARK_HOME = "C:/Users/rezkar/Downloads/spark-2.1.0-bin-
hadoop2.7")
.libPaths(c(file.path(Sys.getenv("SPARK_HOME"), "R", "lib"),
.libPaths()))

#Load SparkR
library(SparkR, lib.loc = SPARK_HOME)

# Initialize SparkSession
sparkR.session(appName = "Example", master = "local[*]", sparkConfig =
list(spark.driver.memory = "8g"))
# Point the data file path:
dataPath<- "C:/Exp/nycflights13.csv"

#Creating DataFrame using external data source API
flightDF<- read.df(dataPath,
header='true',
source = "com.databricks.spark.csv",
inferSchema='true')
printSchema(flightDF)
showDF(flightDF, numRows = 10)
```

```
# Using SQL to select columns of data

# First, register the flights SparkDataFrame as a table
createOrReplaceTempView(flightDF, "flight")
destDF<- sql("SELECT dest, origin, carrier FROM flight")
showDF(destDF, numRows=10)

#And then we can use SparkR sql function using condition as follows:
selected_flight_SQL<- sql("SELECT dest, origin, arr_delay FROM flight
WHERE arr_delay>= 120")
showDF(selected_flight_SQL, numRows = 10)

#Bit complex query: Let's find the origins of all the flights that are
at least 2 hours delayed where the destiantionn is Iowa. Finally, sort
them by arrival delay and limit the count upto 20 and the destinations
selected_flight_SQL_complex<- sql("SELECT origin, dest, arr_delay FROM
flight WHERE dest='IAH' AND arr_delay>= 120 ORDER BY arr_delay DESC
LIMIT 20")
showDF(selected_flight_SQL_complex)

# Stop the SparkSession now
sparkR.session.stop()
```

Summary

In this chapter, we showed some examples of how to write your Spark code in Python and R. These are the most popular programming languages in the data scientist community.

We covered the motivation of using PySpark and SparkR for big data analytics with almost similar ease with Java and Scala. We discussed how to install these APIs on their popular IDEs such as PyCharm for PySpark and RStudio for SparkR. We also showed how to work with DataFrames and RDDs from these IDEs. Furthermore, we discussed how to execute Spark SQL queries from PySpark and SparkR. Then we also discussed how to perform some analytics with visualization of the dataset. Finally, we saw how to use UDFs with PySpark with examples.

Thus, we have discussed several aspects for two Spark's APIs; PySpark and SparkR. There are much more to explore. Interested readers should refer to their websites for more information:

- PySpark: http://spark.apache.org/docs/latest/api/python/
- SparkR: https://spark.apache.org/docs/latest/sparkr.html

Index

O

object-oriented programming (OOP) 43
objects, Scala
  access and visibility 59
  campanion objects 55
  constructors 61
  final keyword 57
  private members 59
  protected members 60
  public members 59
  singleton and companion objects 54
  val keyword 57
OneHotEncoder 445
operators 101
  using, as methods 30
optimization techniques
  about 617
  data serialization 618
  memory tuning 621
option type 140, 144
Out Of Memory (OOM) 610

P

package objects 69
packages 69
PageRank
  about 421
  reference 421
Pair RDD 257
partitioners
  about 280
  HashPartitioner 281
  RangePartitioner 282
partitioning 279
pattern matching
  about 72
  reference 73
PCA
  about 450
  regression analysis 452
  using 452
performance characteristics
  about 152
  memory usage, by collection objects 156,

  157
  of collection objects 153, 155
pivots 309
Platform as a Service (PaaS) 97, 176, 667
Pregel API
  about 414
  connected components 414
  shortest path 421
  shortest paths 416
  traveling salesman problem 415
Principal Component Analysis (PCA) 430
pure functions 101
PySpark configuration
  about 720
  by setting SPARK_HOME 720, 721
  PySpark, setting on Pythons IDEs 722, 723,
  724, 725, 726
  Python shell, using 721, 722
PySpark
  about 195, 720
  configuring 720
  getting started process 726
  installing 720
  UDF, writing on 733, 734, 735, 736, 737,
  738
Python
  about 719

R

R 747
random forests
  used, for classifying MNIST 477
  used, for improving classification accuracy
  475
read-evaluate-print-loop (REPL) 221
reduceByKey
  comparing, with aggregateByKey 276
  comparing, with combineByKey 276
  comparing, with groupByKey 276
Reducer 185
reference
  versus value immutability 46
regression analysis
  about 454
  dataset collection and exploration 452

Made in the USA
Middletown, DE
12 February 2019